McEACHERN

# MACRO ECON⁵

## BRIEF CONTENTS

W9-AQN-586

jannoon028/Shutterstock.com

# CONTENTS

## Part 1
## INTRODUCTION TO ECONOMICS

© Cartoon Network/Everett Collection

# THE **ECON** SOLUTION

## Print + Online

**ECON Macro⁵** delivers all the key terms and core concepts for the **Principles of Macro Economics** course.

**ECON Online** provides the complete narrative from the printed text with additional interactive media and the unique functionality of **StudyBits**—all available on nearly any device!

**What is a StudyBit™?** Created through a deep investigation of students' challenges and workflows, the StudyBit™ functionality of **ECON Online** enables students of different generations and learning styles to study more effectively by allowing them to learn their way. Here's how they work:

**COLLECT WHAT'S IMPORTANT**
Create StudyBits as you highlight text, images or take notes!

WEAK
FAIR
STRONG
UNASSIGNED

**RATE AND ORGANIZE STUDYBITS**
Rate your understanding and use the color-coding to quickly organize your study time and personalize your flashcards and quizzes.

StudyBit™

**TRACK/MONITOR PROGRESS**
Use Concept Tracker to decide how you'll spend study time and study YOUR way!

85%

**PERSONALIZE QUIZZES**
Filter by your StudyBits to personalize quizzes or just take chapter quizzes off-the-shelf.

CORRECT
INCORRECT
INCORRECT
INCORRECT

CENGAGE
Learning®

**ECON Macroeconomics, 5e**
**William A. McEachern, University of Connecticut**

Contributing Author: Steve Trost, Virginia Tech

Vice President, General Manager, 4LTR Press: Neil Marquardt

Product Director, 4LTR Press: Steven E. Joos

Product Manager: Laura Redden

Content/Media Developer: Sarah Dorger

Product Assistant: Lauren Dame

Marketing Manager, Economics: John Carey

Marketing Manager, 4LTR Press: Christopher Walz

Marketing Coordinator: Casey Binder

Senior Content Project Manager: Colleen A. Farmer

Manufacturing Planner: Ron Montgomery

Production Service: MPS Limited

Sr. Art Director: Bethany Casey

Internal Designer: Lou Ann Thesing

Cover Designer: Curio Press, LLC/Lisa Kuhn

Covers and title page Image: jannoon028/Shutterstock.com

Computer and table illustration: iStockPhoto.com/furtaev

Smart Phone illustration: iStockPhoto.com/dashadima

Last ad: Shutterstock.com/Rawpixel.com

Intellectual Property Analyst: Diane Garrity

Intellectual Property Project Manager: Nick Barrows

**Part 2
FUNDAMENTALS OF
MACROECONOMICS**

Universal Images Group Limited/Alamy

**5 Introduction to
Macroeconomics 74**

**6 Tracking the U.S.
Economy 94**

**7 Unemployment
and Inflation 112**

# Part 3
## FISCAL AND MONETARY POLICY

Olivier Douliery/Pool/Corbis

# Part 4
## THE INTERNATIONAL SETTING

iStockphoto.com/Rafael Ramirez

# 19 Economic Development 340

# 1 | The Art and Science of Economic Analysis

© Cartoon Network/Everett Collection

## LEARNING OUTCOMES

After studying this chapter, you will be able to…

**1-1** Explain the economic problem of scarce resources and unlimited wants

**1-2** Describe the forces that shape economic choices

**1-3** Explain the relationship between economic theory and economic reality

**1-4** Identify some pitfalls of economic analysis

**1-5** Describe several reasons to study economics

After finishing this chapter go to **PAGE 15** for **STUDY TOOLS**

**Topics discussed in Chapter 1 include**

- The economic problem
- The scientific method
- Marginal analysis
- Normative versus positive analysis
- Rational self-interest
- Some pitfalls of economic thinking

You have been reading and hearing about economic issues for years—unemployment, inflation, poverty, recessions, federal deficits, college tuition, airfares, stock prices, computer prices, smartphone prices, gas prices. When explanations of such issues go into any depth, your eyes may glaze over and you may tune out, the same way you do when a weather forecaster tries to explain high-pressure fronts colliding with moisture carried in from the coast.

> **"Why are comic-strip and TV characters like those in Adventure Time, The Simpsons, and Family Guy missing a finger on each hand?"**

What many people fail to realize is that economics is livelier than the dry accounts offered by the news media. Economics is about making choices, and you make economic choices every day—choices about whether to get a part-time job or focus on your studies, live in a dorm or off campus, take a course in accounting or one in history, get married or stay single, pack a lunch or buy a sandwich. You already know much more about economics than you realize. You bring to the subject a rich personal experience, an experience that will be tapped throughout the book to reinforce your understanding of the basic ideas.

## 1-1 THE ECONOMIC PROBLEM: SCARCE RESOURCES, UNLIMITED WANTS

Would you like a new car, a nicer home, a smarter phone, tastier meals, more free time, a more interesting social life, more spending money, more leisure, more sleep? Who wouldn't? But even if you can satisfy some of these desires, others keep popping up. *The problem is that although your wants, or desires, are virtually unlimited, the resources available to satisfy these wants are scarce.* A resource is *scarce* when it is not freely available—that is, when its price exceeds zero. Because resources are scarce, you must choose from among your many wants, and whenever you choose, you must forgo satisfying some other wants. The problem of scarce resources but unlimited wants exists to a greater or lesser extent for each of the 7.4 billion people on earth. Everybody—cab driver, farmer, brain surgeon, dictator, shepherd, student, politician—faces the problem. For example, a cab driver uses time and other scarce resources, such as the taxi, knowledge of the city, driving skills, and gasoline, to earn income. That income, in turn, buys housing, groceries, clothing, trips to Disney World, and thousands of other goods and services that help satisfy some of the driver's unlimited wants. **Economics** examines how people use their scarce resources to satisfy their unlimited wants. Let's pick apart the definition, beginning with resources, then goods and services, and finally focus on the heart of the matter—economic choice, which results from scarcity.

> **economics** The study of how people use their scarce resources to satisfy their unlimited wants

## 1-1a Resources

**Resources** are the inputs, or factors of production, used to produce the goods and services that people want. *Goods and services are scarce because resources are scarce.* Resources sort into four broad categories: labor, capital, natural resources, and entrepreneurial ability. **Labor** is human effort, both physical and mental. Labor includes the effort of the cab driver and the brain surgeon. Labor itself comes from a more fundamental resource: *time.* Without time we can accomplish nothing. We allocate our time to alternative uses: We can *sell* our time as labor, or we can *spend* our time doing other things, like sleeping, eating, studying, playing sports, going online, attending class, watching TV, or just relaxing with friends.

**Capital** includes all human creations used to produce goods and services. Economists often distinguish between physical capital and human capital. *Physical capital* consists of factories, tools, machines, computers, buildings, airports, highways, and other human creations used to produce goods and services. Physical capital includes the cab driver's taxi, the surgeon's scalpel, and the building where your economics class meets (or, if you are taking this course online, your computer and online connectors). *Human capital* consists of the knowledge and skill people acquire to increase their productivity, such as the cab driver's knowledge of city streets, the surgeon's knowledge of human anatomy, and your knowledge of economics.

**Natural resources** include all *gifts of nature,* such as bodies of water, trees, oil reserves, minerals, even animals. Natural resources can be divided into renewable resources and exhaustible resources. A *renewable resource* can be drawn on indefinitely if used conservatively. Thus, timber is a renewable resource if felled trees are replaced to regrow a steady supply. The air and rivers are renewable resources if they are allowed sufficient time to cleanse themselves of any pollutants. More generally, biological resources like fish, game, livestock, forests, rivers, groundwater, grasslands, and soil are renewable if managed properly. An *exhaustible resource*—such as oil or coal—does not renew itself and so is available in a limited amount. Once burned, each barrel of oil or ton of coal is gone forever. The world's oil and coal deposits are exhaustible.

A special kind of human skill called **entrepreneurial ability** is the talent required to dream up a new product or find a better way to produce an existing one , organize production, and assume the risk of profit or loss. This special skill comes from an entrepreneur. An **entrepreneur** is a profit-seeking decision maker who starts with an idea, organizes an enterprise to bring that idea to life, and then assumes the risk of operation. An entrepreneur pays resource owners for the opportunity to employ their resources in the firm. Every firm in the world today, such as Ford, Microsoft, Google, and Facebook, began as an idea in the mind of an entrepreneur.

Resource owners are paid **wages** for their labor, **interest** for the use of their capital, and **rent** for the use of their natural resources. Entrepreneurial ability is rewarded by **profit**, which equals the *revenue* from items sold minus the *cost* of the resources employed to make those items. Sometimes the entrepreneur suffers a loss. Resource earnings are usually based on the *time* these resources are employed. Resource payments therefore have a time dimension, as in a wage of $10 *per hour,* interest of 6 percent *per year,* rent of $600 *per month,* or profit of $10,000 *per year.*

## 1-1b Goods and Services

Resources are combined in a variety of ways to produce goods and services. A farmer, a tractor, 50 acres of land, seeds, and fertilizer combine to grow the good: corn. One hundred musicians, musical instruments, chairs, a conductor, a musical score, and a music hall combine to produce the service: Beethoven's *Fifth Symphony.* Corn is a **good** because it is something you can see, feel, and touch; it requires scarce resources to produce; and it satisfies human wants. The book you are now holding, the chair you are sitting in, the clothes you are

---

**resources** The inputs, or factors of production, used to produce the goods and services that people want; consist of labor, capital, natural resources, and entrepreneurial ability

**labor** The physical and mental effort used to produce goods and services

**capital** The buildings, equipment, and human skills used to produce goods and services

**natural resources** All gifts of nature used to produce goods and services; includes renewable and exhaustible resources

**entrepreneurial ability** The imagination required to develop a new product or process, the skill needed to organize production, and the willingness to take the risk of profit or loss

**entrepreneur** A profit-seeking decision maker who starts with an idea, organizes an enterprise to bring that idea to life, and assumes the risk of the operation

**wages** Payment to resource owners for their labor

**interest** Payment to resource owners for the use of their capital

**rent** Payment to resource owners for the use of their natural resources

**profit** Reward for entrepreneurial ability; sales revenue minus resource cost

**good** A tangible product used to satisfy human wants

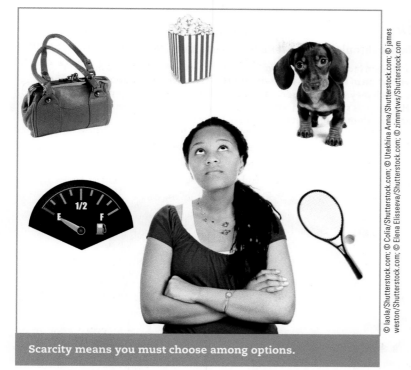

**Scarcity means you must choose among options.**

wearing, and your next meal are all goods. The performance of the *Fifth Symphony* is a **service** because it is intangible, yet it uses scarce resources to satisfy human wants. Lectures, movies, concerts, phone service, wireless connections, yoga lessons, dry cleaning, and haircuts are all services.

Because goods and services are produced using scarce resources, they are themselves scarce. *A good or service is scarce if the amount people desire exceeds the amount available at a zero price.* Because we cannot have all the goods and services we would like, we must continually choose among them. We must choose among more pleasant living quarters, better meals, nicer clothes, more reliable transportation, faster computers, smarter phones, and so on. Making choices in a world of **scarcity** means we must pass up some goods and services. But not everything is scarce. In fact, some things we would prefer to have less of. For example, we would prefer to have less garbage, less spam e-mail, fewer telemarketing calls, and less pollution. Things we want none of even at a zero price are called *bads*, the opposite of goods.

A few goods and services seem *free* because the amount available at a zero price exceeds the amount people want. For example, air and seawater often seem free because we can breathe all the air we want and have all the seawater we can haul away. Yet, despite the old saying "The best things in life are free," most goods and

services are scarce, not free, and even those that appear to be free come with strings attached. For example, *clean* air and *clean* seawater have become scarce. *Goods and services that are truly free are not the subject of economics. Without scarcity, there would be no economic problem and no need for prices.*

Sometimes we mistakenly think of certain goods as free because they involve no apparent cost to us. Napkins seem to be free at Starbucks. Nobody stops you from taking a fistful. Supplying napkins, however, costs the company millions each year and prices reflect that cost. Some restaurants make special efforts to keep napkin use down—such as packing them tightly into the dispenser or making you ask for them. And Starbucks recently reduced the thickness of its napkins.

You may have heard the expression "There is no such thing as a free lunch." *There is no free lunch because all goods and services involve a cost to someone.* The lunch may seem free to you, but it draws scarce resources away from the production of other goods and services, and whoever provides a free lunch often expects something in return. A Russian proverb makes a similar point but with a bit more bite: "The only place you find free cheese is in a mousetrap." Albert Einstein once observed, "Sometimes one pays the most for things one gets for nothing."

## 1-1c Economic Decision Makers and Markets

There are four types of decision makers in the economy: households, firms, governments, and the rest of the world. Their interaction determines how an economy's resources are allocated. *Households* play the starring role. As consumers, households demand the goods and services produced. As resource owners, households supply labor, capital, natural resources, and entrepreneurial ability to firms, governments, and the rest of the world. *Firms, governments,* and *the rest of the world* demand the resources that households supply and then use these resources to supply the goods and services that households demand. The rest of the world

**service** An activity, or intangible product, used to satisfy human wants

**scarcity** Occurs when the amount people desire exceeds the amount available at a zero price includes foreign households, foreign firms, and foreign governments that supply resources and products to U.S. demanders and demand resources and products from U.S. suppliers.

**Markets** are the means by which buyers and sellers carry out exchange at mutually agreeable terms. By bringing together the two sides of exchange, markets determine price, quantity, and quality. Markets are often physical places, such as supermarkets, department stores, shopping malls, yard sales, flea markets, and swap meets. But markets also include other mechanisms by which buyers and sellers communicate, such as classified ads, radio and television ads, telephones, bulletin boards, online sites, and face-to-face bargaining. These market mechanisms provide information about the quantity, quality, and price of products offered for sale. Goods and services are bought and sold in **product markets**. Resources are bought and sold in **resource markets**. The most important resource market is the labor, or job, market. Think about your own experience looking for a job, and you'll already have some idea of that market.

*Exhibit 1*

**The Simple Circular-Flow Model for Households and Firms**

Households earn income by supplying resources to resource markets, as shown in the lower portion of the model. Firms demand these resources to produce goods and services, which they supply to product markets, as shown in the upper portion of the model. Households spend their income to demand these goods and services. This spending flows through product markets as revenue to firms.

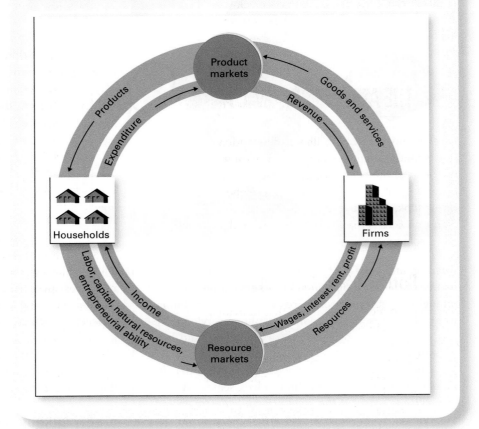

## 1-1d A Simple Circular-Flow Model

Now that you have learned a bit about economic decision makers and markets, consider how all these interact. Such a picture is conveyed by the **circular-flow model**, which describes the flow of resources, products, income, and revenue among economic decision makers. The simple circular-flow model focuses on the primary interaction in a market economy—that between households and firms. Exhibit 1 shows households on the left and firms on the right; please take a look.

Households supply labor, capital, natural resources, and entrepreneurial ability to firms through resource markets, shown in the lower portion of the exhibit. In return, households demand goods and services from firms through product markets, shown on the upper portion of the exhibit. Viewed from the business end, firms demand labor, capital, natural resources, and entrepreneurial ability from households through resource markets, and firms supply goods and services to households through product markets.

The flows of resources and products are supported by the flows of income and expenditure—that is, by the flow of money. So let's add money. The demand and supply of resources come together in resource markets to determine what firms pay for resources. These resource

**market** A set of arrangements by which buyers and sellers carry out exchange at mutually agreeable terms

**product market** A market in which a good or service is bought and sold

**resource market** A market in which a resource is bought and sold

**circular-flow model** A diagram that traces the flow of resources, products, income, and revenue among economic decision makers prices—wages, interest, rent, and profit—flow as *income* to households. The demand and supply of products come together in product markets to determine what households pay for goods and services. These expenditures on goods and services flow as *revenue* to firms. Resources and products flow in one direction—in this case, counterclockwise—and the corresponding payments flow in the other direction—clockwise. What goes around comes around. Take a little time now to trace the logic of the circular flows.

 **1-2  THE ART OF ECONOMIC ANALYSIS**

An economy results as millions of individuals attempt to satisfy their unlimited wants. Because their choices lie at the heart of the economic problem—coping with scarce resources but unlimited wants—these choices deserve a closer look. Learning about the forces that shape economic choices is the first step toward understanding the art of economic analysis.

## 1-2a  Rational Self-Interest

A key economic assumption is that individuals, in making choices, rationally select what they perceive to be in their best interests. By *rational,* economists mean simply that people try to make the best choices they can, given the available time and information. People may not know with certainty which alternative will turn out to be the best. They simply select the alternatives they *expect* will yield the most satisfaction and happiness. In general, **rational self-interest** means that each individual tries to maximize the expected benefit achieved with a given cost or to minimize the expected cost of achieving a given benefit. Thus, economists begin with the assumption that people look out for their self-interest. For example, a physician who owns a pharmacy prescribes 8 percent more drugs on average than a physician who does not own a pharmacy.[1] A physician who owns a nuclear scanner (used to look inside the human body) is seven times more likely to recommend a scan than a physician who does not own a nuclear scanner.[2] And as one more example of self-interest, the *USA Today* weekly football poll asks coaches to list the top

25 teams in the country. It is no surprise that coaches distort their selections to favor their own teams and their own conferences. And, to make their own records look better, coaches inflate the rankings of teams they have beaten.[3]

Rational self-interest should not necessarily be viewed as blind materialism, pure selfishness, or greed. We all know people who are tuned to radio station WIIFM (What's In It For Me?). For most of us, however, self-interest often includes the welfare of our family, our friends, and perhaps the poor of the world. Even so, our concern for others is influenced by our personal cost of that concern. We may readily volunteer to drive a friend to the airport on Saturday afternoon but are less likely to offer a ride if the flight leaves at 6:00 A.M. When we donate clothes to an organization such as Goodwill Industries, they are more likely to be old and worn than brand new. People tend to give more to charities when their contributions are tax deductible and when contributions garner social approval in the community (as when contributor names are made public or when big donors get buildings named after them).[4] Managers donate more company funds to charitable causes when they own less of the company (and, thus, when their personal cost of contributing is lower).[5] TV stations are more likely to donate airtime for public-service announcements during the dead of night than during prime time (which is why, 80 percent of such announcements air between 11:00 P.M. and 7:00 A.M.). In Asia, some people burn money to soothe the passage of a departed loved one. But they burn fake money, not real money.

The notion of self-interest does not rule out concern for others; it simply means that concern for others is influenced by the same economic forces that affect other economic choices. *The lower the personal cost of helping others, the more help we offer.* We don't like to think that our behavior reflects our self-interest, but it usually does. As Jane Austen wrote in *Pride and Prejudice*, "I have been a selfish being all my life, in practice, though not in principle."

1. Brian Chen, Paul Gertler, and Chuh-Yuh Yang, "Moral Hazard and Economies of Scope in Physician Ownership of Complementary Medical Services," NBER Working Paper 19622 (November 2013).

2. Sandeep Jouhar, *Doctored: The Disillusionment of an American Physician*, (Farrar, Straus, and Giroux, 2014), p. 96.

3. Matthew Kotchen and Matthew Potoski, "Conflicts of Interest Distort Public Evaluations: Evidence from the Top 25 Ballots of NCAA Football Coaches," *Journal of Economic Behavior & Organization*, 107 (November 2014): 51–63.

4. Dean Karlan and Margaret McConnell, "Hey Look at Me: The Effect of Giving Circles on Giving," *Journal of Economic Behavior & Organization* (forthcoming).

5. Ing-Haw Cheng, Harrison Hong, and Kelly Shue, "Do Managers Do Good with Other People's Money?" NBER Working Paper No. 19432 (September 2013).

**rational self-interest**
Each individual tries to maximize the expected benefit achieved with a given cost or to minimize the expected cost of achieving a given benefit

## 1-2b Choice Requires Time and Information

Rational choice takes time and requires information, but time and information are themselves scarce and therefore valuable. If you have any doubts about the time and information needed to make choices, talk to someone who recently purchased a home, a car, or a personal computer. Talk to a corporate official trying to decide whether to introduce a new product, sell online, build a new factory, or buy another firm. Or think back to your own experience in choosing a college. You probably talked to friends, relatives, teachers, and guidance counselors. You likely used school catalogs, college guides, and Web sites. You may have even visited some campuses to meet the admissions staff and anyone else willing to talk. The decision took time and money, and it probably involved aggravation and anxiety.

Because information is costly to acquire, we are often willing to pay others to gather and digest it for us. College guidebooks, stock analysts, travel agents, real estate brokers, career counselors, restaurant critics, movie reviewers, specialized Web sites, and *Consumer Reports* magazine attest to our willingness to pay for information that improves our choices. As we'll see next, *rational decision makers continue to acquire information as long as the additional benefit expected from that information exceeds the additional cost of gathering it.*

## 1-2c Economic Analysis Is Marginal Analysis

Economic choice usually involves some adjustment to the existing situation, or status quo. Amazon.com must decide whether to add a new line of products. The school superintendent must decide whether to hire another teacher. Your favorite jeans are on sale, and you must decide whether to buy another pair. You are wondering whether to carry an extra course next term. You just finished lunch and are deciding whether to order dessert.

Economic choice is based on a comparison of the *expected marginal benefit* and the *expected marginal cost* of the action under consideration. **Marginal** means incremental, additional, or extra. Marginal refers to a change in an economic variable, a change in the status quo. *A rational decision maker changes the status quo if the expected marginal benefit from the change exceeds*

**marginal** Incremental, additional, or extra; used to describe a change in an economic variable

When deciding whether to order dessert, ask yourself, "is the marginal benefit higher than the marginal cost?"

*the expected marginal cost.* For example, Amazon.com compares the marginal benefit expected from adding a new line of products (the additional sales revenue) with the marginal cost (the additional cost of the resources required). Likewise, you compare the marginal benefit you expect from eating dessert (the additional pleasure or satisfaction) with its marginal cost (the additional money, time, and calories).

Typically, the change under consideration is small, but a marginal choice can involve a major economic adjustment, as in the decision to quit school and find a job. For a firm, a marginal choice might mean building a plant in Mexico or even filing for bankruptcy. By focusing on the effect of a marginal adjustment to the status quo, the economist is able to cut the analysis of economic choice down to a manageable size. Rather than confront a bewildering economic reality head-on, the economist begins with a marginal choice to see how this choice affects a particular market and shapes the economic system as a whole. Incidentally, to the noneconomist, *marginal* usually means relatively inferior, as in "a movie of marginal quality." Forget that meaning for this course and instead think of *marginal* as meaning incremental, additional, or extra.

## 1-2d Microeconomics and Macroeconomics

Although you have made thousands of economic choices, you probably seldom think about your own economic behavior. For example, why are you reading this book right now rather than doing something else? **Microeconomics** is the study of your economic behavior and the economic behavior of others who make choices about such matters as how much to study and how much to party, how much to borrow and how much to save, what to buy and what to sell. Microeconomics examines individual economic choices and how markets coordinate the choices of various decision makers. Microeconomics explains how price and quantity are determined in individual markets—the market for breakfast cereal, sports equipment, or used cars, for instance.

You have probably given little thought to what influences your own economic choices. You have likely given even less thought to how your choices link up with those made by millions of others in the U.S. economy to determine economy-wide measures such as total production, employment, and economic growth. **Macroeconomics** studies the performance of the economy as a whole. Whereas microeconomics studies the individual pieces of the economic puzzle, as reflected in particular markets, macroeconomics puts all the pieces together to focus on the big picture. Macroeconomics sees the forest, not the trees; the beach, not the grains of sand; and the Rose Bowl parade float, not the individual flowers that shape and color that float.

The national economy usually grows over time, but along the way it sometimes stumbles, experiencing *recessions* in economic activity, as reflected by a decline in production, employment, and other aggregate measures. **Economic fluctuations** are the rise and fall of economic activity relative to the long-term growth trend of the economy. These fluctuations, or *business cycles,* vary in length and intensity, but they usually involve the entire nation and often other nations too. For example, the U.S. economy now produces more than four times as much as it did in 1960, despite experiencing eight recessions since then, including the Great Recession of 2007–2009.

**TO REVIEW:** The art of economic analysis focuses on how people use their scarce resources in an attempt to satisfy their unlimited wants. Rational self-interest guides individual choice. Choice requires time and information and involves a comparison of the expected marginal benefit and the expected marginal cost of alternative actions. Microeconomics looks at the individual pieces of the economic puzzle; macroeconomics fits the pieces together to form the big picture.

## 1-3 THE SCIENCE OF ECONOMIC ANALYSIS

Economists use scientific analysis to develop theories, or models, that help explain economic behavior. An **economic theory**, or **economic model**, is a simplification of economic reality that *is used to make predictions about cause and effect in the real world.* A theory, or model, such as the circular-flow model, captures the important elements of the problem under study but need not spell out every detail and interrelation. In fact, adding more details may make a theory more unwieldy and, therefore, less useful. For example, a wristwatch is a model that tells time, but a watch festooned with extra features is harder to read at a glance and is therefore less useful as a time-telling model. The world is so complex that we must simplify it to make sense of things. Store mannequins simplify the human form (some even lack arms and heads). Comic strips and cartoons simplify a character's anatomy—leaving out fingers (in the case of *Adventure Time*, *The Simpsons*, and *Family Guy*) or a mouth (in the case of *Dilbert*), for instance. You might think of economic theory as a stripped-down, or streamlined, version of economic reality.

A good theory helps us understand a messy and confusing world. Lacking a theory of how things work, our thinking can become cluttered with facts, one piled on another, as in a messy closet. You could think of a good theory as a closet organizer for the mind. A good theory offers a helpful guide to sorting, saving, and understanding information.

> **"**A good theory helps us understand a messy and confusing world.**"**

**microeconomics** The study of the economic behavior in particular markets, such as that for computers or unskilled labor

**macroeconomics** The study of the economic behavior of entire economies, as measured, for example, by total production and employment

**economic fluctuations** The rise and fall of economic activity relative to the long-term growth trend of the economy; also called business cycles

**economic theory, or economic model** A simplification of reality used to make predictions about cause and effect in the real world is widespread enough that people continue to pound on machines that fail to perform (a real problem for the vending machine industry and one reason newer machines are fronted with glass). Yet, if you were to ask these mad pounders to explain their "theory" about how the machine works, they would look at you as if you were crazy.

## 1-3b The Scientific Method

To study economic problems, economists employ a process called the *scientific method,* which consists of four steps, as outlined in Exhibit 2.

### Step One: Identify the Question and Define Relevant Variables

The scientific method begins with curiosity: Someone wants to answer a question. Thus, the first step is to identify the economic question and define the variables relevant to a solution. For example, the question might be, "What is the relationship between the price of Pepsi and the quantity of Pepsi purchased?" In this case, the relevant variables are price and quantity. A **variable** is a measure that can take on different values at different

A good theory can act like a closet organizer for your mind, helping you understand a messy and confusing world.

© iStockphoto.com/Pinopic

## 1-3a The Role of Theory

Most people don't understand the role of theory. Perhaps you have heard, "Oh, that's fine in theory, but in practice it's another matter." The implication is that the theory in question provides little aid in practical matters. People who say this fail to realize that they are merely substituting their own theory for a theory they either do not believe or do not understand. They are really saying, "I have my own theory that works better."

All of us employ theories, however poorly defined or understood. Someone who pounds on the Pepsi machine that just ate a quarter has a crude theory about how that machine works. One version of that theory might be, "The quarter drops through a series of *whatchamacallits,* but sometimes it gets stuck. *If* I pound on the machine, *then* I can free up the quarter and send it on its way." Evidently, this theory

**variable** A measure, such as price or quantity, that can take on different values at different times

*Exhibit 2*

**The Scientific Method: Step-by-Step**

The steps of the scientific method are designed to develop and test hypotheses about how the world works. The objective is a theory that predicts outcomes more accurately than the best alternative theory. A hypothesis is rejected if it does not predict as accurately as the best alternative. A rejected hypothesis can be modified or reworked in light of the test results.

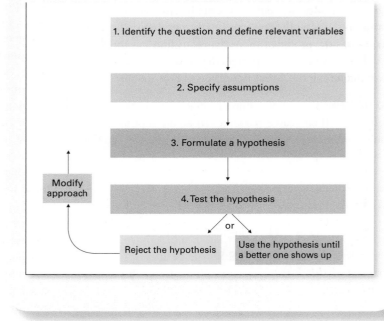

times. The variables of concern become the elements of the theory, so they must be selected with care.

## Step Two: Specify Assumptions

The second step is to specify the assumptions under which the theory is to apply. One major category of assumptions is the **other-things-constant assumption**—in Latin, the *ceteris paribus* assumption. The idea is to identify the variables of interest and then focus exclusively on the relationships among them, assuming that nothing else important changes—that other things remain constant. Again, suppose we are interested in how the price of Pepsi influences the amount purchased. To isolate the relation between these two variables, we assume that there are no changes in other relevant variables such as consumer income, the average daytime temperature, or the price of Coke.

We also make assumptions about how people behave; these are called **behavioral assumptions**. The primary behavioral assumption is rational self-interest. Earlier we assumed that each decision maker pursues self-interest rationally and makes choices accordingly. Rationality implies that each consumer buys the products expected to maximize his or her level of satisfaction. Rationality also implies that each firm supplies the products expected to maximize the firm's profit. These kinds of assumptions are called behavioral assumptions because they specify how we expect economic decision makers to behave—what makes them tick, so to speak.

## Step Three: Formulate a Hypothesis

The third step in the scientific method is to formulate a **hypothesis**, which is a theory about how key variables relate to each other. For example, one hypothesis holds that if the price of Pepsi goes up, other things constant, then the quantity purchased declines. The hypothesis becomes a prediction of what happens to the quantity purchased if the price increases. *The purpose of this hypothesis, like that of any theory, is to help make predictions about cause and effect in the real world.*

If the price of your favorite soft drink rose, would you buy less of it?

## Step Four: Test the Hypothesis

In the fourth step, by comparing its predictions with evidence, we test the validity of a hypothesis. To test a hypothesis, we must focus on the variables in question, while carefully controlling for other effects assumed not to change. The test leads us either to (1) reject the hypothesis, or theory, if it predicts worse than the best alternative theory, or (2) use the hypothesis, or theory, until a better one comes along. If we reject the hypothesis, we can try to go back and modify our approach in light of the results. Please spend a moment now reviewing the steps of the scientific method in Exhibit 2.

## 1-3c Normative Versus Positive

Economists usually try to explain how the economy works. Sometimes they concern themselves not with how the economy *does* work but how it *should* work. Compare these two statements: "The U.S. unemployment rate is 5.6 percent," and "The U.S. unemployment rate should be lower." The first, called a **positive economic statement**, is an assertion about economic reality that can be supported or rejected by reference to the facts. Positive economics, like physics or biology, attempts to understand the world around us as it is. The second, called a **normative economic statement**, reflects an opinion. And an opinion is merely that—it cannot be shown to be true or false by reference to the facts. Positive statements concern what *is;* normative statements concern what, in someone's opinion, *should be*. Positive statements need not necessarily be true, but they must

**other-things-constant assumption** The assumption, when focusing on the relation among key economic variables, that other variables remain unchanged; in Latin, *ceteris paribus*

**behavioral assumption** An assumption that describes the expected behavior of economic decision makers— what motivates them

**hypothesis** A theory about how key variables relate

**positive economic statement** A statement that can be proved or disproved by reference to facts

**normative economic statement** A statement that reflects an opinion, which cannot be proved or disproved by reference to the facts be subject to verification or refutation by reference to the facts. Theories are expressed as positive statements such as "If the price of Pepsi increases, then the quantity demanded decreases."

Most of the disagreement among economists involves normative debates—such as the appropriate role of government—rather than statements of positive analysis. To be sure, many theoretical issues remain unresolved, but economists generally agree on most fundamental theoretical principles—that is, about positive economic analysis. For example, in a survey of 464 U.S. economists, only 6.5 percent disagreed with the statement "A ceiling on rents reduces the quantity and quality of housing available." This is a positive statement because it can be shown to be consistent or inconsistent with the evidence. In contrast, there was much less agreement on normative statements such as "The distribution of income in the United States should be more equal." Half the economists surveyed "generally agreed," a quarter "generally disagreed," and a quarter "agreed with provisos."[6]

Normative statements, or value judgments, have a place in a policy debate such as the proper role of government, provided that statements of opinion are distinguished from statements of fact. In such policy debates, you are entitled to your own opinion, but you are not entitled to your own facts.

## 1-3d Economists Tell Stories

Despite economists' reliance on the scientific method for developing and evaluating theories, economic analysis is as much art as science. Formulating a question, isolating the key variables, specifying the assumptions, proposing a theory to answer the question, and devising a way to test the predictions all involve more than simply an understanding of economics and the scientific method. Carrying out these steps requires good intuition and the imagination of a storyteller. Economists explain their theories by telling stories about how they think the economy works. To tell a compelling story, an economist relies on case studies, anecdotes, parables, the personal experience of the listener, and supporting data. Throughout this book, you'll hear stories that bring you closer to the ideas under consideration. These stories, such as the one about the Pepsi machine, breathe life into economic theory and help you personalize abstract ideas.

**association-is-causation fallacy** The incorrect idea that if two variables are associated in time, one must necessarily cause the other

6. Richard M. Alston et al., "Is There a Consensus among Economists in the 1990s?" *American Economic Review*, 82 (May 1992): 203–209, Table 1.

## 1-3e Predicting Average Behavior

The goal of economic theory is to predict the impact of economic events on economic choices and, in turn, the effect of these choices on particular markets or on the economy as a whole. Does this mean that economists try to predict the behavior of particular consumers or producers? Not necessarily, because a specific individual may behave in an unpredictable way. But the unpredictable actions of numerous individuals tend to cancel one another out, so the *average behavior* of groups can be predicted more accurately. For example, if the federal government cuts personal income taxes, certain households might save the entire tax cut. On average, however, household spending would increase. Likewise, if Burger King cuts the price of Whoppers, the manager can better predict how much sales will increase than how a specific customer coming through the door will respond. *The random actions of individuals tend to offset one another, so the average behavior of a large group can be predicted more accurately than the behavior of a particular individual.* Consequently, economists tend to focus on the average, or typical, behavior of people in groups—for example, as average taxpayers or average Whopper consumers—rather than on the behavior of a specific individual.

## 1-4  SOME PITFALLS OF FAULTY ECONOMIC ANALYSIS

Economic analysis, like other forms of scientific inquiry, is subject to common mistakes in reasoning that can lead to faulty conclusions. Here are three sources of confusion.

### The Fallacy That Association Is Causation

In the past two decades, the number of physicians specializing in cancer treatment increased sharply. At the same time, the incidence of some cancers increased. Can we conclude that physicians cause cancer? No. To assume that event A caused event B simply because the two are associated in time is to commit the **association-is-causation fallacy**, a common error. The fact that one event precedes another or that the two events occur simultaneously does not necessarily mean that one causes the other. Remember: Association is not necessarily causation.

Standing at a concert can help you see better... unless everyone else stands up too! This is an example of the fallacy of composition.

## The Fallacy of Composition

Perhaps you have been to a rock concert where everyone stands to get a better view. At some concerts, most people even stand on their chairs. But even standing on chairs does not improve your view if others do the same, unless you are quite tall. Likewise, arriving early to buy concert tickets does not work if many have the same idea. Earning a college degree to get a better job does not work as well if everyone earns a college degree. These are examples of the **fallacy of composition**, which is an erroneous belief that what is true for the individual, or the part, is also true for the group, or the whole.

## The Mistake of Ignoring the Secondary Effects

In many cities, public officials have imposed rent controls on apartments. The primary effect of this policy, the effect that policy makers focus on, is to keep rents from rising. Over time, however, fewer new apartments get built because renting them becomes less profitable. Moreover, existing rental units deteriorate because owners have plenty of customers anyway. Thus, the quantity and quality of housing may decline as a result of what appears to be a reasonable measure to keep rents from rising. The mistake was to ignore the **secondary effects**, or the unintended consequences, of the policy. Economic actions have secondary effects that often turn out to be more important than the primary effects. Secondary effects may develop more slowly and may not be immediately obvious, but good economic analysis tries to anticipate them and take them into account.

## 1-5 IF ECONOMISTS ARE SO SMART, WHY AREN'T THEY RICH?

Why aren't economists rich? Well, some are, earning over $25,000 per appearance on the lecture circuit. Others top $2 million a year as consultants and expert witnesses.[7] Economists have been appointed to federal cabinet posts, as secretaries of commerce, defense, labor, state, and treasury, for example, and to head the U.S. Federal Reserve System. Economics is the only social science and the only business discipline for which the prestigious Nobel Prize is awarded, and pronouncements by economists are reported in the media daily. A 2015 journal article argued that "the superiority of economists" gives them considerable influence over economic policy.[8] And *The Economist*, a widely respected news weekly from London, has argued that economic ideas have influenced policy "to a degree that would make other social scientists drool."[9]

The economics profession thrives because its models usually do a better job of making economic sense out of a confusing world than do alternative approaches. But not all economists are wealthy, nor is personal wealth the goal of the discipline. In a similar vein, not all doctors are healthy (some even smoke), not all carpenters live in perfectly built homes, not all marriage counselors are happily married, and not all child psychologists have well-adjusted children. Still, those who study economics do reap financial rewards.

Earlier in the chapter, you learned that economic choice involves comparing the expected marginal benefit and the expected marginal cost. Surveys show that students go to college because they believe a college diploma is the ticket to better jobs and higher pay. Put another way, for nearly two-thirds of U.S. high school graduates, the expected marginal benefit of college apparently exceeds the expected marginal cost. The cost of college will be discussed in the next chapter; the focus here is on the benefits of college, particularly expected earnings.

Among college graduates, all kinds of factors affect earnings, such as general

7. As reported by George Anders, "An Economist's Courtroom Bonanza," *Wall Street Journal*, 19 March 2007.

8. Marion Fourcade, Etienne Ollion, and Yann Algan, "The Superiority of Economists," *Journal of Economic Perspectives*, 29 (Winter 2015): 89–114.

9. "The Puzzling Failure of Economics," *The Economist*, 23 August 1997, p. 11.

**fallacy of composition**
The incorrect belief that what is true for the individual, or part, must necessarily be true for the group, or the whole

**secondary effects**
Unintended consequences of economic actions that may develop slowly over time as people react to events

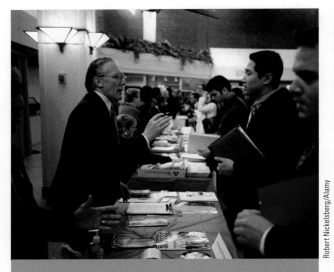

As more people get college degrees, the advantage it gives you in the labor market gets smaller. (Don't worry, it's still worth it.)

Robert Nickelsberg/Alamy

computer majors. Nursing ranked fifth and economics ranked sixth out of the twenty majors listed. Economics had a median pay of $51,400, or 24 percent below the top pay. Elementary education majors held the bottom spot of $33,600, which was only half the top pay.

The dark green bars show the median pay by major for those with 10 to 20 years of job experience. Again, those who had majored in computer engineering led the field with $108,600, an increase of 61 percent over the pay of newer graduates with that degree. Economics majors with 10 to 20 years of job experience saw a 90 percent increase to $97,700. While economics majors with 0 to 5 years experience were paid 25 percent less than the top paying major, among those with at least a decade of job experience, the median pay for economics majors moved up to within 10 percent of the top pay. In fact, economics majors saw their median pay grow more in dollar terms and in percentage terms than did any other major listed. This suggests that those who

ability, effort, occupation, college attended, college major, highest degree earned, appearance, and, yes, luck. PayScale.com collects real-time information on annual pay from its 10 million users. To isolate the effects of a college major on earnings, only workers with a bachelor's as their highest degree are included in the results. Exhibit 3 shows the median earnings in 2015 by major for two groups of college graduates: (1) those with 0 to 5 years of job experience and (2) those with 10 to 20 years of job experience. Majors are listed from the top down by the median annual pay of those with between 0 and 5 years of experience, identified by the light green bars. The top pay of $67,300 went to those who had majored in computer engineering; indeed, the top four slots went to engineering and

*Exhibit 3*
**Median Annual Pay by College Major**

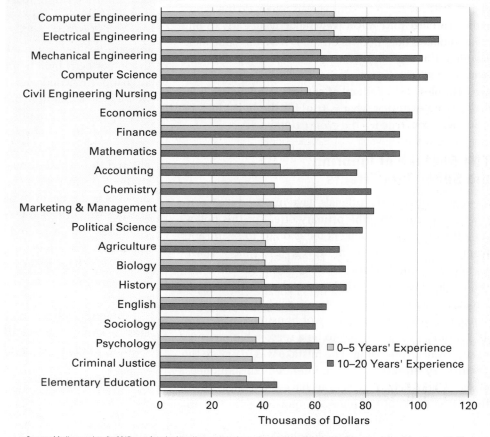

Computer Engineering
Electrical Engineering
Mechanical Engineering
Computer Science
Civil Engineering Nursing
Economics
Finance
Mathematics
Accounting
Chemistry
Marketing & Management
Political Science
Agriculture
Biology
History
English
Sociology
Psychology
Criminal Justice
Elementary Education

☐ 0–5 Years' Experience
■ 10–20 Years' Experience

0    20    40    60    80    100    120
Thousands of Dollars

Sources: Median pay data for 2015 were found at http://www.payscale.com/best-colleges/degrees.asp. For a survey of employment opportunities, go to the U.S. Labor Department's Occupational Outlook Handbook at http://www.bls.gov/oco/.

study economics acquire skills that appreciate with experience. The bump in median pay based on experience for the 19 other majors averaged 67 percent. Elementary education remained the lowest paying major among those with 10 to 20 years of experience. Note that the majors ranked toward the top of the list tend to be more quantitative and analytical. The selection of a relatively more challenging major such as engineering or economics may send a favorable signal to future employers. Nursing majors ranked high right out of school, thanks to strong demand for health care. But nurses with 10 to 20 years of experience earned only 29 percent more than those with only 0 to 5 years of experience. This was the slowest growth rate among the 20 majors.

Incidentally, Exhibit 3 ranks only 20 majors, but Payscale.com ranks 207 majors in all. Median pay for economics majors ranked them in the top 10 percent of that larger group of majors.

Remember, the survey was limited to those whose highest degree was the baccalaureate, so it excluded the many economics majors who went on to pursue graduate studies in law, business administration, economics, public administration, journalism, and other fields (a different study found that lawyers with undergraduate degrees in economics earned more on average than lawyers with other majors).

A number of world leaders majored in economics, including three of the last seven U.S. presidents; Prime Minister Stephen Harper of Canada; billionaire and former president of Chile, Sebastian Pinera (who earned a Ph.D. in economics from Harvard); Turkey's first female prime minister, Tansu Ciller (who earned a Ph.D. in economics from the University of Connecticut); Italy's former prime minister, Mario Monti (who earned a Ph.D. in economics from Yale); Greece's former prime minister, Lucas Papademos (who earned a Ph.D. in economics from MIT); U.S. Supreme Court justices Stephen Breyer and Anthony Kennedy; and former justice Sandra Day O'Connor. Other notable economics majors include billionaire Donald Trump, former Hewlett-Packard president (and billionaire) Meg Whitman, former head of Microsoft (and billionaire) Steve Ballmer, CNN founder (and billionaire) Ted Turner, financial guru (and billionaire) Warren Buffett, Walmart founder (and billionaire) Sam Walton, and Scott Adams, creator of *Dilbert*, the mouthless wonder.

## 1-6 FINAL WORD

This textbook describes how economic factors affect individual choices and how all these choices come together to shape the economic system. Economics is not the whole story, and economic factors are not always the most important. But economic considerations have important and predictable effects on individual choices, and these choices affect the way we live.

Yes, economics is a challenging discipline, but it is also an exciting and rewarding one. The good news is that you already know a lot about economics. To use this knowledge, however, you must cultivate the art and science of economic analysis. You must be able to simplify the world to formulate questions, isolate the relevant variables, and then tell a persuasive story about how these variables relate.

An economic relation can be expressed in words, represented as a table of quantities, described by a mathematical equation, or illustrated as a graph. The appendix to this chapter introduces graphs. You may find a detailed reading of this appendix unnecessary. If you are already familiar with relations among variables, slopes, tangents, and the like, you can probably just browse. But if you have little recent experience with graphs, you might benefit from a more careful reading with pencil and paper in hand.

The next chapter introduces key tools of economic analysis. Subsequent chapters use these tools to explore economic problems and to explain economic behavior that may otherwise seem puzzling. You must walk before you can run, however, and in the next chapter, you will take your first wobbly steps.

## STUDY TOOLS 1

### READY TO STUDY? IN THE BOOK, YOU CAN:

☐ Work the Problems at the end of the chapter.

☐ Rip out the chapter review card for a handy summary of the chapter and key terms.

### ONLINE AT CENGAGEBRAIN.COM YOU CAN:

☐ Collect StudyBits while you read and study the chapter.

☐ Quiz yourself on key concepts.

☐ Prepare for tests with chapter flash cards as well as flash cards that you create.

☐ Watch videos to explore economics further.

# CHAPTER 1 PROBLEMS

*Your instructor can access the answers to these problems online at http://cengagebrain.com.*

## 1-1 Explain the economic problem of scarce resources and unlimited wants

1. *(Definition of Economics)* What determines whether or not a resource is scarce? Why is the concept of scarcity important to the definition of economics?

## 1-2 Describe the forces that shape economic choices

2. *(Rational Self-Interest)* Discuss the impact of rational self-interest on each of the following decisions:
   a. Whether to attend college full time or enter the workforce full time
   b. Whether to buy a new textbook or a used one
   c. Whether to attend a local college or an out-of-town college

3. *(Rational Self-Interest)* If behavior is governed by rational self-interest, why do people make charitable contributions of time and money?

4. *(Marginal Analysis)* The owner of a small pizzeria is deciding whether to increase the radius of delivery area by one mile. What considerations must be taken into account if such a decision is to increase profitability?

5. *(Time and Information)* It is often costly to obtain the information necessary to make good decisions. Yet your own interests can be best served by rationally weighing all options available to you. This requires informed decision making. Does this mean that making uninformed decisions is irrational? How do you determine how much information is the right amount?

## 1-3 Explain the relationship between economic theory and economic reality

6. *(Role of Theory)* What good is economic theory if it can't predict the behavior of a specific individual?

## 1-4 Identify some pitfalls of economic analysis

7. *(Pitfalls of Economic Analysis)* Review the discussion of pitfalls in economic thinking in this chapter. Then identify the fallacy, or mistake in thinking, in each of the following statements:
   a. Raising taxes always increases government revenues.
   b. Whenever there is a recession, imports decrease. Therefore, to stop a recession, we should increase imports.
   c. Raising the tariff on imported steel helps the U.S. steel industry. Therefore, the entire economy is helped.
   d. Gold sells for about $1,200 per ounce. Therefore, the U.S. government could sell all the gold in Fort Knox at $1,200 per ounce to reduce the national debt.

8. *(Association Versus Causation)* Suppose I observe that communities with lots of doctors tend to have relatively high rates of illness. I conclude that doctors cause illness. What's wrong with this reasoning?

## 1-5 Describe several reasons to study economics

9. *(Studying Economics)* According to the text, economics majors on average make more money than most other majors and have more job opportunities. Are these the primary motivations one might have for studying economics? What are your motivations for studying economics?

# APPENDIX

## A1-1 UNDERSTANDING GRAPHS

Take out a pencil and a blank piece of paper. Go ahead. Put a point in the middle of the paper. This is your point of departure, called the **origin**. With your pencil at the origin, draw a straight line off to the right. This line is called the **horizontal axis**. The value of the variable *x* measured along the horizontal axis increases as you move to the right of the origin. Now mark off this line from 0 to 20, in increments of 5 units each. Returning to the origin, draw another line, this one straight north. This line is called the **vertical axis**. The value of the variable *y* measured along the vertical axis increases as you move north of the origin. Mark off this line from 0 to 20, in increments of 5 units each.

Within the space framed by the two axes, you can plot possible combinations of the variables measured along each axis. Each point identifies a value measured along the horizontal, or *x*, axis *and* a value measured along the vertical, or *y*, axis. For example, place point *a* in your graph to reflect the combination where *x* equals 5 units and *y* equals 15 units. Likewise, place point *b* in your graph to reflect 10 units of *x* and 5 units of *y*. Now compare your results with points shown in Exhibit A-1.

A **graph** is a picture showing how variables relate, and a picture can be worth a thousand words. Take a look at Exhibit A-2, which shows the U.S. annual unemployment rate since 1900. The year is measured along the horizontal axis and the unemployment rate is measured as a percentage along the vertical axis. Exhibit A-2 is a *time-series graph,* which shows the value of a variable, in this case the percent of the labor force unemployed, over time. If you had to describe the information presented in Exhibit A-2, the explanation could take many words. The picture shows not only how one year compares to the next but also how one decade compares to another and how the unemployment rate trends over time. The sharply higher unemployment rate during the Great Depression of the 1930s is unmistakable. *Graphs convey information in a compact and efficient way.*

This appendix shows how graphs express a variety of possible relations among variables. Most graphs of interest in this book reflect the relationship between two economic variables, such as the unemployment rate and the year, the price of a product and the quantity demanded, or the price of production and the quantity supplied. Because we focus on just two variables at a time, we usually assume that other relevant variables remain constant.

One variable often depends on another. The time it takes you to drive home depends on your average speed. Your weight depends on how much you eat. The amount of Pepsi you buy depends on the price. A *functional relation* exists between two variables when the value of one variable *depends* on the value of another variable.

*Exhibit A-1*

**Basics of a Graph**

Any point on a graph represents a combination of values of two variables. Here point *a* represents the combination of 5 units of variable *x* (measured on the horizontal axis) and 15 units of variable *y* (measured on the vertical axis). Point b represents 10 units of *x* and 5 units of *y*.

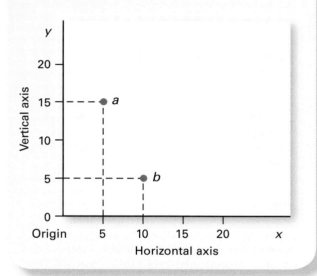

**origin** on a graph depicting two-dimensional space, the zero point

**horizontal axis** line on a graph that begins at the origin and goes to the right and left; sometimes called the *x* axis

**vertical axis** line on a graph that begins at the origin and goes up and down; sometimes called the *y* axis

**graph** a picture showing how variables relate in two-dimensional space; one variable is measured along the horizontal axis and the other along the vertical axis

*Exhibit A-2*

**U.S. Unemployment Rate Since 1900**

A time-series graph depicts the behavior of some economic variable over time. Shown here are U.S. unemployment rates since 1900.

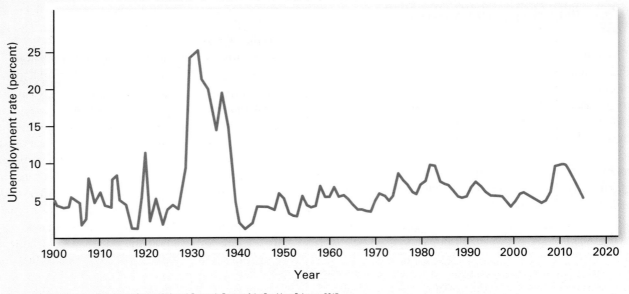

Source: *Historical Statistics of the United States,* 1970; and *Economic Report of the President,* February 2015.

The value of the **dependent variable** depends on the value of the **independent variable**. The task of the economist is to isolate economic relations and determine the direction of causality, if any. Recall that one of the pitfalls of economic thinking is the erroneous belief that association is causation. We cannot conclude that, simply because two events relate in time, one causes the other. There may be no relation between the two events.

## A1-1a Drawing Graphs

Let's begin with a simple relation. Suppose you are planning to drive across the country and want to figure out how far you will travel each day. You plan to average 50 miles per hour. Possible combinations of driving time and distance traveled per day appear in Exhibit A-3. One column lists the hours driven per day, and the next column lists the number of miles traveled per day, assuming an average speed of 50 miles per hour. The

> **dependent variable** a variable whose value depends on that of the independent variable
>
> **independent variable** a variable whose value determines that of the dependent variable

*Exhibit A-3*

**Schedule Relating Distance Traveled to Hours Driven**

| | Hours Driven per Day | Distance Traveled per Day (miles) |
|---|---|---|
| a | 1 | 50 |
| b | 2 | 100 |
| c | 3 | 150 |
| d | 4 | 200 |
| e | 5 | 250 |

distance traveled, the *dependent* variable, depends on the number of hours driven, the *independent* variable. Combinations of hours driven and distance traveled are shown as *a, b, c, d,* and *e.* Each combination is represented by a point in Exhibit A-4. For example, point *a* shows that if you drive for 1 hour, you travel 50 miles. Point *b* indicates that if you drive for 2 hours, you travel 100 miles. By connecting the points, or possible combinations, we create a line running upward and to the right. This makes sense because, the longer you drive, the farther you travel. Assumed constant along this line is your average speed of 50 miles per hour.

**Graph Relating Distance Traveled to Hours Driven**

Points a through e depict different combinations of hours driven per day and the corresponding distances traveled. Connecting these points creates a graph.

Types of relations between variables include the following:

1. As one variable increases, the other increases—as in Exhibit A-4; this is called a **positive**, or **direct**, **relation** between the variables.

2. As one variable increases, the other decreases; this is called a **negative**, or **inverse**, **relation**.

3. As one variable increases, the other remains unchanged; the two variables are said to be *independent*, or *unrelated*.

One of the advantages of graphs is that they easily convey the relation between variables. We do not need to examine the particular combinations of numbers; we need only focus on the shape of the curve.

## A1-1b The Slope of a Straight Line

A more precise way to describe the shape of a curve is to measure its slope. The **slope of a line** indicates how much the vertical variable changes for a given increase in the horizontal variable. Specifically, the slope between any two points along any straight line is the vertical change between these two points divided by the horizontal increase, or

$$\text{Slope} = \frac{\text{Change in the vertical distance}}{\text{Increase in the horizontal distance}}$$

Each of the four panels in Exhibit A-5 indicates a vertical change, given a 10-unit increase in the horizontal variable. In panel (a), the vertical distance increases by 5 units when the horizontal distance increases by 10 units. The slope of the line is therefore 5/10, or 0.5. Notice that the slope in this case is a positive number because the relation between the two variables is positive, or direct. This slope indicates that for every 1-unit increase in the horizontal variable, the vertical variable increases by 0.5 units. The slope, incidentally, does not imply causality; the increase in the horizontal variable does not necessarily *cause* the increase in the vertical variable. The slope simply measures the relation between an increase in the horizontal variable and the associated change in the vertical variable.

In panel (b) of Exhibit A-5, the vertical distance declines by 7 units when the horizontal distance increases by 10 units, so the slope equals −7/10, or −0.7. The slope in this case is a negative number because the two variables have a negative, or inverse, relation. In panel (c), the vertical variable remains unchanged as the horizontal variable increases by 10, so the slope equals 0/10, or 0. These two variables are not related. Finally, in panel (d), the vertical variable can take on any value, although the horizontal variable remains unchanged. Again, the two variables are not related. In this case, any change in the vertical measure, for example a 10-unit change, is divided by 0, because the horizontal value does not change. Any change divided by 0 is mathematically undefined, but as the line tilts toward vertical, its slope gets incredibly large. For practical purposes, we will assume that the slope of this line is not undefined but infinitely large.

## A1-1c The Slope, Units of Measurement, and Marginal Analysis

The mathematical value of the slope depends on the units measured on the graph. For example, suppose copper tubing costs $1 a foot. Graphs depicting the relation between total cost and quantity purchased are shown in Exhibit A-6. In panel (a), the total cost increases by $1 for each 1-foot increase in the amount of tubing purchased. Thus, the slope equals 1/1, or 1. If the cost per foot remains the same but units are

**positive relation (direct relation)** occurs when two variables increase or decrease together; the two variables move in the same direction

**negative relation (inverse relation)** occurs when two variables move in opposite directions; when one increases, the other decreases

**slope of a line** a measure of how much the vertical variable changes for a given increase in the horizontal variable; the vertical change between two points divided by the horizontal increase

## Exhibit A-5

### Alternative Slopes for Straight Lines

The slope of a line indicates how much the vertically measured variable changes for a given increase in the variable measured along the horizontal axis. Panel (a) shows a positive relation between two variables; the slope is 0.5, a positive number. Panel (b) depicts a negative, or inverse, relation. When the x variable increases, the y variable decreases; the slope is 20.7, a negative number. Panels (c) and (d) represent situations in which two variables are unrelated. In panel (c), the y variable always takes on the same value; the slope is 0. In panel (d), the x variable always takes on the same value; the slope is mathematically undefined but we simplify by assuming the slope is infinite.

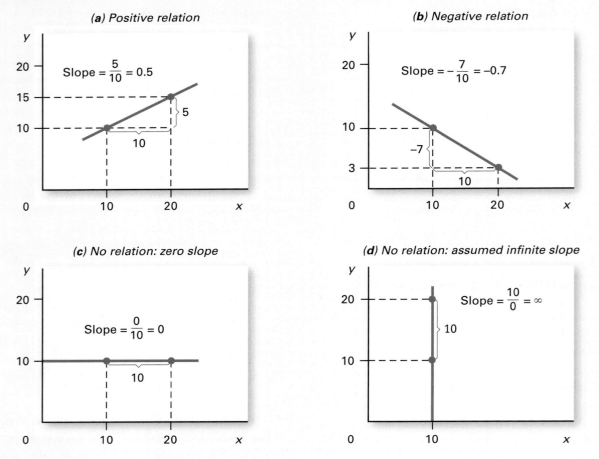

**(a)** Positive relation

$$\text{Slope} = \frac{5}{10} = 0.5$$

**(b)** Negative relation

$$\text{Slope} = -\frac{7}{10} = -0.7$$

**(c)** No relation: zero slope

$$\text{Slope} = \frac{0}{10} = 0$$

**(d)** No relation: assumed infinite slope

$$\text{Slope} = \frac{10}{0} = \infty$$

measured not in *feet* but in *yards*, the relation between total cost and quantity purchased is as depicted in panel (b). Now total cost increases by $3 for each 1-*yard* increase in output, so the slope equals 3/1, or 3. Because different units are used to measure the copper tubing, the two panels reflect different slopes, even though the cost is $1 per foot in each panel. Keep in mind that *the slope depends in part on the units of measurement.*

Economic analysis usually involves *marginal analysis,* such as the marginal cost of one more unit of output. The slope is a convenient device for measuring marginal effects because it reflects the change in total cost, measured along the vertical axis, for each 1-unit change in

output, measured along the horizontal axis. For example, in panel (a) of Exhibit A-6, the marginal cost of another *foot* of copper tubing is $1, which also equals the slope of the line. In panel (b), the marginal cost of another *yard* of tubing is $3, which again is the slope of that line. Because of its applicability to marginal analysis, the slope has special relevance in economics.

### A1-1d The Slopes of Curved Lines

The slope of a straight line is the same everywhere along the line, but the slope of a curved line differs along the curve, as shown in Exhibit A-7. To find the slope of a

## Exhibit A-6

### Slope Depends on the Unit of Measure

The value of the slope depends on the units of measure. In panel (a), output is measured in feet of copper tubing; in panel (b), output is measured in yards. Although the cost is $1 per foot in each panel, the slope is different in the two panels because copper tubing is measured using different units.

**(a)** Measured in feet

**(b)** Measured in yards

## Exhibit A-7

### Slopes at Different Points on a Curved Line

The slope of a curved line varies from point to point. At a given point, such as *a* or *b*, the slope of the curve is equal to the slope of the straight line that is tangent to the curve at the point.

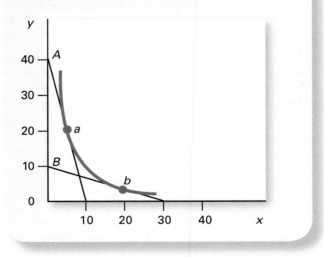

curved line at a particular point, draw a straight line that just touches the curve at that point but does not cut or cross the curve. Such a line is called a tangent to the curve at that point. The slope of the **tangent** gives the slope of the curve at that point. Look at line *A*, which is tangent to the curve at point *a*. As the horizontal value increases

from 0 to 10, the vertical value drops along *A* from 40 to 0. Thus, the vertical change divided by the horizontal change equals $-40/10$, or $-4$, which is the slope of the curve at point *a*. This slope is negative because the vertical value decreases as the horizontal value increases. Line *B*, a line tangent to the curve at point *b*, has the slope $-10/30$, or $-0.33$. As you can see, the curve depicted in Exhibit A-7 gets flatter as the horizontal variable increases, so the value of its slope approaches zero.

Other curves, of course, will reflect different slopes as well as different changes in the slope along the curve. Downward-sloping curves have negative slopes, and upward-sloping curves, positive slopes. Sometimes curves, such as those in Exhibit A-8, are more complex, having both positive and negative ranges, depending on the horizontal value. In the hill-shaped curve, for small values of *x*, there is a positive relation between *x* and *y*, so the slope is positive. As the value of *x* increases, however, the slope declines and eventually becomes negative. We can divide the curve into two segments: (1) the segment between the origin and point *a*, where the slope is positive; and (2) the segment of the curve to the right of point *a*, where the slope is negative. The slope of the curve at point *a* is 0. The U-shaped curve in Exhibit A-8 represents the opposite relation: *x* and *y* are

> **tangent** a straight line that touches a curve at a point but does not cut or cross the curve; used to measure the slope of a curve at a point

## Exhibit A-8

### Curves with Both Positive and Negative Slopes

Some curves have both positive and negative slopes. The hill-shaped curve (in red) has a positive slope to the left of point *a*, a slope of 0 at point *a*, and a negative slope to the right of that point. The U-shaped curve (in blue) starts off with a negative slope, has a slope of 0 at point *b*, and has a positive slope to the right of that point.

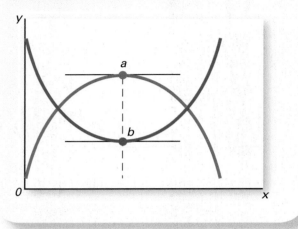

## Exhibit A-9

### Shift of Line Relating Distance Traveled to Hours Driven

Line *T* appeared originally in Exhibit A-5 to show the relation between hours driven and distance traveled per day, assuming an average speed of 50 miles per hour. If the speed averages only 40 miles per hour, the entire relation shifts to the right to T9, indicating that any given distance traveled requires more driving time. For example, 200 miles traveled takes 4 hours at 50 miles per hour but 5 hours at 40 miles per hour. This figure shows how a change in assumptions, in this case, the average speed, can shift the entire relationship between two variables.

negatively related until point *b* is reached; thereafter, they are positively related. The slope equals 0 at point *b*.

## A1-1e Line Shifts

Let's go back to the example of your cross-country trip, where we were trying to determine how many miles you would travel per day. Recall that we measured hours driven per day on the horizontal axis and miles traveled per day on the vertical axis, assuming an average speed of 50 miles per hour. That same relation is shown as line *T* in Exhibit A-8. What happens if the average speed is 40 miles per hour? The entire relation between hours driven and distance traveled would change, as shown by the shift to the right of line *T* to *T'*. With a slower average speed, any distance traveled per day now requires more driving time. For example, 200 miles traveled

requires 4 hours of driving when the average speed is 50 miles per hour (as shown by point *d* on curve *T*), but 200 miles takes 5 hours when your speed averages 40 miles per hour (as shown by point *f* on curve *T'*). Thus, *a change in the assumption about average speed changes the relationship between the two variables observed*. This changed relationship is expressed by a shift of the line that shows how the two variables relate.

That ends our once-over of graphs. Return to this appendix when you need a review.

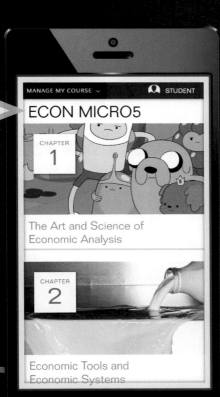

# MICRO
# ECON
## ONLINE

ACCESS TEXTBOOK CONTENT ONLINE—
INCLUDING ON SMARTPHONES!

Includes Videos & Other
Interactive Resources!

Access ECON ONLINE at www.cengagebrain.com

# 2 | Economic Tools and Economic Systems

Gary Bryan/Stone+/Getty Images

## LEARNING OUTCOMES

After studying this chapter, you will be able to...

**2-1** Describe the relationship between choice and opportunity cost

**2-2** Explain how comparative advantage, specialization, and exchange affect economic outcomes (output)

**2-3** Outline how economies function as production systems

**2-4** Describe different economic systems and the decision-making rules that define them

After finishing this chapter go to **PAGE 37** for **STUDY TOOLS**

**Topics discussed in Chapter 2 include**

- Opportunity cost
- Comparative advantage
- Specialization
- Division of labor
- Production possibilities frontier
- Economic systems
- Three economic questions
- Capitalism, command systems, and in between

- Why are you reading this book right now rather than doing something else?
- What is college costing you?
- Why will you eventually major in one subject rather than continue to take courses in various subjects?
- Why is fast food so fast?

- Why is there no point crying over spilled milk?
- Why does common ownership often lead to common neglect?

*These and other questions are addressed in this chapter, which introduces some tools of economic analysis—some tools of the trade.*

Chapter 1 introduced the idea that scarcity forces us to make choices, but the chapter said little about how to make economic choices. This chapter develops a framework for evaluating economic alternatives. First, we consider the cost involved in selecting one alternative over others. Next, we develop tools to explore the choices available to individuals and to the economy as a whole. Finally, we examine the questions that different economies must answer—questions about what goods and services to produce, how to produce them, and for whom to produce them.

> **"Why is there no point crying over spilled milk?"**

## 2-1 CHOICE AND OPPORTUNITY COST

Think about a choice you just made: the decision to begin reading this chapter right now rather than use your time to study for another course, play sports, watch TV, play video games, go online, get some sleep, hang with friends, or do something else. Suppose it's late and your best alternative to reading right now is getting some sleep. The cost of reading is passing up the opportunity of sleep. Because of scarcity, whenever you make a choice, you must pass up another opportunity; you must incur an *opportunity cost*.

### 2-1a Opportunity Cost

What do we mean when we talk about the cost of something? Isn't it what we must give up—must forgo—to get that thing? The **opportunity cost** of the chosen item or activity is *the value of the best alternative that is forgone*. You can think of opportunity cost as the *opportunity lost*. Sometimes opportunity cost can be measured in terms of money, although, as we shall see, money is usually only part of opportunity cost.

How many times have you heard people say they did something because they "had nothing better to do"? They actually mean they had nothing else going on. Yet, according to the idea of opportunity cost, people *always* do what they do because they have nothing better to do. The choice selected seems, at the time, preferable to any other possible alternative. You are reading this chapter right now because you have nothing better to do. In fact, you are attending college for the same reason: College appears more attractive than your best alternative.

### 2-1b Opportunity Cost Is Subjective

Like beauty, opportunity cost is in the eye of the beholder. It is subjective. Only the individual making the choice can identify the most attractive alternative. But the chooser seldom knows the actual value of what was passed up because that alternative is "the road not taken." If you give up an evening of pizza and conversation with friends to work on a research paper, you will never know exactly what you gave up. You know only what you

> **opportunity cost** The value of the best alternative forgone when an item or activity is chosen

*expected*. Evidently, you expected the benefit of working on that paper to exceed the benefit of the best alternative. (Incidentally, focusing on the best alternative forgone makes all other alternatives irrelevant.)

## Calculating Opportunity Cost Requires Time and Information

Economists assume that people rationally choose the most valued alternative. This does not mean you exhaustively assess the value of all possibilities. You assess alternatives as long as the expected marginal benefit of gathering more information about your options exceeds the expected marginal cost (even if you are not aware of making such conscious calculations). In other words, you do the best you can for yourself.

Because learning about alternatives is costly and time consuming, some choices are based on limited or even wrong information. Indeed, some choices may turn out badly (you went for a picnic but it rained; the movie that cost $10 stunk; your new shoes pinched; your new exercise equipment gets no exercise; the stock you bought tanked). Regret about lost opportunities is captured in the common expression "coulda, woulda, shoulda." At the time you made the selection, however, you believed you were making the best use of all your scarce resources, including the time required to gather and evaluate information about your choices.

## Time: The Ultimate Constraint

The Sultan of Brunei is among the richest people on Earth, worth billions based on huge oil revenues that flow into his tiny country. He and his royal family (which has ruled since 1405) live in a palace with 1,788 rooms, including 257 bathrooms and a throne room the size of a football field. The family owns hundreds of cars, including dozens of Rolls-Royces; he can drive any of these or pilot one of his seven planes, including the 747 with gold-plated furniture. Supported by such wealth, the Sultan would appear to have overcome the economic problem of scarcity. Yet, though he can buy just about anything he wants, he lacks the time to enjoy all his stuff. If he pursues one activity, he cannot at the same time do something else. Each activity involves an opportunity cost. Consequently, the Sultan must choose from among the competing uses of his scarcest resource, time. Although your alternatives are less exotic, you too face a time constraint, especially as the college term winds down.

**sunk cost** A cost that has already been incurred, cannot be recovered, and thus is irrelevant for present and future economic decisions

## Opportunity Cost Varies With Circumstance

Opportunity cost depends on your alternatives. This is why you are more likely to study on a Tuesday night than on a Saturday night. The opportunity cost of studying is lower on a Tuesday night, because your alternatives are less attractive than on a Saturday night, when more is going on. Suppose you go to a movie on Saturday night. Your opportunity cost is the value of your best alternative forgone, which might be attending a college game. For some of you, studying on Saturday night may rank well down the list of alternatives—perhaps ahead of reorganizing your closet but behind doing your laundry.

Opportunity cost is subjective, but in some cases, money paid for goods and services is a reasonable approximation. For example, the opportunity cost of the new smartphone you bought is the benefit from spending that $300 on the best forgone alternative. The money measure may leave out some important elements, however, particularly the value of the time involved. For example, watching the latest hit movie costs you not only the $10 admission price but also the time needed to get there, watch the movie, and return home.

Even religious practices are subject to opportunity cost. For example, about half the U.S. population attends religious services at least once a month. In some states, so-called blue laws prohibit retail activity on Sunday. Some states have repealed these laws in recent years, thus raising the opportunity cost of church attendance. Researchers have found that when a state repeals its blue laws, religious attendance declines, as do church donations. These results do not seem to be linked to any decline in religiosity before the repeal.[1]

## 2-1c Sunk Cost and Choice

Suppose you have just finished grocery shopping and are wheeling your cart toward the checkout counters. How do you decide which line to join? Easy. You pick the one with the shortest expected wait. Suppose that line has barely moved for 10 minutes, when you notice that a cashier has opened a new one and invites you to check out. Do you switch to the open cashier, or do you think, "Since I've already spent 10 minutes in this line, I'm staying put"? The 10 minutes you waited represents a **sunk cost**, which is a cost that has already been incurred and cannot be recovered, regardless

---

1. Jonathan Gruber and Daniel Hungerman, "The Church vs. the Mall: What Happens When Religion Faces Increased Secular Competition?" *Quarterly Journal of Economics*, 123 (May 2008): 831–862.

of what you do next. You should ignore sunk costs in making economic choices. Hence, you should switch lines. *Economic decision makers should consider only those costs that are affected by the choice. Sunk costs have already been incurred and are not affected by the choice, so they are irrelevant.* Likewise, you should walk out on a bad movie, even if you spent $10 to get in. Your $10 is gone, and sitting through that stinker only makes you worse off. The irrelevance of sunk costs is underscored by proverbs such as "Don't throw good money after bad," "Let bygones be bygones," "That's water over the dam," and "There's no point crying over spilled milk." The milk has already spilled, so whatever you do now cannot change that. Or, as Shakespeare's Lady Macbeth put it, "Things without all remedy should be without regard: what's done is done." In other words, forget about it.

Now that you have some idea about opportunity cost, let's see how it helps solve the economic problem.

## 2-2 COMPARATIVE ADVANTAGE, SPECIALIZATION, AND EXCHANGE

Suppose you live in a dormitory (and also go to college in the 1950s). You and your roommate have such tight schedules that you each can spare only about an hour a week for mundane tasks like ironing shirts and typing papers (granted, in reality you may not iron shirts or

You should ignore sunk cost when making economic choices.

Does your absolute advantage in both activities mean specialization is no longer a good idea?

type papers, but this example will help you understand some important principles). Each of you must turn in a typed three-page paper every week, and you each prefer ironed shirts when you have the time. Let's say it takes you a half hour to type a handwritten paper. Your roommate is from the hunt-and-peck school and takes about an hour. But your roommate is a talented ironer and can iron a shirt in 5 minutes flat (or should that be, iron it flat in 5 minutes?). You take twice as long, or 10 minutes, to iron a shirt.

During the hour set aside each week for typing and ironing, typing takes priority. If you each do your own typing and ironing, you type your paper in a half hour and iron three shirts in the remaining half hour. Your roommate spends the entire hour typing the paper, leaving no time for ironing. Thus, if you each do your own tasks, the combined output is two typed papers and three ironed shirts.

### 2-2a The Law of Comparative Advantage

Before long, you each realize that total output would increase if you did all the typing and your roommate did all the ironing. In the hour available for these tasks, you type both papers and your roommate irons 12 shirts. As a result of specialization, total output increases by 9 shirts! You strike a deal to exchange your typing for your roommate's ironing, so you each end up with a typed paper and 6 ironed shirts. Thus, *each of you is better off as a result of specialization and exchange.*

By specializing in the task that you each do better, you rely on the **law of comparative advantage**, which states that the individual with the lower opportunity cost of producing a particular output should

**law of comparative advantage** The individual, firm, region, or country with the lowest opportunity cost of producing a particular good should specialize in that good specialize in that output. You face a lower opportunity cost of typing than does your roommate, because in the time it takes to type a paper, you could iron 3 shirts whereas your roommate could iron 12 shirts. And if you face a lower opportunity cost of typing, your roommate must face a lower opportunity cost of ironing (try working that out).

## 2-2b Absolute Advantage Versus Comparative Advantage

The gains from specialization and exchange so far are obvious. A more interesting case arises if you are faster at both tasks. Suppose the example changes only in one respect: Your roommate takes 12 minutes to iron a shirt compared with your 10 minutes. You now have an *absolute advantage* in both tasks, meaning each task takes you less time than it does your roommate. More generally, having an **absolute advantage** means making something using fewer resources than other producers require.

Does your absolute advantage in both activities mean specialization is no longer a good idea? Recall that the law of comparative advantage states that the individual with *the lower opportunity cost* of producing a particular good should specialize in that good. You still take 30 minutes to type a paper and 10 minutes to iron a shirt, so your opportunity cost of typing the paper remains at three ironed shirts. Your roommate takes an hour to type a paper and 12 minutes to iron a shirt, so your roommate could iron five shirts in the time it takes to type a paper. *Because your opportunity cost of typing is lower than your roommate's, you still have a comparative advantage in typing.* Consequently, your roommate must have a comparative advantage in ironing (again, try working this out to your satisfaction). Therefore, you should do all the typing and your roommate, all the ironing. Although you have an absolute advantage in both tasks, your **comparative advantage** calls for specializing in the task for which you have the lower opportunity cost—in this case, typing.

If neither of you specialized, you could type one paper and iron three shirts. Your roommate could still type just the one paper. Your combined output would be two papers and three shirts. If you each specialized according to comparative

**absolute advantage**
The ability to make something using fewer resources than other producers use

**comparative advantage**
The ability to make something at a lower opportunity cost than other producers face

**barter** The direct exchange of one product for another without using money

advantage, in an hour you could type both papers and your roommate could iron five shirts. Thus, specialization increases total output by two ironed shirts. Even though you are better at both tasks than your roommate, you are comparatively better at typing. Put another way, your roommate, although worse at both tasks, is not quite as bad at ironing as at typing.

Don't think that this is just common sense. Common sense would lead you to do your own ironing and typing because you are better at both. *Absolute advantage focuses on who uses the fewest resources, but comparative advantage focuses on what else those resources could produce—that is, on the opportunity cost of those resources.* Comparative advantage is the better guide to who should do what.

The law of comparative advantage applies not only to individuals but also to firms, regions of a country, and entire nations. Individuals, firms, regions, or countries with the lowest opportunity cost of producing a particular good should specialize in producing that good. Because of such factors as climate, workforce skills, natural resources, and capital stock, certain parts of the country and certain parts of the world have a comparative advantage in producing particular goods. From Washington State apples to Florida oranges, from software in India to hardware in Taiwan—*resources are allocated most efficiently across the country and around the world when production and trade conform to the law of comparative advantage.*

## 2-2c Specialization and Exchange

In the previous example, you and your roommate specialized and then exchanged output. No money was involved. In other words, you engaged in **barter**, where products are traded directly for other products. Barter works best in simple economies with little specialization and few traded goods. But for economies with greater specialization, *money* facilitates exchange. Money—coins, bills, checks, and debit cards—is a *medium of exchange* because it is the one thing that everyone accepts in return for goods and services.

Because of specialization and comparative advantage, most people consume little of what they produce and produce little of what they consume. Each individual specializes, then exchanges that product for money, which in turn is exchanged for other products. Did you make anything you are wearing? Probably not. Think about the degree of specialization that went into your cotton shirt. A farmer in a warm climate grew the cotton and sold it to someone who spun it into thread, who

*Exhibit 1*

**Specialization in the Production of Cotton Shirts**

1. Cotton is grown
2. Spun into thread
3. Woven into fabric
4. Sewn into shirts
5. Shipped to a wholesaler
6. Sold to a retailer
7. Bought by a consumer

sold it to someone who wove it into fabric, who sold it to someone who sewed the shirt, who sold it to a wholesaler, who sold it to a retailer, who sold it to you. Many specialists in the chain of production created that shirt. Exhibit 1 traces these steps. *Specialization and exchange create more interdependence in an economy.*

Evidence of specialization is all around us. Shops at the mall specialize in products ranging from luggage to lingerie. Restaurants range from subs to sushi. Or let your fingers do the walking through the help-wanted ads or Craigslist, where you will find thousands of specializations. Without moving a muscle, you can observe the division of labor within a single industry by watching the credits roll at the end of a movie. The credits list scores of specialists—from gaffer (lighting electrician) to assistant location scout. As an extreme example, more than 3,000 specialists helped create the movie *Avatar*.[2] Even TV dramas, such as *NCIS* or *The Walking Dead*, require hundreds of specialists.

Some specialties may seem odd. For example, professional mourners in Taiwan are hired by grieving families to scream, wail, and otherwise demonstrate the deep grief befitting a proper funeral. The sharp degree of specialization is perhaps most obvious online, where the pool of potential customers is so vast that

> **"The degree of specialization is limited by the extent of market."**

individual sites become finely focused. For example, you can find sites specializing in musical bowls, tongue studs, toe rings, brass knuckles, mouth harps, ferret toys, and cat bandanas—just to name a few of the hundreds of thousands of specialty sites. You won't find such precise specialization at the mall. Adam Smith (1723–1790), who is considered the father of economics, said the degree of specialization is limited by the extent of the market. Online sellers draw on the broadest customer base in the world to find a market niche.

## 2-2d Division of Labor and Gains From Specialization

Picture a visit to McDonald's: "Let's see, I'll have a Big Mac, an order of fries, and a chocolate shake." In minutes your order is ready. It would take you much longer to make a homemade version of this meal. Why is the McDonald's meal faster, cheaper, and—for some people—tastier than one you could make yourself? Why is fast food so fast? McDonald's takes advantage of the gains resulting from the **division of labor**. Each worker, rather than preparing an entire meal, specializes in separate tasks. This division of labor allows the group to produce much more.

How is this increase in productivity possible? First, the manager can assign tasks according to *individual preferences and abilities*—that is, according to the law of comparative advantage. The worker with the friendly smile and pleasant personality can handle the customers up front; the one with the strong back but few social graces can handle the heavy lifting out back. Second, a worker who performs the same task again and again gets better at it (experience is a good teacher). The worker filling orders at the drive-through, for example, learns to deal with special problems that arise. As another example, consider the experience gained by someone screening bags at airport security. Experience helps the screener distinguish the harmful from the harmless. Third, specialization means

**division of labor**
Breaking down the production of a good into separate tasks

2. As reported in Hendrik Hertzberg, "And the Oscar Goes To," *The New Yorker*, 15 & 22 February 2010.

no time is lost moving from one task to another. Finally, and perhaps most importantly, the **specialization of labor** allows for the introduction of more sophisticated production techniques—techniques that would not make sense on a smaller scale. For example, McDonald's large shake machine would be impractical in the home. *Specialized machines make each worker more productive.*

To summarize: The specialization of labor (a) takes advantage of individual preferences and natural abilities, (b) allows workers to develop more experience at a particular task, (c) reduces the need to shift among different tasks, and (d) permits the introduction of labor-saving machinery. Specialization and the division of labor occur not only among individuals but also among firms, regions, and, indeed, entire countries. The cotton shirt mentioned earlier might involve growing cotton in one country, turning it into cloth in another, making the shirt in a third, and selling it in a fourth.

We should also acknowledge the downside of specialization. Doing the same thing all day can become tedious. Consider, for example, the assembly line worker whose sole task is to tighten a particular bolt. Such a monotonous job could drive that worker bonkers or lead to repetitive motion injury. Thus, the gains from dividing production into individual tasks must be weighed against any problems caused by assigning workers to repetitive, tedious, and potentially harmful jobs. Fortunately, today many routine tasks, particularly on assembly lines, can be turned over to robots.

© istockphoto.com/EllenMoran

Division of labor puts the "fast" in "fast food."

## 2-3 THE ECONOMY'S PRODUCTION POSSIBILITIES

The focus, up to this point, has been on how individuals choose to use their scarce resources to satisfy their unlimited wants or, more specifically, how they specialize based on comparative advantage. This emphasis on the individual has been appropriate because the economy is shaped by the choices of individual decision makers, whether they are consumers, producers, or public officials. Just as resources are scarce for the individual, they are also scarce for the economy as a whole (no fallacy of composition here). An economy has millions of different resources that can be combined in all kinds of ways to produce millions of different goods and services. This section steps back from the immense complexity of the real economy to develop another simple model, which explores the economy's production options.

### 2-3a Efficiency and the Production Possibilities Frontier or PPF

To get an idea of how well the economy works, you need some perspective; you need a place to stand. Let's develop a model to get some idea of how much an economy can produce with the resources available. What are the economy's production capabilities? Here are the model's assumptions:

1. To simplify matters, output is limited to just two broad classes of products: consumer goods and capital goods.

2. The focus is on production during a given period—in this case, a year.

3. The economy's resources are fixed in both quantity and quality during that period.

4. Society's knowledge about how these resources combine to produce output—that is, the available *technology and know-how*—does not change during the year.

5. Also assumed fixed during the period are the "rules of the game" that facilitate production and exchange. These include such things as the legal system, property rights, tax laws, patent laws, and the manners, customs, and conventions of the market.

The point of these simplifying assumptions is to freeze in time the economy's resources, technology and know-how, and rules of the game so we can focus on the economy's production options. Otherwise, the production possibilities of the economy would be a moving target.

**specialization of labor**
Focusing work effort on a particular product or a single task

*Exhibit 2*

**The Economy's Production Possibilities Frontier**

If the economy uses its available resources and its technology and know-how efficiently to produce consumer goods and capital goods, that economy is on its production possibilities frontier, *AF*. The PPF is bowed out to reflect the law of increasing opportunity cost; the economy must sacrifice more and more units of consumer goods to produce each additional increment of capital goods. Note that more consumer goods must be given up in moving from *E* to *F* than in moving from *A* to *B*, although in each case the gain in capital goods is 10 million units. Points inside the PPF, such as *I*, represent inefficient use of resources. Points outside the PPF, such as *U*, represent unattainable combinations.

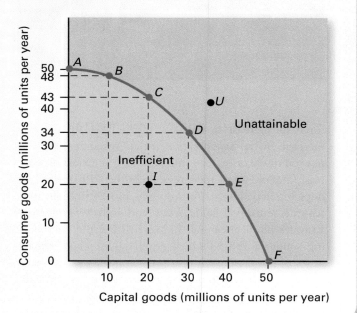

can be produced when all the economy's resources are used efficiently.

## 2-3b Inefficient and Unattainable Production

Points inside the PPF, such as *I* in Exhibit 2, identify combinations that do not employ resources efficiently. Note that *C* yields more consumer goods and no fewer capital goods than *I*. And *E* yields more capital goods and no fewer consumer goods than *I*. Indeed, any point along the PPF between *C* and *E*, such as *D*, yields both more consumer goods and more capital goods than *I*. Hence, combination *I* is *inefficient*. By using resources more efficiently, the economy can produce more of at least one good without reducing the production of the other good. Points outside the PPF, such as *U* in Exhibit 2, identify *unattainable* combinations, given the availability of resources, technology and know-how, and rules of the game. Thus, *the PPF not only shows efficient combinations of production but also serves as the boundary between inefficient combinations inside the frontier and unattainable combinations outside the frontier.*

## 2-3c The Shape of the PPF

Any movement along the PPF involves producing less of one good to produce more of the other. Movements down along the curve indicate that the opportunity cost of more capital goods is fewer consumer goods. For example, moving from point *A* to point *B* *increases* capital production from none to 10 million units but *reduces* consumer units from 50 million to 48 million. Increasing capital goods by 10 million reduces consumer goods only a little. Capital production initially employs resources (such as heavy machinery used to build factories) that produce few consumer goods but are quite productive in making capital.

As shown by the dashed lines in Exhibit 2, each additional 10 million units of capital produced reduce consumer goods by successively

Given the resources, technology and know-how, and rules of the game available in the economy, the **production possibilities frontier**, or **PPF**, identifies possible combinations of the two types of goods that can be produced when available resources are employed efficiently. *Resources are employed efficiently when there is no change that could increase the production of one good without decreasing the production of the other good.* **Efficiency** involves getting the most from available resources.

The economy's PPF for consumer goods and capital goods is shown by the curve *AF* in Exhibit 2. Point *A* identifies the amount produced per year if all the economy's resources are used efficiently to produce consumer goods. Point *F* identifies the amount produced per year if all the economy's resources are used efficiently to produce capital goods. Points along the curve between *A* and *F* identify possible combinations of the two goods that

**production possibilities frontier (PPF)** A curve showing alternative combinations of goods that can be produced when available resources are used efficiently; a boundary line between inefficient and unattainable combinations

**efficiency** The condition that exists when there is no way resources can be reallocated to increase the production of one good without decreasing the production of another; getting the most from available resources larger amounts. The resources used to produce more capital are increasingly better suited to producing consumer goods. *The opportunity cost of making more capital goods increases, because not all resources in the economy are perfectly adaptable to the production of both types of goods.* The shape of the production possibilities frontier reflects the **law of increasing opportunity cost**. If the economy uses resources efficiently, the law of increasing opportunity cost states that each additional increment of one good requires the economy to sacrifice successively larger and larger increments of the other good.

The PPF derives its bowed-out shape from the law of increasing opportunity cost. For example, whereas the first 10 million units of capital have an opportunity cost of only 2 million consumer units, the final 10 million units of capital—that is, the increase from *E* to *F*—have an opportunity cost of 20 million consumer units. Notice that the slope of the PPF shows the opportunity cost of an increment of capital. As the economy moves down the curve, the curve becomes steeper, reflecting the higher opportunity cost of capital goods in terms of forgone consumer goods. The law of increasing opportunity cost also applies when moving from capital goods to consumer goods. Incidentally, if resources were perfectly adaptable to the production of both consumer goods and capital goods, the PPF would be a straight line, reflecting a constant opportunity cost along the PPF.

## 2-3d What Can Shift the PPF?

Any production possibilities frontier assumes the economy's resources, technology and know-how, and rules of the game are fixed during the period under consideration. Over time, however, the PPF may shift if resources, technology and know-how, or the rules of the game change. **Economic growth** is an expansion in the economy's production possibilities as reflected by an outward shift of the PPF.

### Changes in Resource Availability

If people decide to work longer hours, the PPF shifts outward, as shown in panel (a) of Exhibit 3. An increase in the size or health of the labor

Disasters can cause an inward shift or retraction of the PPF.

Angela Harburn/Shutterstock

force, an increase in the skills of the labor force, or an increase in the availability of other resources, such as new oil discoveries, also shifts the PPF outward. In contrast, a decrease of resources shifts the PPF inward, as depicted in panel (b). For example, in 1990 Iraq invaded Kuwait, setting oil fields ablaze and destroying much of Kuwait's physical capital. In West Africa, the encroaching sands of the Sahara destroy thousands of square miles of farmland each year. And in northwest China, a rising tide of wind-blown sand has claimed grasslands, lakes, and forests, and swallowed entire villages, forcing tens of thousands of people to flee.

The new PPFs in panels (a) and (b) appear to be parallel to the original ones, indicating that the resources that changed could produce both capital goods and consumer goods. For example, an increase in electrical power can enhance the production of both, as shown in panel (a). If a resource such as farmland benefits just consumer goods, then increased availability or productivity of that resource shifts the PPF more along the consumer goods axis, as shown in panel (c). Panel (d) shows the effect of an increase in a resource such as construction equipment that is suited only to capital goods.

### Increases in the Capital Stock

An economy's PPF depends in part on the stock of human and physical capital. The more capital an economy produces in one period, the more output can be produced in the next period. Thus, producing more capital goods during this period (for example, more machines in the case of physical capital or more education in the case of human capital) shifts the economy's PPF outward in the next period.

*Exhibit 3*

## Shifts of the Economy's Production Possibilities Frontier

When the resources available to an economy change, the PPF shifts. If more resources become available, if technology and know-how improve, or if the rules of the game create greater stability, the PPF shifts outward, as in panel (a), indicating that more output can be produced. A decrease in available resources or an upheaval in the rules causes the PPF to shift inward, as in panel (b). Panel (c) shows a change affecting consumer goods. More consumer goods can now be produced at any given level of capital goods. Panel (d) shows a change affecting capital goods.

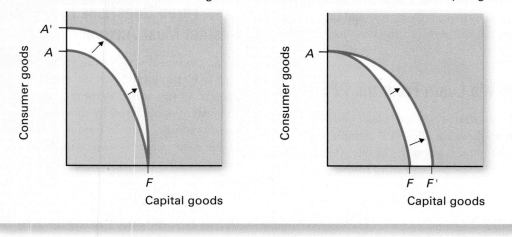

**(a)** *Increase in available resources, better technology, more know-how, or improvement in the rules of the game*

**(b)** *Decrease in available resources or greater uncertainty in the rules of the game*

**(c)** *Change in resources, technology, know-how, or rules that benefits consumer goods*

**(d)** *Change in resources, technology, know-how, or rules that benefits capital goods*

## Technological Change and More Know-how

A technological discovery that employs resources more efficiently could shift the economy's PPF outward. Some discoveries enhance the production of both consumer goods and capital goods, as shown in panel (a) of Exhibit 3. For example, the Internet has increased each firm's ability to find available resources. A technological discovery that benefits consumer goods only, such as more disease-resistant crops, is reflected by a rotation outward of the PPF along the consumer goods axis, as shown in panel (c). Note that point *F* remains unchanged because the breakthrough does not affect the production of capital goods. Panel (d) shows a technological advance in the production of capital goods, such as better software for designing heavy machinery. But even for a given level of technology and a given number of workers, output can increase over time with more know-how. For example, researchers have documented that steel production doubled at a mini-mill even though the technology did not change nor did the number of workers. Through experimentation, workers developed more know-how.[3]

## Improvements in the Rules of the Game

The **rules of the game** are the formal and informal institutions that support the economy—the laws, customs, manners, conventions, and other institutional underpinnings that encourage people to pursue productive activity. A more stable political environment and more reliable property rights increase the incentive to work and to invest, and thus help the economy grow. For example, people have more incentive to work if taxes claim less of their paychecks. People have more incentive to invest if they are confident that their investment will not be appropriated by government, stolen by thieves, destroyed by civil unrest, or blown up by terrorists. Greater certainty and stability in the rules of the game shift the economy's PPF outward. On the other hand, greater uncertainty about the rules of the game reduces the economy's productive capacity, as reflected by an inward shift of the PPF. For example, during the Great Recession of 2007–2009, trust in U.S. institutions such as banks, newspapers, Congress, and big corporations declined and this reduced the economy's productive ability.[4]

## 2-3e What We Learn From the PPF

The PPF demonstrates several ideas introduced so far. The first is *efficiency:* The PPF describes efficient combinations of output, given the economy's resources, technology and know-how, and rules of the game. The second idea is *scarcity:* Given the resources, technology and know-how, and rules of the game, the economy can produce only so much output per period. The PPF slopes downward, because more of one good means less of the other good, thus demonstrating *opportunity cost*. The PPF's bowed-out shape reflects the *law of increasing opportunity cost*, which arises because some resources are not perfectly adaptable to the production of each

type of good. And a shift outward in the PPF reflects *economic growth*.

Finally, because society must somehow select a specific combination of output—a single point—along the PPF, the PPF also underscores the need for *choice*. Selecting a particular combination determines not only the consumer goods available in this period, but also the capital stock available in the next period. One thing the PPF does not tell us is which combination to choose. The PPF tells us only about the costs, not the benefits, of the two goods. To make a selection, we need to know about both costs *and* benefits. How society goes about choosing a particular combination depends on the nature of the economic system, as you will see next.

## 2-4 ECONOMIC SYSTEMS

Each point along the economy's production possibilities frontier is an efficient combination of outputs. Whether the economy produces efficiently and how the economy selects the most preferred combination depends on the decision-making rules employed. But regardless of how decisions are made, each economy must answer three fundamental questions.

### 2-4a Three Questions Every Economic System Must Answer

What goods and services are to be produced? How are they to be produced? And for whom are they to be produced? An **economic system** is the set of mechanisms and institutions that resolve the *what, how,* and *for whom* questions. Some criteria used to distinguish among economic systems are (1) who owns the resources, (2) what decision-making process is used to allocate resources and products, and (3) what types of incentives guide economic decision makers.

### What Goods and Services Are to Be Produced?

Most of us take for granted the incredible number of choices that go into deciding what gets produced—everything from which new kitchen appliances are introduced and which roads get built, to which of the 10,000 movie scripts purchased by U.S. studios each year get to be among the 650 or so movies made. Although different economies resolve these and millions of other questions using different decision-making rules and mechanisms, all economies must somehow make such choices.

---

**economic system** The set of mechanisms and institutions that resolve the what, how, and for whom questions

3. Igal Hendel and Yossi Spiegel, "Small Steps for Workers, a Giant Leap for Productivity." *American Economic Journal: Applied Economics*, 6 February 2014: 73–90.

4. Betsey Stevenson and Justin Wolfers, "Trust in Public Institutions Over the Business Cycle," *American Economic Review*, 101 (May 2011): 281–287.

## How Are Goods and Services to Be Produced?

The economic system must determine how output gets produced. Which resources should be used, and how should they be combined to make stuff? How much labor should be used and at what skill levels? What kinds of machines should be used? What new technology should be incorporated into the latest video games? Should the office complex be built in the city or closer to the interstate highway? Millions of individual decisions determine which resources are employed and how these resources are combined.

## For Whom Are Goods and Services to Be Produced?

Who will actually consume the goods and services produced? The economic system must determine how to allocate the fruits of production among the population. Should everyone receive equal shares? Should the weak and the sick get more? Should it be "first come, first served," so that those willing to wait in line get more? Should goods be allocated according to height? Weight? Religion? Age? Gender? Race? Looks? Strength? Political connections? Lottery? Majority rule? The value of resources supplied? The question "For whom are goods and services to be produced?" is often referred to as the *distribution question*.

Although the three economic questions were discussed separately, they are closely related. The answer to one depends on the answers to the others. For example, an economy that distributes goods and services uniformly to everyone will, no doubt, answer the what-will-be-produced question differently than an economy that somehow allows more personal choice. As we have seen, laws about resource ownership and the role of government determine the "rules of the game"—the set of conditions that shape individual incentives and constraints. Along a spectrum ranging from the freest to the most regimented types of economic systems, *pure capitalism* would be at one end and the *pure command system* at the other.

## 2-4b Pure Capitalism

Under **pure capitalism**, there is no government. The rules of the game include the private ownership of resources and the market distribution of products. Owners have *property rights* to the use of their resources and are therefore free to supply those resources to the highest bidder. **Private property rights** allow individual owners to use resources or to charge others for their use. Any income from supplying labor, capital,

natural resources, or entrepreneurial ability goes to the individual resource owners. Producers are free to make and sell whatever they think will be profitable. Consumers are free to buy whatever goods they can afford. All this voluntary buying and selling is coordinated by unrestricted markets, where buyers and sellers make their intentions known. Market prices guide resources to their most productive use and channel goods and services to the consumers who value them the most.

Under pure capitalism, markets answer the what, how, and for whom questions. That's why capitalism is also referred to as a *market system*. Markets transmit information about relative scarcity, provide individual incentives, and distribute income among resource suppliers. No individual or small group coordinates these activities. Rather, it is the voluntary choices of many buyers and sellers responding only to their individual incentives and constraints that direct resources and products to those who value them the most.

According to Adam Smith, market forces allocate resources as if by an "invisible hand"—an unseen force that harnesses the pursuit of self-interest to direct resources where they earn the greatest reward. According to Smith, *although each individual pursues his or her self-interest, the "invisible hand" of market forces promotes the general welfare*. Capitalism is sometimes called *laissez-faire;* translated from the French, this phrase means "to let do," or to let people do as they choose without government intervention. Thus, under capitalism, voluntary choices based on rational self-interest are made in unrestricted markets to answer the questions what, how, and for whom.

As we will see in later chapters, pure capitalism has its flaws. The most notable market failures are these:

1. No central authority protects property rights, enforces contracts, and otherwise ensures that the rules of the game are followed.

2. People with no resources to sell could starve.

3. Some producers may try to monopolize markets by eliminating the competition.

4. The production or consumption of some goods involves side effects that can harm or benefit people not involved in the market transaction.

5. Firms have no incentive to produce so-called

> **pure capitalism** An economic system characterized by the private ownership of resources and the use of prices to coordinate economic activity in unregulated markets
>
> **private property rights** An owner's right to use, rent, or sell resources or property

*public goods,* such as national defense, because private firms cannot prevent nonpayers from enjoying the benefits of public goods.

6. Market economies experience *economic fluctuations,* which are alternating periods of expansions and recessions in their level of economic activity, especially in employment and production.

Because of these limitations, countries have modified pure capitalism to allow some role for government. Even Adam Smith believed government should play a role. The United States is among the most market-oriented economies in the world today.

## 2-4c Pure Command System

In a **pure command system**, resources are directed and production is coordinated not by market forces but by the "command," or central plan, of government. In theory at least, instead of private property, there is public, or *communal,* ownership of property. That's why central planning is sometimes called *communism.* Government planners, as representatives of all the people, answer the three questions through *central plans* spelling out how much steel, how many cars, and how much housing to produce. They also decide how to produce these goods and who gets them.

In theory, the pure command system incorporates individual choices into collective choices, which, in turn, are reflected in the central plans. Command economies often have names that focus on collective choice, such as the People's Republic of China and the Democratic People's Republic of Korea (North Korea). In practice, the pure command system also has flaws, most notably the following:

1. Running an economy is so complicated and requires so much information that some resources are used inefficiently.

2. Because nobody in particular owns resources, each person has less incentive to employ them in their highest-valued use, so some resources are wasted.

3. Central plans may be more reflective of the preferences of central planners, who in many cases are unelected dictators, than the preferences of society.

4. Because government is responsible for all production, the variety of products tends to be more limited than in a capitalist economy.

5. Each individual has less personal freedom in making economic choices.

6. Because profit has no place in a command economy, people have less incentive to invent new and better products or find more efficient ways to make existing products.

Because of these limitations, countries have modified the pure command system to allow a role for markets. North Korea, a country run for decades by three generations of dictators, is perhaps the most centrally planned economy in the world today.

## 2-4d Mixed and Transitional Economies

No country on earth exemplifies either type of economic system in its pure form. Economic systems have grown more alike over time, with the role of government increasing in capitalist economies and the role of markets increasing in command economies. The United States represents a **mixed system**, with government directly accounting for a little more than one-third of all economic activity. What's more, governments at all levels in the United States regulate the private sector in a variety of ways. For example, local zoning boards determine lot sizes, home sizes, and the types of industries allowed. Federal bodies regulate workplace safety, environmental quality, competitive fairness, food and drug quality, and many other activities.

North Korea is as close as there is to a pure command system.

**pure command system** An economic system characterized by the public ownership of resources and centralized planning

**mixed system** An economic system characterized by the private ownership of some resources and the public ownership of other resources; some markets are regulated by government

Although both ends of the spectrum have moved toward the center, capitalism has gained the most converts in recent decades. Perhaps the benefits of markets are no better illustrated than where a country, as a result of war or political upheaval, became divided by ideology into a capitalist economy and a command economy, such as with Taiwan and China or South Korea and North Korea. In each case, the economies began with similar human and physical resources, but once they went their separate ways, economic growth diverged sharply, with the capitalist economies outperforming the command economies. For example, Taiwan's production per capita in 2015 was four times that of China's, and South Korea's production per capita was 18 times that of North Korea.

Consider the experience of the pilgrims in 1620 while establishing Plymouth Colony. They first tried communal ownership of the land. That turned out badly. Crops were neglected and food shortages developed. After three years of near starvation, the system was changed so that each family was assigned a plot of land and granted the fruits of that plot. Yields increased sharply. The pilgrims learned that people take better care of what they own individually; by contrast, common ownership often leads to common neglect.

Recognizing the incentive power of property rights and markets, some of the most die-hard central planners are now allowing a role for markets. For example, about one-fifth of the world's population lives in China, which grows more market oriented each day, even going so far as to give private property constitutional protection on a par with state property. In a poll of Chinese citizens, 74 percent agreed that "the free enterprise system is the best system on which to base the future of the world." Among Americans polled, 71 percent agreed with that statement.[5] A quarter-century ago, the former Soviet Union dissolved into 15 independent republics; most converted state-owned enterprises into private firms. From Moscow to Beijing, from Hungary to Mongolia, the transition to mixed economies now underway in former command economies will shape the world for decades to come.

Note that nations with freer markets tend to rely more on democratic political systems. Recent research finds that democracy increases economic growth by encouraging investment, increasing schooling, promoting economic reforms, and reducing social unrest.[6]

## 2-4e Economies Based on Custom or Religion

Finally, some economic systems are molded largely by custom or religion. For example, caste systems in India and elsewhere restrict occupational choices. Charging interest is banned under Islamic law. Family relations also play significant roles in organizing and coordinating economic activity. In some countries, businesses are reluctant to hire anyone outside the family because outsiders are less trusted. This limits business growth. Even in the United States, some occupations are still dominated by women, and others by men, largely because of tradition. Your own pattern of consumption and choice of occupation may be influenced by some of these considerations.

## 2-5 FINAL WORD

Although economies can answer the three economic questions in a variety of ways, this book focuses primarily on the mixed market system, such as exists in the United States. This type of economy blends *private choices,* guided by the price system in competitive markets, with *public choices,* guided by democracy in political markets. The study of mixed market systems grows more relevant as former command economies try to develop markets. The next chapter focuses on the economic actors in a mixed economy and explains why and how government gets into the act.

## STUDY TOOLS 2

### READY TO STUDY? IN THE BOOK, YOU CAN:

☐ Work the Problems at the end of the chapter.

☐ Rip out the chapter review card for a handy summary of the chapter and key terms.

### ONLINE AT CENGAGEBRAIN.COM YOU CAN:

☐ Collect StudyBits while you read and study the chapter.

☐ Quiz yourself on key concepts.

☐ Prepare for tests with chapter flash cards as well as flash cards that you create.

☐ Watch videos to explore economics further.

5. As reported in "Capitalism, Comrade," *Wall Street Journal*, 18 January 2006.

6. Daron Acemoglu, et al., "Democracy Does Cause Growth," American Economic Association annual meetings, 3 January 2015.

# CHAPTER 2 PROBLEMS

*Your instructor can access the answers to these problems online at http://cengagebrain.com.*

## 2-1 Describe the relationship between choice and opportunity cost

1. *(Sunk Cost and Choice)* Suppose you go to a restaurant and buy an expensive meal. Halfway through, despite feeling quite full, you decide to clean your plate. After all, you think, you paid for the meal, so you are going to eat all of it. What's wrong with this thinking?

2. *(Opportunity Cost)* You can spend spring break either working at home for $80 per day for five days or go to Florida for the week. If you stay home, your expenses will total about $100. If you go to Florida, the airfare, hotel, food, and miscellaneous expenses will total about $700. What's your opportunity cost of going to Florida?

## 2-2 Explain how comparative advantage, specialization, and exchange affect economic outcomes (output)

3. *(Absolute and Comparative Advantage)* You have the following information concerning the production of wheat and cloth in the United States and the United Kingdom:

**Labor Hours Required to Produce One Unit**

|  | The United Kingdom | The United States |
|---|---|---|
| Wheat | 2 | 1 |
| Cloth | 6 | 5 |

a. What is the opportunity cost of producing a unit of wheat in the United Kingdom? In the United States?
b. Which country has an absolute advantage in producing wheat? In producing cloth?
c. Which country has a comparative advantage in producing wheat? In producing cloth?
d. Which country should specialize in producing wheat? In producing cloth?

4. *(Specialization)* Provide some examples of specialized markets or retail outlets. What makes the Web so conducive to specialization?

## 2-3 Outline how economies function as production systems

5. *(Shape of the PPF)* Suppose a production possibilities frontier includes the following combinations:

| Cars | Washing Machines |
|---|---|
| 0 | 1,000 |
| 100 | 600 |
| 200 | 0 |

a. Graph the PPF, assuming that it has no curved segments.
b. What is the cost of producing an additional car when 50 cars are being produced?

c. What is the cost of producing an additional car when 150 cars are being produced?
d. What is the cost of producing an additional washing machine when 50 cars are being produced? When 150 cars are being produced?
e. What do your answers tell you about opportunity costs?

6. *(Production Possibilities)* Suppose an economy uses two resources (labor and capital) to produce two goods (wheat and cloth). Capital is relatively more useful in producing cloth, and labor is relatively more useful in producing wheat. If the supply of capital falls by 10 percent and the supply of labor increases by 10 percent, how will the PPF for wheat and cloth change?

7. *(Production Possibilities)* There's no reason why a production possibilities frontier could not be used to represent the situation facing an individual. Imagine your own PPF. Right now—today—you have certain resources—your time, your skills, perhaps some capital. And you can produce various outputs. Suppose you can produce combinations of two outputs, call them studying and partying.
a. Draw your PPF for studying and partying. Be sure to label the axes of the diagram appropriately. Label the points where the PPF intersects the axes, as well as several other points along the frontier.
b. Explain what it would mean for you to move upward and to the left along your personal PPF. What kinds of adjustments would you have to make in your life to make such a movement along the frontier?
c. Under what circumstances would your personal PPF shift outward? Do you think the shift would be a "parallel" one? Why, or why not?

8. *(Shifting Production Possibilities)* Determine whether each of the following would cause the national economy's PPF to shift inward, outward, or not at all:
a. An increase in average length of annual vacations
b. An increase in immigration
c. A decrease in the average retirement age
d. The migration of skilled workers to other countries

## 2-4 Describe different economic systems and the decision-making rules that define them

9. *(Economic Systems)* The United States is best described as having a mixed economy. What are some elements of command in the U.S. economy? What are some market elements? What are some traditional elements?

# MICRO ECON ONLINE

## STUDY YOUR WAY WITH STUDYBITS!

Rate and Organize StudyBits

WEAK
FAIR
STRONG
UNASSIGNED

Collect What's Important

Create Flashcards From Your StudyBits

Track/Monitor Your Progress

85%

CORRECT
INCORRECT
INCORRECT
INCORRECT

Personalize Your Quizzes

4LTR PRESS

# 3 | Economic Decision Makers

## LEARNING OUTCOMES

After studying this chapter, you will be able to…

**3-1** Describe the major sources of income and expenditures for households

**3-2** Outline the evolution of production over the centuries from the household to the modern corporation

**3-3** Summarize the seven roles of government in an economy

**3-4** Explain why countries trade with each other and why they sometimes act to restrict that trade

After finishing this chapter go to **PAGE 54** for **STUDY TOOLS**

**Topics discussed in Chapter 3 include**

- Evolution of the household
- Evolution of the firm
- Types of firms
- Role of government
- Taxing and public spending
- International trade and finance

- If we live in the age of specialization, then why haven't specialists taken over all production?

- For example, why do most of us still do our own laundry and perform dozens of other tasks for ourselves?

- If the "invisible hand" of competitive markets is so efficient, why does government get into the act?

- And if specialization based on comparative advantage if such a good idea, why do most nations try to restrict imports?

*Answers to these and other questions are addressed in this chapter, which discusses the four economic decision makers: households, firms, governments, and the rest of the world.*

To develop a better feel for how the economy works, you must become more acquainted with the key players. You already know more about them than you may realize. You grew up in a household. You have dealt with firms all your life, from Sony to Subway. You know much about governments, from taxes to public schools. And you have a growing awareness of the rest of the world, from online sites, to imported goods, to foreign travel. This chapter draws on your abundant personal experience with economic decision makers to consider their makeup and objectives.

> **"If we live in the age of specialization, then why haven't specialists taken over all production?"**

## 3-1 THE HOUSEHOLD

Households play the starring role in a market economy. Their demand for goods and services determines what gets produced. And their supply of labor, capital, natural resources, and entrepreneurial ability produces that output. As demanders of goods and services and suppliers of resources, households make all kinds of choices, such as what to buy, how much to save, where to live, and where to work. Although a household usually consists of several individuals, we will view each household as a single decision maker.

### 3-1a The Evolution of the Household

In earlier times, when the economy was primarily agricultural, a farm household was largely self-sufficient. Each family member often specialized in a specific farm task—cooking meals, making clothes, tending livestock, planting crops, mending fences, and so on. These early households produced what they consumed and consumed what they produced. With the introduction of new seed varieties, better fertilizers, and labor-saving machinery, farm productivity increased sharply.

Fewer farmers were needed to grow enough food to feed a nation. At the same time, the growth of urban factories increased the demand for factory labor. As a result, many workers moved from farms to urban factories, where they became more specialized but less self-sufficient.

Households evolved in other ways. For example, in 1950, only about 15 percent of married women with young children were in the labor force. Since then,

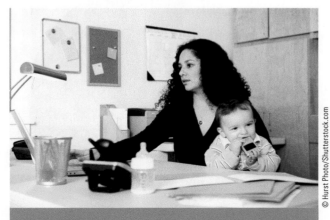

**Seventy percent of women with children under 18 are in the labor force.**

higher levels of education among women and a growing demand for their labor have increased women's earnings, thus raising their opportunity cost of working in the home. This higher opportunity cost contributed to their growing labor force participation. Today, about 70 percent of women with children under 18 are in the labor force.

The rise of two-earner households has reduced specialization in household production—a central feature of the farm family. Households now produce less for themselves and demand more from the market. For example, child-care services and fast-food restaurants have displaced some household production (Americans now consume at least one-third of their calories away from home). Nonetheless, some production still occurs in the home, as we'll explore later.

## 3-1b Households Maximize Utility

There are about 120 million U.S. households. All those who live together under one roof are considered part of the same household. What exactly do households attempt to accomplish in making decisions? Economists assume that people try to maximize their

**utility** The satisfaction received from consumption; sense of well-being

level of satisfaction, sense of well-being, happiness, and overall welfare. In short, households attempt to maximize **utility**. Households, like other economic decision makers, are viewed as rational, meaning that they try to act in their best interests and do not deliberately try to make themselves less happy. Utility maximization depends on each household's subjective goals, not on some objective standard. For example, some households maintain neat homes with well-groomed lawns; others pay little attention to their homes and use their lawns as junkyards.

## 3-1c Households As Resource Suppliers

Households use their limited resources—labor, capital, natural resources, and entrepreneurial ability—in an attempt to satisfy their unlimited wants. They can use these resources to produce goods and services in their homes. For example, they can cook, wash, sew, dust, iron, sweep, vacuum, mop, mow, paint, and fix a leaky faucet. They can also sell these resources in the resource market and use the income to buy goods and services in product markets. The most valuable resource sold by most households is labor.

Panel (a) of Exhibit 1 shows the sources of personal income received by U.S. households in 2014, when personal income totaled $14.9 trillion. As you can

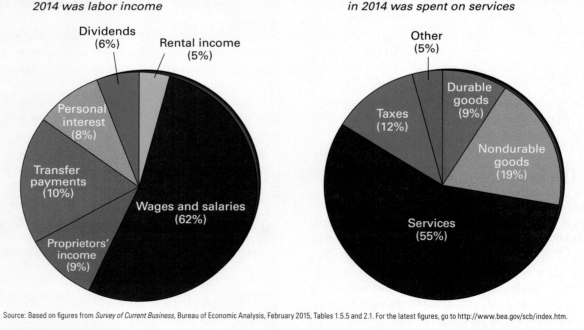

*Exhibit 1*

**Where U.S. Personal Income Comes From and Where It Goes**

**(a)** *More than two-thirds of personal income in 2014 was labor income*

Dividends (6%)
Rental income (5%)
Personal interest (8%)
Transfer payments (10%)
Wages and salaries (62%)
Proprietors' income (9%)

**(b)** *More than half of U.S. personal income in 2014 was spent on services*

Other (5%)
Durable goods (9%)
Taxes (12%)
Nondurable goods (19%)
Services (55%)

Source: Based on figures from *Survey of Current Business*, Bureau of Economic Analysis, February 2015, Tables 1.5.5 and 2.1. For the latest figures, go to http://www.bea.gov/scb/index.htm.

see, 62 percent of personal income came from wages and salaries. A distant second was transfer payments (to be discussed shortly), at 10 percent of personal income, followed by proprietors' income at 9 percent. *Proprietors* are people who work for themselves rather than for employers; farmers, plumbers, and doctors are often self-employed. Proprietors' income should also be considered a form of labor income. *Thus, more than two-thirds of personal income in the United States comes from labor earnings rather than from the ownership of other resources such as capital or natural resources.*

Because of a limited education, disability, discrimination, poor health, caring for small children, limited job opportunities, or just bad luck, some households have few resources that are valued in the market. Society has made the political decision that individuals in such circumstances should receive short-term public assistance. Consequently, the government gives some households **transfer payments**. *Cash transfers* are monetary payments, such as welfare benefits, Social Security, unemployment compensation, and disability benefits. *In-kind transfers* provide for specific goods and services, such as food, health care, and housing.

### 3-1d Households As Demanders of Goods and Services

What happens to personal income once it comes into the household? Most goes to personal consumption, which sorts into three broad spending categories: (1) *durable goods*—that is, goods expected to last three or more years—such as an automobile or a refrigerator; (2) *nondurable goods*, such as food, clothing, and gasoline; and (3) *services*, such as haircuts, air travel, and medical care. As you can see from panel (b) of Exhibit 1, spending on durable goods in 2014 claimed 9 percent of U.S. personal income; nondurables, 19 percent; and services, 55 percent. Taxes claimed 12 percent, and all other categories, including saving, claimed just 5 percent. So more than half of all personal income went for services—the fastest growing sector because many services, such as child care, are shifting from do-it-yourself home production to market purchases.

 **THE FIRM**

Household members once built their own homes, made their own clothes and furniture, grew their own food, and amused themselves with books, games, and hobbies. Over time, however, the efficiency arising from comparative

Specialization and comparative advantage explain why households are no longer self-sufficient.

advantage resulted in a greater specialization among resource suppliers. This section takes a look at firms, beginning with their evolution.

### 3-2a The Evolution of the Firm

Specialization and comparative advantage explain why households are no longer self-sufficient. But why is a firm the natural result? For example, rather than make a woolen sweater from scratch, couldn't a consumer take advantage of specialization by negotiating with someone who produced the wool, another who spun the wool into yarn, and a third who knit the yarn into a sweater? Here's the problem with that model: If the consumer had to visit each of these specialists and reach an agreement, the resulting *transaction costs* could easily erase the gains from specialization. Instead of visiting and bargaining with each specialist, the consumer can pay someone to do the bargaining—an entrepreneur, who hires all the resources necessary to make the sweater. *An entrepreneur, by contracting for many sweaters rather than just one, is able to reduce the transaction costs per sweater.*

**transfer payments**
Cash or in-kind benefits given to individuals by the government

For about 200 years, profit-seeking entrepreneurs relied on "putting out" raw material, like wool and cotton, to rural households that turned this into finished products, like woolen goods made from yarn. The system developed in the British Isles, where workers' cottages served as tiny factories, especially during winter months, when farming chores were few (so the opportunity cost was low). This approach, which came to be known as the *cottage industry system*, still exists in some parts of the world today. You might think of this system as partway between household self-sufficiency and the modern firm.

As the British economy expanded in the 18th century, entrepreneurs began organizing the stages of production under one factory roof. Technological developments, such as waterpower and later steam power, increased the productivity of each worker and helped shift employment from rural areas to urban factories. *Work, therefore, became organized in large, centrally powered factories that (1) promoted a more efficient division of labor, (2) allowed for the direct supervision of production, (3) reduced transportation costs, and (4) facilitated the use of machines far bigger than anything used in the home.* The development of large-scale factory production, known as the **Industrial Revolution**, began in Great Britain around 1750 and spread to the rest of Europe, North America, and Australia.

Production, then, evolved from self-sufficient rural households to the cottage industry system, where specialized production occurred in the household, to production in a firm. Today, entrepreneurs combine resources in firms such as factories, mills, offices, stores, and restaurants. **Firms** are economic units formed by profit-seeking entrepreneurs who combine labor, capital, and natural resources to produce goods and services. Just as we assume that households try to maximize utility, we assume that firms try to *maximize profit*. Profit, the entrepreneur's reward, equals sales revenue minus the cost of production, including the opportunity cost of the entrepreneur's time. Thus,

$$Profit = Revenue - Cost$$

**Industrial Revolution**
Development of large-scale factory production that began in Great Britain around 1750 and spread to the rest of Europe, North America, and Australia

**firms** Economic units formed by profit-seeking entrepreneurs who employ resources to produce goods and services for sale

**sole proprietorship** A firm with a single owner who has the right to all profits but who also bears unlimited liability for the firm's losses and debts

**partnership** A firm with multiple owners who share the profits and bear unlimited liability for the firm's losses and debts

## 3-2b Types of Firms

There are more than 30 million for-profit businesses in the United States. Two-thirds are small retail businesses, small service operations, part-time home-based businesses, and small farms. Each year more than a million new businesses start up and many existing firms fail. A firm is organized in one of three ways: as a sole proprietorship, as a partnership, or as a corporation.

### Sole Proprietorships

The simplest form of business organization is the **sole proprietorship**, a single-owner firm. Examples include self-employed plumbers, farmers, and dentists. Most sole proprietorships consist of just the self-employed proprietor—there are no hired employees. To organize a sole proprietorship, the owner simply opens for business by, for example, making a public announcement or taking out a classified ad announcing availability for plumbing services or whatever. The owner is in complete control. But he or she faces unlimited liability and could lose everything, including a home and other personal assets, to settle business debts or other claims against the business. Also, because the sole proprietor has no partners or other investors, raising enough money to get the business up and running and keep it going can be a challenge. One final disadvantage is that a sole proprietorship usually goes out of business when the proprietor dies or leaves the business. Still, a sole proprietorship is the most common type of business, accounting most recently for 71 percent of all U.S. businesses. Nonetheless, because this type of firm is typically small, proprietorships generate just a tiny portion of all U.S. business sales—only 4 percent. But keep in mind that many of the largest businesses in the world today began as an idea of a sole proprietor.

### Partnerships

A more complicated form of business is the **partnership**, which involves two or more individuals who agree to combine their funds and efforts in return for a share of any profit or loss. Law, accounting, and medical partnerships typify this business form. Partners have strength in numbers and often find it easier than sole proprietors to raise enough funds to get the business going. But partners may not always agree on what's best for the business. Also, each partner usually faces unlimited liability for any debts or claims against the partnership, so one partner could lose everything because of another partner's mistake. Finally, the death or departure of one partner can disrupt the firm's continuity and require a complete reorganization. The partnership is the least common form of U.S. business, making up only 10 percent of all firms and 15 percent of all business sales.

## Corporations

By far the most influential form of business is the corporation. A **corporation** is a legal entity established through articles of incorporation. Shares of stock confer corporate ownership, thereby entitling stockholders to a claim on any profit. A major advantage of the corporate form is that many investors—hundreds, thousands, even millions—can pool their funds, so incorporating represents the easiest way to amass large sums to get a business off the ground. Also, stockholders' liability for any loss is limited to the value of their stock, meaning stockholders enjoy *limited liability*. A final advantage of this form of organization is that the corporation has a life apart from its owners. The corporation survives even if ownership changes hands, and it can be taxed, sued, and even charged with a crime as if it were a person.

The corporate form has some disadvantages as well. A stockholder's ability to influence corporate policy is limited to voting for a board of directors, which oversees the operation of the firm. Each share of stock usually carries with it one vote. The typical stockholder of a large corporation owns only a tiny fraction of the shares and thus has little say. Whereas the income from sole proprietorships and partnerships is taxed only once, corporate income gets whacked twice—first as corporate profits and second as stockholder income, either as corporate dividends or as realized capital gains. A *realized capital gain* is any increase in the market price of a share that occurs between the time the share is purchased and the time it is sold.

A hybrid type of corporation has evolved to take advantage of the limited liability feature of the corporate structure while reducing the impact of double taxation. The *S corporation* provides owners with limited liability, but profits are taxed only once—as income on each shareholder's personal income tax return. To qualify as an S corporation, a firm must have no more than 100 stockholders and no foreign stockholders.

Corporations make up only 19 percent of all U.S. businesses, but because they tend to be much larger than the other two business forms, corporations account for 81 percent of all business sales. Exhibit 2 shows, by business type, the percentage of U.S. firms and the percentage of U.S. sales. *The sole proprietorship is the most important in sheer numbers, but the corporation is the most important in total sales.*

### 3-2c Cooperatives

A **cooperative**, or "co-op" for short, is a group of people who cooperate by pooling

**corporation** A legal entity owned by stockholders whose liability is limited to the value of their stock ownership

**cooperative** An organization consisting of people who pool their resources to buy and sell more efficiently than they could individually

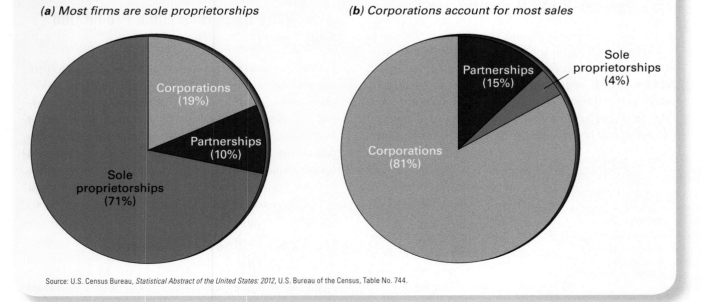

*Exhibit 2*

**Percent Distribution by Type of Firm Based on Number of Firms and Firm Sales**

**(a)** *Most firms are sole proprietorships*

Corporations (19%)
Partnerships (10%)
Sole proprietorships (71%)

**(b)** *Corporations account for most sales*

Partnerships (15%)
Sole proprietorships (4%)
Corporations (81%)

Source: U.S. Census Bureau, *Statistical Abstract of the United States: 2012*, U.S. Bureau of the Census, Table No. 744.

their resources to buy and sell more efficiently than they could independently. Cooperatives try to minimize costs and operate with limited liability of members. The government grants most cooperatives tax-exempt status. There are two types: consumer cooperatives and producer cooperatives.

## Consumer Cooperatives

A *consumer cooperative* is a retail business owned and operated by some or all of its customers in order to reduce costs. Some cooperatives require members to pay an annual fee and others require them to work a certain number of hours each year in the business. Members sometimes pay lower prices than other customers or may share in any revenues that exceed costs. In the United States, consumer cooperatives operate college book stores, credit unions, electric-power facilities, health plans, apartment buildings, and grocery stores.

## Producer Cooperatives

In a *producer cooperative,* producers join forces to buy supplies and equipment and to market their output. Each producer's objective is to reduce costs and increase profits. Federal legislation allows farmers to cooperate without violating antitrust laws (to be discussed later in the chapter). Firms in other industries could not do this legally. Farmers pool their funds to purchase machinery and supplies, provide storage and processing facilities, and transport products to market. Sunkist, for example, is a farm cooperative owned and operated by about 6,000 citrus growers in California and Arizona.

## 3-2d  Not-for-Profit Organizations

So far, you have learned about organizations that try to maximize profits or, in the case of cooperatives, to minimize costs. Some organizations have neither as a goal. **Not-for-profit organizations** engage in charitable, educational, humanitarian, cultural, professional, and other activities, often with a social purpose. Any revenue exceeding cost is plowed back into the organization. Government agencies do not have profit as a goal either, but governments are not included in this definition of not-for-profit organizations.

Like businesses, not-for-profit organizations evolved to help people accomplish their goals. Examples include nonprofit hospitals, private

**not-for-profit organizations** Groups that do not pursue profit as a goal; they engage in charitable, educational, humanitarian, cultural, professional, or other activities, often with a social purpose

Seafood Producers Cooperative (SPC) is a cooperative of over 500 fishermen who harvest their catch in the open ocean at the peak of quality.

schools and colleges, religious organizations, the Red Cross, Greenpeace, charitable foundations, soup kitchens, orchestras, museums, labor unions, and professional organizations. There are about 1.6 million not-for-profit organizations in the United States, and they employ about 12 million workers, or about 8 percent of the U.S. workforce. Not-for-profit hospitals are the largest employers. For example, the Texas Medical Center employs more than 100,000 people, surpassing employment at major corporations such as Apple, Chevron, or Google. But even not-for-profit organizations must somehow pay the bills. Revenue typically includes some combination of voluntary contributions and service charges, such as college tuition and hospital charges. In the United States, not-for-profit organizations are usually exempt from taxes.

## 3-2e  Why Does Household Production Still Exist?

If firms are so efficient at reducing transaction and production costs, why don't they make everything? Why do households still perform some tasks, such as cooking and cleaning? *If a household's opportunity cost of performing a task is below the market price, then the household usually performs that task.* People with a lower opportunity cost of time do more for themselves. For example, janitors are more likely to mow their lawns than are physicians. Let's look at some reasons for household production.

### No Skills or Special Resources Are Required

Some activities require so few skills or special resources that householders find it cheaper to do the jobs themselves. Sweeping the kitchen floor requires only a broom and some time, so it's usually performed by household members. Sanding a wooden floor, however, involves special machinery and expertise, so households hire professionals. Similarly, although you wouldn't hire someone to brush your teeth, dental work is not for amateurs. *Households usually perform domestic chores that demand neither expertise nor special machinery.*

## Household Production Avoids Taxes

Suppose you are deciding whether to pay someone $3,000 to paint your house or do it yourself. If the income tax rate is one-third, you must earn $4,500 before taxes to have the $3,000 after taxes to pay for the job. And the painter who charges you $3,000 nets only $2,000 after paying $1,000 in taxes. Thus, you must earn $4,500 so that the painter can take home $2,000. If you paint the house yourself, no taxes are involved. The tax-free nature of do-it-yourself activity favors household production over market transactions.

> **"Although you wouldn't hire someone to brush your teeth, dental work is not for amateurs."**

## Household Production Reduces Transaction Costs

Getting estimates, hiring a contractor, negotiating terms, and monitoring job performance all take time and require information. Doing the job yourself reduces these transaction costs. Household production also allows for more personal control over the final product than is usually available through the market. For example, some people prefer home cooking because they can prepare home-cooked meals to individual tastes.

Household production often grows during hard times. The economic recession of 2007–2009 prompted some families to shift from market purchases to household production to save money. For example, sales of hair clippers used for home haircuts increased 10 percent in 2008 and 11 percent in 2009.[1]

## Technological Advances Increase Household Productivity

Technological breakthroughs are not confined to market production. Vacuum cleaners, washers and dryers, dishwashers, microwave ovens, and other modern appliances reduce the time and often the skill required to perform household tasks. Also, new technologies such as DVRs, HDTVs, broadband downloads, and computer games enhance home entertainment. The **Information Revolution**

**Information Revolution**
Technological change spawned by the microchip and the Internet that enhanced the acquisition, analysis, and transmission of information

Do it yourself, or pay someone to do it for you?

BuildPix/Construction Photography/Alamy

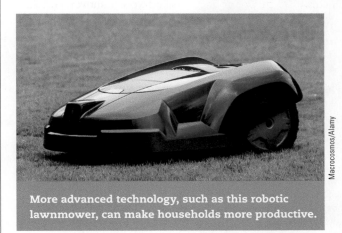

Macrocosmos/Alamy

More advanced technology, such as this robotic lawnmower, can make households more productive.

1. Mary Pilon, "Per Capita Saving: Home Barbering Grows in Recession," *Wall Street Journal*, 31 August 2009.

spawned by the microchip and the Internet has also enhanced the acquisition, analysis, and transmission of information. Indeed, microchip-based technologies have shifted some production from the firm back to the household. Because of technological change, more people can work from their homes.

##  THE GOVERNMENT

You might think that production by households and firms could satisfy all consumer wants. Why must yet another economic decision maker get into the act? After all, governments play some role in every nation on earth.

### 3-3a The Role of Government

Sometimes the unrestrained operation of markets yields undesirable results. Too many of some goods and too few of other goods get produced. This section discusses the sources of **market failure** and how society's overall welfare may be improved through government intervention in the market.

**market failure** A condition that arises when the unregulated operation of markets yields socially undesirable results

**antitrust laws** Prohibitions against price fixing and other anticompetitive practices

**monopoly** A sole supplier of a product with no close substitutes

**natural monopoly** One firm that can supply the entire market at a lower per-unit cost than could two or more firms

**private good** A good, such as pizza, that is both rival in consumption and exclusive

**public good** A good that, once produced, is available for all to consume, regardless of who pays and who doesn't; such a good is nonrival and nonexclusive, such as a safer community

#### Establishing and Enforcing the Rules of the Game

Market efficiency depends on people like you using your resources to maximize your utility. But what if you were repeatedly robbed of your paycheck on your way home from work? Or what if, after you worked two weeks in a new job, your boss called you a sucker and said you wouldn't get paid? Why bother working? The market system would break down if you could not safeguard your private property or if you could not enforce contracts. Governments safeguard private property through police protection and enforce contracts through a judicial system. More generally, governments try to make sure that market participants abide by the rules of the game —

that is, play fair. These rules are established through government laws and regulations and also through the customs and conventions of the marketplace. For example, the U.S. Bureau of Weights and Measures regulates the uniformity of measuring devices to promote confidence in market transactions and to ensure fairness between buyers and sellers in the marketplace.

### Promoting Competition

Although the "invisible hand" of competition usually promotes an efficient allocation of resources, some firms try to avoid competition through *collusion*, which is an agreement among firms to fix the price and carve up the market. Or an individual firm may try to eliminate the competition by using unfair business practices. For example, to drive out local competitors, a large firm may temporarily sell at a price below cost. Government **antitrust laws** try to promote competition by prohibiting collusion and other anticompetitive practices.

### Regulating Natural Monopolies

Competition usually keeps the product price below the price charged by a **monopoly**, a sole supplier to the market. In rare instances, however, a monopoly can produce and sell the product for less than could competing firms. For example, electricity is delivered more efficiently by a single firm that wires the community than by competing firms each stringing its own wires. When it is cheaper for one firm to serve the market than for two or more firms to do so, that one firm is called a **natural monopoly**. Since a natural monopoly faces no competition, it maximizes profit by charging a higher price than would be optimal from society's point of view. A lower price and greater output would improve social welfare. Therefore, the government usually regulates a natural monopoly, forcing it to lower its price and increase output.

### Providing Public Goods

So far this book has been talking about private goods, which have two important features. First, private goods are *rival* in consumption, meaning that the amount consumed by one person is unavailable for others to consume. For example, when you and some friends share a pizza, each slice they eat is no longer available for you. Second, the supplier of a private good can easily exclude those who fail to pay. Only paying customers get pizza. Thus, private goods are said to be *exclusive*. So **private goods**, such as pizza, are both rival in consumption and exclusive. In contrast, **public goods** are *nonrival* in consumption. For example, your family's benefit from a safer neighborhood does not reduce your neighbor's benefit. What's more, once produced, public goods are available to all. Suppliers cannot easily prevent consumption by those who fail to pay. For example, reducing terrorism is *nonexclusive*. It benefits all in the community, regardless of who pays to reduce terrorism and who doesn't. Because public goods are *nonrival* and *nonexclusive*, private firms cannot sell them profitably. The government, however, has the authority to enforce tax collections for public goods. Thus, the government provides public goods and funds them with taxes.

## Dealing With Externalities

Market prices reflect the private costs and private benefits of producers and consumers. But sometimes production or consumption imposes costs or benefits on third parties—on those who are neither suppliers nor demanders in a market transaction. For example, a paper mill fouls the air breathed by nearby residents, but the price of paper usually fails to reflect such costs. Because these pollution costs are outside, or external to, the market, they are called *externalities*. An **externality** is a cost or a benefit that falls on a third party. A negative externality imposes an external cost, such as factory pollution, auto emissions, or traffic congestion. A positive externality confers an external benefit, such as getting a good education, getting inoculated against a disease (thus reducing the possibility of infecting others), or driving carefully. Because market prices usually do not reflect externalities, governments often use taxes, subsidies, and regulations to discourage negative externalities and encourage positive externalities. For example, a polluting factory may face taxes and regulations aimed at curbing that pollution. And because more educated people can read road signs and have options that pay better than crime, governments try to encourage education with free public schools, subsidized higher education, and by keeping people in school until their 16th birthdays.

## A More Equal Distribution of Income

As mentioned earlier, some people, because of poor education, mental or physical disabilities, bad luck, or perhaps the need to care for small children, are unable to support themselves and their families. Because resource markets do not guarantee even a minimum level of

> **"**The supplier of a private good can easily exclude those who fail to pay.**"**

income, transfer payments reflect society's willingness to ensure a basic standard of living to all households. Most Americans agree that government should redistribute income to the poor (note the normative nature of this statement). Opinions differ about who should receive benefits, how much they should get, what form benefits should take, and how long benefits should last.

## Full Employment, Price Stability, and Economic Growth

Perhaps the most important responsibility of government is fostering a healthy economy, which benefits just about everyone. The government—through its ability to tax, to spend, and to control the money supply—attempts to promote full employment, price stability, and economic growth. Pursuing these objectives by taxing and spending is called **fiscal policy**. Pursuing them by regulating the money supply is called **monetary policy**. Macroeconomics examines both policies.

## 3-3b Government's Structure and Objectives

The United States has a *federal system* of government, meaning that responsibilities are shared across levels of government. State governments grant some powers to local governments and surrender some powers to the national, or federal, government. As the system has evolved, the federal government has primary responsibility for national security, economic stability, and promoting market competition. State governments fund public higher education, prisons, and—with aid from the federal government—highways and welfare. Local governments provide primary and secondary education with aid from the state, plus police and fire protection. Here are some distinguishing features of government.

**externality** A cost or a benefit that affects neither the buyer nor seller, but instead affects people not involved in the market transaction

**fiscal policy** The use of government purchases, transfer payments, taxes, and borrowing to influence economy-wide variables such as inflation, employment, and economic growth

**monetary policy** Regulation of the money supply to influence economy-wide variables such as inflation, employment, and economic growth

## Difficulty in Defining Government Objectives

We assume that households try to maximize utility and firms try to maximize profit, but what about governments—or, more specifically, what about government decision makers? What do they try to maximize? One problem is that our federal system consists of not one but many governments—approximately 89,150 separate jurisdictions in all, including 1 nation, 50 states, 3,000 counties, 36,000 cities and towns, 12,900 school districts, and 37,200 special districts. What's more, because the federal government relies on offsetting, or countervailing, powers across the executive, legislative, and judicial branches, government does not act as a single, consistent decision maker. Even within the federal executive branch, there are so many agencies and bureaus that at times they seem to work at cross-purposes. For example, at the same time as the U.S. Surgeon General required health warnings on cigarette packages, the U.S. Department of Agriculture pursued policies to benefit tobacco growers. Given this thicket of jurisdictions, branches, and bureaus, one useful theory of government behavior is that elected officials try to maximize the number of votes they get in the next election. So let's assume that elected officials are vote maximizers. In this theory, vote maximization guides the decisions of elected officials who, in turn, oversee government employees.

## Voluntary Exchange Versus Coercion

Market exchange relies on the voluntary behavior of buyers and sellers. Don't like tofu? No problem— don't buy any. But in political markets, the situation is different. Any voting rule except unanimous consent must involve some government coercion. Public choices are enforced by the police power of the state. Those who don't pay their taxes could go to prison, even though they may object to some programs those taxes support, such as capital punishment or certain military actions.

## No Market Prices

Another distinguishing feature of governments is that public output is usually offered at either a zero price or at some price below the cost of providing it. If you now pay in-state tuition at a public college or university, your tuition probably covers only about half the state's cost of providing your education. Because the revenue side of the government budget is usually separate from the expenditure side, there is no necessary link between the cost of a program and the benefit.

In the private sector, the expected marginal benefit of a product is at least as great as its price; otherwise, nobody would buy it.

## 3-3c The Size and Growth of Government

One way to track the impact of government over time is by measuring government outlays relative to the U.S. *gross domestic product,* or *GDP,* which is the total value of all final goods and services produced in the United States. In 1929, the year the Great Depression began, all government outlays, mostly by state and local governments, totaled about 10 percent of GDP. At the time, the federal government played a minor role. In fact, during the nation's first 150 years, federal outlays, except during war years, never exceeded 3 percent relative to GDP.

The Great Depression, World War II, a change in macroeconomic thinking, and extraordinary measures following the financial crisis of 2008 boosted the share of government outlays to 38 percent of GDP in 2016, with about two-thirds of that by the federal government. In comparison, government outlays relative to GDP that year were 39 percent in Canada and Japan, 41 percent in the United Kingdom, 44 percent in the Germany, 50 percent in Italy, and 56 percent in France. Government outlays by 31 advanced industrial economies averaged 40 percent of GDP in 2016.[2] Thus, government outlays in the United States relative to GDP are slightly below the average of advanced economies.

Let's look briefly at the composition of federal outlays. Since 1960, defense spending has declined from over half of federal outlays to less than one-fifth by 2016, as shown in Exhibit 3. Redistribution—Social Security, Medicare, and welfare programs—has been the mirror image of defense spending, jumping from only about one-fifth of federal outlays in 1960 more than to half by 2016.

## 3-3d Sources of Government Revenue

Taxes provide the bulk of revenue at all levels of government. The federal government relies primarily on the individual income tax, state governments rely on income and sales taxes, and local governments rely on the property tax. Other revenue sources include user charges, such as highway tolls and college tuition, and borrowing. For additional revenue, some states also act as monopolies in certain markets, such as selling lottery tickets and liquor.

2. The Organization of Economic Cooperation and Development, *OECD Economic Outlook,* 97 (May 2015), Total Disbursements, General Government, as a Percent of GDP, at http://stats.oecd.org/index.aspx?queryid=51396.

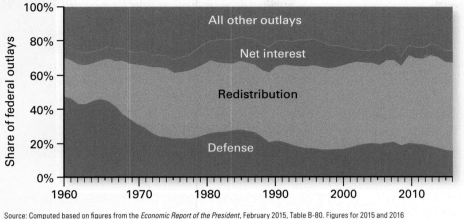

*Exhibit 3*

**Redistribution Has Grown and Defense Has Declined as Share of Federal Outlays: 1960–2016**

Source: Computed based on figures from the *Economic Report of the President*, February 2015, Table B-80. Figures for 2015 and 2016 are estimates based on the President's budget. For the latest figures, go to http://www.whitehouse.gov/administration/eop/cea/economic-report -of-the-President.

Exhibit 4 focuses on the composition of federal revenue since 1960. The share made up by the individual income tax has remained relatively steady, ranging from a low of 42 percent in the mid-1960s to a high of 50 percent in 2001, before averaging about 47 percent from 2011 to 2016. The share from payroll taxes doubled from 16 percent in 1960 to 32 percent in 2016. *Payroll taxes* are deducted from paychecks to support Social Security and Medicare, which fund retirement income and medical care for the elderly. Corporate taxes and revenue from other sources, such as excise (sales) taxes and user charges, have declined as a share of federal revenue since 1960.

## 3-3e Tax Principles and Tax Incidence

The structure of a tax is often justified on the basis of one of two general principles. First, a tax could relate to the individual's ability to pay, so those with a greater ability pay more taxes. Income or property taxes often rely on this **ability-to-pay tax principle**. Alternatively, the **benefits-received tax principle** relates taxes to the benefits taxpayers receive from the government activity funded by the tax. For example, the tax on gasoline funds highway construction and maintenance, thereby linking tax payment to road use, since those who drive more pay more gas taxes.

**Tax incidence** indicates who actually bears the burden of the tax. One way to evaluate tax incidence is by measuring the tax as a percentage of income. Under

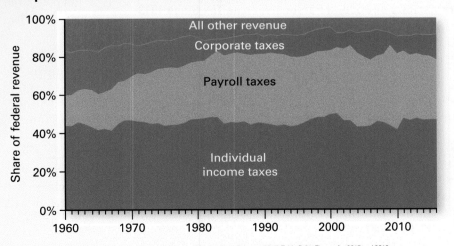

*Exhibit 4*

**Composition of Federal Revenue Between 1960 and 2016**

Source: Computed based on figures from the *Economic Report of the President*, February 2015, Table B-21. Figures for 2015 and 2016 are projections based on the President's budget. For the latest figures, go to http://www.whitehouse.gov/administration/eop/cea/economic-report-of -the-President.

**ability-to-pay tax principle** Those with a greater ability to pay, such as those earning higher incomes or those owning more property, should pay more taxes

**benefits-received tax principle** Those who get more benefits from the government program should pay more taxes

**tax incidence** The distribution of tax burden among taxpayers; who ultimately pays the tax

**proportional taxation**, taxpayers at all income levels pay the same percentage of their income in taxes. A proportional income tax is also called a *flat tax*, since the tax as a percentage of income remains constant, or flat, as income increases. Note that under proportional taxation, although taxes remain constant as a percentage of income, the dollar amount of taxes increases proportionately as income increases.

Under **progressive taxation**, the percentage of income paid in taxes increases as income increases. The **marginal tax rate** indicates the percentage of each additional dollar of income that goes to taxes. Because high marginal rates reduce the after-tax return from working or investing, high marginal rates can reduce people's incentives to work and invest. The seven marginal rates applied to the U.S. personal income tax in 2015 ranged from 10 to 39.6 percent.

The top marginal tax bracket each year during the history of the personal income tax is shown by Exhibit 5. Although the top rate is now lower than it was during most other years, high-income households still pay most of the federal income tax collected. More than 40 percent of U.S. households pay no federal income taxes. According to the U.S. Internal Revenue Service, the top 1 percent of tax filers, based on income, paid 38 percent of all income taxes collected in 2012. Their average tax rate was 23.5 percent. And the top 10 percent of tax filers paid 70 percent of all income taxes collected. Their average tax rate was 18.7 percent. In contrast, the bottom 50 percent of tax filers paid only 2.8 percent of

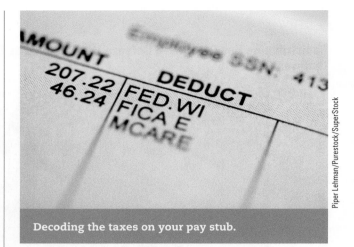

Decoding the taxes on your pay stub.

all income taxes collected. Their tax rate averaged only 3.0 percent. Whether we look at marginal tax rates or average tax rates, the U.S. income tax is progressive. High-income filers pay the overwhelming share of income taxes.

Finally, under **regressive taxation**, the percentage of income paid in taxes decreases as income increases, so the marginal tax rate declines as income increases. Most U.S. *payroll taxes* are regressive, because they impose a flat rate up to a certain level of income, above which the marginal rate drops to zero. For example, Social Security taxes were levied on the first $118,500 of workers' pay in 2015. Employers pay 6.2 percent and employees pay 6.2 percent (the self-employed pay the entire 12.4 percent).

**proportional taxation**
The tax as a percentage of income remains constant as income increases; also called a flat tax

**progressive taxation**
The tax as a percentage of income increases as income increases

**marginal tax rate** The percentage of each additional dollar of income that goes to the tax

**regressive taxation**
The tax as a percentage of income decreases as income increases

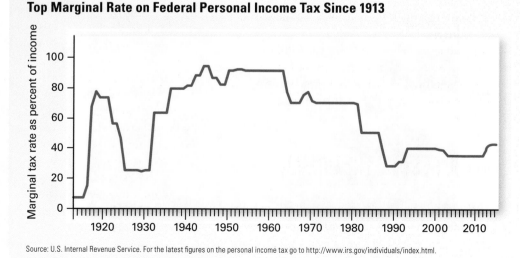

*Exhibit 5*

**Top Marginal Rate on Federal Personal Income Tax Since 1913**

Source: U.S. Internal Revenue Service. For the latest figures on the personal income tax go to http://www.irs.gov/individuals/index.html.

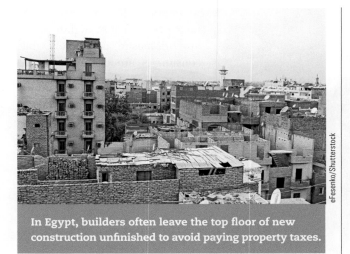

In Egypt, builders often leave the top floor of new construction unfinished to avoid paying property taxes.

eFesenko/Shutterstock

Taxes often do more than fund public programs. Some taxes discourage certain activity. For example, a pollution tax can help clean the air. A tax on gasoline can encourage people to work at home, carpool, or use public transportation. Some taxes have unintended consequences. For example, in Egypt a property tax is not imposed until a new building is completed. To avoid such taxes, builders never finish the job; multistory dwellings are usually missing the top floor. As another example of how taxes can distort the allocation of resources, property taxes in Amsterdam and Vietnam were originally based on the width of the building. As a result, buildings there are extremely narrow. As a final example, in 1696 England levied a property tax based on a dwelling's number of windows. As a consequence, property owners boarded up existing windows and new dwellings had fewer widows. These actions cut ventilation and light, creating health hazards, yet the tax persisted for more than 150 years.[3] Such taxes have unintended consequences distort the efficient allocation of resources.

This discussion of revenue sources brings to a close, for now, our examination of the role of government in the U.S. economy. Government has a pervasive influence on the economy, and its role is discussed throughout the book.

## 3-4 THE REST OF THE WORLD

So far, the focus has been on institutions within the United States—that is, on *domestic* households, firms, and governments. This focus is appropriate because

3. Wallace E. Oates and Robert M. Schwab, "The Window Tax: A Case of Excess Burden," *Journal of Economic Perspectives*, 29 (Winter 2015): 163–180.

our primary objective is to understand the workings of the U.S. economy, still the largest in the world. But the rest of the world affects what U.S. households consume and what U.S. firms produce. For example, Japan and China supply all kinds of manufactured goods to America, thereby affecting U.S. prices, wages, and profits. Likewise, political events in the Middle East can affect what Americans pay for oil. Foreign decision makers, therefore, influence the U.S. economy—what we produce and what we consume. The *rest of the world* consists of the households, firms, and governments in the other 200 or so sovereign nations throughout the world.

### 3-4a International Trade

In the previous chapter, you learned about comparative advantage and the gains from specialization. These gains explain why householders stopped doing everything for themselves and began to specialize. International trade arises for the same reasons. *International trade occurs because the opportunity cost of producing specific goods differs across countries.* Americans import raw materials like crude oil, bauxite (aluminum ore), and coffee beans and finished goods like cameras, computers, and cut diamonds. U.S. producers export sophisticated products like computer software, aircraft, and movies, as well as agricultural products like wheat, corn, and cotton. Farm exports are why America has long been called the "breadbasket of the world."

Trade between the United States and the rest of the world has increased in recent decades. In 1970, U.S. exports of goods and services amounted to only 6 percent of the gross domestic product. That has increased to about 14 percent today. The top 10 destinations for U.S. exports in order of importance are Canada, Mexico, China, Japan, the United Kingdom, Germany, the Netherlands, South Korea, France, and Brazil.

The **merchandise trade balance** equals the value of exported goods minus the value of imported goods. Goods in this case are distinguished from services, which show up in another trade account. For the last quarter century, the United States has imported more goods than it has exported, resulting in a merchandise trade deficit. Just as a household must pay for its spending, so too must a nation. The merchandise trade deficit must be offset by a surplus in one or more of the other *balance-of-payments* accounts. A nation's

**merchandise trade balance** The value during a given period of a country's exported goods minus the value of its imported goods

**balance of payments** is the record of all economic transactions between its residents and residents of the rest of the world.

### 3-4b Exchange Rates

The lack of a common currency complicates trade between countries. How many U.S. dollars buy a Porsche? An American buyer cares only about the dollar cost; the German carmaker cares only about the *euros* received (the common currency of 19 European countries). To facilitate trade funded by different currencies, a market for foreign exchange has developed. **Foreign exchange** is foreign currency needed to carry out international transactions. The supply and demand for foreign exchange comes together in *foreign exchange markets* to determine the exchange rate. The *exchange rate* measures the price of one currency in terms of another. For example, the exchange rate between the euro and the dollar might indicate that one euro exchanges for $1.10. At that exchange rate, a Porsche selling for €100,000 costs $110,000. The exchange rate affects the prices of imports and exports, and thus helps shape the flow of foreign trade.

### 3-4c Trade Restrictions

Despite clear gains from international specialization and exchange, nearly all nations restrict trade to some extent. These restrictions can take the form of (1) **tariffs**, which are taxes on imports; (2) **quotas**, which are limits on the quantity of a particular good that can be imported or exported; and (3) other trade restrictions. If specialization according to comparative advantage is so beneficial, why do most countries restrict trade? Restrictions benefit certain domestic producers that lobby governments for these benefits. For example, U.S. growers of sugarcane have benefited from legislation restricting sugar imports, thereby raising U.S. sugar prices. These higher prices hurt domestic consumers, but consumers are usually unaware of this harm. Trade restrictions interfere with the free flow of products across borders and tend to hurt the overall economy.

Seregam/Shutterstock.com

### 3-5 FINAL WORD

This chapter examined the four economic decision makers: households, firms, governments, and the rest of the world. Domestic households are by far the most important, for they supply resources and demand goods and services.

If you were to stop reading right now, you would already know more economics than most people. But to understand market economies, you must learn how markets work. The next chapter introduces demand and supply.

---

**balance of payments**
A record of all economic transactions during a given period between residents of one country and residents of the rest of the world

**foreign exchange** Foreign money needed to carry out international transactions

**tariff** A tax on imports

**quota** A legal limit on the quantity of a particular product that can be imported or exported

---

# STUDY TOOLS 3

### READY TO STUDY? IN THE BOOK, YOU CAN:

☐ Work the Problems at the end of the chapter.

☐ Rip out the chapter review card for a handy summary of the chapter and key terms.

### ONLINE AT CENGAGEBRAIN.COM YOU CAN:

☐ Collect StudyBits while you read and study the chapter.

☐ Quiz yourself on key concepts.

☐ Prepare for tests with chapter flash cards as well as flash cards that you create.

☐ Watch videos to explore economics further.

# CHAPTER 3 PROBLEMS

*Your instructor can access the answers to these problems online at http://cengagebrain.com.*

## 3-1 Describe the major sources of income and expenditures for households

1. *(Evolution of the Household)* Determine whether each of the following would increase or decrease the opportunity costs for mothers who decide not to work outside the home. Explain your answers.
   a. Higher levels of education for women
   b. Higher unemployment rates for women
   c. Higher average pay levels for women
   d. Lower demand for labor in industries that traditionally employ women

2. *(Household Production)* Many households supplement their food budget by cultivating small vegetable gardens. Explain how each of the following might influence this kind of household production:
   a. Both husband and wife are professionals who earn high salaries.
   b. The household is located in a city rather than in a rural area.
   c. The household is located in a region where there is a high sales tax on food purchases.
   d. The household is located in a region that has a high property tax rate.

3. *(Household Production)* What factors does a householder consider when deciding whether to produce a good or service at home versus buy it in the marketplace?

4. *(Objectives of the Economic Decision Makers)* In economic analysis, what are the assumed objectives of households, firms, and the government?

## 3-2 Outline the evolution of production over the centuries from the household to the modern corporation

5. *(Corporations)* How did the institution of the firm get a boost from the advent of the Industrial Revolution? What type of business organization existed before this?

6. *(Sole Proprietorships)* What are the disadvantages of the sole proprietorship form of business?

7. *(Cooperatives)* How do cooperatives differ from typical businesses?

8. *(Evolution of the Firm)* Explain how production after the Industrial Revolution differed from production under the cottage industry system.

## 3-3 Summarize the seven roles of government in an economy

9. *(Government)* Complete each of the following sentences:
   a. Goods that are nonrival and nonexcludable are known as _____.
   b. _____ are cash or in-kind benefits given to individuals as outright grants from the government.
   c. A(n) _____ confers an external benefit on third parties that are not directly involved in the market transaction.
   d. _____ refers to the government's pursuit of full employment and price stability through variations in taxes and government spending.

10. *(Tax Rates)* Suppose taxes are related to income as follows:

    | Income | Taxes |
    |--------|-------|
    | $1,000 | $200 |
    | $2,000 | $350 |
    | $3,000 | $450 |

    a. What percentage of income is paid in taxes at each level?
    b. Is the tax rate progressive, proportional, or regressive?
    c. What is the marginal tax rate on the first $1,000 of income?
    The second $1,000? The third $1,000?

11. *(Government Revenue)* What are the sources of government revenue in the United States? Which types of taxes are most important at each level of government? Which two taxes provide the most revenue to the federal government?

12. *(Externalities)* Suppose there is an external cost, or negative externality, associated with production of a certain good. What's wrong with letting the market determine how much of this good will be produced?

## 3-4 Explain why countries trade with each other and why they sometimes act to restrict that trade

13. *(International Trade)* Why does international trade occur? What does it mean to run a deficit in the merchandise trade balance?

14. *(International Trade)* Distinguish between a tariff and a quota. Who benefits from and who is harmed by such restrictions on imports?

# 4 | Demand, Supply, and Markets

Stockbyte/Getty Images

## LEARNING OUTCOMES

After studying this chapter, you will be able to…

4-1  Explain why a demand curve slopes downward

4-2  Identify five things which could shift a demand curve to the right or left

4-3  Explain why a supply curve usually slopes upward

4-4  Identify five things which could shift a supply curve to the right or left

4-5  Explain why surpluses push prices down while shortages drive prices up

4-6  Predict the impact of a change in demand or supply on the equilibrium price and quantity

4-7  Describe the result of a government-set price floor and price ceiling on a market

After finishing this chapter go to PAGE 72 for STUDY TOOLS

**Topics discussed in Chapter 4 include**

- Demand and quantity demanded
- Movement along a demand curve
- Shift of a demand curve
- Supply and quantity supplied
- Movement along a supply curve
- Shift of a supply curve
- Markets and equilibrium
- Disequilibrium

- ▶ Why do roses cost more on Valentine's Day than during the rest of the year?
- ▶ Why do TV ads cost more during the Super Bowl ($4.5 million for 30 seconds in 2015) than during *Nick* at *Nite* reruns?
- ▶ Why do hotel room rates double in the host city during Super Bowl weekend?

- ▶ Why do surgeons earn more than butchers?
- ▶ Why do economics majors earn more than most other majors?

*Answers to these and most other economic questions boil down to the workings of demand and supply—the subject of this chapter.*

This chapter introduces demand and supply and shows how they interact in competitive markets. *Demand and supply are the most fundamental and the most powerful of all economic tools*—important enough to warrant a chapter. Indeed, some believe that if you program a computer to answer "demand and supply" to every economic question, you could put many economists out of work. An understanding of the two ideas will take you far in mastering the art and science of economic analysis. Because of the subject matter, this chapter uses more graphs than previous chapters, so you may need to review the Chapter 1 appendix as a refresher.

> " Why do roses cost more on Valentine's Day than during the rest of the year? "

## 4-1 DEMAND

How many six-packs of Pepsi will people buy each month at a price of $4? What if the price is $3? What if it's $5? The answers reveal the relationship between the price of a six-pack and the quantity of Pepsi demanded. Such a relationship is called the *demand* for Pepsi. **Demand** indicates the quantity consumers are both *willing and able* to buy at each price during a given time period, other things constant. Because demand pertains to a specific period—a day, a week, a month—think of demand as the *amounts purchased per period* at each price. Also, notice the emphasis on *willing and able*. You may be *able* to buy a new Harley-Davidson Sportster Forty-Eight that lists for $10,749 because you can afford one, but you may not be *willing* to buy one if motorcycles just don't interest you.

### 4-1a Law of Demand

In 1962, Sam Walton opened his first store in Rogers, Arkansas, with a sign that read, "Wal-Mart Discount City. We sell for less." Now called Walmart, this store chain sells more than any other retailer in the world because prices there are among the lowest around. As a consumer, you understand why people buy more at a lower price. Sell for less, and the world will beat a path to your door. Walmart, for example, sells on average over 20,000 pairs of shoes *an hour*. This relation between the price and the quantity demanded is an economic law. The **law of demand** says that the quantity of a good that consumers are willing and able to buy per period varies inversely, or negatively, with the price, other things equal. Thus, the higher the price, the smaller the quantity demanded; the lower the price, the greater the quantity demanded.

### Demand, Wants, and Needs

Consumer demand and consumer wants are not the same. As we have seen, wants are unlimited. You may want a new Mercedes-Benz SL65 Roadster convertible, but the $215,250 price tag is likely beyond your budget (that is, the quantity you demand at that price is zero). Nor is

**demand** A relation between the price of a good and the quantity that consumers are willing and able to buy per period, other things constant

**law of demand** The quantity of a good that consumers are willing and able to buy per period relates inversely, or negatively, to the price, other things constant demand the same as need. You may need a new muffler for your car, but a price of $300 is just too high for you right now. If, however, the price drops enough—say, to $200—then you may be both willing and able to buy one.

## Substitution Effect of a Price Change

What explains the law of demand? Why, for example, does the quantity demanded increase as the price declines? The explanation begins with unlimited wants confronting scarce resources. Many goods and services can help satisfy particular wants. For example, you can satisfy your hunger with pizza, tacos, burgers, chicken, or hundreds of other foods. Similarly, you can satisfy your desire for warmth in the winter with warm clothing, a home heating system, a trip to Hawaii, or in many other ways. Clearly, some alternatives are more appealing than others (a trip to Hawaii is more fun than warm clothing). In a world without scarcity, everything would be free, so you would always choose the most attractive alternative. Scarcity, however, is the reality, and the degree of scarcity of one good relative to another helps determine each good's relative price.

**substitution effect of a price change** When the price of a good falls, that good becomes cheaper compared to other goods so consumers tend to substitute that good for other goods

**money income** The number of dollars a person receives per period, such as $400 per week

**real income** Income measured by the goods and services it can buy; real income changes when the price changes

**income effect of a price change** A fall in the price of a good increases consumers' real income, making consumers more able to purchase goods; for a normal good, the quantity demanded increases

Notice that the definition of *demand* includes the other-things-constant assumption. Among the "other things" assumed to remain constant are the prices of other goods. For example, if the price of pizza declines while other prices remain constant, pizza becomes relatively cheaper. Consumers are more *willing* to purchase pizza when its relative price falls; they substitute pizza for other goods. This idea is called the **substitution effect of a price change**. On the other hand, an increase in the price of pizza, other things constant, increases the opportunity cost of pizza—that is, the amount of other goods you must give up to buy pizza. This higher opportunity cost causes some consumers to substitute

> **"Sell for less, and the world will beat a path to your door."**

other goods for the now higher-priced pizza, thus reducing their quantity of pizza demanded. Remember that *it is the change in the relative price—the price of one good relative to the prices of other goods—that causes the substitution effect*. If all prices changed by the same percentage, there would be no change in relative prices and no substitution effect.

## Income Effect of a Price Change

A fall in the price of a good increases the quantity demanded for a second reason. Suppose you earn $30 a week from a part-time job, so $30 is your money income. **Money income** is simply the number of dollars received per period, in this case, $30 per week. Suppose you spend all that on pizza, buying three a week at $10 each. What if the price drops to $6? At that lower price, you can now afford five pizzas a week. Your money income remains at $30 per week, but the price drop increases your **real income**—that is, your income measured by what it can buy. The price reduction, other things constant, increases the purchasing power of your income, thereby increasing your *ability* to buy pizza. The quantity you demand will likely increase because of the **income effect of a price change**. You may not increase your quantity demanded to five pizzas, but you could. If you decide to purchase four pizzas a week when the price drops to $6, you would still have $6 remaining to buy other stuff. Thus, the income effect of a lower price increases your real income and thereby increases your ability to buy pizza and other goods, making you better off. The income effect is reflected in Walmart's slogan, which trumpets low prices: "Save money. Live better." Because of the income effect, consumers typically increase their quantity demanded when the price declines.

Conversely, an increase in the price of pizza, other things constant, reduces real income, thereby reducing your ability to buy pizza and other goods. Because of the income effect, consumers typically reduce their quantity demanded when the price increases. The more important the item is as a share of your budget, the bigger the income effect. That's why, for example, consumers cut back on a variety of purchases when the price of gasoline spikes, as it did in 2012. And why those same consumers increase spending on a variety of goods when the price of gasoline falls, as it did in late 2014 and early 2015. Again, note that money income, not real income, is assumed to remain constant along a demand curve. Because a change in price changes your real income, real income varies along a demand curve. The lower the price, the greater your real income.

## 4-1b Demand Schedule and Demand Curve

Demand can be expressed as a *demand schedule* or as a *demand curve*. Panel (a) of Exhibit 1 shows a hypothetical demand schedule for pizza. In describing demand, we must specify the units measured and the period considered. In our example, the unit is a 12-inch regular pizza and the period is a week. The schedule lists possible prices, along with the quantity demanded at each

### Exhibit 1

#### Market Demand Schedule and Market Demand Curve for Pizza

The market demand curve D shows the quantity of pizza demanded, at various prices, by all consumers. Price and quantity demanded are inversely related to other things constant, reflecting the law of demand.

### (a) Demand schedule

|   | Price per Pizza | Quantity Demanded per Week (millions) |
|---|---|---|
| a | $15 | 8 |
| b | 12 | 14 |
| c | 9 | 20 |
| d | 6 | 26 |
| e | 3 | 32 |

### (b) Demand curve

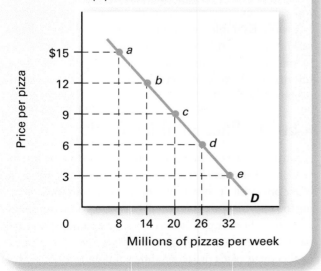

Millions of pizzas per week

price. At a price of $15, for example, consumers demand 8 million pizzas per week. As you can see, the lower the price, other things constant, the greater the quantity demanded. Consumers substitute pizza for other foods. And as the price falls, real income increases, causing consumers to increase the quantity of pizza they demand. If the price drops as low as $3, consumers demand 32 million per week.

The demand schedule in panel (a) appears as a **demand curve** in panel (b), with price measured on the vertical axis and the quantity demanded per week on the horizontal axis. Each price-quantity combination listed in the demand schedule in the left panel becomes a point in the right panel. Point *a*, for example, indicates that if the price is $15, consumers demand 8 million pizzas per week. Connecting points forms the demand curve for pizza, labeled *D*. (By the way, some demand curves are straight lines, some are curved lines, and some are even crooked lines, but for simplicity they all are called demand *curves*.)

A demand curve slopes downward, reflecting the *law of demand:* Price and quantity demanded are inversely related, other things constant. Besides money income, also assumed constant along the demand curve are the prices of other goods. Thus, along the demand curve, the price of pizza changes *relative to the prices of other goods*. The demand curve therefore shows the effect of a change in the *relative price* of pizza—that is, relative to other prices, which do not change.

Take care to distinguish between *demand* and *quantity demanded*. The *demand* for pizza is not a specific amount, but rather the *entire relationship* between price and quantity demanded—represented by the demand schedule or the demand curve. An individual point on the demand curve indicates the **quantity demanded** at a particular price. For example, at a price of $12, the quantity demanded is 14 million pizzas per week. If the price drops from $12 to, say, $9, this is shown in Exhibit 1 by *a movement along the demand curve*—in this case from point *b* to point *c*. Any movement along a demand curve reflects a *change in quantity demanded*, not a change in demand. Got that?

The law of demand applies to the millions of products sold by grocery stores, department stores, clothing stores, shoe stores, drugstores, music stores, bookstores, hardware stores, other retailers,

**demand curve** A curve showing the relation between the price of a good and the quantity consumers are willing and able to buy per period, other things constant

**quantity demanded** The amount of a good consumers are willing and able to buy per period at a particular price, as reflected by a point on a demand curve travel agencies, and restaurants, as well as through mail-order catalogs, Craigslist, classified ads, online sites, stock markets, real estate markets, job markets, flea markets, yard sales, and all other markets. The law of demand applies even to choices that seem more personal than economic, such as whether or not to own a pet. For example, after New York City passed an anti-dog-litter law, law-abiding owners had to follow their dogs around the city with scoopers, plastic bags—whatever would do the job. Because the law in effect raised the personal cost of owning a dog, the quantity of dogs demanded decreased. Some dogs were abandoned, increasing strays in the city. The number of dogs left at animal shelters doubled. The law of demand predicts this inverse relation between cost, or price, and quantity demanded.

It is useful to distinguish between **individual demand**, which is the demand of an individual consumer such as you, and **market demand**, which is the sum of the individual demands of all consumers in the market. In most markets, there are many consumers, sometimes millions. *The market demand curve shows the quantities demanded per period by all consumers at various prices.* Unless otherwise noted, when we talk about demand, we are referring to market demand, as shown in Exhibit 1.

Tough anti-poop laws increase the cost of owning a dog thereby, reducing the quantity of dogs demanded.

**individual demand** The relation between the price of a good and the quantity purchased per period by an individual consumer, other things constant

**market demand** The relation between the price of a good and the quantity purchased per period by all consumers in the market, other things constant; sum of the individual demands in the market

**normal good** A good, such as new clothes, for which demand increases, or shifts rightward, as consumer income rises

**inferior good** A good, such as used clothes, for which demand decreases, or shifts leftward, as consumer income rises

### 4-2 WHAT SHIFTS A DEMAND CURVE?

A demand curve isolates the relation between the price of a good and quantity demanded when other factors that could affect demand remain unchanged. What are those other factors?

Variables that can affect market demand are (1) the money income of consumers, (2) the prices of other goods, (3) consumer expectations, (4) the number or composition of consumers in the market, and (5) consumer tastes. How could changes in each affect demand?

#### 4-2a Consumer Income

Exhibit 2 shows the market demand curve $D$ for pizza. This demand curve assumes a given money income. Suppose consumer income increases. Some consumers are then willing and able to buy more pizza at each price, so market demand increases. The demand curve shifts to the right from $D$ to $D'$. For example, at a price of $12, the amount of pizza demanded increases from 14 million to 20 million per week, as indicated by the movement from point $b$ on demand curve $D$ to point $f$ on demand curve $D'$. In short, *an increase in demand—that is, a rightward shift of the demand curve—means that consumers are willing and able to buy more pizza at each price.*

Goods are classified into two broad categories, depending on how consumers respond to changes in money income. The demand for a **normal good** increases as money income increases. Because pizza is a normal good, its demand curve shifts rightward when money income increases. Most goods are normal. In contrast, demand for an **inferior good** actually decreases as money income increases, so the demand curve shifts leftward. Examples of inferior goods include bologna sandwiches, used furniture, and used clothes. As money income increases, consumers tend to switch from these inferior goods to normal goods (such as roast beef sandwiches, new furniture, and new clothes).

#### 4-2b The Prices of Other Goods

Again, the prices of other goods are assumed to remain constant along a given demand curve. Now let's bring these other prices into play. Consumers have various ways of trying to satisfy any particular want. Consumers choose among substitutes based on relative prices. For example, pizza and tacos are substitutes, though not perfect ones. An increase in the price of tacos, other things constant, reduces the quantity of tacos demanded along a given taco demand

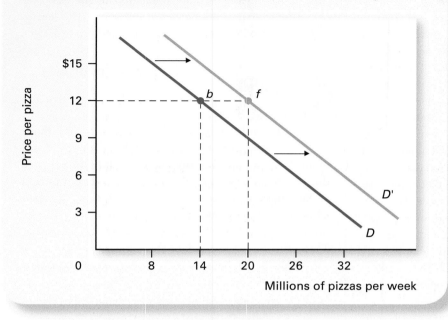

*Exhibit 2*

**An Increase in the Market Demand for Pizza**

An increase of the market demand for pizza is shown by a rightward shift of the curve, indicating that the quantity demanded increases at each price. For example, at a price of $12, quantity demanded increases from 14 million (point *b*) to 20 million (point *f*).

curve. An increase in the price of tacos also increases the demand for pizza, shifting the demand curve for pizza to the right. Two goods are considered **substitutes** if an increase in the price of one shifts the demand for the other rightward.

Goods used in combination are called **complements.** Examples include Pepsi and pizza, milk and cookies, hot dogs and hot-dog buns, cars and gasoline, computer software and hardware, and airline tickets and rental cars. Two goods are considered **complements** if an increase in the price of one decreases the demand for the other, shifting that demand curve leftward. For example, an increase in the price of Pepsi shifts the demand curve for pizza leftward. But most pairs of goods selected at random are *unrelated*—for example, pizza and housing, or milk and gasoline. Still, an increase in the price of an unrelated good reduces the consumers' real income and can thereby reduce the demand for pizza and other goods. For example, a sharp increase in housing prices reduces the income left over for other goods, such as pizza.

## 4-2c Consumer Expectations

Another factor assumed constant along a given demand curve is consumer expectations about factors that influence demand, such as incomes or prices. A change in consumers'

*income expectations* can shift the demand curve. For example, a consumer who learns about a pay raise might increase demand well before the raise takes effect. A college senior who lands that first full-time job may buy a new car even before graduation. Likewise, a change in consumers' *price expectations* can shift the demand curve. For example, if you expect the price of pizza to jump next week, you may buy an extra one today for the freezer, shifting this week's demand for pizza rightward. Or if people come to believe that home prices will climb next year, some will increase their demand for housing now, shifting this year's demand for housing rightward. The expectation of lower prices has the opposite effect. For example, during the recession of 2007–2009, people expected home prices to continue falling, so they put off buying homes, shifting the demand for housing leftward. Such expectations can often be self-fulfilling.

## 4-2d Number or Composition of Consumers

As mentioned earlier, the market demand curve is the sum of the individual demand curves of all consumers in the market. If the number of consumers changes, the demand curve will shift. For example, if the population grows, the demand curve for pizza will shift rightward. Even if total population remains unchanged, demand could shift with a change in the composition of the population. For example, an increase over time in teenagers as a share of the population could shift pizza demand rightward. A baby boom would shift rightward the demand for car seats and baby food. A growing Latino population would affect the demand for Latino foods.

## 4-2e Consumer Tastes

Do you like anchovies on your pizza? How about sauerkraut on your hot dogs? Are you into tattoos and body piercings?

**substitutes** Goods, such as tacos and pizza, that relate in such a way that an increase in the price of one shifts the demand for the other rightward

**complements** Goods, such as Pepsi and pizza, that relate in such a way that an increase in the price of one shifts the demand for the other leftward

Is music to your ears more likely to be rock, country, hip-hop, reggae, R&B, jazz, funk, Latin, gospel, new age, or classical? Choices in food, body art, music, sports, clothing, books, movies, TV shows—indeed, all consumer choices—are influenced by consumer tastes. **Tastes** are nothing more than your likes and dislikes as a consumer. What determines tastes? Your desires for food when hungry and drink when thirsty are largely biological. So too is your desire for comfort, rest, shelter, friendship, love, status, personal safety, and a pleasant environment. Your family background affects some of your tastes—your taste in food, for example, has been shaped by years of home cooking. Other influences include the surrounding culture, peer pressure, and religious convictions. So economists can say a little about the origin of tastes, but they claim no special expertise in understanding how tastes develop and change over time. Economists recognize, however, that tastes have an important impact on demand. For example, although pizza is popular, some people just don't like it and those who are lactose intolerant can't stomach the cheese topping. Thus, most people like pizza but some don't.

In our analysis of consumer demand, *we will assume that tastes are given and are relatively stable.* Tastes are assumed to remain constant along a given demand curve. A change in the tastes for a particular good would shift that good's demand curve. For example, a discovery that the tomato sauce and cheese combination on pizza promotes overall health could change consumer tastes, shifting the demand curve for pizza to the right. But because a change in tastes is so difficult to isolate from changes in other determinants of demand, we should be reluctant to attribute a shift of the demand curve to a change in tastes. We therefore try to rule out other possible reasons for a shift of the demand curve before accepting a change in tastes as the explanation.

**tastes** Consumer preferences; likes and dislikes in consumption; assumed to remain constant along a given demand curve

**movement along a demand curve** A change in quantity demanded resulting from a change in the price of the good, other things constant

**shift of a demand curve** Movement of a demand curve right or left resulting from a change in one of the determinants of demand other than the price of the good

**supply** A relation between the price of a good and the quantity that producers are willing and able to sell per period, other things constant

**law of supply** The amount of a good that producers are willing and able to sell per period is usually directly related to its price, other things constant

**supply curve** A curve showing the relation between price of a good and the quantity producers are willing and able to sell per period, other things constant

That wraps up our look at changes in demand. Before we turn to supply, you should remember the distinction between a **movement along a given demand curve** and a **shift of a demand curve**. A change in *price*, other things constant, causes a *movement along a demand curve*, changing the quantity demanded. A change in one of the determinants of demand other than price causes a *shift of a demand curve*, changing demand.

## 4-3 SUPPLY

Just as demand is a relation between price and quantity demanded, supply is a relation between price and quantity supplied. **Supply** indicates how much producers are *willing and able* to offer for sale per period at each possible price, other things constant. The **law of supply** states that the quantity supplied is usually directly related to its price, other things constant. Thus, the lower the price, the smaller the quantity supplied; the higher the price, the greater the quantity supplied.

### 4-3a Supply Schedule and Supply Curve

Exhibit 3 presents the market *supply schedule* and the market **supply curve** *S* for pizza. Both show the quantities supplied per week at various possible prices by the thousands of pizza makers in the economy. As you can see, price and quantity supplied are directly, or positively, related. Producers have a profit incentive to offer more at a higher price than at a lower price, so the supply curve slopes upward.

Here are two reasons why producers offer more for sale when the price rises. First, as the price increases, other things constant, a producer becomes more *willing* to supply the good. Prices act as signals to existing and potential suppliers about the rewards for producing various goods. A higher pizza price attracts resources from lower-valued uses. *A higher price makes producers more willing to increase quantity supplied.*

Second, higher prices also increase the producer's *ability* to supply the good. The law of increasing opportunity cost, as noted in Chapter 2, states that the opportunity cost of producing more of a particular good rises as output increases—that is, the *marginal cost* of production increases as output increases. Because producers face a higher marginal cost for additional output, they need to get a higher price for that output to be *able* to increase the quantity supplied. *A higher*

## Exhibit 3

### The Market Supply Schedule and Market Supply Curve for Pizza

The market supply curve *S* shows the quantities of pizza supplied, at various prices, by all pizza makers. Price and quantity supplied are directly related.

**(a) Supply schedule**

| Price per Pizza | Quantity Supplied per Week (millions) |
|---|---|
| $15 | 28 |
| 12 | 24 |
| 9 | 20 |
| 6 | 16 |
| 3 | 12 |

**(b) Supply curve**

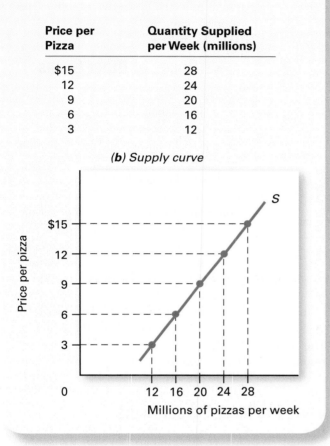

On the other hand, a lower price makes production less attractive, so suppliers are less willing and less able to offer the good. For example, a mining company "reacted quickly to steep copper price declines in 2008 by curbing production at its North American sites and implementing layoffs at its mines and corporate headquarters."[1]

As with demand, we distinguish between *supply* and *quantity supplied*. *Supply* is the entire relationship between prices and quantities supplied, as reflected by the supply schedule or supply curve. **Quantity supplied** refers to a particular amount offered for sale at a particular price, as reflected by a point on a supply curve. We also distinguish between **individual supply**, which is the supply of an individual producer, and **market supply**, which is the sum of individual supplies of all producers in the market. Unless otherwise noted, the term *supply* refers to market supply.

 **4-4**  # WHAT SHIFTS A SUPPLY CURVE?

The supply curve isolates the relation between the price of a good and the quantity supplied, other things constant. Assumed constant along a supply curve are the determinants of supply other than the price of the good, including (1) the state of technology and know-how, (2) the prices of resources, (3) the prices of other goods, (4) producer expectations, and (5) the number of producers in the market. Let's see how a change in each affects the supply curve.

## 4-4a State of Technology and Know How

Recall from Chapter 2 that the state of technology and know-how represents the economy's knowledge about how to combine resources efficiently. Along a given supply curve, technology and know-how are assumed to remain unchanged. If a better technology or a better production process is discovered, production costs will fall, so suppliers will be more willing and able to supply the good at each price.

1. Andrew Johnson, "Freeport Outsourcing Will Cut 60 Valley Jobs," *Arizona Republic*, 23 February 2010.

*price makes producers more able to increase quantity supplied.* As a case in point, a higher price for gasoline increases a producer's ability to extract oil from tar sands, to drill deeper, and to explore in less accessible areas, such as the remote jungles of the Amazon, the stormy waters of the North Sea, or the frozen tundra above the Arctic Circle. For example, at a market price of $45 per barrel, extracting oil from tar sands is unprofitable, but at a price of $50 per barrel, such production is profitable.

Thus, a higher price makes producers more *willing* and more *able* to increase quantity supplied. Producers are more *willing* because production becomes more attractive than other uses of the resources involved. Producers are more *able* because they can afford to cover the higher marginal cost that typically results from increasing output.

**quantity supplied** The amount offered for sale per period at a particular price, as reflected by a point on a supply curve

**individual supply** The relation between the price of a good and the quantity an individual producer is willing and able to sell per period, other things constant

**market supply** The relation between the price of a good and the quantity all producers are willing and able to sell per period, other things constant

*Exhibit 4*

**An Increase in the Market Supply of Pizza**

An increase in the market supply of pizza is reflected by a rightward shift of the supply curve, from *S* to *S'*. Quantity supplied increases at each price. For example, at a price of $12, the quantity supplied increases from 24 million pizzas (point *g*) to 28 million pizzas (point *h*).

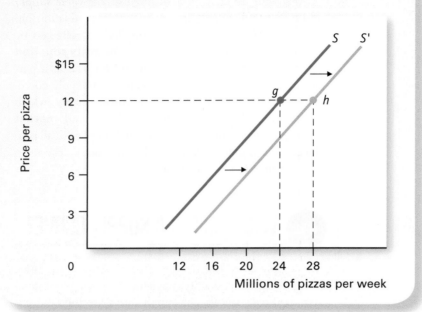

pizza. The supply curve for pizza shifts rightward, as shown in Exhibit 4. On the other hand, an increase in the price of a resource reduces supply, meaning a shift of the supply curve leftward. For example, a higher price of mozzarella increases the cost of making pizza. Higher production costs decrease supply, as reflected by a leftward shift of the supply curve.

## 4-4c Prices of Other Goods

Nearly all resources have alternative uses. The labor, building, machinery, ingredients, and knowledge needed to run a pizza business could produce other goods instead. A drop in the price of one of these other goods, with the price of pizza unchanged, makes pizza production more attractive. For example, if the price of Italian bread declines, some bread makers become pizza makers so the supply of pizza increases, shifting the supply curve of pizza rightward as in Exhibit 4. On the other hand, if the price of Italian bread increases, supplying pizza becomes relatively less attractive compared to supplying Italian bread. The opportunity cost of supplying pizza increases. As resources shift from pizza to bread, the supply of pizza decreases, or shifts to the left.

## 4-4d Producer Expectations

Changes in producer expectations can shift the supply curve. For example, if pizza makers expect higher pizza prices in the future, some will expand operations now, thereby shifting the supply curve rightward. If, however, a good can be easily stored (crude oil, for example, can be left in the ground), expecting higher prices in the future might prompt some producers to *reduce* their current supply while awaiting the higher price. Thus, an expectation of higher prices in the future could either increase or decrease current supply, depending on the good. More generally, any change affecting future profitability, such as a change in business taxes, could shift the supply curve now.

## 4-4e Number of Producers in the Market

Because market supply sums the amounts supplied at each price by all producers in that market, market

For example, new techniques helped Marathon Oil cut drilling time for a new well from 56 days in 2006 to only 24 days in 2009.[2] Consequently, supply will increase, as reflected by a rightward shift of the supply curve. In our pizza example, suppose a new, high-tech oven that costs the same as existing ovens can bake pizza in half the time. Such a breakthrough would shift the market supply curve rightward, as from *S* to *S'* in Exhibit 4, indicating that more is supplied at each possible price. For example, at a price of $12, the amount supplied increases from 24 million to 28 million pizzas per week, as shown in Exhibit 4 by the movement from point *g* to point *h*. In short, *an increase in supply—that is, a rightward shift of the supply curve—means that producers are willing and able to sell more pizza at each price.*

## 4-4b Resource Prices

The prices of resources employed to make the good affect the cost of production and therefore the supply of the good. For example, suppose the price of mozzarella cheese falls. This reduces the cost of making pizza, so producers are more willing and better able to supply

2. Ben Casselman, "Oil Industry Boom—in North Dakota," *Wall Street Journal*, 26 February 2010.

supply depends on the number of producers in that market. If that number increases, supply will increase, shifting the supply curve to the right. If the number of producers decreases, supply will decrease, shifting the supply curve to the left. As an example of increased supply, the number of gourmet coffee bars has more than quadrupled in the United States since 1990 (think Starbucks), shifting the supply curve of gourmet coffee to the right.

Finally, note again the distinction between a **movement along a supply curve** and a **shift of a supply curve**. A change in *price*, other things constant, causes *a movement along a supply curve,* changing the quantity supplied. A change in one of the determinants of supply other than price causes a *shift of a supply curve,* changing supply.

You are now ready to bring demand and supply together.

By locating together, stores reduce transaction costs for consumers.

## 4-5 DEMAND AND SUPPLY CREATE A MARKET

Demanders and suppliers have different views of price. Demanders pay the price and suppliers receive it. Thus, a higher price is bad news for consumers but good news for producers. As the price rises, consumers reduce their quantity demanded along the demand curve and producers increase their quantity supplied along the supply curve. How is this conflict between producers and consumers resolved?

### 4-5a Markets

Markets sort out differences between demanders and suppliers. A *market,* as you know from Chapter 1, includes all the arrangements used to buy and sell a particular good or service. Markets reduce **transaction costs**—the costs of time and information required for exchange. For example, suppose you are looking for a summer job. One approach might be to go from employer to employer looking for openings. But this could have you running around for days or weeks. A more efficient strategy would be to pick up a copy of the local newspaper or go online and look for job openings. Classified ads and Web sites, which are elements of the job market, reduce the transaction costs of bringing workers and employers together.

The coordination that occurs through markets takes place not because of some central plan but because of Adam Smith's "invisible hand." For example,

auto dealers in your community tend to locate together, usually on the outskirts of town, where land is cheaper. The dealers congregate not because they all took an economics course or because they like one another's company but because grouped together they become a more attractive destination for car buyers. A dealer who makes the mistake of locating away from the others misses out on a lot of business. Similarly, stores locate together so that more shoppers will be attracted by the call of the mall. From Orlando theme parks to Broadway theaters to Las Vegas casinos, suppliers in a particular market tend to congregate to attract demanders. Some groupings can be quite specialized. For example, shops in Hong Kong that sell dress mannequins cluster along Austin Road. And diamond merchants in New York City congregate within the same few blocks.

### 4-5b Market Equilibrium

To see how a market works, let's bring together market demand and market supply. Exhibit 5 shows the market for pizza, using schedules in panel (a) and curves in panel (b). Please take a look now. Suppose the price initially is $12. At that price,

**movement along a supply curve** Change in quantity supplied resulting from a change in the price of the good, other things constant

**shift of a supply curve** Movement of a supply curve left or right resulting from a change in one of the determinants of supply other than the price of the good

**transaction costs** The costs of time and information required to carry out market exchange producers supply 24 million pizzas per week, but consumers demand only 14 million, resulting in an *excess quantity supplied*, or a **surplus**, of 10 million pizzas per week. Producers compete by dropping the price. Suppliers don't like getting stuck with unsold pizzas. Competition among producers puts downward pressure on the price, as shown by the arrow pointing down in the graph. As the price falls, producers reduce their quantity supplied and consumers increase their quantity demanded. The price continues to fall as long as quantity supplied exceeds quantity demanded.

Alternatively, suppose the price initially is $6. You can see from Exhibit 5 that at that price consumers demand 26 million pizzas but producers supply only 16 million, resulting in an *excess quantity demanded*, or a **shortage**, of 10 million pizzas per week. Consumers compete to buy pizza, which is in short supply. Consumer competition forces the price higher. Profit-maximizing producers and eager consumers create market pressure for a higher price, as shown by the arrow pointing up in the graph. As the price rises, producers increase their quantity supplied and consumers reduce their quantity demanded. The price continues to rise as long as quantity demanded exceeds quantity supplied.

Thus, *a surplus creates downward pressure on the price, and a shortage creates upward pressure.* As long as quantity demanded differs from quantity supplied, this

> **"A surplus creates downward pressure on the price, and a shortage creates upward pressure."**

difference forces a price change. Note that a shortage or a surplus depends on the price. There is no such thing as a general shortage or a general surplus, only a

**surplus** At a given price, the amount by which quantity supplied exceeds quantity demanded; a surplus usually forces the price down

**shortage** At a given price, the amount by which quantity demanded exceeds quantity supplied; a shortage usually forces the price up

---

### Exhibit 5

### Equilibrium in the Pizza Market

Market equilibrium occurs at the price where quantity demanded equals quantity supplied. This is shown at point c, where the price is $9 and the quantity is 20 million pizzas per week . Above the equilibrium price, quantity supplied exceeds quantity demanded. This creates a surplus, which puts downward pressure on the price. Below the equilibrium price, quantity demanded exceeds quantity supplied. The resulting shortage puts upward pressure on the price.

**(a) Market schedules**

| | Millions of Pizzas per Week | | | |
|---|---|---|---|---|
| Price per Pizza | Quantity Demanded | Quantity Supplied | Surplus or Shortage | Effect on Price |
| $15 | 8 | 28 | Surplus of 20 | Falls |
| 12 | 14 | 24 | Surplus of 10 | Falls |
| 9 | 20 | 20 | Equilibrium | Remains the same |
| 6 | 26 | 16 | Shortage of 10 | Rises |
| 3 | 32 | 12 | Shortage of 20 | Rises |

**(b) Market curves**

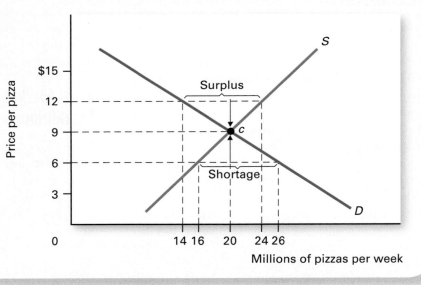

shortage or a surplus at a particular price.

To repeat, buyers prefer a lower price and sellers prefer a higher price. A market reaches equilibrium when the quantity demanded equals quantity supplied. In **equilibrium**, the independent plans of buyers and sellers exactly match, so market forces exert no pressure for change. In Exhibit 5, the demand and supply curves intersect at the *equilibrium point,* identified as point *c*. The *equilibrium price* is $9 per pizza, and the *equilibrium quantity* is 20 million per week. At that price and quantity, the market *clears*. Because there is no shortage or surplus, there is no pressure for the price to change. The demand and supply curves form an "x" at the intersection. You could say that the equilibrium point is found where "x" marks the spot.

Markets indicate the price, quantity, and variety of goods available to you—from the latest social network to the smartest phone. You should be interested in equilibrium prices because they are what you usually pay for the thousands of goods and services you consume.

A market finds equilibrium through the independent actions of thousands, or even millions, of buyers and sellers. In one sense, the market is personal because each consumer and each producer makes a personal decision about how much to buy or sell at a given price. In another sense, the market is impersonal because it requires no conscious communication or coordination among consumers or producers. The price does all the talking. *Impersonal market forces synchronize the personal and independent decisions of many individual buyers and sellers to achieve equilibrium price and quantity.* Prices reflect relative scarcity. For example, to rent a 26-foot truck one way from San Francisco to Austin, U-Haul recently charged $3,236. Its one-way charge for that same truck from Austin to San Francisco was just $399. Why the difference? Far more people wanted to move from San Francisco to Austin than vice versa, so U-Haul had to pay its own employees to drive the empty trucks back from Texas. Rental rates reflected that extra cost.

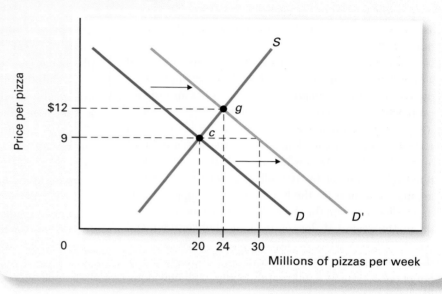

*Exhibit 6*

**Effects of an Increase in Market Demand**

An increase in demand is shown by a shift of the demand curve rightward from *D* to *D'*. Quantity demanded exceeds quantity supplied at the original price of $9 per pizza; this shortage puts upward pressure on the price. As the price rises, quantity supplied increases along supply curve S, and quantity demanded decreases along demand curve *D'*. When the new equilibrium price of $12 is reached at point *g*, quantity demanded once again equals quantity supplied.

## 4-6 CHANGES IN EQUILIBRIUM PRICE AND QUANTITY

Equilibrium occurs when the plans of demanders and suppliers exactly match. Once a market reaches equilibrium, that price and quantity remain stable until something affects demand or supply. A change in any non-price determinant of demand or supply usually changes equilibrium price and quantity in a predictable way, as you'll see.

### 4-6a Shifts of the Demand Curve

In Exhibit 6, demand curve *D* and supply curve *S* intersect at point *c* to yield the initial equilibrium price of $9 and the initial equilibrium quantity of 20 million 12-inch regular pizzas per week. Now suppose that one of the determinants of demand changes in a way that increases demand, shifting the demand curve to the right

> **equilibrium** The condition that exists in a market when the plans of buyers match those of sellers, so quantity demanded equals quantity supplied and the market clears

from $D$ to $D'$. Any of the following could shift the demand for pizza rightward: (1) an increase in the money income of consumers (because pizza is a normal good); (2) an increase in the price of a substitute, such as tacos, or a decrease in the price of a complement, such as Pepsi; (3) a change in consumer expectations that causes people to demand more pizzas now; (4) a growth in the number of pizza consumers; or (5) a change in consumer tastes—based, for example, on a discovery that the tomato sauce on pizza has antioxidant properties that improve overall health.

After the demand curve shifts rightward to $D'$ in Exhibit 6, the amount demanded at the initial price of $9 is 30 million pizzas, which exceeds the amount supplied of 20 million by 10 million pizzas. Competition among consumers for the limited quantity supplied puts upward pressure on the price. As the price increases, the quantity demanded decreases along the new demand curve $D'$, and the quantity supplied increases along the existing supply curve $S$ until the two quantities are equal once again at equilibrium point $g$. The new equilibrium price is $12, and the new equilibrium quantity is 24 million pizzas per week. Thus, given an upward-sloping supply curve, an increase in demand increases both equilibrium price and quantity. For example, an increase in demand explains why roses cost more on Valentine's Day, why TV ads cost more on the Super Bowl broadcast, and why hotel rooms cost more in the host city during Super Bowl weekend.

A decrease in demand would initially create a surplus. Competition among producers to sell pizzas would lower both equilibrium price and quantity. These results can be summarized as follows: *Given an upward-sloping supply curve, a rightward shift of the demand curve increases both equilibrium price and quantity and a leftward shift decreases both equilibrium price and quantity.*

## 4-6b Shifts of the Supply Curve

Let's now consider shifts of the supply curve. In Exhibit 7, as before, we begin with demand curve $D$ and supply curve $S$ intersecting at point $c$ to yield an equilibrium price of $9 and an equilibrium quantity of 20 million pizzas per week. Suppose one of the determinants of supply changes, increasing supply from $S$ to $S'$. Changes that could shift the supply curve rightward include (1) a technological breakthrough in pizza ovens; (2) a reduction in the price of a resource such as mozzarella cheese; (3) a decline in the price of another good such as Italian bread; (4) a change in expectations that encourages pizza makers to expand production now; or (5) an increase in the number of pizzerias.

After the supply curve shifts rightward in Exhibit 7, the amount supplied at the initial price of $9 increases from 20 million to 30 million, so producers now supply 10 million more pizzas than consumers demand. Pizza makers compete to sell the surplus by lowering the price. As the price falls, the quantity supplied declines along the new

### Exhibit 7

**Effects of an Increase in Market Supply**

An increase in supply is shown by a shift of the supply curve rightward, from $S$ to $S'$. Quantity supplied exceeds quantity demanded at the original price of $9 per pizza, putting downward pressure on the price. As the price falls, quantity supplied decreases along supply curve $S'$, and quantity demanded increases along demand curve $D$. The new equilibrium price of $6 is reached at point $d$, where quantity demanded once again equals quantity supplied.

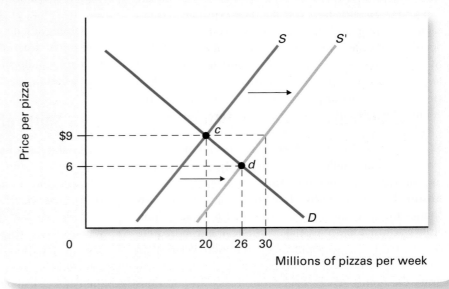

## Exhibit 8

### Effects of an Increase in Both Demand and Supply

When both demand and supply increase, the equilibrium quantity also increases. The effect on price depends on which curve shifts more. In panel (a), the demand curve shifts more, so the price rises. In panel (b), the supply curve shifts more, so the price falls.

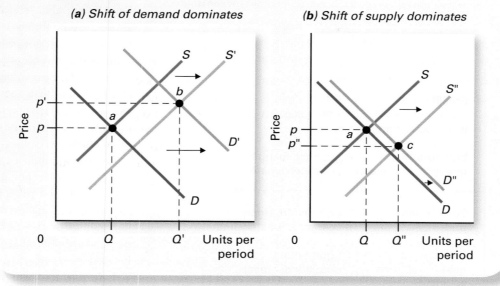

*(a)* Shift of demand dominates

*(b)* Shift of supply dominates

supply curve and the quantity demanded increases along the existing demand curve until a new equilibrium point *d* is established. The new equilibrium price is $6, and the new equilibrium quantity is 26 million pizzas per week. In short, an increase in supply reduces the price and increases the quantity. This recent *Wall Street Journal* headline captures the idea: "Global Oil Glut Sends Prices Plunging."[3] On the other hand, a decrease in supply increases the price but decreases the quantity. As a case in point, a recent worldwide shortage af baby eels, an Asian delicacy, rocketed the price to more than $2,000 per pound.[4] Thus, *given a downward-sloping demand curve, a rightward shift of the supply curve decreases price but increases quantity, and a leftward shift increases price but decreases quantity.*

## 4-6c Simultaneous Shifts of Demand and Supply Curves

As long as only one curve shifts, we can say how equilibrium price and quantity will change. If both curves shift, however, the outcome is less obvious. For example, suppose both demand and supply increase, or shift rightward, as in Exhibit 8. Note that in panel (a),

3. Written by Russell Gold, this story appeared in October 14, 2014.

4. Clark Canfield, "Candia Man Cited for 41 Pounds of Illegal Eels in Maine," *Concord Monitor*, 9 April 2013.

demand shifts more than supply, and in panel (b), supply shifts more than demand. In both panels, equilibrium quantity increases. The change in equilibrium price, however, depends on which curve shifts more. If demand shifts more, as in panel (a), equilibrium price increases. For example, between 1995 and 2005, the demand for housing increased more than the supply, so both price and quantity increased. But if supply shifts more, as in panel (b), equilibrium price decreases. For example, in the last decade, the supply of personal computers has increased more than the demand, so price has decreased and quantity has increased.

Conversely, if both demand and supply decrease, or shift leftward, equilibrium quantity decreases. But, again, we cannot say what will happen to equilibrium price unless we examine relative shifts. (You can use Exhibit 8 to consider decreases in demand and supply by viewing *D′* and *S′* as the initial curves.) If demand shifts more, the price will fall. If supply shifts more, the price will rise.

If demand and supply shift in opposite directions, we can say what will happen to equilibrium price. Equilibrium price will increase if demand increases and supply decreases. Equilibrium price will decrease if demand decreases and supply increases. Without reference to particular shifts, however, we cannot say what will happen to equilibrium quantity.

## Exhibit 9

### Effects of Shifts of Both Demand and Supply

When the demand and supply curves shift in the same direction, equilibrium quantity also shifts in that direction. The effect on equilibrium price depends on which curve shifts more. If the curves shift in opposite directions, equilibrium price will move in the same direction as demand. The effect on equilibrium quantity depends on which curve shifts more.

|  | **Shift of demand** | |
|---|---|---|
|  | Demand increases | Demand decreases |
| **Supply increases** | Equilibrium price change is indeterminate.<br><br>Equilibrium quantity increases. | Equilibrium price falls.<br><br>Equilibrium quantity change is indeterminate. |
| **Supply decreases** | Equilibrium price rises.<br><br>Equilibrium quantity change is indeterminate. | Equilibrium price change is indeterminate.<br><br>Equilibrium quantity decreases. |

*(Row label on left: **Shift of supply**)*

These results are no doubt confusing, but Exhibit 9 summarizes the four possible combinations of changes. Using Exhibit 9 as a reference, please take the time right now to work through some changes in demand and supply to develop a feel for the results.

## 4-7 DISEQUILIBRIUM

**disequilibrium** The condition that exists in a market when the plans of buyers do not match those of sellers; a temporary mismatch between quantity supplied and quantity demanded as the market seeks equilibrium

**price floor** A minimum legal price below which a product cannot be sold; to have an impact, a price floor must be set above the equilibrium price

A surplus exerts downward pressure on the price, and a shortage exerts upward pressure. Markets, however, don't always reach equilibrium quickly. During the time required to adjust, the market is said to be in disequilibrium. **Disequilibrium** is usually temporary as market forces push toward equilibrium. But sometimes, often as a result of government intervention, when market forces are suppressed, disequilibrium can last a while, perhaps decades, as we will see next.

## 4-7a Price Floors

Sometimes public officials force a price above the equilibrium level. For example, the federal government regulates some agriculture prices in an attempt to ensure farmers a higher and more stable income than they would otherwise earn. To achieve a higher price, the government imposes a **price floor**, or a *minimum* selling price that is above the equilibrium price. Panel (a) of Exhibit 10 shows the effect of a $2.50 per gallon price floor for milk. At that price, farmers supply 24 million gallons per week, but consumers demand only 14 million gallons, yielding a surplus of 10 million gallons. This surplus milk will pile up on store shelves, eventually souring. To take it off the market, the government usually agrees to buy the surplus milk. The federal government, in fact, has spent billions buying and storing surplus agricultural products over the years. Note, to have an impact, a price floor must be set *above* the equilibrium price. A price floor set at or below the equilibrium price wouldn't matter (how come?). Price floors distort markets and reduce economic welfare.

The U.S. government often buys surplus milk that results from a price floor imposed above the equilibrium market price.

*Exhibit 10*

**Effects of Price Floors and Price Ceilings**

A price floor set above the equilibrium price results in a surplus, as shown in panel (a). A price floor set at or below the equilibrium price has no effect. A price ceiling set below the equilibrium price results in a shortage, as shown in panel (b). A price ceiling set at or above the equilibrium price has no effect.

**(a) Price floor for milk**

**(b) Price ceiling for rent**

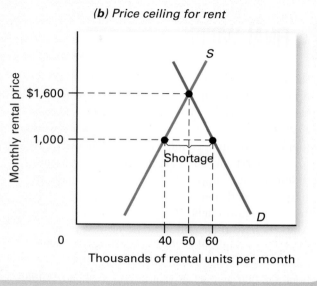

## 4-7b Price Ceilings

Sometimes public officials try to keep a price below the equilibrium level by setting a **price ceiling**, or a *maximum* selling price. Concern about the rising cost of rental housing in some cities prompted city officials to impose rent ceilings. Panel (b) of Exhibit 10 depicts the demand and supply of rental housing. The vertical axis shows monthly rent, and the horizontal axis shows the quantity of rental units. The equilibrium, or market-clearing, rent is $1,600 per month, and the equilibrium quantity is 50,000 housing units. Suppose city officials set a maximum rent of $1,000 per month. At that ceiling price, 60,000 rental units are demanded, but only 40,000 supplied, resulting in a housing shortage of 20,000 units. Because of the price ceiling, the rental price no longer rations housing to those who value it the most. Other devices emerge to ration housing, such as long waiting lists, personal connections, and the willingness to make under-the-table payments, such as "key fees," "finder's fees," high security deposits, and the like. To have an impact, a price ceiling must be set *below* the equilibrium price. A price ceiling set at or above equilibrium wouldn't matter. (Again, why not?) Price floors and ceilings distort markets and reduce economic welfare.

Government intervention is not the only source of market disequilibrium. Sometimes, when new products are introduced or when demand

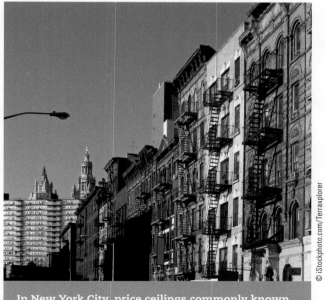

In New York City, price ceilings commonly known as "rent control" help contribute to acute housing shortages.

**price ceiling** A maximum legal price above which a product cannot be sold; to have an impact, a price ceiling must be set below the equilibrium price suddenly changes, it takes a while to reach equilibrium. For example, popular toys and best-selling books sometimes sell out. On the other hand, some products attract few customers and pile up unsold on store shelves, awaiting a "clearance sale."

## 4-8 FINAL WORD

Demand and supply are the building blocks of a market economy. Although a market usually involves the interaction of many buyers and sellers, few markets are consciously designed. Just as the law of gravity works whether or not we understand Newton's principles, market forces operate whether or not participants understand demand and supply. These forces arise naturally, much the way car dealers cluster on the outskirts of town to attract more customers.

Markets have their critics. Some observers may be troubled, for example, that Boston Patriots quarterback Tom Brady earns a salary that could pay 675 new schoolteachers $40,000 a year; or that corporate head Ralph Lauren earned enough in a recent year to pay for 1,600 new schoolteachers; or that U.S. consumers spend more than $60 billion a year on their pets.[5] On your next trip to the supermarket, notice how much shelf space goes to pet products—often an entire aisle. PetSmart, a chain store, sells over 12,000 different pet items. Veterinarians offer cancer treatment, cataract removal, root canals,

kidney transplants, even acupuncture. Kidney dialysis for a pet can cost over $75,000 per year.

In a market economy, consumers are kings and queens. Consumer sovereignty rules, deciding what gets produced. Those who don't like the market outcome usually look to government for a solution through price ceilings and price floors, regulations, income redistribution, and public finance more generally.

5. Arlene Weintraub, "The Rising Cost of Health Care—for Cats and Dogs," *Bloomberg Business*, 17 February 2015 at http://www.bloomberg.com/news /articles/2015-02-17/the-rising-costs-of-health-care-for-cats-and-dogs.

## STUDY TOOLS 4

### READY TO STUDY? IN THE BOOK, YOU CAN:

☐ Work the Problems at the end of the chapter.

☐ Rip out the chapter review card for a handy summary of the chapter and key terms.

### ONLINE AT CENGAGEBRAIN.COM YOU CAN:

☐ Collect StudyBits while you read and study the chapter.

☐ Quiz yourself on key concepts.

☐ Prepare for tests with chapter flash cards as well as flash cards that you create.

☐ Watch videos to explore economics further.

# CHAPTER 4 PROBLEMS

*Your instructor can access the answers to these problems online at http://cengagebrain.com.*

## 4-1 Explain why a demand curve slopes downward

1. *(Shifting Demand)* Using demand and supply curves, show the effect of each of the following on the market for cigarettes:
   a. A cure for lung cancer is found.
   b. The price of cigars increases.
   c. Wages increase substantially in states that grow tobacco.
   d. A fertilizer that increases the yield per acre of tobacco is discovered.
   e. There is a sharp increase in the price of matches, lighters, and lighter fluid.
   f. More states pass laws restricting smoking in restaurants and public places.

2. *(Substitutes and Complements)* For each of the following pair of goods, determine whether the goods are substitutes, complements, or unrelated:
   a. Peanut butter and jelly
   b. Private and public transportation
   c. Coke and Pepsi
   d. Alarm clocks and automobiles
   e. Golf clubs and golf balls

## 4-2 Identify five things which could shift a demand curve to the right or left

3. *(Demand Shifters)* List five things that are held constant along a market demand curve, and identify the change in each that would shift that demand curve to the right—that is, that would increase demand.

## 4-3 Explain why a supply curve usually slopes upward

4. *(Supply)* Why is a firm willing and able to increase the quantity supplied as the product price increases?

5. *(Supply)* What is the law of supply? Give an example of how you have observed the law of supply at work. What is the relationship between the law of supply and the supply curve?

## 4-4 Identify five things which could shift a supply curve to the right or left

6. *(Supply Shifters)* List the five things that are held constant along a market supply curve, and identify the change in each that would shift that supply curve to the right—that is, that would increase supply.

7. *(Demand and Supply)* How do you think each of the following affected the world price of oil? (Use demand and supply analysis.)
   a. Tax credits were offered for expenditures on home insulation.
   b. The Alaskan oil pipeline was completed.
   c. The ceiling on the price of oil was removed.
   d. Oil was discovered in the North Sea.
   e. Sport utility vehicles and minivans became popular.
   f. The use of nuclear power declined.

8. *(Demand and Supply)* What happens to the equilibrium price and quantity of ice cream in response to each of the following? Explain your answers.
   a. The price of dairy cow fodder increases.
   b. The price of beef decreases.
   c. Concerns arise about the high fat content of ice cream. Simultaneously, the price of sugar (used to produce ice cream) increases.

## 4-5 Explain why surpluses push prices down while shortages drive prices up

9. *(Market Surplus)* Why would firms accept a lower price if there is a market surplus?

10. *(Market Shortage)* Why would firms raise the price if there is a market shortage, and why would some consumers pay that higher price. At what point would firms stop raising the price?

## 4-6 Predict the impact of a change in demand or supply on the equilibrium price and quantity

11. *(Equilibrium)* "If a price is not an equilibrium price, there is a tendency for it to move to its equilibrium level. Regardless of whether the price is too high or too low to begin with, the adjustment process will increase the quantity of the good purchased." Explain, using a demand and supply diagram.

12. *(Equilibrium)* Assume the market for corn is depicted as in the table that appears below.
    a. Complete the table below.
    b. What market pressure occurs when quantity demanded exceeds quantity supplied? Explain.
    c. What market pressure occurs when quantity supplied exceeds quantity demanded? Explain.
    d. What is the equilibrium price?
    e. What could change the equilibrium price?
    f. At each price in the first column of the table below, how much is sold?

| Price per Bushel | Quantity Demanded (millions of bushels) | Quantity Supplied (millions of bushels) | Surplus/ Shortage | Will Price Rise or Fall? |
|---|---|---|---|---|
| $1.80 | 320 | 200 | _____ | _____ |
| 2.00 | 300 | 230 | _____ | _____ |
| 2.20 | 270 | 270 | _____ | _____ |
| 2.40 | 230 | 300 | _____ | _____ |
| 2.60 | 200 | 330 | _____ | _____ |
| 2.80 | 180 | 350 | _____ | _____ |

13. *(Market Equilibrium)* Determine whether each of the following statements is true, false, or uncertain. Then briefly explain each answer.
    a. In equilibrium, all sellers can find buyers.
    b. In equilibrium, there is no pressure on the market to produce or consume more than is being sold.
    c. At prices above equilibrium, the quantity exchanged exceeds the quantity demanded.
    d. At prices below equilibrium, the quantity exchanged is equal to the quantity supplied

14. *(Changes in Equilibrium)* What are the effects on the equilibrium price and quantity of steel if the wages of steelworkers rise and, simultaneously, the price of aluminum rises?

## 4-7 Describe the result of a government-set price floor or price ceiling on a market

15. *(Price Floor)* There is considerable interest in whether the minimum wage rate contributes to teenage unemployment. Draw a demand and supply diagram for the unskilled labor market, and discuss the effects of a minimum wage. Who is helped and who is hurt by the minimum wage law?

# 5 | Introduction to Macroeconomics

Universal Images Group Limited/Alamy

## LEARNING OUTCOMES

After studying this chapter, you will be able to...

**5-1** Explain what's special about a national economy compared to regional, state, or local economies

**5-2** Describe the phases of the business cycle

**5-3** Explain the shapes of the aggregate demand curve and the aggregate supply curve, and how they interact to determine real GDP and the price level for a nation

**5-4** Identify the five eras of the U.S. economy, and describe briefly what went on during each

After finishing this chapter go to **PAGE 91** for **STUDY TOOLS**

**Topics discussed in Chapter 5 include:**

- The national economy
- Economic fluctuations
- Aggregate demand
- Aggregate supply
- Equilibrium price level and aggregate output
- A brief history of the U.S. economy
- Demand-side economics
- Stagflation
- Supply-side economics
- The Great Recession of 2007–2009

- ▶ What's the big idea in macroeconomics?

- ▶ Why is its focus the national economy?

- ▶ How do we measure the economy's performance over time?

- ▶ Which has more impact on your standard of living, the economy's short-term ups and downs or the long-term growth trend?

- ▶ What's the difference between demand-side economics and supply-side economics?

- ▶ How has the economic role of government evolved during the last century?

- ▶ How is learning about the macroeconomy like learning about the weather?

*Answers to these and other questions are addressed in this chapter, which introduces macroeconomics.*

**M**acroeconomics looks at the big picture—not the demand for Apple Watches but the demand for everything produced in the economy; not the price of gasoline but the average price of all goods and services produced in the economy; not consumption by the Martinez household but consumption by all households; not investment by Google but investment by all firms in the economy.

> **"Which has more impact on your standard of living, the economy's short-term ups and downs or the long-term growth trend?"**

Macroeconomists develop and test theories about how the economy as a whole works—theories that can help predict the impact of economic policies and events. Macroeconomists are concerned not only with what determines such big-picture indicators as production, employment, and the price level but also with understanding how and why they change over time. Macroeconomists are especially interested in what makes an economy grow, because a growing economy creates more jobs and more goods and services—in short, more growth means a rising standard of living. What determines the economy's ability to use resources productively, to adapt, to grow? This chapter begins exploring such questions.

## 5-1 THE NATIONAL ECONOMY

Macroeconomics concerns the overall performance of the *economy*. The term **economy** describes the structure of economic activity, in a community, a region, a country, a group of countries, or the world. We could talk about the Chicago economy, the Illinois economy, the Midwest economy, the U.S. economy, the North American economy, or the world economy. We measure an economy in different ways, such as the amount produced, the number of people working, or their total income. The most common yardstick is *gross product,* which measures the market value of all final goods and services produced in a particular geographical region during a given period, usually one year.

If the focus is the Illinois economy, we consider the *gross state product*. If the focus is the U.S. economy, we consider the **gross domestic product**, or **GDP**, which measures the market value of all final goods and services produced in the United States during a given period, usually a year. GDP adds up production of the economy's incredible variety of

**economy** The structure of economic activity in a community, a region, a country, a group of countries, or the world

**gross domestic product (GDP)** The market value of all final goods and services produced in the nation during a particular period, usually a year goods and services, from trail bikes to pedicures. We can use the gross domestic product to compare different economies at the same time or to track the same economy over time. We could also consider the **gross world product**, which measures the value of all final goods and services produced in the world during a given period, usually a year. Just as a point of reference, the gross world product was estimated to be about $105 trillion in 2014, up 3.3 percent from the year before.[1] The United States, with 4.5 percent of the world's population in 2014, accounted for 17 percent of gross world product. The focus of macroeconomics is usually the national economy.

## 5-1a What's Special About the National Economy?

The national economy deserves special attention. Here's why: If you were to drive west on Interstate 10 in Texas, you would hardly notice the crossing into New Mexico. But if, instead, you took the Juarez exit south into Mexico, you would be stopped at the border and asked for identification, and you and your vehicle could be searched. You would become quite aware of crossing an international border. Like most other countries, the United States and Mexico usually allow people and goods to move more freely *within* their borders than *across* their borders.

The differences between the United States and Mexico are far greater than the differences between Texas and New Mexico. For example, each country has its own standard of living and currency, its own culture and language, its own communication and transportation system, its own system of government, and its own "rules of the game"—that is, its own laws, regulations, customs, manners, and ways of doing business both within and across its borders.

Macroeconomics typically focuses on the performance of the national economy, including how the national economy interacts with other national economies around the world. The U.S. economy is the largest

The United States and Mexico usually allow people and goods to move more freely within their borders than across their borders.

> **"We can use the gross domestic product to compare different economies at the same time or to track the same economy over time."**

and most complex in world history, with about 120 million households, more than 30 million for-profit businesses, and about 89,150 government jurisdictions. The world economy includes about 200 sovereign nations, ranging in population from Liechtenstein, with only 37,000 people, to China, with 1.4 billion, or about 38,000 Liechtensteins. These numbers offer snapshots, but the economy is a motion picture, a work in progress—too complex to capture in snapshots. That's why we use theoretical models to focus on key relationships. To help you get your mind around the economy, let's begin with a simple analogy.

## 5-1b The Human Body and the U.S. Economy

Consider the similarities and differences between the human body and the economy. The body consists of millions of cells, each performing particular functions yet each linked to the entire body. Similarly, the U.S. economy is composed of millions of decision makers, each acting with some independence yet each connected with the economy as a whole. The economy, like the body, is continually renewing itself, with new households, new businesses, a changing cast of public officials, and new foreign competitors and customers. Blood circulates throughout the body, facilitating the exchange

**gross world product**
The market value of all final goods and services produced in the world during a given period, usually a year

1. Central Intelligence Agency, *World Factbook*, at https://www.cia.gov/library /publications/the-world-factbook/; and The World Bank at http://data.worldbank.org/.

of oxygen and vital nutrients among cells. Similarly, *money* circulates throughout the economy, facilitating the exchange of resources and products among individual economic units. In fact, blood and money are each called a *medium of exchange*. In Chapter 1, we saw that the movement of money, products, and resources throughout the economy follows a *circular flow*, as does the movement of blood, oxygen, and nutrients throughout the body.

Like a human body, the economy is made up of millions of parts that interact with each other to keep the whole system running.

Matthew Cole/Shutterstock.com

## Flow and Stock Variables

Just as the same blood recirculates as a medium of exchange in the body, the same dollars recirculate as a medium of exchange in the economy to finance transactions. The dollars you spend on bagels are spent by the baker on butter and then spent by the dairy farmer on work boots. Dollars *flow* through the economy. To measure a flow, we use a **flow variable**, which is an amount per period of time, such as your average spending per week or your heartbeats per minute. In contrast, a **stock variable** is an amount measured at a particular point in time, such as the amount of money you have with you right now or your current weight.

## Testing New Theories

Physicians and other natural scientists test their theories using controlled experiments. Macroeconomists, however, have no laboratories and little ability to run economy-wide experiments of any kind. Granted, they can study different economies around the world, but each economy is unique, so comparisons are tricky. Controlled experiments also provide the natural sciences with something seldom available to economists—the chance, or serendipitous, discovery (such as penicillin). Macroeconomists studying the U.S. economy have only one patient, so they can't introduce particular policies in a variety of alternative settings. You can't squeeze economies into a test tube. Cries of "Eureka!" are seldom heard from macroeconomists. An economy consisting of hundreds of millions of individual actors is a complicated thing. As Nobel Prize-winning physicist Murray Gell-Mann once observed, "Think how hard physics would be if particles could think."

## 5-1c Knowledge and Performance

Throughout much of history, little was known about how the human body works, yet many people still enjoyed good health. For example, the fact that blood circulates in the body was not established until 1638; it took scientists another 150 years to figure out why. Similarly, over the millennia, various complex economies developed and flourished, although at the time there was little understanding about how an economy worked.

The economy is much like the body: As long as it functions smoothly, policy makers need not understand how it works. But if a problem arises—severe unemployment, high inflation, or sluggish growth, for example—we must know how a healthy economy works before we can consider whether anything can be done. We need not know every detail of the economy, just as we need not know every detail of the body. But we must understand essential relationships among key variables. For example, does the economy work well on its own, or does it often perform poorly? If it performs poorly, are there public-policy remedies? Can we be sure that a proposed remedy would not do more harm than good? When doctors didn't understand how the human body worked, their attempted "cures" were often worse than the diseases. Much of the history of medicine describes misguided efforts to deal with disease. For example, when George Washington became ill in 1799, doctors drained half his blood, believing that this bloodletting would cure

**flow variable** A measure of something per period of time, such as your spending per week

**stock variable** A measure of something at a point in time, such as the amount of money you have with you right now him. Instead, he died. The best doctors in the land couldn't help Washington because they did not understand how the human body works.

Even today, medical care is based on less scientific evidence than you might think. According to one study, only one in seven medical interventions was supported by reliable scientific evidence.[2] For example, acetaminophen (e.g., Tylenol) is a popular pain reliever, but nobody really knows how it works. According to an old saying, "Nature heals and the doctor collects the fee." Or as Voltaire wrote, "The art of medicine consists of amusing the patient while nature cures the disease."

Likewise, policy makers may adopt the wrong prescription because of a flawed theory about how the economy works. At one time, for example, a nation's economic vitality was thought to spring from the stock of precious metals accumulated in the public treasury. This theory spawned a policy called **mercantilism**, which held that, as a way of accumulating gold and silver, a nation should try to export more than it imports. To pursue this, nations restricted imports by such barriers as tariffs and quotas. But these restrictions led to retaliations by other countries, reducing international trade and the gains from specialization. Another flawed economic theory prompted President Herbert Hoover to introduce a major tax *increase* during the Great Depression. Economists have since learned that such a policy does more harm than good. Debates about the effectiveness of government policies were widespread as officials reacted to the crushing recession of 2007–2009, now known as the Great Recession.

We turn now to the performance of the U.S. economy.

2. As reported by Sherwin Nuland, "Medical Fads: Bran, Midwives and Leeches," *New York Times*, 25 January 1995.

## 5-2 ECONOMIC FLUCTUATIONS AND GROWTH

The U.S. economy and other industrial market economies historically have experienced alternating periods of expansion and contraction in economic activity. As noted in Chapter 1, *economic fluctuations* are the rise and fall of economic activity relative to the long-term growth trend of the economy. These fluctuations, or *business cycles*, vary in length and intensity, yet some features appear common to all. The ups and downs usually involve the entire nation and often many other economies around the world, and they affect nearly all dimensions of economic activity, not just production and employment.

© JustASC/Shutterstock.com

### 5-2a U.S. Economic Fluctuations

Perhaps the easiest way to understand the business cycle is to examine its components. During the 1920s and 1930s, Wesley C. Mitchell, director of the National Bureau of Economic Research (NBER), analyzed business cycles, noting that the economy has two phases: *expansions* and *contractions*. During an **expansion**, the economy grows as reflected by rising output, employment, income, and other aggregate measures. During a **contraction**, the economy declines as reflected by falling output, employment, income, and other aggregate measures. A contraction might be so sharp as to be called a **depression**, which is a severe and prolonged reduction in the nation's economic activity, as occurred during the 1930s. A milder contraction is called a **recession**, which is a period of decline in economic activity lasting more than a few months, as reflected by falling output employment, income, and other aggregate measures. The U.S. economy experienced both recessions and depressions before World War II. Since then, there have been recessions but no depressions, so things have improved.

Despite these ups and downs, the U.S. economy has grown dramatically over the long term. Although economic activity is measured in a variety of ways, if we had to settle on a single indicator, *output* best captures what's going on. The economy in 2014 produced 15 times more output than it did in 1929. Output is measured by real

GDP, the value of final goods and services after stripping away changes due to **inflation**, which is an increase in the economy's average price level. Production increased because of (1) increases in the amount and quality of resources, especially labor and capital; (2) better technology and know-how; and (3) improvements in the *rules of the game* that facilitate production and exchange, such as property rights, patent laws, the legal system, and market practices.

Exhibit 1 shows the long-term growth trend in economic activity as an upward-sloping straight line. Economic fluctuations reflect movements around this growth trend. A contraction begins after the previous expansion has reached a *peak,* or high point, and continues until the economy reaches a *trough,* or low point. The period between a peak and trough is a *contraction,* and the period between a trough and subsequent peak is an *expansion.* Note that expansions last longer than contractions, but the length of the full cycle varies.

> **❝Because of seasonal fluctuations and random disturbances, the economy does not move smoothly through phases of the business cycle.❞**

Analysts at the NBER have tracked the U.S. economy back to 1854. Since then, the nation has experienced 33 peak-to-trough-to-peak cycles. No two have been exactly alike. During the 22 business cycles prior to 1945, expansions averaged 29 months and contractions 21 months. During the 11 cycles since 1945, expansions stretched twice as long to 57 months, and recessions fell by nearly half to 11 months—so expansions averaged nearly five years and recessions nearly one year. Thus, since 1945 expansions are longer and recessions are shorter. Both developments have been hugely beneficial for economic growth and the U.S. standard of living. The longest expansion on record lasted ten years, from March 1991 to March 2001. The longest contraction lasted five and a half years, from 1873 to 1879.

Exhibit 2 shows annual percentage changes in real GDP since 1929. Years of declining real GDP are shown as red bars and years of increasing real GDP as blue bars. The big decline during the Great Depression of the early 1930s and the sharp jump during World War II stand in stark contrast. Growth since 1929 has averaged 3.3 percent a year.

The intensity of U.S. economic fluctuations varies across regions. A recession hits hardest those regions that produce more capital goods, such as heavy machinery, and durable goods, such as appliances, furniture, and automobiles. The demand for these goods falls more during hard times than does the demand for other goods and services, such as breakfast cereal, electricity, and haircuts. Recessions also hit hardest those states that rely on more housing construction such as Arizona, California, Florida, and Nevada.

Because of seasonal fluctuations and random disturbances, the economy does not move smoothly through phases of the business cycle. Economists can't always distinguish a temporary drop in economic activity from the beginning of a downturn. A drop in economic activity may result from a temporary

**inflation** An increase in the economy's average price level

## *Exhibit 1*

### Hypothetical Business Cycles

Business cycles reflect movements of economic activity around a trend line that shows long-term growth. An expansion (shaded in blue) begins when the economy starts to grow and continues until the economy reaches a peak. After an expansion has peaked, a contraction (shaded in pink) begins and continues until the economy reaches a trough.

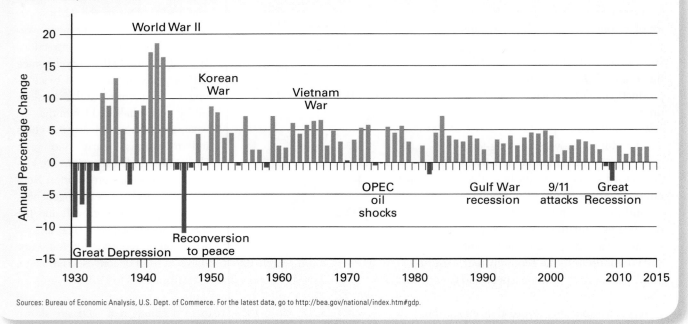

*Exhibit 2*

**Annual Percentage Change in U.S. Real GDP Since 1929**

Years of declining real GDP are shown as red bars and years of growth as blue bars. Note that the year-to-year swings in output became less pronounced after World War II.

Sources: Bureau of Economic Analysis, U.S. Dept. of Commerce. For the latest data, go to http://bea.gov/national/index.htm#gdp.

slowdown, such as a snowstorm or a poor growing season. Turning points—peaks and troughs—are thus identified by the NBER only after the fact. Because a recession means economic activity declines for more than a few months (two quarters, or six months, is sometimes used as a rule of thumb), and because the official announcement that a recession has begun is not made until months after that, we sometimes don't know for sure when a recession starts until a year later (as was the case with the recession that began in December 2007). Likewise, a recession's end is sometimes not announced until a year or more after it's over (for example, the Great Recession ended in June 2009, but the official announcement of that fact did not come until 15 months later).

## 5-2b The Global Economy

As noted, fluctuations usually involve the entire nation. Indeed, major economies around the world often fluctuate together. Though business cycles are not perfectly synchronized across countries, a link is usually apparent. Economies are related through international trade, finance, and migration, and ties grow stronger each year. For example, U.S. exports as a share of U.S.

output are now double what they were four decades ago. Consider the experience of two leading economies—the United States and the United Kingdom, nations separated by the Atlantic Ocean. Exhibit 3 shows for each country the year-to-year percentage changes in real GDP since 1978. Again, *real* means that the effects of inflation have been erased, so remaining changes reflect *real* changes in the total value of goods and services produced each year.

If you spend a minute looking at the annual changes, you will notice the similarities. For example, both economies went into recession in the early 1980s, grew strongly for the rest of the decade, entered another recession in 1991, then recovered for the rest of that decade. After a short recession in 2001, both economies grew until the Great Recession of 2007–2009, when they both took a dive. After that, both economies recovered.

One problem with the linkage across economies is that a slump in another major economy can worsen a recession in the United States and vice versa. For example, the Great Recession of 2007–2009 affected economies around the world, increasing unemployment and cutting production. Trouble in seemingly

*Exhibit 3*

**U.S. and U.K. Annual Growth Rates in Output Are Similar**

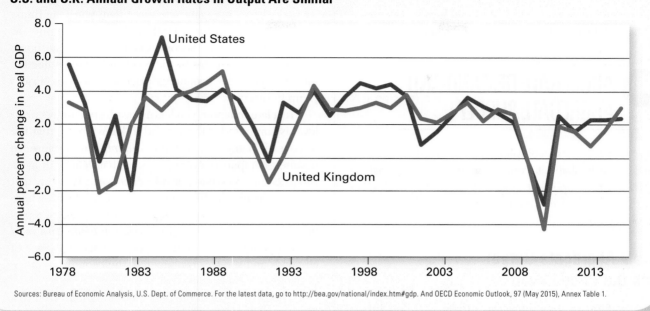

Sources: Bureau of Economic Analysis, U.S. Dept. of Commerce. For the latest data, go to http://bea.gov/national/index.htm#gdp. And OECD Economic Outlook, 97 (May 2015), Annex Table 1.

minor economies, such as Greece, can sometimes spill over and drag down other economies with them. On the brighter side, economic strength abroad can give the U.S. economy a lift, as reflected by the recent headline "IMF Says Asia to Lead Growth in 2015."[3] The point is that the U.S. economy depends more and more on what's going on with the rest of the world and vice versa.

## 5-2c Leading Economic Indicators

Certain events foreshadow a turning point in economic activity. Months before a recession is fully under way, changes in leading economic indicators point to the coming storm. In the early stages of a recession, business slows down, orders for machinery and computers slip, and the stock market, anticipating lower profits, turns down. Consumer confidence in the economy also begins to sag, so households spend less, especially on big-ticket items like homes and automobiles. Unsold goods start piling up. All these signs are called **leading economic indicators** because they usually predict, or *lead to,* a downturn. Likewise, upturns in leading indicators point to an economic recovery. But leading indicators cannot predict precisely *when* a turning point will occur, or even

3. This headline appeared above a story written by Elaine Kurtenbach in *The Arizona Republic,* 8 May 2015.

*whether* one will occur. Sometimes leading indicators sound a false alarm.

Some economic indicators measure what's going on in the economy right now. **Coincident economic indicators** are those measures that reflect expansions, contractions, peaks, and troughs as they occur. Coincident indicators include total employment, personal income, and industrial production. And some economic indicators measure what has already happened. **Lagging economic indicators** follow, or trail, changes in overall economic activity. Lagging indicators, which look at the economy through the rearview mirror, include interest rates, the unemployment rate, and how long people remain unemployed.

Our introduction to business cycles has been largely mechanical, focusing on the history and measurement of these fluctuations. We have not

**leading economic indicators** Variables that predict or lead to a recession or recovery; examples include consumer confidence, stock market prices, business investment, and big-ticket purchases, such as automobiles and homes

**coincident economic indicators** Variables that reflect peaks and troughs in economic activity as they occur; examples include employment, personal income, and industrial production

**lagging economic indicators** Variables that follow, or trail, changes in overall economic activity; examples include the interest rate, the unemployment rate, and the average duration of unemployment discussed why economies fluctuate, in part because such a discussion requires firmer footing in macroeconomic theory and in part because the causes remain in dispute. In the next section, we begin to build a macroeconomic framework by introducing a key model of analysis.

## 5-3 AGGREGATE DEMAND AND AGGREGATE SUPPLY

The economy is so complex that we need to simplify matters, or to abstract from the millions of relationships to isolate the important ones. We must step back from all the individual economic transactions to survey the resulting mosaic.

### 5-3a Aggregate Output and the Price Level

Let's begin with something you already know. Picture a pizza. Now picture food more generally. Food, of course, includes not just pizza but thousands of other items. Although food is more general than pizza, you probably have no difficulty picturing food. Now make the leap from food to all goods and services produced in the economy— food, housing, clothing, entertainment, transportation, health care, and so on. Economists call this **aggregate output**. Because *aggregate* means total, aggregate output is the total amount of goods and services produced in the economy during a given period. Because output is measured per period, it's a flow measure. The best measure of aggregate output is *real GDP*, which you'll soon learn more about.

Just as we can talk about the demand for pizza, or the demand for food, we can talk about the demand for aggregate output. **Aggregate demand** is the relationship between the average price of aggregate output

**aggregate output** A composite measure of all final goods and services produced in an economy during a given period; real GDP

**aggregate demand** The relationship between the economy's price level and aggregate output demanded, with other things constant

**price level** A composite measure reflecting the prices of all goods and services in the economy relative to prices in a base year

**real gross domestic product (real GDP)** The economy's aggregate output measured in dollars of constant purchasing power

**aggregate demand curve** A curve representing the relationship between the economy's price level and real GDP demanded per period, with other things constant

in the economy and the quantity of aggregate output demanded. The average price of aggregate output is called the economy's **price level**. You are more familiar with these aggregate measures than you may think. Headlines refer to the growth of aggregate output—as in "Growth Slows in Second Quarter." News accounts also report on changes in the "cost of living," reflecting movements in the economy's price level—as in "Prices Jump in June."

In a later chapter, you learn how the economy's price level is computed. All you need to know now is that the price level in any year is an *index number*, or a reference number, comparing average prices that year with average prices in some base, or reference, year. If we say that the price level is higher, we mean compared with where it was. In Chapter 4, we talked about the price of a particular product, such as pizza, *relative to the prices of other products*. Now we talk about the *average price* of all goods and services produced in the economy *relative to the price level in some base year*.

The price level in the *base year* is standardized to a benchmark value of 100, and price levels in other years are expressed relative to the base-year price level. For example, in 2014, the U.S. price level, or price index, was 108.3, indicating that the price level that year was 8.3 percent higher than its value of 100 in the base year of 2009. The price level, or price index, is used not only to compare prices over time but also to compare real aggregate output over time. Economists use the *price index* to eliminate year-to-year changes in GDP due solely to changes in the price level. What's left is the change in real output—the change in the amount of goods and services produced. After adjusting GDP for price level changes, we end up with what is called the **real gross domestic product**, or **real GDP**. So the price index (1) shows how the economy's price level changes over time and (2) is used to figure out real GDP each year. You'll get a better idea of these two roles as we discuss the U.S. economy.

### 5-3b Aggregate Demand Curve

In Chapter 4, you learned about the demand for a particular product, such as pizza. Now let's talk about the demand for our composite measure of output—aggregate output, or real GDP. The **aggregate demand curve** shows the relationship between the price level in the economy and real GDP demanded, other things constant. Exhibit 4 shows a hypothetical aggregate demand curve, *AD*. The vertical axis measures an index of the economy's price level relative to a 2009 base-year price level of 100. The horizontal axis shows real GDP, which measures

## Exhibit 4
### U.S. Aggregate Demand Curve

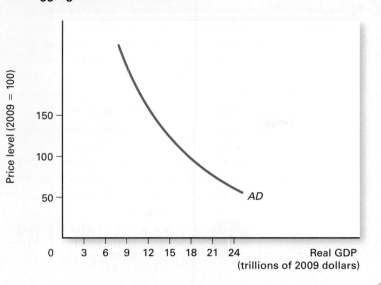

output in dollars of constant purchasing power (here we use 2009 prices).

The aggregate demand curve in Exhibit 4 reflects an inverse relationship between the price level in the U.S. economy and real GDP demanded. Aggregate demand sums demands of the four economic decision makers: households, firms, governments, and the rest of the world. As the price level increases, other things constant, households demand less housing and furniture, firms demand fewer trucks and tools, governments demand less computer software and military hardware, and the rest of the world demands less U.S. grain and U.S. aircraft.

The reasons behind this inverse relationship get a closer look in later chapters, but here's a quick summary. Real GDP demanded depends in part on household *wealth*. Some wealth is usually held in bank accounts and in currency. An increase in the price level, other things constant, decreases the purchasing power of bank accounts and currency. Households are therefore poorer when the price level increases, so the quantity of real GDP they demand decreases. Conversely, a reduction in the price level increases the purchasing power of bank accounts and currency. Because

> **"Aggregate demand sums demands of the four economic decision makers: households, firms, governments, and the rest of the world."**

households are richer as the price level decreases, the quantity of real GDP they demand increases.

Factors held constant along a given aggregate demand curve include the price levels in other countries as well as the exchange rates between the U.S. dollar and foreign currencies. When the U.S. price level increases, U.S. products become more expensive relative to foreign products. Consequently, households, firms, and governments both here and abroad decrease the quantity of U.S. products demanded. On the other hand, a lower U.S. price level makes U.S. products cheaper relative to foreign products, so the quantity of U.S. products demanded increases.

Consider the demand for a particular product versus aggregate demand. If the price of a particular product, such as pizza, increases, quantity demanded declines in part because pizza becomes more costly compared to substitutes. If the U.S. economy's price level increases, the quantity of U.S. real GDP demanded declines in part because U.S. products become more costly compared to foreign products.

### 5-3c Aggregate Supply Curve

The **aggregate supply curve** shows how much U.S. producers are willing and able to supply at each price level, other things constant. How does quantity supplied respond to changes in the price level? The upward-sloping aggregate supply curve, *AS*, in Exhibit 5 shows a positive relationship between the price level and the quantity of real GDP supplied. Assumed constant along an aggregate supply curve are (1) resource prices, (2) the state of technology and know-how, and (3) the rules of the game that provide production incentives, such as patents, tax rates, and business practices. With regard to resource prices, wage rates are typically

**aggregate supply curve** A curve representing the relationship between the economy's price level and real GDP supplied per period, with other things constant

CHAPTER 5: Introduction to Macroeconomics    83

*Exhibit 5*

**U.S. Aggregate Demand and Aggregate Supply in 2014**

The total output of the economy and its price level are determined at the intersection of the aggregate demand and aggregate supply curves. This point reflects real GDP and the price level for 2014, using 2009 as the base year.

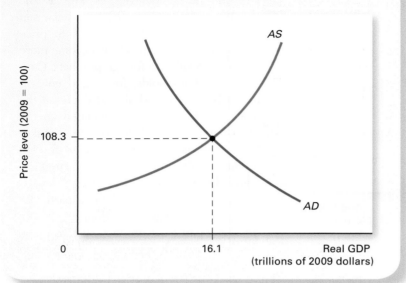

quantity demanded would not match quantity supplied.

Incidentally, although employment is not measured directly along the horizontal axis, firms usually must hire more workers to produce more output. So higher levels of real GDP can be beneficial because (1) more goods and services become available in the economy, and (2) more people are employed. Perhaps the best way to understand aggregate demand and aggregate supply is to apply these tools to the U.S. economy. The following section simplifies U.S. economic history to review changes in the price and output levels over time.

## 5-4 A BRIEF HISTORY OF THE U.S. ECONOMY

The history of the U.S. economy can be divided roughly into five economic eras: (a) before and during the Great Depression, (b) after the Great Depression to the early 1970s, (c) from the early 1970s to the early 1980s, (d) from the early 1980s to 2007, and (e) the Great Recession of 2007–2009 and beyond. The first era suffered from recessions and depressions, culminating in the Great Depression of the 1930s. These depressions were often accompanied by a falling price level. The second era was one of generally strong economic growth, with only moderate increases in the price level. The third era saw both high unemployment and high inflation at the same time, a troubling combination. The fourth era was more like the second, with good economic growth on average and only moderate increases in the price level. And the fifth era brought us the worst recession since the Great Depression. It remains to be seen whether the Great Recession turns out to be just a temporary setback or has long-term consequences for the United States and the world.

assumed to be constant along the aggregate supply curve. With wages constant, firms find a higher price level more profitable, so they increase real GDP supplied. *As long as the prices firms receive for their products rise faster than their cost of production, firms find it profitable to expand output, so real GDP supplied varies directly with the economy's price level.*

### 5-3d Equilibrium Real GDP

The aggregate demand curve intersects the aggregate supply curve to determine the equilibrium levels of price and real GDP in the economy. Exhibit 5 offers a rough depiction of aggregate demand and aggregate supply in 2014. Equilibrium real GDP that year was about $16.1 trillion (measured in dollars of 2009 purchasing power). The equilibrium price level was 108.3 (compared with a price level of 100 in the base year of 2009). At any other price level,

> **❝As long as the prices firms receive for their products rise faster than their cost of production, firms find it profitable to expand output, so real GDP supplied varies directly with the economy's price level.❞**

## 5-4a The Great Depression and Before

Before World War II, the U.S. economy alternated between hard times and prosperity. As noted earlier, the longest contraction on record occurred between 1873 and 1879, when 80 railroads went bankrupt and most of the nation's steel mills shut down. During the 1890s, the economy contracted about half the time, and the unemployment rate topped 18 percent. In October 1929, the stock market crash began what was to become the deepest, though not the longest, economic contraction in our nation's history, the Great Depression of the 1930s.

In terms of aggregate demand and aggregate supply, the Great Depression can be viewed as a shift to the left of the aggregate demand curve, as shown in Exhibit 6. $AD_{1929}$ depicts the aggregate demand curve in 1929, before the onset of the depression. Real GDP in 1929 was $1,057 billion (measured in dollars of 2009 purchasing power), and the price level was 9.9 (relative to a 2009 base-year price level of 100). By 1933, aggregate demand shifted leftward, decreasing to $AD_{1933}$. Why did aggregate demand decline? Though economists still debate the exact causes, most agree that the stock market crash of 1929 was the trigger. From there, grim business expectations cut investment,

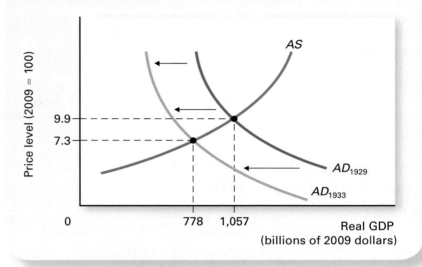

*Exhibit 6*

### The Decrease in U.S. Aggregate Demand From 1929 to 1933

The Great Depression of the 1930s can be represented by a shift to the left of the aggregate demand curve, from $AD_{1929}$ to $AD_{1933}$. In the resulting depression, real GDP fell from $1,057 billion to $778 billion, and the price level dropped from 9.9 to 7.3, measured relative to a price level of 100 in the base year 2009.

consumer spending fell, banks failed, the nation's money supply shrank by one-third, and world trade was severely restricted by high tariffs. All this contributed to a big decline in aggregate demand. The aggregate supply curve probably also shifted somewhat during this period, but the drop in aggregate demand was the dominant force.

Because of the decline in aggregate demand, both the price level and real GDP dropped. Real GDP fell 26 percent, from $1,057 billion in 1929 to $778 billion in 1933, and the price level fell 26 percent, from 9.9 to 7.3. As real GDP declined, unemployment soared from

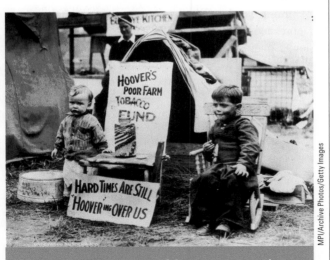

The size and persistence of the Great Depression led to increased government involvement in the economy.

MPI/Archive Photos/Getty Images

> **"Higher levels of real GDP can be beneficial because (1) more goods and services become available in the economy, and (2) more people are usually employed."**

only 3 percent of the labor force in 1929 to 25 percent in 1933, the highest U.S. rate ever recorded.

Before the Great Depression, macroeconomic policy was based primarily on the *laissez-faire* philosophy of Adam Smith. Smith, you may recall, argued in his famous book, *The Wealth of Nations*, that if people are allowed to pursue their self-interest in free markets, resources would be guided as if by an "invisible hand" to produce the most efficient and most valued level of aggregate output. Although the U.S. economy suffered many sharp contractions even before the Great Depression, most economists of the day viewed these as a natural phase of the economy—unfortunate for those who lost jobs and savings but ultimately therapeutic and self-correcting.

## 5-4b The Age of Keynes: After the Great Depression to the Early 1970s

The Great Depression was so deep that it stimulated new thinking about how the economy worked (or didn't work). In 1936, John Maynard Keynes (1883–1946) published *The General Theory of Employment, Interest, and Money,* the most famous economics book of the 20th century. In it, he argued that aggregate demand was inherently unstable, in part because investment decisions were often guided by the unpredictable "animal spirits" of business expectations. If businesses grew pessimistic about the economy, they would invest less, which would reduce aggregate demand, output, and employment. For example, investment spending dropped more than 80 percent between 1929 and 1933. Keynes saw no natural market forces operating to ensure that the economy, even if allowed a reasonable time to adjust, would get output and employment growing again.

*Keynes proposed that the government jolt the economy out of its depression by increasing aggregate demand.* He recommended an expansionary fiscal policy to help offset a contraction. The government could achieve this stimulus either directly by increasing its own spending, or indirectly by cutting taxes to stimulate consumption and investment. But either action would likely create a federal budget deficit. A **federal budget deficit** is a flow variable that measures,

**federal budget deficit**
A flow variable measuring the amount by which federal government outlays exceed federal government revenues in a particular period, usually a year

**demand-side economics**
Macroeconomic policy that focuses on shifting the aggregate demand curve as a way of promoting full employment and price stability

for a particular period, the amount by which federal outlays exceed federal revenues.

To understand what Keynes had in mind, imagine federal budget policies that would increase the aggregate demand shown in Exhibit 6, shifting the aggregate demand curve to the right, back to its original position. Such a shift would raise real GDP, which would increase employment. According to the Keynesian prescription, the miracle drug of fiscal policy—changes in government spending and taxes—could compensate for what he viewed as the instability of private-sector spending, especially investment. If demand in the private sector declined, Keynes said the government should pick up the slack. We can think of the Keynesian approach as **demand-side economics** because it focused on how changes in aggregate demand might promote full employment. Keynes argued that government stimulus could shock the economy out of its depression. Once investment returned to normal levels, and the economy started growing on its own, the government's shock treatment would no longer be necessary.

The U.S. economy bounced back beginning in 1933, growing four years in a row (see Exhibit 2 again). The outbreak of World War II boosted employment to fight for the country and to make tanks, ships, aircraft, and the like. Federal government spending increased from 7 percent of GDP in 1940 to 46 percent in 1944. The explosion of output and sharp drop in unemployment seemed to confirm the powerful role government spending could play in the economy. But the increase in government spending, with no significant increase in tax rates, created large federal deficits during the war.

Immediately after the war, memories of the Great Depression were still vivid. Trying to avoid another depression, Congress approved the *Employment Act of 1946,* which imposed a clear responsibility on the federal government to promote "maximum employment, production, and purchasing power." The act also required the president to appoint a *Council of Economic Advisers,* a three-member team of economists to provide economic advice and report on the economy.

The economy seemed to prosper during the 1950s largely without added stimulus from fiscal policy. The 1960s, however, proved to be the *golden age of Keynesian economics,* a period when fiscal policy makers thought they could "fine-tune" the economy for top performance—just as a mechanic fine-tunes a racecar. During the early 1960s, nearly all advanced economies around the world enjoyed low unemployment and healthy growth with only modest inflation.

The U.S. economy was on such a roll that toward the end of the 1960s some economists believed the business cycle was history. As a sign of the times, the name of a federal publication, *Business Cycle Developments,* was changed to *Business Conditions Digest.* In the early 1970s, however, the business cycle returned with a fury. Worse yet, the problems of recession were compounded by higher inflation, which increased during the recessions of 1973–1975 and 1980. Prior to that, high inflation had been limited primarily to periods of expansion—that is, to boom times. Confidence in demand-side policies was shaken, and the expression "fine-tuning" dropped from the economic vocabulary. What ended the golden age of Keynesian economics?

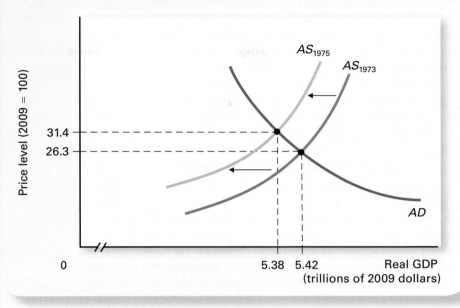

*Exhibit 7*

**U.S. Stagflation From 1973 to 1975**

The stagflation of the mid-1970s can be represented as a leftward shift of the aggregate supply curve from $AS_{1973}$ to $AS_{1975}$. Aggregate output fell from $5.42 trillion in 1973 to $5.38 trillion in 1975, for a decline of about $40 billion (stagnation). The price level rose from 26.3 to 31.4, for an increase of 19 percent (inflation).

## 5-4c Stagflation: 1973–1975 and 1979–1980

During the late 1960s, federal spending increased on both the war in Vietnam and social programs at home. This combined stimulus increased aggregate demand enough that in 1968 the *inflation rate,* the annual percentage increase in the price level, rose to 4.4 percent, after averaging only 2.0 percent during the previous decade. Inflation climbed to 4.9 percent in 1969 and to 5.3 percent in 1970. These rates were so alarming at the time that in 1971, President Richard Nixon imposed ceilings on prices and wages. Those ceilings were eliminated in 1973, about the time that crop failures around the world caused grain prices to soar. To compound these problems, Organization of the Petroleum Exporting Countries (OPEC) cut its supply of oil to world markets, so oil prices jumped. Crop failures plus the OPEC action reduced aggregate supply, shown in Exhibit 7 by the leftward shift of the aggregate supply curve from $AS_{1973}$ to $AS_{1975}$. This resulted in **stagflation**, meaning a *stag*nation, or a contraction, in the economy's aggregate output and in*flation*, or increase, in the economy's price level. Real GDP declined between 1973 and 1975, and

unemployment climbed from 4.9 percent to 8.5 percent. During the same two-year period, the price level jumped by 19 percent.

Stagflation hit again five years later, stoked again by more OPEC cutbacks. Between 1979 and 1980, real GDP declined but the price level increased by 9.1 percent. Macroeconomics has not been the same since. Because stagflation was on the supply side, not on the demand side, the demand-management prescriptions of Keynes seemed ineffective. Increasing aggregate demand might reduce unemployment but would worsen inflation.

## 5-4d Somewhat Normal Times: 1980 to 2007

Increasing aggregate supply seemed an appropriate way to combat stagflation, for such a move would both lower the price level and increase output and employment. Attention thus turned from aggregate demand to aggregate supply. A key idea behind **supply-side economics** was that the

**stagflation** A contraction, or stagnation, of a nation's output accompanied by inflation in the price level

**supply-side economics** Macroeconomic policy that focuses on a rightward shift of the aggregate supply curve through tax cuts or other changes to increase production incentives federal government, by lowering tax rates, would increase after-tax wages, which would provide incentives to increase the supply of labor and other resources. According to advocates of the supply-side approach, the resulting increase in aggregate supply would achieve the happy result of expanding real GDP and reducing the price level. You can get the idea behind supply-side economics in Exhibit 7 by picturing the aggregate supply curve as shifting back to the right from $AS_{1975}$ to $AS_{1973}$. Such a move would increase real GDP while lowering the price level. But this was easier said than done.

In 1981, to provide economic incentives to increase aggregate supply, President Ronald Reagan and Congress cut personal income tax rates by an average of 23 percent to be phased in over three years. They believed that lower tax rates would increase aggregate supply, thereby expanding output and employment. They hoped that higher tax revenue from a larger economy would more than make up for the revenue lost by the cut in tax rates. In other words, the tax cutters hoped that the government's smaller share of a bigger pie would exceed what had been its larger share of a smaller pie.

But even before the tax cut took effect, recession hit, contracting output and pushing the unemployment rate up to 10 percent. Once the recession ended in late 1982, the economy began to grow, and this growth continued for the rest of the decade. Between 1982 and 1990 employment grew 19 percent and real GDP grew 38 percent, an indication that each worker was producing more. But the growth in federal spending exceeded the growth in federal tax revenues during this period, so federal budget deficits increased. Deficits worsened with the onset of a recession in 1990–1991, which was brought on by the first war in the Persian Gulf. Annual deficits accumulated as a growing federal debt. The **federal debt** is a stock variable that measures the net accumulation of prior federal deficits. But robust economic growth during the 1990s boosted employment by 15 percent and real GDP by 40 percent, again an indication that output per worker was growing nicely. The expanding economy combined with a booming stock market to increase tax revenue enough to yield a federal budget surplus by the end of the 1990s.

By early 2001, the U.S. economic expansion had lasted ten years to become the longest on record. Then the economy slipped into a short recession aggravated by the terrorist attacks of September 11, 2001. The recession lasted only eight months, but the recovery was slow and uneven. President George W. Bush pushed through tax cuts "to get the economy moving again." But the tax cuts and

**federal debt** A stock variable that measures the net accumulation of annual federal deficits

spending programs increased the federal budget deficit, which exceeded $400 billion in 2004. Still, employment grew 7 percent between 2000 and 2007, and real GDP grew 18 percent. That growth helped cut the budget deficit to $161 billion by 2007. In fact, during the quarter century between 1982 and 2007, employment grew 47 percent and real GDP grew 128 percent, quite an impressive performance and the envy of the world. Then things went bad.

## 5-4e The Great Recession of 2007–2009 and Beyond

By late 2007, the expansion that began in late 2001 had lasted six years, about average for expansions since World War II. So it was not that surprising when the expansion peaked in December 2007; then the recession began, this time precipitated by declining home prices and rising foreclosures, as more borrowers failed to make their mortgage payments. With home prices falling, fewer were getting built, meaning fewer jobs in residential construction, furnishings, and other industries that rely on the housing sector. During the first eight months of the recession, U.S. job losses averaged 151,000 a month, in line with monthly losses during the prior two recessions. In early 2008, Washington tried to stimulate aggregate demand with a $117 billion tax rebate, but the result was disappointing. The softer economy and tax cuts nearly tripled the federal deficit from $161 billion in 2007 to $459 billion in 2008; at the time this deficit seemed huge.

Fears about the effect of rising home foreclosures on the banking system fed into a full-scale global financial panic in September 2008, triggered by the collapse of Lehman Brothers, a Wall Street investment bank. An *investment bank* is a financial institution that helps businesses raise financial capital. Because Lehman Brothers was the largest bankruptcy in U.S. history, financial

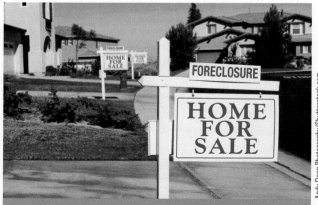

Falling home prices led to an unprecedented number of foreclosures — a key cause of the Great Recession.

institutions grew reluctant to lend, so credit dried up—a major problem for an economy that relies a lot on credit. Businesses cut investments sharply. Consumers cut their spending in the face of sliding home prices, mounting job losses, and a collapsing stock market. You could picture all this as a leftward shift of the aggregate demand curve. These events unfolded against the backdrop of a presidential election. Is it any wonder that voters in 2008 went for "hope and change?"

After the collapse of Lehman Brothers and the freezing up of financial flows around the world, policy makers were emboldened to enact some extraordinary measures to shore up confidence in financial institutions, open up the flow of credit, and stimulate consumer spending. These included two huge programs: (1) the $700 billion Troubled Asset Relief Program, or TARP, aimed at stabilizing financial institutions, and (2) the $787 billion American Recovery and Reinvestment Act, or the stimulus bill, aimed at increasing aggregate demand (the estimated cost would rise to $831 billion). The effects of these programs are still being debated today and will be discussed in later chapters. One point to underscore now is just how extraordinary these measures were. What we know for sure is that these rescue programs tripled the federal deficit from $459 billion in 2008 to $1.4 trillion in 2009.

We also know that during the 12 months following the failure of Lehman Brothers, job losses averaged 565,000 a month, nearly four times the average during the two prior recessions and during the first eight months of 2008. Job losses on that scale had not been experienced since the Great Depression. Altogether, employment fell by 8.4 million between December 2007 and December 2009, a drop of 6.1 percent. Despite the sizable job losses, real GDP didn't fall that much. Because those who still had jobs were more productive, output dropped only about 2 percent between 2007 and 2009, and the price level hardly budged. The recession ended in June 2009. By the third quarter of 2009, real GDP was growing again, though the unemployment rate remained stubbornly high deep into 2012. Events during the recession of 2007–2009 traumatized the economy. Lasting 18 months, what

has come to be called the Great Recession was the longest of the 11 recessions since World War II. This recession will be discussed in the course of the following chapters.

Focusing on the ups and downs of the economy can miss the point that the U.S. economy over the long run has been an incredible creator of jobs and output—one of the most productive economies in the world. To underscore that point, we close with a look at U.S. economic growth since 1929.

## 5-4f U.S. Economic Growth Since 1929

Points in Exhibit 8 trace the U.S. real GDP and price level for each year since 1929. Aggregate demand and aggregate supply curves are shown for 2014, but all points in the series reflect such intersections. Years of growing GDP are indicated as blue points and years of declining GDP as red ones. Despite the Great Depression of the 1930s and the 11 recessions since World War II, the long-term growth in output is unmistakable. Real GDP, measured along the horizontal axis in 2009 constant dollars, grew from about $1.1 trillion in 1929 to about $16.1 trillion in 2014—an elevenfold increase and an average annual growth rate of 3.3 percent. The price index also rose, but not quite as fast, rising from 9.9 in 1929 to 105 in 2012—almost an elevenfold increase and an average inflation rate of 2.9 percent per year. Note that what matters here is the growth in real GDP, because that nets out the effects of inflation (inflation is mostly troublesome noise in the economy). Since 1982, annual output declined only three times—in 1991, in 2008, and in 2009.

Because the U.S. population is growing all the time, the economy must create more jobs just to employ the additional people entering the workforce. For example, the U.S. population grew from 122 million in 1929 to 319 million in 2014, a rise of 162 percent. Fortunately, employment grew even faster, from 47 million in 1929 to 146 million in 2014, for a growth of 211 percent. So, since 1929, employment grew more than enough to keep up with a rising population. Despite the

> **"Focusing on the ups and downs of the economy can miss the point that the U.S. economy over the long run has been an incredible creator of jobs and output—one of the most productive economies in the world."**

## Exhibit 8

### Tracking U.S. Real GDP and Price Level Since 1929

As you can see, both real GDP and the price level trended higher since 1929. Blue points indicate years of growing real GDP, and red points are years of declining real GDP. Real GDP in 2014 was 15 times greater than in 1929.

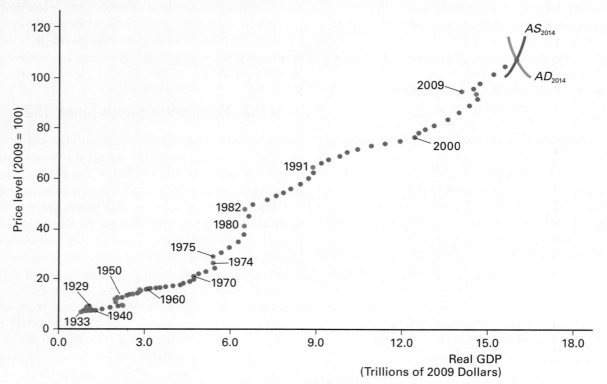

recessions, the United States has been an impressive job machine over the long run.

Not only did the number employed more than triple since 1929, the average education of workers increased as well. Other resources, especially capital, also rose

sharply. What's more, the level of technology and know-how improved steadily, thanks to breakthroughs such as the personal computer and the Internet. The availability of more and higher-quality human capital and physical capital increased the productivity of each

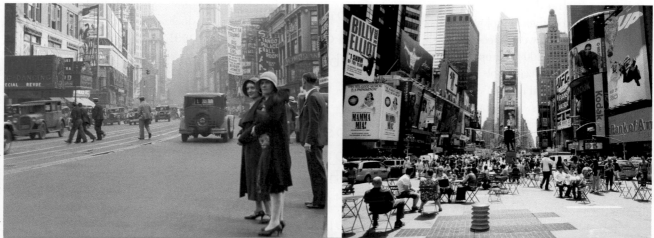

Real GDP per capita rose sixfold between 1929 and 2012. The impact of such economic growth is clearly seen in these two photos of Times Square in New York.

worker, contributing to the fifteenfold jump in real GDP since 1929.

Real GDP is important, but the best measure of the average standard of living is an economy's **real GDP per capita**, which tells us how much an economy produces on average per resident. Because real GDP grew much faster than the population, real GDP *per capita* jumped nearly sixfold between 1929 and 2014. The United States is one of the largest economies in the world and a leader among major economies in output per capita.[4]

## 5-5  FINAL WORD

Because macroeconomists have no test subjects and cannot rely on luck, they hone their craft by developing models of the economy and then searching for evidence to support or reject these models. In this sense, macroeconomics is retrospective, always looking at recent developments for hints about which model works best. The macroeconomist is like a traveler who can see only the road behind and must find the way ahead using a collection of poorly drawn maps. The traveler must continually check each map (or model) against the landmarks to see whether one map is more consistent with the terrain than the others. Each new batch of information about the economy causes macroeconomists to shuffle through their "maps" to check their models.

Macroeconomics often emphasizes what can go wrong with the economy. Sagging output, high unemployment, and rising inflation capture much of the attention, and we'll examine those problems in the next two chapters. But perhaps the most important performance measure is economic growth, and we'll devote a chapter to that after you learn more about real GDP, unemployment, and inflation.

Finally, learning about the macro economy is like learning about the weather. You may not be able to change the weather, but knowing what's coming will help you cope with it better—for example, by bringing an umbrella if rain is on the way. Likewise, you may not be able to change macroeconomic conditions, but knowing what's coming will help you adapt to them better—for example, by deciding to pursue graduate studies rather than dive into a poor job market. A knowledge of macroeconomics will give you an edge in coping with a complex economic environment.

**real GDP per capita** Real GDP divided by the population; the best measure of an economy's standard of living

4. "GDP and the Economy," *Survey of Current Business* 95 (April 2015); *Economic Report of the President*, February 2015; *Economic Report of the President*, January 1980; and *OECD Economic Outlook* 97 (May 2015). For the latest real GDP and price level data, go to http://bea.gov/. For the latest population data, go to http://www.census.gov. For the latest employment data, go to http://www.bls.gov.

## STUDY TOOLS 5

### READY TO STUDY? IN THE BOOK, YOU CAN:

☐ Work the Problems at the end of the chapter.

☐ Rip out the chapter review card for a handy summary of the chapter and key terms.

### ONLINE AT CENGAGEBRAIN.COM YOU CAN:

☐ Collect StudyBits while you read and study the chapter.

☐ Quiz yourself on key concepts.

☐ Prepare for tests with chapter flash cards as well as flash cards that you create.

☐ Watch videos to explore economics further.

# CHAPTER 5 PROBLEMS

*Your instructor can access the answers to these problems online at http://cengagebrain.com.*

**5-1 Explain what's special about a national economy compared to regional, state, or local economies**

1. *(The National Economy)* Why do economists pay more attention to national economies (for example, the U.S. or Canadian economies) than to state or provincial economies (such as California or Ontario)?

**5-2 Describe the phases of the business cycle**

2. *(Economic Fluctuations)* Describe the various components of fluctuations in economic activity over time. Because economic activity fluctuates, how is long-term growth possible?

**5-3 Explain the shapes of the aggregate demand curve and the aggregate supply curve, and how they interact to determine real GDP and the price level for a nation**

3. *(Aggregate Demand and Supply)* Review the information on demand and supply curves in Chapter 4. How do the aggregate demand and aggregate supply curves presented in this chapter differ from the market curves of Chapter 4?

4. *(Aggregate Demand and Supply)* Determine whether each of the following would cause a shift of the aggregate demand curve, a shift of the aggregate supply curve, neither, or both. Which curve shifts, and in which direction? What happens to aggregate output and the price level in each case?
   a. The price level changes.
   b. Consumer confidence declines.
   c. The supply of resources increases.
   d. The wage rate increases.

**5-4 Identify the five eras of the U.S. economy, and describe briefly what went on during each**

5. *(Five Eras of U.S. Economy)* Identify the five eras of the U.S. economy beginning with the Great Depression and before.

6. *(Supply-Side Economics)* One supply-side measure introduced by the Reagan administration was a cut in income tax rates. Use an aggregate demand/aggregate supply diagram to show what effect was intended. What might happen if such a tax cut also shifted the aggregate demand curve?

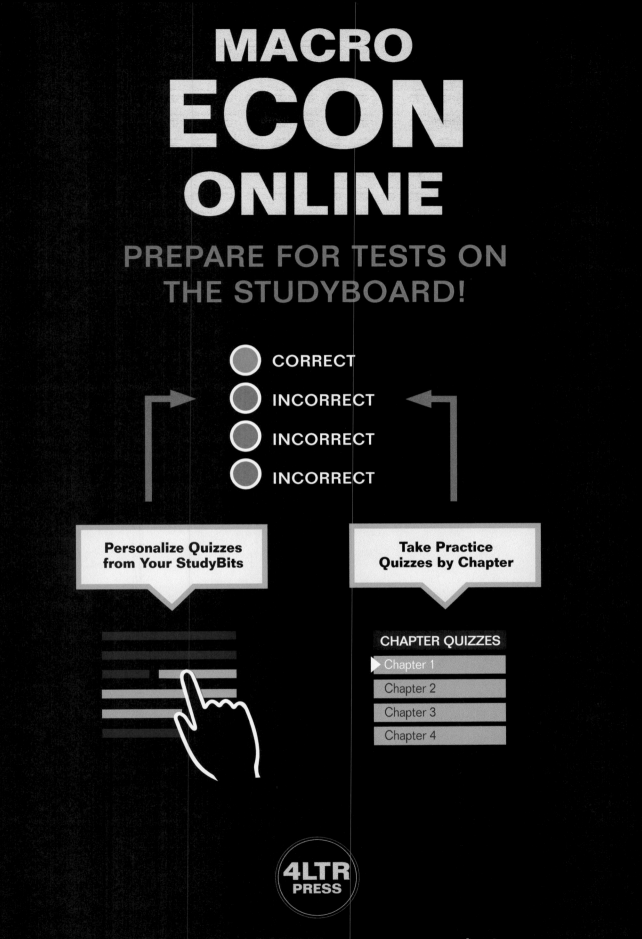

# 6 | Tracking the U.S. Economy

Mark Summerfield/Alamy

## LEARNING OUTCOMES

After studying this chapter, you will be able to…

**6-1** Describe the two ways of computing GDP and explain why they are equivalent

**6-2** Trace through the circular-flow model, explaining each of the 10 steps along the way

**6-3** Identify the limitations of the national income accounting system

**6-4** Define a price index and explain why is it useful

After finishing this chapter go to **PAGE 109** for **STUDY TOOLS**

**Topics discussed in Chapter 6 include:**

- National income accounts
- Expenditure approach to GDP
- Income approach to GDP
- Circular flow of income and expenditure
- Leakages and injections
- Limitations of national income accounting
- Consumer price index
- GDP price index

- How do we track one of the most complex economies in world history?

- What's gross about the gross domestic product? What's domestic about it?

- If you make yourself a tuna sandwich, how much does your effort add to the gross domestic product?

- Because prices change over time, how can we compare the economy's production in one year with that in other years?

*Answers to these and other questions are addressed in this chapter, which introduces an economic scorecard for one of the largest economies in world history. That scorecard is the national income accounting system, which reduces a huge network of economic activity to a few aggregate measures.*

As you will see, aggregate output is measured either by the spending on that output or by the income derived from producing it. In this chapter, we examine each approach and learn why they are equivalent. The major components and important equalities built into the national income accounts are offered here as another way of understanding how the economy works—not as a foreign language to be mastered before the next exam. The emphasis is more on economic intuition than on accounting precision.

> **"How do we track one of the most complex economies in world history?"**

## 6-1 THE PRODUCT OF A NATION

How do we measure the economy's performance? During much of the 17th and 18th centuries, when the dominant economic policy was mercantilism, many thought that economic prosperity was best measured by the *stock* of precious metals a nation accumulated in the public treasury. Mercantilism led to restrictions on international trade, with the unintended consequence of reducing the gains from comparative advantage. In the latter half of the 18th century, François Quesnay became the first to measure economic activity as a *flow*. In 1758, he published his *Tableau Économique*, which described the *circular flow* of output and income through different sectors of the economy. His insight was likely inspired by his knowledge of blood's circular flow in the body—Quesnay was court physician to King Louis XV of France.

> **"GDP can be measured either by total spending on U.S. production or by total income received from that production."**

Rough measures of national income were developed in England two centuries ago, but detailed calculations built up from microeconomic data were refined in the United States during the Great Depression. The resulting *national income accounting system* organizes huge quantities of data collected from a variety of sources across America. These data are summarized, assembled into a coherent framework, and reported by the federal government. The conception and implementation of these accounts has been hailed as one of the greatest achievements of the 20th century. The U.S. national income accounts are the most widely copied and most highly regarded in the world and earned their developer, Simon Kuznets, the Nobel Prize in 1971 for "giving quantitative precision to economic entities."

### 6-1a National Income Accounts

How do the national income accounts keep track of the economy's incredible variety of goods and services, from hiking boots to Pilates classes? The *gross domestic product,* or GDP, measures the market value of all final goods and services produced during a year by resources located in the United States, regardless of who owns the resources. For example, GDP includes production in the United States by foreign firms, such as a Toyota plant in Kentucky, but excludes foreign production by U.S. firms, such as a Ford plant in Mexico.

© iStockphoto.com /RiverNorthPhotography

GDP estimates are computed each quarter by the Bureau of Economic Analysis in Washington, D.C. On computation day, staff members follow a process that dates back half a century. The office is in "lockup." Communications with the outside are shut down—no cell phones or land lines can be used. Office drapes are drawn. Only certain people are allowed in and out. To estimate GDP, the staff draws on more than 10,000 streams of data describing economic activity. Nobody speaks the final GDP estimate aloud for fear that it could be overheard and exploited in securities markets. Once they estimate GDP and its components, they write a press release, make hundreds of copies, then lock all but one in a safe for distribution to the media the next morning at 8:30 A.M. Eastern Time. The single copy not locked away is delivered to the head of the president's Council of Economic Advisers, so he or she can give the president a heads-up. But despite all the security and formality, we should keep in mind that the GDP reported is still just an estimate, one that will be revised twice more each quarter as more data become available.

The national income accounts are based on the simple fact that *one person's spending is another person's income.* GDP can be measured either by total spending on U.S. production or by total income received

from that production. The **expenditure approach** adds up spending on all final goods and services produced in the United States during the year. The **income approach** adds up earnings during the year by those who produce all that output. In the *double-entry bookkeeping system* used to track the economy, spending on aggregate output is recorded on one side of the ledger and income from producing that aggregate output is recorded on the other side.

Gross domestic product includes only **final goods and services**, which are goods and services sold to the final, or end, user. A toothbrush, a pair of contact lenses, and a bus ride are examples of final goods and services. Whether a sale is to the final user depends on who buys the product. When you buy chicken for dinner, that's reflected in GDP. When KFC buys chicken, however, that's not counted in GDP because KFC is not the final consumer. Only after the chicken is prepared, fried, and sold by KFC is the transaction counted in GDP.

**Intermediate goods and services** are those purchased for additional processing and resale, like KFC's chicken purchase. This change may be imperceptible, as when a grocer buys canned goods to restock shelves. Or the intermediate goods can be dramatically altered, as when an artist transforms a $100 canvas and $30 in oil paints into a work of art that sells for $5,000. Sales of intermediate goods and services are excluded from GDP to avoid the mistake of **double counting**, which is counting an item's value more than once. For example, suppose the grocer buys a can of tuna for $1.00 and sells it for $1.50. If GDP counted both the intermediate transaction of $1.00 and the final transaction of $1.50, the recorded value of $2.50 would exceed its final value by $1.00. Hence, GDP counts only the market value of the final sale. As another example, in a recent year Walmart paid $287 billion for products it sold for

$375 billion. If GDP counted both Walmart's intermediate transactions and final transactions, Walmart's impact on GDP would be $287 billion too high. GDP also ignores most of the secondhand value of used goods, such as existing homes, used cars, and used textbooks. These goods were counted in GDP when they were produced. But just as the services provided by the grocer and by Walmart are captured in GDP, so are the services provided by real estate agents, used-car dealers, and used-book sellers.

## 6-1b GDP Based on the Expenditure Approach

As noted already, one way to measure GDP is to add up spending on all final goods and services produced in the economy during the year. The easiest way to understand the spending approach is to sort aggregate expenditure into its components: consumption, investment, government purchases, and net exports. **Consumption**, or more specifically, *personal consumption expenditures*, consists of purchases of final goods and services by households during the year. Consumption is the largest spending category, averaging 68 percent of U.S. GDP during the past decade. Along with *services* such as dry cleaning, haircuts, and air travel, consumption includes *nondurable goods*, such as soap and soup, and *durable goods*, such as furniture and kitchen appliances. Durable goods are expected to last at least three years.

**Investment**, or more specifically, *gross private domestic investment*, consists of spending on new construction, new capital goods, new software, and on net additions to inventories. The most important investment is **physical capital**, such as new buildings and new machinery. Investment also includes new **residential construction**. Although it fluctuates a lot from year to year, investment averaged 16 percent of U.S. GDP this past decade. More generally, investment consists of spending on current production that is not used for current consumption. A firm's net increase in inventories also counts as investment because it represents current production not used for current consumption. **Inventories** are stocks of goods in process, such as computer parts, and stocks of finished goods, such as new computers awaiting sale. Inventories help manufacturers cope with unexpected changes in the supply of their resources or in the demand for their products.

Although investment includes purchasing a new residence, it excludes purchases of *existing* buildings and machines and purchases of financial assets, such as stocks and bonds. Existing buildings and machines were counted in GDP when they were produced. Stocks and bonds are not investments themselves but simply indications of ownership.

**Government purchases**, or more specifically, *government consumption and gross investment,* include government spending for goods and services—from clearing snowy roads to clearing court dockets, from buying library books to paying teachers. Government purchases averaged 20 percent of U.S. GDP during the last decade. Government purchases, and therefore GDP, exclude transfer payments, such as Social Security, welfare benefits, and unemployment insurance. Such payments are not true purchases by the government or true earnings by the recipients.

The final spending component, net exports, reflects international trade in goods and services. Goods, or *merchandise,* include physical items such as wheat and machinery (stuff you can load on a ship). Services, or so-called *invisibles,* include intangible items, such as international travel and education. Foreign purchases of U.S. goods and services are counted as part of U.S. GDP. But U.S. purchases of foreign goods and services are subtracted from U.S. GDP. **Net exports** equal the value of U.S. exports of goods and services minus the value of U.S. imports of goods and services. U.S. imports have exceeded U.S. exports nearly every year since the 1960s, meaning U.S. net exports have been negative. During the last decade, net exports averaged a negative 4 percent of GDP.

**Aggregate expenditure** is total spending on final goods and services in an economy during a given period, usually a year. With the expenditure approach, the nation's aggregate expenditure sums

**consumption** Household purchases of final goods and services, except for new residences, which count as investment

**investment** The purchase of new plants, new software, new equipment, new buildings, and new residences, plus net additions to inventories

**physical capital** Manufactured items used to produce goods and services; includes new plants and new equipment

**residential construction** Building new homes or dwelling places

**inventories** Producers' stocks of finished and in-process goods

**government purchases** Spending for goods and services by all levels of government; government outlays minus transfer payments

**net exports** The value of a country's exports minus the value of its imports

**aggregate expenditure** Total spending on final goods and services in an economy during a given period, usually a year; the sum of consumption, investment, government purchases, and net exports consumption, $C$; investment, $I$; government purchases, $G$; and net exports, which is the value of exports, $X$, minus the value of imports, $M$, or $(X - M)$. Summing these yields aggregate expenditure, or GDP:

$$C + I + G + (X - M) = \text{Aggregate expenditure} = \text{GDP}$$

## 6-1c Composition of Aggregate Expenditure

Now that we have introduced each component of aggregate spending, let's get a better idea of spending over time. Exhibit 1 shows the composition of spending in the United States since 1959. As you can see, consumption's share of GDP appears stable from year to year, but the long-term trend shows an increase from an average of 62 percent during the 1960s to 68 percent during the most recent decade. Investment fluctuates more year to year but with little long-term trend up or down; investment averaged 15 percent of GDP during the 1960s and 16 percent during the most recent

decade. But, as you can see in the exhibit, investment's share of GDP dropped sharply during the recession of 2007–2009.

Government purchases declined from an average of 22 percent of GDP during the 1960s to an average of 20 percent during the last decade, due primarily to decreases in defense spending. Remember, government purchases do not include transfer payments, which have grown faster than government purchases. Net exports averaged a surplus of 1 percent in the 1960s but were in deficit nearly every year since then, averaging a minus 4 percent of GDP during the last decade. Negative net exports mean that the sum of consumption, investment, and government purchases exceeds GDP, the amount produced in the U.S. economy. Americans are spending more than they make, and they are covering the difference by borrowing from abroad. U.S. spending exceeds U.S. GDP by the amount shown as negative net exports. Because the spending components must sum to GDP, *negative* net exports are expressed in Exhibit 1 by the red portion

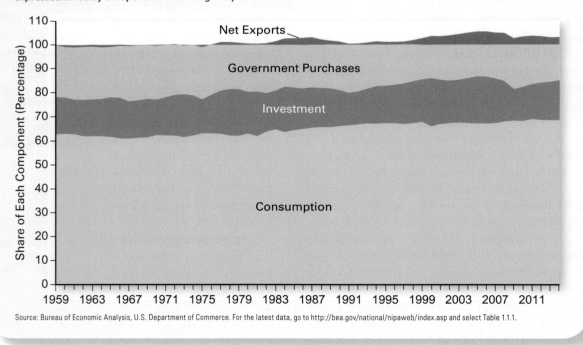

*Exhibit 1*

**U.S. Spending Components as Percent of GDP Since 1959**

The composition of U.S. GDP has not changed that much since 1959. Consumption's share edged up from an average of 62 percent during the 1960s to 68 percent during the most recent decade. Investment has fluctuated from year to year but with no clear long-term trend up or down. Government purchases declined slightly from an average of 22 percent of GDP during the 1960s to an average of 20 percent in the most recent decade. And net exports have become more negative, expressed in red by that portion exceeding 100 percent of GDP.

Source: Bureau of Economic Analysis, U.S. Department of Commerce. For the latest data, go to http://bea.gov/national/nipaweb/index.asp and select Table 1.1.1.

of spending that exceeds 100 percent of GDP. Thus, during the last five-and-a-half decades, consumption's share of total spending increased and government purchases decreased. Investment's share bounced around and net exports' share turned negative, meaning that imports exceeded exports.

## 6-1d GDP Based on the Income Approach

The expenditure approach sums, or aggregates, spending on production. The income approach sums, or aggregates, income arising from that production. Again, double-entry bookkeeping ensures that the value of aggregate output equals the aggregate income paid for resources used to produce that output: the wages, interest, rent, and profit arising from production. The price of a Hershey's candy bar reflects the income earned by resource suppliers along the way. **Aggregate income** equals the sum of all the income earned by resource suppliers in the economy. Thus, we can say that

Aggregate expenditure = GDP = Aggregate income

A product usually goes through several stages involving different firms on its way to the consumer. A wooden desk, for example, starts as raw timber, which is typically cut by one firm, milled by another, made into a desk by a third, and retailed by a fourth. We avoid double counting either by including only the market value of the desk when sold to the final user or by *summing the value added at each stage of production*. The **value added** by each firm equals that firm's selling price minus payments for inputs from other firms. The value added at each stage is the income earned by resource suppliers at that stage. *The value added at all stages sums to the market value of the final good, and the value added for all final goods sums to GDP based on the income approach*. For example, suppose you buy a wooden desk for $200. This final market value gets added directly into GDP. Consider the history of that desk. Suppose the tree that gave its life for your studies was cut into a log and sold to a miller for $20, who converted the log to lumber that sold for

> **"The value added at all stages sums to the market value of the final good, and the value added for all final goods sums to GDP based on the income approach."**

$50 to a desk maker, who made the desk and sold it for $120 to a retailer, who sold it to you for $200.

Column (1) of Exhibit 2 lists the selling price at each stage of production. If all these transactions were added up, the sum of $390 would exceed the $200 market value of the desk. To avoid double counting, we include only the value added at each stage, listed in column (3) as the difference between the purchase price and the selling price at that stage. Again, *the value added at each stage equals the income earned by those who supply their resources at that stage*. For example, the $80 in value added by the retailer consists of income to resource suppliers at that stage, from the salesperson to the janitor who cleaned the showroom to the trucker who provided "free delivery" of your desk. The value added at all stages totals $200, which is both the final market value of the desk and the total income earned by all resource suppliers along the way.

To reinforce your understanding of the equality of income and spending, let's return to something introduced in Chapter 1, the circular-flow model.

## Exhibit 2

### Computing Value Added for a New Desk

The value added at each stage of production is the sale price at that stage minus the cost of intermediate goods purchased from other firms, or column (1) minus column (2). The value added at each stage sums to the market value of the final good, shown at the bottom of column (3).

| Stage of Production | (1) Sale Value | (2) Cost of Intermediate Goods | (3) Value Added (3) = (1) − (2) |
|---|---|---|---|
| Logger | $ 20 | ––––– | $20 |
| Miller | 50 | $ 20 | 30 |
| Manufacturer | 120 | 50 | 70 |
| Retailer | 200 | 120 | 80 |
| | | Market value of final good | $200 |

**aggregate income** All earnings of resource suppliers in an economy during a given period, usually a year

**value added** At each stage of production, the selling price of a product minus the cost of intermediate goods purchased from other firms

## 6-2 CIRCULAR FLOW OF INCOME AND EXPENDITURE

The model in Exhibit 3 outlines the circular flow of income and spending in the economy for not only households and firms, as was the case in Chapter 1, but also for governments and the rest of the world. The main stream flows clockwise around the circle, first as income from firms to households (in the lower half of the circle), and then as spending from households back to firms (in the upper half of the circle). For each flow of money, there is an equal and opposite flow of products or resources. Here we follow the money.

### 6-2a Income Half of the Circular Flow

To develop a circular flow of income and spending, we must make some simplifying assumptions. Specifically, by assuming that physical capital does not wear out (i.e., no capital depreciation occurs) and that firms pay out all profits to firm owners (i.e., firms retain no earnings), we can say that *GDP equals aggregate income*. The circular flow is a continuous process, but the logic of the model is clearest if we begin at juncture (1) in Exhibit 3, where U.S. firms make production decisions. After all, production must occur before output can be sold and income earned. As Henry Ford explained, "It is not the employer who pays the wages—the employer only handles the money. It is the product that pays wages." Households supply their labor, capital, natural resources, and entrepreneurial ability to make products that firms sell to pay wages, interest, rent, and profit. Production of aggregate output, or GDP, gives rise to an equal amount of aggregate income.

Thus, at juncture (1), aggregate output equals aggregate income. But not all that income is available to spend. At juncture (2), governments collect taxes. Some of these tax dollars return as transfer payments to the income stream at juncture (3). By subtracting taxes and adding transfers, we transform aggregate income into **disposable income**, *DI*, which flows to households at juncture (4). Disposable income is take-home pay, which households can spend or save.

The bottom half of this circular flow is the *income half* because it focuses on the income arising from production. Aggregate income is the total income from producing GDP, and disposable income is the income remaining after taxes are subtracted and transfers added. To simplify the discussion, we define **net taxes**, *NT*, as taxes minus transfer payments. So *disposable income equals GDP minus net taxes*. Put another way, we can say that aggregate income equals disposable income plus net taxes:

$$\text{GDP} = \text{Aggregate income} = DI + NT$$

At juncture (4), firms have produced output and have paid resource suppliers, and governments have collected taxes and made transfer payments. With the resulting disposable income in hand, households now decide how much to spend and how much to save. Because firms have already produced the output and have paid resource suppliers, firms wait to see how much consumers want to spend. Any unsold production gets added to firm inventories.

### 6-2b Expenditure Half of the Circular Flow

Disposable income splits at juncture (5). Part is spent on consumption, *C*, and the rest is saved, *S*. Thus,

$$DI = C + S$$

*Consumption remains in the circular flow and is the biggest aggregate expenditure, about 68 percent of the total.* Household saving flows to **financial markets**, which consist of banks and other financial institutions that link savers to borrowers. For simplicity, Exhibit 3 shows households as the only savers, though governments, firms, and the rest of the world could save as well (e.g., savings from China finance U.S. borrowers). The primary borrowers are firms and governments, but households borrow too, particularly for new homes, and the rest of the world also borrows. In reality, financial markets should be connected to all four economic decision makers, but we have simplified the flows to keep the model from looking like a plate of spaghetti.

In our simplified model, firms pay resource suppliers an amount equal to the entire value of output. With nothing left for investment—that is, with no retained earnings—firms must borrow to finance purchases of physical capital plus any increases in their inventories. Households also borrow to purchase new homes. Therefore, investment, *I*, consists of spending on new capital by firms, including inventory changes, plus spending on residential construction. Investment enters the circular flow at juncture (6), so aggregate spending at that point totals $C + I$.

**disposable income (DI)** The income households have available to spend or to save after paying taxes and receiving transfer payments

**net taxes (NT)** Taxes minus transfer payments

**financial markets** Banks and other financial institutions that facilitate the flow of funds from savers to borrowers

*Exhibit 3*

## Circular Flow of Income and Expenditure

The circular-flow model captures important relationships in the economy. The bottom half depicts the income arising from production. At juncture (1), GDP equals aggregate income. Taxes leak from the flow at (2), but transfer payments enter the flow at (3). Taxes minus transfers equal net taxes, *NT*. Aggregate income minus net taxes equals disposable income, *DI*, which flows to households at juncture (4). The top half of the model shows the flow of expenditure. At (5), households either spend disposable income or save it. Consumption enters the spending flow directly. Saving leaks from the spending flow into financial markets, where it is channeled to borrowers. At (6), investment enters the spending flow. At (7), government purchases enter the spending flow. At (8), imports leak from the spending flow, and at (9), exports enter the spending flow. Consumption plus investment plus government purchases plus net exports add up to the aggregate expenditure on GDP received by firms at (10).

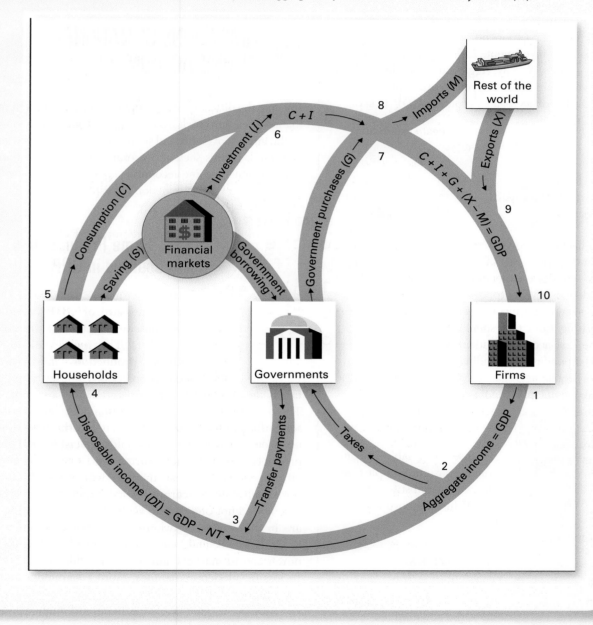

Governments must also borrow whenever they incur deficits, that is, whenever their total *outlays*—transfer payments plus purchases of goods and services—exceed their revenues. Government purchases of goods and services, represented by *G*, enter the spending stream in the upper half of the circular flow at juncture (7). Remember that *G excludes* transfer payments, which already entered the stream as income at juncture (3).

Some spending by households, firms, and governments goes for imports. Because spending on imports flows to foreign producers, spending on imports, $M$, leaks from the circular flow at juncture (8). But the rest of the world buys U.S. products, so foreign spending on U.S. exports, $X$, enters the spending flow at juncture (9). Net exports, the impact of the *rest of the world* on aggregate expenditure, equal exports minus imports, $X - M$, which can be positive, negative, or zero. In recent decades, net exports have been negative.

The upper half of the circular flow, the *expenditure half*, tracks the four components of aggregate expenditure: consumption, $C$; investment, $I$; government purchases, $G$; and net exports, $X - M$. Aggregate expenditure flows into firms at juncture (10). Aggregate expenditure equals the market value of aggregate output, or GDP. In short,

$$C + I + G + (X - M) = \text{Aggregate expenditure}$$
$$= \text{GDP}$$

### 6-2c Leakages Equal Injections

Let's step back now to view the big picture. In the upper half of the circular flow, aggregate expenditure is total spending on U.S. output. In the lower half, aggregate income is the income arising from that spending. This is the first accounting identity. Aggregate expenditure (spending by each sector) equals aggregate income (disposable income plus net taxes), or

$$C + I + G + (X - M)$$
$$= DI + NT$$

Because disposable income equals consumption plus saving, we can substitute $C + S$ for $DI$ in the above equation to yield

$$C + I + G + (X - M)$$
$$= C + S + NT$$

After subtracting $C$ from both sides and adding $M$ to both sides, the equation reduces to

$$I + G + X = S + NT + M$$

Note that **injections** into the main stream occur at various points around the circular

"Injections into the circular flow equal leakages from the flow."

flow. Investment, $I$, government purchases, $G$, and exports, $X$, are *injections* of spending into the circular flow. At the same time, some of the circular-flow leaks from the main stream. Saving, $S$, net taxes, $NT$, and imports, $M$, are **leakages** from the circular flow. As you can see from the equation, *injections into the circular flow equal leakages from the flow*. This injections-leakages equality demonstrates a second accounting identity based on double-entry bookkeeping.

## 6-3 LIMITATIONS OF NATIONAL INCOME ACCOUNTING

Imagine the difficulty of developing an accounting system that must capture such a complex and dynamic economy. In the interest of clarity and simplicity, certain features get neglected. In this section, we examine some limitations of the national income accounting system, beginning with production not captured by GDP.

### 6-3a Some Production Is Not Counted in GDP

With some minor exceptions, the official measure of GDP includes only those products that are sold in markets. This ignores all do-it-yourself production—child care, meal preparation, house-cleaning, family laundry, and home maintenance and repair. Thus, an economy in which householders are largely self-sufficient has a lower GDP than an otherwise similar economy in which households specialize and sell products to one another. During the 1950s, more than 80 percent of American mothers with small children remained at home caring for the family, but all this care added not one cent to GDP. Today most mothers are in the workforce, where their labor gets counted in GDP. Meals, child care, and the like are now often purchased in markets and thus get reflected in GDP. In less developed economies, more economic activity is do-it-yourself.

GDP also ignores off-the-books production. The term **underground economy** describes market activity that goes unreported because either it's illegal or because people want to evade taxes on otherwise legal activity. Although there is no official measure of the underground economy, most economists agree that it is

**injection** Any spending other than by households or any income other than from resource earnings; includes investment, government purchases, exports, and transfer payments

**leakage** Any diversion of income from the domestic spending stream; includes saving, taxes, and imports

**underground economy** Market transactions that go unreported either because they are illegal or because people involved want to evade taxes

The labor of mother who is employed is reflected in GDP; the labor of a mother who stays at home is not.

leisure is not reflected in GDP because it is not directly bought and sold in a market. The quality and variety of products available have also improved on average over the years because of technological advances and greater competition. For example, the magazine *Consumer Reports* has found a consistent improvement in the quality of automobiles over time. Yet most of these improvements are not reflected in GDP. Recording systems, computers, tires, running shoes, cell phones, and hundreds of other products have gotten better over the years. Also, new products are being introduced all the time, such as smart phones, e-readers, social networks, and energy drinks. *The gross domestic product fails to capture changes in the availability of leisure time and often fails to reflect changes in the quality of products or in the availability of new products.*

substantial. A federal study suggests the equivalent of 15 percent of U.S. GDP is underground production; this amounted to about $2.7 trillion in 2015. Incidentally, in 2014, Britain and Italy began including spending on prostitution and illegal drugs in their GDP estimates.[1]

For some economic activity, income must be *imputed*, or assigned a value, because market exchange does not occur. For example, included in GDP is an *imputed rental income* from home ownership, even though no rent is actually paid or received by those in owner-occupied housing. Also included in GDP is an imputed dollar amount for (1) wages paid *in kind*, such as an employer's payment for employees' medical insurance, and (2) food produced by a farm family for its own consumption. *GDP therefore includes some economic production that does not involve market exchange.*

> **"The gross domestic product fails to capture changes in the availability of leisure time and often fails to reflect changes in the quality of products or in the availability of new products."**

### 6-3b Leisure, Quality, and Variety

The average U.S. workweek is much shorter now than it was a century ago, so people work less to produce today's output. People also retire earlier and live longer after retirement. As a result of a shorter workweek and earlier retirement, more leisure is available. But

1. Ricardo Lopez, "Britain, Italy Count Prostitution, Drugs in GDP Estimates," *Los Angeles Times*, 30 May 2014.

### 6-3c What's Gross About Gross Domestic Product?

Again, a nation's physical capital consists of its buildings, machines, vehicles, computers, and all the other equipment used to produce GDP. In the course of producing GDP, some capital wears out, such as the delivery truck that finally dies, and some capital becomes obsolete, such as an aging computer that no longer runs the latest software. A new truck that logs 100,000 miles its first year has been subject to wear and tear, and therefore has a diminished value as a resource. A truer picture of the *net* production that actually occurs during a year is found by subtracting this capital *depreciation* from GDP. **Depreciation** measures the value of the capital stock that is used up or becomes obsolete in the production process. Gross domestic product is called "gross" because it fails to take into account this depreciation. **Net domestic product** equals gross domestic product minus depreciation, the capital stock used up in the production process.

We now have two measures of investment. *Gross investment* is the value of all

**depreciation** The value of capital stock used up to produce GDP or that becomes obsolete during the year

**net domestic product** Gross domestic product minus depreciation investment during a year and is used in computing GDP. *Net investment* equals gross investment minus depreciation. The economy's production possibilities depend on what happens to net investment. If net investment is positive—that is, if gross investment exceeds depreciation—the economy's capital stock increases, so its contribution to output increases as well. If net investment is zero, the capital stock remains constant, as does its contribution to output. And if net investment is negative, the capital stock declines, as does its contribution to output.

As the names imply, *gross* domestic product reflects gross investment and *net* domestic product reflects net investment. But estimating depreciation involves some guesswork. For example, what is the appropriate measure of depreciation for the roller coasters at Six Flags, the metal display shelves at Target, or the parking lots at the Mall of America in Minnesota?

## 6-3d GDP Does Not Reflect All Costs

Some production and consumption degrades the quality of our environment. Trucks and automobiles pump pollution into the atmosphere, which could contribute to climate change. Housing developments displace scenic open space and forests. Paper mills foul the lungs and burn the eyes. Oil spills foul the coastline. Coal-fired electric plants pollute the air. More generally, U.S. mortality rates increase during economic expansion, in part, because of the increased air pollution that comes with more traffic and greater output.[2] These negative externalities—costs that fall on those not directly involved in the transactions—are mostly ignored in GDP calculations, even though they diminish the quality of life now and in the future. Recent research suggests that the external costs of some production, such as oil- and coal-fired electricity generation, could exceed the value added by these firms.[3] To the extent that growth in GDP generates negative externalities, a rising GDP may not be as attractive as it would first appear.

Although the national income accounts reflect the depreciation of buildings, machinery, vehicles, and other manufactured capital, this accounting ignores the depletion of natural resources, such as standing timber, oil reserves, fish stocks, and soil fertility. So national income accounts reflect depreciation of the physical capital stock but not the natural capital stock. For example, intensive farming may raise productivity and boost GDP temporarily, but this depletes soil fertility. Worse still, some

2. Garth Heutel and Christopher Ruhm, "Air Pollution and Procyclical Mortality," *Journal of the Association of Environmental and Resource Economists* (forthcoming).

3. Nicholas Muller, Robert Mendelsohn, and William Nordhaus, "Environmental Accounting for Pollution in the United States Economy," *American Economic Review*, 101 (August 2011): 1649–1675.

GDP, as currently measured, does not take into account externalities, such as oils spills, that impose a cost on society.

production may speed the extinction of certain plants and animals. The U.S. Commerce Department is now in the process of developing so-called *green accounting*, or *green GDP*, trying to register the impact of production on air pollution, water pollution, soil depletion, and the loss of other natural resources.

## 6-3e GDP and Economic Welfare

In computing GDP, the market price of output is the measure of its value. Therefore, each dollar spent on handguns or cigarettes is counted in GDP the same as each dollar spent on baby formula or preventive health care. Positive economic analysis tries to avoid making value judgments about *how* people spend their money. Because GDP, as a number, provides no information about its composition, some economists question whether GDP is the best measure of the nation's economic welfare.

Despite the limitations of official GDP estimates, GDP offers a useful snapshot of the U.S. economy at a point in time. Inflation, however, clouds comparability over time. In the next section, we discuss how to adjust GDP for changes in the economy's price level.

## 6-4 ACCOUNTING FOR PRICE CHANGES

As noted earlier, the national income accounts are based on the market values of final goods and services produced in a particular year. Initially, gross domestic product measures the value of output in *nominal dollars*—that is, in the dollar values at the time production occurs. When GDP is based on nominal dollars, the national income accounts measure the *nominal value* of national output. Thus, **nominal GDP** is based on the prices prevailing when production takes place. National income accounts based on nominal dollars allow for comparisons among income or expenditure components in a particular year. Because the economy's average price level changes over time, however, nominal-dollar comparisons across years can be misleading. For example, between 1979 and 1980, nominal GDP increased by about 9 percent. That sounds impressive, but the economy's average price level rose more than 9 percent. So the growth in nominal GDP came entirely from inflation. Real GDP, or GDP measured in terms of the goods and services produced, in fact declined. If nominal GDP increases in a given year, part of this increase may simply reflect inflation—pure hot air. To make meaningful comparisons of GDP across years, we must take out the hot air, or *deflate* nominal GDP. We focus on *real* changes in production by eliminating changes due solely to inflation.

### 6-4a Price Indexes

To compare the price level over time, let's first establish a point of reference, a base year to which prices in other years can be compared. An *index number* compares the value of some variable in a particular year to its value in a base year, or reference year. Think about the simplest of index numbers. Suppose bread is the only good produced in an economy. As a reference point, let's look at its price in some specific year. The year selected is called the **base year**; prices in other years are expressed relative to the base-year price.

Suppose the base year is 2014, when a loaf of bread in our simple economy sold for $2.50. Let's say the price of bread increased to $2.60 in

*Exhibit 4*

**Hypothetical Example of a Price Index (base year = 2014)**

The price index equals the price in the current year divided by the price in the base year, all multiplied by 100.

| Year | (1)<br>Price of Bread in<br>Current Year | (2)<br>Price of Bread in<br>Base Year | (3)<br>Price Index<br>(3) = [(1)/(2)] × 100 |
|---|---|---|---|
| 2014 | $2.50 | $2.50 | 100 |
| 2015 | 2.60 | 2.50 | 104 |
| 2016 | 2.80 | 2.50 | 112 |

2015 and to $2.80 in 2016. We construct a **price index** by dividing each year's price by the price in the base year and then multiplying by 100, as shown in Exhibit 4. For 2014, the base year, we divide the base price of bread by itself, $2.50/$2.50, or 1, so the price index in 2014 equals 1 × 100 = 100. *The price index in the base period is always 100.* The price index in 2015 is $2.60/$2.50, or 1.04, which when multiplied by 100 equals 104. In 2016, the index is $2.80/$2.50, or 1.12, which when multiplied by 100 equals 112. Thus, the index is 4 percent higher in 2015 than in the base year and 12 percent higher in 2016 than in the base year. The price index permits comparisons across years. For example, what if you were provided the indexes for 2015 and 2016 and asked what happened to the price level between the two years? By dividing the 2016 price index by the 2015 price index, 112/104, you find that the price level rose 7.7 percent.

This section has shown how to develop a price index assuming we already know the price level each year. Determining the price level is a bit more involved, as we'll now see.

iStockphoto.com/NoDerog

**nominal GDP** GDP based on prices prevailing at the time of production

**base year** The year with which other years are compared when constructing an index; the index equals 100 in the base year

**price index** A number that shows the average price of products; changes in a price index over time show changes in the economy's average price level

## Exhibit 5

**Hypothetical Market Basket Used to Develop the Consumer Price Index**

The cost of a market basket in the current year, shown at the bottom of column (5), sums the quantities of each item in the basket, shown in column (1), times the price of each item in the current year, shown in column (4).

| Product | (1) Quantity in Market Basket | (2) Prices in Base Year | (3) Cost of Basket in Base Year (3) = (1) × (2) | (4) Prices in Current Year | (5) Cost of Basket in Current Year (5) = (1) × (4) |
|---|---|---|---|---|---|
| Twinkies | 365 packages | $ 1.30/package | $474.50 | $ 1.20 | $438.00 |
| Fuel Oil | 500 gallons | 3.00/gallon | 1,500.00 | 3.25 | 1,625.00 |
| Cable TV | 12 months | 50.00/month | 600.00 | 50.00 | 600.00 |
| | | | $2,574.50 | | $2,663.00 |

## 6-4b Consumer Price Index

The price index most familiar to you is the **consumer price index, or CPI**, which measures changes over time in the cost of buying a "market basket" of goods and services purchased by a typical family. For simplicity, suppose a typical family's market basket for the year includes 365 packages of Twinkies, 500 gallons of heating oil, and 12 months of cable TV. Prices in the base year are listed in column (2) of Exhibit 5. The total cost of each product in the base year is found by multiplying price by quantity, as shown in column (3). The cost of the market basket in the base year is shown at the bottom of column (3) to be $2,574.50.

Prices in the current year are listed in column (4). Notice that not all prices changed by the same percentage since the base year. The price of fuel oil increased, but the price of Twinkies declined. The cost of that same basket in the current year is $2,663.00, shown as the sum of column (5). To compute the consumer price index for the current year, we simply divide the cost in the current year by the cost of that same basket in the base year, $2,663.00/$2,574.50, and then multiply by 100. This yields a price index of 103.4. We could say that between the base period and the current year, the "cost of living" increased by 3.4 percent.

The federal government uses the 36 months of 1982,

> **"To the extent that the CPI ignores quality improvements, it overstates the true extent of inflation."**

**consumer price index, or CPI** A measure of inflation based on the cost of a fixed market basket of goods and services

1983, and 1984 as the base period for calculating the CPI for a market basket consisting of hundreds of goods and services. The CPI is reported monthly based on prices collected from about 23,000 sellers across the country in 87 metropolitan areas. In reality, each household consumes a unique market basket, so we could theoretically develop about 120 million CPIs—one for each household.

Exhibit 6 shows the relative importance of major spending categories in the CPI market basket in 2015. As you can see, housing claimed the largest share, accounting for 33.0 percent of all consumer spending. Next was food, at 14.4 percent. Your market basket would likely differ from the official CPI mix. For example, you probably spend more than 3.1 percent of your budget on education.

## 6-4c Problems With the CPI

There is no perfect way to measure changes in the price level. As we have already seen, the quality and variety of some products are improving all the time, so some price increases may be as much a reflection of improved quality as of inflation. The CPI does not account very well for new products with more and better features than the products they replace. A price index that properly accounts for product upgrades could shave an average of 0.8 percentage points from the current CPI measure.[4] Thus, there is a *quality bias* in the CPI, because it assumes that the quality of the market basket remains relatively constant over time. *To the extent that the CPI ignores quality improvements, it overstates the true extent of inflation.* Those who come up with the CPI each month try to make some quality adjustments.

But the CPI tends to overstate inflation for another reason. Recall that the CPI holds constant over time the kind and amount of goods and services in the typical

4. Christian Broda and David Weinstein, "Product Creation and Destruction: Evidence and Price Implications," *American Economic Review*, 100 (June 2010): 691–723.

## Exhibit 6

### Relative Importance of Items in CPI Market Basket

- Communication, 3.4%
- Education, 3.1%
- Recreation, 3.8%
- Clothing, 3.3%
- Transportation, 10.9%
- Medical Care, 7.8%
- Other, 12.9%
- Food, 14.4%
- Energy, 7.4%
- Housing, 33.0%

Source: "Consumer Price Index–February 2015," Bureau of Labor Statistics, 24 March 2015, at http://www.bls.gov/news.release/pdf/cpi.pdf.

Home Depot's lower prices do not necessarily mean a reduction in the cost of living.

©iStockphoto.com/Igor Aronov

market basket. Because not all items in the basket experience the same rate of price change, relative prices change over time. A rational household would respond to changes in relative prices by buying less of the more expensive products and more of the cheaper products. The CPI allows for some substitution within narrow categories (e.g., shoppers in Chicago can switch among choices of ground beef based on price), but consumers can't easily switch across categories because the point of the CPI is to look at price changes over time for a given market basket. Because the CPI holds the market basket constant for long periods, the CPI is slow to incorporate consumer responses to changes in relative prices. *The CPI calculations, by not allowing households to shift away from goods that have become more costly, overestimates the true extent of inflation experienced by the typical household.*

The CPI has also failed to keep up with the consumer shift toward discount stores such as Walmart, Costco, and Home Depot. Government statisticians consider goods sold by discounters as different from goods sold by regular retailers. Hence, the discounter's lower price does not necessarily translate into a reduction in the cost of living, but simply as a different consumer purchase decision.

Finally, the CPI overstates inflation because it includes an item in the market basket only after the product becomes widely used. By that time, the major price drops have already occurred. For example, the first portable video recorder and camera, the Ampex VR-3000 Backpack, weighed over 40 pounds and sold for $65,000 when it was introduced in 1967 (or about $465,000 in 2015 dollars). Now, for less than $100, you can buy a high definition video camera that fits in a vest pocket. The CPI captured few of the major price drops. The same is true for all kinds of new products, such as the cell phone, which began as big as a brick and priced north of $1,000. Only after the price of cell phones fell far enough for wider adoption did they make it into the CPI basket.

Experts conclude that the CPI has overestimated inflation by more than 1 percentage point per year. This problem is of more than academic concern because changes in the CPI determine changes in tax brackets and in an array of payments, including wage agreements that include a cost-of-living adjustment, Social Security benefits totaling about $900 billion annually, welfare benefits, even alimony. In fact, about one-third of federal outlays are tied to changes in the CPI. Just a 1 percentage point correction in the upward bias of the CPI would save the federal budget about $100 billion annually by 2020.

Overstating the CPI also distorts other measures, such as wages, that use the CPI to adjust for inflation. For example, based on the official CPI,

©dwori/Shutterstock.com

*Exhibit 7*

## U.S. Gross Domestic Product in Nominal Dollars and Chained (2009) Dollars Since 1929

Real GDP, the red line, shows the value of output measured in chained (2009) dollars. The blue line measures GDP in nominal dollars of each year shown. The two lines intersect in 2009, when real GDP equaled nominal GDP. Year-to-year changes in nominal-dollar GDP reflect changes in both real GDP and in the price level. Year-to-year changes in chained-dollar GDP reflect changes in real GDP only. Nominal-dollar GDP grows faster than chained-dollar GDP. Prior to 2009, nominal-dollar prices are less than chained-dollar prices, so nominal-dollar GDP is less than chained-dollar GDP.

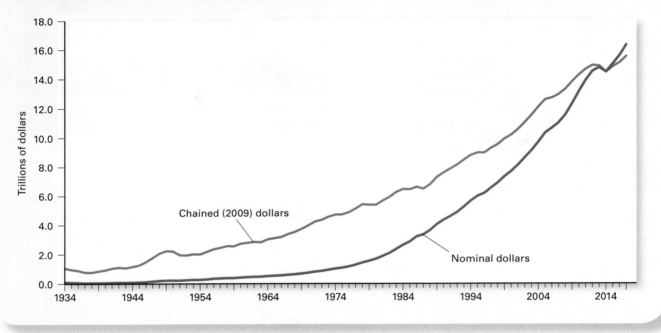

the average real wage in the U.S. economy fell by a total of about 2 percent in the last two decades. But if the CPI overstated inflation by at least 1 percent per year, as many researchers now believe, then the average real wage, instead of dropping by 2 percent, actually increased by about 20 percent. The Bureau of Labor Statistics, the group that estimates the CPI, is now working on these problems and has introduced an experimental version of the CPI that would reduce measured inflation. One experiment uses scanner data at supermarkets to find out how consumers respond, for example, to a rise in the price of romaine lettuce relative to iceberg lettuce, two products assumed to be reasonable substitutes for one another.

## 6-4d The GDP Price Index

**GDP price index** A comprehensive inflation measure of all goods and services included in the gross domestic product

A price index is a weighted sum of various prices. Whereas the CPI focuses on just a sample of consumer purchases, a more complex and more comprehensive price index, the **GDP price index**, measures the average price of all goods and services produced in the economy. To calculate the GDP price index, we use the formula

$$\text{GDP price index} = \frac{\text{Nominal GDP} \times 100}{\text{Real GDP}}$$

where nominal GDP is the dollar value of GDP in a particular year measured in prices of that same year, and real GDP is the dollar value of GDP in a particular year measured in base-year prices. The challenge is finding real GDP in a particular year. Any measure of real GDP is constructed as the weighted sum of thousands of different goods and services produced in the economy. The question is what weights, or prices, to use. Prior to 1995, the Bureau of Economic Analysis (BEA) used prices for a particular base year (most recently 1987) to estimate real GDP. In this case, the quantity of each output in a particular year was valued by using the 1987 price of each output. So real GDP in, say, 1994 was the sum of 1994 output valued at 1987 prices.

## 6-4e Moving From Fixed Weights to Chain Weights

Estimating real GDP by using prices from a base year yields an accurate measure of real GDP as long as the year in question is close to the base year. But BEA used prices that prevailed in 1987 to value production from 1929 to 1995. In early 1996, BEA switched from a fixed-price weighting system to a **chain-weighted system**, using a complicated process that changes price weights from year to year. All you need to know is that the chain-weighted real GDP adjusts the weights more or less continuously from year to year, reducing the bias caused by a fixed-price weighting system.

Even though the chain-type index adjusts the weights from year to year, any index, by definition, must still use some year as an anchor, or reference point—that is, any index must answer the question, "Compared to what?" To provide such a reference point, BEA measures U.S. real GDP and its components in *chained (2009) dollars*. Exhibit 7 presents nominal-dollar estimates of GDP as well as chained (2009) dollar estimates of real GDP. The blue line indicates nominal-dollar GDP since 1929. The red line indicates real GDP since 1929, or GDP measured in chained (2009) dollars. The two lines intersect in 2009, because that's when real GDP equaled nominal GDP. Nominal GDP is below real GDP in years prior to 2009 because real GDP is based on chained (2009) prices, which on average are higher than prices prior to 2009. Nominal GDP reflects growth in real GDP and in the price level. Chained-dollar GDP reflects growth only in real GDP. So nominal-dollar GDP grows faster than chained-dollar GDP.

## 6-5 FINAL WORD

This chapter discussed how GDP is measured and how it's adjusted for changes in the price level over time. The national income accounts have limitations, but they offer a reasonably accurate picture of the economy at a point in time as well as year-to-year movements in the economy. Subsequent chapters will refer to the distinction between real and nominal values.

> **chain-weighted system** An inflation measure that adjusts the weights from year to year in calculating a price index, thereby reducing the bias caused by a fixed-price weighting system

# STUDY TOOLS 6

### READY TO STUDY? IN THE BOOK, YOU CAN:

☐ Work the Problems at the end of the chapter.

☐ Rip out the chapter review card for a handy summary of the chapter and key terms.

### ONLINE AT CENGAGEBRAIN.COM YOU CAN:

☐ Collect StudyBits while you read and study the chapter.

☐ Quiz yourself on key concepts.

☐ Prepare for tests with chapter flash cards as well as flash cards that you create.

☐ Watch videos to explore economics further.

# CHAPTER 6 PROBLEMS

*Your instructor can access the answers to these problems online at http://cengagebrain.com.*

## 6-1 Describe the two ways of computing GDP and explain why they are equivalent

1. *(Income Approach to GDP)* How does the income approach to measuring GDP differ from the expenditure approach? Explain the meaning of *value added* and its importance in the income approach. Consider the following data for the selling price at each stage in the production of a 5-pound bag of flour sold by your local grocer. Calculate the final market value of the flour.

| Stage of Production | Sale Price |
|---|---|
| Farmer | $0.30 |
| Miller | 0.50 |
| Wholesaler | 1.00 |
| Grocer | 1.50 |

2. *(Expenditure Approach to GDP)* Given the following annual information about a hypothetical country, answer questions a through d.

| | Billions of Dollars |
|---|---|
| Personal consumption expenditures | $200 |
| Personal taxes | 50 |
| Exports | 30 |
| Depreciation | 10 |
| Government purchases | 50 |
| Gross private domestic investment | 40 |
| Imports | 40 |
| Government transfer payments | 20 |

   a. What is the value of GDP?
   b. What is the value of net domestic product?
   c. What is the value of net investment?
   d. What is the value of net exports?

3. *(Investment)* Given the following data, answer questions a through c.

| | Billions of Dollars |
|---|---|
| New residential construction | $500 |
| Purchases of existing homes | 250 |
| Sales value of newly issued stocks and bonds | 600 |
| New physical capital | 800 |
| Depreciation | 200 |
| Household purchases of new furniture | 50 |
| Net change in firms' inventories | 100 |
| Production of new intermediate goods | 700 |

   a. What is the value of gross private domestic investment?
   b. What is the value of net investment?
   c. Are any intermediate goods counted in gross investment?

## 6-2 Trace through the circular-flow model, explaining each of the 10 steps along the way

4. *(Circular-Flow Model)* First describe in general terms the point of the circular-flow model. Next describe the 10 steps along the way.

5. *(Leakages and Injections)* What are the leakages from and injections into the circular flow? How are leakages and injections related in the circular flow?

## 6-3 Identify the limitations of the national income accounting system

6. *(National Income Accounts)* What relevant aspects of the economy are not reflected in the national income accounting system.

7. *(Limitations of National Income Accounting)* Explain why each of the following should be taken into account when GDP data are used to compare the "level of well-being" in different countries:
   a. Population levels
   b. The distribution of income
   c. The amount of production that takes place outside of markets
   d. The length of the average workweek
   e. The level of environmental pollution

## 6-4 Define a price index and explain why is it useful

8. *(Consumer Price Index)* Calculate a new consumer price index for the data in the following exhibit. Assume that current-year prices of Twinkies, fuel oil, and cable TV are $0.95/package, $1.25/gallon, and $15.00/month, respectively. Calculate the current year's cost of the market basket and the value of the current year's price index. What is this year's percentage change in the price level compared to the base year?

| Product | (1) Quantity in Market Basket | (2) Prices in Base Year | (3) Cost of Basket in Base Year (3) · (1) · (2) | (4) Prices in Current Year | (5) Cost of Basket in Current Year (5) · (1) · (4) |
|---|---|---|---|---|---|
| Twinkies | 365 packages | $ 0.89/package | $ 324.85 | $ 0.79 | $ 288.35 |
| Fuel oil | 500 gallons | 1.00/gallon | 500.00 | 1.50 | 750.00 |
| Cable TV | 12 months | 30.00/month | 360.00 | 30.00 | 360.00 |
| | | | $1,184.85 | | $1,398.35 |

9. *(Consumer Price Index)* Given the following data, what was the value of the consumer price index in the base year? Calculate the annual rate of consumer price inflation in 2015 in each of the following situations:
   a. The CPI equals 200 in 2014 and 240 in 2015.
   b. The CPI equals 150 in 2014 and 175 in 2015.
   c. The CPI equals 325 in 2014 and 340 in 2015.
   d. The CPI equals 325 in 2014 and 315 in 2015.

# 7 | Unemployment and Inflation

©iStockphoto.com/Andrew Penner

## LEARNING OUTCOMES

After studying this chapter, you will be able to…

**7-1** Describe what the unemployment rate measures, and summarize four sources of unemployment

**7-2** Outline the pros and cons of unemployment insurance

**7-3** Define inflation and describe the two sources of inflation

**7-4** Explain how unanticipated inflation harms some individuals and harms the economy as a whole

After finishing this chapter go to PAGE 131 for STUDY TOOLS

**Topics discussed in Chapter 7 include:**

- Measuring unemployment
- Frictional, structural, seasonal, and cyclical unemployment
- Full employment
- Sources and consequences of inflation
- Relative price changes
- Nominal and real interest rates

- What's so bad about unemployment?

- Who among the following would be counted as unemployed: a college student who is not working, a bank teller displaced by an automatic teller machine, Jennifer Lawrence between movies, and baseball slugger Miguel Cabrera in the off-season?

- Why is unemployment a problem for the individual and for the economy?

- What type of unemployment might be healthy for the economy?

- Why is the unemployment rate for young adults much higher than for other age groups?

- What's so bad about inflation?

- Why is anticipated inflation less of a problem than unanticipated inflation?

*These and other questions are answered in this chapter, where we explore two macroeconomic problems: unemployment and inflation.*

To be sure, unemployment and inflation are not the only problems an economy could face. Sluggish growth and widespread poverty are others. But low unemployment and low inflation go a long way toward reducing other economic ills. Although unemployment and inflation are often related, each is discussed separately. The causes of each and the relationship between the two will become clearer as you learn more about how the economy works.

**"Why is unemployment a problem for the individual and for the economy?"**

This chapter shows that not all unemployment or all inflation harms the economy. Even in a healthy economy, a certain amount of unemployment reflects the voluntary choices of workers and employers seeking their best options. And moderate inflation that is fully anticipated creates fewer distortions than does unanticipated inflation.

## 7-1 UNEMPLOYMENT: ITS MEASURE AND SOURCES

"They scampered about looking for work....They swarmed on the highways. The movement changed them; the highways, the camps along the road, the fear of hunger and the hunger itself, changed them. The children without dinner changed them, the endless moving changed them."[1] There is no question, as John Steinbeck wrote in *The Grapes of Wrath*, a novel set in the Great Depression, that a long stretch of unemployment profoundly affects the jobless and their families. The most obvious loss is a steady paycheck, but the unemployed often lose self-esteem and part of their identity as well. Losing a job also means losing connections to coworkers. According to psychologists, in terms of stressful events,

the loss of a good job ranks only slightly below a divorce or the death of a loved one.

Even some economists argue that the other effects of unemployment can have a more serious impact on an individual's well-being than the loss of income itself.[2] Job losses worsen health in both men and women, in part because those out of work tend to smoke more cigarettes.[3] More generally, unemployment appears to be linked to a greater incidence of crime and to a variety of afflictions, including heart disease, suicide, and clinical depression.[4] People out of work also report a greater

1. John Steinbeck, *The Grapes of Wrath* (Viking, 1939), p. 293.

2. See, for example, John Helliwell and Haifang Huang, "New Measures of the Costs of Unemployment: Evidence From the Subjective Well-Being of 3.3 Million Americans," *Economic Inquiry*, 52 (October 2014): 1485–1502.

3. Sandra Black, Paul Devereux, and Kjell Salvanes, "Losing Heart? The Effect of Job Displacement on Health," *Industrial Labor Relations Review* (forthcoming).

4. For a study linking a higher incidence of suicides to recessions, see Christopher Ruhm, "Are Recessions Good for Your Health?" *Quarterly Journal of Economics*, 115 (May 2000): 617–650. Clinical depression is also higher among the unemployed, as demonstrated in Frederick Zimmerman and Wayne Katon, "Socioeconomic Status, Depression Disparities, and Financial Strain: What Lies Behind the Income-Depression Relationship," *Health Economics*, 14 (December 2005): 1197–1215.

CHAPTER 7: Unemployment and Inflation 113

To be counted as "unemployed," you must be actively looking for a job. Those not looking for jobs are simply not in the labor force.

kpatylka/Shutterstock.com

level of sadness, which decreases dramatically if they find jobs.[5] And U.S. workers who experience a national economic recession in their 50s have a shorter lifespan because of long spells of unemployment and lost health insurance.[6] No matter how often people complain about their jobs, they rely on those same jobs not only for their livelihood but for part of their personal identity. When strangers meet, one of the first questions asked is "what do you do for a living?" Alfred Marshall, the most famous economist of the 19th century, wrote that a job is often the main object of our thoughts and intellectual development.

In addition to the personal costs, unemployment imposes a cost on the economy as a whole because fewer goods and services are produced. When those who are willing and able to work can't find jobs, their labor is lost forever. *This lost income and output coupled with the economic and psychological cost*

**66 This lost income and output coupled with the economic and psychological cost of unemployment on the individual and the family are the real costs of unemployment. 99**

*of unemployment on the individual and the family are the real costs of unemployment.* As we begin our analysis, keep in mind that the national unemployment rate reflects millions of individuals with their own stories. As President Harry Truman once remarked, "It's a recession when your neighbor loses his job; it's a depression when you lose your own." For some lucky people, unemployment is a brief vacation between jobs. For some others, a long stretch can have a lasting effect on family stability, economic welfare, self-esteem, and personal identity. Because young adults have higher unemployment rates than others in the labor force, this section should be of special interest to some of you.

## 7-1a Measuring Unemployment

The unemployment rate is the most widely reported measure of the nation's economic health. What does the unemployment rate measure? What are the sources of unemployment? How has unemployment changed over time? These are some of the questions explored in this section. Let's first see how to measure unemployment.

We begin with the U.S. *civilian noninstitutional adult population*, which consists of all civilians 16 years of age and older, except those in prison, in mental hospitals, or in homes for the aged. The adjective *civilian* means the definition excludes those in the military. From here on, references to the *adult population* will mean the civilian noninstitutional adult population. The **labor force** consists of the people in the adult population who are either working or looking for work. *Those who want a job but can't find one are unemployed.* The Bureau of Labor Statistics interviews 60,000 households monthly (which translates into about 110,000 individuals) and counts people as unemployed if they have no job but want one *and* have looked for work at least once during the preceding four weeks. Thus, the college student, the displaced bank teller, actress Jennifer Lawrence, and baseball player Miguel Cabrera in the off-season would all be counted as unemployed if they wanted a job and looked for work in the previous month. The **unemployment rate** measures the percentage of those in the labor force who are unemployed. Hence, the unemployment rate, which is

**labor force** Those 16 years of age and older who are either working or looking for work

**unemployment rate** The number unemployed as a percentage of the labor force

5. Alan Krueger and Andreas Miller, "Time Use, Emotional Well-Being, and Unemployment: Evidence From Longitudinal Data," *American Economic Review*, 102 (May 2012): 594–599.

6. Courtney Coile, Phillip Levine, and Robin McKnight, "Recessions, Older Workers, and Longevity: How Long Are Recessions Good for Your Health?" *American Economic Journal: Economic Policy*, 6 (August 2014): 92–119.

reported monthly, equals the number unemployed—that is, people without jobs who are looking for work—divided by the number in the labor force.

Only a fraction of adults who are not working are considered unemployed. The others may have retired, are students, are caring for children at home, or simply don't want to work. Others may be unable to work because of long-term illness or disability. Some may have become so discouraged by a long, unfruitful job search that they have given up in frustration. These **discouraged workers** have, in effect, dropped out of the labor force, so they are not counted as unemployed. Finally, about one-third of those working part time would prefer to work full time, yet all part-timers are counted as employed. Because the official unemployment rate does not include discouraged workers and counts all part-time workers as employed, it may underestimate the true extent of unemployment in the economy. Later we'll consider some reasons why the unemployment rate may exaggerate the true extent of unemployment.

These definitions are illustrated in Exhibit 1, where circles represent the various groups, and the numbers (in millions) of individuals in each category and subcategory are shown in parentheses. The circle on the left depicts the entire U.S. labor force in February 2015, including both employed and unemployed people. The circle on the right represents those in the adult population who, for whatever reason, are not working. These two circles combine to show the adult population. The overlapping area identifies the number of *unemployed* workers—that is, people in the labor force who are not working. The unemployment rate is found by dividing the number unemployed by the number in the labor force. In February 2015, 8.7 million people were unemployed in a labor force of 157.0 million, yielding an unemployment rate of 5.5 percent (= 8.7/157.0).

## 7-1b Labor Force Participation Rate

The productive capability of any economy depends in part on the proportion of adults in the labor force, measured as the *labor force participation rate*. In Exhibit 1, the U.S. adult population equals those in the labor force (157.0 million) plus those not in the labor force (92.9 million)—a total of 249.9 million people. The **labor force participation rate** therefore equals the number in the labor force divided by the adult population, or 62.8 percent (=157.0/249.9). So, on average, one out of three adults is in the labor force. The labor force participation rate increased from 60 percent in 1970 to 67 percent in 1990, but declined after the Great Recession, as many dropped out of the labor market because jobs were hard to find. In fact, the labor force participation rate in February 2015 was among the lowest in decades.

One striking development since World War II has been the convergence in the labor force participation rates of men and women. In 1950, only

### Exhibit 1

**The Adult Population Sums the Employed, the Unemployed, and Those Not in the Labor Force: February 2015 (in millions)**

The labor force, depicted by the left circle, consists of those employed plus those unemployed. Those not working, depicted by the right circle, consists of those not in the labor force and those unemployed. The adult population sums the employed, the unemployed, and those not in the labor force.

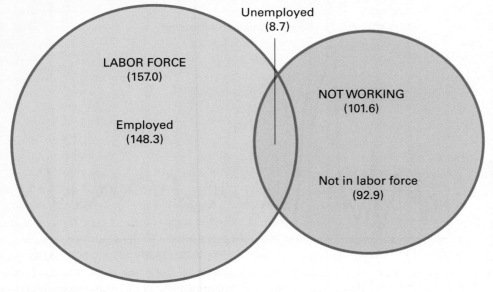

Source: Figures are for February 2015 from the U.S. Bureau of Labor Statistics. For the latest data, go to http://www.bls.gov/news.release/empsit.toc.htm.

**discouraged workers** Those who drop out of the labor force in frustration because they can't find work

**labor force participation rate** The labor force as a percentage of the adult population

34 percent of adult women were in the labor force. Today, 57 percent are, with the greatest increase among younger women. The labor force participation rate among men has declined from 86 percent in 1950 to 69 percent today, primarily because of earlier retirement. The participation rate is higher among white males, at 72 percent, than black males, at 67 percent, but higher among black females, at 62 percent, than white females, at 57 percent. Finally, the participation rate climbs with education—from only 45 percent for those lacking a high school diploma to 75 percent among those with at least a bachelor's degree.

## 7-1c Unemployment Over Time

Exhibit 2 shows the U.S. unemployment rate since 1900, with shaded bars to indicate periods of recession or depression. As you can see, rates rise during contractions and fall during expansions. Most striking is the jump during the Great Depression of the 1930s, when the rate topped 25 percent. Note that the rate trended upward from the end of World War II in the mid-1940s until the early 1980s; then it backed down, from a high of 10 percent in 1982 to a low of 4 percent in 2000. With the recession of 2001, the rate gradually increased to 6 percent by 2003, then declined into 2007. But the global financial crisis of 2008 and sharp U.S. recession boosted the rate to 10 percent by the end of 2009.

Let's examine some of the broad trends over the last three decades. Why did the unemployment rate trend down from 9.7 percent in 1982 to only 4.0 percent in 2000? First, the overall economy was on a roll during that period, interrupted by only a brief recession in the early 1990s triggered by the first war in Iraq. The number employed increased by 37 million between 1982 and 2000, making the U.S. economy an incredible job machine and the envy of the world.

The unemployment rate also trended down because there were fewer teenagers in the workforce. Teenagers have an unemployment rate about three times that of adults, so the declining share of teenage workers helped cut the overall unemployment rate.

But job growth between 2000 and 2015 was hobbled by a mild recession in 2001 and the Great Recession of 2007–2009, when unemployment exceeded 10.0 percent. That rate gradually came down to 5.5 percent by early 2015. More troubling was that the labor force participation rate dropped from 66.3 percent in February 2007 to 62.8 percent in February 2015. If the labor force participation rate had remained constant, the labor force in early 2015 would have been 5.7 million workers greater than it turned out to be.

## 7-1d Duration of Unemployment

A given unemployment rate tells us little about how long people have been unemployed. In February 2015, with the unemployment rate at 5.5 percent, the average duration of unemployment was 32 weeks, down from 39 weeks in 2012, which had been the longest since the Great Depression. The 32 week average in early 2015 was still double the average of previous three decades. Some people were unemployed longer than others in February 2015: 28 percent were unemployed less than

*Exhibit 2*

**The U.S. Unemployment Rate Since 1900**

Since 1900, the unemployment rate has fluctuated widely, rising during contractions and falling during expansions. During the Great Depression of the 1930s, the rate spiked to 25 percent.

Sources: U.S. Census Bureau, *Historical Statistics of the United States: Colonial Times to 1970* (U.S. Government Printing Office, 1975); *Economic Report of the President*, February 2015; and U.S. Bureau of Labor Statistics. Figure for 2015 is estimated . For the latest unemployment rate, go to http://www.bls.gov/news/release/empsit.toc.htm.

## Exhibit 3
### Unemployment Rates and Educational Attainment

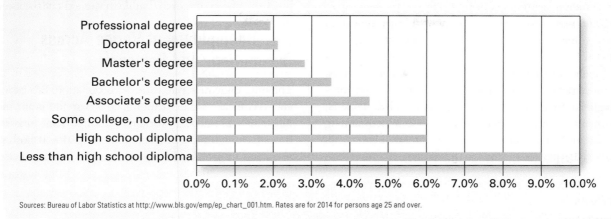

Sources: Bureau of Labor Statistics at http://www.bls.gov/emp/ep_chart_001.htm. Rates are for 2014 for persons age 25 and over.

5 weeks, 26 percent 5–14 weeks, 15 percent 15–26 weeks, and 31 percent 27 weeks or longer. Those out of work 27 weeks or longer are called the **long-term unemployed**, and are of special concern to policy makers. Thus, about 3 in 10 of those looking for work in February 2015 were long-term unemployed. Reported another way, that month, 1.7 percent of the labor force consisted of the long-term unemployed. In 2007, prior to the financial crisis and Great Recession, only 0.8 percent of the labor force were long-term unemployed. Researchers have found that the longer someone remains unemployed the more difficult it becomes to find work. Thus, a long stretch of unemployment reduces the chances of finding a job.[7]

## 7-1e Unemployment Among Various Groups

The unemployment rate also says nothing about who is unemployed. The overall rate masks wide differences in the labor force based on education, race, gender, and age. Exhibit 3 shows the unemployment rate in 2014 based on educational attainment for people age 25 and older. For example, the unemployment rate for those with less than a high school diploma was 9.0 percent. From there, the rate drops as education increases. The lowest rate was 1.9 percent, for those with a professional degree. Note that the rate among those with some college but no degree was 6.0 percent, the same as those with just a high school diploma. So education provides some insurance against unemployment, especially if you finish college. (But timing is important, even for college graduates. Not only do those who

graduate from college during a recession have a harder time finding that first job, but their job opportunities can be limited for years.)[8]

Unemployment also differs based on race and ethnicity; in February 2015, the rate was 4.7 percent among white workers, 10.4 percent among African Americans, 6.6 percent among those of Hispanic ethnicity, and 4.0 percent among Asian workers. (According to the 2010 Census, half of those over 25 years of age who identified themselves as Asian had at least a bachelor's degree, compared to only 28 percent for the entire U.S. population over 25.) Finally, the unemployment rate in February 2015 was 5.2 percent among males 20 and older and 4.9 percent among females 20 and older, but 17.1 percent among workers 16 to 19 years of age.

Why is the unemployment rate among teenage workers so much higher than among other workers? Teenagers enter the labor force with little education or job experience, so they take unskilled jobs and are first to be laid off if the economy slows down (last hired, first fired). Teenagers also move in and out of the labor force more frequently as they juggle school demands. Even those who have left school often shop around more than workers 20 and older, quitting one job in search of a better one.[9]

The unemployment rate is higher among black workers for several reasons. The black workforce is on average younger, and younger workers tend to experience higher

7. Kory Kroft, Fabian Lange, and Matthew Notowidigdo, "Duration Dependence and Labor Market Conditions: Evidence from a Field Experiment," *Quarterly Journal of Economics*, 128 (August 2013): 1123–1167.

8. Philip Oreopoulos, Till von Wachter, and Andrew Heisz, "The Short- and Long-Term Career Effects of Graduating in a Recession," *American Economic Journal: Applied Economics*, 4 (January 2012): 1–29.

9. Martin Gervais et al. "What Should I Be When I Grow Up? Occupation and Unemployment Over the Life Cycle," NBER Working Paper No. 20628 (October 2014).

**long-term unemployed**
Those looking for work for 27 weeks or longer

unemployment rates. A smaller than average percentage of black workers graduated from college. Black workers tend to live in areas harder hit by recessions. And racial discrimination is also a contributing factor.

Unemployment rates for different groups appear in Exhibit 4. Each panel shows the rate by race and by gender since 1972. Panel (a) shows the rates for workers 20 and older, and panel (b) the rates for 16- to 19-year-old workers. Periods of recession are shaded pink. As you can see, rates are higher among black workers than among white workers, and rates are higher among teenage workers than among those 20 and older. During recessions, rates climbed for all groups. Rates peaked during the recession of 1982 and then trended down to 2000. The rate rose with the recession of 2001 and more sharply with the Great Recession of 2007–2009. Exhibit 4 shows that the unemployment rate among black men was more than double that among white men.

## 7-1f Unemployment Varies Across Occupations and Regions

The unemployment rate varies by occupation. Professional and technical workers experience lower unemployment rates than blue-collar workers. Construction workers at times face high rates because that occupation is both seasonal and subject to wide swings over the business cycle.

### Exhibit 4
**Unemployment Rates for Various Groups**

Different groups face different unemployment rates. The unemployment rate is higher for black workers than for white workers and higher for teenagers than for those age 20 years and older.

*(a) 20 years of age or older*

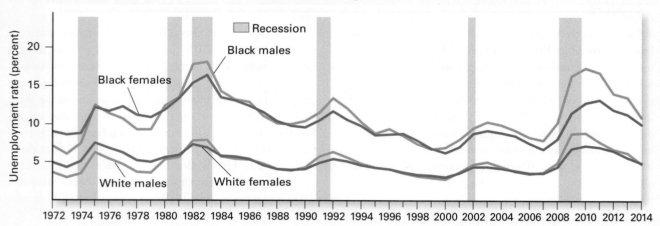

*(b) 16 to 19 years of age*

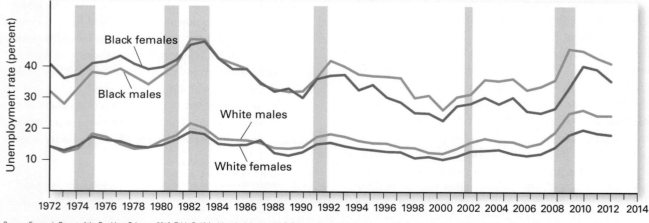

Source: *Economic Report of the President*, February 2013, Table B-43 for historical data; and U.S. Bureau of Labor Statistics for recent years. For the latest data, go to http://www.bls.gov/news .release/empsit.toc.htm. A breakout by race was not available for teenagers in 2013 and 2014.

Partly because certain occupations dominate labor markets in certain regions, unemployment rates also vary by region. For example, the unemployment rates in New Jersey, Rhode Island, and West Virginia in February 2015 were double those in the upper Midwest farm states of Nebraska, North Dakota, and South Dakota. Even within a state, unemployment can vary widely. For example, the California city of El Centro had an unemployment rate of 20.0 percent, more than four times that of San Francisco.

Exhibit 5 shows unemployment rates for 27 major metropolitan areas in February 2015. As you can see, Washington, DC had the highest unemployment rate, at 8.1 percent. This was more than double the rate for Minneapolis and Honolulu. The point is that *the national unemployment rate masks differences across states and even within an individual state*. Still, most cities in Exhibit 5 had rates between 4.0 percent and 6.0 percent.

## 7-1g International Comparisons of Unemployment

How do U.S. unemployment rates compare with those around the world? Exhibit 6 shows rates since 1980 for the United States, Japan, and the average of four major European economies (France, Germany, Italy, and the United Kingdom). During the decades before the Great Recession, unemployment trended down in the United States, trended up in Japan, and remained high in Europe. During the Great Recession of 2007–2009, the unemployment rate spiked in the United States, even briefly exceeding the average in Europe. The rate in Japan remained relatively low. In recent years, the U.S. rate has dropped.

Since 1980 the unemployment rate in Europe has averaged 8.3 percent versus a U.S. average of 6.4 percent. Why have rates averaged higher in Europe? The ratio of unemployment benefits to average pay is higher

*Exhibit 5*
**Unemployment Rates Differ Across U.S. Metropolitan Areas**

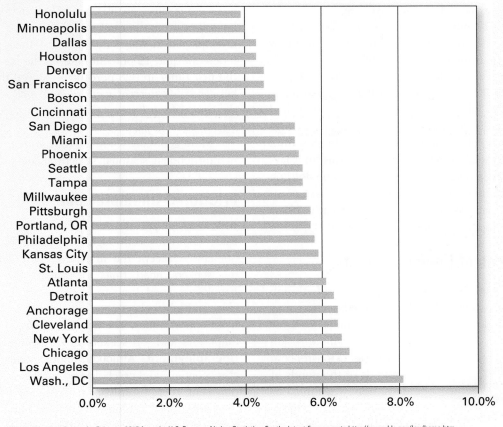

Source: Based on figures for February 2015 from the U.S. Bureau of Labor Statistics. For the latest figures, go to http://www.bls.gov/lau/home.htm.

*Exhibit 6*

**Unemployment Rates Increased After the Global Financial Crisis of 2008**

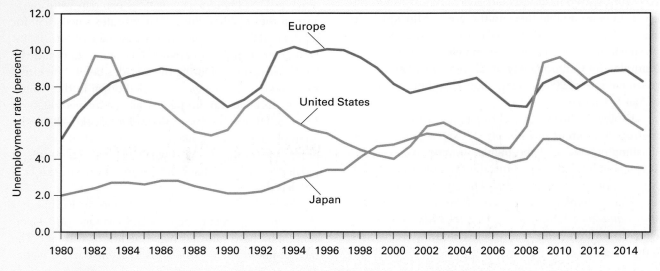

Source: Based on standardized rates in Figures for 2015 are projections. *OECD Economic Outlook*, 97 (May 2015); and *Economic Report of the President*, February 2015. Figures for Europe are the averages for France, Germany, Italy, and the United Kingdom. For the latest international data, go to http://www.bls.gov/fls/home.htm.

in Europe than in the United States, and unemployment benefits last longer there, sometimes years. So those collecting unemployment benefits have less incentive to find work. What's more, government regulations have made European employers more reluctant to hire new workers because firing them can be difficult.

Historically, unemployment has been low in Japan, averaging only 3.5 percent since 1980, because many firms there offer job security for life. In a system called *shukatsu*, Japanese companies typically hire most workers right out of school and expect them to stay until retirement. Both labor laws and social norms limit layoffs in Japan. As a result, some employees who do little or no work are still carried on company payrolls. Unemployment has increased there since the early 1990s because more Japanese firms went bankrupt.

### 7-1h Sources of Unemployment

Pick up any metropolitan newspaper and thumb through the classifieds. The help-wanted section may include hundreds of jobs, from accountants to X-ray technicians. Online job sites such as Monster.com list hundreds of thousands of openings. Why, when millions are unemployed, are so many jobs available? To understand this, we must think about all the reasons why people are unemployed. They may be looking for a first job, or they may be reentering the labor force after an absence. They may have quit or been fired from their last job. Fifty-two percent of those unemployed in February 2015 lost their previous job, 8 percent quit, 12 percent entered the labor market for the first time, and 28 percent reentered the labor market. *Thus, 48 percent were unemployed either because they quit jobs or because they were just joining or rejoining the labor force.*

More generally, there are four sources of unemployment: frictional, seasonal, structural, and cyclical.

### Frictional Unemployment

Just as employers do not always hire the first applicant who comes through the door, job seekers do not always accept the first offer. Both employers and job seekers need time to explore the job market. Employers need time to learn about the talent available, and job seekers need time to learn about employment opportunities. The time required to bring together employers and job seekers is the source of **frictional unemployment**. Although unemployment often creates economic and psychological hardships, not all unemployment is necessarily bad. Frictional unemployment does not usually last long and it results in a better match between workers and jobs, so the entire economy works more efficiently. Workers switch jobs to find better fits;

**frictional unemployment** Unemployment that occurs because job seekers and employers need time to find each other the resulting *churn* makes the labor market more efficient. Policy makers and economists are not that concerned about frictional unemployment. In recent years, however, there has less job switching. This reduces frictional unemployment but makes for a less dynamic and less flexible economy.[10]

## Seasonal Unemployment

Unemployment caused by seasonal changes in labor demand during the year is called **seasonal unemployment**. During cold winter months, demand for farm hands, lifeguards, landscapers, and construction workers shrinks, as it does for dozens of other seasonal occupations. Likewise, tourism in winter destinations such as Miami and Phoenix melts in the heat of summer. The Christmas season increases the demand for sales clerks, postal workers, and Santa Clauses. Those in seasonal work realize their jobs disappear in the off-season. Some even choose such work to complement their lifestyles or academic schedules. To eliminate seasonal unemployment, we would have to outlaw winter and abolish Christmas. Monthly employment data are *seasonally adjusted* to smooth out the unemployment bulges that result from seasonal factors. Policy makers and economists are not that concerned about seasonal unemployment.

## Structural Unemployment

A third reason why job vacancies and unemployment coexist is that unemployed workers often do not have the skills in demand or do not live where their skills are demanded. For example, the Lincoln Electric Company in Ohio took a long time filling 200 openings because few among the thousands who applied could operate computer-controlled machines. Unemployment arising from a mismatch of skills or geographic location is called **structural unemployment**. *Structural unemployment occurs because changes in tastes, technology,*

The unemployment rate usually falls before the holiday season as stores hire temporary workers.

AP Images/Gary He

> "Although most frictional unemployment is short term and voluntary, structural unemployment poses more of a problem because workers must either develop the skills demanded in the local job market or look elsewhere."

*taxes, and competition reduce the demand for certain skills and increase the demand for other skills.* In our dynamic economy, some workers, such as coal miners in West Virginia, are stuck with skills no longer demanded. Likewise, golf carts replaced caddies, ATMs replaced bank tellers, and office technology is replacing clerical staff. For example, because of email, voice mail, text messages, word processors, smart phones, and other electronic devices, the number of secretaries, typists, and administrative assistants in the United States has fallen by more than half over the past two decades. Structural unemployment may also arise from a change in tastes and preferences. For example, because Americans smoke less, some tobacco farmers had to grow other crops or find other work. And because Americans buy fewer newspapers, employment in that industry as well as the paper industry has declined.

Although most frictional unemployment is short term and voluntary, structural unemployment poses more of a problem because workers must either develop the skills

**seasonal unemployment** Unemployment caused by seasonal changes in the demand for certain kinds of labor

**structural unemployment** Unemployment because (1) the skills demanded by employers do not match those of the unemployed, or (2) the unemployed do not live where the jobs are

10. Ryan Decker et al., "The Role of Entrepreneurship in U.S. Job Creation and Economic Dynamism," *Journal of Economic Perspectives*, 28 (Summer 2014): 3–24.

demanded in the local job market or look elsewhere. Moving is not easy. Most people out of work prefer to remain near friends and relatives. Those laid off from good jobs hang around in hopes of getting rehired. Married couples with one spouse still employed may not want to give up that job to look for two jobs elsewhere. Finally, available jobs may be in regions where the living cost is much higher. So those structurally unemployed often stay put. U.S. interstate migration has slowed since the 1980s, which could worsen structural unemployment.[11] Some researchers concluded that, as a result of the Great Recession, structural unemployment in the U.S. economy between 2006 and 2010 increased by 1.75 percentage points.[12] Some federal retraining programs aim to reduce structural unemployment. Policy makers and economists are very much concerned about structural unemployment.

## Cyclical Unemployment

As output declines during recessions, firms reduce their demand for nearly all resources, including labor. **Cyclical unemployment** increases during recessions and decreases during expansions. Between 1932 and 1934, when unemployment averaged about 24 percent because of the Great Depression, there was clearly much cyclical unemployment. Between 1942 and 1945, when unemployment averaged less than 2 percent because of the demands of World War II, there was no cyclical unemployment. Cyclical unemployment means the economy is operating inside its production possibilities frontier. Government policies that stimulate aggregate demand aim to reduce cyclical unemployment. Policy makers and economists worry about cyclical unemployment.

 **7-2** OTHER UNEMPLOYMENT ISSUES

**cyclical unemployment** Unemployment that fluctuates with the business cycle, increasing during recessions and decreasing during expansions

**full employment** Employment level when there is no cyclical unemployment

**unemployment benefits** Cash transfers to those who lose their jobs and actively seek employment

Thus far we have discussed measures of unemployment, rates among various demographic groups, and sources of unemployment. Now we'll consider some other issues of unemployment.

11. Raven Molloy, Christopher Smith, and Abigail Wozniak, "Internal Migration in the United States," *Journal of Economic Perspectives*, 25 (Summer 2011): 173–196.

12. Marcello Estevao and Evridiki Tsounta, " Has the Great Recession Raised U.S. Structural Unemployment?" IMF Working Paper (May 2011); and Aysegul Sahin et al.,"Mismatch Unemployment," *American Economic Review*, 104 (November 2014): 3529–3564.

### 7-2a The Meaning of Full Employment

In a dynamic economy such as ours, changes in product demand and in technology continually alter the supply and demand for particular types of labor. Thus, even in a healthy economy, there is some frictional, structural, and seasonal unemployment. The economy is viewed as operating at *full employment* if there is no cyclical unemployment. When economists talk about "full employment," they do not mean zero unemployment but low unemployment, with estimates ranging from 4 to 6 percent. Even when the economy is at **full employment**, there is some frictional, structural, and seasonal unemployment. As noted earlier, nearly half of those unemployed in February 2015 had quit their previous job or were new entrants or reentrants into the labor force. We can't expect people to find jobs overnight. Many in this group would be considered frictionally unemployed.

### 7-2b Unemployment Compensation

As noted at the outset, unemployment often involves an economic and psychological hardship. For a variety of reasons, however, the burden of unemployment on the individual and the family may not be as severe today as it was during the Great Depression. Today, many households have two or more workers in the labor force, so if one loses a job, another may still have one—a job that could provide health insurance and other benefits for the family. *Having more than one family member in the labor force cushions the shock of unemployment.* And those just out of school who can't find work can usually move back home, an option that helps cushion unemployment.[13]

Moreover, unlike the experience during the Great Depression, most who lose jobs now collect unemployment benefits. In response to the Great Depression, Congress passed the Social Security Act of 1935, which provided unemployment insurance financed by a tax on employers. Unemployed workers who meet certain qualifications can receive **unemployment benefits** for up to six months, provided they actively look for work. During recessions, benefits usually extend beyond six months in states with especially high unemployment. During and following the Great Recession of 2007–2009, the extension of benefits was nationwide, and many states offered benefits for up to two years. Benefits go primarily to people who have lost jobs. Those just entering or reentering the labor force are not covered, nor are those who quit

13. Greg Kaplan, "Moving Back Home: Insurance Against Labor Market Risk," *Journal of Political Economy*, 120 (June 2014): 446–512.

Having more than one family member in the labor force helps cushion the shock of unemployment.

RYO/a.collectionRF/amanaimages/Corbis

their last job or those fired for just cause, such as excessive absenteeism or theft. In 2014 only 27 percent of the unemployed received benefits. Why so low? Recall that nearly a third of the unemployed most recently were out of work for 27 weeks or longer. This group would have run out of unemployment benefits, which typically last six months. And nearly half of the unemployed were not eligible in the first place because they either quit their job or were just entering or reentering the labor force.

> **"Evidence suggests that those collecting unemployment benefits remain out of work weeks longer than those without benefits."**

Unemployment benefits replace on average about half of a person's take-home pay, with a higher percentage for those who lost lower-paying jobs. Benefits vary by state but averaged about $340 per week in 2015. That year, Massachusetts had the highest maximum benefits, at $700 per week, and Mississippi, the lowest, at $235 per week. Because these benefits reduce the opportunity cost of remaining unemployed, they may reduce the incentives to find work. For example, if faced with a choice between washing dishes for $350 per week and collecting $250 per week in unemployment benefits, which would you choose? Evidence suggests that those collecting unemployment benefits remain out of work weeks longer than those without benefits. Many leave the labor force once their benefits run out.[14] In a 2014 Harris Survey of 1,500 unemployed Americans, 82 percent said they would "search harder and wider" once their unemployment compensation ran out. Forty-eight percent said they "haven't had to look for work as hard" because of their unemployment benefits, and 62 percent agreed that those benefits "allowed me to take time for myself."[15]

There is also evidence that after receiving government-provided health insurance, people reduced their labor supply.[16] And unemployment spells are longer after receiving an Earned Income Tax Credit refund (based on work the previous year) than unemployment spells during other times of the year.[17] So unemployment insurance and other safety-net programs reduce the urgency of finding work, thereby increasing unemployment.[18] There is also the possibility of fraud, with some collecting unemployment benefits who are, in fact, working.[19] On the plus side, because beneficiaries need not take the first job that comes along, unemployment insurance allows for a higher-quality job search. As a result of a higher-quality search, there is a better match between job skills and job requirements, and this promotes economic efficiency.

14. See, for example, David Card, Raj Chetty, and Andrea Weber, "Cash-on-Hand and Competing Models of Intertemporal Behavior: New Evidence from the Labor Markets," *Quarterly Journal of Economics*, 122 (November 2007): 1511–1560; and Kory Kroft and Matthew Notowidigdo, "Should Unemployment Insurance Vary With the Unemployment Rate? Theory and Evidence," *Review of Economic Studies* (forthcoming).

15. Bob Funk, "Clear Evidence on Disincentives to Work," *Wall Street Journal*, 9 November 2014.

16. Laura Dague, Thomas DeLiere, and Lindsey Leininger, "The Effect of Public Insurance Coverage for Childless Adults on Labor Supply," NBER Working Paper No. 20111 (May 2014).

17. Sara LaLumia, "The EITC, Tax Refunds, and Unemployment Spells," *American Economic Journal*: Economic Policy, 5 (May 2013): 190–221

18. Kurt Mitman and Stanislav Rabinovich, "Do Changes in Unemployment Insurance Explain the Emergence of Jobless Recoveries," *American Economic Association annual meetings*, 3 January 2014.

19. David L. Fuller, B. Ravikumar, and Yuzhe Zhang, "Unemployment Insurance Fraud and Optimal Monitoring," *American Economic Journal*: Macroeconomics, 7 (April 2015): 249–290.

## 7-2c Problems with Official Unemployment Figures

Official unemployment statistics are not problem free. We already discussed discouraged workers, those who have dropped out of the labor force in frustration. The U.S. Labor Department also keeps track of a second group of people who wanted a job but did not look for work in the prior four weeks. This group faced transportation problems, family problems, or other snags that kept them from looking for work. It wasn't that they were frustrated with their search; they just got sidetracked with some personal issues. Discouraged workers and this group that got sidetracked are considered *marginally attached to the labor force*. Not counting discouraged workers and others marginally attached to the labor force as unemployed understates unemployment. Official employment data also ignore the problem of **underemployment**, which arises because people are counted as employed even if they can find only part-time work or are overqualified for their jobs, as when someone with a Ph.D. in literature can find only a clerk's position. Counting overqualified and part-time workers as employed tends to understate the actual amount of unemployment. The federal government has another measure of unemployment, called *U-6*, which counts as unemployed those marginally attached to the labor force and those working part time who would prefer to work full time. In February 2015, the U-6 unemployment rate was 11.0 percent, or double the official unemployment rate that month.

On the other hand, because unemployment insurance benefits and most welfare programs require recipients to seek work, some people may go through the motions of looking for a job just to qualify for these benefits. If they do not in fact want a job, counting them as unemployed overstates actual unemployment. Likewise, some people who would prefer to work part time can find only full-time jobs, and some forced to work overtime and weekends would prefer to work less. To the extent that people must work more than they would prefer, the official unemployment rate overstates the actual rate. Finally, people in the underground economy may not admit they have jobs because they are breaking the law. For example, someone working off the books or someone selling illegal drugs may not admit to being employed.

On net, because discouraged workers and others marginally attached to the labor force aren't counted as unemployed and because underemployed workers are counted as employed, *most experts agree that the official U.S. unemployment rate underestimates unemployment.* Still, the size of this underestimation may not be huge, even in the wake of a recession. For example, counting discouraged workers as unemployed would have raised the unemployment rate in April 2012 from 8.1 percent to 8.7 percent. Adding in others who were marginally attached to the labor force would have raised the rate to 9.6 percent. There are no estimates of what the unemployment rate would be if we subtracted those looking for work only to qualify for government benefits.

Despite these qualifications and limitations, the U.S. unemployment rate is a useful measure of trends across demographic groups, across regions, and over time.

We turn next to inflation.

## 7-3 INFLATION: ITS MEASURE AND SOURCES

As noted already, *inflation* is a sustained increase in the economy's average price level, and we have already discussed inflation in different contexts. If the price level bounces around—moving up one month, falling back the next month—any particular increase in the price level would not necessarily be called inflation in a meaningful sense. We typically measure inflation on an annual basis. The annual *inflation rate* is the percentage increase in the average price level from one year to the next. Extremely high inflation, as occurred recently in Zimbabwe (where prices at the end of 2008 were *150 million times* higher than they were at the beginning of that year), is called **hyperinflation**.

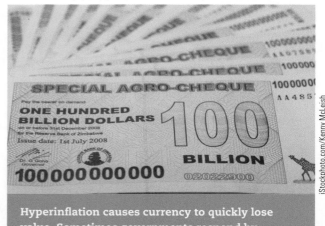

Hyperinflation causes currency to quickly lose value. Sometimes governments respond by printing money in larger and larger denominations.

**underemployment** Workers are overqualified for their jobs or work fewer hours than they would prefer

**hyperinflation** A very high rate of inflation

A sustained *decrease* in the average price level is called **deflation**, as occurred in the United States during the Great Depression and in 2009. Japan, Hong Kong, and Taiwan have also experienced deflation in recent years. And a reduction in the rate of inflation is called **disinflation**, as occurred in the United States from 1981 to 1986, 1991 to 1994, 2000 to 2002, and 2011–2015.

In this section, we first consider two sources of inflation. Then, we examine the extent and consequences of inflation in the United States and around the world.

## 7-3a Two Sources of Inflation

Inflation is a sustained increase in the economy's price level. Inflation results from an increase in aggregate demand, a decrease in aggregate supply, or both. Panel (a) of Exhibit 7 shows that an increase in aggregate demand raises the economy's price level from *P* to *P'*. In such cases, a shift to the right of the aggregate demand curve *pulls up* the price

> **❝Inflation is a sustained increase in the economy's price level; it results from an increase in aggregate demand, a decrease in aggregate supply, or both.❞**

level. Inflation resulting from increases in aggregate demand is called **demand-pull inflation**. To generate continuous demand-pull inflation, the aggregate demand curve would have to keep shifting out along a given aggregate supply curve. Rising U.S. inflation during the late 1960s came from demand-pull inflation, when federal spending for the Vietnam War and expanded social programs boosted aggregate demand.

Alternatively, inflation can arise from reductions in aggregate supply, as shown in panel (b) of Exhibit 7, where a leftward shift of the aggregate supply curve raises the price level. For example, crop failures and OPEC price hikes reduced aggregate supply between 1973 and 1975, thereby raising the price level in the economy. Inflation stemming

**deflation** A sustained decrease in the price level

**disinflation** A reduction in the rate of inflation

**demand-pull inflation** A sustained rise in the price level caused by a rightward shift of the aggregate demand curve

---

*Exhibit 7*

### Inflation Caused by Shifts of Aggregate Demand and Aggregate Supply Curves

Panel (a) illustrates demand-pull inflation. An outward shift of the aggregate demand to *AD'* "pulls" the price level up from *P* to *P'*. Panel (b) shows cost-push inflation. A decrease of aggregate supply to *AS'* "pushes" the price level up from *P* to *P'*.

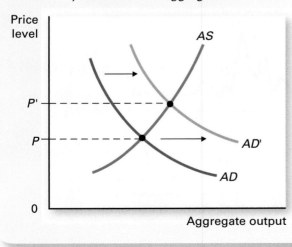

*(a)* Demand-pull inflation: inflation caused by an increase of aggregate demand

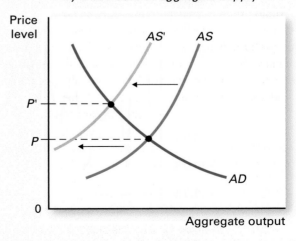

*(b)* Cost-push inflation: inflation caused by a decrease of aggregate supply

from decreases in aggregate supply is called **cost-push inflation**, suggesting that increases in the cost of production *push up* the price level. Prices increase and real GDP decreases, a combination identified earlier as *stagflation*. Again, to generate sustained and continuous cost-push inflation, the aggregate supply curve would have to keep shifting left along a given aggregate demand curve.

**cost-push inflation** A sustained rise in the price level caused by a leftward shift of the aggregate supply curve

## 7-3b Historical Look at Inflation and the Price Level

The consumer price index is the inflation measure you most often encounter, so it gets the most attention here. As you learned in the previous chapter, the *consumer price index*, or *CPI*, measures the cost of a market basket of consumer goods and services over time. Exhibit 8 shows prices in the United States since 1913, using the consumer price index. Panel (a) shows the price *level*, measured by an index number relative to the base period of 1982 to 1984.

*Exhibit 8*

**Consumer Price Index Since 1913**

Panel (a) shows that, despite fluctuations, the price level, as measured by the consumer price index, was lower in 1940 than in 1920. The price level began rising in the 1940s. Panel (b) shows the annual rate of change in the price level.

*(a) Consumer Price Index*

*(b) Annual Percentage Change*

Source: The CPI home page of the U.S. Bureau of Labor Statistics is at http://www.bls.gov/cpi/home.htm. Go there for the latest figures.

As you can see, the price level was lower in 1940 than in 1920. Since 1940, however, it has risen steadily, especially during the 1970s.

People are concerned less about the price level and more about year-to-year changes in that level. The lower panel shows the annual *rate of change* in the CPI, or the annual rate of *inflation* or *deflation*. The 1970s and early 1980s were not the only periods of high inflation. Inflation exceeded 10 percent from 1916 to 1919 and in 1947—periods associated with world wars. Prior to the 1950s, high inflation was war related and was usually followed by deflation. Such an inflation-deflation cycle stretches back over the last two centuries. In fact, between the Revolutionary War and World War II, the price level fell in about as many years as it rose. At the end of World War II, the price level was about where it stood at the end of the Civil War.

So fluctuations in the price level are nothing new. But prior to World War II, years of inflation and deflation balanced out over the long run. Therefore, people had good reason to believe the dollar would retain its purchasing power over the long term. Since the end of World War II, however, the CPI has increased by an average of 3.5 percent per year. That may not sound like much, but it translates into a tenfold increase in the consumer price index since 1947. *Inflation erodes confidence in the value of the dollar over the long term.*

## 7-3c Inflation Across Metropolitan Areas

Inflation rates differ across regions mostly because of differences in housing prices, which rise or fall more in some places than in others. But most prices, such as for automobiles, refrigerators, or jeans, do not differ that much across regions. The federal government tracks separate CPIs for each of 27 U.S. metropolitan areas. Based on these CPIs, the average annual inflation rate from 2010 to 2014 is presented in Exhibit 9. Annual inflation averaged from a low of 1.7 percent in Philadelphia to a high of 2.8 percent in Denver. Incidentally, the U.S. CPI also grew at an average annual rate of 2.1 percent between 2010 and 2014. Again, the metropolitan inflation rate is heavily influenced by what's happening in the local housing market. Housing markets were strong throughout the United States during

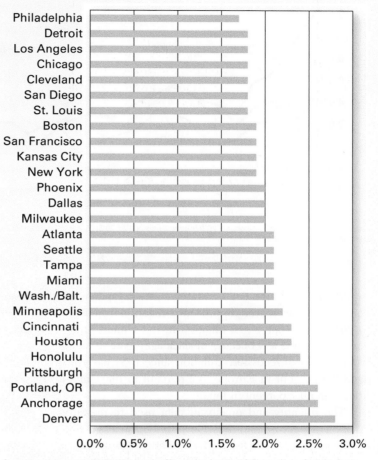

*Exhibit 9*

**Average Annual Inflation from 2010 to 2014 Differed Across U.S. Metropolitan Areas**

Source: Annual averages for 2010 to 2014 based on CPI estimates from the U.S. Bureau of Labor Statistics. For the latest figures go to http://www.bls.gov/cpi/home.htm and find "Regional Resources."

the years observed, but they were stronger in Denver than in Philadelphia.

## 7-3d International Comparisons of Inflation

Exhibit 10 shows annual inflation based on the GDP price index since 1981 in the United States, Japan, and Europe, represented here as the average of four major nations (France, Germany, Italy, and the United Kingdom). All three economies show a similar trend, with declining inflation, or disinflation, during the first half of the 1980s, rising inflation during the second half of the 1980s to a peak in the early 1990s, and then another trend lower. The overall trend since 1980 has been toward lower inflation. Inflation rates in Europe were

*Exhibit 10*

**Inflation Rates in Major Economies Have Trended Lower Over the Past Three Decades**

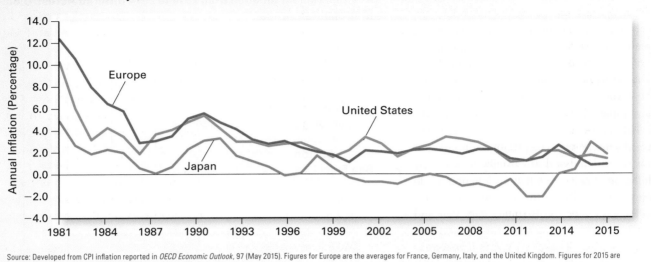

Source: Developed from CPI inflation reported in *OECD Economic Outlook*, 97 (May 2015). Figures for Europe are the averages for France, Germany, Italy, and the United Kingdom. Figures for 2015 are projections. For the latest data, go to http://www.bls.gov/fls/home.htm.

similar to those in the United States. Rates in Japan were consistently lower, even dipping into deflation from 2005 to 2011. In recent years, inflation in the United States and Europe was low because of slack aggregate demand from the global recession. Inflation since 1981 has averaged 3.5 percent in Europe, 3.2 percent in the United States, and 0.7 percent in Japan.

The quantity and quality of data used to measure inflation vary across countries. Governments in less-developed countries sample fewer products and measure prices only in the capital city. Although thousands of items are sampled to determine the U.S. consumer price index, as few as 30 might be sampled in some developing countries.

## 7-4 EFFECTS OF INFLATION

We have defined inflation, considered sources of inflation, traced the record of inflation over the last century, and examined inflation both across metropolitan areas and across countries. Now let's consider some effects of inflation.

### 7-4a Anticipated Versus Unanticipated Inflation

What is the effect of inflation on the economy? *Unanticipated inflation* creates more problems than *anticipated inflation*. To the extent that inflation is higher or lower than anticipated, it arbitrarily creates winners and

losers in the economy. For example, suppose inflation is expected to be 3 percent next year, and you and your employer agree to a 4 percent increase in your nominal, or money, wage. You both expect your *real* wage—that is, your wage measured in dollars of constant purchasing power—to increase by 1 percent. If inflation turns out to be 3 percent, as expected, you and your employer are both satisfied. After all, that's the wage your employer offered and you accepted. If inflation turns out to be 5 percent, your real wage will fall by 1 percent, so you are a loser and your employer a winner. If inflation turns out to be only 1 percent, your real wage will increase by 3 percent, so you are a winner and your employer a loser.

More generally, if inflation is higher than expected, the losers are those who agreed to sell at a price that anticipated lower inflation and the winners are those who agreed to pay that price. If inflation is lower than expected, the situation is reversed: The losers are those who agreed to pay a price that anticipated higher inflation, and the winners are those who agreed to sell at that price. *The arbitrary gains and losses arising from unanticipated inflation are partly why inflation is so unpopular.* Inflation just doesn't seem fair.

### 7-4b The Transaction Costs of Variable Inflation

During long periods of price stability, people correctly believe they can predict future prices and can therefore plan accordingly. If inflation changes unexpectedly, however, the future is cloudier, so planning gets harder. Uncertainty about inflation undermines money's ability to link the present with the future. U.S. firms dealing with the rest of the world face an added burden. They must not only anticipate U.S. inflation; they must also guess how the value of the dollar will change relative to foreign currencies. Inflation uncertainty and the resulting exchange-rate uncertainty complicate international transactions. In this more uncertain environment, companies with international ties must shift attention from production decisions to anticipating the effects of inflation and exchange-rate changes on the firm's finances. Market transactions, particularly long-term contracts, become more complicated as inflation becomes more unpredictable. Some economists believe that the high and variable U.S. inflation during the 1970s and early 1980s cut economic growth during those periods.

> **"The arbitrary gains and losses arising from unanticipated inflation are one reason inflation is so unpopular."**

## 7-4c Inflation Obscures Relative Price Changes

Even with no inflation, some prices would increase and some would decrease, reflecting normal activity in particular markets. For example, since the mid-1980s the U.S. price level has more than doubled, yet the prices of flat-screen TVs, computers, long-distance phone service, and many other products have declined sharply. Prices for education and for hospital care increased more than fivefold. Because the prices of various goods change by different amounts, *relative prices* change. Consider price changes over a longer period. In the last hundred years, consumer prices overall increased about 2000 percent, but the price of a hotel room in New York City jumped 7500 percent, while the price of a three-minute phone call from New York to Chicago dropped 99 percent. Whereas the economy's price level describes the exchange rate between a market basket and *money*, relative prices describe the exchange rate among goods— that is, how much one good costs compared to another.

Inflation does not necessarily cause a change in relative prices, but it can obscure that change. During periods of volatile inflation, there is greater uncertainty about the price of one good relative to another—that is, about relative prices. But relative price changes are important signals for allocating the economy's resources efficiently.

If all prices moved together, suppliers could link the selling prices of their goods to the overall inflation rate. Because prices usually do not move in unison, however, tying a particular product's price to the overall inflation rate may result in a price that is too high or too low based on market conditions. The same is true of agreements to link wages with inflation. If the price of an employer's product grows more slowly than the rate of inflation in the economy, the employer may be hard-pressed to increase wages by the rate of inflation. Consider the problem confronting oil refiners who signed labor contracts agreeing to pay their workers cost-of-living wage increases. In some years, those employers had to increase wages at a time when the price of oil was falling like a rock.

## 7-4d Inflation and Interest Rates

No discussion of inflation would be complete without some mention of the interest rate. **Interest** is the dollar amount paid by borrowers to lenders. Lenders must be rewarded for forgoing present consumption, and borrowers are willing to pay a premium to spend now. The **interest rate** is the amount paid per year as a percentage of the amount borrowed. For example, an interest rate of 5 percent means $5 per year on a $100 loan. The greater the interest rate, other things constant, the greater the reward for lending money. The amount of money people are willing to lend, called *loanable funds*, increases as the interest rate rises, other things constant. The supply curve for loanable funds therefore slopes upward, as indicated by curve S in Exhibit 11.

These funds are demanded by households, firms, and governments to finance homes, buildings, machinery, college, and other major purchases. The lower the interest rate, other things constant, the cheaper the cost of borrowing. So the quantity of loanable funds demanded increases as the interest rate decreases, other things constant. That is, the interest rate and the quantity of loanable funds demanded are inversely related. The demand curve therefore slopes downward, as indicated by curve *D* in Exhibit 11. The downward-sloping demand

**interest** The dollar amount paid by borrowers to lenders

**interest rate** Interest per year as a percentage of the amount loaned

## Exhibit 11

### The Market for Loanable Funds

The upward-sloping supply curve, *S*, shows that more loanable funds are supplied at higher interest rates. The downward-sloping demand curve, *D*, shows that the quantity of loanable funds demanded is greater at lower interest rates. The two curves intersect to determine the market interest rate, *i*.

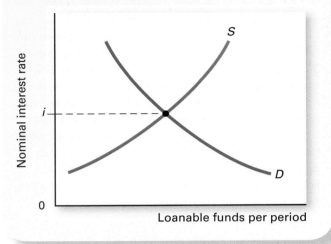

curve and the upward-sloping supply curve intersect to yield the equilibrium nominal rate of interest, *i*.

The **nominal interest rate** measures interest in terms of the current dollars paid. The nominal rate is the one that appears on the loan agreement; it is the rate discussed in the news media and is often of political significance. The **real interest rate** equals the nominal rate minus the inflation rate:

$$\text{Real interest rate} = \text{Nominal interest rate} - \text{Inflation rate}$$

For example, if the nominal interest rate is 5 percent and the inflation rate is 3 percent, the real interest rate is 2 percent. With no inflation, the nominal rate and the real rate would be identical. But with inflation, the nominal rate exceeds the real rate. If inflation is unexpectedly high—higher, for example, than the nominal interest rate—then the real interest rate would be negative. In this case, the nominal interest earned for lending money would not even cover the loss of spending power caused by inflation. Lenders would lose

**nominal interest rate** The interest rate expressed in dollars of current value (that is, not adjusted for inflation) as a percentage of the amount loaned; the interest rate specified on the loan agreement

**real interest rate** The interest rate expressed in dollars of constant purchasing power as a percentage of the amount loaned; the nominal interest rate minus the inflation rate

purchasing power. This is why lenders and borrowers are concerned more with the real rate than with the nominal rate. The real interest rate, however, is known only after the fact—that is, only after inflation actually occurs.

Because the future is uncertain, lenders and borrowers must form expectations about inflation, and they base their willingness to lend and borrow on those expectations. The higher the *expected* inflation, the higher the nominal rate of interest that lenders require and that borrowers are willing to pay. Lenders and borrowers base their decisions on the *expected* real interest rate, which equals the nominal rate minus the expected inflation rate.

Although the discussion has implied that there is only one market rate of interest, there are many rates. Rates differ depending on such factors as the duration of the loan, tax treatment of interest, and the risk the loan will not be repaid.

## 7-4e Why Is Inflation So Unpopular?

Whenever the price level increases, spending must increase just to buy the same amount of goods and services. If you think of inflation only in terms of spending, you consider only the problem of paying those higher prices. But if you think of inflation in terms of the higher money income that results, you see that higher prices mean higher receipts for resource suppliers, usually including higher nominal wages for workers. When viewed from the income side, inflation is not so bad.

If every higher price is received by some resource supplier, why are people so troubled by inflation? People view their higher incomes as well-deserved rewards for their labor, but they see inflation as a penalty that unjustly robs them of purchasing power. Most people do not stop to realize that unless they are producing more with each hour of labor, higher

**When prices rise faster than money income, real income falls and people can afford to buy less.**

wages *must* result in higher prices. Prices and wages are simply two sides of the same coin. To the extent that nominal wages on average keep up with inflation, workers retain their purchasing power.

Presidents Ford and Carter could not control inflation and were turned out of office. Inflation slowed significantly during President Reagan's first term, and he won reelection easily. During the 1988 election, George H. W. Bush won in part by reminding voters what inflation was in 1980, the last time a Democrat was president. But he lost his bid at reelection in part because inflation spiked to 6.0 percent in 1990, the highest in nearly a decade. Inflation remained under 3.0 percent during President Clinton's first term, and he was reelected easily. In the presidential elections of 2000, 2004, 2008, and 2012, inflation remained low enough not to be a campaign issue.

As noted earlier, unanticipated inflation creates winners and losers in the economy. The perceived unfairness and arbitrariness of these gains and losses are more reasons why people hate inflation. Finally, although inflation affects everyone to some extent, it hits hardest those whose incomes are fixed in nominal terms. For example, pensions are often fixed amounts and are eroded by inflation. And retirees who rely on fixed nominal interest income also see their incomes shrunk by inflation. But the benefits paid by the largest pension program, Social Security, are adjusted annually for changes in the CPI. Thus, Social Security recipients get a cost-of-living adjustment, or a **COLA**.

**TO REVIEW:** anticipated inflation is less of a problem than unanticipated inflation. Unanticipated inflation arbitrarily redistributes income and wealth from one group to another, reduces the ability to make long-term plans, and forces people to focus more on money and prices. The more unpredictable inflation becomes the harder it is to negotiate long-term contracts. Productivity suffers because people must spend more time coping with inflation, leaving less time for production.

## 7-5 FINAL WORD

This chapter has focused on unemployment and inflation. Although we have discussed them separately, they are related in ways that will unfold in later chapters. Politicians sometimes add the unemployment rate to the inflation rate to come up with what they refer to as the "misery index." In 1980, for example, an unemployment rate of 7.1 percent combined with a CPI increase of 12.5 percent to yield a misery index of 19.6—a number that helps explain why President Carter was not reelected. By 1984 the misery index dropped to 11.8, and by 1988 to 9.6; Republicans retained the White House in both elections. In 1992, the index climbed slightly to 10.4 percent, spelling trouble for President George H. W. Bush. And in 1996, the index fell back to 8.4 percent, helping President Clinton's reelection. During the election of 2000, the misery index was down to 7.7, which should have helped Al Gore, the candidate of the incumbent party. But during the campaign, Gore distanced himself from President Clinton and thus was not able to capitalize on the strong economy. In the 2004 election, the misery index remained about the same as in 2000, which helps explain why challenger John Kerry had difficulty making much of an issue of the economy. A misery index of 10.4 right before the 2008 election helped defeat the incumbent party and put Barack Obama in office. The misery index showed no improvement in 2012, and this made President Obama's reelection more of a challenge.

**COLA** Cost-of-living adjustment; an increase in wages or transfer payments tied to increases in the price level

## STUDY TOOLS 7

### READY TO STUDY? IN THE BOOK, YOU CAN:

☐ Work the Problems at the end of the chapter.

☐ Rip out the chapter review card for a handy summary of the chapter and key terms.

### ONLINE AT CENGAGEBRAIN.COM YOU CAN:

☐ Collect StudyBits while you read and study the chapter.

☐ Quiz yourself on key concepts.

☐ Prepare for tests with chapter flash cards as well as flash cards that you create.

☐ Watch videos to explore economics further.

# CHAPTER 7 PROBLEMS

*Your instructor can access the answers to these problems online at http://cengagebrain.com.*

## 7-1 Describe what the unemployment rate measures, and summarize four sources of unemployment

1. *(Measuring Unemployment)* Determine the impact on each of the following if 2 million unemployed workers decide to return to school full time and stop looking for work:
   a. The labor force participation rate
   b. The size of the labor force
   c. The unemployment rate

2. *(Measuring Unemployment)* Suppose that the U.S. non-institutional adult population is 230 million and the labor force participation rate is 67 percent.
   a. What would be the size of the U.S. labor force?
   b. If 85 million adults are not working, what is the unemployment rate?

3. *(Types of Unemployment)* Determine whether each of the following would be considered frictional, structural, seasonal, or cyclical unemployment:
   a. A UPS employee who was hired for the Christmas season is laid off after Christmas.
   b. A worker is laid off due to reduced aggregate demand in the economy.
   c. A worker in a DVD rental store becomes unemployed as video-on-demand cable service becomes more popular.
   d. A new college graduate is looking for employment.

## 7-2 Outline the pros and cons of unemployment insurance

4. *(Unemployment Insurance)* What are the pros and cons of unemployment insurance?

5. *(The Meaning of Full Employment)* When the economy is at full employment, is the unemployment rate at zero percent? Why or why not? How would a more generous unemployment insurance system affect the full employment figure?

## 7-3 Define inflation and describe the two sources of inflation

6. *(Two Sources of Inflation)* Using aggregate supply and aggregate demand, demonstrate two sources of inflation.

7. *(Inflation)* Here are some recent data on the U.S. consumer price index:

| Year | CPI | Year | CPI | Year | CPI |
|------|------|------|------|------|------|
| 2013 | 233.5 | 1999 | 166.6 | 2006 | 201.6 |
| 2014 | 237.1 | 2000 | 172.2 | 2007 | 207.3 |
| 1994 | 148.2 | 2001 | 177.1 | 2008 | 215.3 |
| 1995 | 152.4 | 2002 | 179.9 | 2009 | 214.5 |
| 1996 | 156.9 | 2003 | 184.0 | 2010 | 218.1 |
| 1997 | 160.5 | 2004 | 188.9 | 2011 | 226.3 |
| 1998 | 163.0 | 2005 | 195.3 | 2012 | 230.3 |

Compute the inflation rate for each year 1995–2014 and determine which were years of inflation. In which years did deflation occur? In which years did disinflation occur? Was there hyperinflation in any year?

8. *(Sources of Inflation)* Using the concepts of aggregate supply and aggregate demand, explain why inflation usually increases during wartime.

9. *(Inflation and Interest Rates)* Using a demand-supply diagram for loanable funds (like the exhibit below), show what happens to the nominal interest rate and the equilibrium quantity of loans when both borrowers and lenders increase their estimates of the expected inflation rate from 2 percent to 4 percent.

**The Market for Loanable Funds**

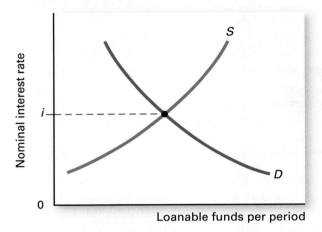

## 7-4 Explain how unanticipated inflation harms some individuals and harms the economy as a whole

10. *(Anticipated Versus Unanticipated Inflation)* If actual inflation exceeds anticipated inflation, who will lose purchasing power and who will gain? How does unanticipated inflation harm the economy?

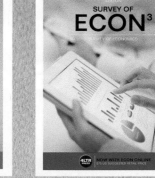

# 8 | Productivity and Growth

## LEARNING OUTCOMES

After studying this chapter, you will be able to…

**8-1** Describe how we measure labor productivity, and explain why is it important for a nation's standard of living

**8-2** Summarize the history of U.S. labor productivity changes since World War II, and explain why these changes matter

**8-3** Evaluate the evidence that technological change increases the unemployment rate

After finishing this chapter go to **PAGE 150** for **STUDY TOOLS**

**Topics discussed in Chapter 8 include:**

- Labor productivity
- The production function
- U.S. productivity and growth
- Rules of the game
- Technological change and unemployment
- Research and development
- Industrial policy
- Income and happiness

- Why is the standard of living so much higher in some countries than in others?
- How does an economy increase its living standard?
- Why is the long-term growth rate more important than short-term fluctuations in economic activity?
- What's labor productivity, why is it important, and why has it varied so much over time?

- What's been the impact of computers and the Internet on labor productivity?

*Answers to these and other questions are addressed in this chapter, which focuses on arguably the most important criteria for judging an economy's performance—productivity and growth.*

The single most important determinant of a nation's standard of living in the long run is the productivity of its resources. Even seemingly low growth in productivity, if sustained for years, can have a substantial effect on the standard of living—that is, on the availability of goods and services per capita. Growing productivity is therefore critical to a rising standard of living and has kept the U.S. economy a world leader.

> **"Why is the long-term growth rate more important than short-term fluctuations in economic activity?"**

You may not realize it, but you now live in one of the most technologically innovative times in human history. Each day brings faster computers, smarter phones, higher-definition video, more sophisticated social media, more effective medicines, more automated machines, and other breakthroughs that raise your productivity and your standard of living.

Economic growth is a complicated process, one that even experts do not yet fully understand. Since before Adam Smith wrote about *The Wealth of Nations*, economists have puzzled over what makes some economies thrive while others founder. Because a market economy is not the product of conscious design, it does not reveal its secrets readily, nor can it be easily manipulated in pursuit of growth. We can't simply push here and pull there to achieve the desired result. Changing the economy is not like remodeling a home by knocking out a wall to expand the kitchen. Because we have no clear blueprint of the economy, we cannot make changes to specifications.

Still, there is much economists do know. In this chapter, we first develop a few simple models to examine productivity and growth. Then, we use these models to help explain why some nations are rich and some poor. The U.S. performance gets special attention, particularly compared with other major economies around the world. We close with some controversies of technology and growth.

## 8-1 THE THEORY OF PRODUCTIVITY AND GROWTH

Two centuries ago, 90 percent of the American workforce was in agriculture, where the hours were long and rewards unpredictable. Other workers had it no better, toiling from sunrise to sunset for a wage that bought just the bare necessities. Most people had little intellectual stimulation and little contact with the outside world. A skilled worker's home in 1800 was described as follows: "Sand sprinkled on the floor did duty as a carpet. . . . What a stove was he did not know. Coal he had never seen. Matches he had never heard of. . . . He rarely tasted fresh meat. . . . If the food of a [skilled worker] would now be thought coarse, his clothes would be thought abominable."[1]

1. E. L. Bogart, *The Economic History of the United States* (Longmans Green, 1912), pp. 157–158.

Over the last two centuries, there has been an incredible increase in the U.S. *standard of living* as measured by the amount of goods and services available on average per person. Note that economic progress was unusual during the long sweep of history. For example, people of Shakespearean England had a living standard little better than those of ancient Greece, who lived nearly two thousand years earlier.

An economy's standard of living grows over the long run because of (1) increases in the amount and quality of resources, especially labor and capital; (2) better technology and know-how; and (3) improvements in the *rules of the game* that facilitate production and exchange, such as tax laws, property rights, patent laws, the legal system, and the manners, customs, and conventions of the market. Perhaps the easiest way to introduce economic growth is by beginning with something you have already read about, the production possibilities frontier.

## 8-1a Growth and the Production Possibilities Frontier

The *production possibilities frontier*, or *PPF*, first introduced in Chapter 2, shows what the economy can produce if available resources are used efficiently. Let's briefly review the assumptions made in developing the frontier shown in Exhibit 1. During the period under consideration, usually a year, the quantity of resources in the economy and the level of technology and know-how are assumed to be fixed. Also assumed fixed during the period are the rules of the game that facilitate production and exchange. We classify all production into two broad categories—in this case, consumer goods and capital goods. Capital goods are used to produce other goods. For example, the economy can bake pizzas and make pizza ovens. Pizzas are consumer goods, and ovens are capital goods.

When resources are employed efficiently, the production possibilities frontier *CI* in each panel of Exhibit 1 shows the possible combinations of consumer goods and capital goods that can be produced in a given year. Point *C* depicts the quantity of consumer goods produced if all the economy's resources are employed efficiently to produce them. Point *I* depicts the same for capital goods. Points inside the frontier are inefficient combinations, and points outside the frontier are unattainable combinations, given the resources, technology and know-how, and rules of the game. The production possibilities frontier is bowed out because resources are not perfectly adaptable to the production of both goods; some resources are specialized.

*Economic growth is shown by an outward shift of the production possibilities frontier*, as reflected in each panel of Exhibit 1. What can cause growth? An increase in resources, such as a growth in the labor supply or in the capital stock, shifts the frontier outward from one period to the next. Labor supply can increase either because of population growth or because the existing population works more. The capital stock increases if the economy produces more capital this year than it uses up. The more capital produced this year, on net, the more the economy grows, as reflected by an outward shift of the production frontier next year.

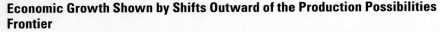

### Exhibit 1

**Economic Growth Shown by Shifts Outward of the Production Possibilities Frontier**

An economy that produces more capital goods will grow more, as reflected by a shift outward of the production possibilities frontier. More capital goods are produced in panel (b) than in panel (a), so the PPF shifts out more in panel (b).

(a) Lower growth

(b) Higher growth

Breakthroughs in technology also shift out the frontier by making more efficient use of resources. Technological change often improves the quality of capital, but it can enhance the productivity of any resource. And technological change can free up resources for other uses. For example, the development of synthetic dyes in the 19th century freed up millions of acres of agricultural land around the world that had been growing dye crops such as madder (red) and indigo (blue). The development of fiber-optic cable and cellular technology freed up the world's largest stock of copper in the form of existing telephone wires strung on poles.

Finally, any improvement in the rules of the game that nurtures production and exchange promotes growth and expands the frontier. For example, the economy can grow as a result of improved patent laws that encourage more inventions[2] or legal reforms that reduce transaction costs. Extending the length of patent protection could lead to more research and development (R&D), more inventions, and more innovations.

Thus, *the economy grows because of a greater availability of resources, an improvement in the quality of resources, technological change that makes better use of resources, or improvements in the rules of the game that enhance production.*

The amount of capital produced this year shapes the PPF next year. For example, in panel (a) of Exhibit 1, the economy has chosen point $A$ from possible points along $CI$. The capital produced this year shifts the PPF out to $C'I'$ next year. But if more capital goods are produced this year, as reflected by point $B$ in panel (b), the PPF shifts farther out next year, to $C''I''$. An economy that produces more capital this year is said to *invest* more in capital. As you can see, to invest more, people must give up some consumer goods this year. Thus, the opportunity cost of producing more capital goods this year is producing fewer consumer goods. More generally, we can say that people must *save* more

> **"**An economy grows because of a greater availability of resources, an improvement in the quality of resources, technological change that makes better use of resources, or improvements in the rules of the game that enhance production.**"**

now—that is, forgo some current consumption—to invest in capital. *Investment cannot occur without saving.* Economies that save more can invest more, as we'll see later. But let's get back to production.

## 8-1b What is Productivity?

**Production** *is a process that transforms resources into goods and services.* Resources coupled with technology and know-how produce output. Productivity measures how efficiently resources are turned into goods and services. In simplest terms, the greater the productivity, the more can be produced from a given amount of resources, and the farther out the production possibilities frontier. Economies that use resources more efficiently create a higher standard of living, meaning that more goods and services are produced per capita.

**Productivity** is defined as the ratio of total output to a specific measure of input. Productivity usually reflects an average, expressing total output divided by the amount of a particular kind of resource employed to produce that output. For example, **labor productivity** is the output per unit of labor and measures total output divided by the hours of labor employed to produce that output.

We can talk about the productivity of any resource, such as labor, capital, or natural resources. When agriculture accounted for most output in the economy, land productivity, such as bushels of grain per acre, was a key measure of economic welfare. Where soil was rocky and barren, people were poorer than where soil was fertile and fruitful. Even today, soil productivity determines the standard of living in some economies. Industrialization and trade, however, have liberated many from

**production** A process that transforms resources into goods and services

**productivity** The ratio of a specific measure of output, such as real GDP, to a specific measure of input, such as labor; in this case productivity measures real GDP per hour of labor

**labor productivity** Output per unit of labor; measured as real GDP divided by the hours of labor employed to produce that output

2. For evidence of how the greater protection of intellectual property stimulates technological change, see Sunil Kanwar and Robert Evenson, "Does Intellectual Property Protection Spur Technological Change?" *Oxford Economic Papers*, 55 (April 2003): 235–264.

Labor accounts for about 70 percent of production costs.

dependence on soil fertility. Today, some of the world's most productive economies have little land or have land of poor fertility. For example, Japan has only 2 percent as much land per capita as Russia, but Japan's GDP per capita is 50 percent higher than Russia's.

## 8-1c Labor Productivity

Labor is the resource most commonly used to measure productivity. Why labor? First, labor accounts for most production cost—about 70 percent on average. Second, labor is more easily measured than other inputs, whether we speak of hours per week or full-time workers per year. Statistics about employment and hours worked are more readily available and more reliable than those about other resources.

But the resource most responsible for increasing labor productivity is capital. As introduced in Chapter 1, the two broad categories are human capital and physical capital. *Human capital* is the accumulated knowledge, skill, and experience of the labor force. As workers acquire more human capital, their productivity and their incomes grow. That's why surgeons earn more than butchers and accountants earn more than file clerks. You are reading this book right now to enhance your human capital. *Physical capital* includes the machines, buildings, roads, airports, communication networks, and

**per-worker production function** The relationship between the amount of capital per worker in the economy and average output per worker

other human creations used to produce goods and services. Think about digging a ditch with bare hands versus using a shovel. Now switch the shovel for a backhoe. More physical capital obviously makes diggers more productive. Or consider picking oranges with bare hands versus using a picking machine that combs the trees with steel bristles. In less than 15 minutes that machine can pick 18 tons of oranges from 100 trees, catch the fruit, and drop it into storage carts. Without the machine, that job would take four workers all day.[3] The operator of the picking machine is at least 128 times more productive than someone picking oranges by hand.

In poorer countries labor is cheap and capital dear, so producers substitute labor for capital. For example, in India a beverage truck makes its rounds festooned with workers so as to minimize the time the truck, the valuable resource, spends at each stop. In the United States, where labor is more costly (compared with capital), the truck makes its rounds with just the driver. As another example, in Haiti, the poorest country in the Western Hemisphere, a ferry service could not afford to rebuild a dock, so it hired workers to carry passengers on their shoulders through the water to and from the ferry.[4]

As an economy accumulates more capital per worker, labor productivity increases and the standard of living grows. The most productive combination of all is human capital combined with physical capital. For example, one certified public accountant with a computer and specialized software can sort out a company's finances more quickly and more accurately than could a thousand high-school-educated file clerks using just pencils and paper.

## 8-1d Per-Worker Production Function

We can express the relationship between the amount of capital per worker and the output per worker as an economy's **per-worker production function**. Exhibit 2 shows the amount of capital per worker, measured along the horizontal axis, and average output per worker, or labor productivity, measured along the vertical axis, other things constant—including the amount of labor, the level of technology and know-how, and rules of the game. Any point on the production function, *PF*, shows the average output per worker on the vertical axis for each level of capital per worker on the horizontal axis. For example, with $k$ units of capital per

3. Eduardo Porter, "In Florida Groves, Cheap Labor Means Machines," *New York Times*, 22 March 2004.

4. This example was noted by Tyler Cowen in "The Ricardo Effect in Haiti," 23 February 2004, http://www.marginalrevolution.com.

## Exhibit 2

### Per-Worker Production Function

The per-worker production function, *PF*, shows a direct relationship between the amount of capital per worker, *k*, and the output per worker, *y*. The bowed shape of *PF* reflects the law of diminishing marginal returns from capital, which holds that as more capital is added to a given number of workers, output per worker increases but at a diminishing rate and eventually could turn negative.

**New capital and technological change leads to greater output as well as rising labor productivity.**

worker, the average output per worker in the economy is *y*. The curve slopes upward from left to right because an increase in capital per worker helps each worker produce more output. For example, bigger trucks make truck drivers more productive.

An increase in the amount of capital per worker is called **capital deepening** and is one source of rising productivity. *Capital deepening contributes to labor productivity and economic growth.* As the quantity of capital per worker increases, output per worker increases but at a diminishing rate, as reflected by the shape of the per-worker production function. The diminishing slope of this curve reflects the *law of diminishing marginal returns from capital*, which says that beyond some level of capital per worker, increases in capital add less and less to output per worker. For example, increasing the size of trucks beyond some point has diminishing returns as trucks become too large to negotiate some public roads. Thus, given the amount of labor, the level of technology and know-how, and the rules of the game, additional gains from more capital per worker eventually diminish and could turn negative.

## 8-1e Technological Change and Know-How

Held constant along a per-worker production function is the economy's level of technology and know-how.

Technological change and better know-how usually improve the *quality* of capital and represent additional sources of increased productivity. For example, a tractor is more productive than a horse-drawn plow, a word processor more productive than a typewriter, and an Excel spreadsheet more productive than pencil and paper. Bill Gates, founder of Microsoft, noted that putting an hour of video online cost about $400 in the late 1990s but only two cents in 2013.[5] Better technology and know-how are reflected in Exhibit 3 by an upward rotation of the per-worker production function from *PF* to *PF′*. As a result of a technological breakthrough, more is produced at each level of capital per worker. For example, if there are *k* units of capital per worker, a major breakthrough in technology increases the output per worker in the economy from *y* to *y′*.

Simon Kuznets, who won a Nobel Prize in Economics in part for his analysis of economic growth, claimed that technological change and the ability to apply such breakthroughs to all aspects of production are the driving forces behind economic growth in market economies. Kuznets argued that changes in the *quantities* of labor and capital account for only one-tenth of the increase in economic growth. Nine-tenths came from improvements in the *quality* of these inputs. For example, by manipulating metallic structures at the nanometer level (a billionth of a meter), scientists are developing material that has the strength and lightness of titanium but at a tenth of the cost.[6] As technological breakthroughs

5. "Catching On At Last," *The Economist*, 29 June 2013, pp. 24–25.

6. "Wings of Steel," *The Economist*, 7 February 2015. p. 77.

**capital deepening** An increase in the amount of capital per worker; one source of rising labor productivity

Exhibit 3

## Impact of a Technological Breakthrough on the Per-Worker Production Function

A technological breakthrough increases output per worker at each level of capital per worker. Better technology makes workers more productive. This is shown by an upward rotation of the per-worker production function from *PF* to *PF'*. An improvement in know-how or the rules of the game would have a similar effect.

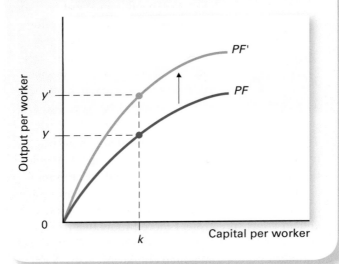

become *embodied* in new capital, resources are combined more efficiently, increasing total output. *From the wheel to the assembly-line robot, capital embodies the fruits of discovery and drives economic growth.*

But even for a given level of technology and a given number of workers, output can increase over time by improved know-how. As mentioned in Chapter 2, researchers have documented a doubling of steel production at a mini-mill with no change in technology or in the number of workers. Through experimentation, workers collectively developed more know-how and thereby became more productive.[7]

Thus, two kinds of changes in capital improve worker productivity: (1) an increase in the *quantity* of capital per worker, as reflected by a movement along the per-worker production function, and (2) an improvement in the *quality* of capital per worker, as reflected by technological change and know-how that rotates the curve upward. More capital per worker and better capital per worker result in more output per worker, which, over time,

**rules of the game** The laws, customs, manners, conventions, and other institutional elements that determine transaction costs and thereby affect people's incentive to undertake production and exchange

translates into more output per capita, meaning a higher standard of living.

## 8-1f Rules of the Game

Perhaps the most elusive ingredients for productivity and growth are the **rules of the game**, the formal and informal institutions that promote economic activity: the laws, customs, manners, conventions, and other institutional elements that encourage people to undertake productive activity. A stable political environment and a system of well-defined property rights are important. It's been said that capital goes where it's welcome and remains where it is well treated. Less is invested in human and physical capital if people believe the fruits of their investment could be seized by the government, stolen by thieves, destroyed by civil unrest, or blown up by terrorists. For example, countries whose colonizers established strong property rights hundreds of years ago have, on average, much higher incomes today than countries whose colonizers did not.[8] And recent research finds that economies grow faster if people are more trusting and more trustworthy.[9] After all, one sign of an advanced economy is a willingness to participate in impersonal market exchange. More generally, some countries are more inviting to talented people than other countries. For example, one recent study found that 38 percent of scientists working in the United States came from abroad (China and India are the two biggest sources of scientists). On the other hand, only 5 percent of the scientists in Japan came from abroad.[10]

Improvements in the rules of the game could result in more output for each level of capital per worker, thus reflected by a rotation up in the per-worker production function, as shown in Exhibit 3. On the other hand, a deterioration in the rules of the game would rotate down the per-worker production function. As an example, "Capital flight out of Russia has been high, blamed in part on a lack of confidence in the country's respect for property rights and on persistent, rampant corruption."[11]

We tend to think that laws are the backbone of market exchange, but we should not underestimate the role of manners, customs, and conventions. According to the

7. Igal Hendel and Yossi Spiegel, "Small Steps for Workers, a Giant Leap for Productivity," *American Economic Journal: Applied Economics*, 6 (January 2014): 73–90.

8. Daron Acemoglu, Simon Johnson, and James A. Robinson, "The Colonial Origins of Comparative Development," *American Economic Review*, 91 (December 2001): 1369–1401.

9. Yann Algan and Pierre Cahuc, "Inherited Trust and Growth," *American Economic Review*, 100 (December 2010): 2060–2092.

10. Chiara Franzoni, Giuseppe Scellato, and Paula Stephan, "Foreign Born Scientists: Mobility Patterns in Sixteen Countries," *Nature Biotechnology*, 30 (December 2012): 1250-1253, at http://www.nature.com/nbt/journal/v30/n12/pdf/nbt.2449.pdf.

11. Megan Davies and Melissa Akins, "Russian Risks Bear Down on Oligarch Fridman," Reuters, 6 June 2012.

18th-century British philosopher Edmund Burke, "Manners are of more importance than law....The law touches us but here and there and now and then. Manners are what vex or soothe, corrupt or purify, exalt or debase, barbarize or refine us, by a constant, steady, uniform and insensible operation like that of the air we breathe in."[12] The Russian proverb, "Custom is stronger than law," makes a similar point.

Simply put, a more stable political climate could benefit productivity just like a technological improvement could. Conversely, events that foster instability can harm an economy's productivity and rotate the per-worker production function downward. The terrorist attacks on the World Trade Center and Pentagon were such destabilizing events. According to Albert Abadie, a Harvard economist, the attack affected "the spinal cord of any favorable business environment"— the ability of business and workers "to meet and communicate effectively without incurring risks."[13] The 9/11 attacks increased the vacancy rates of tall buildings even in cities other than New York, such as Chicago's Sears Tower, making that capital less productive.[14] As other examples, a greater threat to airport security adds to the time and cost of flying. Shops in countries plagued by suicide bombers must hire security guards to deter such horror, and this increases the cost of doing business. And the mortgage meltdown of 2007–2009 reduced the trust that one bank had in another, thereby freezing up credit markets and increasing the cost of borrowing.

Advanced economies have developed a reliable and respected system of property rights, customs, and conventions that nurture productive activity. These successful economies have also cultivated the social capital that helps an economy run more smoothly. **Social capital** consists of the shared values and trust that promote cooperation in the economy. At the national level, social capital could be reflected in a sense of common

> **"More capital per worker and better capital per worker result in more output per worker, which, over time, translates into more output per capita, meaning a higher standard of living."**

purpose. For example, despite the Great Recession, polls show that Americans remain among the most patriotic people in the world. In a recent survey, 83 percent said they were "extremely" or "very" proud to be Americans.[15] At the local level, social capital could be expressed by a neighborhood crime watch, and there is evidence that such efforts help reduce property crime.[16]

Low-income economies typically have poorly defined property rights, less social capital, and in the extreme, customs and conventions where violence, bribery, and government corruption are common. Worse still, civil wars have ravaged some of the poorest countries on Earth. Such violence and uncertainty make people less willing to invest in their own future or in the future of their country. In short, as the Nobel Prize winner Kenneth Arrow noted, "Virtually every commercial transaction has within itself an element of trust, certainly any transaction conducted over a period of time."[17] Economies do not work as well where there is less trust, less social capital.

Now that you have some idea about the theory of productivity and growth, let's look at them in practice, beginning with the vast difference in performance among economies around the world. Then we will turn to the United States.

## 8-2 PRODUCTIVITY AND GROWTH IN PRACTICE

Differences in the standard of living among countries are vast. To give you some idea, per capita output in the United States, a world leader among major economies, is about 90 times that of the world's poorest countries. Poor countries are poor because they experience low labor productivity. We can sort the world's economies into two broad

12. Edmund Burke, *Letters to Parliament*, 2nd ed. (Rivington, 1796), p. 105.

13. As quoted in Greg Ip and John McKinnon, "Economy Likely Won't See Gain From War Against Terrorism," *Wall Street Journal*, 25 September 2001.

14. Alberto Abadie and Sofia Dermisi, "Is Terrorism Eroding Agglomeration Economies in Central Business Districts? Lessons From the Office Real Estate Market in Downtown Chicago," *Journal of Urban Economics*, 64 (September 2008): 451–463.

15. Lexington, "Where Has All the Greatness Gone?" *The Economist*, 17 July 2010.

16. Paolo Buonanno, Daniel Montolio, and Paolo Vanin, "Does Social Capital Reduce Crime?" *Journal of Law & Economics*, 52 (February 2009): 145–170.

17. "Gifts and Exchanges," *Philosophy & Public Affairs*, 1 (Summer 1972): 343–362.

**social capital** The shared values and trust that promote cooperation in the economy groups. **Industrial market countries**, or *developed countries,* make up about 18 percent of the world's population. They consist of the economically advanced capitalist countries of Western Europe, North America, Australia, New Zealand, and Japan, plus the newly industrialized Asian countries of Taiwan, South Korea, Hong Kong, and Singapore. Industrial market countries were usually the first to experience long-term economic growth during the 19th century, and today have the world's highest standards of living based on abundant human and physical capital. Industrial market countries produce more than half the world's output. The rest of the world, the remaining 82 percent of the world's population, consists of **developing countries**, which have a lower standard of living because they have less human and physical capital. Many workers in developing countries are farmers. Because farming methods there are often primitive, labor productivity is low and most people barely subsist, much like Americans two centuries ago.

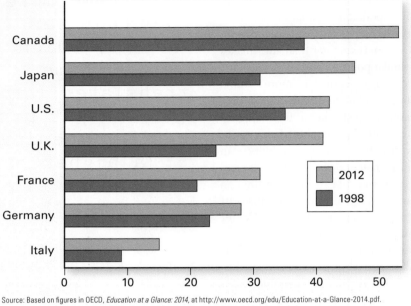

*Exhibit 4*

**Percent of Population Ages 25 to 64 with at Least a Post–High School Degree: 1998 and 2012**

The share of the U.S. population ages 25 to 64 with at least a degree beyond high school increased from 35 percent in 1998 to 42 percent in 2012. The United States slipped from second among the seven major industrial market economies in 1998 to third in 2012.

Source: Based on figures in OECD, *Education at a Glance: 2014,* at http://www.oecd.org/edu/Education-at-a-Glance-2014.pdf.

## 8-2a Education and Economic Development

Another important source of productivity is human capital—the skill, experience, and education of workers. If knowledge is lacking, other resources may not be used efficiently. *Education makes workers aware of the latest production techniques and more receptive to new approaches and methods.* Exhibit 4 shows the percentage of the population ages 25 to 64 who have at least a degree beyond high school. Figures are presented for the United States and six other industrial market economies, together called the *Group of Seven,* or G-7 (sometimes Russia is added to form the G-8, but Russia is not yet an industrial market economy). In 1998, 35 percent of the U.S. adult population had at least a degree beyond high school, ranking second behind Canada. The U.S. percentage grew to 42 by 2012, though America slipped to third behind Canada and Japan.

Not shown in Exhibit 4 are developing countries, which have far lower education levels. For example, only 13 percent of those in Brazil between the ages of 25 and 64 had a degree beyond high school in 2012. And while the literacy rate exceeds 95 percent in industrial market economies, nearly half the adults in the world's poorest countries can't read or write.

**industrial market countries** The economically advanced capitalist countries of Western Europe, North America, Australia, New Zealand, and Japan, plus the newly industrialized Asian economies of Taiwan, South Korea, Hong Kong, and Singapore

**developing countries** Countries with a lower living standard because of less human and physical capital per worker

*Exhibit 5*

**Long-Term Trend in U.S. Labor Productivity Growth: Annual Average by Decade**

Annual productivity growth, measured as the growth in real output per work hour, is averaged by decade. For the entire period since 1870, labor productivity grew at an average of 2.1 percent per year. Note the big dip during the Great Depression of the 1930s and the big bounce back during World War II. Productivity growth slowed during the 1970s and 1980s but recovered slightly during the 1990s and 2000s.

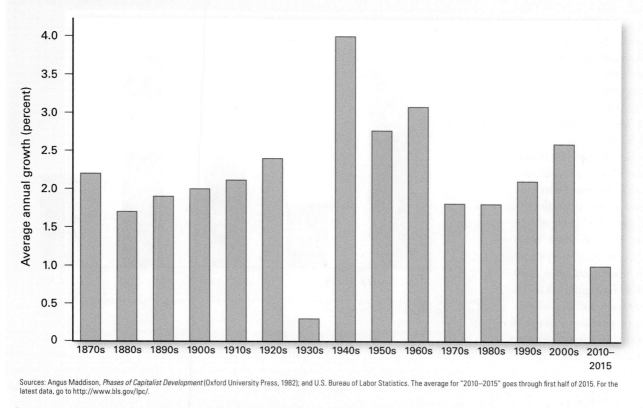

Sources: Angus Maddison, *Phases of Capitalist Development* (Oxford University Press, 1982); and U.S. Bureau of Labor Statistics. The average for "2010–2015" goes through first half of 2015. For the latest data, go to http://www.bls.gov/lpc/.

## 8-2b U.S. Labor Productivity

What has been the record of labor productivity in the United States? Exhibit 5 offers a long-run perspective, showing growth in real output per work hour for the last 145 years. Annual productivity growth is averaged by decade (except for the most recent period, which averages 2010 to 2015). The huge dip during the Great Depression and the strong rebound during World War II are unmistakable. Growth slowed during the 1970s and 1980s but has recovered somewhat during the 1990s and 2000s. However, during the most recent period, 2010 to 2015, labor productivity growth dropped to just 1.0 percent, among the slowest on record. Labor productivity has grown an average of 2.1 percent per year since 1870. This may not impress you, but because of the power of compounding, output per hour has jumped more than 1,900 percent during the period. To put this in perspective, if a roofer in 1870 could shingle one roof

If a roofer in the 1870s could shingle one roof in a day, today's roofer could shingle more than 20 in a day.

in a day, today's roofer could shingle more than 20 roofs in a day.

Over long periods, small differences in productivity can make huge differences in the economy's ability to produce and therefore in the standard of living. For example, if productivity grew only 1.0 percent per year instead of 2.1 percent, output per work hour since 1870 would have increased by only 323 percent, not 1,936 percent. On the other hand, if productivity grew 2.6 percent per year (the average from 2000 to 2010), output per work hour since 1870 would have jumped about 4,000 percent! The wheels of progress seem to grind slowly but they grind very fine, and the cumulative effect is powerful.

So far, we have averaged productivity growth for all workers. Productivity has grown more in some industries than in others. In ocean shipping, for example, cargo carried per worker hour is about 100 times greater now than in 1900, for an average annual growth of 4.1 percent. On the other hand, makers of wooden office furniture are only about three times more productive today than in 1900, for an average annual growth in productivity of only 1.0 percent. Consider productivity gains in TV journalism. Not long ago, a TV reporter covering a story would need a camera operator, a sound technician, and a broadcast editor. Now, because of technological advances in the size, quality, and ease of use of equipment, most TV reporters set up their own cameras on the scene, shoot their own footage, and do their own editing. One person can do what used to take four to accomplish. And because of technological advances in car manufacturing, some automakers can now produce twice as many vehicles per worker as they did a decade ago.[18]

Recent research suggests an additional reason for the growth in U.S. labor productivity: A reduction in racial and gender discrimination since 1960 has made labor markets more efficient, as African Americans and women entered professions where they could be more productive. Researchers argue that these more open labor markets, by allocating labor more efficiently, have accounted for 15 to 20 percent of U.S. economic growth since 1960.[19]

*Exhibit 6*

**U.S. Labor Productivity Growth Since 1947**

The growth in labor productivity declined from an average of 2.8 percent per year between 1947 and 1973 to only 0.9 percent between 1973 and 1982. A jump in the price of oil contributed to three recessions during that stretch, and new environmental and workplace regulations, though necessary and beneficial, slowed down productivity growth temporarily. The information revolution powered by the computer chip and the Internet has boosted productivity between 1982 and 2005.

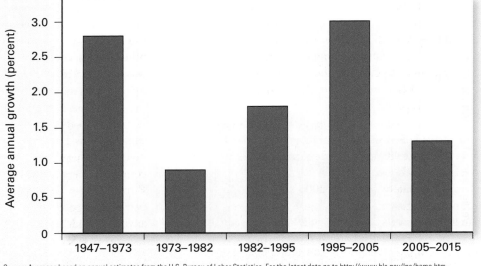

Source: Averages based on annual estimates from the U.S. Bureau of Labor Statistics. For the latest data go to http://www.bls.gov/lpc/home.htm. Average for 2005–2015 is through the first half of 2015.

## 8-2c Slowdown and Rebound in Productivity Growth

You can see in Exhibit 5 that productivity growth slowed to 1.8 percent per year during the 1970s and 1980s, increased to 2.1 percent during the 1990s and to 2.6 percent in the 2000s. But between 2010 and 2015, labor productivity managed a growth rate of only 1.2 percent. By breaking the data down into intervals other than decades, we can get a better feel for years since World War II. Exhibit 6 offers average annual growth for five periods. Labor productivity growth averaged 2.8 percent per year between 1947 and 1973; these could be called the golden years of productivity growth. But, between 1973 and 1982, productivity growth slowed to only about a third of that, averaging just 0.9 percent. Why the slowdown? First, as a

18. "The Third Industrial Revolution," *The Economist*, 21 April 2012.

19. Chang-Tai Hsieh et al. "The Allocation of Talent and U.S. Economic Growth," American Economic Association annual meetings, 4 January 2013.

result of the actions of the Organization of the Petroleum Exporting Countries (OPEC), oil prices jumped between 1973 and 1974 and again between 1979 and 1980, boosting inflation and contributing to stagflation and three recessions. Second, federal legislation in the early 1970s necessary to protect the environment and improve workplace safety slowed the growth of labor productivity.

Fortunately, productivity rebounded off the 1973–1982 low, averaging 1.8 percent from 1982 to 1995 and 3.0 percent from 1995 to 2005. Why the rebound? The information revolution powered by the computer chip and the Internet started paying off. One study of industrial economies found that the greater the penetration of broadband Internet service, the higher the economic growth per capita.[20]

The U.S. dominance in computer technology carries over to U.S. multinational firms, which experienced higher productivity growth after 1995 than did multinationals from other countries.[21]

Unfortunately, between 2005 and 2015, U.S. labor productivity growth averaged just 1.3 percent, or less than half the average for 1995 to 2005. Some economists argue that the boost to productivity provided by information technology was just temporary, and the recent slowdown indicates that boost has now run its course.[22]

Higher labor productivity growth can make up for output lost from most recessions. For example, if over the next decade U.S. labor productivity grows an average of 3.0 percent per year (the average from 1995 to 2005) instead of 1.3 percent (the average from 2005 to 2015), that higher growth would add about $3.3 trillion to real GDP in the tenth year—more than enough to make up for the output lost during the worst recession since the Great Depression. *This cumulative power of productivity growth is why economists pay so much attention to long-term growth.*

One final point before we move on: The U.S. Bureau of Labor Statistics measures labor productivity in only about 60 percent of all industries, leaving out some of the newest ones. So labor productivity is not a foolproof measure of what's going on throughout the economy.

## 8-2d Output Per Capita

As noted earlier, the best measure of an economy's standard of living is output per capita. *Output per capita*, or

20. Nina Czernich et al. "Broadband Infrastructure and Economic Growth," *Economic Journal*, 121 (May 2011): 505–532.

21. Nicholas Bloom, Raffaella Sadun, and John Van, "Americans Do IT Better: U.S. Multinationals and the Productivity Miracle," *American Economic Review*, 102 (March 2012): 167–201.

22. John Fernald and Bing Wang, "The Recent Rise and Fall of Rapid Productivity Growth," *FRBSF Economic Letter*, 9 February 2015, http://www.frbsf.org/economic-research/publications/economic-letter/2015/february/economic-growth-information-technology-factor-productivity/.

GDP divided by the population, indicates how much an economy produces on average per resident.

How does U.S. output per capita compare with that of other industrial countries? Exhibit 7 compares GDP per capita in 2014 for the United States and the six other G-7 countries plus China. Local currencies have been converted to U.S. dollars of 2014 purchasing power. With GDP per capita of $54,800 in 2014, the United States stood alone at the top, with a per capita GDP 23 percent above second-ranked Germany. Thus, the United States produced more per capita than any other major economy. GDP per capita for the world was about $16,100 in 2014. Hence, U.S. per capita income was more than three times the world average.

Of course, U.S. output per capita is far greater than in less developed economies. For example, U.S. output per capita is more than four times that of China and more than nines time that of India. The United States has an open and competitive economy, where successful firms can thrive. Firms in less developed countries often remain small because of government regulations and a fear of hiring anyone outside the family for lack of trust. One economist joked that if Walmart's founder, Sam Walton, had started in India, he would have only five stores by now, they would all be called "Sam Walton's Family Market," and each store would be managed by one of his sons or sons-in-law.[23]

**TO REVIEW:** U.S. labor productivity growth has averaged 2.1 percent per year since 1870. Productivity growth slowed between 1973 and 1982, because of spikes in energy prices and the implementation of necessary but costly environmental and workplace regulations. After 1982 labor productivity growth picked up, especially between 1995 and 2005, due primarily to breakthroughs in information technology. But the boost from information technology seemed to wane during the 2005 to 2015 decade, when the rate averaged less than half that of the decade from 1995 to 2005. Still, in 2014, U.S. GDP per capita was the highest among major economies, was more than three times the world average, and was four times that of China.

## 8-3 OTHER ISSUES OF TECHNOLOGY AND GROWTH

In this section, we consider some other issues of technology and growth, beginning with the question whether technological change creates unemployment.

23. Drawn from an "Interview with Nicholas Bloom," *Econ Focus: Federal Reserve Bank of Richmond*, 18 (Second Quarter 2014): 22–26.

*Exhibit 7*

**U.S. GDP Per Capita in 2014 Was Highest of G-7 Economies and Four Times China's**

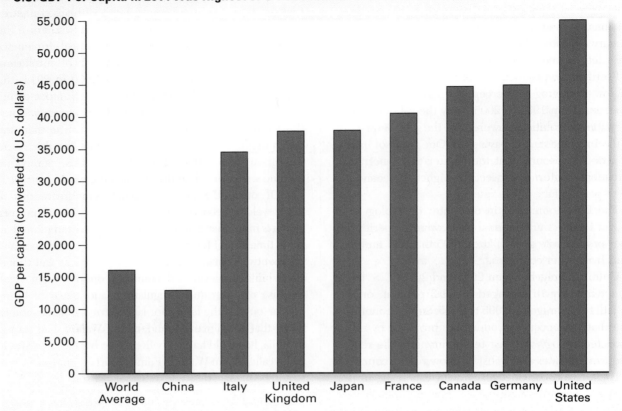

Source: Based on 2014 dollar estimates from the OECD at http://www.oecd.org/home/; and *The World Factbook 2015:* at https://www.cia. gov/library/publications/the-world-factbook/index.html. Estimates have been adjusted across countries using the purchasing power of the local currency in 2014.

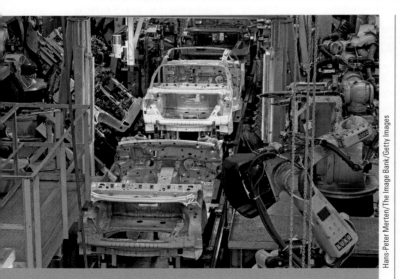

While machines may displace workers in the short run, those displaced workers normally find new jobs elsewhere. As a result, new technology does not lead to overall higher rates of unemployment.

Hans-Peter Merten/The Image Bank/Getty Images

## 8-3a Does Technological Change Lead to Unemployment?

Because technological change usually reduces the labor needed to produce a given amount of output, some observers fear technological change increases unemployment. True, technological change can create dislocations as displaced workers try to find jobs elsewhere. But technological change can also create new products and job opportunities and make existing products more affordable. For example, the assembly line cut the cost of automobiles, making them more affordable for the average household. This increased the quantity of automobiles demanded, boosting production and employment. Even in industries where machines displace some workers, those who keep their jobs become more productive, so they earn more. And *because human wants are unlimited, displaced workers usually find jobs producing other goods and services demanded in a growing economy.*

Although job data from the 19th century are sketchy, there is no evidence that the unemployment rate is any higher today than it was in 1870. Since then, worker productivity per hour has increased more than 1,900 percent, and the length of the average workweek has been cut nearly in half. Although technological change may displace some workers in the short run, long-run benefits include higher real incomes and more leisure—in short, a higher standard of living.

If technological change causes unemployment, then the spurt in productivity growth from 1995 to 2005 should have increased unemployment compared to the slow-growth years from 1973 to 1982. But the unemployment rate, the share of the workforce looking for jobs, averaged 7.0 percent during 1973 to 1982, compared to only 5.1 percent from 1995 to 2005. What's more, the unemployment rate increased during the slowdown in labor productivity growth after 2005. And if technological change causes unemployment, then unemployment rates should be lower in economies where the latest technology has not yet been adopted, such as in developing countries. But unemployment is far worse there, and those fortunate enough to find work earn little because they are not very productive.

Again, there is no question that technological change sometimes creates job dislocations and hardships in the short run, as workers scramble to adjust to a changing world. Because of technological progress, labor is becoming less important in some types of production. For example, the $499 charged for the first-generation iPad included only about $33 of manufacturing labor. And the final assembly in China accounted for just $8 of that $33.[24] Some workers with specialized skills made obsolete by technology may be unable to find jobs that pay as well as the ones they lost. These dislocations are one price of progress. Over time, however, most displaced workers find other jobs, often in new industries created by technological change. In a typical month of expansion, the U.S. economy sheds about

> **"Most displaced workers find other jobs, often in new industries created by technological change."**

> **"Basic research yields a higher return to society as a whole than does applied research."**

3.8 million jobs but creates about 4 million new ones.

Although unemployment may not have increased because of technological change, researchers have found that advances in information technology during the last three decades have reduced the cost of investment goods, encouraging some firms to substitute capital for labor. The lower cost of investment goods has contributed to a decline in labor's share of total income in most countries and in most industries.[25] Because of the broad advances in technology, some companies can become successful with few workers. For example, Oculus VR, makers of virtual reality headsets, had only 75 employees in 2014, when it was purchased by Facebook for $2 billion.[26]

## 8-3b Research and Development

As noted several times already, a prime contributor to labor productivity growth has been an improvement in the quality of human and physical capital. Human capital has benefited from better education, better health care, and more job training. Better technology embodied in physical capital has also helped labor productivity. For example, because of extensive investments in cellular transmission, new satellites, and fiber-optic technology, labor productivity in the telecommunications industry has increased by an average of 5.5 percent per year during the past three decades.

Improvements in technology arise from scientific discovery, which is the fruit of research. We can distinguish between basic research and applied research. **Basic research**, the search for knowledge

24. "The Third Industrial Revolution," *The Economist*, 21 April 2012.

25. Loukas Karabarbounis and Brent Neiman, "The Global Decline of the Labor Share," *Quarterly Journal of Economics*, 129 (February 2014): 61–103.

26. Simon Parkin, "What Zuckerberg Sees in Oculus Rift," *MIT Technology Review*, 26 March 2014, at http://www .technologyreview.com/news/525881 /what-zuckerberg-sees-in-oculus-rift/.

**basic research** The search for knowledge without regard to how that knowledge will be used

## Exhibit 8

### R&D Spending as a Percentage of GDP for G-7 Economies During the 1980s, 1990s, and in 2013

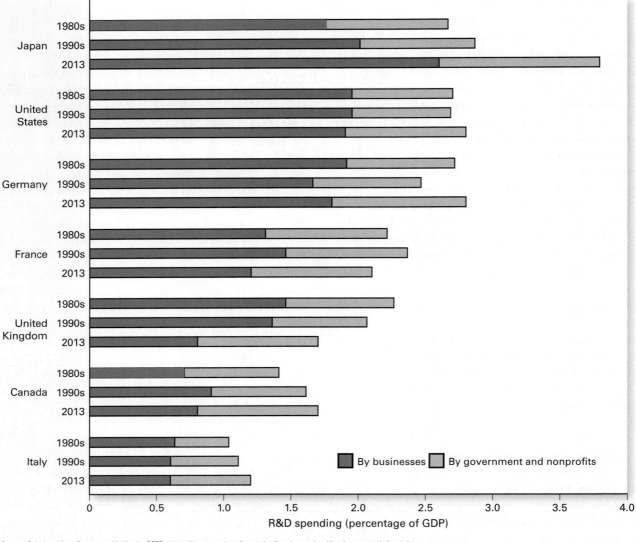

Source: Calculated from figures provided by the OECD at http://www.oecd.org/innovation/inno/researchanddevelopmentstatisticsrds.htm.

without regard to how that knowledge will be used, is a first step toward technological advancement. In terms of economic growth, however, scientific discoveries are of little value until they are implemented, which requires applied research. **Applied research** seeks to answer particular questions or to apply scientific discoveries to the development of specific products. Because technological breakthroughs may or may not have commercial possibilities, the payoff is less immediate with basic

**applied research**
Research that seeks answers to particular questions or to apply scientific discoveries to develop specific products

research than with applied research. *Yet basic research yields a higher return to society as a whole than does applied research.*

Because technological change is the fruit of R&D, investment in R&D improves productivity through technological discovery. One way to track R&D spending is to measure it relative to gross domestic product, or GDP. Exhibit 8 shows R&D spending as a share of GDP for the United States and the six other G-7 economies. Overall R&D spending in the United States has remained relatively constant, averaging 2.7 percent of GDP in the 1980s and 1990s, and 2.8 percent in 2013. During the 1990s, the United States ranked second among the major economies, behind Japan; in 2013 the United States tied with Germany for second place behind Japan.

Bar segments in the chart distinguish between R&D by businesses (shown as dark blue segments) and R&D by governments and nonprofit institutions (shown as light blue segments). Business R&D is more likely to target applied research and innovations. R&D spending by governments and nonprofits, such as universities, may generate basic knowledge that has applications in the long run (e.g., the Internet sprang from R&D spending on national defense). R&D by U.S. businesses was about 1.9 percent of GDP in all three periods. Again, only Japan had higher business R&D than the United States in the 1990s and in 2013. In short, the United States devotes more resources to R&D than most other advanced economies, and this helps America maintain a higher standard of living. Incidentally, manufacturers undertake more R&D than most other types of producers. Manufacturing accounts for only 11 percent of U.S. GDP but is responsible for 68 percent of R&D spending.[27]

## 8-3c Industrial Policy

Policy makers have debated whether the government should become more involved in shaping an economy's technological future. One concern is that technologies of the future will require huge sums to develop, sums that an individual firm cannot easily raise and put at risk. Another concern is that the benefits of some technological breakthroughs spill over to other firms and other industries, but the firm that develops the breakthrough may not be in a position to reap benefits from these spillover effects, so individual firms may underinvest in such research. For example, the majority of the important drug discoveries in the last decade came from basic research.[28] Yet drug companies are often reluctant to invest in these long-term projects.[29] One possible solution is more government involvement in economic planning.

**Industrial policy** is the idea that government, using taxes, subsidies, regulations, and coordination of the private sector, could help nurture the industries and technologies of the future to give domestic industries an advantage over foreign competitors. The idea is to secure a leading role for domestic industry in the world economy. One example of European industrial policy is Airbus Industrie,

European manufacturer Airbus has the direct support of a four-nation aircraft consortium that promotes policies favorable to Airbus.

a four-nation aircraft consortium. With an estimated $20 billion in government aid, the aircraft maker has become Boeing's main rival. When Airbus seeks aircraft orders around the world, it can draw on government backing to promise favorable terms, such as landing rights at key European airports and an easing of regulatory constraints. U.S. producers get less government backing.

For decades, U.S. industrial policy was aimed at creating the world's most advanced military production capacity. With the demise of the Soviet Union, however, defense technologies became less important, but wars in Iraq and Afghanistan shifted some attention back to military applications. Some argue that U.S. industrial policy should shift from a military to a civilian focus. Many state governments are also trying to identify what industries to support. Economists have long recognized that firms in some industries gain a performance advantage by *clustering*—that is, by locating in a region already thick with firms in the same industry or in related industries. For example, new entrants to an industry can hire experienced workers from established firms.[30] New entrants can also buy other specialized factors of production from local suppliers.[31] And new entrants can benefit from local knowledge about industry know-how, such as which production methods work best.[32]

27. "Manufacturing and Innovation: Back to Making Stuff," *The Economist*, 21 April 2012.

28. Dan Hurley, "Why Are So Few Block Buster Drugs Invented Today?" *New York Times*, 13 November 2014.

29. Eric Budish, Benjamin N. Roin, and Heidi Williams, "Do Firms Underinvest in Long-Term Research? Evidence from Cancer Clinical Trials," *American Economic Review* (forthcoming).

30. Andrey Stoyonov and Nikolay Zubanov, "Productivity Spillovers Across Firms Through Worker Mobility," *American Economic Journal: Applied Economics*, 4 (April 2012): 168–198.

31. Ejaz Ghani, William Kerr, and Stephen O'Connell, "Spatial Determinants of Entrepreneurship in India," *Regional Studies*, 48 (June 2014): 1071–1089.

32. Glenn Ellison, Edward Glaeser, and William Kerr, "What Causes Agglomeration? Evidence From Coagglomeration Patterns," *American Economic Review*, 100 (June 2010): 1195–1213.

**industrial policy** The view that government—using taxes, subsidies, and regulations—should nurture the industries and technologies of the future, thereby giving these domestic industries an advantage over foreign competition

Clusters such as Hollywood studios, Wall Street brokers, Broadway theaters, Las Vegas casinos, Boston colleges, Orlando theme parks, and Silicon Valley software makers facilitate communication and promote healthy competition among cluster members. The flow of information and cooperation between firms, as well as the competition among firms in close proximity, stimulates regional innovation and propels growth. Thus, by locating in a region already settled with similar firms, a firm can also tap into established local markets for specialized labor and for other inputs. Research into patent activity suggests that know-how in one firm spills over to other firms in the locality.[33] And there is some evidence that an industrial policy that nurtures younger and more productive enterprises can boost productivity growth in the economy.[34]

But skeptics wonder whether the government should be trusted to identify productive enterprises and to pick the industry clusters that will lead the way. Critics of industrial policy believe that markets allocate scarce resources better than governments do. For example, European governments' costly attempt to develop the supersonic transport Concorde never became cost efficient. Airbus also ran into financial difficulties, and sponsoring governments tried to distance themselves from the company. As a U.S. example, in the early 1980s, the U.S. government spent $1 billion to help military contractors develop a high-speed computer circuit. But Intel, a company getting no federal aid, was the first to develop the circuit. The 2009 federal stimulus program included funds to promote green energy, such as a $527 million loan to Solyndra, a California maker of solar panels. In 2011, that company went bankrupt, leaving taxpayers on the hook for the loan. Some other green energy companies getting federal aid also went bankrupt. The federal government's promotion of green energy sources such as solar panels and biofuels is an example of industrial policy.

There is also concern that an industrial policy could evolve into a government giveaway program. Rather than going to the most promising technologies, the money and the competitive advantages would go to the most politically connected. Critics also wonder why government should sponsor corporate research when beneficiaries may share their expertise with foreign companies or even build factories abroad. Most economists would prefer to let Microsoft, General Electric, Google, Apple, or some start-up bet its own money on the important technologies of the future. Note that the advantages of clustering create an economic impetus for firms in certain industries to group together. Most clusters form on their own, without government direction or support.

## 8-4  FINAL WORD

Productivity and growth depend on the supply and quality of resources, the level of technology and know-how, and the rules of the game that nurture production and exchange. These elements tend to be correlated with one another. An economy with an unskilled and poorly educated workforce usually is deficient in physical capital, in the latest technology and know-how, and in the institutional support that promotes production and exchange, including social capital. Similarly, an economy with a high-quality workforce likely excels in the other sources of productivity and growth.

We should distinguish between an economy's standard of living, as measured by output per capita, and improvements in that standard of living, as measured by the growth in output per capita. Growth in output per capita can occur when labor productivity increases or when the number of workers in the economy grows faster than the population. *In the long run, productivity growth and the growth in workers relative to the growth in population will determine whether or not the United States continues to enjoy one of the world's highest standards of living.*

## STUDY TOOLS 8

33. Yasusada Murata et al., "Localized Knowledge Spillovers and Patent Citations: A Distance-Based Approach," *Review of Economics and Statistics*, 96 (Issue 5, 2014): 967–983.

34. Philippe Aghion et al., "Industrial Policy and Competition," *American Economics Journal: Macroeconomics* (forthcoming).

# CHAPTER 8 PROBLEMS

*Your instructor can access the answers to these problems online at http://cengagebrain.com.*

## 8-1 Describe how we measure labor productivity, and explain why is it important for a nation's standard of living

1.  *(Measuring Labor Productivity)* How do we measure labor productivity? How do changes in labor productivity affect the U.S. standard of living?

2.  *(Growth and the PPF)* Use the production possibilities frontier (PPF) to demonstrate economic growth.

    a. With consumption goods on one axis and capital goods on the other, show how the combination of goods selected this period affects the PPF in the next period.

    b. Extend this comparison by choosing a different point on this period's PPF and determining whether that combination leads to more or less growth.

## 8-2 Summarize the history of U.S. labor productivity changes since World War II and explain why these changes matter

3.  *(Labor Productivity)* Identify at least four definable periods of labor productivity growth beginning right after World War II. During which periods was productivity growth lowest and why? (Refer to Exhibit 6 in the chapter.)

4.  *(Long-Term Productivity Growth)* Suppose that two nations start out in 2016 with identical levels of output per work hour—say, $100 per hour. In the first nation, labor productivity grows by 1 percent per year. In the second, it grows by 2 percent per year. Use a calculator or a spreadsheet to determine how much output per hour each nation will be producing 20 years later, assuming that labor productivity growth rates do not change. Then, determine how much each will be producing per hour 100 years later. What do your results tell you about the effects of small differences in productivity growth rates?

## 8-3 Evaluate the evidence that technological change increases the unemployment rate

5.  *(Technological Change)* Does technological change create unemployment? What's the evidence?

6.  *(Technological Change and Unemployment)* What are some examples, other than those given in the chapter, of technological change that has caused unemployment? And what are some examples of new technologies that have created jobs? How do you think you might measure the net impact of technological change on overall employment and GDP in the United States?

# 9 | Aggregate Demand

Romakoma/Shutterstock.com

## LEARNING OUTCOMES

After studying this chapter, you will be able to…

**9-1** Explain what a consumption function illustrates and interpret its slope

**9-2** Describe what can shift the consumption function up or down

**9-3** Explain why investment varies more than consumption from year to year

**9-4** Describe how the aggregate expenditure line determines the quantity of aggregate output demanded

**9-5** Determine the simple spending multiplier and explain its relevance

**9-6** Summarize the relationship between the aggregate expenditure line and the aggregate demand curve

After finishing this chapter go to **PAGE 170** for **STUDY TOOLS**

**Topics discussed in Chapter 9 include:**

- Consumption and income
- The consumption function
- Marginal propensity to consume
- Marginal propensity to save
- Life-cycle model of consumption and saving
- Income-expenditure model
- Aggregate expenditure line
- Simple spending multiplier
- Aggregate demand curve

Your economic success depends in part on the overall performance of the economy. When the economy grows, job opportunities expand, so your chances of finding a good job increase. When the economy contracts, job opportunities shrink, and so do your job prospects. Thus, you have a personal stake in the economy's success.

> **"When driving through a neighborhood new to you, how can you guess the income of the residents?"**

Consumption is the most important component of aggregate expenditure, accounting for about 68 percent of the total. We discuss how consumption and the other spending components relate to income in the economy. We then see how a change in the economy's price level affects aggregate spending. All this is aimed at getting to the economy's aggregate demand curve. In the next chapter, we develop the aggregate supply curve and see how the two curves interact to determine the economy's equilibrium levels of price and output.

## 9-1 CONSUMPTION

What if a college friend invited you home for the weekend? On your first visit, you would get some idea of the family's standard of living. Is their house a mansion, a modest rental, or in between? Do they drive a new BMW or take the bus? The simple fact is that consumption tends to reflect income. Although some people can temporarily live beyond their means and others still have the first nickel they ever earned, in general, consumption depends on income. *The positive and stable relationship between consumption and income, both for the household and for the economy as a whole, is a fundamental point of this chapter.*

A key decision in the circular-flow model developed three chapters back was how much households spent and how much they saved. Consumption depends primarily on income. Although this relationship seems obvious, the link between consumption and income will help you understand how the economy works. Let's look at this link in the U.S. economy over time.

**Consumption, especially of luxury items, is usually a good indicator of income.**

Car Culture/Collection Mix: Subjects/Getty Images

### 9-1a Consumption and Income

Exhibit 1 shows the relationship between consumption and income in the United States since 1959; disposable income is measured along the horizontal axis and

*Exhibit 1*

## U.S. Consumption and Disposable Income Since 1959

Consumption is on the vertical axis and disposable income on the horizontal axis. Notice that each axis measures trillions of 2009 dollars. For example, in 2000, identified by the red point, disposable income was $8.9 trillion and consumption $8.2 trillion. There is a clear and direct relationship over time between disposable income and consumption. As disposable income increases, so does consumption.

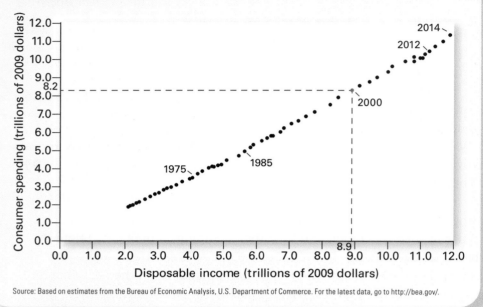

Source: Based on estimates from the Bureau of Economic Analysis, U.S. Department of Commerce. For the latest data, go to http://bea.gov/.

prevents you from both spending and saving the same dollar. So consumption depends on disposable income. *Consumption is the dependent variable and disposable income is the independent variable*. Because consumption depends on income, we say that consumption is a *function* of income. Exhibit 2 presents for the economy a hypothetical **consumption function**, which shows that consumption increases with disposable income, assuming other determinants of consumption remain constant. Again, both consumption and disposable income are in real terms, or in inflation-adjusted dollars. Notice that this hypothetical consumption function reflects the historical relationship between consumption and income shown in Exhibit 1.

consumption along the vertical axis. Notice that each axis measures the same units: trillions of 2009 dollars. Each year is depicted by a point that reflects two flow variables: disposable income and consumption. For example, the combination for 2000 identified by the red point, shows that when disposable income (measured along the horizontal axis) was $8.9 trillion, consumption (measured along the vertical axis) was $8.2 trillion.

As you can see, there is a clear and direct relationship between consumption and disposable income. You need little imagination to figure out that by connecting the dots, you could trace a line relating consumption to income. This relationship has special significance in macroeconomics.

## 9-1b The Consumption Function

After examining the link between consumption and income, we found it to be quite stable. Based on their disposable income, households decide how much to consume and how much to save. Scarcity

> **"There is a clear and direct relationship between consumption and disposable income."**

## 9-1c Marginal Propensities to Consume and to Save

In Chapter 1, you learned that economic analysis focuses on activity at the margin. For example, what happens to consumption if income changes by a certain amount? Suppose U.S. households receive another billion dollars in disposable income. Some is spent on consumption, and the rest is saved. The fraction of the additional income that is spent is called the marginal propensity to consume. More precisely, the **marginal propensity to consume**, or **MPC**, equals the change in consumption divided by the change in income. Likewise, the fraction of that additional income that is saved is called the marginal propensity to save. More precisely, the

**consumption function**
The relationship in the economy between consumption and income, other things constant

**marginal propensity to consume (MPC)** The fraction of a change in income that is spent on consumption; the change in consumption divided by the change in income that caused it

## Exhibit 2

### The Consumption Function

The consumption function, C, shows the relationship between consumption and disposable income, other things constant.

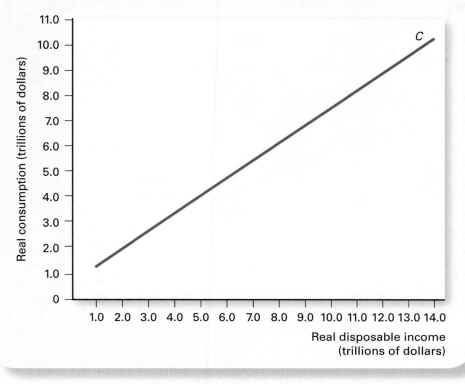

## 9-1d The MPC Is the Slope of the Consumption Function

You may recall from the appendix to Chapter 1 that the slope of a straight line is the vertical distance between any two points divided by the horizontal distance between those same two points. Consider, for example, the slope between points *a* and *b* on the consumption function in Exhibit 3, where the delta symbol (Δ)

> **marginal propensity to save (MPS)** The fraction of a change in income that is saved; the change in saving divided by the change in income that caused it

**marginal propensity to save**, or **MPS**, equals the change in saving divided by the change in income.

For example, if U.S. income increases by $0.5 trillion, suppose consumption increases by $0.4 trillion and saving increases by $0.1 trillion. The marginal propensity to consume equals the change in consumption divided by the change in income. In this case, the change in consumption is $0.4 trillion and the change in income is $0.5 trillion, so the marginal propensity to consume is 0.4/0.5, or 4/5. Income not spent is saved. Saving increases by $0.1 trillion as a result of the $0.5 trillion increase in income, so the marginal propensity to save equals 0.1/0.5, or 1/5. Because disposable income is either spent or saved, the marginal propensity to consume plus the marginal propensity to save must sum to 1.

In our example, 4/5 + 1/5 = 1. We can say more generally that $MPC + MPS = 1$.

## Exhibit 3

### The Marginal Propensity to Consume and the Consumption Function

The slope of the consumption function equals the marginal propensity to consume. For the straight-line consumption function, the slope is the same at all levels of income and is given by the change in consumption divided by the change in disposable income that causes it. Thus, the marginal propensity to consume equals ΔC/ΔDI, or 0.4/0.5 = 4/5.

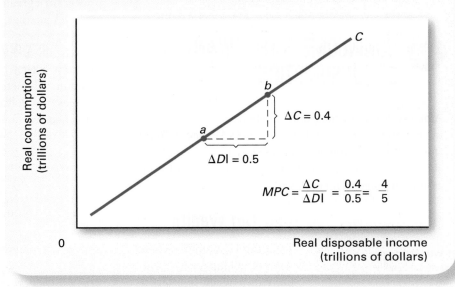

means "change in." The horizontal distance between these points shows the change in disposable income, denoted as $\Delta DI$—in this case, $0.5 trillion. The vertical distance shows the change in consumption, denoted as $\Delta C$—in this case, $0.4 trillion. The slope equals the vertical distance divided by the horizontal distance, or 0.4/0.5, which equals the marginal propensity to consume of 4/5.

Thus, the marginal propensity to consume is measured graphically by the slope of the consumption function. After all, the slope is nothing more than the increase in consumption divided by the increase in income. Because the slope of any straight line is constant everywhere along the line, the MPC for any linear, or straight-line, consumption function is constant at all incomes. We assume here for convenience that the consumption function is a straight line, though it need not be.

> **"The marginal propensity to consume is measured graphically by the slope of the consumption function."**

## 9-2 NONINCOME DETERMINANTS OF CONSUMPTION

Along a given consumption function, consumer spending depends on disposable income in the economy, other things constant. Now let's see what factors are held constant and how changes in them could shift the entire consumption function up or down.

### 9-2a Net Wealth

**net wealth** The value of assets minus liabilities

Given the economy's income, an important influence on consumption is each household's net wealth—that is, the value of all assets that each household owns minus any liabilities, or debts. Net wealth is a *stock* variable. Consumption and income are *flow* variables. Your family's assets may include a home, furnishings, automobiles, bank accounts, corporate stocks and bonds, cash, and the value of any pensions. Your family's liabilities, or debts, may include a mortgage, car loans, student loans, credit card balances, and the like.

Net wealth is assumed to be constant along a given consumption function. A decrease in net wealth would make consumers less inclined to spend and more inclined to save at each income level. To see why, suppose prices fall sharply on the stock market. Stockholders are poorer than they were, so they spend less. For example, the stock market crash of 2008 combined with the slide in home prices to cut the net wealth of U.S. households from $64.5 trillion in 2007 to $54.5 trillion in 2009.[1] As a result, people spent less and saved more at each income level. Consumption as a share of disposable income fell from 95 percent in 2007 to 92 percent in 2009. Compared to families surveyed in 2007, families surveyed in 2009 expressed a greater desire to build up savings as a buffer against hard times.[2] The sharp drop in stockholder wealth thus reduced consumption and contributed to the Great Recession.[3]

Some economists believe that changing home prices had a greater impact on consumption than changing stock market prices.[4] Between 2006 and 2008, the average price of homes in the United States dropped 22 percent, and this drop in net wealth reduced consumption at each income level. Our original consumption function is depicted as line $C$ in Exhibit 4. If net wealth declines, the consumption function shifts from $C$ down to $C'$, because households now spend less and save more at every income level.

1. Figures are from Board of Governors of the Federal Reserve System, *Flow of Funds Accounts of the United States: 2005 to 2009* (March 11, 2010), Table B.100, at http://www.federalreserve.gov/RELEASES/z1/Current/annuals/a2005–2009.

2. Jesse Bricker et al., "Drowning or Weathering the Storm? Changes in Family Finances From 2007 to 2009," Chapter 10 in *Measuring Wealth and Financial Intermediation and Their Links to the Real World*, C. Hulten and M. Reinsdorf, eds. (University of Chicago Press, 2015).

3. Roger Farmer, "The Stock Market Crash of 2008 Caused the Great Recession: Theory and Evidence," *Journal of Economic Dynamics and Control*, 36 (Issue 5, 2012): 693–707.

4. Karl Case, John Quigley, and Robert Shiller, "Wealth Effects Revisited 1975–2012," *Critical Finance Review*, 2 (July 2013): 101–128.

## Exhibit 4

### Shifts of the Consumption Function

A downward shift of the consumption function, such as from C to C', can be caused by a decrease in net wealth, an increase in the price level, an unfavorable change in consumer expectations, or an increase in the interest rate. An upward shift, such as from C to C", can be caused by an increase in net wealth, a decrease in the price level, a favorable change in expectations, or a decrease in the interest rate.

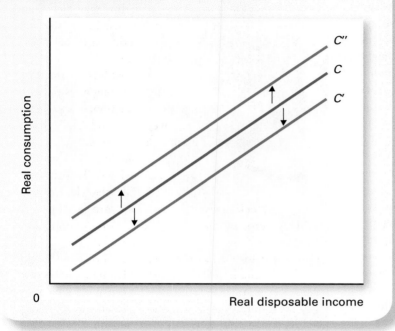

## 9-2b The Price Level

Another variable that affects the consumption function is the price level prevailing in the economy. As we have seen, net wealth is an important determinant of consumption. The greater the net wealth, other things constant, the greater the consumption at each income level. Some household wealth is held as money, such as cash and bank accounts. When the price level changes, so does the real value of cash and bank accounts.

For example, suppose your wealth consists of a $20,000 bank account. If the economy's price level increases by 5 percent, your bank account buys about 5 percent less in real terms. You feel poorer because you are poorer. To rebuild the real value of your money holdings to some desired comfort level, you decide to spend less and save more. *An increase in the price level reduces the purchasing power of money holdings, causing households to consume less and save more at each income level.* So the consumption function would shift downward from C to C', as shown in Exhibit 4.

Conversely, should the price level fall, as it did frequently before World War II, in 2009, and recently in Japan, Hong Kong, and Taiwan, the real value of money holdings increases. Households would be wealthier, so they decide to consume more and save less at each income level. For example, if the price level declined by 5 percent, your $20,000 bank account would then buy about 5 percent more in real terms. A drop in the price level would shift the consumption function from C up to C". *At each income level, a change in the price level influences consumption by affecting the real value of money holdings.*

## 9-2c The Interest Rate

Interest is the reward savers earn for deferring consumption and the cost borrowers pay for current spending power. When graphing the consumption function, we assume a given interest rate in the economy. If the interest rate increases, other things constant, savers or lenders are rewarded more, and borrowers are charged more. The higher the interest rate, the less is spent on those items typically purchased on credit, such as cars and major appliances. Thus, at a higher interest rate, households save more, borrow less, and spend less. Greater saving at each income level means less

Conversely, suppose stock prices increase sharply. This increase in net wealth increases the desire to spend. For example, stock prices surged in 1999, increasing stockholders' net wealth. Consumers spent 93 percent of disposable income that year compared with an average of about 90 percent during the first half of the decade. Purchases of homes and cars soared. Because of an increase in net wealth, the consumption function in Exhibit 4 shifts from C up to C", reflecting households' desire to spend more at each income level. Research by the Federal Reserve indicates that consumer spending eventually rises or falls between three to five cents for every dollar rise or fall in the value of stock market holdings.

Again, it is a change in net wealth, not a change in disposable income, that shifts the consumption function. A change in disposable income, other things constant, means a movement along a given consumption function, not a shift of that function. Be mindful of the difference between a movement along the consumption function, which results from a change in income, and a shift of the consumption function, which results from a change in one of the nonincome determinants of consumption, such as net wealth.

consumption. Simply put, *a higher interest rate, other things constant, shifts the consumption function downward.* Conversely, *a lower interest rate, other things constant, shifts the consumption function upward.*

### 9-2d  Consumer Expectations

Expectations influence economic behavior in a variety of ways. For example, suppose as a college senior you land a good job that starts after graduation. Your consumption probably jumps long before the job actually begins because you expect an increase in your income. You might buy a car, for example. On the other hand, a worker who gets a layoff notice to take effect at the end of the year likely reduces consumption immediately, well before the actual layoff. More generally, if people grow more concerned about their job security, they reduce consumption at each income level.

A change in expectations about price levels or interest rates also affects consumption. For example, any change that leads householders to expect higher car prices or higher borrowing costs in the future prompts some to buy a new car now. On the other hand, any change leading householders to expect lower car prices or lower borrowing costs in the future causes some to defer a car purchase. Thus, expectations affect spending, and a change in expectations can shift the consumption function. This is why economic forecasters monitor consumer confidence so closely.

Sometimes people find they need to save more for the future. For example, each Chinese household now is more personally responsible for housing, education, and health care—items that in the past were more of a government responsibility. What's more, China's "one-child policy" meant that parents would have to rely less on their offspring for support in old age.[5] This increased the need to save. As a consequence, the average saving rate as a percentage of income among urban households in China jumped from 7 percent in 1995 to 25 percent in 2005.[6]

**TO REVIEW:** Keep in mind the distinction between *a movement along a given consumption function*, which results from a change in income, and a *shift of the consumption function,* which results from a change in one of the factors assumed to remain constant along the consumption function.

How would your spending change if you were expecting an increase in income?

Caro/Alamy

### 9-2e  The Life-Cycle Model of Consumption and Saving

Do people with high income save a larger fraction of their income than those with low income? Both theory and evidence suggest they do. The easier it is to make ends meet, the more income is left over to save. Does it follow from this that richer economies save more than poorer ones—that economies save a larger fraction of total disposable income as they grow? In his famous book, *The General Theory of Employment, Interest, and Money*, published in 1936, John Maynard Keynes drew that conclusion. But as later economists studied the data—such as that presented earlier in Exhibit 1—it became clear that Keynes was wrong. *The fraction of disposable income saved in an economy seems to stay constant as the economy grows.*

So how can it be that richer people save more than poorer people, yet richer countries do not necessarily save more than poorer ones? Several answers have been proposed. One of the most important is

5. Dennis Tao Yang, Junsen Zhang, and Shaojie Zhou, "Why Are Saving Rates So High in China?" in *Capitalizing China, Joseph Fan and Randall Morck, eds. (University of Chicago Press, 2013)*: 249–278. and Chadwick C. Curtis, Steven Lugauer, and Nelson C. Mark, "Demographic Patterns and Household Saving in China," *American Economic Journal: Macroeconomics,* 7 (April 2015): 58–94.

6. Marcos Chamon and Eswar S. Prasad, "Why Are Saving Rates of Urban Households in China Rising?" *American Economic Journal: Macroeconomics,* 2 (January 2010): 93–130.

the **life-cycle model of consumption and saving**. According to this model, young people tend to borrow to finance education and home purchases. In middle age, people pay off debts and save more. In old age, they draw down their savings, or *dissave*. Some people still have substantial wealth at death, because they are not sure when death will occur and because some parents want to bequeath wealth to their children. And some people die in debt. But on average net savings over a person's lifetime tend to be small. The life-cycle hypothesis suggests that the saving rate for an economy as a whole depends on, among other things, the relative number of savers and dissavers in the population.

A problem with the life-cycle hypothesis is that the elderly do not seem to draw down their assets as much as the theory predicts. One reason, already mentioned, is that some want to leave bequests to children. Another reason is that the elderly seem particularly concerned about covering unpredictable expenses such as divorce, health problems, and living much longer than average. Because of such uncertainty, many elderly spend less and save more than the life-cycle theory predicts. Researchers have found that those elderly who have not experienced a divorce or health problems continue to build their net wealth well into old age.[7]

Other evidence that seems at odds with the life-cycle hypothesis comes from a study of National Football League (NFL) players. The theory predicts that players should save during their peak earning years in the NFL to help them get by when they can no longer play. But a high bankruptcy rate among former players suggests they saved little during their years of high pay.[8] Still, the life-cycle hypothesis offers an interesting theory about consumption patterns over a lifetime.

We turn next to the other component of aggregate expenditure, with a special emphasis on investment. Keep in mind that our immediate goal is to understand the relationship between aggregate expenditure and income.

> *"Keep in mind the distinction between a movement along a given consumption function, which results from a change in income, and a shift of the consumption function, which results from a change in one of the factors assumed to remain constant along the consumption function."*

7. James Poterba, Steven Venti, and David Wise, "The Composition and Drawdown of Wealth in Retirement," *Journal of Economic Perspectives*, 25 (Fall 2011): 95–118.
8. Kyle Carlson et al., "Bankruptcy Rates Among NFL Players with Short-Lived Income Spikes," *American Economic Review*, 105 (May 2015): 381–384.

## 9-3 OTHER SPENDING COMPONENTS

While consumption is the most important spending component and the one that gets the most attention here, aggregate spending also includes investment, government purchases, and net exports. Here we look briefly at how each relates to income.

### 9-3a Investment

The second component of aggregate expenditure is investment, or, more precisely, *gross private domestic investment*. Again, by *investment* we do not mean buying stocks, bonds, or other financial assets. Investment consists of spending on (1) new factories, office buildings, malls, and new equipment, such as computers and software; (2) new housing; and (3) net increases to inventories. People invest now expecting of a future return. Because the return is in the future, a would-be investor must estimate how much a particular investment will yield this year, next year, the year after, and in all years during the productive life of the investment. *Firms buy new capital goods only if they expect this investment to yield a higher return than other possible uses of their funds.*

### Investment Demand Curve

The market interest rate is the opportunity cost of investing in capital. More is invested when the opportunity cost of borrowing is lower, other things constant. A downward-sloping investment demand curve for the entire economy can be derived, with some qualifications, from a horizontal summation of each firm's downward-sloping investment demand curves. The

**life-cycle model of consumption and saving** Young people borrow, middle agers pay off debt and save, and older people draw down their savings; on average, net savings over a lifetime is usually little or nothing

## Exhibit 5

**Investment Demand Curve for the Economy**

The investment demand curve for the economy sums the investment demanded by each firm at each interest rate. At lower interest rates, other things constant, more investment projects become profitable for individual firms, so total investment in the economy increases

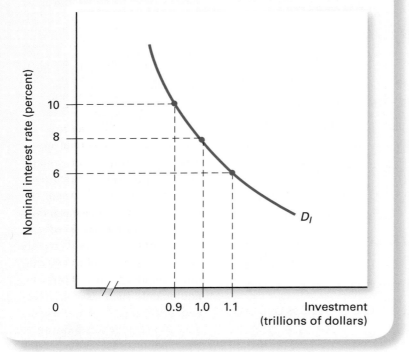

what Keynes called the "animal spirits" of business. Examples of factors that could affect business expectations, and thus investment demand, include wars, technological changes, tax changes, and destabilizing events such as terrorist attacks or financial crises.

## Investment and Income

To integrate the discussion of investment with our earlier analysis of consumption, we need to know if and how investment varies with income in the economy. Whereas we were able to present evidence relating consumption to income over time, the link between investment and income is weaker. Investment in a particular year shows little relation to income that year. *Investment depends more on interest rates and business expectations than on the current income level.* One reason investment is less related to income is that some investments, such as a new power plant or an oil pipeline, take years to build. And investment, once in place, is expected to last for years, sometimes decades. The investment decision is thus said to be *forward looking*, based more on expected profit than on current income in the economy.

economy's *investment demand curve* is depicted as $D_I$ in Exhibit 5, which shows the inverse relationship between the quantity of investment demanded and the market interest rate, other things—including business expectations—held constant. For example, in Exhibit 5, when the market rate of interest is 8 percent, the quantity of investment demanded is $1.0 trillion. If the interest rate rises to 10 percent, investment declines to $0.9 trillion, and if the rate falls to 6 percent, investment increases to $1.1 trillion.

Assumed constant along the investment demand curve are business expectations about the economy. If firms grow more optimistic about profit prospects, the demand for investment increases, so the investment demand curve shifts to the right. Investment demand depends primarily on

> **"Investment depends more on interest rates and business expectations than on the prevailing income level."**

So how does the amount firms plan to invest relate to income? The simplest assumption is that *investment* is unrelated to income. For example, suppose that, given current business expectations and a market interest rate of 8 percent, firms plan to invest $1.0 trillion per year, regardless of the economy's income level.

Now that we have examined consumption and investment, let's take a look at their year-to-year variability. Although consumption averaged 68 percent of GDP and investment only 16 percent of GDP during the most recent decade, Exhibit 6 illustrates that investment varies much more from year to year than consumption does. In fact, investment spending variations account for nearly all the variability in real GDP. This is why economic forecasters pay special attention to the business outlook and investment plans.

## Exhibit 6

### Annual Percentage Changes in U.S. Real GDP, Consumption, and Investment

Investment varies much more year-to-year than consumption does and accounts for nearly all the variability in real GDP. This is why economic forecasters pay special attention to the business outlook and investment plans.

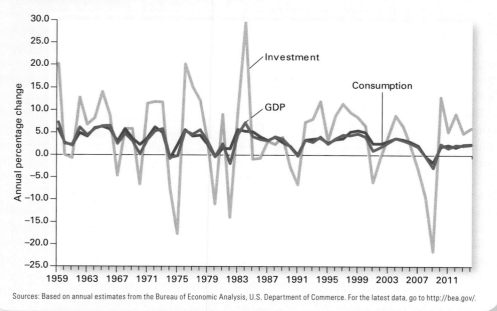

Sources: Based on annual estimates from the Bureau of Economic Analysis, U.S. Department of Commerce. For the latest data, go to http://bea.gov/.

To fund government outlays, governments impose taxes. Taxes vary directly with income; as income increases, so do taxes. *Net taxes* equal taxes minus transfers. Because taxes tend to increase with income but transfers tend to decrease with income, for simplicity, let's assume that net taxes do not vary with income. Thus, we assume that *net taxes* are independent of income.

Net taxes affect aggregate spending indirectly by changing disposable income, which in turn changes consumption. We saw from the discussion of the circular flow that by subtracting

## 9-3b Government Purchases

The third component of aggregate expenditure is government purchases of goods and services. Federal, state, and local governments buy thousands of goods and services, ranging from weapon systems to traffic lights to education. During the most recent decade, government purchases in the United States accounted for 20 percent of GDP, most of that by state and local governments. Decisions about government purchases are largely under the control of public officials, such as the decision to build an interstate highway, boost military spending, or hire more teachers. These spending decisions do not depend directly on income in the economy. We therefore assume that *government purchases* are independent of income.

As noted earlier, government purchases represent only one of the two government outlays; the other is *transfer payments,* such as for Social Security, welfare benefits, and unemployment insurance. Government outlays equal government purchases plus transfer payments. Transfer payments, which make up more than a third of government outlays, are outright grants from governments to households and are thus not considered part of aggregate expenditure. Transfer payments vary inversely with income—as income increases, transfer payments decline.

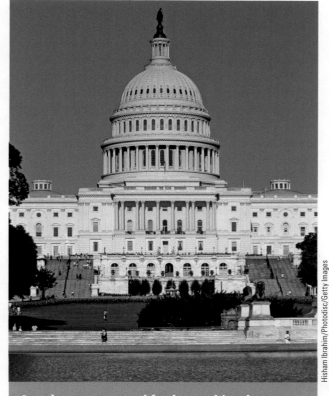

In order to operate and fund everything the government does, taxes need to be collected.

Hisham Ibrahim/Photodisc/Getty Images

net taxes, we transform real GDP into *disposable income*. Disposable income is take-home pay—the income households can spend or save. We examine the impact of net taxes in the next few chapters.

### 9-3c Net Exports

The rest of the world affects aggregate expenditure through imports and exports and has a growing influence on the U.S. economy. The United States, with less than one-twentieth of the world's population, accounts for about one-eighth of the world's imports and one-ninth of the world's exports. How do imports and exports relate to the economy's income? When incomes rise, Americans spend more on all normal goods, including imports. Higher incomes lead to more spending on Persian rugs, French wine, German cars, Chinese toys, European vacations, African safaris, and thousands of other foreign goods and services.

How do U.S. exports relate to the economy's income? U.S. exports depend on the income of foreigners, not on U.S. income. U.S. disposable income does not affect Europe's purchases of U.S. smartphones or Africa's purchases of U.S. grain. Because our exports are insensitive to U.S. income but our imports tend to increase with income, *net exports*, which equal the value of exports minus the value of imports, tend to decline as U.S. incomes increase. For simplicity, we will assume that net exports are independent of income.

If exports exceed imports, net exports are positive; if imports exceed exports, net exports are negative; and if exports equal imports, net exports are zero. U.S. net exports have been negative nearly every year during the past three decades.

> **"If exports exceed imports, net exports are positive; if imports exceed exports, net exports are negative; and if exports equal imports, net exports are zero."**

### 9-4 AGGREGATE EXPENDITURE AND INCOME

The big idea so far in this chapter is that consumption depends on income, other things constant; this link is one of the most stable in all of macroeconomics. Let's build on that connection to learn how total spending in the economy changes with income. If we try to confront the economy head-on, it soon becomes a bewildering maze, which is why we make progress by starting with simple models. We continue to assume, as we did in developing the circular-flow model, that there is no capital depreciation and no business saving. Thus, we can say that *each dollar of spending translates directly into a dollar of income*. Therefore, gross domestic product, or GDP, equals aggregate income.

### 9-4a Components of Aggregate Expenditure

When income increases, consumption increases. As noted already, the marginal propensity to consume indicates the fraction of each additional dollar of income that is spent on consumption. For example, if the marginal propensity to consume is 4/5 (four-fifths), spending increases by $4 for every $5 increase in income. The consumption function shows how much consumption increases with income.

For simplicity, we continue to assume that investment, government purchases, and net exports are independent of the economy's income level.

If we add to the consumption function, investment, government purchases, and net exports, we get the aggregate expenditure line presented in Exhibit 7 as $C + I + G + (X - M)$. Real GDP is measured on the horizontal axis, and aggregate expenditure is measured on the vertical axis. The **aggregate expenditure line** shows how much households, firms, governments, and the rest of the world plan to spend on U.S. output at each level of real GDP, or real income, assuming a given price level in the economy. Again, the only spending component that varies with real GDP is consumption. Because only consumption varies with income, the slope of the aggregate expenditure line equals the marginal propensity to consume. Please give that a little thought.

### 9-4b Real GDP Demanded

Let's begin developing the aggregate demand curve by asking how much aggregate output would be demanded at a given price level. By finding the quantity demanded

**aggregate expenditure line** A relationship tracing, for a given price level, spending at each level of income, or real GDP; the total of $C + I + G + (X - M)$ at each level of income, or real GDP

## Exhibit 7

### Deriving the Real GDP Demanded for a Given Price Level

Real GDP demanded for a given price level is found where aggregate expenditure equals aggregate output—that is, where spending equals the amount produced, or real GDP. This occurs at point *e*, where the aggregate expenditure line intersects the 45-degree line.

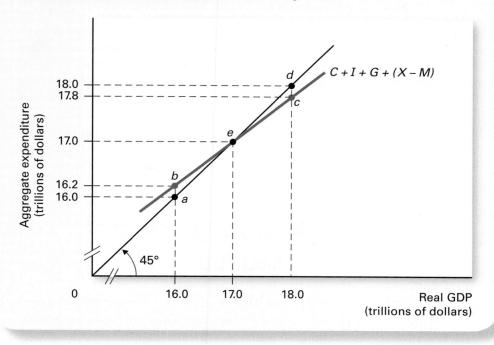

The special feature of this line is that any point along it is the same distance from each axis. Thus, the 45-degree line identifies all points where spending equals real GDP. *Aggregate output demanded at a given price level occurs where aggregate expenditure, measured along the vertical axis, equals real GDP, measured along the horizontal axis.* In Exhibit 7, this occurs at point *e*, where the aggregate expenditure line intersects the 45-degree line. At point *e*, the amount people spend equals the amount produced. We conclude that, at a price level of 110, the quantity of real GDP demanded equals $17.0 trillion.

at a given price level, we'll end up identifying a single point on the aggregate demand curve. We begin by considering the relationship between aggregate spending in the economy and aggregate income. To get us started, suppose that the price level in the economy is 110, or 10 percent higher than in the base-year price level. We want to find out how much is spent at various levels of real income, or real GDP. By *real* GDP, we mean GDP measured in terms of real goods and services produced. Exhibit 7 combines the relationships introduced earlier—consumption, investment, government purchases, and net exports. Although the entries are hypothetical, they bear some relation to current levels in the U.S. economy.

Real GDP, measured along the horizontal axis in Exhibit 7, can be viewed in two ways—as the value of *aggregate output* and as the *aggregate income* generated by that output. Because real GDP or aggregate income is measured on the horizontal axis, and aggregate expenditure is measured on the vertical axis, this graph is often called the **income-expenditure model**. To gain perspective on the relationship between income and expenditure, we use a handy analytical tool: the 45-degree ray from the origin.

### 9-4c What If Spending Exceeds Real GDP?

To find the real GDP demanded at the given price level, consider what happens if real GDP is initially less than $17.0 trillion. As you can see from Exhibit 7, when real GDP is less than $17.0 trillion, the aggregate expenditure line is above the 45-degree line, indicating that spending exceeds the amount produced (again, give this a little thought). For example, if real GDP is $16.0 trillion, spending is $16.2 trillion, as indicated by point *b* on the aggregate expenditure line, so spending exceeds output by $0.2 trillion. When the amount people want to spend exceeds the amount produced, something has to give. Ordinarily what gives is the price, but remember that we are seeking the real GDP demanded for a given price level, so the price level is assumed to remain constant, at least for now. What gives in this model are *inventories*.

**income-expenditure model** A relationship that shows how much people plan to spend at each income level; this model identifies, for a given price level, where the amount people plan to spend equals the amount produced in the economy

Unplanned reductions in inventories cover the $0.2 trillion shortfall in output. Because firms can't draw down inventories indefinitely, *inventory reductions* prompt firms to produce more output. That increases employment and consumer income, leading to more spending. As long as spending exceeds output, firms increase production to make up the difference. This process of more output, more income, and more spending continues until spending equals real GDP, an equality achieved at point *e* in Exhibit 7.

When output reaches $17.0 trillion, spending exactly matches output, so no unintended inventory adjustments occur. More importantly, when output reaches $17.0 trillion, the amount people want to spend equals the amount produced and equals the total income generated by that production. Earlier we assumed a price level of 110. Therefore, $17.0 trillion is the real GDP demanded at that price level.

### 9-4d What If Real GDP Exceeds Spending?

To reinforce the logic of the model, consider what happens when the amount produced exceeds the amount people want to spend. Notice in Exhibit 7 that, to the right of point *e*, spending indicated on the aggregate expenditure line falls short of production. For example, suppose real GDP is $18.0 trillion. Spending, as indicated by point *c* on the aggregate expenditure line, is $0.2 trillion less than real GDP, indicated by point *d* on the 45-degree line. Because real GDP exceeds spending, unsold goods accumulate. This swells inventories by $0.2 trillion more than firms planned on. Rather than allow inventories to pile up indefinitely, firms cut production, which reduces employment and income. As an example of such behavior, a recent news account read, "General Motors will

> **"Unplanned inventory buildups cause firms to cut production until the amount they produce equals aggregate spending."**

> **"Inventory reductions prompt firms to produce more output."**

idle two assembly plants in a move to trim inventories in the wake of slowing sales." *Unplanned inventory buildups* cause firms to cut production until the amount they produce equals aggregate spending, which occurs, again, where real GDP is $17.0 trillion. Given the price level, real GDP demanded is found where the amount people spend equals the amount produced. *For a given price level, there is only one point along the aggregate expenditure line at which spending equals real GDP.*

We have now discussed the forces that determine real GDP demanded for a given price level. In the next section, we examine changes that can alter spending plans.

### 9-5 THE SIMPLE SPENDING MULTIPLIER

We just used the aggregate expenditure line to find real GDP demanded for a particular price level. In this section, we continue to assume that the price level stays the same as we trace the effects of other changes that could affect spending plans. Like a stone thrown into a still pond, the effects of any change in spending ripple through the economy, generating changes in aggregate output that could exceed the initial change in spending.

### 9-5a An Increase in Spending

Let's consider the effect of an increase in one of the components of spending. Suppose that firms become more optimistic about profit prospects and decide to increase their investment from $1.0 trillion to $1.1 trillion per year, other things constant.

What happens to real GDP demanded? An instinctive response is to say that real GDP demanded increases by $0.1 trillion as well. The idea of the circular flow is central to an understanding of the adjustment process. Recall that production yields income, which generates spending. We can think of each trip around the circular flow as a "round" of income and spending.

#### Round One

OK, so planned spending now exceeds the amount produced by $0.1 trillion, or $100 billion. Initially, firms supply this increased investment spending by drawing down their inventories. John Deere, for example, satisfies the increased demand for tractors by drawing down tractor inventories. But reduced inventories prompt firms to expand production by $100 billion. This generates $100 billion more income. The income-generating process does not stop there, however, because those who earn this additional income spend some of it and save the rest, leading to round two of spending and income.

## Round Two

Given a marginal propensity to consume of 0.8, those who earn the additional $100 billion spend $80 billion on toasters, backpacks, gasoline, restaurant meals, and thousands of other goods and services. They save the other $20 billion. Firms respond by increasing their output by $80 billion. Thus, the $100 billion in new income increases real GDP by $80 billion during round two.

## Round Three and Beyond

We assume that four-fifths of the $80 billion earned during round two gets spent during round three and one-fifth gets saved. Thus, $64 billion is spent during round three on still more goods and services. The remaining $16 billion gets saved. The added spending causes firms to increase output by $64 billion. Round three's additional production generated $64 billion more income, which sets up subsequent rounds of spending, output, and income. *As long as spending exceeds output, production increases, thereby creating more income, which generates still more spending.*

Exhibit 8 summarizes the multiplier process, showing the first three rounds, round 10, and the cumulative effect of all rounds. The new spending from each round is shown in the second column, and the accumulation of new spending appears in the third column. For example, the cumulative new spending as of the third round totals $244 billion—the sum of the first three rounds of spending ($100 billion + $80 billion + $64 billion). The new saving from each round appears in the fourth column, and the accumulation

> **"As long as spending exceeds output, production increases, thereby creating more income, which generates still more spending."**

of new saving appears in the final column. All this develops with the price level assumed to remain unchanged.

### 9-5b Using the Simple Spending Multiplier

In our model, consumers spend four-fifths of the change in income each round, with each fresh round equal to the change in spending from the previous round times the marginal propensity to consume, or the MPC. This goes on round after round, leaving less and less to fuel more spending and income. At some point, the new rounds of income and spending become so small that they disappear and the process stops. The question is, by how much does total spending increase? We can get some idea of the total by working through a limited number of rounds. For example, as shown in Exhibit 8, total new spending after 10 rounds sums to $446.3 billion. But calculating the exact total for all rounds would require us to work through an infinite number of rounds—an impossible task.

Fortunately, we can borrow a shortcut from mathematicians, who have shown that the sum of an infinite number of rounds, each of which is MPC times the previous round, equals $1/(1 - MPC)$ times the initial change. Translated, the cumulative spending change equals $1/(1 - MPC)$, which, in our example, was $1/0.2$, or 5, times the

*Exhibit 8*

**Tracking the Rounds of Spending Following a $100 Billion Increase in Investment (billions of dollars)**

| Round | New Spending This Round | Cumulative New Spending | New Saving This Round | Cumulative New Saving |
|---|---|---|---|---|
| 1 | 100 | 100 | — | — |
| 2 | 80 | 180 | 20 | 20 |
| 3 | 64 | 244 | 16 | 36 |
| ⋮ | ⋮ | ⋮ | ⋮ | ⋮ |
| 10 | 13.4 | 446.3 | 3.35 | 86.6 |
| ⋮ | ⋮ | ⋮ | ⋮ | ⋮ |
| ∞ | 0 | 500 | 0 | 100 |

initial increase in spending, which was $100 billion. In short, the increase in investment eventually boosts real GDP demanded by five times $100 billion, or $500 billion—and again, all this happens with the price level assumed to remain unchanged.

**The simple spending multiplier** is the factor by which real GDP demanded changes for a given initial change in spending.

$$\text{Simple spending multiplier} = \frac{1}{1 - MPC}$$

The simple spending multiplier provides a shortcut to the total change in real GDP demanded. This multiplier depends on the MPC. The larger the MPC, the larger the simple spending multiplier. That makes sense—the more people spend from each dollar of fresh income, the more total spending increases. For example, if the MPC was 0.9 instead of 0.8, the denominator of the multiplier formula would equal 1.0 minus 0.9, or 0.1, so the multiplier would be 1/0.1, or 10. With an MPC of 0.9, a $0.1 trillion investment increase would boost real GDP demanded by $1.0 trillion. On the other hand, an MPC of 0.5 would yield a denominator of 0.5 and a multiplier of 2. So a $0.1 trillion investment increase would raise real GDP demanded by $0.2 trillion.

Let's return to what started all this. The $0.1 trillion rise in investment raised real GDP demanded by $0.5 trillion. Note that real GDP demanded would have increased by the same amount if consumers had decided to spend $0.1 trillion more at each income level. Aggregate demand likewise would have increased if government purchases or net exports increased $0.1 trillion at each income level. *The change in aggregate output demanded depends on how much the aggregate expenditure line shifts, not on which spending component causes the shift.*

In our example, investment increased by $0.1 trillion in the year in question. *If this greater investment is not sustained the following year, real GDP demanded would fall back.* For example, if investment returns to its initial level, other things constant, real GDP demanded would return to $17.0 trillion. Finally, recall from the earlier discussion that the MPC and the MPS sum to 1, so 1 minus the MPC equals the MPS. With this information, we can define the simple spending multiplier in terms of the MPS as follows:

$$\text{Simple spending multiplier} = \frac{1}{1 - MPC} = \frac{1}{MPS}$$

We can see that the smaller the MPS, the less leaks from the spending stream as saving. Because less is saved, more gets spent each round, so the spending multiplier is greater. Incidentally, this spending multiplier is called "simple" because consumption is the only spending component that varies with income.

## 9-6 THE AGGREGATE DEMAND CURVE

In this chapter, we have identified the quantity demanded *for a given price level*. But what happens if the price level changes? As you will see, for each price level, there is a unique aggregate expenditure line, which yields a unique real GDP demanded. By altering the price level, we find a different real GDP demanded. By pairing a price level with the real GDP demanded at that price level, we can derive the aggregate demand curve.

### 9-6a A Higher Price Level

What is the effect of a higher price level on the quantity of real GDP demanded? Recall that consumers hold many assets that are fixed in dollar terms, such as currency and bank accounts. A higher price level decreases the real value of these money holdings. This cuts consumer wealth, making people less willing to spend at each income level. For reasons that will be explained in a later chapter, a higher price level also tends to increase the market interest rate, and a higher interest rate reduces investment. Finally, a higher U.S. price level, other things constant, means that foreign goods become relatively cheaper for U.S. consumers, and U.S. goods become more expensive abroad. So imports rise and exports fall, decreasing net exports. Therefore, *a higher price level reduces consumption, investment,*

> **"**A higher price level reduces consumption, investment, and net exports, which all reduce aggregate spending.**"**

**simple spending multiplier** The ratio of a change in real GDP demanded to the initial change in spending that brought it about; the numerical value of the simple spending multiplier is $1/(1 - MPC)$; called "simple" because only consumption varies with income

## Exhibit 9

### Changing the Price Level to Find the Aggregate Demand Curve

At the initial price level of 110, the aggregate expenditure line is *AE*, which identifies real GDP demanded of $17.0 trillion. This combination of a price level of 110 and a real GDP demanded of $17.0 trillion determines one combination (point *e*) on the aggregate demand curve in panel (b). At the higher price level of 120, the aggregate expenditure line shifts down to *AE'*, and real GDP demanded falls to $16.5 trillion. This price-quantity combination is identified as point *e'* in panel (b). At the lower price level of 100, the aggregate expenditure line shifts up to *AE"*, which increases real GDP demanded. This combination is plotted as point *e"* in panel (b). Connecting points *e*, *e'*, and *e"* in panel (b) yields the downward-sloping aggregate demand curve *AD*, which shows the inverse relation between the price level and real GDP demanded.

**(a)** Aggregate expenditure lines for different price levels

**(b)** Aggregate demand curve

and net exports, which all reduce aggregate spending. This decrease in spending reduces real GDP demanded.

Exhibit 9 represents two different ways of expressing the effects of a change in the price level on real GDP demanded. Panel (a) offers the income-expenditure model, and panel (b) offers the aggregate demand curve, showing the inverse relationship between the price level and real GDP demanded. The idea is to find the real GDP demanded for a given price level in panel (a), and then show that price-quantity combination as a point on the aggregate demand curve in panel (b). The two panels measure real GDP on the horizontal axes. At the initial price level of 110 in panel (a), the aggregate expenditure line, now denoted simply as *AE*, intersects the 45-degree line at point *e* to yield real GDP demanded of $17.0 trillion. Panel (b) shows more directly the link between real GDP demanded and the price level. As you can see, when the price level is 110, the quantity of real GDP demanded is $17.0 trillion. This combination is identified by point *e* on the aggregate demand curve.

What if the price level increases from 110 to, say, 120? As you've just learned, an increase in the price level reduces consumption, investment, and net exports. This reduction in spending is reflected in panel (a) by a downward shift of the aggregate expenditure line from *AE* to *AE′*. As a result, real GDP demanded declines from $17.0 trillion to $16.5 trillion. Panel (b) shows that an increase in the price level from 110 to 120 decreases real GDP demanded from $17.0 trillion to $16.5 trillion, as reflected by the movement from point *e* to point *e′*.

## 9-6b A Lower Price Level

The opposite occurs if the price level falls. At a lower price level, the value of bank accounts, currency, and other money holdings increases. Consumers on average are wealthier and thus spend more at each income level. A lower price level also tends to decrease the market interest rate, which increases investment. Finally, a lower U.S. price level, other things constant, makes U.S. products cheaper abroad and foreign products relatively more expensive here, so exports increase and imports decrease. *Because of a decline in the price level, consumption, investment, and net exports increase at each income level.*

When prices fall, we feel like we have more money even if we don't. That's what is called an increase in "real income" or income in terms of what we can buy with the money we have.

Refer again to Exhibit 9 and suppose the price level declines from 110 to, say, 100. This increases spending at each income level, as reflected by an upward shift of the spending line from *AE* to *AE″* in panel (a). An increase in spending increases real GDP demanded from $17.0 trillion to $17.5 trillion, as indicated by the intersection of the top aggregate expenditure line with the 45-degree line at point *e″*. This same price decrease can be viewed more directly in panel (b). As you can see, when the price level decreases to 100, real GDP demanded increases to $17.5 trillion.

The aggregate expenditure line and the aggregate demand curve present real output from different perspectives. The aggregate expenditure line shows, for a given price level, how spending relates to income, or the amount produced in the economy. Real GDP demanded is found where spending equals income, or the amount produced. The aggregate demand curve shows, for various price levels, the quantities of real GDP demanded.

## 9-6c The Multiplier and Shifts in Aggregate Demand

Now that you have some idea of how changes in the price level shift the aggregate expenditure line to generate the aggregate demand curve, let's reverse course and return to the situation where the price level is assumed to remain constant. What we want to do now is trace through the effects of a shift of a spending component on aggregate demand, assuming the price level does not change. For example, suppose that a jump in business confidence spurs a $0.1 trillion increase in investment at each real GDP level. Each panel of Exhibit 10 shows a different way of expressing the effects of an increase in spending on real GDP demanded, assuming the price level remains unchanged. Panel (a) presents the income-expenditure model and panel (b), the aggregate demand model. Again, the two panels measure real GDP on the horizontal axes. At a price level of 110 in panel (a), the aggregate expenditure line, $C + I + G + (X - M)$, intersects the 45-degree line at point *e* to yield $17.0 trillion in real GDP demanded. Panel (b) shows more directly the link between real GDP demanded and the price level. As you can see, when the price level is 110, real GDP demanded is $17.0 trillion, identified as point *e* on the aggregate demand curve.

Exhibit 10 shows how a shift of the aggregate expenditure line relates to a shift of the aggregate demand curve, given a constant price level. In panel (a), a $0.1 trillion increase in investment shifts the aggregate expenditure line up by $0.1 trillion. Because of the multiplier effect, real GDP demanded climbs from $17.0 trillion to $17.5 trillion. Panel (b) shows the effect of the increase in spending on the aggregate demand curve,

© Minerva Studio/Shutterstock.com

*Exhibit 10*

## A Shift of the Aggregate Expenditure Line That Shifts the Aggregate Demand Curve

A shift of the aggregate expenditure line at a given price level shifts the aggregate demand curve. In panel (a), an increase in investment of $0.1 trillion, with the price level constant at 110, causes the aggregate expenditure line to increase from $C + I + G + (X - M)$ to $C + I' + G + (X - M)$. As a result, real GDP demanded increases from $17.0 trillion to $17.5 trillion. In panel (b), the aggregate demand curve has shifted from $AD$ out to $AD'$. At the prevailing price level of 110, real GDP demanded has increased by $0.5 trillion.

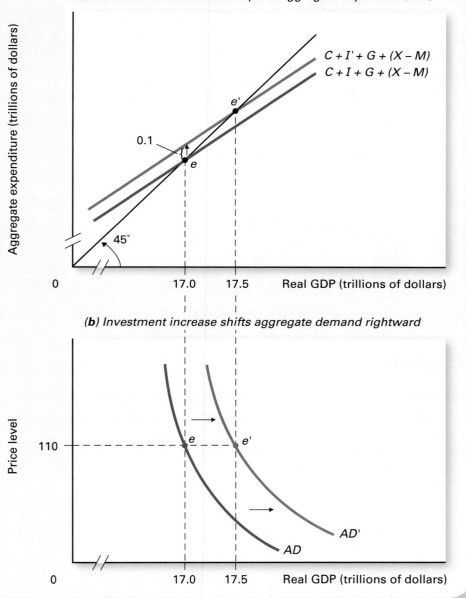

**(a) Investment increase shifts up the aggregate expenditure line**

**(b) Investment increase shifts aggregate demand rightward**

which shifts to the right, from $AD$ to $AD'$. At the prevailing price level of 110, real GDP demanded increases from $17.0 trillion to $17.5 trillion as a result of the $0.1 trillion increase in investment.

As noted earlier in the chapter, the simple spending multiplier is the ratio of a change in real GDP demanded to the initial change in spending that brought it about. Here the change in real GDP demanded is $0.5 trillion, and the change that brought it about is the $0.1 trillion increase in investment. So the simple spending multiplier is 5.

Our discussion of the simple spending multiplier exaggerates the actual effect we might expect. For one thing, we have assumed that the price level remains constant. As we shall see in the next chapter, incorporating aggregate supply into the analysis reduces the multiplier because of the resulting price change. Moreover, as income increases, there are leakages from the circular flow in addition to saving, such as higher income taxes and additional imports; these leakages reduce the multiplier. Finally, although we have presented the process in a timeless framework, the spending multiplier takes time to work through rounds—perhaps a year or more.

**TO REVIEW:** For a given price level, the aggregate expenditure line relates spending plans to income, or real GDP. Real GDP demanded is found where the amount people plan to spend equals the amount produced. A change in the price level shifts the aggregate expenditure line, changing real GDP demanded. Changes in the price level and consequent changes in real GDP demanded generate points along an aggregate demand curve. But at a given price level, changes in spending plans, such as changes in investment, consumption, or government purchases, shift the aggregate demand curve.

## 9-7 FINAL WORD

This chapter began with the relationship between consumption and income. Simply put, consumption increases with income, other things constant. We used this link to develop the aggregate expenditure line and the quantity of real GDP demanded for a given price level.

> **" For a given price level, the aggregate expenditure line relates spending plans to income. "**

These models, in turn, helped shape the aggregate demand curve, the goal of the chapter.

Three ideas central to this chapter are (1) certain forces determine the quantity of real GDP demanded at a given price level; (2) changes in the price level change the quantity of real GDP demanded; and these price-quantity combinations generate the aggregate demand curve; and (3) at a given price level, changes in spending plans shift the aggregate demand curve. The simple multiplier provides a crude but exaggerated idea of how a change in spending plans affects real GDP demanded.

# STUDY TOOLS 9

# CHAPTER 9 PROBLEMS

*Your instructor can access the answers to these problems online at http://cengagebrain.com.*

## 9-1 Explain what a consumption function illustrates and interpret its slope

1. *(Consumption)* Use the following data to answer the questions below:

   Consumption

   | Real Disposable Income (billions) | Expenditures (billions) | Saving (billions) |
   |---|---|---|
   | $100 | $150 | $_____ |
   | $200 | $200 | _____ |
   | $300 | $250 | _____ |
   | $400 | $300 | _____ |

   a. Graph the consumption function, with consumption spending on the vertical axis and disposable income on the horizontal axis.

   b. If the consumption function is a straight line, what is its slope?

   c. Fill in the saving column at each level of income. If the saving function is a straight line, what is its slope?

2. *(MPC and MPS)* If consumption increases by $12 billion when disposable income increases by $15 billion, what is the value of the MPC? What is the relationship between the MPC and the MPS? If the MPC increases, what must happen to the MPS? How is the MPC related to the consumption function? How is the MPS related to the saving function?

3. *(Consumption and Saving)* Suppose that consumption equals $500 billion when disposable income is $0 and that each increase of $100 billion in disposable income causes consumption to increase by $70 billion. Draw a graph of the consumption function using this information. What is the slope of the consumption function?

## 9-2 Describe what can shift the consumption function up or down

4. *(Consumption Function)* How would an increase in each of the following affect the consumption function?

   a. Net taxes
   b. The interest rate
   c. Consumer optimism, or confidence
   d. The price level
   e. Consumers' net wealth
   f. Disposable income

5. *(Life-Cycle Hypothesis)* According to the life-cycle hypothesis, what is the typical pattern of saving and spending for an individual over his or her lifetime? What impact does this pattern have on the saving rate in the overall economy?

## 9-3 Explain why investment varies more than consumption from year to year

6. *(Investment)* Why does investment vary more than consumption from year to year?

7. *(Investment)* Why would the following investment expenditures increase as the interest rate declines?

   a. Purchases of a new plant and equipment
   b. Construction of new housing
   c. Increase of inventories

## 9-4 Describe how the aggregate expenditure line determines the quantity of aggregate output demanded

8. *(Aggregate Expenditure)* What are the components of aggregate expenditure? In the model developed in this chapter, which components vary with changes in the level of real GDP? What determines the slope of the aggregate expenditure line?

9. *(GDP Demanded)* How is the aggregate expenditure line used to identify real GDP demanded assuming a given price level?

## 9-5 Determine the simple spending multiplier and explain its relevance

10. *(Simple Spending Multiplier)* For each of the following values for the MPC, determine the size of the simple spending multiplier and the total change in real GDP demanded following a $10 billion decrease in spending:

    a. $MPC = 0.9$
    b. $MPC = 0.75$
    c. $MPC = 0.6$

11. *(Simple Spending Multiplier)* Suppose that the MPC is 0.8 and that $17 trillion of real GDP is currently being demanded. The government wants to increase real GDP demanded to $18 trillion at the given price level. By how much would it have to increase government purchases to achieve this goal?

12. *(Investment and the Multiplier)* This chapter assumes that investment is autonomous. What would happen to the size of the multiplier if investment increases as real GDP increases? Explain.

## 9-6 Summarize the relationship between the aggregate expenditure line and the aggregate demand curve

13. *(Shifts of Aggregate Demand)* Assume the simple spending multiplier equals 3. Determine the size and direction of any changes of the aggregate expenditure line, real GDP demanded, and the aggregate demand curve for each of the following changes in spending:

    a. Spending rises by $8 billion at each income level.
    b. Spending falls by $5 billion at each income level.
    c. Spending rises by $20 billion at each income level.

# 10 | Aggregate Supply

## LEARNING OUTCOMES

After studying this chapter, you will be able to...

**10-1** Explain what determines the shape and position of the short-run aggregate supply curve

**10-2** Describe the market forces that push the economy toward its potential output in the long run

**10-3** Explain why shifts of the aggregate demand curve change the price level in the long run but do not change potential output

**10-4** Summarize what can shift an economy's potential output in the long run

After finishing this chapter go to **PAGE 187** for **STUDY TOOLS**

**Topics discussed in Chapter 10 include:**

- Expected price level and long-term contracts
- Potential output
- Short-run aggregate supply curve
- Long-run aggregate supply curve
- Expansionary gap
- Recessionary gap
- Changes in aggregate supply
- Beneficial supply shocks
- Adverse supply shocks

- How do producers react when the economy's price level increases?

- When the economy is already operating at full employment, how can it produce more?

- What's your normal capacity for academic work, and when do you exceed that effort?

- What valuable piece of information do employers and workers lack when they negotiate wages?

- Why do employers and workers fail to agree on pay cuts that could save jobs?

*These and other questions are answered in this chapter, which develops the aggregate supply curve in the short run and in the long run.*

U p to this point, we have focused on aggregate demand. We have not yet examined in any detail aggregate supply, a much-debated topic. The debate involves the shape of the aggregate supply curve and the reasons for that shape. This chapter develops a single, coherent approach to aggregate supply. Although the focus continues to be

**"When the economy is already operating at full employment, how can it produce more?"**

on economic aggregates, you should keep in mind that aggregate supply reflects billions of production decisions made by millions of individual resource suppliers and firms in the economy. Each firm operates in its own little world, dealing with its own suppliers and customers, and keeping a watchful eye on existing and potential competitors.

Yet each firm recognizes that success also depends on the performance of the economy as a whole. The theory of aggregate supply described here must be consistent with both the microeconomic behavior of individual suppliers and the macroeconomic behavior of the economy as a whole.

## 10-1 AGGREGATE SUPPLY IN THE SHORT RUN

*Aggregate supply* is the relationship between the economy's price level and the amount of output firms are willing and able to supply, with other things constant. Assumed constant along a given aggregate supply curve are resource prices, the state of technology and know-how, and the rules of the game—the formal and informal institutions that structure production incentives, such as the system of property rights, patent laws, tax systems, respect for laws, and the customs and conventions of the marketplace. The greater the supply of resources, the better the technology and know-how, and the more effective the rules of the game, the greater the aggregate supply. Let's begin with the key resource—labor.

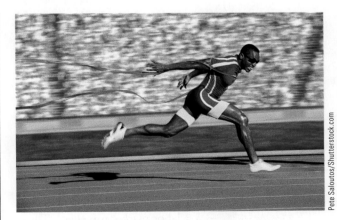
Pete Saloutos/Shutterstock.com

### 10-1a Labor and Aggregate Supply

Labor is the most important resource, accounting for about 70 percent of production costs. The supply of labor in an economy depends on the size and abilities of the adult population and their preferences for work versus leisure. Along a given labor supply curve—that is, for a given adult population with given abilities and preferences for work and leisure—the quantity of labor supplied depends on the wage. The higher the wage, other things constant, the more labor supplied.

So far, so good. But things start getting complicated once we recognize that the purchasing power of any given nominal wage depends on the economy's price level. *The higher the price level, the less any given money wage purchases, so the less attractive that wage is to workers.* Consider wages and the price level over time. Suppose a worker in 1970 was offered a job paying $20,000 per year. That salary may not impress you today, but its real purchasing power back then would exceed $80,000 in today's dollars. Because the price level matters, we must distinguish between the **nominal wage**, or money wage, which measures the wage in dollars of the year in question (such as 1970), and the **real wage**, which measures the wage in constant dollars—that is, dollars measured by the goods and services they buy. A higher real wage means workers can buy more goods and services.

Both workers and employers care more about the real wage than about the nominal wage. The problem is that nobody knows for sure how the price level will change during the life of the wage agreement, so labor contracts must be negotiated in terms of nominal wages, not real wages. Some resource prices, such as wages set by long-term contracts, remain in force for extended periods, often for two or three years. Workers as well as other resource suppliers must therefore negotiate based on the *expected* price level.

Even where there are no explicit labor contracts, there is often an implicit agreement that the wage, once negotiated, will not change for a while. For example, in many firms the standard practice is to revise wages annually. So wage agreements may be either *explicit* (based on a labor contract) or *implicit* (based on labor market practices). These explicit and implicit agreements are difficult to renegotiate while still in effect, even if the price level in the economy turns out to be higher or lower than expected.

**nominal wage** The wage measured in dollars of the year in question; the dollar amount on a paycheck

**real wage** The wage measured in dollars of constant purchasing power; the wage measured in terms of the quantity of goods and services it buys

**potential output** The economy's maximum sustainable output, given the supply of resources, technology and know-how, and rules of the game; the output level when there are no surprises about the price level

**natural rate of unemployment** The unemployment rate when the economy produces its potential output

## 10-1b Potential Output and the Natural Rate of Unemployment

Here's how resource owners and firms negotiate resource price agreements for a particular period, say, a year. Firms and resource suppliers expect a certain price level to prevail in the economy during the year. You could think of this as the *consensus* view for the upcoming year. Based on consensus expectations, firms and resource suppliers reach agreements on resource prices, such as wages. For example, firms and workers may expect the price level to increase 3 percent next year, so they agree on a nominal wage increase of 4 percent, which would increase the real wage by 1 percent. If these price-level expectations are realized, the agreed-on nominal wage translates into the expected real wage, so everyone is satisfied with the way things work out—after all, that's what they willingly negotiated. When the actual price level turns out as expected, we call the result the economy's potential output. *Potential output is the amount produced when there are no surprises about the price level.* So, at the agreed-on real wage, workers are supplying the quantity of labor they want and firms are hiring the quantity of labor they want. Both sides are content with the outcome.

We can think of **potential output** as the economy's maximum sustainable output, given the supply of resources, the state of technology and know-how, and the formal and informal production incentives offered by the rules of the game. Potential output is also referred to by other terms, including the *natural rate of output* and the *full-employment rate of output*.

The unemployment rate that occurs when the economy produces its potential gross domestic product (GDP) is called the **natural rate of unemployment**. That rate prevails when cyclical unemployment is zero. When the economy produces its potential output, the number of job openings equals the number of people unemployed for frictional, structural, and seasonal reasons. Widely accepted estimates of the natural rate range from about 4 percent to about 6 percent of the labor force. Some economists believe that, in the aftermath of the Great Recession, the natural rate of unemployment increased toward the higher end of that range.[1] The Federal Reserve estimated the natural rate in 2015 as between 5.0 and 5.2 percent.

Potential output provides a reference point, an anchor, for the analysis in this chapter. *When the price-level expectations of both workers and firms are fulfilled, the economy*

---

1. See, for example, Murat Tasci and Saeed Zaman, "Unemployment After the Recession: A New Natural Rate?" *Economic Commentary*, September 2010, at http://www.clevelandfed.org/research/commentary/2010/2010-11.cfm.

*produces its potential output.* Complications arise, however, when the actual price level differs from expectations, as we'll see next.

## 10-1c What If the Actual Price Level Is Higher Than Expected?

As you know, each firm's goal is to maximize profit. Profit equals total revenue minus total cost. Suppose workers and firms agree on a wage. What if the economy's price level turns out to be higher than expected? What happens *in the short run* to real GDP supplied? The **short run** in macroeconomics is a period during which some resource prices remain fixed by explicit or implicit agreements. Does output in the short run exceed the economy's potential, fall short of that potential, or equal that potential?

Because the prices of many resources are fixed for the duration of contracts, firms welcome a higher than expected

> " Potential output is also referred to by other terms, including the *natural rate of output* and the *full-employment rate of output.* "

price level. After all, the selling prices of their products, on average, are higher than expected, while the costs of at least some of the resources they employ remain constant. *A price level that is higher than expected results in a higher profit per unit, so firms have a profit incentive in the short run to increase production beyond the economy's potential level.*

At first it might appear odd to talk about producing beyond the economy's potential, but remember that potential output means not zero unemployment but the natural rate of unemployment. Even in an economy producing its potential output, there is some unemployed labor and some unused production capacity. If you think of potential GDP as the economy's *normal capacity,* you get a better idea of how production can temporarily exceed that capacity. For example, during World War II, the United States pulled out all the stops to win the war. Factories operated around the clock. Overtime was common. The unemployment rate dropped below 2 percent—well under its natural rate. People worked longer and harder for the war effort than they normally would have.

Think about your own study habits. During most of the term, you display your normal capacity for academic work. As the end of the term draws near, however, you may shift into a higher gear, finishing term papers, studying late into the night for final exams, and generally running yourself ragged trying to pull things together. During those final frenzied days of the term, you study beyond your normal capacity, beyond the schedule you follow on a regular or sustained basis. We often observe workers exceeding their normal capacity for short bursts: fireworks technicians around the Fourth of July, accountants at tax time, farmers at harvest time, and elected officials toward the end of a campaign or legislative session. Similarly, firms and their workers are able, *in the short run,* to push output beyond the economy's potential. But that higher rate of output is not normal and not sustainable in the long run.

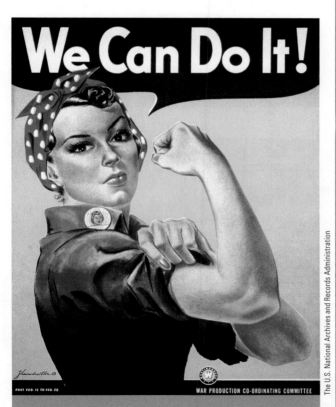

Starting during World War II, women entered the work force at higher and higher rates. This led to an increase in potential output of the U.S. economy.

The U.S. National Archives and Records Administration

## 10-1d Why Costs Rise When Output Exceeds Potential

The economy is flexible enough to expand output beyond potential GDP, but

**short run** In macroeconomics, a period during which some resource prices, especially those for labor, remain fixed by explicit or implicit agreements as output expands, the cost of additional output increases. Although many workers are bound by contracts, wage agreements may require overtime pay for extra hours or weekends. As the economy expands and the unemployment rate declines, additional workers are harder to find. Retirees, homemakers, and students may require extra pay to draw them into the labor force. If few additional workers are available or if workers require additional pay for overtime, the nominal cost of labor increases as output expands in the short run, even though most wages remain fixed by implicit or explicit agreements.

As production increases, the demand for nonlabor resources increases too, so the prices of those resources in markets where prices are flexible—such as the market for oil—will increase, reflecting their greater scarcity. Also, as production increases, firms use their machines and trucks more intensively, so equipment wears out faster and is more prone to breakdowns. Thus, the nominal cost per unit of output rises when production is pushed beyond the economy's potential output. But *because some resource prices are fixed by contracts, the economy's price level rises faster than the per-unit production cost, so firms still find it profitable to increase the quantity supplied.*

When the economy's actual price level exceeds the expected price level, the real value of an agreed-on nominal wage declines. We might ask why workers would be willing to increase the quantity of labor they supply when the price level is higher than expected. One answer is that labor agreements require workers to do so, at least until workers have a chance to renegotiate.

In summary: If the price level is higher than expected, firms have a profit incentive to increase the quantity of goods and services supplied. At higher rates of output, however, the per-unit cost of additional output increases. Firms expand output as long as the revenue from additional production exceeds the cost of that production.

> **"A price level that is higher than expected results in a higher profit per unit, so firms have a profit incentive in the short run to increase production beyond the economy's potential level."**

## 10-1e What If the Actual Price Level Is Lower Than Expected?

We have learned that if the price level is greater than expected, firms expand output in the short run, but as they do, the marginal cost of production increases. Now let's look at the effects of a price level that turns out to be lower than expected. Again, suppose that firms and resource suppliers have reached an agreement based on an expected price level. If the price level turns out to be lower than expected, firms find production less profitable, as reflected in the headline, "Consumer Price Drop Squeezes Profits."[2] The prices firms receive for their output are on average lower than they expected, yet many of their production costs, such as nominal wages, do not fall.

Because production is less profitable when prices are lower than expected, firms reduce their quantity supplied, so the economy's output is below its potential. As a result, some workers are laid off, some work fewer hours, and unemployment exceeds the natural rate. Not only is less labor employed, but machines go unused, delivery

**Construction of things like new factories and office buildings may speed up or slow down depending on whether the actual price level is higher or lower than expected.**

© iStockphoto.com/GreenPimp

2. Sudeep Reddy and Dana Mattioli, "Consumer Price Drop Squeezes Profits," *Wall Street Journal*, 18 June 2010.

trucks sit idle, and entire plants may shut down—for example, automakers sometimes halt production for weeks. Cyclical unemployment increases.

Just as some costs increase in the short run when output is pushed beyond the economy's potential, some costs decline when output falls below that potential. As resources become unemployed, resource prices decline in markets where prices are flexible.

**TO REVIEW:** If the economy's price level turns out to be higher than expected, firms maximize profit by increasing the quantity supplied beyond the economy's potential output. As output expands, the per-unit cost of additional production increases, but firms expand production as long as prices rise more than costs. If the economy's price level turns out to be lower than expected, firms produce less than the economy's potential output because prices fall more than costs. All of this is a long way of saying that *there is a direct relationship in the short run between the actual price level and real GDP supplied.*

## 10-1f The Short-Run Aggregate Supply Curve

What we have been describing so far traces out the **short-run aggregate supply (SRAS) curve**, which shows the relationship between the actual price level and real GDP supplied, other things constant. Again, the *short run* in this context is the period during which some resource prices, especially those for labor, are fixed by implicit or explicit agreements. For simplicity, we can think of the short run

> **"There is a direct relationship in the short run between the actual price level and real GDP supplied."**

aggregate supply curve at point *a*. If the economy produces its potential output, unemployment is at the *natural rate*.

as the duration of labor contracts, which are based on the expected price level.

Suppose the expected price level is 110. The short-run aggregate supply curve in Exhibit 1, $SRAS_{110}$, is based on that expected price level (hence the subscript 110). If the price level turns out as expected, producers supply the economy's *potential output*, which in Exhibit 1 is $17.0 trillion. Although not shown in the exhibit, the aggregate demand curve would intersect the

**short-run aggregate supply (SRAS) curve** A curve that shows a direct relationship between the actual price level and real GDP supplied in the short run, other things constant, including the expected price level

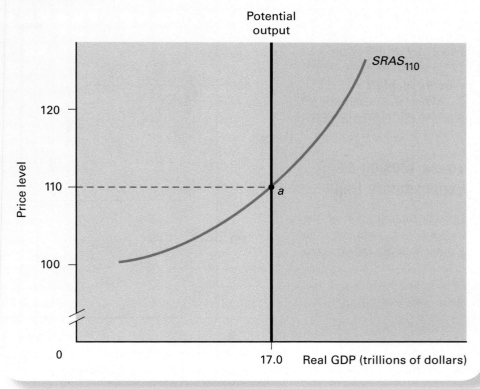

*Exhibit 1*

**Short-Run Aggregate Supply Curve**

The short-run aggregate supply curve is based on a given expected price level, in this case, 110. Point a shows that if the actual price level equals the expected price level of 110, firms supply potential output. If the actual price level exceeds 110, quantity supplied exceeds potential. If the actual price level is below 110, quantity supplied is less than potential. Output levels that fall short of the economy's potential are shaded pink; output levels that exceed the economy's potential are shaded blue.

Nobody is surprised, and all are content with the outcome. There is no tendency to move away from point *a* even if workers and firms could renegotiate wages.

In Exhibit 1, output levels that fall short of the economy's potential are shaded pink, and output levels that exceed the economy's potential are shaded blue. The slope of the short-run aggregate supply curve depends on how sharply the marginal cost of production rises as real GDP expands. If costs increase modestly as output expands, the supply curve is relatively flat. If these costs increase sharply as output expands, the supply curve is relatively steep. Much of the controversy about the short-run aggregate supply curve involves its shape. Shapes range from flat to steep. Notice that the short-run aggregate supply curve becomes steeper as output increases, because some resources become scarcer and thus more costly as output increases.

price level of 110. The short-run aggregate supply curve for that expected price level is $SRAS_{110}$. Given this short-run aggregate supply curve, the equilibrium price level and real GDP depend on the aggregate demand curve. The actual price level would equal the expected price level only if the aggregate demand curve intersects the aggregate supply curve at point *a*—that is, where the short-run quantity equals potential output. Point *a* reflects potential output of $17.0 trillion and a price level of 110, which is the expected price level.

But what if aggregate demand turns out to be greater than expected, such as $AD'$, which intersects the short-run aggregate supply curve $SRAS_{110}$ at point *b*? Point *b* is the **short-run equilibrium**, reflecting a price level of 115 and a real GDP of $17.2 trillion. The actual price level in the short run is higher than expected, and output exceeds the economy's potential of $17.0 trillion.

## 10-2 FROM THE SHORT RUN TO THE LONG RUN

This section begins with the price level exceeding expectations in the short run to see what happens in the long run. The long run is long enough that firms and resource suppliers can renegotiate all agreements based on knowledge of the actual price level. *So in the long run, there are no surprises about the economy's price level.*

### 10-2a Closing an Expansionary Gap

Let's begin our look at the long-run adjustment in Exhibit 2 with an expected

**short-run equilibrium**
The price level and real GDP that result when the aggregate demand curve intersects the short-run aggregate supply curve

*Exhibit 2*

**Long-Run Adjustment When the Price Level Exceeds Expectations**

If the expected price level is 110, the short-run aggregate supply curve is $SRAS_{110}$. If the actual price level turns out as expected, the quantity supplied is the potential output of $17.0 trillion. But here the price level ends up higher than expected, and output exceeds potential, as shown by the short-run equilibrium at point *b*. The amount by which actual output exceeds the economy's potential output is called the expansionary gap. In the long run, price-level expectations and nominal wages will be revised upward. Costs will rise and the short-run aggregate supply curve will shift leftward to $SRAS_{120}$. Eventually, the economy will move to long-run equilibrium at point *c*, thus closing the expansionary gap.

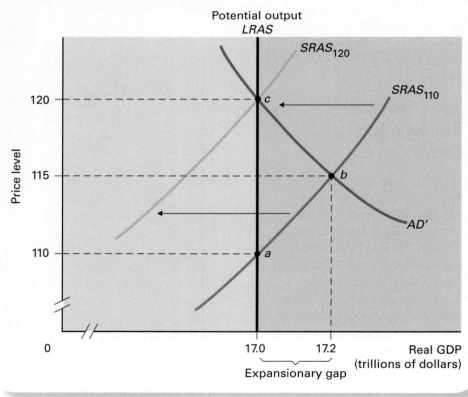

The amount by which short-run output exceeds the economy's potential is called an **expansionary gap**. In Exhibit 2, that gap is the short-run output of $17.2 trillion minus potential output of $17.0 trillion, or $0.2 trillion. When real GDP exceeds its potential, the unemployment rate is less than its natural rate. Employees are working overtime, machines are being pushed to their limits, and farmers are sandwiching extra crops between usual plantings. Remember that the nominal wage was negotiated based on an expected price level of 110; because the actual price level is higher, that nominal wage translates into a lower-than-expected real wage. As we will see, output exceeding the economy's potential creates inflationary pressure. *The more that short-run output exceeds the economy's potential, the larger the expansionary gap and the greater the upward pressure on the price level.*

What happens in the long run? The **long run** is a period during which firms and resource suppliers know all about market conditions, particularly aggregate demand and the actual price level, and have the time to renegotiate resource payments based on that knowledge. Because the higher-than-expected price level cuts the real value of the nominal wage originally agreed to, workers try to negotiate a higher nominal wage at their earliest opportunity. Workers and other resource suppliers negotiate higher nominal payments, raising production costs for firms, so

> **"Actual output can exceed the economy's potential in the short run but not in the long run."**

Production exceeding the economy's potential creates inflationary pressure, which causes the short-run aggregate supply curve to shift to the left, reducing output, increasing the price level, and closing the expansionary gap.

Chris Batson/Alamy

the short-run aggregate supply curve shifts leftward, resulting in cost-push inflation. In the long run, the expansionary gap causes the short-run aggregate supply curve to shift leftward to $SRAS_{120}$, which results in an expected price level of 120. Notice that the short-run aggregate supply curve shifts until the equilibrium output equals the economy's potential output. *Actual output can exceed the economy's potential in the short run but not in the long run.*

As shown in Exhibit 2, the expansionary gap is closed by long-run market forces that shift the short-run aggregate supply curve from $SRAS_{110}$ left to $SRAS_{120}$. Whereas $SRAS_{110}$ was based on resource contracts reflecting an expected price level of 110, $SRAS_{120}$ is based on resource contracts reflecting an expected price level of 120. At point $c$ the expected price level and the actual price level are identical, so the economy is not only in short-run equilibrium, but is also in **long-run equilibrium**. Consider all the equalities that hold at point $c$: (1) the expected price level equals the actual price level; (2) the quantity supplied in the short run equals potential output, which also equals the quantity supplied in the long run; and (3) the quantity supplied equals the quantity demanded. Looked at another way, *long-run equilibrium occurs where the aggregate demand curve intersects the vertical line drawn at potential output.* Point $c$ continues to be the equilibrium point unless there is some change in aggregate demand or in aggregate supply.

Note that the situation at point $c$ is no different *in real terms* from what had been expected at point $a$. At both points, firms supply the economy's potential output of $17.0 trillion. The same amounts of labor and other resources are employed, and although the price level, the nominal wage, and other nominal resource payments are higher at point $c$, the real wage and the real return to other resources are the same as they would have been at point $a$. For example, suppose the nominal wage averaged

**expansionary gap**
The amount by which actual output in the short run exceeds the economy's potential output

**long run** In macroeconomics, a period during which wage contracts and resource price agreements can be renegotiated; there are no surprises about the economy's actual price level

**long-run equilibrium** The price level and real GDP that occur when (1) the actual price level equals the expected price level, (2) real GDP supplied equals potential output, and (3) real GDP supplied equals real GDP demanded

$22 per hour when the expected price level was 110. If the expected price level increased from 110 to 120, an increase of 9.1 percent, the nominal wage would also increase by that same percentage to an average of $24 per hour, leaving the real wage unchanged. With no change in real wages between points *a* and *c*, firms demand enough labor and workers supply enough labor to produce $17.0 trillion in real GDP.

Thus, if the price level turns out to be higher than expected, the short-run response is to increase quantity supplied. But production exceeding the economy's potential creates inflationary pressure. In the long run this causes the short-run aggregate supply curve to shift to the left, reducing output, increasing the price level, and closing the expansionary gap.

If an increase in the price level were predicted accurately year after year, firms and resource suppliers would build these expectations into their long-term agreements. The price level would move up each year by the expected amount, but the economy's output would remain at potential GDP, thereby skipping the round-trip beyond the economy's potential and back.

## 10-2b Closing a Recessionary Gap

Let's begin again with an expected price level of 110 as presented in Exhibit 3, where blue shading indicates output exceeding potential and pink shading indicates output below potential. If the price level turned out as expected, the resulting equilibrium combination would occur at *a*, which would be both a short-run and a long-run equilibrium. Suppose this time that the aggregate

demand curve intersects the short-run aggregate supply curve to the left of potential output, yielding a price level below that expected. The intersection of the aggregate demand curve, *AD″*, with *SRAS₁₁₀* yields the short-run equilibrium at point *d*, where the price level is below expectations and production is less than the economy's potential. The amount by which actual output falls short of potential GDP is called a **recessionary gap**. In this case, the recessionary gap is $0.2 trillion, and unemployment exceeds its natural rate.

Because the price level is less than expected, the nominal wage, which was based on the expected price level of 110 and not the actual price level of 105, translates into a higher real wage in the short run. What happens in the long run? With the price level lower than expected, employers are no longer willing to pay as high a nominal wage. And with the unemployment rate higher

**recessionary gap** The amount by which actual output in the short run falls short of the economy's potential output

### Exhibit 3

### Long-Run Adjustment When the Price Level Is Below Expectations

When the actual price level is below expectations, as indicated by the intersection of the aggregate demand curve *AD″* with the short-run aggregate supply curve *SRAS₁₁₀*, short-run equilibrium occurs at point *d*. Production below the economy's potential opens a recessionary gap of $0.2 trillion. If prices and wages are flexible enough in the long run, nominal wages will be renegotiated lower. As resource costs fall, the short-run aggregate supply curve eventually shifts rightward to *SRAS₁₀₀* and the economy moves to long-run equilibrium at point *e*, with output increasing to the potential level of $17.0 trillion.

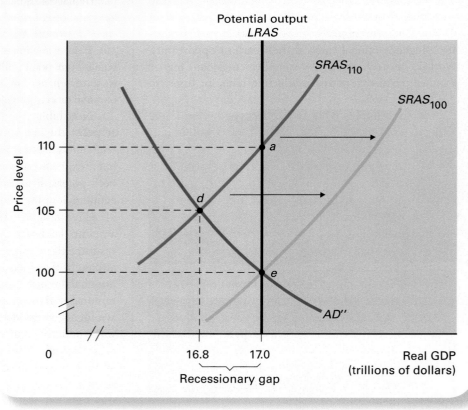

than the natural rate, more workers are competing for jobs, putting downward pressure on the nominal wage. If the price level and the nominal wage are flexible enough, the combination of a lower price level and a pool of unemployed workers competing for jobs should make workers more willing to accept lower nominal wages next time wage agreements are negotiated.

If firms and workers negotiate lower nominal wages, the cost of production decreases, shifting the short-run aggregate supply curve rightward, leading to price deflation and greater output. The short-run supply curve continues to shift rightward until it intersects the aggregate demand curve where the economy produces its potential output. This is reflected in Exhibit 3 by a rightward shift of the short-run aggregate supply curve from SRAS110 to SRAS100. *If the price level and nominal wage are flexible enough, the short-run aggregate supply curve shifts rightward until the economy produces its potential output.* The new short-run aggregate supply curve is based on an expected price level of 100. Because the expected price level and the actual price level are now identical, the economy is in long-run equilibrium at point *e*.

Although the nominal wage is lower at point *e* than that originally agreed to when the expected price level was 110, the real wage is the same at point *e* as it was at point *a*. Because the real wage is the same, the amount of labor that workers supply is the same and real output is the same. All that has changed between points *a* and *e* are nominal measures—the price level, the nominal wage, and other nominal resource prices.

We conclude that when incorrect expectations cause firms and resource suppliers to overestimate the actual price level, output in the short run falls short of the economy's potential. As long as wages and prices are flexible enough, however, firms and workers should be able to renegotiate wage agreements based on a lower expected price level. The negotiated drop in the nominal wage shifts the short-run aggregate supply curve to the right until the economy once again produces its potential output. If wages and prices are not flexible, they will not adjust quickly to a recessionary gap, so shifts of the short-run aggregate supply curve may be slow to move the economy to its potential output. The economy can therefore get stuck at an output and employment level below its potential.

> **"Closing an expansionary gap involves inflation and closing a recessionary gap involves deflation."**

## 10-3 AGGREGATE SUPPLY IN THE LONG RUN

We are now in a position to provide an additional interpretation of the pink- and blue-shaded areas of our exhibits. If a short-run equilibrium occurs in the blue-shaded area, that is, to the right of potential output, then market forces in the long run increase nominal resource costs, shifting the short-run aggregate supply to the left. If a short-run equilibrium occurs in the pink-shaded area, then market forces in the long run reduce nominal resource costs, shifting the short-run aggregate supply curve to the right. *Closing an expansionary gap involves inflation and closing a recessionary gap involves deflation.*

### 10-3a Tracing Potential Output

If wages and prices are flexible enough, the economy produces its potential output in the long run, as indicated in Exhibit 4 by the vertical line drawn at the economy's potential GDP of $17.0 trillion. This vertical line is called the economy's **long-run aggregate supply (LRAS) curve**. *The long-run aggregate supply curve depends on the supply of resources in the economy, the level of technology and know-how, and the production incentives provided by the formal and informal institutions of the economic system.*

In Exhibit 4, the initial price level of 110 is determined by the intersection of *AD* with the long-run aggregate supply curve. If the aggregate demand curve shifts out to *AD′*, then in the long run, the equilibrium price level increases to 120 but equilibrium output remains at $17.0 trillion, the economy's potential GDP. Conversely, a decline in aggregate demand from *AD* to *AD″*, in the long run, leads only to a fall in the price level from 110 to 100, with no change in output. Note that these long-run movements are more like tendencies than smooth and timely adjustments. It may take a long time for resource prices to adjust, particularly when the economy faces a recessionary gap. But as long as wages and prices are flexible,

> **long-run aggregate supply (LRAS) curve** A vertical line at the economy's potential output; aggregate supply when there are no surprises about the price level and all resource contracts can be renegotiated

*Exhibit 4*

## Long-Run Aggregate Supply Curve

In the long run, when the actual price level equals the expected price level, the economy produces its potential. In the long run, $17.0 trillion in real GDP is supplied regardless of the actual price level. As long as wages and prices are flexible enough, the economy's potential GDP is consistent with any price level. Thus, shifts of the aggregate demand curve, in the long run, do not affect potential output. The long-run aggregate supply curve, *LRAS*, is a vertical line at potential GDP.

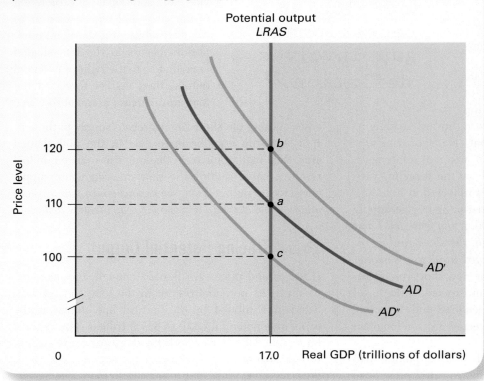

the economy's potential GDP is consistent with any price level. *In the long run, equilibrium output equals long-run aggregate supply, which is also potential output. The equilibrium price level depends on the aggregate demand curve.*

## 10-3b Wage Flexibility and Employment

What evidence is there that a vertical line drawn at the economy's potential GDP depicts the long-run aggregate supply curve? Except during the Great Depression, unemployment over the last century has varied from year to year but typically has returned to what would be viewed as a natural rate of unemployment—again, estimates range from 4 percent to 6 percent.

An *expansionary* gap creates a labor shortage that eventually results in a higher nominal wage and a higher price level. But a *recessionary* gap does not necessarily generate enough downward pressure to lower the nominal wage. Studies indicate that nominal wages are slow

to adjust to high unemployment. Nominal wages have declined in particular industries; during the 1980s, for example, nominal wages fell in airlines, steel, and trucking. But seldom have we observed actual declines in nominal wages across the economy, especially since World War II. Nominal wages do not adjust downward as quickly or as substantially as they adjust upward, and the downward response that does occur tends to be slow and modest. Consequently, we say that nominal wages tend to be "sticky" in the downward direction.[3] *Because nominal wages fall slowly, if at all, the supply-side adjustments needed to close a recessionary gap may take so long as to seem ineffective.* What, in fact, usually closes a recessionary gap is an increase in aggregate demand as the economy pulls out of its funk. For example, consider the U.S. economy's recovery from the Great Recession of 2007–2009. Here's how *The Wall Street Journal* reported events: "U.S. factories that were idled during the recession are now humming with activity. Office and apartment buildings have less empty space. Unemployment is falling, while wages and benefits are growing slowly."[4]

Although the nominal wage seldom falls, an actual decline in the nominal wage is not necessary to close a recessionary gap. All that's needed is a fall in the real wage. And *the real wage falls if the prices increase more than nominal wages.* For example, if the price level increases by 4 percent and the nominal wage increases by 3 percent, the real wage falls by 1 percent. If the real wage falls enough, firms demand enough additional labor to produce the economy's potential output. More generally, total

3. For evidence on sticky wages, see Alessandro Barattieri , Susanto Basu, and Peter Gottschalk, "Some Evidence on the Importance of Sticky Wages," *American Economic Journal: Macroeconomics*, 6 (January 2014): 70–101.

4. Pedro Nicolaci da Costa, "Decline in 'Slack' Helps Fed Gauge Recovery," *Wall Street Journal*, 10 August 2014.

*Exhibit 5*

**The U.S. Output Gap: Red Bars Show Actual Output Below Potential Output and Blue Bars Show Actual Output Exceeding Potential Output**

The output gap each year equals actual GDP minus potential GDP as a percentage of potential GDP. When actual output exceeds potential output, the output gap is positive and the economy has an expansionary gap, as shown by the blue bars. When actual output falls short of potential output, the output gap is negative and the economy suffers a recessionary gap, as shown by the red bars. Note that the economy need not be in recession for actual output to fall below potential output.

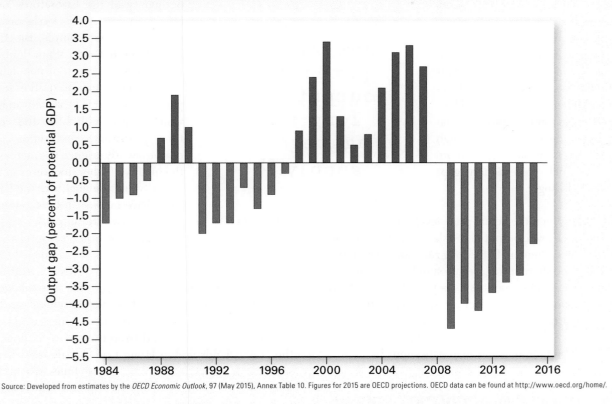

Source: Developed from estimates by the *OECD Economic Outlook*, 97 (May 2015), Annex Table 10. Figures for 2015 are OECD projections. OECD data can be found at http://www.oecd.org/home/.

compensation falls if employers cut back on employee benefits such as health insurance or paid time off.

Let's look at estimates of actual and potential GDP. Exhibit 5 measures actual GDP minus potential GDP as a percentage of potential GDP for the United States. When actual output exceeds potential output, the output gap is positive and the economy has an expansionary gap. For example, actual output in 2000 was 3.4 percent above potential output, amounting to an expansionary gap that year of about $410 billion (in 2009 dollars). When actual output falls short of potential output, the output gap is negative and the economy suffers a recessionary gap. For example, actual output in 2009 was 4.7 percent below potential output, amounting to a recessionary gap of about $710 billion (in 2009 dollars). If actual output equals potential output, there is no output gap, as was the case in 2008. Note that the economy need not be in recession for actual output to fall short of potential output. For example, from 2010 to 2015, real GDP expanded, yet actual output was below potential output. As long as unemployment exceeds its natural rate, the economy suffers a recessionary gap.

Employers and employees would have been better off if these recessionary gaps had been reduced or eliminated. After all, more people would have jobs to produce more goods and services, thereby increasing the nation's standard of living. If workers and employers fail to reach an agreement that seems possible and that all would prefer, then they have failed to coordinate in some way. Recessionary gaps can thus be viewed as resulting from a **coordination failure**.

If employers and workers can increase output and employment by agreeing to lower nominal wages, why don't they? As we have already seen, some workers are

**coordination failure** A situation in which workers and employers fail to achieve an outcome that all would prefer operating under long-term contracts, so wages aren't very flexible, particularly in the downward direction. But if long-term contracts are a problem, why not negotiate shorter ones? First, negotiating contracts is costly and time consuming (e.g., airline union contracts take an average of 1.3 years to negotiate). Longer contracts reduce the frequency, and thus reduce the average annual cost, of negotiations. Second, long-term contracts reduce the frequency of strikes, lockouts, and other labor disputes. Thus, both workers and employers gain from longer contracts, even though such contracts make wages more sticky and make recessionary gaps more likely to linger.

> **"Shifts of the aggregate demand curve change the price level but do not affect potential output, or long-run aggregate supply."**

**TO REVIEW:** When the actual price level differs from the expected price level, output in the short run departs from the economy's potential. In the long run, however, market forces shift the short-run aggregate supply curve until the economy once again produces its potential output. Thus, surprises about the price level change real GDP in the short run but not in the long run. Shifts of the aggregate demand curve change the price level but do not affect potential output, or long-run aggregate supply.

 ## 10-4 CHANGES IN AGGREGATE SUPPLY

In this section, we consider factors other than changes in the expected price level that may affect aggregate supply. We begin by distinguishing between long-term trends in aggregate supply and **supply shocks**, which are unexpected events that affect aggregate supply, sometimes only temporarily.

### 10-4a What if Aggregate Supply Increases?

The economy's potential output is based on the willingness and ability of households to supply resources to firms, the level of technology and know-how, and the institutional underpinnings of the economic system. Any change in these factors could affect the economy's

**supply shocks**
Unexpected events that affect aggregate supply, sometimes only temporarily

potential output. Changes in the economy's potential output over time were introduced in Chapter 8, which focused on U.S. productivity and growth. The supply of labor may change over time because of a change in the size, composition, or quality of the labor force or a change in preferences for labor versus leisure. For example, the U.S. labor force has more than doubled since 1948 as a result of population growth and a growing labor force participation rate, especially among women with children. At the same time, job training, education, and on-the-job experience has increased the quality of labor. Increases in the quantity and the quality of the labor force have increased the economy's potential GDP, or long-run aggregate supply.

The quantity and quality of other resources also change over time. The capital stock—machines, buildings, and trucks—increases when gross investment exceeds capital depreciation. And the capital stock improves with technological breakthroughs. Even the quantity and quality of land can be increased—for example, by claiming land from the sea, as is done in the Netherlands and in Hong Kong, or by revitalizing soil that has lost its fertility. These increases in the quantity and quality of resources increase the economy's potential output.

> **"The economy's potential output is based on the willingness and ability of households to supply resources to firms, the level of technology, and the institutional underpinnings of the economic system."**

*Exhibit 6*

**Effect of a Gradual Increase in Resources on Aggregate Supply**

A gradual growth in the supply of resources increases the potential GDP—in this case, from $17.0 trillion to $17.5 trillion. The long-run aggregate supply curve shifts to the right.

By adding to available productive resources, oil discoveries in Alaska increased aggregate supply.

Finally, institutional changes that define property rights more clearly or make contracts more enforceable, such as the introduction of clearer patent and copyright laws, will increase the incentives to undertake productive activity, thereby increasing potential output. *Changes in the labor force, in the quantity and quality of other resources, and in the institutional arrangements of the economic system tend to occur gradually.* Exhibit 6 depicts a gradual shift of the economy's potential output from $17.0 trillion to $17.5 trillion. The long-run aggregate supply curve shifts from *LRAS* out to *LRAS'*.

In contrast to the gradual, or long-run, changes that often occur in the supply of resources, *supply shocks* are unexpected events that change aggregate supply, sometimes only temporarily. **Beneficial supply shocks** increase aggregate supply; examples include (1) abundant harvests that increase the food supply; (2) discoveries of natural resources, such as oil in Alaska or the North Sea; (3) technological breakthroughs that allow firms to combine resources more efficiently, such as faster computers or the Internet; and (4) sudden changes in the economic system that promote more production, such as tax cuts that stimulate production incentives or stricter limits on frivolous product liability lawsuits.

Exhibit 7 shows the effect of a beneficial supply shock from a technological breakthrough. The beneficial supply shock shown here shifts the short-run and long-run aggregate supply curves rightward. Along the aggregate demand curve, *AD*, the equilibrium combination of price and output moves from point *a* to point *b*. *For a given aggregate demand curve, the happy outcome of a beneficial supply shock is an increase in output and a decrease in the price level.* The new equilibrium at point *b* is a short-run and a long-run equilibrium in the sense that there is no tendency to move from that point as long as whatever caused the beneficial effect continues, and a technological discovery usually has a lasting effect. Likewise, substantial new oil discoveries usually benefit the economy for a long time. On the other hand, an unusually favorable growing season won't last. When a normal growing season returns, the short-run and long-run aggregate supply curves return to their original equilibrium position—back to point *a* in Exhibit 7.

## 10-4b What if Aggregate Supply Decreases?

**Adverse supply shocks** are sudden, unexpected events that reduce aggregate supply, sometimes only temporarily. For example, a drought

**beneficial supply shocks** Unexpected events that increase aggregate supply, sometimes only temporarily

**adverse supply shocks** Unexpected events that reduce aggregate supply, sometimes only temporarily

## Exhibit 7

### Effects of a Beneficial Supply Shock on Aggregate Supply

A beneficial supply shock that has a lasting effect, such as a breakthrough in technology, permanently shifts both the short-run and the long-run aggregate supply curves to the right. A beneficial supply shock lowers the price level and increases output, as reflected by the change in equilibrium from point *a* to point *b*. A temporary beneficial supply shock shifts the aggregate supply curves only temporarily.

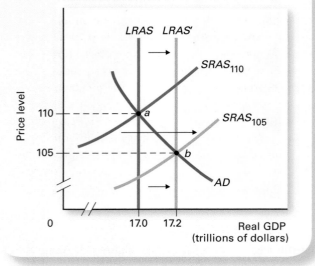

## Exhibit 8

### Effects of an Adverse Supply Shock on Aggregate Supply

Given the aggregate demand curve, an adverse supply shock, such as a drought, shifts the short-run and long-run aggregate supply curves to the left, increasing the price level and reducing real GDP, a movement called stagflation. This change is shown by the move in equilibrium from point *a* to point *c*. If the shock is just temporary, the shift of the aggregate supply curves will be temporary.

could reduce the supply of a variety of resources, such as food, building materials, and water-powered electricity. An overthrow of a government could destabilize the economy. Terrorist attacks could shake the institutional underpinnings of the economy, as occurred in America, England, Spain, and the Middle East. Such attacks add to the cost of doing business—everything from airline screening to building security.

An adverse supply shock is depicted as a leftward shift of both the short-run and long-run aggregate supply curves, as shown in Exhibit 8, moving the equilibrium combination from point *a* to point *c* and reducing potential output from $17.0 trillion to $16.8 trillion. As mentioned earlier, the combination of reduced output and a higher price level is often referred to as stagflation. The United States encountered stagflation during the 1970s, when the economy was rocked by a series of adverse supply shocks, such as crop failures around the globe and the oil price hikes by the Organization of the Petroleum Exporting Countries (OPEC)

> **hysteresis** The theory that the natural rate of unemployment depends in part on the recent history of unemployment; a long period of high unemployment can increase the natural rate of unemployment

in 1974 and again in 1979. If the effect of the adverse supply shock is temporary, such as a poor growing season, the aggregate supply curve returns to its original position once things return to normal. But some economists question an economy's ability to bounce back from a prolonged period of high unemployment, as discussed next.

## 10-4c Hysteresis and the Natural Rate of Unemployment

Between World War II and the mid-1970s, unemployment in Western Europe was low. From 1960 to 1974, for example, the unemployment rate in France never got as high as 4 percent. The worldwide recession of the mid-1970s, however, jacked up unemployment rates. But unemployment continued to climb in Europe long after the recession ended, topping 10 percent during the 1990s. In February 2015, the unemployment rate in the 19 countries of the eurozone averaged 11.3 percent, twice the rate in the United States.

Some observers claim that the natural rate of unemployment has increased in Europe, and they have borrowed a term from physics, **hysteresis** (pronounced *his-ter-eé-sis*), to argue that the natural rate of unemployment depends in part on the recent history of unemployment. *The longer the actual unemployment rate remains above what had been the natural rate, the more the natural rate itself increases.* For example, those unemployed can lose valuable job skills, such as an out-of-work computer programmer who loses touch with the latest developments. As weeks of unemployment stretch into months and years, the shock and stigma may diminish, so the work ethic weakens. What's more, some European countries offer generous unemployment benefits indefinitely, reducing the hardship of unemployment. On average, unemployment benefits in Western Europe replace 60 to 80 percent of lost pay versus about 50 percent in the United States. Some Europeans have collected unemployment benefits *for more than a decade*.

Another explanation for high unemployment in Europe is that legislation introduced there in the 1970s made it more difficult to lay off workers. In most European countries, job dismissals must be approved by worker councils, which consider such factors as the worker's health, marital status, and number of dependents. Severance pay has also become mandatory and can amount to a year's pay or more. With layoffs difficult and costly, hiring became almost an irreversible decision for an employer, so firms have become reluctant to add workers, particularly untested workers with little experience. Regardless of the explanation, the result has been high unemployment in Europe, particularly among young workers.

## 10-5 FINAL WORD

This chapter explains why the aggregate supply curve slopes upward in the short run and is vertical at the economy's potential output in the long run. Firms and resource suppliers negotiate contracts based on the economy's expected price level, which depends on expectations about aggregate demand. Unexpected changes in the price level can move output in the short run away from its potential level. But if firms and resource suppliers fully adjust to price surprises, the economy in the long run moves toward its potential output. Potential output is the anchor for analyzing aggregate supply in the short run and long run.

## STUDY TOOLS 10

### READY TO STUDY? IN THE BOOK, YOU CAN:

☐ Work the Problems at the end of the chapter.

☐ Rip out the chapter review card for a handy summary of the chapter and key terms.

### ONLINE AT CENGAGEBRAIN.COM YOU CAN:

☐ Collect StudyBits while you read and study the chapter.

☐ Quiz yourself on key concepts.

☐ Prepare for tests with chapter flash cards as well as flash cards that you create.

☐ Watch videos to explore economics further.

# CHAPTER 10 PROBLEMS

Your instructor can access the answers to these problems online at http://cengagebrain.com.

## 10-1 Explain what determines the shape and position of the short-run aggregate supply curve

1. *(Natural Rate of Unemployment)* What is the relationship between potential output and the natural rate of unemployment?

   a. If the economy currently has a frictional unemployment rate of 2 percent, structural unemployment of 2 percent, seasonal unemployment of 0.5 percent, and cyclical unemployment of 2 percent, what is the natural rate of unemployment? Where is the economy operating relative to its potential GDP?

   b. What happens to the natural rate of unemployment and potential GDP if cyclical unemployment rises to 3 percent with other types of unemployment unchanged from part (a)?

   c. What happens to the natural rate of unemployment and potential GDP if structural unemployment falls to 1.5 percent with other types of unemployment unchanged from part (a)?

2. *(Real Wages)* In the accompanying exhibit, how does the real wage rate at point *c* compare with the real wage rate at point *a*? How do nominal wage rates compare at those two points? Explain your answers.

**Long-Run Adjustment When the Price Level Exceeds Expectations**

## 10-2 Describe the market forces that push the economy toward its potential output in the long run

3. *(Expansionary and Recessionary Gaps)* Answer questions a through f on the basis of the following graph:

   a. If the actual price level exceeds the expected price level reflected in long-term contracts, real GDP equals _____ and the actual price level equals _____ in the short run.

   b. The situation described in part (a) results in a(n) _____ gap equal to _____.

   c. If the actual price level is lower than the expected price level reflected in long-term contracts, real GDP equals _____ and the actual price level equals _____ in the short run.

   d. The situation described in part (c) results in a(n) _____ gap equal to _____.

   e. If the actual price level equals the expected price level reflected in long-term contracts, real GDP equals _____ and the actual price level equals _____ in the short run.

   f. The situation described in part (e) results in a(n) _____ gap equal to _____.

4. *(Long-Run Adjustment)* The ability of the economy to eliminate any imbalances between actual and potential output is sometimes called self-correction. Using an aggregate supply and aggregate demand diagram, show why this self-correction process involves only temporary periods of inflation or deflation.

## 10-3 Explain why shifts of the aggregate demand curve change the price level in the long run but do not change potential output

5. *(Changes in Aggregate Supply)* List three factors that can change the economy's potential output. What is the impact of shifts of the aggregate demand curve on potential output? Illustrate your answers with a diagram.

## 10-4 Summarize what can shift an economy's potential output in the long run

6. *(Supply Shocks)* Give an example of an adverse supply shock and illustrate graphically. Now do the same for a beneficial supply shock.

# 11 | Fiscal Policy

Olivier Douliery/Pool/Corbis

## LEARNING OUTCOMES

After studying this chapter, you will be able to...

**11-1** Describe the discretionary fiscal policies to close a recessionary gap and an expansionary gap

**11-2** Summarize fiscal policy from the Great Depression to stagflation

**11-3** Identify some reasons why discretionary fiscal policy may not work very well

**11-4** Summarize fiscal policy during the 1980s and 1990s. When and why did the federal budget show a surplus?

**11-5** Summarize fiscal policy during and after the Great Recession.

After finishing this chapter go to **PAGE 203** for **STUDY TOOLS**

**Topics discussed in Chapter 11 include:**

- Theory of fiscal policy
- Discretionary fiscal policy
- Automatic stabilizers
- Fiscal policy in practice
- Limits of fiscal policy
- Deficits, surpluses, then more deficits
- Fiscal policy response to the Great Recession

- What is the appropriate role of fiscal policy in the economy?
- Can fiscal policy reduce swings in the business cycle?
- Why did fiscal policy fall on hard times for a quarter century, and what brought it back to life?
- Does fiscal policy affect aggregate supply?

*Answers to these and other questions are addressed in this chapter, which examines the theory and practice of fiscal policy.*

President Obama claimed on February 17, 2010, that "it is largely thanks to the Recovery Act that a second depression is no longer a possibility." The Japanese government cut taxes and increased spending to stimulate its troubled economy. These are examples of fiscal policy, which focuses on the effects of taxing and public spending on aggregate economic activity.

In this chapter, we examine the role of fiscal policy in moving the economy to its potential output. We review U.S. fiscal policy and discuss limitations to its effectiveness. The Great Recession had a major impact on the economy. We'll consider the fiscal response to that calamity.

A more complex model of fiscal policy appears in the online appendix to this chapter.

> **"U.S. President Barack Obama claimed on February 17, 2010, that 'it was largely thanks to the Recovery Act that a second depression is no longer a possibility.'"**

## 11-1  THEORY OF FISCAL POLICY

Our macroeconomic model so far has viewed government as passive. But government purchases and transfer payments at all levels in the United States total more than $7.0 trillion a year, making government an important player in the economy. From highway construction to unemployment compensation to income taxes to federal deficits, fiscal policy affects the economy in myriad ways. We now move fiscal policy to center stage. As introduced in Chapter 3, *fiscal policy* refers to government purchases, transfer payments, taxes, and borrowing as they affect macroeconomic variables such as real gross domestic product (GDP), employment, the price level, and economic growth. When economists study fiscal policy, they usually focus on the federal government, although governments at all levels affect the economy.

### 11-1a Fiscal Policy Tools

The tools of fiscal policy sort into two broad categories: automatic stabilizers and discretionary fiscal policy.

**Automatic stabilizers** are revenue and spending programs in the federal budget that automatically adjust with the ups and downs of the economy to stabilize disposable income and, consequently, consumption and real GDP. For example, the federal income tax is an automatic stabilizer because (1) once adopted, it requires no congressional action to operate year after year, so it's *automatic*, and (2) it reduces the drop in disposable income during recessions and reduces the jump in disposable income during expansions, so it's a *stabilizer*, a smoother. **Discretionary fiscal policy**, on the other hand, requires the deliberate manipulation of government purchases, transfer payments, and taxes to promote macroeconomic goals like full employment, price stability, and economic growth. President Obama's 2009 stimulus plan, which was enacted by congress, is

**automatic stabilizers** Structural features of government spending and taxation that reduce fluctuations in disposable income, and thus consumption, over the business cycle

**discretionary fiscal policy** The deliberate manipulation of government purchases, taxation, and transfer payments to promote macroeconomic goals, such as full employment, price stability, and economic growth an example of discretionary fiscal policy. Discretionary fiscal policy usually requires congressional approval. Some discretionary policies are temporary, such as one-time tax cuts or government spending increases to fight a recession. President Bush's 2001 and 2008 one-time tax rebates are examples. Let's next consider how, in theory, fiscal policy can be used to close a recessionary gap and an expansionary gap.

## 11-1b Discretionary Fiscal Policy to Close a Recessionary Gap

What if the economy produces less than its potential? Suppose the aggregate demand curve *AD* in Exhibit 1 intersects the aggregate supply curve at point *e''*, yielding the short-run output of $16.5 trillion and price level of 105. Output falls short of the economy's potential, opening up a recessionary gap of $0.5 trillion. Unemployment exceeds the natural rate. If markets adjusted naturally to high unemployment, the short-run aggregate supply curve would shift rightward in the long run to achieve equilibrium at the economy's potential output, point *e*. History suggests, however, that wages and other resource prices could be slow to respond to a recessionary gap.

Suppose policy makers believe that natural market forces will take too long to return the economy to potential output. They also believe that the appropriate increase in government purchases, decrease in net taxes, or some combination of the two could increase aggregate demand just enough to return the economy to its potential output. A $0.2 trillion increase in government purchases reflects an **expansionary fiscal policy** that increases

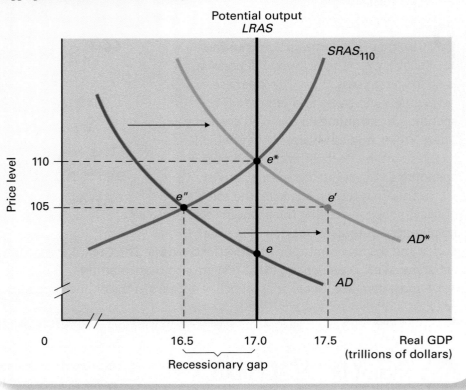

*Exhibit 1*

**Discretionary Fiscal Policy to Close a Recessionary Gap**

The aggregate demand curve *AD* and the short-run aggregate supply curve, *SRAS*$_{110}$, intersect at point *e''*. Output falls short of the economy's potential. The resulting recessionary gap could be closed by discretionary fiscal policy that increases aggregate demand by just the right amount. An increase in government purchases, a decrease in net taxes, or some combination could shift aggregate demand out to *AD\**, moving the economy out to its potential output at *e\**.

aggregate demand, as shown in Exhibit 1 by the rightward shift from *AD* to *AD\**. If the price level remained at 105, the additional spending would increase the quantity demanded from $16.5 to $17.5 trillion. This increase of $1.0 trillion reflects the simple spending multiplier effect, given a constant price level.

At the original price level of 105, however, excess quantity demanded causes the price level to rise. As the price level rises, real GDP supplied increases, but real GDP demanded decreases along the new aggregate demand curve. The price level rises until quantity

> **expansionary fiscal policy** An increase in government purchases, decrease in net taxes, or some combination of the two aimed at increasing aggregate demand enough to reduce unemployment and return the economy to its potential output; fiscal policy used to close a recessionary gap

**"An expansionary fiscal policy aims to close a recessionary gap"**

demanded equals quantity supplied. In Exhibit 1, the new aggregate demand curve intersects the aggregate supply curve at $e^*$, where the price level is 110, the one originally expected, and output equals potential GDP of $17.0 trillion. Note that *an expansionary fiscal policy aims to close a recessionary gap.*

The intersection at point $e^*$ is not only a short-run equilibrium but also a long-run equilibrium. If fiscal policy makers are accurate enough (or lucky enough), the appropriate fiscal stimulus can close the recessionary gap and foster a long-run equilibrium at potential GDP. But the increase in output results in a higher price level. What's more, if the federal budget was in balance before the fiscal stimulus, an increase in government spending creates a budget deficit. In fact, the federal government has run deficits in all but four years since 1960.

*Exhibit 2*

**Discretionary Fiscal Policy to Close an Expansionary Gap**

The aggregate demand curve $AD'$ and the short-run aggregate supply curve, $SRAS_{110}$, intersect at point $e'$, resulting in an expansionary gap of $0.5 trillion. Discretionary fiscal policy aimed at reducing aggregate demand by just the right amount could close this gap without inflation. An increase in net taxes, a decrease in government purchases, or some combination could shift the aggregate demand curve back to $AD^*$ and move the economy back to potential output at point $e^*$.

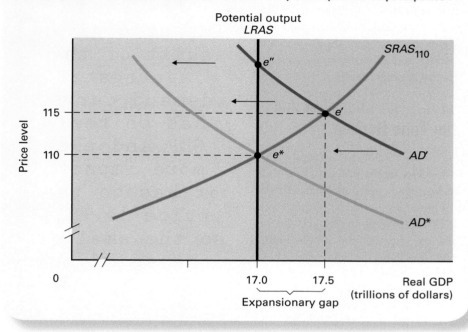

What if policy makers overshoot the mark and stimulate aggregate demand more than necessary to achieve potential GDP? In the short run, real GDP exceeds potential output. In the long run, the short-run aggregate supply curve shifts back until it intersects the aggregate demand curve at potential output, increasing the price level further but reducing real GDP to potential output.

## 11-1c Discretionary Fiscal Policy to Close an Expansionary Gap

Suppose output exceeds potential GDP. In Exhibit 2, the aggregate demand curve, $AD'$, intersects the aggregate supply curve to yield short-run output of $17.5 trillion, an amount exceeding the potential of $17.0 trillion. The economy faces an expansionary gap of $0.5 trillion. Ordinarily, this gap would be closed by a leftward shift of the short-run aggregate supply curve, which would return the economy to potential output but at a higher price level, as shown by point $e''$.

But the use of discretionary fiscal policy introduces another possibility. By reducing government purchases, increasing net taxes, or employing some combination of the two, the government can implement a **contractionary fiscal policy** to reduce aggregate demand. This could move the economy to potential output without the resulting inflation. If the policy succeeds, aggregate demand in Exhibit 2 shifts leftward from $AD'$ to $AD^*$, establishing a new equilibrium at point $e^*$. Again, with just the right reduction in aggregate demand, output falls to $17.0 trillion, the potential GDP. Closing an expansionary gap through fiscal policy rather than through natural market forces results in a lower price level, not a higher one. Increasing net taxes or reducing government purchases also reduces a government deficit or increases a surplus. So a contractionary fiscal policy could reduce inflation and reduce a federal deficit. Note that *a contractionary fiscal policy aims to close an expansionary gap.*

Such precisely calculated expansionary and contractionary fiscal policies are difficult to achieve. Their

**contractionary fiscal policy** A decrease in government purchases, increase in net taxes, or some combination of the two aimed at reducing aggregate demand enough to return the economy to potential output without worsening inflation; fiscal policy used to close an expansionary gap proper execution assumes that (1) potential output is accurately gauged, (2) the relevant spending multiplier can be predicted accurately, (3) aggregate demand can be shifted by just the right amount, (4) various government entities can somehow coordinate their fiscal efforts, and (5) the shape of the short-run aggregate supply curve is known and remains unaffected by the fiscal policy itself.

### 11-1d The Multiplier and the Time Horizon

In the short run, the aggregate supply curve slopes upward, so a shift of aggregate demand changes both the price level and the output level. When aggregate supply gets in the act, we find that the simple multiplier overstates the amount by which output changes. The exact change of equilibrium output in the short run depends on the steepness of the aggregate supply curve, which in turn depends on how sharply production costs increase as output expands. *The steeper the short-run aggregate supply curve, the less impact a given shift of the aggregate demand curve has on real GDP and the more impact it has on the price level, so the smaller the spending multiplier.*

If the economy is already producing its potential, then in the long run, any change in fiscal policy aimed at stimulating aggregate demand increases the price level but does not affect output. Thus, *if the economy is already producing its potential, the spending multiplier in the long run is zero.*

### 11-2 FISCAL POLICY UP TO THE STAGFLATION OF THE 1970S

**classical economists**
A group of 18th- and 19th-century economists who believed that economic downturns corrected themselves through natural market forces

Now that you have some idea of how fiscal policy can work in theory, let's take a look at fiscal policy in practice, beginning with the approach used before the Great Depression.

> "The steeper the short-run aggregate supply curve, the less impact a given shift of the aggregate demand curve has on real GDP and the more impact it has on the price level, so the smaller the spending multiplier."

### 11-2a Before the Great Depression

Before the 1930s, discretionary fiscal policy was seldom used to influence the macroeconomy. Public policy was shaped by the views of **classical economists**, who advocated *laissez-faire*, the belief that free markets were the best way to achieve economic prosperity. Classical economists did not deny that depressions and high unemployment occurred from time to time, but they argued that the sources of such crises lay outside the market system, in the effects of wars, tax increases, poor growing seasons, natural disasters, changing tastes, and the like. Such external shocks could reduce output and employment, but classical economists also believed that natural market forces, such as changes in prices, wages, and interest rates, could correct these problems.

Simply put, classical economists argued that if the economy's price level was too high to sell all that was produced, prices would fall until the quantity supplied equaled the quantity demanded. If wages were too high to employ all who wanted to work, wages would fall until the quantity of labor supplied equaled the quantity demanded. And if the interest rate was too high to invest all that had been saved, interest rates would fall until the amount invested equaled the amount saved.

So the classical approach implied that natural market forces, through flexible prices, wages, and interest rates, would move the economy toward potential GDP. There appeared to be no need for government intervention. What's more, the government, like households, was expected to live within its means. The idea of government running a deficit year after year was considered immoral. Thus, before the onset of the Great Depression, most economists believed that discretionary fiscal policy could do more harm than good. Besides, the federal government itself was a bit player in the economy. At the onset of the Great Depression, for example, all U.S. federal outlays were only about 3 percent relative to GDP (compared to about 22 percent today).

## 11-2b The Great Depression and World War II

Although classical economists acknowledged that capitalistic, market-oriented economies could experience high unemployment from time to time, the depth and duration of the Depression strained belief in the economy's ability to heal itself. The Great Depression was marked by four consecutive years of contraction during which unemployment reached 25 percent. Investment plunged 80 percent. Many factories sat idle. With vast unemployed resources, output and income fell well short of the economy's potential.

The stark contrast between the natural market adjustments predicted by classical economists and the years of high unemployment during the Great Depression represented a collision of theory and fact. In 1936, John Maynard Keynes, of Cambridge University in England, published *The General Theory of Employment, Interest, and Money,* a book that challenged the classical view and touched off what would later be called the Keynesian revolution. *Keynesian theory and policy were developed*

> **"As a result of the Great Depression, the objective of fiscal policy was no longer to balance the budget but to promote full employment with price stability even if budget deficits resulted."**

*in response to the problem of high unemployment during the Great Depression.* Keynes's main quarrel with the classical economists was that prices and wages did not seem to be flexible enough to ensure the full employment of resources. According to Keynes, prices and wages were relatively inflexible in the downward direction—they were "sticky"—so natural market forces would not return the economy to full employment in a timely fashion. Keynes also believed business expectations could at times become so grim that even very low interest rates would not spur firms to invest all that consumers might save.

Three developments in the years following the Great Depression bolstered the use of discretionary fiscal policy in the United States. The first was the influence of Keynes's *General Theory,* in which he argued that natural forces would not necessarily close a recessionary gap. Keynes thought the economy could get stuck well below its potential, requiring the government to increase aggregate demand to boost output and employment. The second development was the impact of World War II on output and employment. The demands of war greatly increased production and erased cyclical unemployment during the war years, pulling the U.S. economy out of its depression. The third development, largely a consequence of the first two, was the passage of the **Employment Act of 1946**, which gave the federal government responsibility for promoting full employment and price stability.

Prior to the Great Depression, the dominant fiscal policy was a balanced budget. During 1929, the year the stock market crashed, and 1930, the first full year of the Great Depression, the federal budget yielded surpluses. Indeed, to reduce a deficit in 1932, federal tax rates were raised. In the wake of Keynes's *General Theory* and World War II, however, policy makers grew more receptive to the idea that fiscal policy could improve economic stability. The objective of fiscal policy was no longer to balance the budget, but instead to promote full

ESVB0257460   Detroit, Michigan: Closed assembly-lines at the Ford factory in Detroit due to a downturn in sales. 1929   ©Scherl / SV-Bilderdienst / The Image Works

Scherl/SZ Photo/The Image Works

**During the Great Depression, unemployment reached 25 percent, investment fell by 80 percent, and many factories, such as this Ford factory, sat idle.**

**Employment Act of 1946**  Law that assigned to the federal government the responsibility for promoting full employment and price stability employment with price stability even if budget deficits resulted.

## 11-2c Automatic Stabilizers

This chapter so far has focused mostly on discretionary fiscal policy—conscious decisions by public policy makers to change taxes and government spending to achieve the economy's potential output. Now let's get a clearer picture of automatic stabilizers. *Automatic stabilizers smooth out fluctuations in disposable income over the business cycle by stimulating aggregate demand during recessions and dampening aggregate demand during expansions.* Consider the federal income tax. The federal income tax system is progressive, meaning that the fraction of income paid in taxes increases as a taxpayer's income increases. During an economic expansion, employment and incomes rise, moving some taxpayers into higher tax brackets. As a result, taxes claim a growing fraction of income. This slows the growth in disposable income and, hence, slows the growth in consumption. Therefore, the progressive income tax relieves some of the inflationary pressure that might otherwise arise as output increases during an economic expansion. Conversely, when the economy is in recession, output declines, and employment and incomes fall, moving some people into lower tax brackets. As a result, taxes take a smaller bite out of income, so disposable income does not fall as much as GDP. Thus, the progressive income tax cushions declines in disposable income, in consumption, and in aggregate demand.

Another automatic stabilizer is unemployment insurance. During economic expansions, the system automatically increases the flow of unemployment insurance taxes from the income stream into the unemployment insurance fund, thereby moderating consumption and aggregate demand. During contractions, unemployment increases and the system reverses itself.

> **"Automatic stabilizers smooth out fluctuations in disposable income over the business cycle by stimulating aggregate demand during recessions and dampening aggregate demand during expansions."**

Unemployment payments automatically flow from the insurance fund to the unemployed, increasing disposable income and propping up consumption and aggregate demand. Likewise, welfare payments automatically increase during hard times as more people become eligible. *Because of these automatic stabilizers, GDP fluctuates less than it otherwise would, and disposable income varies proportionately less than does GDP.* Because disposable income varies less than GDP does, consumption also fluctuates less than GDP does (as was shown in an earlier chapter's case study).

The progressive income tax, unemployment insurance, and welfare benefits were initially designed not so much as automatic stabilizers but as income redistribution programs. Their roles as automatic stabilizers were secondary effects of the legislation. Automatic stabilizers do not eliminate economic fluctuations, but they do reduce their magnitude. The stronger and more effective the automatic stabilizers are, the less need for discretionary fiscal policy. Because of the greater influence of automatic stabilizers, *the economy is more stable today than it was during the Great Depression and before.* As a measure of just how successful these automatic stabilizers have become in cushioning the impact of recessions, consider this: Since 1948, real GDP declined 10 years, but real consumption fell only four years—in 1974, 1980, 2008, and 2009. *Without much fanfare, automatic stabilizers have been quietly doing their work, keeping the economy on a more even keel.*

## 11-2d From the Golden Age to Stagflation

The 1960s were the Golden Age of fiscal policy. John F. Kennedy was the first president to propose a federal budget deficit to stimulate an economy experiencing a recessionary gap. Fiscal policy was also used on occasion to provide an extra kick to an expansion already under way, as in 1964, when Kennedy's successor, Lyndon B. Johnson, cut income tax rates to keep an expansion alive. *This tax cut, introduced to stimulate business investment, consumption, and employment, was perhaps the shining example of fiscal policy during the Golden Age.* The tax cut seemed to work wonders, increasing disposable income and consumption. The unemployment rate dropped under 5 percent for the first time in seven years, the inflation rate dipped under 2 percent, and the federal budget deficit in 1964 equaled only 0.9 percent of GDP (compared with an average of 3.4 percent between 1980 and 2015).

Discretionary fiscal policy is a demand-management policy; the objective is to increase or decrease aggregate demand to smooth economic fluctuations. But the 1970s brought a different problem—stagflation, the double trouble of higher inflation and higher unemployment resulting from a decrease in aggregate supply. The aggregate supply curve shifted left because of crop failures around the world, sharply higher OPEC-driven oil prices, and other adverse supply shocks. Demand-management policies are ill suited to cure stagflation because an increase of aggregate demand would increase inflation, whereas a decrease of aggregate demand would increase unemployment.

> "Discretionary fiscal policy is a demand-management policy; the objective is to increase or decrease aggregate demand to smooth economic fluctuations."

## 11-3 LIMITS ON FISCAL POLICY'S EFFECTIVENESS

Other concerns besides stagflation also caused policy makers and economists to question the effectiveness of discretionary fiscal policy. These concerns included the difficulty of estimating the natural rate of unemployment, the time lags involved in implementing fiscal policy, the distinction between current income and permanent income, and the possible feedback effects of fiscal policy on aggregate supply. We consider each in turn.

### 11-3a Estimating the Natural Rate of Unemployment

As discussed in the previous chapter, the unemployment that occurs when the economy is producing its potential GDP is called the *natural rate of unemployment*. Before adopting discretionary policies, public officials must correctly estimate this natural rate. Suppose the economy is producing its potential output of $17.0 trillion, as in Exhibit 3, where the natural rate of unemployment is 5.0 percent. Also suppose that public officials mistakenly believe the natural rate to be

*Exhibit 3*

**When Discretionary Fiscal Policy Overshoots Potential Output**

If public officials underestimate the natural rate of unemployment, they may attempt to stimulate aggregate demand even if the economy is already producing its potential output, as at point *a*. This expansionary policy yields a short-run equilibrium at point *b*, where the price level and output are higher and unemployment is lower, so the policy appears to succeed. But the resulting expansionary gap will, in the long run, reduce the short-run aggregate supply curve from $SRAS_{110}$ to $SRAS_{120}$, eventually reducing output to its potential level of $17.0 trillion while increasing the price level to 120. Thus, attempts to increase production beyond potential GDP lead only to inflation in the long run.

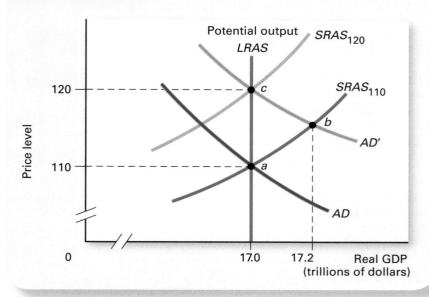

4.0 percent, and they attempt to reduce unemployment and increase real GDP through discretionary fiscal policy. As a result of their policy, the aggregate demand curve shifts to the right, from $AD$ to $AD'$. In the short run, this stimulation of aggregate demand expands output to $17.2 trillion and reduces unemployment to 4.0 percent, so the policy appears successful. But stimulating aggregate demand opens up an expansionary gap, which in the long run results in a leftward shift of the short-run aggregate supply curve. This reduction in aggregate supply pushes up prices and reduces real GDP to $17.0 trillion, the economy's potential. Thus, policy makers initially believe their plan worked, but pushing production beyond the economy's potential leads only to inflation in the long run.

Given the effects of fiscal policy, particularly in the short run, we should not be surprised that elected officials might try to use it to get reelected. Research suggests that public officials use fiscal policy to boost their reelection chances. This has created what some argue is a **political business cycle**, which results from the economic fluctuations that occur when discretionary policy is manipulated for political gain. During an election year, incumbent presidents use expansionary policies to stimulate the economy. For example, a study of 18 industrial economies over three decades found that incumbents boosted healthcare spending during election years.[1] There is also evidence that municipal officials, just before an election, spend more on those public goods most visible to the electorate, such as city parks.[2]

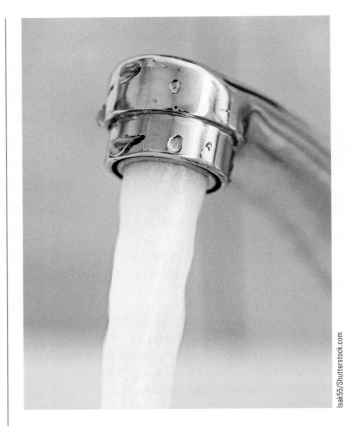

Isak55/Shutterstock.com

## 11-3b Lags in Fiscal Policy

The time required to approve and implement fiscal legislation may hamper its effectiveness and weaken discretionary fiscal policy as a tool of macroeconomic stabilization. Even if a fiscal prescription is appropriate for the economy when proposed, the months

> **"The time required to approve and implement fiscal legislation may hamper its effectiveness."**

and sometimes years required to approve and implement legislation means the medicine could do more harm than good. The policy might kick in only after the economy has already turned itself around. Because a recession is not usually identified until at least six months after it begins, and because the 11 recessions since 1945 lasted only 11 months on average, discretionary fiscal policy allows little room for error (more about timing problems in a later chapter).

## 11-3c Discretionary Fiscal Policy and Permanent Income

It was once believed that discretionary fiscal policy could be turned on and off like a water faucet, stimulating or dampening the economy at the right time by just the right amount. Given the marginal propensity to consume, tax changes could increase or decrease disposable income to bring about desired change in consumption. A more recent view suggests that people

**political business cycles** Economic fluctuations that occur when discretionary policy is manipulated for political gain

1. Niklas Potrafke, "The Growth of Public Health Expenditures in OECD Countries: Do Government Ideology and Electoral Motives Matter?" *Journal of Health Economics*, 29 (December 2010): 797–810.

2. Linda Veiga and Francisco Veiga, "Political Business Cycles at the Municipal Level," *Public Choice*, 131 (April 2007): 45–64.

base their consumption decisions not merely on changes in their current income but also on changes in their permanent income.

**Permanent income** is the income a person expects on average over the long term. Altering tax rates does not affect consumption much if people view the change as only temporary. For example, one-time tax rebates seem to have had little impact on consumption. The stimulative effects of the $117 billion tax-rebate program in early 2008 were disappointing. Surveys showed that only about 20 percent of households spent most of their rebate check. Other households saved most of it or paid down debt.[3] The *temporary* nature of the tax cuts meant that households faced only a small increase in their permanent income. Because permanent income changed little, consumption changed little. In short, *to the extent that consumers base spending decisions on their permanent income, attempts to fine-tune the economy with temporary tax changes are less effective.*

> **"To the extent that consumers base spending decisions on their permanent income, attempts to fine-tune the economy with temporary tax changes are less effective."**

There would be no change in aggregate demand and thus no change in equilibrium real GDP, simply a redistribution of disposable income from the employed to the unemployed.

But could the program affect labor supply? Higher unemployment benefits reduce the opportunity cost of not working, so some job seekers may decide to search at a more leisurely pace. Meanwhile, higher tax rates reduce the opportunity cost of leisure, so some with jobs may decide to work fewer hours. In short, the supply of labor could decrease as a result of higher unemployment benefits funded by higher taxes on earnings. A decrease in the supply of labor would decrease aggregate supply, reducing the economy's potential GDP.

Both automatic stabilizers, such as unemployment insurance, welfare benefits, and the progressive income tax, and discretionary fiscal policies, such as legislated changes in tax rates, may affect individual incentives to work, spend, save, and invest, although these effects are usually unintended consequences. We should keep these secondary effects in mind when we evaluate fiscal policies. It was concern about the effects of taxes on the supply of labor that motivated the tax cuts approved in 1981, when President Reagan and Congress agreed on a 23 percent reduction in average income tax rates to increase aggregate supply. But government spending grew faster than tax revenue, causing higher budget deficits, which stimulated aggregate demand. The incentive effects of the tax cuts on aggregate supply and the stimulus effects of deficit spending on aggregate demand both contributed to the longest peacetime expansion to that point in the nation's history.

# 11-4   FISCAL POLICY FROM 1980 TO 2007

After examining fiscal policy up through the era of stagflation and considering limitations of fiscal policy, you are in a position to look at fiscal policy in recent decades.

## 11-4a Fiscal Policy During the 1980s

So far we have limited the discussion of fiscal policy to its effect on aggregate demand. Fiscal policy may also affect aggregate supply, although this is usually unintentional. For example, suppose the government increases unemployment benefits, paid for by higher taxes on earnings. If the marginal propensity to consume is the same for both groups, the increased spending by beneficiaries just offsets the reduced spending by workers.

## 11-4b 1990 to 2007: From Deficits to Surpluses Back to Deficits

The large federal budget deficits of the 1980s and first half of the 1990s reduced the use of discretionary fiscal policy as a tool for economic

> **permanent income**
> Income that individuals expect to receive on average over the long term

3. See Matthew Shapiro and Joel Slemrod, "Did the 2008 Tax Rebates Stimulate Spending?" *American Economic Review*, 99 (May 2009): 374–379; and Kanishka Misra and Paolo Surico, "Consumption, Income Changes, and Heterogeneity: Evidence from Two Fiscal Stimulus Programs," *American Economic Journal: Macroeconomics*, 6 (October 2014): 84–106.

stabilization. Because deficits were already high during economic expansions, it was hard to justify increasing deficits to stimulate the economy. For example, President Clinton proposed a modest stimulus package in early 1993 to help the recovery that was already under way. His opponents blocked the measure, arguing that it would increase the budget deficit. President George W. Bush's tax cuts during his first term were widely criticized by the opposition as budget-busting sources of a widening deficit.

Clinton did not get his way with his stimulus package, but in 1993, he did manage to substantially increase taxes on high-income households, a group that pays the lion's share of federal income taxes (the top 10 percent of earners pay about 70 percent of federal income taxes collected). The Republican Congress elected in 1994 imposed more discipline on federal spending as part of their plan to balance the budget. Meanwhile, the economy experienced a strong recovery fueled by growing consumer spending, rising business optimism based on technological innovation, market globalization, and the strongest stock market in history. The confluence of these events—higher taxes on the rich, more spending discipline, and a strengthening economy—changed the dynamic of the federal budget. Tax revenues gushed into Washington, growing an average of 8.3 percent per year between 1993 and 1998; meanwhile, federal outlays remained in check, growing only 3.2 percent per year. By 1998, that one-two punch knocked out the federal deficit, a deficit that only six years earlier reached a record at the time of $290 billion. The federal surplus grew from $69 billion in 1998 to $236 billion in 2000.

But in early 2001, the economy suffered a recession, so newly elected President George W. Bush pushed through an across-the-board $1.35 trillion, ten-year tax cut to "get the economy moving again." Then on September 11, 2001, 19 men in four hijacked airplanes ended thousands of lives and reduced the chances of a strong economic recovery. Although the recession lasted only eight months, the recovery was weak, and jobs did not start coming back until the second half of 2003, nearly two years after the recession officially ended. But, between 2003 and 2007, the economy added more than 8 million jobs. By late 2007, the economic expansion, which began in late 2001, had lasted six years, somewhat longer than average for expansions after World War II. The economy peaked in December 2007. The strengthening economy helped cut the federal deficit from $413 billion in 2004 to $161 billion in 2007. Then the economy fell apart.

## 11-5 FISCAL POLICY DURING AND AFTER THE GREAT RECESSION

After peaking in December 2007, the U.S. economy entered a recession, this time precipitated by declining home prices and rising foreclosure rates, as more borrowers failed to make their mortgage payments. The recession began quietly. Many economists doubted that one was even underway (the starting date of December 2007 would not be officially announced until a year later). But as a precaution, Congress and President Bush enacted a $168 billion plan in early 2008 to stimulate the softening economy. The centerpiece was a $117 billion one-time tax rebate of up to $600 for individual filers and up to $1,200 for joint filers. Probably because the tax cuts were temporary, the results were disappointing and the stimulation minimal. As noted already, surveys showed that most households saved the rebate or used it to pay down debt; the marginal propensity to consume from rebate money was estimated to be less than one-third.

After a quiet start, the recession gathered steam. Job losses jumped six fold from an average of 31,000 a month during the first quarter of 2008 to an average of 191,000 a month in the second quarter. Then things got worse. In the third quarter, monthly job losses averaged 334,000.

### 11-5a The Financial Crisis

The problems of falling home prices and rising default rates that simmered throughout 2007 and the first half of 2008 reached a boiling point in September 2008 when Lehman Brothers, the nation's fourth-largest investment bank, with assets of over $600 billion and about 25,000 employees, filed for what became the largest bankruptcy in U.S. history. The financial crisis froze credit markets around the world. Nobody wanted to lend for fear that the borrower might go bankrupt.

Facing financial chaos, public policy makers were emboldened to take some extraordinary measures. The first of these was the Troubled Asset Relief Program, or TARP, passed in October 2008 and aimed at unfreezing financial flows by investing what ultimately totaled to $426 billion in financial institutions and two car makers (these investments became known derisively as "bailouts"). Nearly all of that money was eventually paid back with interest to the U.S. Treasury. TARP, to be discussed in a later chapter, helped calm credit markets, but the economy and the stock market continued to worsen. In the fourth quarter of 2008, real GDP fell 8.2 percent from the previous quarter (at an annualized rate), the largest drop in many decades, and job losses averaged 662,000 a month, or 21 times the average during the first three months of the year. The unemployment rate in 2008 climbed from 5.0 percent in January to 7.4 percent in December, at the time the highest in nearly two decades.

## 11-5b President Obama's Stimulus Package

With the economy bleeding jobs, policy makers had a sense of urgency if not panic. On February 17, 2009, newly-elected President Barack Obama signed the **American Recovery and Reinvestment Act**, a $787 billion package of tax benefits and spending programs aimed at stimulating aggregate demand. The president called the measure "the most sweeping economic recovery package in our history." He predicted the measure would "create or save three and a half million jobs over the next two years." The projected cost would later rise to $831 billion, or about $7,000 per U.S. household.

> **"The rationale for deficit spending is that unemployed labor and idle capital will be put to work."**

According to the White House Website Recovery.gov, which was created to track the stimulus package and its consequences, 37 percent funded tax cuts, 28 percent funded entitlements (such as Medicaid), and 35 percent funded grants, contracts, and loans. Most of the tax cuts were one-time reductions for individuals. Grants, contracts, and loans included some "shovel-ready" infrastructure projects, such as bridges and roads, but these projects were slow to get underway and they represented just a small fraction of stimulus spending (only 4 percent of stimulus funds went to the Federal Highway Administration for road and bridge projects).

The stimulus package was all deficit spending. The rationale for deficit spending is that unemployed labor and idle capital will be put to work. And if the spending multiplier exceeds 1.0, a dollar of government spending should produce more than a dollar of new output and income. Thus, the effectiveness of any stimulus program depends on the size of the tax and spending multipliers. During the debate on the measure, one group of economists argued that the multipliers were less than 1.0 and another group, including the president's economists, argued they were greater than 1.0. Unfortunately, because of chronic deficits since the early 1980s, discretionary fiscal policies had not been used much, at least not explicitly, so few researchers had attempted to measure those effects, and not all those researchers have tried to estimate multipliers.

Still, recent research suggests that *permanent* tax cuts had more of an impact on the economy than spending increases, and of those studies that tried to estimate a government spending multiplier, the average was less than 1.0. For example, a recent study of more than one hundred developing countries between 1970 and 2010 estimated a government spending multiplier of only 0.4.[4]

## 11-5c Fiscal Policy Since 2007

To gain some perspective on fiscal policy during and after the Great Recession, which began in December 2007,

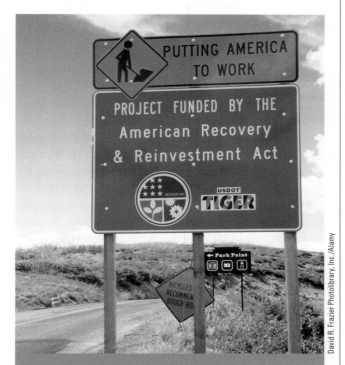

*David R. Frazier Photolibrary, Inc./Alamy*

A small portion of the funds associated with the American Recovery and Reinvestment Act went to direct creation of new jobs through building and improving infrastructure.

4. Aart Kraay, "Government Spending Multipliers in Developing Countries: Evidence from Lending by Official Creditors." *American Economic Journal: Macroeconomics*, 6 (October 2014): 170–208.

**American Recovery and Reinvestment Act**
At an estimated cost of $831 billion, the largest stimulus measure in U.S history; enacted in February 2009

*Exhibit 4*

**Federal Outlays Funded by Revenue and by Borrowing: 2007–2014 (billions of nominal dollars)**

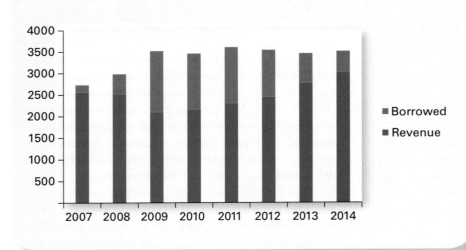

let's look at federal spending and federal deficits during the period. The height of each bar of Exhibit 4 shows nominal federal spending from 2007 through 2014. The blue portion of each bar shows the amount funded by federal revenue sources, such as taxes, charges, and the like. The red portion of each bar shows the amount that was borrowed—that is, deficit financing. For example, in 2007, $2,567 billion of federal spending came from federal revenue and $161 billion was borrowed. Thus, 6 percent of spending that year was borrowed. Real GDP in 2007 increased by 1.8 percent.

Federal spending rose 9.3 percent in 2008, the first full year of the Great Recession. Fifteen percent of federal spending was borrowed in 2008. Real GDP declined 0.3 percent, and 3.6 million jobs were lost. Because of the $831 billion stimulus program signed by President Obama in February 2009, federal spending in 2009 rose 17.8 percent. That's the fastest peacetime growth rate in federal spending since the Great Depression. Of the $3,518 billion spent in 2009, $1,413 had to be borrowed. You can see from Exhibit 4 that the federal deficit grew in 2009 because spending increased and revenue decreased. Alongside the stimulus plan in 2009, automatic stabilizers kicked in to boost spending and reduce revenue. As a result, 40 percent of spending in 2009 had to be borrowed, the highest share of deficit financing since World War II. Despite all the fiscal stimulus coming from a 17.8 percent increase in spending and a $1,413 billion

deficit, real GDP in 2009 declined by 2.8 percent, and the economy lost 5.1 million jobs. Supporters of the stimulus program said the economy would have been much worse without the stimulus. For example, President Obama claimed that this stimulus package prevented another Great Depression.[5]

In 2010, 37 percent of federal spending was borrowed. Real GDP that year rose 2.5 percent, and 1.1 million jobs were added back, making 2010 the first full year of economic recovery. But four years of trillion-dollar deficits seemed to limit federal spending between 2009 and 2014. Notice in Exhibit 4 that after the jump in federal outlays in 2009, nominal federal spending remained relatively flat through 2014. In inflation-adjusted dollars, federal spending actually declined. The share of spending coming from borrowed funds fell, too, from 40 percent in 2009 to 14 percent in 2014. Thus, any fiscal stimulus offered by the federal budget declined between 2009 and 2014, both because real federal spending declined and because deficit spending as a share of total spending declined.

Economists will be debating for years the actual impact of fiscal policy during this period. After the 2.8 percent drop in 2009, real GDP growth averaged 2.2 percent a year between 2010 and 2014. By April 2014 the economy had added all the jobs lost during the Great Recession, and by April 2015 had added another 3 million, for a net job growth of 2.2 percent. Despite that performance, this was still one of the weakest economic recoveries on record (during a comparable period following the sharp recession of 1982, real GDP grew an average of 4.6 percent a year, and after quickly recovering jobs lost during the recession, the economy added 14 million more, for a net job growth of 15.3 percent).

Advocates of the stimulus package argue that the weak recovery showed just how bad off the economy was and just how much this fiscal stimulus was needed. Some said the federal government did not borrow enough or

5. Ross Covin, "Obama Stimulus Plan Halted Economic Freefall: White House," Reuters, 17 February 2010.

spend enough. Another group of economists believe that the fiscal stimulus was not very effective because the government spending multiplier was less than 1.0 and because the large deficits and accumulating debt created an uncertain business climate, a climate that put a damper on economic growth and job creation.

The stimulus measure was never very popular. During his State of the Union address early in the election year of 2012, President Obama did not mention it, nor did he bring it up much during his successful campaign for a second term that year. Regardless of the effect of these deficits on real GDP and employment, what we do know is that federal debt grew $6.7 trillion between 2008 and 2014. The first $6.7 trillion of federal debt took the nation more than 220 years to accumulate, as it did by the end of 2003. Implications of a growing federal debt will be discussed in the next chapter.

It is said that geologists learn more about the nature of the Earth's crust from one major upheaval, such as a huge earthquake or major volcanic eruption, than from a dozen lesser events. The recession of 2007–2009 traumatized the economy and the economics profession.

Events will be dissected for years to develop a clearer understanding of how the economy works and what went wrong.

## 11-6 FINAL WORD

This chapter discussed fiscal policy in theory and in practice. It also examined several factors that reduce the effectiveness of fiscal policy. In the short run, the aggregate supply curve slopes upward, so the impact on equilibrium output of any change in aggregate demand is blunted by a change in the price level. In the long run, aggregate supply is a vertical line, so if the economy is already producing at its potential, the spending multiplier is zero. To the extent that consumers respond primarily to changes in their permanent incomes, temporary changes in taxes affect consumption less, so the tax multiplier is smaller. Various lags in fiscal policy also limit its effectiveness. Discretionary fiscal policy is presented in greater detail in the online appendix.

# STUDY TOOLS 11

### READY TO STUDY? IN THE BOOK, YOU CAN:

☐ Work the Problems at the end of the chapter.

☐ Rip out the chapter review card for a handy summary of the chapter and key terms.

### ONLINE AT CENGAGEBRAIN.COM YOU CAN:

☐ Collect StudyBits while you read and study the chapter.

☐ Quiz yourself on key concepts.

☐ Prepare for tests with chapter flash cards as well as flash cards that you create.

☐ Watch videos to explore economics further.

# CHAPTER 11 PROBLEMS

*Your instructor can access the answers to these problems online at http://cengagebrain.com.*

## 11-1 Describe the discretionary fiscal policies to close a recessionary gap and an expansionary gap

1. *(Fiscal Policy)* Define *fiscal policy*. Determine whether each of the following, other factors held constant, would, in the short run, lead to an increase, a decrease, or no change in the level of real GDP demanded:
   a. A decrease in government purchases
   b. An increase in net taxes
   c. A reduction in transfer payments
   d. A decrease in the marginal propensity to consume

2. *(Recessionary Gap)* What is a recessionary gap? What fiscal policy might close that gap? Show with a graph.

3. *(Expansionary Gap)* What is an expansionary gap? What fiscal policy might close that gap? Show with a graph.

4. *(Changes in Government Purchases)* Assume that government purchases decrease by $10 billion, with other factors held constant, including the price level. Calculate the change in the level of real GDP demanded for each of the following values of the MPC. Then, calculate the change if the government, instead of reducing its purchases, increased autonomous net taxes by $10 billion.
   a. 0.9
   b. 0.8
   c. 0.75
   d. 0.6

5. *(Fiscal Multipliers)* Explain the difference between the government purchases multiplier and the net tax multiplier. If the MPC falls, what happens to the tax multiplier?

6. *(Multipliers)* Suppose investment, in addition to having an autonomous component, also has a component that varies directly with the level of real GDP. How would this affect the size of the spending multiplier?

7. *(Fiscal Policy)* Chapter 11 shows that increased government purchases, with taxes held constant, can eliminate a recessionary gap. How could a tax cut achieve the same result?

8. *(Fiscal Policy with an Expansionary Gap)* Using the aggregate demand–aggregate supply model, illustrate an economy with an expansionary gap. If the government is to close the gap by changing government purchases, should it increase or decrease those purchases? In the long run, what happens to the level of real GDP as a result of government intervention? What happens to the price level? Illustrate this on an *AD–AS* diagram, assuming that the government changes its purchases by exactly the amount necessary to close the gap.

## 11-2 Summarize fiscal policy from the Great Depression to stagflation

9. *(Evolution of Fiscal Policy)* What did classical economists assume about the flexibility of prices, wages, and interest rates? What did this assumption imply about the self-correcting tendencies in an economy in recession? What disagreements did Keynes have with classical economists?

10. *(Fiscal Policy)* Was fiscal policy effective when the U.S. economy was experiencing stagflation during the 1970s? Why or why not?

## 11-3 Identify some reasons why discretionary fiscal policy may not work very well

11. *(Fiscal Policy Effectiveness)* Determine whether each of the following would make fiscal policy more effective or less effective:
    a. A decrease in the marginal propensity to consume
    b. Shorter lags in the effect of fiscal policy
    c. Consumers suddenly becoming more concerned about permanent income than about current income
    d. More accurate measurement of the natural rate of unemployment

## 11-4 Summarize fiscal policy during the 1980s and 1990s. When and why did the federal budget show a surplus?

12. What are some reasons why the federal government showed a surplus in the late 1990s? Why did that surplus disappear?

## 11-5 Summarize fiscal policy during and after the Great Recession.

13. *(Fiscal Policy During the Great Recession)* Using the aggregate demand–aggregate supply model, illustrate what President Obama was trying to accomplish with the $831 billion stimulus program. What were some costs and benefits of this program?

# 12 | Federal Budgets and Public Policy

## LEARNING OUTCOMES

After studying this chapter, you will be able to...

**12-1** Summarize how federal spending priorities have changed since the 1960s

**12-2** Explain why the federal budget has been in deficit in most years since the Great Depression

**12-3** Outline what has happened to the federal debt in recent decades and how it compares with debt levels in other countries

**12-4** Describe how a giant federal debt could have a negative impact on the economy

After finishing this chapter go to **PAGE 223** for **STUDY TOOLS**

**Topics discussed in Chapter 12 include:**

- The federal budget process
- Rationale for deficit spending
- Impact of federal deficits
- Crowding out and crowding in
- The short-lived budget surplus
- Federal debt
- The sustainability of federal debt

- How big is the U.S. federal budget, and where does the money go?
- Why is the federal budget process such a tangled web?
- In what sense is the federal budgeting process at odds with discretionary fiscal policy?
- How is a sluggish economy like an empty restaurant?

- Why has the federal budget been in deficit most years?
- What is the federal debt, and who owes it to whom?
- Can a nation run deficits year after year and decade after decade?

*Answers to these and other questions are examined in this chapter, which considers federal budgeting in theory and practice.*

The word *budget* derives from the Old French word *bougette*, which means "little bag." The federal budget is now about $4,000,000,000,000—$4 trillion a year. That's big money! If this "little bag" held $100 bills, it would weigh 42,000 *tons*! These $100 bills could paper over a 24-lane highway stretching from northern Maine to southern California. A $4 trillion stack of $100 bills would tower 2,600 miles high. Here's another way to appreciate the size of the federal budget: If all 4,600 tons of gold stored in Fort Knox were sold at the mid-2015 price of $1,100 per ounce, the proceeds would fund the federal government for only about two weeks.

> "How big is the federal budget, and where does the money go?"

Government budgets have a tremendous impact on the economy. Government outlays at all levels amount to about 38 percent relative to gross domestic product (GDP). Our focus in this chapter will be the federal budget, beginning with the budget process. We then look at federal deficits. We also examine the national debt and its impact on the economy. At some point, a giant federal debt could cripple the nation. Because you and your classmates will inherit liability for the federal debt, you may have a particular interest in this material.

## 12-1 THE FEDERAL BUDGET PROCESS

The **federal budget** is a plan of outlays and revenues for a specified period, usually a year. Federal *outlays* include both government purchases and transfer payments. Exhibit 1 shows U.S. federal outlays by major category since 1960. As you can see, the share of outlays going to national defense dropped from over half in 1960 to only 15 percent in 2016. Social Security's share has grown every decade. Medicare, medical care for the elderly, was introduced in 1965 and has also grown sharply. In fact, Social Security and Medicare, programs aimed primarily at the elderly, combined for 38 percent of federal outlays in 2016. For the last two decades, welfare spending, which consists of cash and in-kind transfer payments, has remained relatively stable, and in 2016 accounted for almost 14 percent of federal outlays. And, thanks to record low interest rates, interest payments on the federal debt were a little over 7 percent of federal outlays in 2016, down from 15 percent as recently as 1996. So 52 percent, or more than half the federal budget, redistributes income (Social Security, Medicare, and welfare); 15 percent goes for national defense; 7 percent services the federal debt; and the remaining 25 percent pays for everything else in the federal budget—from environmental protection to federal prisons to federal education aid. Note that the spike in "All Other Outlays" in 2009 was caused by the $831 billion stimulus package passed early that year.

Since the 1960s, the federal government has shifted its focus from national defense to income redistribution. Again, U.S. federal outlays in 2016 totaled about $4 trillion, or about $12,200 per capita.

**federal budget** A plan for federal government outlays and revenues for a specified period, usually a year

*Exhibit 1*

**Defense's Share of Federal Outlays Declined Since 1960 and Redistribution Increased**

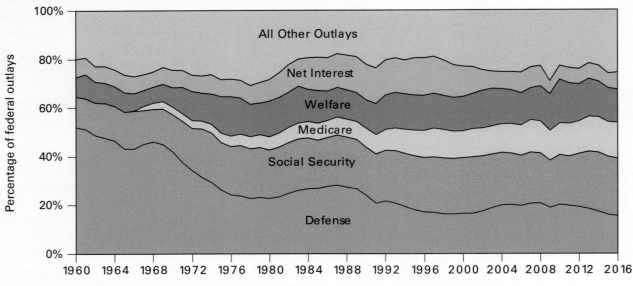

Sources: Computed based on budget totals from *Economic Report of the President*, February 2015, Table B-21; and the Office of Management and Budget. For the most recent year, go to http://www .gpoaccess.gov/eop/. Percentage shares for 2015 and 2016 are estimates based on the president's budget.

## 12-1a Presidential and Congressional Roles

The president's budget proposal begins to take shape a year before it is submitted to Congress, with each agency preparing a budget request. In late January or early February, the president submits to Congress *The Budget of the U.S. government,* a pile of books detailing spending and revenue proposals for the upcoming fiscal year, which begins October 1. At this stage, the president's budget is little more than detailed suggestions for congressional consideration. About the same time, the president's Council of Economic Advisers sends Congress the *Economic Report of the President*, which offers the president's take on the economy.

Budget committees in both the House and the Senate rework the president's budget until they agree on total outlays, spending by major category, and expected

> **"Social Security and Medicare outlays have grown sharply, while welfare spending has remained relatively stable."**

**budget resolution** A congressional agreement about total outlays, spending by major category, and expected revenues; it guides spending and revenue decisions by the many congressional committees and subcommittees

revenues. This agreement, called a **budget resolution**, guides spending and revenue decisions made by the many congressional committees and subcommittees. The budget cycle is supposed to end before October 1, the start of the new fiscal year. Before that date, Congress should have approved detailed plans for outlays along with revenue projections. Thus, the federal budget has a congressional gestation period of about nine months—though, as noted, the president's budget usually begins taking shape a year before it's submitted to Congress.

The size and composition of the budget and the difference between outlays and revenues measure the budget's fiscal impact on the economy. *When outlays exceed revenues, the budget is in deficit. A deficit stimulates aggregate demand in the short run but increases the federal debt and reduces national saving, which in the long run could impede economic growth. Alternatively, when revenues exceed outlays, the federal budget is in surplus. A surplus dampens aggregate demand in the short run but reduces the federal debt and boosts domestic saving, which in the long run could promote economic growth.*

> **"When outlays exceed revenues, the budget is in deficit. A deficit stimulates aggregate demand in the short run but increases the federal debt and reduces national saving, which in the long run could impede economic growth."**

## 12-1b Problems With the Federal Budget Process

The federal budget process sounds good on paper, but it does not work that well in practice. Here are some problems.

### Continuing Resolutions Instead of Budget Decisions

Congress often ignores the timetable for developing and approving a budget. Because deadlines are frequently missed, budgets typically run from year to year based on **continuing resolutions**, which are agreements to allow agencies, in the absence of an approved budget, to spend at the rate of the previous year's budget. Poorly conceived programs continue through sheer inertia; successful programs cannot expand. For example, beginning in 2009, the U.S. Senate failed to pass a budget for three years in a row. During that stretch, the federal government was funded by one continuing resolution after another, and all this was accompanied by huge budget deficits.

### Lengthy Budget Process

You can imagine the difficulty of using the budget as a tool of discretionary fiscal policy when the budget process takes so long and relies on continuing resolutions. Given that the average recession since World War II has lasted only eleven months and that budget preparations begin more than a year and a half before the budget takes effect, planning discretionary fiscal measures to reduce economic fluctuations is difficult if not impossible. That's one reason why attempts to stimulate an ailing economy often seem so halfhearted; by the time Congress and the president agree on a fiscal remedy, the economy has usually recovered on its own.

### Uncontrollable Spending Categories

Congress has only limited control over much of the budget. *Most federal outlays are determined by existing laws.* For example, once Congress establishes eligibility criteria, **entitlement programs,** such as Social Security, Medicare, and Medicaid, take on lives of their own, with each annual appropriation simply reflecting the amount required to support the expected number of entitled beneficiaries. Healthcare reform introduced another major entitlement program, the cost of which has not yet been fully calculated. Congress has no say in such appropriations unless it chooses to change benefits or eligibility criteria. Most entitlement programs have such politically powerful constituencies that Congress is reluctant to mess with the structure.

> **"Most federal outlays are determined by existing laws."**

### Overly Detailed Budget

The federal budget is divided into thousands of accounts and subaccounts, which is why it fills volumes. To the extent that the budget is a way of making political payoffs, such micromanagement allows elected officials to reward friends and punish enemies with great precision. For example, a recent budget included $176,000 for the Reindeer Herders Association in Alaska, $400,000 for the Southside Sportsman Club in New York, and $5 million for an insect-rearing facility in Mississippi. By budgeting in such detail, Congress may lose sight of the big picture. When economic conditions change or when the demand for certain public goods shifts, the federal government

**continuing resolutions** Budget agreements that allow agencies, in the absence of an approved budget, to spend at the rate of the previous year's budget

**entitlement programs** Guaranteed benefits for those who qualify for government transfer programs such as Social Security and Medicare cannot easily reallocate funds. Detailed budgeting is not only time consuming, but it also reduces the flexibility of discretionary fiscal policy and is subject to political abuse.

## 12-1c Possible Budget Reforms

Some reforms might improve the budget process. First, the annual budget could become a two-year budget, or *biennial budget*. As it is, Congress spends nearly all of the year working on the budget, and even then sometimes fails to pass one, as noted already. The executive branch is always dealing with three budgets: administering an approved budget, defending a proposed budget before congressional committees, and preparing the next budget for submission to Congress. With a two-year budget, Congress would not be continually involved with budget deliberations, and cabinet members could focus more on running their agencies (many states have adopted two-year budgets). A two-year budget, however, would require longer-term economic forecasts and would be less useful than a one-year budget as a tool of discretionary fiscal policy.

Another possible reform would be to simplify the budget document by concentrating only on major groupings and eliminating line items. Each agency head would receive a total budget, along with the discretion to allocate that budget in a manner consistent with the perceived demands for agency services. The drawback is that agency heads may have different priorities than those of elected representatives. On the plus side, elected officials would be less able to insert favorite pork-barrel projects into the budget.

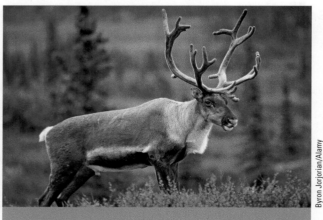

A recent federal budget included $176,000 for the Reindeer Herders Association in Alaska.

Byron Jorjorian/Alamy

# 12-2 FISCAL IMPACT OF THE FEDERAL BUDGET

When government outlays—government purchases plus cash and in-kind transfer programs—exceed government revenue, the result is a *budget deficit*, a flow measure already introduced. Although the federal budget was in surplus from 1998 to 2001, before that it had been in deficit every year but one since 1960. After 2001 the budget slipped back into the red, where it remains. To place federal deficits in perspective, let's first examine the economic rationale for deficit financing.

## 12-2a The Rationale for Deficits

Deficit financing has been justified for outlays that increase the economy's productivity—capital outlays for investments such as highways, waterways, and dams. The cost of these capital projects should be borne in part by future taxpayers, who will also benefit from these investments. Thus, there is some justification for shifting some of the cost of capital projects to future taxpayers. State and local governments issue debt to fund capital projects, such as schools and infrastructure. But the federal government does not issue bonds to fund specific capital projects.

Before the Great Depression, federal deficits occurred primarily during wartime. Because wars often impose great hardship on the population, public officials have been understandably reluctant to tax citizens still more to finance war-related spending. Deficits during wars were largely self-correcting, however, because military spending dropped after a war, but tax revenue did not.

The Great Depression led John Maynard Keynes to argue that public spending should offset any drop in private spending. As you know by now, Keynes argued that a federal budget deficit would stimulate aggregate demand. As a result of the Great Depression, automatic stabilizers were also introduced, which increased public outlays during recessions and decreased them during expansions. Deficits increase during recessions because tax revenues decline while spending programs such as unemployment benefits and welfare increase. For example, between 2007 and 2009, corporate tax revenue fell 62 percent but welfare spending jumped 45 percent. An economic expansion reverses these flows. As the economy picks up, so do personal income and corporate profits, boosting tax revenue. Unemployment compensation and welfare spending decline. Thus, federal deficits usually fall during the recovery stage of the business cycle.

## 12-2b Budget Philosophies and Deficits

Several budget philosophies have emerged over the years. Prior to the Great Depression, fiscal policy focused on maintaining an **annually balanced budget,** except during wartime. Because tax revenues rise during expansions and fall during recessions, an annually balanced budget means that spending increases during expansions and declines during recessions. But such a pattern magnifies fluctuations in the business cycle, overheating the economy during expansions and increasing unemployment during recessions.

A second budget philosophy calls for a **cyclically balanced budget**, meaning that deficits during recessions are paid for by surpluses during expansions. Such a fiscal policy dampens swings in the business cycle without increasing the federal debt. Nearly all state governments have "rainy day" funds to build up budget surpluses during the good times for use during hard times.

A third budget philosophy is **functional finance**, which says that policy makers should be concerned less with balancing the budget annually, or even over the business cycle, and more with ensuring that the economy produces its potential output. If the budgets needed to keep the economy producing its potential involve chronic deficits, so be it. Since the Great Depression, budgets in this country have seldom balanced. *Although budget deficits have been larger during recessions than during expansions, the federal budget has been in deficit in all but 14 years since 1929.* One major problem with functional finance is that chronic deficits accumulate into a federal debt that at some point could cripple an economy.

## 12-2c Federal Deficits Since the Birth of the Nation

Between 1789, when the U.S. Constitution was adopted, and 1929, the year the Great Depression started, the federal budget was in deficit 33 percent of the time, primarily during war years. After a war, government spending dropped more than government revenue. Thus, deficits arising during wars were largely self-correcting once the wars ended.

Since the onset of the Great Depression, however, federal budgets have been in deficit in 84 percent of the years. Exhibit 2 shows federal

**annually balanced budget** Budget philosophy prior to the Great Depression; aimed at matching annual revenues with outlays, except during times of war

**cyclically balanced budget** A budget philosophy calling for budget deficits during recessions to be financed by budget surpluses during expansions

**functional finance** A budget philosophy using fiscal policy to achieve the economy's potential GDP, rather than balancing budgets either annually or over the business cycle

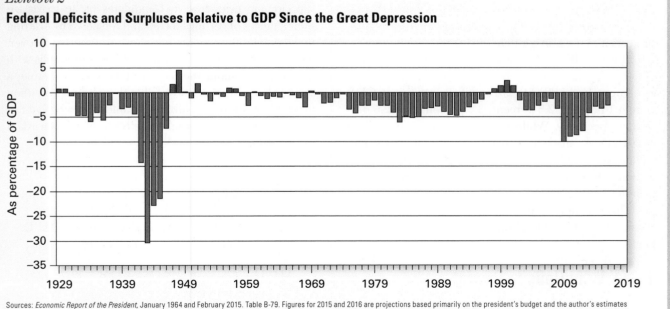

*Exhibit 2*

**Federal Deficits and Surpluses Relative to GDP Since the Great Depression**

Sources: *Economic Report of the President*, January 1964 and February 2015. Table B-79. Figures for 2015 and 2016 are projections based primarily on the president's budget and the author's estimates of GDP. For the latest data, go to http://www.gpoaccess.gov/eop/.

deficits and surpluses as a percentage of GDP since 1929. Unmistakable are the huge deficits during World War II, which dwarf deficits in other years. Turning now to the last few decades, we see the relatively large deficits of the 1980s. These resulted from large tax cuts along with higher defense spending. Supply-side economists argued that tax cuts would stimulate enough economic activity to keep tax revenues from falling. Unspecified cuts in federal spending were supposed to erase a projected deficit, but Congress never made the promised cuts. In short, the president and Congress cut tax rates but not expenditures.

As the economy improved during the 1990s, the deficit decreased and then disappeared, turning into a surplus by 1998. But a recession in 2001, tax cuts, and higher federal spending turned surpluses into deficits. A weak recovery and the cost of fighting the war against terrorism worsened the deficits to 3.5 percent relative to GDP by 2003. But over the next four years, a stronger economy along with a rising stock market increased federal revenue enough to drop the deficit to about 1.2 percent relative to GDP in 2007.

Because of the global financial crisis and the Great Recession of 2007–2009, federal deficits relative to GDP swelled to levels not seen since World War II. The recession reduced revenues and expanded outlays, especially the $831 billion American Reinvestment and Recovery Act, more popularly known as the stimulus program. The 2009 deficit was $1.4 trillion, or 9.8 percent relative to GDP. Deficits topped $1 trillion each year through 2012. Relative to GDP, deficits were 8.6 percent in 2010, 8.4 percent in 2011, and 6.7 percent in 2012. Except for World War II, these were the largest deficits in the nation's history relative to GDP, even larger than during the Great Depression. From 2009 to 2012, about 36 cents of every dollar of federal spending had to be borrowed, much of it from foreigners. From 2013 to 2016, deficits relative to GDP were 4.1 percent, 2.8 percent, 3.2 percent, and 2.5 percent, respectively. While moderate compared to 2009 to 2012 levels, these four years still added more than $2 trillion to the federal debt. The President's budget projection, which some called optimistic, add another $4.4 trillion to federal debt between 2017 and 2024.

That's a short history of federal deficits. Now let's consider why the federal budget has been in deficit so long.

## 12-2d Why Deficits Persist

As we have seen, recent deficits climbed as the global financial crisis spilled into the wider economy, decreasing tax revenues and increasing government outlays. But

Spirit of america/Shutterstock.com

**Candidates try to maximize their chance of getting elected by offering budgets long on benefits but short on taxes.**

why has the budget been in deficit for all but 14 years since 1929? The most obvious answer is that, unlike budgeters in 49 states, federal officials are not required to balance the budget. But why deficits rather than balanced budgets or even surpluses? One widely accepted model of the public sector assumes that elected officials try to maximize their political support, including votes and campaign contributions. Voters like spending programs but hate paying taxes, so public spending wins support and taxes lose it. Candidates try to maximize their chances of getting elected and reelected by offering budgets long on benefits but short on taxes. Moreover, members of Congress push their favorite programs with little concern about the overall budget. For example, a senator from Mississippi was able to include $1.5 billion in a budget for an amphibious assault ship to be built in his hometown of Pascagoula. The Navy never even asked for the ship.

> ❝Voters like spending programs but hate paying taxes, so public spending wins support and taxes lose it.❞

## 12-2e Deficits, Surpluses, Crowding Out, and Crowding In

What effect do federal deficits and surpluses have on interest rates? Recall that interest rates affect investment, a critical component of economic growth. What's more, year-to-year fluctuations in investment are a primary source of shifts in the aggregate demand curve. Let's look at the impact of government deficits and surpluses on investment.

> ❝Higher interest rates discourage, or *crowd out*, some private investment, reducing the stimulating effect of the government's deficit.❞

Suppose the federal government increases spending without raising taxes, thereby increasing the budget deficit. How will this affect national saving, interest rates, and investment? An increase in the federal deficit reduces the supply of national saving, leading to higher interest rates. Higher interest rates discourage, or *crowd out*, some private investment, reducing the stimulating effect of the government's deficit. The extent of **crowding out** is a matter of debate. Some economists argue that although government deficits may displace some private-sector borrowing, expansionary fiscal policy results in a net increase in aggregate demand, leading to greater output and employment in the short run. Others believe that the crowding out is more extensive, so borrowing from the public in this way results in little or no net increase in aggregate demand and output.

Although crowding out is likely to occur to some degree, there is another possibility. If the economy is operating well below its potential, the additional fiscal stimulus provided by a higher government deficit could encourage some firms to invest more. Recall that an important determinant of investment is business expectations. Government stimulus of a weak economy could put a sunny face on the business outlook. As expectations grow more favorable, firms become more willing to invest. This ability of government deficits to stimulate private investment is sometimes called **crowding in**, to distinguish it from crowding out. Between 1993 and 2013, the Japanese government pursued deficit spending that averaged 6.5 percent relative to GDP as a way of getting that flat economy going, but with only limited success.

Were you ever reluctant to patronize a restaurant because it was too crowded? You simply did not want to put up with the hassle and long wait and were thus "crowded out." Similarly, high government deficits may "crowd out" some investors by driving up interest rates. On the other hand, did you ever pass up an unfamiliar restaurant because the place seemed dead—it had no customers? Perhaps you wondered why? If you had seen just a few customers, you might have stopped in—you might have been willing to "crowd in." Similarly, businesses may be reluctant to invest in a seemingly lifeless economy. The economic stimulus resulting from deficit spending could encourage some investors to "crowd in."

## 12-2f The Twin Deficits

To finance the huge deficits, the U.S. Treasury must sell a lot of government IOUs. To get people to buy more of these Treasury securities, the government must offer higher interest rates, other things constant. So funding a higher deficit pushes up the market interest rates, other things constant. With U.S. interest rates higher, foreigners find Treasury securities more attractive. But to buy them, foreigners must first exchange their currencies for dollars. This greater demand for dollars causes the dollar to appreciate relative to foreign currencies. The rising value of the dollar makes foreign goods cheaper in the United States and U.S. goods more expensive abroad. Thus, U.S. imports increase and U.S. exports decrease, so the trade deficit increases.

Higher trade deficits

> **crowding out** The displacement of interest-sensitive private investment that occurs when higher government deficits drive up market interest rates

> **crowding in** The potential for government spending to stimulate private investment in an otherwise dead economy

© Thinkstock Images/Getty Images; Photodisc/Getty Images

mean that foreigners have dollars left over after they buy all the U.S. goods and services they want. With these accumulated dollars, foreigners buy U.S. assets, including U.S. government securities, and thereby help fund federal deficits. The increase in funds from abroad is both good news and bad news for the U.S. economy. The supply of foreign saving increases investment spending in the United States over what would have occurred in the absence of these funds. Ask people what they think of foreign investment in their town; they will likely say it's great. But foreign funds to some extent simply offset a decline in U.S. saving. Such a pattern could pose problems in the long run. The United States has surrendered a certain amount of control over its economy to foreign investors. And the return on foreign investments in the United States flows abroad. For example, a growing share of the federal government's debt is now owed to foreigners, as discussed later in the chapter.

America was once the world's leading creditor. Now it's the lead debtor nation, borrowing huge sums from abroad, helping in the process to fund the federal deficit. Some critics blame U.S. fiscal policy as reflected in the large federal deficits for the switch from creditor to debtor nation. Japan and China are big buyers of U.S. Treasury securities. A debtor country becomes more beholden to those countries that supply credit.

## 12-2g A Short-Lived Budget Surplus Then More Deficits

Exhibit 3 summarizes the federal budget since 1970, showing outlays relative to GDP as the red line and revenues relative to GDP as the blue line. These percentages offer an overall look at the federal government's role in the economy. Between 1970 and 2016, federal outlays averaged 20.4 percent and revenues averaged 17.4 percent relative to GDP. When outlays exceed revenues, the federal budget is in deficit, measured each year by the vertical distance between the blue and red lines. Thus, on average, the federal budget has had a deficit of 3.0 percent relative to GDP. The pink shading shows the annual deficit as a percent of GDP between 1970 and 2016. In the early 1990s, federal outlays started to decline relative to GDP, while revenues increased. This shrank the deficit and, by 1998, created a surplus, as indicated by the blue shading. Specifically, the deficit in 1990, which amounted to 3.8 percent relative to GDP, became a surplus by 1998, which lasted through 2001. What turned a hefty deficit into a surplus, and why has the surplus turned back into an even bigger deficit?

### Tax Increases

With concern about the deficits of the 1980s growing, Congress and President George H. W. Bush agreed in 1990 to a package of spending cuts and tax increases aimed

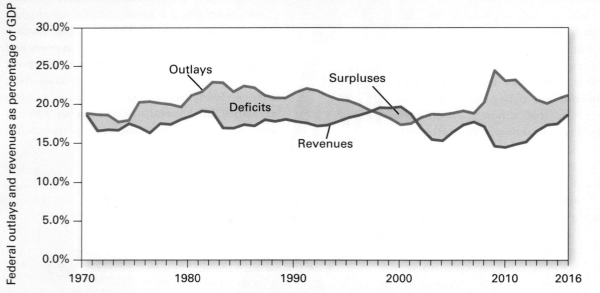

*Exhibit 3*

**The Great Recession of 2007–2009 Cut Federal Revenues and Increased Federal Outlays, Resulting in Huge Deficits**

Sources: *Economic Report of the President*, February 2015, Tables B-2 and B-21, and the Office of Management and Budget. Figures for 2015 and 2016 are projections based primarily on the president's budget. For the latest data, go to http://www.gpoaccess.gov/eop/.

at trimming budget deficits. Ironically, those tax increases not only may have cost President Bush reelection in 1992 (because they violated his 1988 election promise of "no new taxes"), but they also began the groundwork for erasing the budget deficit, for which President Bill Clinton was able to take credit. For his part, President Clinton increased taxes on high-income households in 1993, boosting the top marginal tax rate from 31 percent to 40 percent. The economy also enjoyed a vigorous recovery during the 1990s, fueled by rising worker productivity, growing consumer spending, globalization of markets, and a strong stock market. The combined effects of higher taxes on the rich and a strengthening economy raised federal revenue from 17.8 percent of GDP in 1990 to 20.1 percent in 2000. That may not seem like much of a difference, but it translated into an additional $240 billion in federal revenue in 2000.

## Slower Growth in Federal Outlays

Because of spending discipline imposed by the 1990 legislation, growth in federal outlays slowed compared to the 1980s. What's more, the collapse of the Soviet Union reduced U.S. military commitments abroad. Between 1990 and 2000, the number of military personnel dropped by one-third and defense spending dropped 30 percent in real terms. An additional impetus for slower spending growth came from Republicans, who attained congressional majority in 1994. Between 1994 and 2000, domestic spending grew little in real terms. Another beneficial development was a drop in interest rates, which fell to their lowest level in thirty years, saving billions in interest charges on the federal debt. In short, federal outlays dropped from 21.6 percent relative to GDP in 1990 to 17.4 percent in 2000. Again, if federal outlays remained the same percentage of GDP in 2000 as in 1990, federal spending in 2000 would have been $430 billion higher than it was.

## A Reversal of Fortune in 2001

Thanks to the tax-rate increases and the strong economy, revenues gushed into Washington, growing an average of 8.4 percent per year between 1993 and 2000. Meanwhile, federal outlays remained in check, growing only 3.5 percent per year. By 2000, that combination created a federal budget surplus of $236 billion, quite a turnaround from a deficit that had topped $290 billion in 1992. But in 2001 unemployment increased, the stock market sank, and terrorists crashed jets into buildings and spread anthrax. All this slowed federal revenues and accelerated federal spending. To counter the recession and cope with terrorism, Congress and the president cut taxes and increased federal spending. As a result, the federal budget surplus returned to a deficit by 2002 and has been in the red ever since. The era of federal budget surpluses was short-lived.

## Trillion-Dollar Deficits

The financial crisis of 2008 and the Great Recession of 2007–2009 increased budget deficits for two reasons. On the revenue side, falling employment, income, and profits cut tax receipts. Discretionary tax cuts reduced revenue even more. Revenues dropped from 17.7 percent relative to GDP in 2007 to only 14.6 percent in 2009. On the spending side, automatic stabilizers such as unemployment benefits and welfare payments increased federal outlays, as did discretionary spending such as bailouts and the $831 billion stimulus plan. Federal outlays jumped from 18.8 percent relative to GDP in 2007 to 24.4 percent in 2009. The federal deficit climbed from $161 billion in 2007 to $459 billion in 2008 to $1.4 trillion in 2009. Even after the recession ended, the federal deficit remained stub-bornly high, topping $1.0 trillion in 2010, 2011, and 2012.

## Sequestration

Faced with large deficits and a growing debt far into the future, policy makers looked for ways to slow the growth of spending. In 2011, President Barack Obama and Congressional leaders agreed that if their efforts to curb spending failed, automatic cuts would kick in. That alternative, called **sequestration**, seemed so crude and so broad that officials believed that just the threat of it would force them to adopt a more rational strategy. But guess what? Congress and the president couldn't agree on how to slow spending growth, so sequestration took hold. Sequestration refers to automatic cuts to certain categories of federal spending between 2012 and 2021 to slow spending growth by a total of $1.1 trillion. Some major programs such as Social Security, Medicaid, federal pensions, and veterans benefits were exempt. Defense spending was cut the most.

The cuts amounted to about $85 billion a year, or about 2.4 percent of the budget. That does not sound like much, but with some major programs exempt, other programs got

**sequestration**
Automatic cuts to certain categories of federal spending enacted in 2011 to reduce the growth of federal spending from 2012 to 2021

*Exhibit 4*

**Government Outlays as a Percentage of GDP in 1997 and 2016**

Government outlays relative to GDP increased in 7 of the 10 industrial economies between 1997 and 2016. The 10-country average increased slightly from 42 percent to 43 percent. In the United States, the percentage increased from 36 to 38.

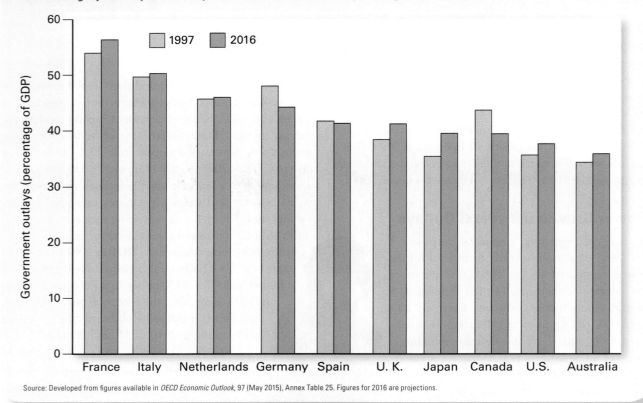

Source: Developed from figures available in *OECD Economic Outlook,* 97 (May 2015), Annex Table 25. Figures for 2016 are projections.

hammered. Compared to pre-sequester spending levels, defense was cut by an average of 9 percent a year, for a total of $454 billion between 2012 and 2021. Nondefense spending programs that were not exempt were cut by 6.5 percent a year, for a total of $294 billion. In a separate action, Medicare was cut by 2 percent, or $170 billion. Because less would be borrowed as a result of sequestration, interest payments on the debt would be cut by $170 billion. The sequester helped keep federal spending flat in 2012, 2013, and 2014 (see Exhibit 4 in the previous chapter).

Few liked the sequester, but alternative ways of cutting the growth in spending did not emerge. With defense spending particularly hard hit, policy makers looked for ways of getting around the sequester. In May 2015, Congress created a separate account not subject to the sequester to augment defense spending.[1] As a result of this breach of sequestration, the law may lose its effectiveness.

1. Nick Timoras, "U.S. Posts Biggest Monthly Surplus in Seven Years," *Wall Street Journal,* 13 May 2015.

### 12-2h The Relative Size of the Public Sector

So far, we have focused on the federal budget, but a fuller picture includes state and local governments as well. For added context, we can look at government budgets over time compared to other major economies. Exhibit 4 shows government outlays at all levels relative to GDP in 10 industrial economies in 1997 and in 2016. Government outlays in the United States relative to GDP increased from 36 percent in 1997 to 38 percent in 2016. Despite the increase, the United States is projected to have a smaller public sector in 2016 than all but one of the other listed countries. Outlays relative to GDP increased in seven of the major economies and decreased in three. The 10-country average increased slightly from 42 percent to 43 percent. Government grew the most in Japan, rising from 35 percent relative to GDP in 1997 to 39 percent in 2016. Two decades of trying to stimulate the Japanese economy swelled the public sector. Government spending shrank the most in Canada, dropping from 44 percent to 39 percent relative to GDP.

*Exhibit 5*

**Federal Debt Held by the Public as Percent of GDP Spiked Because of World War II and the Great Recession**

The huge cost of World War II rocketed federal debt from 44 percent of GDP in 1940 to over 100 percent by 1946. During the next few decades, GDP grew faster than federal debt so by 1980, federal debt had dropped to only 26 percent of GDP. But high deficits in recent years increased federal debt to 75 percent relative to GDP by 2016. That's double the percentage in 2007 and the highest since the early 1950s.

Source: Figures for 2015 and 2016 are estimated based on the president's 2016 budget proposal. Computed by the author based on fiscal year figures from the *Economic Report of the President*, February 2013, Table B-79; and Economic Report of the President, February 2015, Table B-22; plus updates from budget deliberations. For the latest data, go to http://www.gpoaccess.gov/eop/.

Let's now turn our attention to a consequence of federal deficits—a sizable federal debt.

# 12-3 THE NATIONAL DEBT IN PERSPECTIVE

Federal deficits add up. It took 39 presidents, six wars, the Great Depression, and more than 200 years for the federal debt to reach $1 trillion, as it did in 1981. It took only five presidents and 35 years for that debt to increase more than fivefold in real terms, as it did by 2016. The federal deficit is a flow variable measuring the amount by which outlays exceed revenues in a particular year. The federal debt, or the **national debt**, is a stock variable measuring the net accumulation of past deficits, the amount owed by the federal government. This section puts the national debt in perspective by looking at (1) changes over time, (2) U.S. government debt levels compared with those in other countries, (3) interest payments on the national debt, (4) who bears the burden of the national debt, and (5) what impact does the national debt have on the nation's future. Note that the national debt ignores the projected liabilities of Social Security, Medicare, and other healthcare entitlements or other federal retirement programs. If these liabilities were included, the national debt would more than triple.

## 12-3a
## Measuring the National Debt

In talking about the national debt, we should distinguish between the gross debt and debt held by the public. The *gross debt* includes U.S. Treasury securities purchased by various federal agencies. Because the federal government owes this debt to itself, analysts often focus instead on *debt held by the public*, which includes U.S. Treasury securities held by households, firms, banks (including Federal Reserve Banks), and foreign entities. As of 2015, the gross federal debt stood at $18.6 trillion, and the debt held by the public stood at $13.5 trillion.

One way to measure debt over time is relative to the economy's production and income, or GDP (just as a bank might compare the size of a mortgage to a borrower's income). Exhibit 5 shows federal debt held by the public relative to GDP. The cost of World War II ballooned the debt from 44 percent relative to GDP in 1940 to 109 percent in 1946. After the war, the economy grew much faster than the debt, so by 1980, debt fell to only 26 percent relative to GDP. But high deficits in the 1980s and early 1990s nearly doubled debt to 49 percent relative to GDP by 1993. Budget surpluses from 1998 to 2001 cut debt to 33 percent relative to GDP by 2001. A recession, a stock market slump, tax cuts, and higher federal spending increased debt to 37 percent relative to GDP in 2004, where it remained through 2007. Deficits from the 2007–2009 recession increased federal debt relative to GDP. Public debt was projected to climb to 75 percent relative to GDP by 2016. That's double the percentage in 2007 and the highest since the early 1950s, after World War II. For the next

**national debt** The net accumulation of federal budget deficits

Social Security and Medicare create a big hole in the budget.

AP Images/Moises Castillo

their financial statements, as required by private accounting boards and by federal laws. As of 2015, the federal government should have $25 trillion set aside and earning interest to cover the Social Security retirement benefits of current workers beyond what payroll taxes would cover.

## 12-3b International Perspective on Public Debt

Exhibit 5 shows federal debt relative to GDP over time, but how does the United States compare with other major economies around the world? Because different economies have different fiscal structures—for example some rely more on a central government—we should consider the debt at all government levels. Exhibit 6 compares the net government debt in the United States relative to GDP with those of nine other industrial countries. *Net debt* includes outstanding liabilities of federal, state, and local governments minus government financial assets, such as loans to students and farmers, securities,

decade, the federal debt held by the public is projected by the President's budget assumptions to grow at about the same rate as GDP. If that turns out the be the case, then public debt as a percentage of GDP will remain at about 75 percent. Research suggests that once debt levels top 80 percent relative to GDP, lenders begin demanding higher interest payments, which could trigger still higher debt.[2]

But, again, this measure of the debt ignores the fact that the federal government is on the hook to pay Social Security and Medicare benefits that will create a big hole in the budget. Why are these other debts ignored? The U.S. Congress exempts itself from including the cost of promised retirement benefits in the budget. Yet firms as well as state and local governments include retirement commitments in

> **"Net debt for all levels of government in the United States was projected to be 86 percent of GDP in 2014."**

2. David Greenlaw et al., "Crunch Time: Fiscal Crises and the Role of Monetary Policy," NBER Working Paper No. 19297 (August 2013).

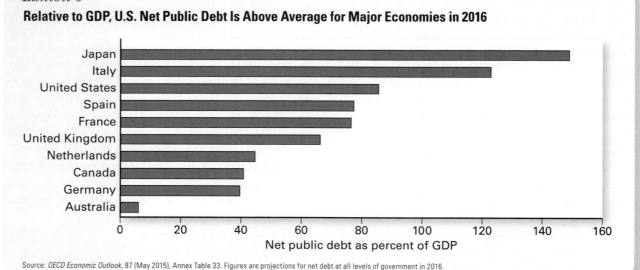

*Exhibit 6*

**Relative to GDP, U.S. Net Public Debt Is Above Average for Major Economies in 2016**

Source: *OECD Economic Outlook*, 97 (May 2015), Annex Table 33. Figures are projections for net debt at all levels of government in 2016.

*Exhibit 7*

**Interest Payments on Federal Debt Held by the Public as Percent of Federal Outlays Peaked in 1996**

After remaining relatively constant during the 1960s and 1970s, interest payments as a share of federal outlays climbed during the 1980s and early 1990s because of growing deficits and higher interest rates. After peaking in 1996 at 15.4 percent of outlays, interest payments declined first because of budget surpluses and later because of record-low interest rates.

Source: Computed by the author based on figures found in the *Economic Report of the President*, February 2015. Figures for 2015 and 2016 are estimates based on the president's budget. For the latest figures, go to http://www.gpoaccess.gov/eop/.

are short term, nearly half the debt is refinanced every year. Based on a $13.5 trillion debt held by the public in 2015, a 1 percentage point increase in the nominal interest rate ultimately increases interest costs by $135 billion a year.

Exhibit 7 shows interest on the federal debt held by the public as a percent of federal outlays since 1960. After remaining relatively constant for two decades, interest payments climbed in the 1980s because growing deficits added to the debt and because of higher interest rates. Interest payments peaked at 15.4 percent of outlays in 1996, when the U.S. Treasury had to offer a 6.4 percent annual interest rate to sell 10-year bonds. Interest payments then began falling first because of budget surpluses and later because of lower interest rates. By 2015, interest payments were only 1 percent of outlays, because the interest rate on 10-year Treasury bonds dropped below 1.8 percent. Interest's share of federal outlays will climb as debt grows and as interest rates rise from historic lows of recent years. For example, if the average interest rate paid by the federal government in 2015 was 5.0 percent, instead of about 2.0 percent, annual interest payments on public debt of 13.5 trillion in 2016 would rise from 6.1 percent of federal outlays to 16.1 percent of federal outlays.

cash on hand, and foreign exchange on reserve. Net debt for the 10 nations was projected to average 72 percent relative to GDP in 2016, below the U.S. figure of 86 percent (remember this is for all levels of government, not just the federal level). Australia was the lowest with only a 6 percent net debt relative to GDP, and Japan was the highest at 150 percent relative to GDP. Much of Japan's debt has been taken on since 2000 as the government borrowed to fund efforts to stimulate the ailing economy. The United States ranked third highest among the 10 industrialized nations, the same ranking as a decade ago. Thus, although the United States ranks low in public outlays relative to GDP, the country ranks high in public debt relative to GDP. That's because we have been running big deficits for decades, and really big ones lately. Net public debt has been increasing in many countries around the world to levels not seen since World War II. The average among the 30 most advanced economies more than doubled from 35 percent in 2000 to 72 percent in 2016. No question, governments on average have been taking on more debt, in part because of the Great Recession of 2007–2009.

## 12-3c Interest Payments on the National Debt

Purchasers of federal securities range from individuals who buy $25 U.S. savings bonds to institutions that buy $1 million Treasury securities. Because most Treasury securities

 ## FEDERAL DEBT AND THE ECONOMY

In light of the giant deficits of recent years, a growing federal debt has become central to the debate about fiscal policy effectiveness. Let's consider some economic implications of high deficits and an accumulating debt.

## 12-4a Are Persistent Deficits Sustainable?

Given that deficits have been with us so long, we might ask: How long can the country run a deficit? The short answer is: As long as lenders are willing to finance that deficit at reasonable interest rates. And that depends on the confidence that lenders have about getting repaid. At some point, chronic deficits may accumulate into such a debt that lenders demand an extremely high interest rate or refuse to lend at all. As interest rates rise, debt service costs could eat up the budget.

U.S. government securities have been considered the safest in the world, and this has helped us finance our chronic deficits and rising debt. Ironically, the global financial crisis of 2008 encouraged investors around the globe to buy U.S. securities as they sought safety. This "flight to quality" drove down the interest rate the U.S. government had to pay, thus reducing the cost of servicing our debt. But that could change. Greece had little trouble borrowing until 2010, when the financial community decided the government debt there had become too high and therefore too risky.

Indebted countries such as Greece, Ireland, Spain, and Portugal all received rescue packages from international institutions, yet they continued to struggle, some with violent public protests against deficit-cutting remedies that reduced public spending and increased taxes. One sign of possible problems in the United States was the downgrading of the nation's credit risk by the chief credit-rating agency in 2011. For the first time in 70 years, debt issued by some U.S. "government entities" such as the Federal Farm Credit System and the Federal Deposit Insurance Corporation was judged to be more risky.[3]

Countries can continue to run deficits as long as the cost of servicing the resulting debt remains manageable. Suppose that debt service, which consists almost entirely of interest payments, remains at 10 percent or less of the federal budget. Something like that would appear to be sustainable (since 1960, U.S. debt service payments have averaged 9.8 percent of federal outlays). More generally, government could still run a deficit year after year, and the dollar amount of the deficit might even rise. As long as the economy is growing at least as fast as the debt service payments, those deficits should be manageable. But the

**debt ceiling** A limit on the total amount of money the federal government can legally borrow

3. Alan Zibel and Tess Stynes, "S&P Cuts U.S. Government Entities," *Wall Street Journal*, 8 August 2011.

> " Countries can continue to run deficits as long as the cost of servicing the resulting debt remains manageable. "

trillion-dollar deficits experienced between 2009 and 2012 were not sustainable.

## 12-4b The Debt Ceiling and Debt Default

The **debt ceiling** is a limit on the total amount of money the federal government can legally borrow. About a century ago, Congress set the first debt ceiling and raised it whenever necessary, more than 80 times in all. The ceiling was largely a formality—until early 2011, that is, when the federal government faced sharply rising debt from giant deficits for years to come. In early 2011, the gross debt ceiling stood at $14.3 trillion. The federal government actually hit that ceiling in May of that year, but the U.S. Treasury was able to buy time by suspending payments to some retirement funds. At the time, the government was borrowing about 40 cents of each dollar spent, so without additional borrowing the Treasury would run out of money. The limit would be reached in early August.

If the debt ceiling had not been raised, the U.S. government would have missed some debt-service payments and would be in default. This would have triggered a cascade of troubles, not the least of which would be a sharply higher cost of borrowing or even an inability to borrow. Difficulty rolling over the more than $200 billion of debt that came due each month would cripple federal finances.

A default on what had been considered the securest investment in the world would also be catastrophic for world financial markets. Not only would the federal cost of borrowing increase sharply but also market interest rates would spike to reflect a riskier economy, so interest on everything from car loans to home loans would rise. Credit flows could dry up. Unemployment would jump as businesses cut jobs in the face of growing uncertainty.

Both Democrats and Republicans in Congress agreed in August 2011 that the debt ceiling should be raised. Before approving a higher debt ceiling, Republicans wanted to reduce future deficits by cutting spending. Democrats focused more on tax increases, especially on high-income households. In the end, the two sides came together enough to raise the debt ceiling and avert a fiscal crisis for a while.

## 12-4c Who Bears the Burden of the Debt?

Deficit spending is a way of billing future taxpayers for current spending. The national debt raises moral questions about the right of one generation to bequeath to the next generation the burden of its borrowing. To what extent do deficits and debt shift the burden to future generations? Let's examine two arguments about the burden of the federal debt.

### We Owe It to Ourselves

It is often argued that the debt is not a burden to future generations because, although future generations must service the debt, those same generations receive the payments. It's true that if U.S. citizens forgo present consumption to buy bonds, they or their heirs will be repaid, so debt service payments stay in the country. Thus, future generations both service the debt and receive the payments. In that sense, the debt is not a burden on future generations. It's all in the family, so to speak.

### Foreign Ownership of Debt

But the "we-owe-it-to-ourselves" argument does not apply to that portion of the national debt owed to foreigners. Foreigners who buy U.S. Treasury securities forgo present consumption and are paid back in the future. Foreign buyers reduce the amount of current consumption that Americans must sacrifice to finance a deficit. *A reliance on foreigners, however, increases the burden of the debt on future generations of Americans because future debt service payments no longer remain in the country.* Foreigners held nearly half of all federal debt held by the public in 2015, more than triple the share of two decades ago. So the burden of the debt on future generations of Americans has increased both absolutely and relatively.

Exhibit 8 shows the top ten foreign holders of U.S. Treasury securities in February 2015, when foreigners held a total of $6,163 billion of U.S. federal debt. China and Japan were tied for the lead with $1,224 billion,

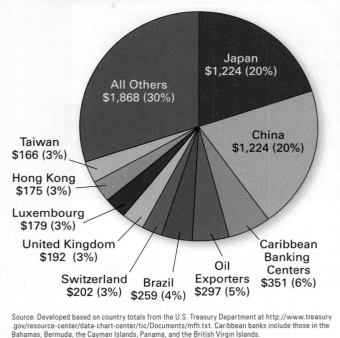

*Exhibit 8*

**Largest Foreign Holders of U.S. Treasury Securities as of February 2015 (in billions and as percent of foreign holdings)**

Japan $1,224 (20%)
All Others $1,868 (30%)
China $1,224 (20%)
Taiwan $166 (3%)
Hong Kong $175 (3%)
Luxembourg $179 (3%)
United Kingdom $192 (3%)
Switzerland $202 (3%)
Brazil $259 (4%)
Oil Exporters $297 (5%)
Caribbean Banking Centers $351 (6%)

Source: Developed based on country totals from the U.S. Treasury Department at http://www.treasury.gov/resource-center/data-chart-center/tic/Documents/mfh.txt. Caribbean banks include those in the Bahamas, Bermuda, the Cayman Islands, Panama, and the British Virgin Islands.

or 20 percent of foreign-held U.S. federal debt each. Together, Asian countries (including some not shown) had more than half of foreign-held federal debt. Despite the growth in federal debt, U.S. Treasury securities are considered the safest in the world because they are backed by the U.S. government. Whenever there is trouble around the world, investors flock to U.S. Treasury securities in a "flight to quality." Some other countries have proven to be less trustworthy borrowers. Argentina, Mexico, and Russia, for example, all defaulted on some national debt.

## 12-4d Crowding Out and Capital Formation

As we have seen, government borrowing can drive up interest rates, crowding out some private investment. The long-run effect of deficit spending depends on how the government spends the borrowed funds. If the funds are invested in better highways and a more educated workforce, this could enhance productivity in the long run. If, however, borrowed dollars go toward current expenditures such as more farm subsidies or higher retirement benefits, less capital formation results. With

Federal spending on infrastructure has declined in recent decades, leaving roads and bridges, such as this collapsed bridge in Minnesota, in dire need of repair.

JOSHUA LOTT/Reuters/Landov

## 12-4e The National Debt and Economic Growth

Finally, what's the impact of the national debt on economic growth? Researchers have identified major public debt episodes in the advanced economies around the world since the early 1800s.[4] A major episode is one where the ratio of public debt to GDP exceeds 90 percent for at least five years in a row. Researchers found that the economy grows at least one percentage point less annually during these periods than during other periods. What's more, the growth slowdown can last a long time. Among the 26 episodes the researchers identified, 20 lasted more than a decade (five of the six shorter episodes were immediately after World Wars I and II). Across all 26 instances, the average duration of the slowdown was about 23 years. Thus the cumulative shortfall in output from a high national debt is potentially huge.

Perhaps most telling for the United States is that economic growth declines are significant even in the many episodes where debtor countries were able to secure continual access to capital markets at relatively low real interest rates. This suggests that the growth-reducing effects of high public debt are apparently not transmitted entirely through high real interest rates on that debt. Chairwoman of the Federal Reserve System, Janet Yellen, has noted that government officials need to "significantly improve their structural fiscal balance during good times so they have more space to provide stimulus when times turn bad."[5]

Government deficits of one generation can affect the standard of living of the next. Note again that our current measure of the national debt does not capture all burdens passed on to future generations. As mentioned earlier, if the unfunded liabilities of government retirement programs, especially Medicare, were included, this would more than triple the national debt.

less investment today, there will be less capital in the future, thus hurting labor productivity and our future standard of living.

> **"The long-run effect of deficit spending depends on how the government spends the borrowed funds."**

Ironically, despite the large federal deficits during the last few decades, public investments in roads, bridges, and airports—so-called *public capital*—declined, perhaps because a growing share of the federal budget goes toward income redistribution, especially for the elderly. On average, the United States spent 3 percent of GDP building and maintaining the public infrastructure between 1950 and 1970. Since 1980 that share has averaged only 2 percent. Some argue that declining investment in the public infrastructure slows productivity growth. For example, the failure to invest sufficiently in airports and in the air traffic control system has led to congested air travel and flight delays, a problem compounded by the threat of terrorism. The $831 billion stimulus package approved in February 2009 was supposed to fund "shovel-ready" infrastructure improvements such as repairing crumbling roads and bridges. But surprisingly little went into such programs.

## 12-5 FINAL WORD

John Maynard Keynes introduced the idea that federal deficit spending is an appropriate fiscal policy when private aggregate demand is insufficient to achieve potential output. The federal budget has not been the

4. Carmen Reinhart, Vincent Reinhart, and Kenneth Rogoff, "Public Debt Overhangs: Advanced Economy Episodes Since 1800," *Journal of Economic Perspectives*, 26 (Summer 2012): 69–86.

5. Jon Hilsenrath, "What the Big Economies Got Right, or Wrong, After Crisis," *Wall Street Journal*, 24 November 2014.

same since. Beginning in 1960, the federal budget was in deficit every year but one until 1998. And beginning in the early 1980s, large federal deficits dominated the fiscal policy debate. A major policy issue for the coming decade will be how to address high federal deficits and a growing debt. The difficulties that other nations faced in addressing their national debts suggest the kind of political challenge the United States could encounter.

Monetary policy is the regulation of the money supply by the Federal Reserve. The next few chapters introduce money and financial institutions, review monetary policy, and discuss the impact of monetary and fiscal policy on economic stability and growth. Once we bring money into the picture, we consider yet another reason why the simple spending multiplier is overstated.

# STUDY TOOLS 12

## READY TO STUDY? IN THE BOOK, YOU CAN:

☐ Work the Problems at the end of the chapter.

☐ Rip out the chapter review card for a handy summary of the chapter and key terms.

## ONLINE AT CENGAGEBRAIN.COM YOU CAN:

☐ Collect StudyBits while you read and study the chapter.

☐ Quiz yourself on key concepts.

☐ Prepare for tests with chapter flash cards as well as flash cards that you create.

☐ Watch videos to explore economics further.

# CHAPTER 12 PROBLEMS

*Your instructor can access the answers to these problems online at http://cengagebrain.com.*

## 12-1 Summarize how federal spending priorities have changed since the 1960s

1.  *(Changing Budget Priorities)* What spending category claimed the largest share of federal outlays during the 1960s? How about during the most recent decade?
2.  *(The Federal Budget Process)* Why does the budget require a forecast of the economy? Under what circumstances would actual government spending and tax revenue fail to match the budget as approved?

## 12-2 Explain why the federal budget has been in deficit in most years since the Great Depression

3.  *(Budget Philosophies)* Explain the differences among an annually balanced budget, a cyclically balanced budget, and functional finance. How does each affect economic fluctuations?
4.  *(Chronic Deficits)* Why has the federal budget been in deficit in all but 14 years since 1929?

## 12-3 Outline what has happened to the federal debt in recent decades and how it compares with debt levels in other countries

5.  *(Federal Debt)* What has happened to the federal debt since 2008 as measured relative to GDP?
6.  *(Net Public Debt)* What's the level of net public debt (for federal, state, and local governments) relative to U.S. GDP? How does the United States measure compare with that of other major economies?
7.  *(Debt Measures)* What's the difference between gross federal debt and federal debt held by the public?
8.  *(The National Debt)* Try the following exercises to better understand how the national debt is related to the government's budget deficit.

a. Assume that the gross national debt initially is equal to $3 trillion and the federal government then runs a deficit of $300 billion.
   i. What is the new level of gross national debt?
   ii. If 100 percent of the deficit is financed by the sale of securities to federal agencies, what happens to the amount of debt held by the public? What happens to the level of gross debt?
   iii. If GDP increased by 5 percent in the same year that the deficit is run, what happens to gross debt as a percentage of GDP? What happens to the level of debt held by the public as a percentage of GDP?

b. Now suppose that the gross national debt initially is equal to $2.5 trillion and the federal government then runs a deficit of $100 billion.
   i. What is the new level of gross national debt?
   ii. If 100 percent of this deficit is financed by the sale of securities to the public, what happens to the level of debt held by the public? What happens to the level of gross debt?
   iii. If GDP increases by 6 percent in the same year as the deficit is run, what happens to gross debt as a percentage of GDP? What happens to the level of debt held by the public as a percentage of GDP?

## 12-4 Describe how a giant federal debt could have a negative impact on the economy

9.  *(Crowding Out and Capital Formation)* In earlier chapters, we've seen that the government can try to increase GDP in the short run by running a budget deficit. What are some longterm effects of deficit spending?
10. *(Sustainability of Federal Debt)* Are large federal deficits and a growing federal debt sustainable? What can be learned from the experiences of other countries?

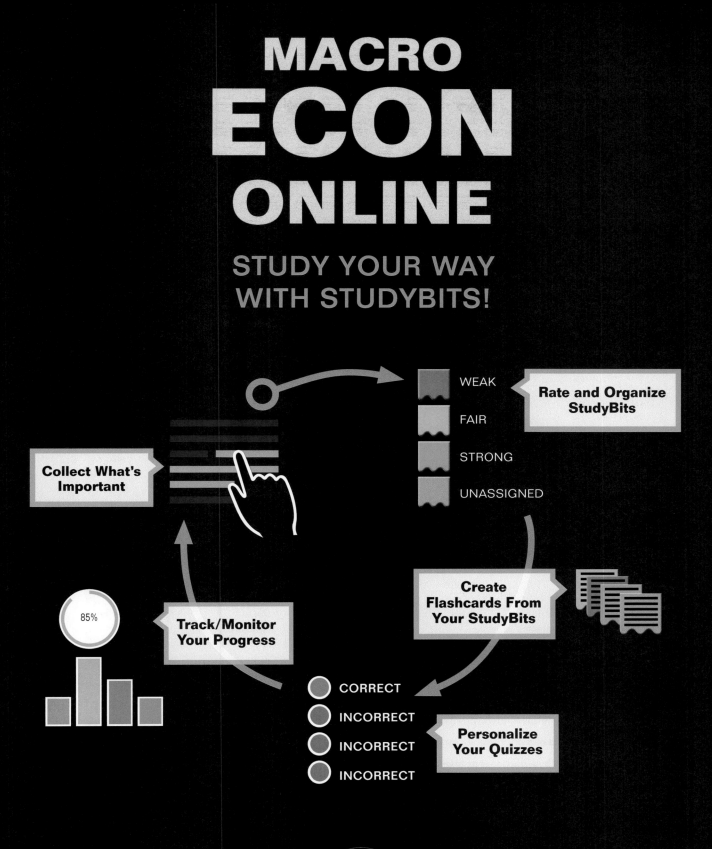

# MACRO ECON ONLINE

## STUDY YOUR WAY WITH STUDYBITS!

# 13 | Money and the Financial System

## LEARNING OUTCOMES

After studying this chapter, you will be able to…

**13-1** Identify three functions of money and six qualities of the ideal money

**13-2** Explain what is meant by a fractional reserve banking system

**13-3** Describe the Fed, summarize its two mandated objectives, and outline some of its other goals

**13-4** Describe subprime mortgages and the role they played in the financial crisis of 2008

After finishing this chapter go to **PAGE 245** for **STUDY TOOLS**

**Topics discussed in Chapter 13 include:**

- Barter
- Functions of money
- Commodity money and fiat money
- The Federal Reserve System
- Depository institutions
- U.S. banking structure
- Subprime mortgages
- Mortgage-backed securities

© iStockphoto.com/Creativeye99

- Why are you willing to exchange a piece of paper bearing Alexander Hamilton's portrait and the number 10 in each corner for a pepperoni pizza with extra cheese?

- Why do dimes and quarters have notched edges?

- If Russia can't pay its bills, why don't officials there simply print more rubles?

- Because money is banned in federal prisons, what do inmates use instead?

- What's the difference between the *Fed* and the *Feds*?

- Why was someone able to cash a check written on a clean but frayed pair of underpants?

*These and other questions are answered in this chapter, which introduces money and banking.*

The word *money* comes from the name of the goddess (*Juno Moneta*) in whose temple Rome's money was coined. Money has come to symbolize all personal and business finance. You can read *Money* magazine and the "Money" section of *USA Today*, and visit Websites such as www.moneyfactory.gov, the site for the federal agency that prints money (a Google search for "money" returned about three billion hits). You can watch TV shows such as *Your Money, Mad Money, Fast Money,* and *Strictly Money*.

> **"If Russia can't pay its bills, why don't officials there simply print more rubles?"**

With money, you can articulate your preferences—after all, money talks. And when it talks, it says a lot, as in, "Put your money where your mouth is" and "Show me the money." Money is the grease that lubricates the wheels of market exchange (in fact, an old expression, "grease the palm," means to pay someone a tip or a bribe). Just as grease makes for an easier fit among gears, money reduces the friction—the transaction costs—of exchange. Too little leaves some parts creaking; too much gums up the works.

This chapter is obviously about money. We begin with the birth of money and trace its evolution in broad strokes from primitive economies to our own. Then we turn to developments in the United States, particularly the financial crisis of 2008, which was arguably the most important economic event since the Great Depression.

## 13-1 THE BIRTH OF MONEY

In the beginning, there was no money. The earliest families were largely self-sufficient. Each produced all it consumed and consumed all it produced, so there was little need for exchange. Without exchange, there was no need for money. When specialization first emerged, as some people went hunting and others took up farming, hunters and farmers had to trade. Thus, the specialization of labor resulted in exchange, but the assortment of goods traded was limited enough that people could easily exchange their products directly for other products—a system called *barter*.

## 13-1a Barter and the Double Coincidence of Wants

Barter depends on a **double coincidence of wants**, which occurs when each trader is willing to exchange his or her product for something the other trader has to offer. If a hunter was willing to exchange hides for a farmer's corn, that was a coincidence. But if the farmer was also willing to exchange corn for the hunter's hides, that was a double coincidence—a *double coincidence of wants*. As long as specialization was

> **double coincidence of wants** Two traders are willing to exchange their products directly

limited, to, say, two or three goods, mutually beneficial trades were relatively easy to come by—that is, trade wasn't much of a coincidence. As specialization increased, however, finding the particular goods that each trader wanted became more difficult.

In a barter system, traders must not only discover a double coincidence of wants; they must also agree on an exchange rate. How many bushels of corn should the hunter get for a hide? If only two goods are traded, only one exchange rate needs to be worked out. As the variety of goods traded increases, however, exchange rates multiply. Specialization increased the transaction costs of barter. A huge difference in the values of the units to be exchanged also made barter difficult. For example, a hunter wanting to buy a home that exchanged for 1,000 hides would be hard-pressed finding a home seller needing that many. High transaction costs of barter gave birth to money.

### 13-1b The Earliest Money and its Functions

Nobody actually recorded the emergence of money. We can only speculate about how it first came into use. Through experience with barter, traders may have found they could always find buyers for certain goods. If a trader could not find a good that he or she desired personally, some other good with a ready market could be accepted instead. So traders began to accept a certain good not for immediate consumption, but because that good could be easily traded later. For example, corn might have become acceptable because traders knew that it was always in demand. As one good became generally accepted in return for all other goods, that good began to function as **money**. *Any commodity that acquires*

**money** Anything that is generally accepted in exchange for goods and services

**medium of exchange** Anything that facilitates trade by being generally accepted by all parties in payment for goods or services

**commodity money** Anything that serves both as money and as a commodity; money that has intrinsic value such as gold or silver coins

**unit of account** A common unit for measuring the value of each good or service

> **"Money fulfills three important functions: a medium of exchange, a unit of account, and a store of value."**

*a high degree of acceptability throughout an economy becomes money.*

Money fulfills three important functions: a *medium of exchange,* a *unit of account,* and a *store of value.* Let's consider each.

### Medium of Exchange

Separating the sale of one good from the purchase of another requires an item acceptable to all involved in the transactions. If a society, by luck or by design, can find a commodity that everyone accepts in exchange for whatever is sold, traders can save time, disappointment, and sheer aggravation. Suppose corn takes on this role, a role that clearly goes beyond its role as food. We then call corn a medium of exchange because it is accepted in exchange by all buyers and sellers, whether or not they want corn to eat. A **medium of exchange** is anything that is generally accepted in payment for goods and services. The person who accepts corn in exchange for some product believes corn can be traded later for whatever is desired.

In this example, corn is both a *commodity* and *money,* so we call it **commodity money**. The earliest money was commodity money. Gold and silver have been used as money for at least four thousand years. Cattle served as money, first for the Greeks, then for the Romans. In fact, the word *pecuniary* (meaning "of or relating to money") comes from the Latin word for cattle, *pecus.* Likewise, the word *fee* comes from the Old English word *feoh,* which also meant cattle. Roman soldiers received part of their pay in salt bricks; the salt portion was called the *salarium,* the origin of the word *salary.* Also used as money were wampum (strings of polished shells) and tobacco in colonial America, tea pressed into small cakes in Russia, rice in Japan, and palm dates in North Africa. Note that commodity money is a good, not a service; a service is intangible and cannot be held for later exchange.

### Unit of Account

A commodity such as corn that grows to be widely accepted becomes a **unit of account**, a standard on which prices are based. The price of hides or shoes or pots is measured in bushels of corn. Thus, corn serves not only as a medium of exchange; it also becomes a common denominator, a yardstick, for *measuring the value* of each product exchanged in the economy. Rather than having to determine exchange rates among all products, as required with a barter economy, people can price everything using a single measure, such as corn. For example, if a pair of shoes sells for 2 bushels of corn and a 5-gallon pot sells for 1 bushel of corn, then a pair of shoes has the same value in exchange as two 5-gallon pots.

## Store of Value

Because people do not want to buy something every time they sell something, the purchasing power acquired through a sale must somehow be preserved. Money serves as a **store of value** when it retains purchasing power over time. The better it preserves purchasing power, the better money serves as a store of value, and the more willing people are to accept it and hold it. Consider again the distinction between a stock and a flow. Recall that a *stock* is an amount measured at a particular point in time, such as the amount of food in your refrigerator or the amount of money you have with you right now. In contrast, a *flow* is an amount per unit of time, such as the calories you consume per day or the income you earn per week. *Money* is a stock and *income* is a flow. Don't confuse money with income. The role of money as a stock is best reflected by money's role as a store of value.

## 13-1c Properties of the Ideal Money

The introduction of commodity money reduced the transaction costs of exchange compared with barter, but commodity money also involves some transaction costs. First, if the commodity money is perishable, as is corn, it must be properly stored or its quality deteriorates; even then, it won't maintain its quality for long. U.S. coins have a projected life of 30 years (a $1 note, 6 years). So the ideal money should be *durable*.

Second, if the commodity money is bulky, major purchases can become unwieldy. For example, truckloads of corn would be needed to purchase a home selling for 5,000 bushels of corn. So the ideal money should be *portable*, or easily carried. Dollar notes are easier to carry than dollar coins, which may explain why dollar coins never became popular in the United States, despite several attempts to introduce them.

Third, some commodity money was not easily divisible into smaller units. For example, when cattle served as money, any price involving a fraction of a cow posed an exchange problem. So the ideal money should be *divisible*.

Fourth, if commodity money like corn is valued equally in exchange, regardless of its quality, people will eat the best corn and trade away the rest. As a result, the quality remaining in circulation will decline, reducing its acceptability. To avoid this problem, the ideal money should be of *uniform quality*.

Fifth, commodity money often ties up otherwise valuable resources, so it has a higher opportunity cost than, say, paper money. For example, corn that is used for money cannot at the same time be used for corn on the cob, corn flour, popcorn, corn chips, corn oil, or biofuel. So the ideal money should have *a low opportunity cost*.

> **"The ideal money is durable, portable, divisible, of uniform quality, has a low opportunity cost, and is relatively stable in value."**

If the supply or demand for money fluctuates unpredictably, so will the economy's price level, and this is the final problem with commodity money. For example, if a bumper crop increases the supply of corn, more corn will be required to purchase other goods. This we call *inflation*. Likewise, any change in the demand for corn *as food* from, say, the growing popularity of corn chips, would affect the exchange value of corn. Erratic fluctuations in the market for corn limit its usefulness as money, particularly as a unit of account and a store of value. So the ideal money *should maintain a relatively stable value over time*. Money supplied by a responsible issuing authority is likely to retain its value better over

**store of value** Anything that retains its purchasing power over time

## Exhibit 1
### Six Properties of Ideal Money

| Quality | Rationale | Good Examples | Bad Examples |
|---|---|---|---|
| 1. Durable | Money should not wear out quickly | Paper money; coins; sea shells | Strawberries; seafood |
| 2. Portable | Money should be easy to carry, even relatively large sums | Diamonds; paper money | Lead bars; corn |
| 3. Divisible | Market exchange is easier if denominations support a range of possible prices | Honey; paper money and coins | Cattle; diamonds |
| 4. Uniform Quality | If money is not of uniform quality, people will hoard the best and spend the rest, reducing the quality in circulation | Salt bricks; paper money; coins | Diamonds |
| 5. Low Opportunity Cost | The fewer resources tied up in creating money, the more available for other uses | Iron coins; paper money | Gold coins; diamonds; corn |
| 6. Stable Value | People are more willing to accept and hold money if they believe it will keep its value over time | Anything whose supply can be limited by the issuing authority, such as paper money | Farm crops |

time than money whose supply depends on uncontrollable forces of nature such as good or bad growing seasons.

What all this boils down to is that the ideal money is durable, portable, divisible, of uniform quality, has a low opportunity cost, and is relatively stable in value. These qualities are reinforced in Exhibit 1, which also lists the rationale, good examples, and bad examples. Please spend a minute now reviewing the table.

## Mackerel Economics in Federal Prisons[1]

The economist R. A. Radford spent several years in prisoner-of-war camps in Italy and Germany during World War II, and he wrote about his experience. Although economic activity was sharply limited, many features of a normal economy were found in the prison life he observed. For example, in the absence of any official currency behind bars, cigarettes came to serve all three roles of money: medium of exchange, unit of account, and store of value. Cigarettes were of uniform quality, of limited supply (they came in rations from the International Red Cross), reasonably durable, and individually could support small transactions or, in packs, larger ones. Prices measured in cigarettes became fairly uniform and well known throughout a camp of up to 50,000 prisoners of many nationalities and languages.

Now fast-forward half a century to the U.S. federal prison system. Prisoners are not allowed to hold cash. Whatever money sent by relatives or earned from prison jobs (at 40 cents an hour) goes into a prisoner's commissary account, which allows an inmate to buy items such as snacks and toiletries. In the absence of cash, to trade among themselves, federal prisoners also came to settle on cigarettes as their commodity money (despite official prohibitions against trade of any kind among inmates). Cigarettes served as the informal money until 2004, when smoking was banned in all federal prisons.

Once the ban took effect, the urge to trade created incentives to come up with some other commodity money. Prisoners tried other items sold at the commissary including postage stamps, cans of tuna, and Power Bars, but none of that seemed to catch on. Eventually prisoners settled on cans of mackerel, a bony, oily fish. So inmates informally use "macks"—as the commodity money came to be called—to settle gambling debts, to buy services from other inmates (such as haircuts, ironing, shoe shining, and cell cleaning), and to buy goods from other inmates (including special foods prepared with items from the commissary and illicit items such as home-brewed "prison hooch"). At those federal prisons where the commissary opens only one day a week, some prisoners fill the void by running mini-commissaries out of their lockers.

After wardens banned cans (because they could be refashioned into makeshift knives), the commodity

1. R. A. Radford, "The Economic Organization of a P.O.W. Camp," *Economica*, 12 (November 1945): 189–201; Justin Scheck, "Mackerel Economics in Prisons Leads to Appreciation of the Oily Fillets," *Wall Street Journal*, 2 October 2008; and Ben Paynter, "Prison Economics," *Wired*, 31 January 2011, at http://www.wired.com /magazine/2011/01 /st_prisoncurrencies/

money quickly shifted from cans of mackerel to plastic-and-foil pouches of mackerel. The mack is considered a good stand-in for the dollar because each pouch costs about $1 at the commissary, yet most prisoners, aside from weight-lifters seeking extra protein, would rather trade macks than eat them. The foil packets are also small enough to be carried around in pockets, so they are portable. And the mack is durable; unopened, a foil packet is good for years.

Wardens try to discourage the mackerel economy by limiting the amount of food prisoners can stockpile. Those caught using macks as money can lose commissary privileges, can be reassigned to a less desirable cell, or can even spend time in the "hole." Still, market forces are so powerful that the mackerel economy survives in many federal prisons. Most state prisons have now banned smoking, and the mack has become the coin of the realm there too.

## 13-1d Coins

The division of commodity money into units was often natural, as in bushels of corn or heads of cattle. When rock salt was used as money, it was cut into uniform bricks. Because salt was usually of consistent quality, a trader had only to count the bricks to determine the amount of money. When silver and gold were used as money, both their quantity and quality were open to question. First, the amount had to be weighed, so transactions required scales. Second, because precious metals could be *debased* with cheaper metals, the quality of the metal had to be determined with each exchange. This was a nuisance.

This quantity and quality control problem was addressed by coining precious metals. *Coinage determined both the quantity and the quality of the metal.* Coins allowed payment by count rather than by weight. A flat surface on which this money was counted came to be called the *counter,* a term still used today. Initially, an image was stamped on only one side of a coin, leaving the other side blank. But people began shaving precious metal from the blank side. To prevent this, images were stamped on both sides. But another problem arose because bits of metal could still be clipped from the coin's edge. To prevent clipping, coins were bordered with a well-defined rim. If you have a dime or a quarter, notice the notches, or tiny serrations, on the edge. These serrations, throwbacks from the time when these coins were silver or gold, reduced the chances of "getting clipped."

**Token money** is money whose face value exceeds its production cost. Some coins and all paper money now in circulation in the United States are token money. For example, the 25-cent coin costs the U.S. Mint only about 12 cents to make. Minting 25-cent coins nets the U.S. Treasury hundreds of millions of dollars a year. But the penny and even the nickel now cost more to mint than they are worth in exchange.

## 13-2 MONEY AND BANKING

For thousands of years, commodity money facilitated market exchange. Money existed long before banks did. Now we explore how banking developed a special role in supplying a nation's money.

## 13-2a Early Banking

You have been around banks all your life, so you know more about them than you may think. But before we get to what you know, here's some background about how banking got started. The word *bank* comes from the Italian word *banca,* meaning "bench," which was a money changer's table. Banking spread from Italy to England, where London goldsmiths offered safekeeping for money and other valuables. The goldsmith gave depositors their money back on request, but because deposits by some tended to offset withdrawals by others, the amount of idle cash, or gold, in the vault changed little over time. Goldsmiths found that they could earn interest by lending from this pool of idle cash.

Goldsmiths offered depositors safekeeping, but visiting the goldsmith to get money to pay for each purchase became a nuisance. For example, a farmer might visit the goldsmith to withdraw enough money to buy a horse. The farmer would then pay the horse trader, who would promptly deposit the receipts with the goldsmith. Thus, money took a round-trip from goldsmith to farmer to horse trader and back to goldsmith. Because depositors soon grew tired of visiting the goldsmith

**token money** Money whose face value exceeds its cost of production

© R. Mackay Photography/Shutterstock.com

every time they needed money, they began instructing the goldsmith to pay someone from their account. The payment amounted to moving gold from one stack (the farmer's) to another stack (the horse trader's). *These written instructions to the goldsmith were the first checks.* **Checks** have since become official looking, but they need not be, as evidenced by the actions of a Montana man who paid a speeding fine with instructions written on clean but frayed underpants. The Western Federal Savings and Loan of Missoula honored the "check."

By combining the ideas of cash loans and checks, the goldsmith soon discovered how to make loans by check. Rather than lend idle cash, the goldsmith could simply create a checking balance for the borrower. *The goldsmith could extend a loan by creating an account against which the borrower could write checks. In this way goldsmiths, or banks, were able to create a medium of exchange, or to "create money."* This money, based only on an entry in the goldsmith's ledger, was accepted because of the public's confidence that these claims would be honored.

The total claims against the goldsmith consisted of claims by people who had deposited their money plus claims by borrowers for whom the goldsmith had created deposits. Because these claims exceeded the value of gold on reserve, this was the beginning of a **fractional reserve banking system**, a system in which bank reserves amounted to just a fraction of total deposits. The *reserve ratio* measured reserves as a percentage of total claims against the goldsmith, or total deposits. For example, if the goldsmith had reserves of $6,000 but deposits of $10,000, the reserve ratio would be 60 percent. The goldsmith was relying on the fact that not everyone would ask for their deposits at the same time.

## 13-2b Bank Notes and Fiat Money

Another way a bank could create money was by issuing bank notes. **Bank notes** were pieces of paper promising the bearer specific amounts of gold or silver when the notes were presented to the issuing bank for redemption. In London, goldsmith bankers introduced bank notes about the same time they introduced checks. *Whereas checks could be redeemed only if endorsed by the payee, notes could be redeemed by anyone who presented them.* Paper money was often "as good as gold," because the bearer could redeem it for gold. In fact, paper money was more convenient than gold because it was less bulky and more portable.

The amount of paper money issued by a bank depended on that bank's estimate of the fraction of notes that would be redeemed. The higher the redemption rate, the fewer notes could be issued based on a given amount of reserves. Initially, these promises to pay were issued by private individuals or banks, but over time, governments took a larger role in printing and circulating notes. Once paper money became widely accepted, it was perhaps inevitable that governments would begin issuing **fiat money**, which derives its status as money from the power of the state, or by *fiat.* Fiat (pronounced "feé at") money is money because the government says so. The word *fiat* is from Latin and means "so be it." Fiat money is not redeemable for anything other than more fiat money; it is not backed by something of intrinsic value. You can think of fiat money as mere paper money. It is acceptable not because it is intrinsically useful or valuable—as is corn or gold—but because the government says it's money. Fiat money is declared **legal tender** by the government, meaning that you are making a valid and legal offer when you pay with such money. *Gradually, people came to accept fiat money because they believed that others would accept it as well.* The currency issued in the United States and throughout most of the world is fiat money.

A well-regulated system of fiat money is more efficient for an economy than commodity money. Fiat money uses only paper and ink (a $1 note costs about 5 cents to make; a $100 note, about 12 cents),[2] but commodity money ties up something intrinsically valuable. Paper money makes up only part of the money supply. Modern money also includes checking accounts, which are electronic entries in bank computers.

## 13-2c The Value of Money

Money has grown increasingly more abstract—from a physical commodity, to a piece of paper representing a claim on a physical commodity, to a piece of paper of no intrinsic value, to an electronic entry representing a claim on a piece of paper of no intrinsic value. So why does money have value? The commodity feature of early

**check** A written order instructing the bank to pay someone from an amount deposited

**fractional reserve banking system** Bank reserves amount to only a fraction of funds on deposit with the bank

**bank notes** Originally, pieces of paper promising a specific amount of gold or silver to anyone who presented them to issuing banks for redemption; today, Federal Reserve notes are mere paper money

**fiat money** Money not redeemable for any commodity; its status as money is conferred initially by government decree but eventually by common experience

**legal tender** Currency that constitutes a valid and legal offer of payment of debt

2. "How Much Does It Cost to Produce Currency and Coins?" Board of Governors of the Federal Reserve System, at http://www.federalreserve.gov/faqs/currency_12771.htm.

money bolstered confidence in its acceptability. Commodities such as corn, tobacco, and gold had value in use even if for some reason they became less acceptable in exchange. When paper money came into use, its acceptability was initially fostered by the promise to redeem it for gold or silver. But because most paper money throughout the world is now fiat money, there is no promise of redemption. So why can a piece of paper bearing the portrait of Alexander Hamilton and the number 10 in each corner be exchanged for a pizza or anything else selling for $10? *People accept these pieces of paper because, through experience, they believe that others will do the same.* The acceptability of money, which we now take for granted, is based on decades of experience with the stability of its value and with the willingness of others to accept it as payment. As we will soon see, when money's value becomes questionable, so does its acceptability.

The *purchasing power* of money is the rate at which it exchanges for goods and services. The higher the price level in the economy, the less can be purchased with each

People accept money as payment for goods and services because they believe others will do the same.

dollar, so the less each dollar is worth. The purchasing power of each dollar over time varies inversely with the economy's price level. As the price level increases, the purchasing power of money falls. To measure the purchasing power of the dollar in a particular year, you first compute the price index for that year and then divide 100 by that price index. For example, relative to the base period of 1982 through 1984, the consumer price index for 2015 was 238. The purchasing power of a dollar was therefore 100/238, or $0.42, measured in 1982–1984 dollars. Exhibit 2 shows the steady decline in the purchasing power of the dollar since 1960, when it was worth $3.38

> **"People accept these pieces of paper because, through experience, they believe that others will do the same."**

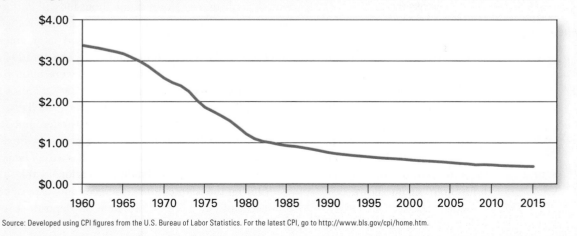

*Exhibit 2*

**Purchasing Power of $1.00 Measured in 1982–1984 Constant Dollars**

An increase in the price level over time reduces what $1.00 buys. Since 1960 the price level has risen every year except 2009, so the purchasing power of $1.00 (measured in 1982–1984 constant dollars) has fallen from $3.38 in 1960 to $0.42 in 2015.

Source: Developed using CPI figures from the U.S. Bureau of Labor Statistics. For the latest CPI, go to http://www.bls.gov/cpi/home.htm.

in 1982–1984 dollars. Put another way, as measured by the CPI, the value of a dollar—that is, what it could buy—fell by 88 percent between 1960 and 2015.

### 13-2d When Money Performs Poorly

One way to understand the functions of money is to look at instances where money did not perform well. In an earlier chapter, we mentioned hyperinflation in Zimbabwe. With prices growing by the hour, money no longer served as a reliable store of value, so workers couldn't wait to exchange their money for goods or for some "hard" currency—that is, a more stable currency. If inflation gets high enough, people no longer accept the nation's money and instead resort to some other means of exchange. On the other hand, if the supply of money dries up or if the price system is not allowed to function properly, barter may be the only alternative.

When the official currency fails to serve as a medium of exchange because of price controls or hyperinflation or when cash hoarding dries up money in circulation, some other means of exchange emerges. But this diverts more resources from production to exchange. A poorly functioning monetary system increases the transaction costs of exchange. *No machine increases the economy's productivity as much as properly functioning money.* Indeed, it seems hard to overstate the value of a reliable monetary system. This is why we pay so much attention to money and banking.

Let's turn now to the development of money and banking in the United States.

## 13-3 FINANCIAL INSTITUTIONS IN THE UNITED STATES

You have already learned about the origin of modern banks: Goldsmiths lent money from deposits held for safekeeping. So you already have some idea of how banks work. Recall from the circular-flow model that household saving flows into financial markets, where it is lent to investors. Financial institutions, such as banks, mortgage companies, and finance companies, accumulate funds from savers and lend them to borrowers. Financial institutions, or **financial intermediaries**, earn a profit by "buying low and selling high"—that is, by paying a lower interest rate to savers than they charge borrowers.

### 13-3a Commercial Banks and Thrifts

A wide variety of financial intermediaries respond to the economy's demand for financial services. **Depository institutions**—such as commercial banks, savings banks, and credit unions—obtain funds primarily by accepting customer *deposits*. Depository institutions play a key role in providing the nation's money supply. Depository institutions can be classified broadly into commercial banks and thrift institutions.

Commercial banks are the oldest, largest, and most diversified of depository institutions. They are called **commercial banks** because historically they made loans primarily to *commercial* ventures, or businesses, rather than to households. Commercial banks hold most deposits in the United States. **Thrift institutions**, or **thrifts**, include savings banks and credit unions. Historically, savings banks specialized in making home mortgage loans. Credit unions, which are more numerous but smaller than savings banks, extend loans only to their "members" to finance homes or other major consumer purchases, such as new cars. For the most part, this chapter will ignore credit unions, which are numerous but small and specialized.

### 13-3b Birth of the Fed

Before 1863, banks in the United States were chartered by the states in which they operated, so they were called *state banks*. These banks, like the English goldsmiths, issued bank notes. Notes from thousands of different banks circulated and most were redeemable for gold. The National Banking Act of 1863 and later amendments created a new system of federally chartered banks called *national banks*. National banks were authorized to issue notes and were regulated by the Office of the Comptroller of the Currency, part of the U.S. Treasury. State bank notes were taxed out of existence, but state banks survived by creating checking accounts for borrowers. To this day, the United States has a *dual banking system* consisting of state banks and national banks.

During the 19th century, the economy experienced a number of panic "runs" on banks by depositors seeking to withdraw their money. A panic was usually set off by the failure of some prominent financial institution.

Fearful customers besieged their banks. Borrowers wanted additional loans and extensions of credit, and depositors wanted their money back. *As many depositors tried to withdraw their money, they couldn't because each bank held only a fraction of its deposits as cash reserves.* To reduce such panics, Congress created the **Federal Reserve System** in 1913 as the central bank and monetary authority of the United States.

Nearly all industrialized countries had formed central banks by 1900—such as the Bundesbank in Germany, the Bank of Japan, and the Bank of England, which has been around since 1694. But the American public's suspicion of monopoly power led to the establishment of not one central bank but separate banks in each of 12 Federal Reserve districts around the country. The new banks were named after the cities in which they were located—the Federal Reserve Banks of Boston, New York, Chicago, San Francisco, and so on, as shown in Exhibit 3 (which district are you in?). *Throughout most of its history, the United States had what is called a decentralized banking system. The Federal Reserve Act moved the country toward a system that was partly centralized and partly decentralized.* All national banks had to join the Federal Reserve System and thus were subject to new regulations issued by *the Fed,* as it came to be called (don't confuse *the Fed* with *the Feds,* shorthand for the Federal Bureau of Investigation and other federal crime fighters). For state banks, membership was voluntary, and, to avoid the new regulations, most did not join.

## 13-3c Powers of the Federal Reserve System

The Federal Reserve was authorized to ensure sufficient money and credit in the banking system as needed to support a growing economy. The power to issue bank notes was taken away from national banks and turned over to Federal Reserve banks. (Take out a $1 note and notice what it says across the top: "FEDERAL RESERVE NOTE." On the front of a $1 note, the seal to the left of George Washington's portrait identifies which Federal Reserve bank issued the note.) The Federal Reserve was also granted other powers: *to buy and sell government securities, to extend loans to member banks, to clear checks in the banking system, and to require that member banks hold reserves equal to at least some specified fraction of their deposits.*

Federal Reserve banks do not deal with the public directly. Each may be thought of as a bankers' bank. Reserve banks hold deposits of member banks, just as depository institutions hold deposits of the public, and they extend loans to member banks, just as depository institutions extend loans to the public. The name *reserve bank* comes from the responsibility to hold member bank *reserves* on deposit.

**Reserves** are funds that banks have on hand or on deposit with the Fed to promote banking safety, to facilitate interbank transfers of funds, to satisfy the cash

---

*Exhibit 3*

**The Twelve Federal Reserve Districts**

The map shows by color the area covered by each of the 12 Federal Reserve districts. Black dots note the locations of the Federal Reserve bank in each district. Identified with a white star is the Board of Governors headquarters in Washington, DC.

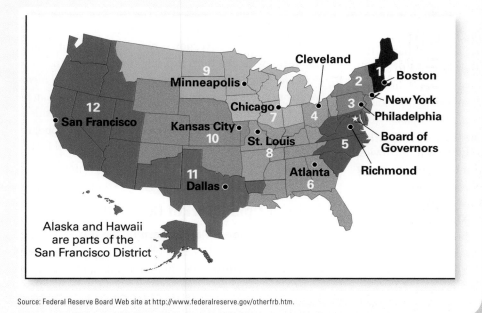

Alaska and Hawaii are parts of the San Francisco District

Source: Federal Reserve Board Web site at http://www.federalreserve.gov/otherfrb.htm.

---

**Federal Reserve System, or the Fed** The central bank and monetary authority of the United States

**reserves** Funds that banks use to satisfy the cash demands of their customers and the reserve requirements of the Fed; reserves consist of cash held by banks plus deposits at the Fed demands of their customers, and to comply with Federal Reserve regulations. By holding bank reserves, a Reserve bank can clear a check written by a depositor at one bank and deposited at another bank, much like the goldsmith's moving of gold reserves from the farmer's account to the horse trader's account. Reserve banks are also authorized to lend to banks in need of reserves; the interest rate charged is called the *discount rate*.

A member bank is required to own stock in its district Federal Reserve bank, and this entitles the bank to a 6 percent annual dividend. Any additional profit earned by the Reserve banks is turned over to the U.S. Treasury. So, technically, the Reserve banks are owned by the member banks in the district, but in practice the Fed is a not-for-profit, independent agency of the federal government. When the Fed chair gets grilled, it's by Congress, not by member banks.

## 13-3d Banking Troubles During the Great Depression

From 1913 to 1929, both the Federal Reserve System and the national economy performed relatively well. But the stock market crash of 1929 was followed by the Great Depression, creating a new set of problems for the Fed, such as bank runs caused by panicked depositors. The Fed, however, dropped the ball by failing to act as a lender of last resort—that is, the Fed did not lend banks the money they needed to satisfy deposit withdrawals in cases of runs on otherwise sound banks. In fact, banks were discouraged from borrowing from the Fed; such borrowing came with a stigma, a sign of weakness, and this contributed to the banking panic of the day.[3] Many banks did not survive. Between 1930 and 1933, about 10,000 banks failed—about one-third of all U.S. banks. Most depositors at the failed banks lost everything. Banking panics, lost savings, and bank failures fueled the rising unemployment and lost output during the period.[4]

In his first inaugural address in 1933, newly elected President Franklin D. Roosevelt said, "The only thing we have to fear is fear itself," a statement especially apt for a fractional reserve banking system. Most banks were sound as long as people had confidence in the safety of their deposits. But if many depositors tried to withdraw their money, they could not do so because each bank held only a fraction of deposits as reserves. Bank legislation passed during the Great Depression shored up the banking system and centralized power with the Fed in Washington. Here are some features of that legislation.

*Bank legislation passed under President Franklin Roosevelt shored up the banking system and centralized power with the Fed in Washington.*

### Board of Governors

The *Board of Governors*, which consists of seven members appointed by the president and confirmed by the Senate, became responsible for setting and implementing the nation's monetary policy. *Monetary policy*, a term introduced in Chapter 3, is the regulation of the economy's money supply and interest rates to promote macroeconomic objectives. The Board of Governors now oversees the 12 Reserve banks, making the system more centralized. Each governor serves a 14-year nonrenewable term, with one term expiring every even-numbered year. *The long tenure is designed to insulate board members from political pressure.* A new U.S. president can be sure of appointing only two members during a presidential term, so a new president could not change monetary policy that much. One governor is also appointed by the U.S. president to chair the Board for a four-year term, with no limit on reappointments.

### Federal Open Market Committee

The **Federal Open Market Committee (FOMC)** makes decisions about the key tool of monetary policy, **open-market operations**—the Fed's buying and selling of

**Federal Open Market Committee** The 12-member group that makes decisions about open-market operations—purchases and sales of U.S. government securities by the Fed that affect the money supply and interest rates; consists of the seven Board governors plus five of the 12 presidents of the Reserve banks

**open-market operations** Purchases and sales of government securities by the Fed in an effort to influence the money supply

3. Gary Gorton and Andrew Metrick, "The Federal Reserve and Panic Prevention: The Role of Financial Regulation and Lender of Last Resort," *Journal of Economic Perspectives*, 27 (Fall 2013): 45–64.

4. Andrew J. Jalil, "A New History of Banking Panics in the United States, 1925–1929: Construction and Implications," *American Economic Journal: Macroeconomics* (forthcoming).

government securities (tools of monetary policy are examined in the next chapter). The FOMC consists of the 7 board governors plus 5 of the 12 presidents of the Reserve banks; the chair of the Board of Governors heads the group. Because the New York Federal Reserve bank carries out open-market operations, that bank's president always sits on the FOMC. The structure of the Federal Reserve System is presented in Exhibit 4. The FOMC and, less significantly, the Federal Advisory Committee (which consists of a banker from each of the 12 Reserve bank districts) advise the board.

> **"The Federal Reserve System has a variety of tools to regulate the money supply."**

## Regulating the Money Supply

Because reserves amount to just a fraction of deposits, the United States has a *fractional reserve* banking system, as already noted. The Federal Reserve System has a variety of tools to regulate the money supply,

including (1) conducting open-market operations—buying and selling U.S. government securities; (2) setting the discount rate—the interest rate charged by Reserve banks for loans to member banks; and (3) setting legal reserve requirements for member banks. We examine these long-standing tools in greater detail in the next two chapters and discuss additional tools developed to deal with the financial crisis of 2008.

## Deposit Insurance

Panic runs on banks stemmed from fears about the safety of bank deposits. The *Federal Deposit Insurance Corporation (FDIC)* was established in 1933 to insure the first $2,500 of each deposit account. Today the insurance ceiling is $250,000 per depositor per bank. Over 90 percent of all banks now purchase FDIC insurance, and deposits at FDIC-insured institutions totaled

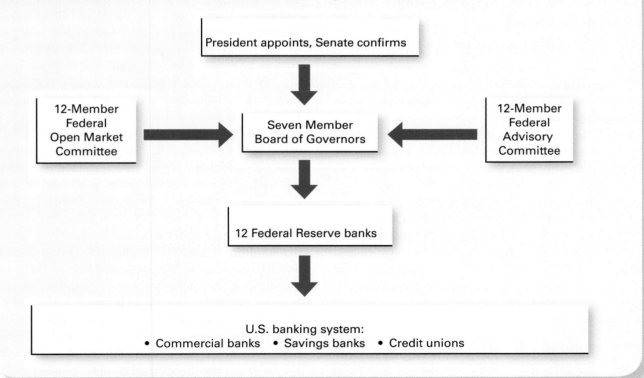

*Exhibit 4*

**Organization Chart of the Federal Reserve System**

Members of the Board of Governors are appointed by the president and confirmed by the Senate. The seven board members also belong to the 12-member Federal Open Market Committee, which advises the board. The Board of Governors controls the Reserve banks in each of the 12 districts, which in turn control the U.S. banking system.

President appoints, Senate confirms

12-Member Federal Open Market Committee

Seven Member Board of Governors

12-Member Federal Advisory Committee

12 Federal Reserve banks

U.S. banking system:
• Commercial banks  • Savings banks  • Credit unions

$10.6 trillion in 2015. Other insurance programs take care of the rest. *Deposit insurance, by calming fears about the safety of bank deposits, worked wonders to reduce bank runs.*

## Goals of the Fed

The Fed's primary goals, its legal mandates, are price stability and maximum employment. Stable prices promote greater certainty, make economic planning easier, and help savers retain their spending power over time. Maximum employment means that jobs are easier to find so more people have money to spend.

Thus, price stability and maximum employment motivate Fed actions. But over the years, the Fed has accumulated additional responsibilities. Here are four frequently mentioned goals of the Fed: (1) economic growth, (2) interest rate stability, (3) financial market stability, and (4) exchange rate stability. *All these goals boil down to low inflation; high employment; economic growth; and stability in interest rates, financial markets, and exchange rates.* As we will see, not all of these objectives can be achieved simultaneously.

## 13-3e Banks Lost Deposits When Inflation Increased

Prior to the 1930s, banks could own corporate stocks and bonds, financial assets that fluctuated widely in value and contributed to instability of the banking system. Reforms enacted during the Great Depression limited bank assets primarily to loans and government securities—bonds issued by federal, state, and local governments. A *bond* is an IOU, so a government bond is an IOU from the government. Also, bank failures during the 1930s were thought to have resulted in part from fierce interest-rate competition among banks for customer deposits. To curb such competition, the Fed was empowered to set a ceiling on interest rates that banks could pay depositors.

These restrictions made banking a heavily regulated industry. Banks lost much of their freedom to wheel and deal, and the federal government insured most deposits. The assets banks could acquire were carefully limited, as were the interest rates they could offer depositors (checking deposits earned no interest).

> **"The Fed's primary goals, its legal mandates, are price stability and maximum employment."**

**money market mutual fund** A collection of short-term interest-earning assets purchased with funds collected from many shareholders

Banking thus became a highly regulated, even stuffy, industry. The term "banker's hours" was applied derisively to someone who had a short workday.

Ceilings on interest rates reduced interest-rate competition for deposits *among* banks. But a surge of inflation during the 1970s increased interest rates in the economy. When market interest rates rose above what banks could legally offer depositors, many withdrew their deposits and put them into higher-yielding alternatives. In 1972, Merrill Lynch, a major brokerage house, introduced an account combining a **money market mutual fund** with limited check-writing privileges. Money market mutual fund shares are claims on a portfolio, or collection, of short-term interest-earning assets. These mutual funds, as financial intermediaries, became stiff competition for bank deposits, especially checkable deposits, which at the time paid no interest at banks.

## 13-3f Banking Deregulation

In response to the loss of deposits and other problems, Congress tried to ease regulations, giving banks greater discretion in their operations. For example, interest-rate ceilings for deposits were eliminated, and all depository institutions were allowed to offer money market deposit accounts. Such deposits jumped from only $8 billion in 1978 to $200 billion in 1982. Some states, like California and Texas, also deregulated state-chartered savings banks. The combination of deposit insurance, unregulated interest rates, and wider latitude in the kinds of assets that savings banks could purchase gave them a green light to compete for large deposits in national markets. Savings banks had been restricted to residential lending, but the 1982 legislation allowed them to make commercial loans. Once-staid financial institutions moved into the fast lane.

Banks could wheel and deal but with the benefit of deposit insurance. The combination of deregulation and deposit insurance encouraged some on the verge of failing to take bigger risks—to "bet the bank"—because their depositors would be protected by deposit insurance. This created a *moral hazard,* which in this case was the tendency of bankers to take unwarranted risks in making loans because deposits were insured. Banks that were virtually bankrupt—so-called zombie banks—were able to attract deposits because of deposit insurance. Zombie banks, by offering higher interest rates, also drew deposits away from healthier banks. Meanwhile, because deposits were insured, most depositors paid less attention to their banks' health. Thus, *deposit insurance, originally introduced during the Great Depression to prevent bank panics, caused depositors to become complacent about the safety of their deposits. Worse still, it caused those who ran troubled banks to take wild gambles to survive.*

## 13-3g Banks on the Ropes

Many of these gambles didn't pay off, particularly loans to real estate developers, and banks lost a ton of money. The insolvency and collapse of a growing number of banks prompted Congress in 1989 to approve what was then the largest financial bailout of any U.S. industry—a measure that would eventually cost about $180 billion in today's dollars. Taxpayers paid 80 percent of the total, and banks paid the remaining 20 percent through higher deposit insurance premiums. The money was spent to close down failing banks, pay off insured depositors, and find healthier banks to take over the deposit accounts. Exhibit 5 shows the number of bank failures in the United States by year since 1980. About 3,000 banks failed between the early 1980s and early 1990s, with 1989 the peak.

## 13-3h Banks Recover

As failed banks disappeared or merged with stronger banks, the industry got healthier. Bank profits grew four-fold during the 1990s. Although the number of commercial banks fell by half since the mid-1980s, the United States, with about 5,600 Federal Deposit Insurance Corporation (FDIC)-insured commercial banks in early 2015, still had more than any other country. Other major economies have fewer than 1,000 commercial banks (Japan and Canada, for example, have fewer than 100 banks each, though most have many branches). The large number of U.S. banks reflects past restrictions on **bank branches**, which are additional offices that carry out banking operations. Again, Americans, fearing monopoly power, did not want any one bank to become too large or powerful. The combination of intrastate and interstate restrictions on branching spawned the many commercial banks that exist today, most of which are relatively small. For example, the bottom 98 percent of U.S. commercial banks in 2015 held just 20 percent of all deposits. Branching restrictions create inefficiencies, because banks cannot achieve optimal size and cannot easily diversify their portfolios

> **bank branches** A bank's additional offices that carry out banking operations

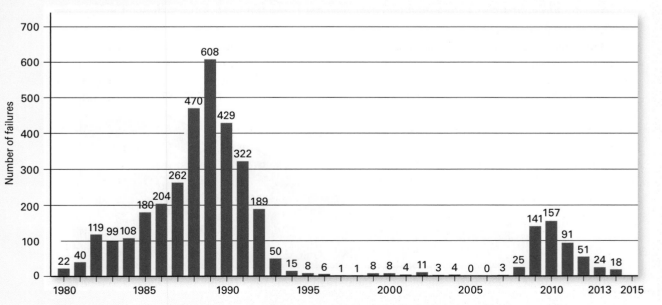

*Exhibit 5*

**U.S. Bank Failures Peaked in 1989**

Sources: Based on annual reports from the Federal Deposit Insurance Corporation. For the latest figures, go to http://www.fdic.gov/bank/individual/failed/banklist.html.

of loans across different regions. Branching restrictions were one reason for bank failures during the Depression. Such restrictions meant a bank made loans primarily in one community—it had all its eggs in that basket. Geographic expansion reduces bank risks.[5]

In recent years, federal legislation has lifted some restrictions on interstate branching and on the kinds of assets that banks can own. Two developments allowed banks to get around branching restrictions: bank holding companies and mergers. A **bank holding company** is a corporation that may own several different banks. The *Gramm-Leach-Bliley Act* of 1999 repealed some Depression-era restrictions on the kinds of assets a bank could own. A holding company can provide other services that banks are not authorized to offer, such as financial advising, leasing, insurance, credit cards, and securities trading. Thus, holding companies blossomed. About 90 percent of the nation's checking deposits are in banks owned by holding companies. But in the aftermath of the recent financial crises, policy makers restricted the kinds of assets a bank can own and trade, as you'll soon see.

Another important development that allowed banks to expand their geographical reach is *bank mergers,* which have spread the presence of some banks across the country. Banks are merging because they want more customers and expect the higher volume of transactions to reduce operating costs per customer. Nationwide banking is also seen as a way of avoiding the concentration of bad loans that sometimes occurs in one geographical area. The merger movement was initially fueled by a rising stock market and by federal legislation that facilitates consolidation of merged banks. More recently, some banks weakened by the financial crisis have been forced to merge with stronger banks to survive.

Bank holding companies and bank mergers have reduced the number of banks, but increased the number of branches. Exhibit 6 shows the number of commercial banks and bank branches in the United States since 1934. The number of banks, as indicated by "main offices," remained relatively constant between 1934 and 1982 but has since fallen by more than half as a result of failures, mergers, and holding companies. The number of bank branches increased steadily, however, more than doubling since 1982. So the number of branches per bank increased. In 1982, the average U.S. commercial bank had about three branches; by 2014, it had about 14 branches. But with the spread of online banking and growth of cash-back opportunities using debit cards, banks face less market pressure now to expand the number of branches or even ATMs.

**bank holding company**
A corporation that owns banks

5. Martin Goetz, Luc Laeven, and Ross Levine, "Does the Geographic Expansion of Bank Assets Reduce Risk?" NBER Working Paper No. 20758 (December 2014).

*Exhibit 6*

**Number of Commercial Banks Declined over the Last Three Decades, but the Number of Branches Has Grown**

Sources: Figures are for FDIC-insured commercial banks in the United States based on Federal Deposit Insurance Corporation and the Federal Reserve Bank data.

## 13-4 BANKING DURING AND AFTER THE GREAT RECESSION OF 2007–2009

The biggest financial development in recent years has been the introduction of the subprime mortgage, which contributed to the financial crisis of 2008 and the Great Recession. Here's what happened.

### 13-4a Subprime Mortgages and Mortgage-Backed Securities

Prior to 2000, only a credit worthy, or *prime*, borrower could get a home mortgage. But new statistical techniques and better computers supposedly increased a lender's ability to assess the risk of a **subprime mortgage**, which is a mortgage for a borrower with a not-so-good credit rating. Any household with a credit history could be assigned a numerical credit score, and this score could be used to predict how likely that borrower would be to default on mortgage payments. Borrowers more likely to default would pay a higher interest rate to compensate the lender for their higher risk. Hundreds of mortgages could then be bundled together based on credit scores into a **mortgage-backed security**, which represents a claim on the monthly payments made on those mortgages. The idea is that subprime mortgages could be blended with other mortgages in whatever proportion needed to arrive at a particular level of default risk for the security. And a securities-rating agency could look at the mix of mortgages and assign that security an overall credit rating. A higher proportion of subprime loans would result in a higher-risk security, but would also yield a higher return for investors. Investors could choose securities based on their tolerance for risk. Mortgage-backed securities opened up new sources of financing for subprime borrowers.

After the U.S economy recovered from the recession of 2001, subprime mortgages grew in popularity. Fueled by lending sources coming into the United States from places like China, the sub prime market became a trillion-dollar business by 2007. This development was considered good for America because it gave more households access to mortgage credit. Subprime borrowers might pay higher interest rates than prime borrowers, but at least they could get mortgages. The availability of subprime mortgages turned some renters into homeowners, a group presumably more committed to the community. Indeed, federal regulators pressured financial institutions into lending to groups that before the advent of subprime mortgages had been underserved.

Subprime loans increased the demand for housing, which raised housing prices, which, in turn, fueled a boom in subprime loans in a reinforcing cycle. As home prices rose, many borrowers saw this as an opportunity to refinance. Based on the rising value of their homes, they would take out a bigger mortgage, use most of that money to pay off the old one, and still have money left over. Of course, monthly mortgage payments would increase too, but rising home prices meant that, in a pinch, the house could always be sold to pay off the mortgage. After all, home prices had been marching higher for at least two decades. Mortgage-backed securities were considered a safe investment offering an attractive return. They were sold around the world. Banks and other financial institutions bought a lot of them. What could go wrong?

### 13-4b Bad Incentives Fueled the Financial Crisis of 2008

A subprime mortgage typically originated with a mortgage broker (two-thirds originated this way). The mortgage was then sold to an underwriter who bundled it with other mortgages and sold them as a mortgage-backed security to investors, the source of financing in the deal. Once the mortgage was originated, that mortgage broker earned a fee and soon lost interest in whether the borrower was good for the money. Research indicates that the riskier the loan, the higher the interest rate, and the more the broker made on that loan. Brokers had an incentive to encourage borrowers to apply for mortgages they could not afford, and some brokers falsified information on mortgage applications to make sure they would get approved. Some borrowers also exaggerated their income if there was no income verification (these became known as "liar's loans"). Making everything worse was lax regulation of mortgage originators, who were not required to tell borrowers whether or not they could afford the loans. Some borrowers clearly could not afford their loans. Research suggests that about a third of subprime loans should not have been made in the first place.[6]

Meanwhile, banks and other financial institutions were earning attractive fees creating and selling mortgage-backed securities. Underwriters of mortgage-backed securities usually had little incentive to

**subprime mortgage** Mortgage for a borrower with a not-so-good credit rating

**mortgage-backed security** A claim on payments made on the many mortgages bundled into this financial instrument

6. Sumit Agarwal et al. "Predatory Lending and the Subprime Mortgage," *Journal of Financial Economics*, 113 (July 2014): 29–52.

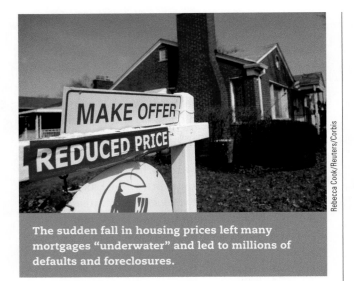

The sudden fall in housing prices left many mortgages "underwater" and led to millions of defaults and foreclosures.

Rebecca Cook/Reuters/Corbis

make sure that those who bought the securities would ultimately get paid.[7] Worse yet, the credit-rating agencies that evaluated these securities also had a conflict of interest. They earned their fees by assessing the riskiness of these securities. But underwriters could shop around for the credit-rating agency that offered the highest rating. Thus, mortgage-backed securities tended to get better ratings than they deserved—that is, the securities were actually more risky than their credit ratings indicated.

As housing prices rose and the profitability of converting mortgages into securities increased, underlying credit standards fell. Riskier borrowers could get mortgages with little trouble. The size of the mortgages increased, as did the loan-to-value ratio, meaning that instead of borrowing up to 80 percent of a home's value, home buyers could borrow 90 or even 100 percent of its value. And borrowers could often take out a second mortgage to pay for the down payment, so they ended up needing little or no money down to buy a house. In 2001 half of all mortgages required down payments of 20 percent or less; by 2006 at least half required down payments of only 10 percent or less, and a quarter of mortgages had no down payment requirements at all.

Bundling hundreds of mortgages into a single mortgage-backed security made

**Troubled Asset Relief Program, or TARP**
Government program that invested in financial institutions and automakers to help stabilize financial markets

> **"Policy makers had not seen anything like this in their lifetimes."**

for a complicated investment, and this worsened the incentive problems. Yet as long as home prices were rising, everyone was happy—the borrower, the mortgage originator, the banker who underwrote and sold the mortgage-backed security, the credit-rater, and the investor who found the yield attractive. But housing prices reached a level that in retrospect was far out of whack with fundamentals of the housing market. After peaking in 2006, housing prices began to fall. Between 2006 and the middle of 2008, U.S. home prices plunged 22 percent on average. With housing prices tumbling, all the corners cut in the mortgage market soon became obvious. Many mortgages slipped "underwater," meaning that borrowers owed more than the house was worth. Such borrowers had an incentive to stop making payments. Many did, and defaults rose sharply, leading to millions of foreclosures.

Mortgage-backed securities quickly turned into "troubled assets." Because nobody wanted them, their value plummeted. Rising home foreclosures fed into the full-scale global financial panic in September 2008. The collapse of a major investment bank, Lehman Brothers, signaled that other financial institutions could soon follow. Nobody wanted to lend money they might not get back. Credit dried up. Panic spread to consumers, who cut consumption because of falling home prices, mounting job losses, and a collapsing stock market.

### 13-4c The Troubled Asset Relief Program

Policy makers had not seen anything like this in their lifetimes. By early October 2008, a consensus had formed around a stopgap measure to help unfreeze credit markets and stabilize the banks. The **Troubled Asset Relief Program**, or **TARP**, authorized the U.S. Treasury to purchase up to $700 billion in mortgage-backed securities. The idea was to buy these illiquid, difficult-to-value assets and get them off the banks' books. Treasury officials soon decided that TARP money would not be used to buy troubled assets but instead would be invested directly into financial institutions that were sound except for their troubled assets. The idea was to infuse new financial capital into these financial institutions to prevent more failures and to get banks lending again. The failure of Lehman Brothers was such a shock to financial markets that policy makers wanted to prevent other financial giants from collapsing. A trillion-dollar

7. See, for example, Benjamin Keys et al. "Did Securitization Lead to Lax Screening? Evidence from Subprime Loans," *Quarterly Journal of Economics*, 125 (February 2010): 307–362.

institution such as AIG, with its financial ties to hundreds of other financial institutions, had become **too big to fail**—that is, its failure would have been such a disaster for the wider economy that failure had to be prevented, even if it required a financial bailout.

TARP money was used to buy stakes in banks large and small. (TARP money also bought government stakes in General Motors and Chrysler to keep the car makers operating.) Once financial markets stabilized a bit and the stock market recovered some ground, the value of the Treasury's investment increased (ultimately, the Treasury would get its money back with interest from all except the automakers, where the loss amounted to about $9 billion). But housing prices continued to fall, homes continued to slip under water, and banks continued to suffer from mortgage defaults. Underwater loans were greatest in Nevada, Arizona, Florida, Michigan, and California.

All these troubles contributed to a spike in bank failures. As was shown in Exhibit 5, failures climbed from 25 in 2008 to 157 in 2010. By 2014, failures declined to just 18. Because of failures and mergers, the number of banks in the United States declined from about 18,000 in 1984 to about 6,500 in 2015. Eighty-seven percent were commercial banks, and 13 percent were savings banks. Commercial banks account for the overwhelming share of deposits. The troubles created by subprime mortgages, mortgage-backed securities, and other financial problems prompted regulatory reform. That's discussed next.

### 13-4d The Dodd–Frank Act of 2010

In 2010, President Obama signed into law the most sweeping overhaul of financial regulations since the Great Depression. The **Dodd-Frank Wall Street Reform and Consumer Protection Act**, named for its sponsors in the Senate and House, took 18 months to develop and will take many years to implement. The legislation, which was 2,300 pages long, authorized 10 regulatory agencies to write and interpret hundreds of new rules governing financial markets.

Some provisions aim to remedy the incentive problems already discussed. To ensure that borrowers can repay a home loan, a mortgage originator must verify income, credit history, and job status. Mortgage originators cannot be paid more for funneling borrowers to riskier loans. To ensure that issuers of mortgage-backed securities are sensitive to the risk of these assets, issuers must retain at least 5 percent of the credit risk associated with the mortgages. And credit-rating agencies will be subject to new regulations.

For the first time, the law authorizes the Federal Reserve to regulate companies other than banks—such as insurance companies and investment firms—if they are engaged mostly in financial activities. The law imposes other regulations on banks, limiting their ability to trade on their own behalf and restricting their investments in hedge funds and private equity funds, which tend to be riskier.

The law establishes the *Financial Stability Oversight Council*, a super-regulator that monitors Wall Street's largest firms and other market participants to spot and respond to emerging systemic risks. The nine-member panel, led by the Treasury Department, includes regulators from other agencies. Regulators get new authority to seize and liquidate troubled financial firms if their failure would jeopardize the nation's financial stability (such as with AIG). The idea is that reducing systemic risk and maintaining financial stability become regulatory objectives. A new *Bureau of Consumer Financial Protection* has broad powers to write consumer-protection rules for banks and other firms that offer financial services.

*Financial regulators get more funding, more information, and more power.* Supporters say the law will reduce the likelihood of another financial crisis and will handle it better if one should occur. Others aren't so sure. Some economists argue that there are many ways a firm can take risks, and banning one form of risk-taking just shifts traders to other kinds of risk. For example, at a high enough interest rate, a bank may be willing to lend to extremely risky borrowers. What other unintended consequences will the new regulations create? Will regulations stifle financial innovation? Will U.S. financial institutions lose business to foreign competitors? Will the availability of credit be impaired by increased uncertainty and costs? Will new financial products be developed that make the regulations irrelevant? Will credit flows get choked by regulatory bureaucracy and politics? More generally, how will capitalism change if government regulators can seize and liquidate any financial institution? It's said that the military is often planning for the previous war. Are regulators, the same ones who allowed all this to happen in the first place, gearing up to prevent the next financial crisis?

There have been 17 financial crises in the United States since 1792. That's an average of one every 13 years. Researchers have traced how financial crises affected real per capita income. After examining one hundred such crises in 12 countries beginning in 1790, researchers concluded that it usually took years for per capita income to recover to its pre-crisis level. For example, six years after the onset of the recent financial crisis, only Germany and the United States (out of the 12 nations studied) had surpassed their 2007-2008 peaks of real per capita income.[8]

8. Carmen Reinhart and Kenneth Rogoff, "Recovery from Financial Crises: Evidence from 100 Episodes." *American Economic Review*, 104 (May 2014): 50–55.

### 13-4e Top Banks in America and the World

The financial crisis of 2008 and the recession rattled the banking world. Let's take a look at the biggest banks in America and in the world. Exhibit 7 (a) shows the top 10 U.S. banks based on their U.S. assets at the end of 2014. Notice the wide range in size, with the top bank

*Exhibit 7*

**Top 10 Banks in America and in the World**

Among America's top 10 banks (based on U.S. assets) in panel (a), size differs sharply, with the top bank about eight times larger than the tenth-ranked bank. Among the world's top 10 banks (based on worldwide assets) in panel (b), only one, JPMorgan Chase, is American.

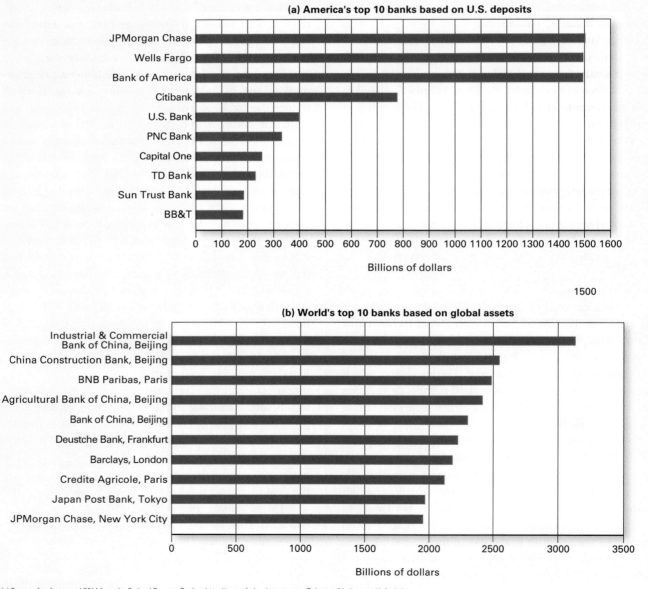

(a) America's top 10 banks based on U.S. deposits

Billions of dollars

(b) World's top 10 banks based on global assets

Billions of dollars

(a) Source: As of year-end 2014 from the Federal Reserve Bank at http://www.federalreserve.gov/Releases/Lbr/current/default.htm.
(b) Source: "Top Banks in the World," Accuity, available at http://www.accuity.com/useful-links/bank-rankings/. Figures are for November 2014.

holding over eight times the assets as the bank ranked tenth. The top banks grew mostly through mergers and acquisitions. Because of the subprime mortgage and global financial crises of September 2008, some big banks that were in trouble had to be taken over by healthier banks. For example, Wachovia, in 2008 the nation's third-largest bank, had to merge with Wells Fargo, then the nation's fourth largest. And Washington Mutual, at the time the sixth-largest bank, was seized by the FDIC after a 10 day bank run during which depositors withdrew $16 billion, or about 10 percent of all deposits. The FDIC arranged for Washington Mutual to be acquired by JPMorgan Chase. You can see from panel (a) of Exhibit 7 that JPMorgan Chase most recently ranked first in assets among U.S. banks, and Wells Fargo ranked second.

How big are U.S. banks on the world stage? Not very. Only one U.S. bank ranks among the top 10 based on worldwide assets. As shown by Exhibit 7 (b), China is home to four of the world's five largest banks. France has two in the top 10. Thus, the United States has the second largest economy in the world (slightly below China) but has only one bank among the top 10 in the world. This partly reflects America's lingering fear of big banks. Some U.S. banks may be considered "too big to fail," but all but JPMorgan Chase are still too small to rank among the world's top 10.

## 13-5 FINAL WORD

Money has grown increasingly more abstract over time, moving from commodity money to paper money that represented a claim on some commodity, such as gold, to paper money with no intrinsic value. As you will see, paper money constitutes only a fraction of the money supply. Modern money also consists of electronic entries in the banking system's computers. So money has changed from a physical commodity to an electronic entry. Money today does not so much change hands as change electronic accounts.

## STUDY TOOLS 13

### READY TO STUDY? IN THE BOOK, YOU CAN:

- ☐ Work the Problems at the end of the chapter.

- ☐ Rip out the chapter review card for a handy summary of the chapter and key terms.

### ONLINE AT CENGAGEBRAIN.COM YOU CAN:

- ☐ Collect StudyBits while you read and study the chapter.
- ☐ Quiz yourself on key concepts.

- ☐ Prepare for tests with chapter flash cards as well as flash cards that you create.
- ☐ Watch videos to explore economics further.

# CHAPTER 13 PROBLEMS

*Your instructor can access the answers to these problems online at http://cengagebrain.com.*

## 13-1 Identify three functions of money and six qualities of the ideal money

1. *(Functions of Money)* What are three functions of money?
2. *(Ideal Money)* What are six qualities of the ideal money?
3. *(Origins of Banking)* Discuss the various ways in which London goldsmiths functioned as early banks.
4. *(Types of Money)* Complete each of the following sentences:
   a. A product that serves both as money and as a commodity is _____.
   b. Some coins and all paper money circulating in the United States have face values that exceed the value of the materials from which they are made. Therefore, they are forms of _____.
   c. If the government declares that creditors must accept a form of money as payment for debts, the money becomes _____.
   d. A common unit for measuring the value of every good or service in the economy is known as a(n) _____.
5. *(Fiat Money)* Most economists believe that the better fiat money serves as a store of value, the more acceptable it is. What does this statement mean? How could people lose faith in money?
6. *(The Value of Money)* When the value of money was based on its gold content, new discoveries of gold were frequently followed by periods of inflation. Explain.

## 13-2 Explain what is meant by a fractional reserve banking system

7. *(Depository Institutions)* What is a depository institution, and what types of depository institutions are found in the United States? How do they act as intermediaries between savers and borrowers? Why do they play this role?

8. *(Depository Institutions)* Explain why a bank typically holds as reserves only a fraction of its deposit liabilities? In light of this arrangement, why is it important that depositors have confidence in their bank's health?

## 13-3 Describe the Fed, summarize its two mandated objectives, and outline some of its other goals

9. *(Federal Reserve System)* What are the main powers and responsibilities of the Federal Reserve System? What are its two mandates and some of it's other goals?

## 13-4 Describe subprime mortgages and the role they played in the financial crisis of 2008

10. *(Subprime Mortgages)* What are subprime mortgages, and what role did they play in the financial crisis of 2008?
11. *(Bank Deregulation)* Some economists argue that deregulating the interest rates that could be paid on deposits combined with deposit insurance led to the insolvency of many depository institutions during the 1980s. On what basis do they make such an argument?

# MACRO ECON ONLINE

## PREPARE FOR TESTS ON THE STUDYBOARD!

CORRECT

INCORRECT

INCORRECT

INCORRECT

**Personalize Quizzes from Your StudyBits**

**Take Practice Quizzes by Chapter**

CHAPTER QUIZZES

Chapter 1

Chapter 2

Chapter 3

Chapter 4

4LTR PRESS

# 14 | Banking and the Money Supply

Matthias Kulka/Corbis

## LEARNING OUTCOMES

After studying this chapter, you will be able to...

**14-1** Explain why using a debit card is like using cash, but using a credit card is not

**14-2** Explain why a bank is in a better position to lend your savings than you are

**14-3** Describe how banks create money

**14-4** Summarize the Fed's tools of monetary policy

After finishing this chapter go to **PAGE 263** for **STUDY TOOLS**

**Topics discussed in Chapter 14 include:**

- Money aggregates
- Checkable deposits
- Debit cards
- Bitcoin
- Balance sheets
- Money creation
- The money multiplier
- Tools of the Fed

- How do banks create money?
- Why are banks called First Trust or Security National rather than Benny's Bank or Loans 'R' Us?
- How is the Fed both literally and figuratively a money machine?
- Why are we so interested in banks, anyway?

- After all, isn't banking a business like any other, such as dry cleaning, auto washing, or home remodeling?
- Why not devote a chapter to the home-remodeling business?

*Answers to these and related questions are provided in this chapter, which examines banking and the money supply.*

In this chapter, we take a closer look at the unique role banks play in the economy. Banks are special in macroeconomics because, like the London goldsmith, they can convert a borrower's IOU into money, one key to a healthy economy. Because regulatory reforms have eliminated many of the distinctions between commercial banks and thrift institutions, all depository institutions are usually referred to more simply as banks.

> **"How is the Fed both literally and figuratively a money machine?"**

We begin by going over the definitions of money, from the narrow to the broad view. Then, we look at how banks work and how they create money. We also consider the Fed in more detail. As you will see, the Fed attempts to control the money supply directly by issuing currency and indirectly by regulating bank reserves.

## 14-1 MONEY AGGREGATES

When you think of money, what comes to mind is probably currency—dollar notes and coins. But as you learned in the last chapter, dollar notes and coins account for only part of the money supply. In this section, we consider two definitions of money.

### 14-1a Narrow Definition of Money: M1

Suppose you have some cash with you right now—dollar notes and coins. These are part of the money supply as narrowly defined. If you were to deposit this cash in your checking account, you could then write a check or use a debit card directing your bank to pay someone from your account. **Checkable deposits** are bank deposits that allow the account owner to draw down that account with a check or a debit card. Checkable deposits are included in the narrow definition of money. Banks hold a variety of checkable deposits. In recent years, financial institutions have developed other kinds of accounts that carry check-writing privileges but also earn interest.

**Money aggregates** are measures of the money supply defined by the Federal Reserve. The narrow definition, called **M1**, consists of currency (including coins) held by the nonbanking public, checkable deposits, and traveler's checks. Note that currency in bank vaults is not counted as part of the money supply because it is not being used as a medium of exchange—it's just sitting there out of circulation. But checkable deposits are money because their owners can write checks or use debit cards to tap them. Checkable deposits are the liabilities of the issuing banks, which stand ready to convert them into cash. But unlike cash, checks are not legal tender, as signs that say "No Checks!" attest.

The currency circulating in the United States consists mostly of Federal Reserve notes, which are produced by the U.S. Bureau of Engraving

**checkable deposits**
Bank deposits that allow the account owner to write checks to third parties; debit cards can also access these deposits and transmit them electronically

**money aggregates**
Measures of the economy's money supply

**M1** The narrow measure of the money supply, consisting of currency and coins held by the nonbanking public, checkable deposits, and traveler's checks

A menu of a restaurant in Ecuador, where prices are in U.S. dollars.

and Printing and are issued by and are liabilities of the 12 Federal Reserve banks. Nearly one-third of the Fed's liabilities consist of Federal Reserve notes. The Fed spends about $600 million a year printing, storing, and distributing notes. Because Federal Reserve notes are redeemable for nothing other than more Federal Reserve notes, U.S. currency is *fiat money*. The other component of currency is coins, manufactured by the U.S. Mint, which sells these coins to Federal Reserve banks at face value. Like paper money, some U.S. coins are token money because the face value of the coins exceeds the cost of production (though the cost of minting the penny and the nickel now exceed their face values). The U.S. Mint, a division of the U.S. Treasury, reaps any profit from coin production (in 2013 this amounted to $289 million, mostly from quarters).

About half of Federal Reserve notes are held abroad.[1] Some countries, such as Panama, Ecuador, and El Salvador, use U.S. dollars as their currency. In other countries, especially those that have experienced high inflation, U.S. dollars circulate alongside the local currency. In Vietnam, for example, some high-end restaurants list prices in U.S. dollars, not in dong, the national

1. Ruth Judson, "Crisis and Calm: Demand for U.S. Currency at Home and Abroad," Board of Governors of the Federal Reserve System, International Finance Discussion Paper No. 1058 (November 2012) at http://www.federalreserve.gov/PubS/ifdp/2012/1058/ifdp1058.pdf.

**savings deposits** Bank deposits that earn interest but have no specific maturity date

**time deposits** Bank deposits that earn a fixed interest rate if held for the specified period, which can range from several months to several years; also called certificates of deposit

currency. Dollars circulating abroad are, in fact, a good deal for Americans because a $100 note that costs only about 12 cents to print can be "sold" to foreigners for $100 worth of goods and services. It's as if these countries were granting us an interest-free loan during the period the $100 note circulates abroad, usually years.

## 14-1b Broader Definition of Money: M2

Economists regard currency and checkable deposits as money because each serves as a medium of exchange, a unit of account, and a store of value. Some other financial assets perform the store-of-value function and can be converted into currency or to checkable deposits. Because these are so close to money, they are called near-monies and are included under a broader definition.

**Savings deposits** earn interest but have no specific maturity date. Banks often allow depositors to shift funds from savings accounts to checking accounts by phone, ATM card, or online, so distinctions between narrow and broad definitions of money have become blurred. **Time deposits** (also called *certificates of deposit*, or *CDs*) earn a fixed rate of interest if held for a specified period, ranging from several months to several years. Premature withdrawals are penalized by forfeiture of some interest. Neither savings deposits nor time deposits serve directly as media of exchange, so they are not included in M1, the narrow definition of money.

*Money market mutual fund accounts*, mentioned in the previous chapter, are another component of money when defined more broadly. But, because of restrictions on the minimum balance, on the number of checks that can be written per month, and on the minimum amount

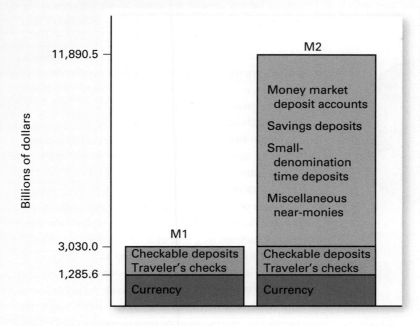

*Exhibit 1*

**Two Measures of the Money Supply (Week of May 4, 2015)**

Source: Based on seasonally adjusted averages for the week from the Federal Reserve Board. For the latest data, go to http://www.federalreserve.gov/releases/h6/Current/.

of each check, these popular accounts are not viewed as money as narrowly defined.

Recall that M1 consists of currency (including coins) held by the nonbanking public, checkable deposits, and traveler's checks. **M2** includes M1 as well as savings deposits, small-denomination time deposits, money market mutual fund accounts, and other miscellaneous near-monies. Exhibit 1 shows the size and relative importance of each money aggregate. As you can see, compared to M1, M2 is nearly four times larger. Thus, the narrow definition of money is only a fraction of the broader aggregate. But distinctions between M1 and M2 become less meaningful as banks allow depositors to transfer funds from one account to another.

## 14-1c Credit Cards and Debit Cards: What's the Difference?

You may be curious why the narrow definition includes funds accessed by debit cards but not funds accessed by credit cards. After all, most sellers accept credit cards as

> **"The credit card has not eliminated your use of money, but merely delayed it."**

readily as they accept cash, checks, or debit cards (online sellers even prefer credit cards), and credit cards finance about 30 percent of all consumer purchases. Credit cards offer an easy way to get a loan from the card issuer. If you buy an airline ticket with a credit card, the card issuer lends you the money to pay for the ticket. You don't need money until you repay the credit card issuer. The credit card has not eliminated your use of money, but merely delayed it.

On the other hand, when you use your debit card, you tap directly into your checking account, paying with electronic money—part of M1. Debit cards get their name because they *debit*, or draw down, your checking account immediately. A **debit card**, also called a check card or bank card, is issued by a bank, sometimes jointly with Visa, MasterCard, or other major card issuers. Even though debit cards look like credit cards, and even may bear a name such as Visa, they are not credit cards.

Many people prefer debit cards to checks because no checkbook is required and payments are made directly and immediately. Transactions using debit cards and other electronic transfers now exceed payments by check. Debit cards usually require a personal identification number, or PIN, to use. In that regard, debit cards are safer than credit cards, which could be used more easily by a thief. But debit cards have some disadvantages. Whereas a debit card draws down your checking account immediately, credit cards provide a grace period between a purchase and required payment. And about half of credit card users prefer to borrow beyond the grace period—that is, to carry a balance from month to month. Also, because debit cards immediately reduce your checking account, you can't dispute a bill or withhold payment as you can

**M2** A money aggregate consisting of M1 plus savings deposits, small-denomination time deposits, money market mutual funds, and other near-monies

**debit card** Cards that tap directly into the depositor's bank account to fund purchases; also called check cards

## Exhibit 2

### U.S. Consumer Payments as a Share of Spending: 2013 and 2018

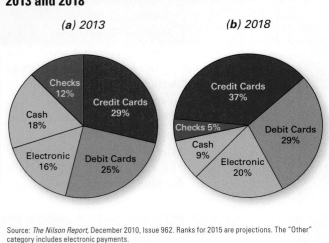

*(a) 2013*

*(b) 2018*

Source: *The Nilson Report*, December 2010, Issue 962. Ranks for 2015 are projections. The "Other" category includes electronic payments.

after using a credit card and you can't stop payment as you can after writing a check. Still, debit cards, which came from nowhere a few years ago, are used by most of households today.

How often have you heard a store clerk ask, "Will that be cash or charge?" Exhibit 2 shows how consumers chose to pay for their purchases in 2013 and how they are projected to pay in 2018. Based on the dollar volume of purchases, cash and checks will decline as a share of the total, while credit cards, debit cards, and electronic payments will increase. Cash and checks combined are projected to fall from 30 percent of all payments in 2013 to only 14 percent in 2018. The share of other types of payments combined are projected to increase from 70 percent in 2013 to 86 percent in 2018. Of course, credit-card balances are ultimately paid off with money.

### 14-1d  Is Bitcoin Money?

New forms of payments are being tried every day. For example, some people use smartphones as debit cards. Online payments are executed by systems such as Square, which operates like a credit card, and PayPal, which can be used like either a credit card or a debit card. These transactions are still settled in traditional currencies, such as the U.S. dollars, through the banking system. But some new digital currencies, such as bitcoin, once they are initially purchased with traditional currencies, can fund some transactions without further reliance on traditional currencies or the banking system. A bitcoin user gets a digital wallet with a private key that serves as

a password. With computers or mobile apps, users can send bitcoin to one another.

Bitcoin account holders need not use their real names, so they can buy or sell goods anonymously. This makes bitcoin attractive for drug dealings and other illegal activities. But the safety of bitcoin is a question. A bitcoin account can be hacked, destroyed by a virus, or mistakenly deleted. For example, a British man in 2013 accidently discarded a hard drive containing bitcoin worth $9 million at the time.[2] And in 2014, hackers stole $460 million in bitcoin from the world's largest bitcoin exchange, Mt. Gox, driving that exchange into bankruptcy.[3]

Is bitcoin really money? Since its inception, the dollar cost of one bitcoin has ranged from as low as six cents to as high as $971.45. Wide fluctuations relative to traditional currencies undermine bitcoin's functions as a unit of account and as a store of value. Bitcoin also lacks access to banking systems and deposit insurance. According to one economist who has studied the matter, bitcoin behaves more like a speculative investment than a currency.[4] And even as a speculative investment, bitcoin is more volatile than nearly any other asset one could find.

True, bitcoin is a medium of exchange as long as you can find others willing to accept this type of electronic payment. But it's not good as a unit of account or a store of value. So it's not so good as money. As of June 13, 2015, there were 14.3 million bitcoin in circulation throughout the world. Based on an exchange value of $231.33 per bitcoin on that date, the dollar value of bitcoin in circulation was $3.3 billion. By way of comparison, the supply of M1 at the time was about $3.0 trillion, or about 900 times greater. Bitcoin or another new currency could some day replace traditional currencies, but probably not soon.

### 14-2  HOW BANKS WORK

Banks attract deposits from savers to lend to borrowers, earning a profit on the difference between the interest paid depositors and the interest charged borrowers. Savers need a safe place for their money, and borrowers need credit; banks try to earn a profit by serving both groups. To inspire depositor confidence, a bank usually presents an image of trust and assurance with an impressive building,

2. "Bitcoin Worth $9M Buried in Garbage Dump," *CNN Money*, 29 November 2013, at http://money.cnn.com/2013/11/29/news/bitcoin-haul-landfill/index.html.

3. Robert McMillan, "The Inside Story of Mt. Gox, Bitcoins $460 Million Disaster," *Wired*, 3 March 2014, at http://www.wired.com/2014/03/bitcoin-exchange/.

4. David Yermack, "Is Bitcoin A Real Currency? An Economic Appraisal," in *Handbook of Digital Currency: Bitcoin, Innovation, Financial Instruments, and Big Data*, David Lee Kuo Chuen, ed. (Academic Press, 2015): 31–44.

a big safe often visible from the lobby, and a name that sounds serious. Banks are more apt to be called Fidelity Trust, First National, or U.S. Bankcorp than Benny's Bank, Loans 'R' Us, or Loadsamoney. In contrast, *finance companies* are financial intermediaries that do not get their funds from depositors, so they can choose names aimed more at borrowers—names such as Household Finance, Lending Tree, and The Money Store. Likewise, mortgage companies do not rely on depositors, so they pick names aimed at home buyers, names such as Lender's Depot, Quicken Loans, and Cheap Mortgages.

## 14-2a Banks Are Financial Intermediaries

*By bringing together both sides of the money market, banks serve as financial intermediaries, or as go-betweens.* They gather various amounts from savers and repackage these funds into the amounts demanded by borrowers. Some savers need their money next week, some next year, some only after retirement. Likewise, borrowers need credit for different lengths of time. Banks, as intermediaries, offer desirable durations to both groups. In short, *banks reduce the transaction costs of channeling savings to creditworthy borrowers.* Here's how.

> **"The economy is more efficient because banks develop expertise in evaluating creditworthiness, structuring loans, and enforcing loan contracts."**

### Coping with Asymmetric Information

Banks, as lenders, try to identify borrowers who are willing to pay interest and are able to repay their loans. But borrowers have more reliable information about their own credit history and financial plans than do lenders. Thus, in the market for loans, there is **asymmetric information**—an inequality in what's known by each party to the transaction. Asymmetric information is unequal information. This wouldn't be a problem if borrowers could be trusted to report relevant details to lenders. Some borrowers, however, have an incentive to suppress important information, such as other debts outstanding, a troubled financial history, or plans to use the borrowed money to fund a risky venture. Because of their experience and expertise in evaluating loan applicants, banks can better cope with asymmetric information than could an individual saver. Banks also know more about lending agreements than do individual savers. Thus, savers, rather than lending their money directly, are better

off depositing their money in banks, and letting banks do the lending. *The economy is more efficient because banks develop expertise in evaluating creditworthiness, structuring loans, and enforcing loan contracts.*

### Reducing Risk through Diversification

By developing a diversified portfolio of assets rather than lending funds to a single borrower, banks reduce the risk to each individual saver. A bank, in effect, lends a tiny fraction of each saver's deposits to each of its many borrowers. If one borrower fails to repay a loan, it hardly affects a large, diversified bank. Certainly such a default does not represent the personal disaster it would if one saver's entire nest egg had been loaned directly to that defaulting borrower.

Yet, as noted in the previous chapter, a bank can get into financial trouble if many borrowers fail to repay their loans. For example, when housing prices collapsed in 2007 and 2008, many borrowers owed the bank more than their homes were worth. Some borrowers stopped making mortgage payments. These homes went into foreclosure and banks suffered heavy losses. The problem of these bad loans rippled through the economy and contributed to the global financial crisis of September 2008 and the Great Recession of 2007–2009, the worst downturn since the Great Depression.

## 14-2b Starting a Bank

We could consider the operation of any type of depository institution (commercial bank, savings bank, or credit union), but let's focus on commercial banks because they are the most important in terms of total assets. What's more, the operating principles also apply to other depository institutions. Suppose some business leaders in your hometown want to open a commercial bank called Home Bank. To obtain a *charter*, or the right to operate, they must apply to the state banking authority in the case of a state bank or to the U.S. Comptroller of the Currency in the case of a national bank.

**asymmetric information**
A situation in which one side of the market has more reliable information than the other side

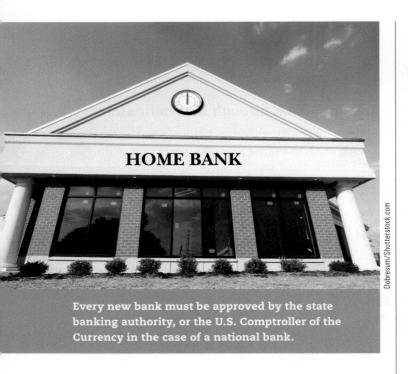

Every new bank must be approved by the state banking authority, or the U.S. Comptroller of the Currency in the case of a national bank.

## Exhibit 3
### Home Bank's Initial Balance Sheet

| Assets | | Liabilities and Net Worth | |
|---|---|---|---|
| Building and furniture | $450,000 | Net worth | $500,000 |
| Stock in district Fed | 50,000 | | |
| Total | $500,000 | Total | $500,000 |

The chartering agency reviewing the application judges the quality of management, the need for another bank in the community, the proposed bank's funding, and the likely success of the bank. Note that a proposed restaurant would not be subject to such scrutiny, but a failed restaurant is not nearly as problematic for a community as a failed bank.

Suppose the founders plan to invest $500,000 in the bank, and they so indicate on their application for a national charter. If their application is approved, they incorporate, issuing themselves shares of stock—certificates of ownership. Thus, they exchange $500,000 for shares of stock in the bank. These shares are called the *owners' equity*, or the **net worth**, of the bank. Part of the $500,000, say $50,000, is used to buy shares in their district Federal Reserve bank. So Home Bank is now a member of the Federal Reserve System. With the remaining $450,000, the owners acquire and furnish the bank building.

To focus our discussion, we examine the bank's **balance sheet**, presented in Exhibit 3. As the name implies, a balance sheet shows a balance between the two sides of the bank's accounts. The left side lists the bank's assets. An **asset** is any physical property or financial claim owned by the bank. At this early stage, assets include the building and equipment owned by Home Bank plus its stock in the district Federal Reserve bank. The right side lists the bank's liabilities and net worth. A **liability** is an amount the bank owes. So far the bank owes nothing, so the right side includes only the net worth of $500,000. The two sides of the ledger must always be equal, or in *balance*, which is why it's called a *balance sheet*. So assets must equal liabilities plus net worth:

$$\text{Assets} = \text{Liabilities} + \text{Net worth}$$

The bank is now ready for business. Opening day is the bank's lucky day, because the first customer carries in a briefcase full of $100 notes and deposits $1,000,000 into a new checking account. In accepting this cash, the bank promises to repay the depositor that amount. The deposit therefore is an amount the bank owes—it's a liability of the bank. As a result of this deposit, the bank's assets increase by $1,000,000 in cash and its liabilities increase by $1,000,000 in checkable deposits. Exhibit 4 shows the effects of this transaction on Home Bank's balance sheet. The right side now shows two claims on the bank's assets: claims by the owners, called net worth, and claims by nonowners, called liabilities, which at this point consist of checkable deposits.

## Exhibit 4
### Home Bank's Balance Sheet after $1,000,000 Deposit into Checking Account

| Assets | | Liabilities and Net Worth | |
|---|---|---|---|
| Cash | $1,000,000 | Checkable deposits | $1,000,000 |
| Building and furniture | 450,000 | Net worth | 500,000 |
| Stock in district Fed | 50,000 | | |
| Total | $1,500,000 | Total | $1,500,000 |

**net worth** Assets minus liabilities; also called owners' equity

**balance sheet** A financial statement at a given point in time showing assets on one side and liabilities and net worth on the other side; because assets must equal liabilities plus net worth, the two sides of the statement must balance, hence the name

**asset** Anything of value that is owned

**liability** Anything that is owed to other people or institutions

## 14-2c Reserve Accounts

Where do we go from here? As mentioned in the previous chapter, banks are required by the Fed to set aside, or to hold in reserve, a percentage of their checkable deposits. The dollar amount that must be held in reserve is called **required reserves**—checkable deposits multiplied by the required reserve ratio. The **required reserve ratio** dictates the minimum proportion of deposits the bank must hold in reserve. The current reserve requirement is 10 percent on checkable deposits (other types of deposits have no reserve requirement). All depository institutions are subject to the Fed's reserve requirements. Reserves are held either as cash in the bank's vault, which earns the bank no interest, or as deposits at the Fed, where reserves earn a small rate of interest (most recently, one quarter of one percent, or 0.25 percent). Home Bank must therefore hold $100,000 as reserves, or 10 percent times $1,000,000.

Suppose Home Bank deposits $100,000 in a reserve account with its district Federal Reserve bank. Home Bank's reserves now consist of $100,000 in required reserves on deposit with the Fed and $900,000 in **excess reserves** held as cash in the vault. Home Bank earns no interest on cash in its vault. Excess reserves, however, can be used to make loans or to purchase interest-bearing assets, such as government bonds. By law, the bank's interest-bearing assets are limited primarily to loans and to government securities. (Note that if a bank is owned by a holding company, the holding company has broader latitude in the kinds of assets it can own.)

## 14-2d Liquidity Versus Profitability

Like the early goldsmiths, modern banks must be prepared to satisfy depositors' requests for funds. A bank loses reserves whenever a depositor withdraws cash, writes a check that gets deposited in another bank, or uses a debit card that ultimately shifts deposits to another bank. The bank must be in a position to satisfy all depositor demands, even if many ask for their money at the same time. Required reserves are not meant to be used to meet depositor requests for funds; therefore, banks often hold excess reserves or other assets, such as government bonds, that can be easily liquidated, or converted to cash, to satisfy any unexpected demand for

cash. Banks may also want to hold excess reserves in case a valued customer needs immediate credit.

The bank's portfolio manager must therefore structure assets with an eye toward liquidity but must not forget that survival also depends on profitability. **Liquidity** is the ease with which an asset can be converted into cash without a significant loss of value. *The objectives of liquidity and profitability are at odds*. For example, more liquid assets yield lower interest rates than less liquid assets do. The most liquid asset is cash in the bank's vault, but such reserves earn no interest.

At one extreme, suppose a bank is completely liquid, holding all its assets as cash in its vault. Such a bank would have no difficulty meeting depositors' demands for funds. This bank is playing it safe—too safe. The bank earns no interest and will fail. At the other extreme, suppose a bank uses all its excess reserves to acquire high-yielding but illiquid assets, such as long-term home loans. Such a bank runs into problems whenever withdrawals exceed new deposits. There is a trade-off between liquidity and profitability. The portfolio manager's task is to strike the right balance between liquidity, or safety, and profitability.

Because vault cash earns no interest, banks prefer to hold reserves at the Fed. Any bank short of required reserves at the end of the day can borrow from a bank that has excess reserves at the Fed. The **federal funds market** provides for day-to-day lending and borrowing among banks of excess reserves on account at the Fed. These funds usually do not leave the Fed—instead, they shift among accounts. For example, suppose that at the end of the business day, Home Bank has excess reserves of $100,000 on account with the Fed and wants to lend that amount to another bank that finished the day short $100,000 in required reserves. These two banks are

**required reserves** The dollar amount of reserves a bank is obligated by regulation to hold as cash in the bank's vault or on account at the Fed

**required reserve ratio** The ratio of reserves to deposits that banks are obligated by regulation to hold

**excess reserves** Bank reserves exceeding required reserves

**liquidity** A measure of the ease with which an asset can be converted into money without a significant loss of value

**federal funds market** A market for overnight lending and borrowing of reserves among banks; the interbank market for reserves on account at the Fed brought together by a broker who specializes in the market for federal funds—that is, the market for reserves at the Fed. The interest rate paid on this loan is called the **federal funds rate**; this is the rate the Fed targets as a tool of monetary policy, but more on that later.

 ## 14-3 HOW BANKS CREATE MONEY

Let's now discuss how the Fed, Home Bank, and the banking system as a whole can create fiat money. Excess reserves are the raw material the banking system uses to create money. Again, our discussion focuses on commercial banks because they are the largest and most important depository institutions, although thrifts operate the same way.

### 14-3a Creating Money through Excess Reserves

Suppose Home Bank has already used its $900,000 in excess reserves to make loans and buy government bonds and has no excess reserves left. In fact, let's assume there are no excess reserves in the banking system. With that as a point of departure, let's walk through the money creation process.

### Round One

To start, suppose the Fed buys a $1,000 U.S. government bond from a securities dealer, with the transaction handled by the dealer's bank—Home Bank. The Fed pays the dealer by crediting Home Bank's reserve account with $1,000, so Home Bank can increase the dealer's checking account by $1,000. Where does the Fed get these reserves? It makes them up—creates them out of thin air, out of electronic ether! The securities dealer has exchanged one asset, a U.S. bond, for another asset, checkable deposits. A U.S. bond is not money, but checkable deposits are, so the money supply increases by $1,000 in this first round. Exhibit 5 shows changes in Home Bank's balance sheet as a result of the Fed's bond purchase. On the assets side, Home Bank's reserves at the Fed increase by $1,000. On the liabilities side, checkable deposits increase by $1,000. Of the dealer's $1,000 checkable deposit, Home Bank must set aside $100 in required reserves (based on a 10 percent required reserve ratio). The remaining $900 becomes excess reserves, which can fuel a further increase in the money supply.

**federal funds rate** The interest rate charged in the federal funds market; the interest rate banks charge one another for overnight borrowing; the Fed's target interest rate

*Exhibit 5*

### Changes in Home Bank's Balance Sheet after the Fed Buys a $1,000 Bond from Securities Dealer

| Assets | | Liabilities and Net Worth | |
|---|---|---|---|
| Reserves at Fed | +$1,000 | Checkable deposits | +$1,000 |

### Round Two

Suppose Home Bank is your regular bank, and you apply for a $900 loan to help pay student fees. Home Bank approves your loan and increases your checking account by $900. *Home Bank has converted your promise to repay the loan, your IOU, into a $900 checkable deposit. Because checkable deposits are money, this action increases the money supply by $900.* The money supply has increased by a total of $1,900 to this point—the $1,000 increase in the securities dealer's checkable deposits and now the $900 increase in your checkable deposits. In the process, what had been $900 in Home Bank's excess reserves now back up its loan to you. As shown in Exhibit 6, Home Bank's loans increase by $900 on the assets side because your IOU becomes the bank's asset. On the bank's liabilities side, checkable deposits increase by $900 because the bank has increased your account by that amount. In short, Home Bank has created $900 in checkable deposits based on your promise to repay the loan.

When you write a $900 check for student fees, your college promptly deposits the check into its checking account at Merchants Trust, which increases the college's account by $900, and sends your check to the Fed. The Fed transfers $900 in reserves from Home Bank's account to Merchants Trust's account.

> **"Home Bank has converted your promise to repay the loan, your IOU, into a $900 checkable deposit. Because checkable deposits are money, this action increases the money supply by $900."**

The Fed then sends the check to Home Bank, which reduces your checkable deposits by $900. The Fed has thereby "cleared" your check by settling the claim that Merchants Trust had on Home Bank. Your $900 in checkable deposits at Home Bank has become your college's $900 in checkable deposits at Merchants Trust. The total increase in the money supply to this point is still $1,900.

*Exhibit 6*

### Changes in Home Bank's Balance Sheet after Lending $900 to You

| Assets | | Liabilities and Net Worth | |
|---|---|---|---|
| Loans | +$900 | Checkable deposits | +$900 |

## Round Three

Merchants Trust now has $900 more in reserves on deposit with the Fed. After setting aside $90 as required reserves, or 10 percent of your college's checkable deposit increase, the bank has $810 in excess reserves. Suppose Merchants Trust lends this $810 to an English major starting a new business called "Note This," an online note-taking service for students in large classes. Exhibit 7 shows assets at Merchants Trust are up by $810 in loans, and liabilities are up by $810 in checkable deposits. At this point, checkable deposits in the banking system, and the money supply in the economy, are up by a total of $2,710 (= $1,000 + $900 + $810), all springing from the Fed's original $1,000 bond purchase.

The $810 loan is spent at the college bookstore, which deposits the check in its account at Fidelity Bank. Fidelity credits the bookstore's checkable deposits with $810 and sends the check to the Fed for clearance. The Fed reduces Merchants Bank's reserves by $810 and increases Fidelity's by the same. The Fed then sends the check to Merchants, which reduces the English major's checkable deposits by $810. So checkable deposits are down by $810 at Merchants and up by the same amount at Fidelity. Checkable deposits are still up by $2,710, as the $810 in checkable deposits has simply shifted from Merchants Trust to Fidelity Bank.

*Exhibit 7*

### Changes in Merchants Trust's Balance Sheet after Lending $810 to English Major

| Assets | | Liabilities and Net Worth | |
|---|---|---|---|
| Loans | +$810 | Checkable deposits | +$810 |

## Round Four and Beyond

We could continue the process with Fidelity Bank setting aside $81 in required reserves and lending $729 in excess reserves, but you get some idea of money creation by now. Notice the pattern of deposits and loans. Each time a bank gets a fresh deposit, 10 percent goes to required reserves. The rest becomes excess reserves, which fuel new loans or other asset acquisitions. The borrower writes a check, which the recipient deposits in a checking account, thereby generating excess reserves to support still more loans. Because this example began with the Fed, the Fed can rightfully claim, "The buck starts here"—a slogan that appeared on a large plaque in the Federal Reserve chairman's office.

**TO REVIEW:** An individual bank can lend no more than its excess reserves. When the borrower spends those funds, reserves at one bank usually fall, but total reserves in the banking system do not. The recipient bank uses most of the new deposit to extend more loans, creating more checkable deposits. The potential expansion of checkable deposits in the banking system therefore equals some multiple of the initial increase in reserves. Note that our example assumes that banks do not allow excess reserves to sit idle, that borrowed funds do not idle in checking accounts, and that the public does not hold some of the newly created money as cash. If excess reserves remained just that or if borrowed funds idled in checking accounts, they would not fuel an expansion of the money supply. And if people chose to hold borrowed funds in cash rather than in checking accounts, that idle cash would not add to reserves in the banking system.

## 14-3b A Summary of the Rounds

Let's review the money creation process: *The initial and most important step is the Fed's injection of $1,000 in fresh reserves into the banking system.* By buying the bond from the securities dealer, the Fed immediately increased the money supply by $1,000. Home Bank set aside $100 as required reserves and lent you its $900 in excess reserves. You paid your college fees, and the $900 ended up in your college's checkable account. This fueled more money creation, as shown in a series of rounds of Exhibit 8. As you can see, during each round, the increase in checkable deposits (column 1) minus the increase in required reserves (column 2) equals the potential increase in loans (column 3). Checkable deposits in this example can potentially increase by as much as $10,000.

In our example, money creation results from the Fed's $1,000 bond purchase from the securities dealer,

## Exhibit 8

### Summary of the Money Creation Resulting from the Fed's Purchase of $1,000 U.S. Government Bond

| Bank | (1)<br>Increase in<br>Checkable<br>Deposits | (2)<br>Increase in<br>Required<br>Reserves | (3)<br>Increase in<br>Loans<br>(3) = (1) − (2) |
|---|---|---|---|
| Round 1. Home Bank | $ 1,000 | $ 100 | $ 900 |
| Round 2. Merchants Trust | 900 | 90 | 810 |
| Round 3. Fidelity Bank | 810 | 81 | 729 |
| All remaining rounds | 7,290 | 729 | 6,561 |
| Totals | $ 10,000 | $ 1,000 | $ 9,000 |

but excess reserves would also have increased if the Fed purchased a $1,000 bond from Home Bank, lent Home Bank $1,000, or freed up $1,000 in excess reserves by lowering the reserve requirement.

What if the Fed paid the securities dealer in cash? By exchanging Federal Reserve notes, which become part of the money supply in the hands of the public, for a U.S. bond, which is not part of the money supply, the Fed would have increased the money supply by $1,000. Once the securities dealer put this cash into a checking account—or spent the cash, so the money ended up in someone else's checking account—the banking system's money creation process would have been off and running.

## 14-3c Requirements and Money Expansion

The banking system as a whole eliminates excess reserves by expanding the money supply. With a 10 percent reserve requirement, the Fed's initial injection of $1,000 in fresh reserves could support up to $10,000 in new checkable deposits in the banking system as a whole, *assuming no bank holds excess reserves, borrowed funds don't sit idle, and people don't want to hold more cash.*

The multiple by which the money supply increases as a result of an increase in the banking system's reserves is called the **money multiplier**. The **simple money multiplier** equals the reciprocal of the required reserve ratio, or $1/r$, where $r$

**money multiplier** The multiple by which the money supply changes as a result of a change in fresh reserves in the banking system

**simple money multiplier** The reciprocal of the required reserve ratio, or $1/r$; the maximum multiple of fresh reserves by which the money supply can increase

is the reserve ratio. In our example, the reserve ratio was 10 percent, or 0.1, so the reciprocal is 1/0.1, which equals 10. The formula for the multiple expansion of money supply can be written as follows:

$$\text{Change in the money supply} = \text{Change in fresh reserves} \times 1/r$$

Again, the simple money multiplier assumes that banks hold no excess reserves, that borrowers do not let the funds sit idle, and that people do not want to hold more cash. The higher the reserve requirement, the greater the fraction of deposits that must be held as reserves, so the smaller the money multiplier. A reserve requirement of 20 percent instead of 10 percent would mean each bank must set aside twice as much in required reserves. The simple money multiplier in this case would be 1/0.2, which equals 5. The maximum possible increase in checkable deposits resulting from an initial $1,000 increase in fresh reserves would therefore be $1,000 × 5, or $5,000. *Excess reserves fuel the deposit expansion process, and a higher reserve requirement drains this fuel from the banking system, thereby reducing the amount of new money that can be created.*

On the other hand, with a reserve requirement of only 5 percent, banks would set aside less for required reserves, leaving more excess reserves available for

> **"Excess reserves fuel the deposit expansion process, and a higher reserve requirement drains this fuel from the banking system, thereby reducing the amount of new money that can be created."**

loans. The simple money multiplier in that case would be 1/0.05, or 20. With $1,000 in fresh reserves and a 5 percent reserve requirement, the banking system could increase the money supply by a maximum of $1,000 × 20, which equals $20,000. Thus, the change in the required reserve ratio affects the banking system's ability to create money.

In summary, money creation usually begins with the Fed injecting new reserves into the banking system. An individual bank lends an amount no greater than its excess reserves. The borrower's spending ends up in someone else's checking account, fueling additional loans. *The fractional reserve requirement is the key to the multiple expansion of checkable deposits.* If each $1 deposit had to be backed by $1 in required reserves, the money multiplier would be reduced to 1, which is no multiplier at all.

## 14-3d Limitations on Money Expansion

Various leakages from the multiple expansion process reduce the size of the money multiplier, which is why $1/r$ is called the *simple* money multiplier. You could think of "simple" as meaning maximum. To repeat, our example assumes (1) that banks do not let excess reserves sit idle, (2) that borrowers do something with the money, and (3) that people do not choose to increase their cash holdings. How realistic are these assumptions? With regard to the first, banks have a profit incentive to make loans or buy some higher interest-bearing asset with excess reserves. Granted, banks earn some interest on reserves deposited with the Fed, but the rate is typically much less than could be earned on loans or on most other interest-bearing assets. The second assumption is also easy to defend. Why would people borrow money if they didn't need it for something? The third assumption is trickier. Cash may sometimes be preferable to checking accounts because cash is more versatile, so people may choose to hold some of the newly created money as cash. To the extent that people prefer to hold idle cash, this drains reserves from the banking system. With less excess reserves, banks are less able to make loans, reducing the money multiplier. Incidentally, for the money multiplier to operate, a particular bank need not use excess reserves in a specific way; it could use them to pay all its employees a Christmas bonus, for that matter. As long as the money ends up as checkable deposits in the banking system, away we go with the money expansion process.

## 14-3e Contraction of the Money Supply

We have already outlined the money creation process, so the story of how the Federal Reserve System can reduce bank reserves, thereby reducing the money supply, can be a brief one. Again, we begin by assuming there are no excess reserves in the system and the reserve requirement is 10 percent. Suppose the Fed *sells* a $1,000 U.S. bond to a securities dealer and gets paid with a check drawn on the security dealer's account at Home Bank. So the Fed gets paid by drawing down Home Bank's reserves at the Fed by $1,000. The Fed has thereby reduced the money supply by $1,000 in this first round.

Because the dealer's checking account was reduced by $1,000, Home Bank no longer needs to hold $100 in required reserves. But Home Bank is still short $900 in required reserves (remember, when we started, there were no excess reserves in the banking system). To replenish reserves, Home Bank must recall loans (ask for repayment before the due date), or sell some other asset. As the poet Robert Frost wryly observed, "A bank is a place where they lend you an umbrella in fair weather and ask for it back when it begins to rain." Suppose the bank calls in $900 loaned to a local business, and the loan is repaid with a check written against Merchants Bank. When the check clears, Home Bank's reserves are up by $900, just enough to satisfy its reserve requirement, but Merchants Bank's reserves and checkable deposits are down by $900. Checkable deposits are now down $1,900 as a result of the Fed's purchase of a $1,000 bond. Because there were no excess reserves at the outset, the loss of $900 in reserves leaves Merchants $810 short of its required level of reserves, forcing that bank to get more reserves.

And so it goes down the line. The Fed's sale of government bonds reduces bank reserves, forcing banks to recall loans or to somehow replenish reserves. This reduces checkable deposits each additional round. *The maximum possible effect is to reduce the money supply by the original reduction in bank reserves times the simple money multiplier, which again equals 1 divided by the reserve requirement, or 1/r.* In our example, the Fed's sale of $1,000 in U.S. bonds could reduce the money supply by as much as $10,000.

Now that you have some idea how fractional reserve banking works, we are in a position to summarize the Federal Reserve's role in the economy.

## 14-4 THE FED'S TOOLS OF MONETARY CONTROL

As mentioned in the previous chapter, in its capacity as a bankers' bank, the Fed clears checks for, extends loans to, and holds deposits of banks. More than half of the narrow definition of money (M1) consists of checkable deposits. The Fed's control over checkable deposits works indirectly through its control over reserves in the banking system. You are already familiar with the Fed's three oldest tools for controlling reserves: (1) open-market operations, or the buying and selling of U.S. government bonds; (2) the discount rate, which is the interest rate the Fed charges for loans it makes to banks; and (3) the required reserve ratio, which is the minimum fraction of reserves that banks must hold against deposits. Let's examine each of these in more detail, then look at some other tools that emerged during the recent financial crisis.

> **"To increase the money supply, the Fed directs the New York Fed to buy U.S. bonds."**

**open-market purchase** The purchase of U.S. government bonds by the Fed to increase the money supply

**open-market sale** The sale of U.S. government bonds by the Fed to reduce the money supply

**discount rate** The interest rate the Fed charges banks that borrow reserves

### 14-4a Open-Market Operations and the Federal Funds Rate

The Fed carries out open-market operations whenever it buys or sells U.S. government bonds in the open market. The term "open market" here means that securities dealers compete to do business with the Fed based on price in an *open market*. Decisions about open-market operations are made by the Federal Open Market Committee, or FOMC, which meets every six weeks and during emergencies. To increase the money supply, the Fed directs the New York Fed to buy U.S. bonds. This is called an **open-market purchase**. To reduce the money supply, the New York Fed is directed to carry out an **open-market sale**. Open-market operations are relatively easy to carry out. They require no change in laws or regulations and can be executed in any amount—large or small—chosen by the Fed. Their simplicity and ease of use make them the tool of choice for the Fed.

Through open-market operations, the Fed influences bank reserves and the *federal funds rate*, which is the interest rate banks charge one another for borrowing excess reserves at the Fed, typically just for a day or two. Banks that need reserves can borrow excess reserves from other banks, paying the federal funds rate of interest. The federal funds rate serves as a good indicator of the "tightness" of monetary policy. For example, suppose the Fed buys U.S. bonds in the open market and thereby increases reserves in the banking system. As a result, more banks have excess reserves. Demand for excess reserves in the federal funds market falls and supply increases, so the federal funds rate—the interest rate for borrowing reserves in this market—declines. We can expect this lower federal funds rate to spread quickly to the economy at large. The excess reserves that have created the lower federal funds rate prompt banks to lower short-term interest rates in general, and this increases the quantity of loans demanded by the public.

### 14-4b The Discount Rate

The second monetary policy tool available to the Fed is the **discount rate**, which is the interest rate the Fed charges for loans it makes to banks. Banks borrow from the Fed to satisfy their reserve requirements. A lower discount rate reduces the cost of borrowing, encouraging banks to borrow reserves from the Fed. The Fed usually does not encourage banks to borrow, but the Fed considers itself as the "lender of last resort," and a lender during a financial crisis, as occurred between 2007 and 2010 when some homeowners defaulted on their mortgages.

> **"A lower discount rate reduces the cost of borrowing, encouraging banks to borrow reserves from the Fed."**

There are actually two discount rates. The *primary discount rate* is usually one percentage point above the federal funds rate. Thus, discount borrowing is less attractive than borrowing through the federal funds market. But during a financial crisis, the Fed could lower the primary discount rate to supply liquidity to the banking system as it did 12 times between August 2007 and December 2008. The Fed charges more interest on loans to banks considered less sound than to other banks. This *secondary discount rate* is usually about one-half a percentage point higher than the primary discount rate.

The Fed uses the discount rate more as a signal to financial markets about its monetary policy than as a tool for increasing or decreasing the money supply. The discount rate might also be thought of as an emergency tool for injecting liquidity into the banking system in the event of some financial crisis, such as the global credit crisis of 2008. Discount loans outstanding jumped from only $2 billion in August 2007, before the trouble started, to more than $130 billion in April 2009, when the economy was in a sharp recession. (Because of huge excess reserves held in the banking system, discount loans have since nearly disappeared—only about $100 million in May, 2015.) Banks would prefer to borrow reserves from other banks in the federal funds market rather than borrow reserves directly from the Fed.

### 14-4c Reserve Requirements

The Fed also influences the money supply through reserve requirements, which are regulations regarding the minimum amount of reserves that banks must hold to back up deposits. Reserve requirements determine how much money the banking system can create with each dollar of fresh reserves. If the Fed increases the reserve requirement, then banks have less excess reserves to lend out. This reduces the banking system's ability to create money. On the other hand, a lower reserve requirement increases the banking system's ability to create money. Reserve requirements can be changed by a simple majority vote of the Board of Governors. But changes in the reserve requirement disrupt the banking system, so the Fed seldom makes such changes. As noted already, the current reserve requirement is 10 percent on checkable deposits and zero on other deposits; these have not changed in years. Some countries such as Australia, Canada, and the United Kingdom have no reserve requirement. Banks there still hold reserves to deal with everyday cash requirements and can borrow from their central banks (at relatively high rates) if necessary.

> **"A lower reserve requirement increases the banking system's ability to create money."**

### 14-4d Responding to Financial Crises

The Fed, through its regulation of financial markets, also tries to prevent major disruptions and financial panics. For example, during the uncertain days

The United States Federal Reserve building in Washington, DC.

following the terrorist attacks of September 11, 2001, people used their ATM cards and debit cards to load up on cash. Some hoarded cash. To ensure the banking system had sufficient liquidity, the Fed bought all the government securities offered for sale, purchasing a record $150 billion worth in two days.[5] The Fed also eased some regulations to facilitate bank clearances, especially for banks struck during the attacks.

Likewise, when financial crises threatened in 1987, 1989, 1998, 2007, and 2008, the Fed worked to ensure the financial system had sufficient liquidity. For example, to calm fears during a rash of mortgage defaults in 2007 and 2008, the Fed lowered the discount rate from 6.25 percent to only 0.25 percent and encouraged banks to borrow from the Fed. To help banks improve their balance sheets, the Fed also began paying interest on bank reserves held at the Fed. To keep mortgage rates low, the Fed invested more than a $1 trillion in mortgage-backed securities. And to help prevent the insurance giant AIG from collapsing, the Fed invested more than $90 billion in the company. As a general approach, Ben Bernanke, Fed chairman at the time, announced that the Fed would provide sufficient liquidity to reduce the harm of mortgage defaults on the overall economy. To prevent cash shortages during a crisis, the Fed stockpiles extra cash in bank vaults around the country and around the world.

## 14-4e The Fed Is a Money Machine

One way to get a better idea of the Fed is to review its balance sheet, shown as Exhibit 9, with assets on the left and liabilities and net worth on the right. Because of the mortgage crisis and global financial meltdown of 2008, investors were reluctant to buy mortgage-backed securities. So the Fed stepped in and began buying them in late 2008. As of May 13, 2015, these securities still accounted for 40 percent of the Fed's assets. U.S. government securities were 55 percent of Fed assets (during normal times they might account for 90 percent of assets). These IOUs from the federal government result from open-market operations, and they earn the

5. Anita Rachavan, Susan Pulliam, and Jeff Opdyke, "Banks and Regulators Drew Together to Calm Rattled Markets after Attack," *Wall Street Journal*, 18 October 2001.

*Exhibit 9*

**Federal Reserve Bank Balance Sheet as of May 13, 2015 (Billions)**

| Assets | | Liabilities and Net Worth | |
|---|---|---|---|
| U.S. Treasury securities | $2,460.3 | Depository institution reserves | 2,643.8 |
| Mortgage-backed securities | 1,743.8 | Federal Reserve notes outstanding | 1,320.0 |
| Other federal agency securities | 35.9 | U.S. Treasury balance | 205.4 |
| Foreign currencies | 20.2 | Other liabilities | 274.5 |
| Discount loans to depository institutions | 0.1 | Net worth | 58.1 |
| Bank buildings | 2.2 | | |
| Other assets | 239.3 | | |
| Total | $4,501.8 | Total | $4,501.8 |

Source: Federal Reserve Bank at http://www.federalreserve.gov/releases/h41/Current/.

Fed interest. Other assets include foreign currencies, most of which the Fed acquired during the financial crisis as foreign central banks swapped their currencies for U.S. dollars. Note that nearly all the Fed's assets earn interest.

Federal Reserve notes are literally IOUs that pay no interest.

On the other side of the ledger, Federal Reserve notes outstanding account for about 30 percent of Fed liabilities. These notes—U.S. currency—are IOUs from the Fed and are therefore liabilities of the Fed, but the Fed pays no interest on these notes. Thus, nearly all the Fed's assets earn interest, whereas one of the Fed's primary liabilities—Federal Reserve notes—requires no interest payments by the Fed. The Fed does pay interest on excess reserves it holds on deposit, but that rate has been extremely low—again, just 0.25 percent since early 2009. *The Fed is therefore both literally and figuratively a money machine. It is literally a money machine because it supplies the economy with Federal Reserve notes; it is figuratively a money machine because most assets earn interest, but a main liability requires no interest payments.* The Fed also earns revenue from discount lending to banks and from other services it provides banks. After covering its operating costs, paying a small amount of interest on bank reserves at the Fed, and paying a 6 percent dividend to the member banks, the Fed turns over any remaining income to the federal government. In early 2015, the Fed sent the U.S. Treasury its 2014 operating surplus of $97 billion, a record amount.

On the right side of the ledger, you can see that depository institutions' reserves at the Fed totaled $2,643.8 billion (mostly in excess reserves). This reflects a huge jump in recent years. One reason for the increase is that in late 2008, the Fed began paying a small amount of interest on excess bank reserves held by the Fed, as noted already. Also, because of the financial crisis, banks grew reluctant to make loans, preferring instead to let their excess reserves collect interest at the Fed. You can also see that the Fed held deposits of the U.S. Treasury, a reminder that the Fed is the federal government's banker.

## 14-5 FINAL WORD

Banks play a unique role in the economy because they can transform someone's IOU into a checkable deposit, and a checkable deposit is money. The banking system's ability to expand the money supply depends on the amount of excess reserves in that system. In our example, it was the purchase of a $1,000 U.S. bond that started the ball rolling. The Fed can also increase reserves by lowering the discount rate enough to stimulate bank borrowing from the Fed (although the Fed changes the discount rate more to signal its policy than to alter the money supply). By reducing the required reserve ratio, the Fed not only instantly creates excess reserves in the banking system but also increases the money multiplier. In practice, the Fed rarely changes the reserve requirement because of the disruptive effect of such a change on the banking system. Finally, by purchasing long-term assets such as mortgage-backed securities, the Fed helped stabilize banks during and after the financial crisis, put reserves in the banking system, and lowered long-term interest rates to promote investment and help the housing market.

In the next chapter, we consider how monetary policy affects the economy.

## STUDY TOOLS 14

# CHAPTER 14 PROBLEMS

*Your instructor can access the answers to these problems online at http://cengagebrain.com.*

## 14-1 Interpret why using a debit card is like using cash, but using a credit card is not

1. *(Credit vs. Debit Cards)* Explain why using a debit card is just like using cash, while using a credit card is different.

2. *(Monetary Aggregates)* Calculate M1 and M2 using the following information:

| | |
|---|---|
| Large-denomination time deposits | $304 billion |
| Currency and coin held by the non-banking public | $438 billion |
| Checkable deposits | $509 billion |
| Small-denomination time deposits | $198 billion |
| Traveler's checks | $18 billion |
| Savings deposits | $326 billion |
| Money market mutual fund accounts | $637 billion |

## 14-2 Explain why a bank is in a better position to lend your savings than you are

2. *(Bank Expertise)* Why are banks in a better position to make loans than would be a typical saver? Describe a bank's expertise in this area.

3. *(Reserve Accounts)* Suppose that a bank's customer deposits $4,000 in her checking account. The required reserve ratio is 0.25. What are the required reserves on this new deposit? What is the largest loan that the bank can make on the basis of the new deposit? If the bank chooses to hold reserves of $3,000 on the new deposit, what are the excess reserves on the deposit?

## 14-3 Describe how banks create money

4. *(Money Creation)* Suppose Bank A, which faces a reserve requirement of 10 percent, receives a $1,000 cash deposit from a customer.
   a. Assuming that it wishes to hold no excess reserves, determine how much the bank should lend. Show your answer on Bank A's balance sheet.
   b. Assuming that the loan shown in Bank A's balance sheet is redeposited in Bank B, show the changes in Bank B's balance sheet if it lends out the maximum possible.
   c. Repeat this process for three additional banks: C, D, and E.

   d. Using the simple money multiplier, calculate the total change in the money supply resulting from the $1,000 initial deposit.
   e. Assume Banks A, B, C, D, and E each wish to hold 5 percent excess reserves. How would holding this level of excess reserves affect the total change in the money supply?

5. *(Money Multiplier)* Suppose that the Federal Reserve lowers the required reserve ratio from 0.10 to 0.05. How does this affect the simple money multiplier, assuming that excess reserves are held to zero and there are no currency leakages? What are the money multipliers for required reserve ratios of 0.15 and 0.20?

6. *(Money Creation)* Show how each of the following would initially affect a bank's assets and liabilities.
   a. Someone makes a $10,000 deposit into a checking account.
   b. A bank makes a loan of $1,000 by establishing a checking account for $1,000.
   c. The loan described in part (b) is spent.
   d. A bank must write off a loan because the borrower defaults.

7. *(Money Creation)* Show how each of the following *initially* affects bank assets, liabilities, and reserves. Do *not* include the results of bank behavior resulting from the Fed's action. Assume a required reserve ratio of 0.05.
   a. The Fed purchases $10 million worth of U.S. government bonds from a bank.
   b. The Fed loans $5 million to a bank.
   c. The Fed raises the required reserve ratio to 0.10.

## 14-4 Summarize the Fed's tools of monetary policy

8. *(Monetary Tools)* What tools does the Fed have to pursue monetary policy. Which tool does it use the most?

9. *(Monetary Control)* Suppose the money supply is currently $500 billion and the Fed wishes to increase it by $100 billion.
   a. Given a required reserve ratio of 0.25, what should it do?
   b. If it decided to change the money supply by changing the required reserve ratio, what change should it make? Why may the Fed be reluctant to change the reserve requirement?

# MACRO
# ECON
# ONLINE

## REVIEW FLASHCARDS ANYTIME, ANYWHERE!

**Create Flashcards from Your StudyBits**

**Review Key Term Flashcards Already Loaded on the StudyBoard**

**4LTR**
PRESS

Access ECON ONLINE at www.cengagebrain.com

# 15 | Monetary Theory and Policy

Bloomberg/Getty Images

## LEARNING OUTCOMES

After studying this chapter, you will be able to…

**15-1** Explain how the demand and supply of money determine the market interest rate

**15-2** Outline the steps between an increase in the money supply and an increase in equilibrium output

**15-3** Describe the relevance of velocity's stability on monetary policy

**15-4** Summarize the specific policies the Fed pursued during and after the Great Recession

After finishing this chapter go to **PAGE 281** for **STUDY TOOLS**

**Topics discussed in Chapter 15 include:**

- Demand and supply of money
- Money in the short run
- Federal funds rate
- Money in the long run
- Velocity of money
- Monetary policy targets
- Stress test
- Quantitative Easing

- Why do people maintain checking accounts and have cash in their pockets, purses, wallets, desk drawers, piggy banks, coffee cans—wherever?

- In other words, why do people hold money?

- How does the stock of money in the economy affect your ability to find a job, get a student loan, buy a car, or pay credit card bills?

- What have economic theory and the historical record taught us about the relationship between the amount of money in the economy and other macroeconomic variables?

*Answers to these and related questions are addressed in this chapter, which examines monetary theory and policy in the short run and in the long run*

The amount of money in the economy affects you in a variety of ways, but to understand these effects, we must dig a little deeper. So far, we have focused on how banks create money. But a more fundamental question is how money affects the economy, a topic called *monetary theory*. Monetary theory explores the effect of the money supply on the economy's price level, employment, and growth. The Fed's control over the money supply is called *monetary policy*. In the short run, changes in the money supply affect the economy by working through changes in the interest rate. In the long run, changes in the money supply affect the price level. Monetary policy affects the interest you pay on a car loan and the interest you earn on a bank account.

> **"How does the stock of money in the economy affect your ability to find a job?"**

## 15-1 THE DEMAND AND SUPPLY OF MONEY

Let's begin by reviewing the important distinction between the *stock of money* and the *flow of income*. How much money do you have with you right now? That amount is a *stock*—an amount measured at a point in time. Income, in contrast, is a *flow*—an amount measured per period of time. Income is a measure of how much money you receive per period. Income has no meaning unless the period is specified. You would not know whether to be impressed that a friend earned $400 unless you knew whether this was per month, per week, per day, or per hour.

The **demand for money** is a relationship between the interest rate and how much money people choose to hold. Keep in mind that the quantity of money held is a stock measure. It may seem odd at first to be talking about the demand for money. You might think people would demand all the money they could get their hands

on. But remember that money, the stock, is not the same as income, the flow. People express their demand for income by selling their labor and other resources. People express their demand for money by holding some of their wealth as money rather than holding other assets that earn more interest.

But we are getting ahead of ourselves. The question is: Why do people demand money? Why do people have money with them, stash money around the house, and have money in checking accounts? The most obvious reason people demand money is that money is a convenient medium of exchange. *People demand money to make purchases.*

### 15-1a The Demand for Money

Because barter represents an insignificant portion of exchange in the modern industrialized economy, households, firms, governments, and foreigners need

> **demand for money**
> The relationship between the interest rate and how much money people choose to hold

People demand money to make purchases.

money to conduct their daily transactions. Consumers need money to buy products, and firms need money to buy resources. *Money allows people to carry out economic transactions more easily and more efficiently.* With credit cards, the short-term loan delays the payment of money, but all accounts must eventually be settled with money.

The greater the value of transactions to be financed in a given period, the greater the demand for money. So the more active the economy is—that is, the more goods and services exchanged, reflected by real output—the more money demanded. Obviously an economy with a real GDP of $17 trillion needs more money than an economy half that size. Also, the higher the economy's price level, the greater the demand for money. The more things cost on average, the more money is needed to buy them. Shoppers in economies suffering from hyperinflation need mountains of cash.

You demand the money needed to fund your normal spending in the course of the day or week, and you may need money for unexpected expenditures. If you plan to buy lunch tomorrow, you will carry enough money to pay for it. But you may also want to be able to pay for other possible contingencies. For example, you could have car trouble or you could come across a sale on a favorite item. You can use checks, debit cards, or credit cards for some of these unexpected purchases, but you still feel safer with some extra cash. You may have a little extra cash with you right now for who knows what. Even *you* don't know.

The demand for money is rooted in money's role as a medium of exchange. But as we have seen,

> **"The quantity of money demanded varies inversely with the market interest rate."**

money is more than a medium of exchange; it is also a store of value. People save for a new home, for college, for retirement. People can store their purchasing power as money or as some other financial assets, such as corporate and government bonds. When people buy bonds and other financial assets, they are lending their money and are paid interest for doing so.

The demand for any asset is based on the services it provides. The big advantage of money as a store of value is its liquidity: Money can be immediately exchanged for whatever is for sale. In contrast, other financial assets, such as corporate or government bonds, must first be *liquidated*, or exchanged for money, which can then be used to buy goods and services. Money, however, has one major disadvantage when compared to other financial assets. Money in the form of currency and traveler's checks earns no interest, and the rate earned on checkable deposits is well below that earned on other financial assets; in recent years that rate has been close to zero. So holding wealth as money means giving up some interest. For example, suppose a business could earn 3 percent more interest by holding financial assets other than money. The opportunity cost of holding $1 million as money rather than as some other financial asset would amount to $30,000 per year. *The interest forgone is the opportunity cost of holding money.*

### 15-1b Money Demand and Interest Rates

When the market interest rate is low, other things constant, the cost of holding money—the cost of maintaining liquidity—is low, so people hold more of their wealth in the form of money. Such was the case in 2015, when the interest paid on savings deposits and time deposits was close to zero. When the interest rate is high, the cost of holding money is high, so people hold less of their wealth in money and more in other financial assets that pay higher interest. Thus, *other things constant, the quantity of money demanded varies inversely with the market interest rate.*

The money demand curve $D_m$ in Exhibit 1 shows the quantity of money people demand at alternative interest rates, other things constant. Both the quantity of money and the interest rate are in nominal terms. *The money demand curve slopes downward because the lower the interest rate, the lower the opportunity cost of holding money.* Movements along the curve reflect the effects of changes in the interest rate

## Exhibit 1

**Demand for Money**

The money demand curve, $D_m$, slopes downward. As the interest rate falls, other things constant, so does the opportunity cost of holding money; the quantity of money demanded increases.

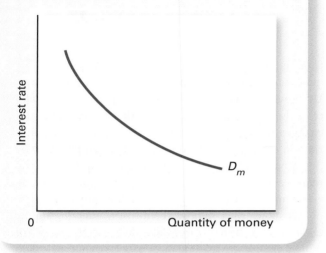

## Exhibit 2

**Effect of an Increase in the Money Supply**

Because the money supply is determined by the Federal Reserve, it can be represented by a vertical line. At point $a$, the intersection of the money supply, $S_m$, and the money demand, $D_m$, determines the market interest rate, $i$. Following an increase in the money supply to $S'_m$, the quantity of money supplied exceeds the quantity demanded at the original interest rate, $i$. The new equilibrium occurs at point $b$.

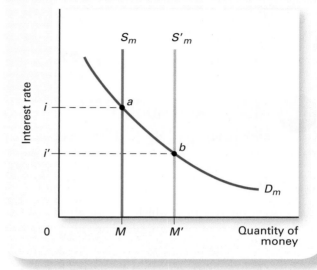

on the quantity of money demanded. Assumed constant along the curve are the price level and real GDP. If either increases, the demand for money increases, as reflected by a rightward shift of the money demand curve.

## 15-1c The Supply of Money and the Equilibrium Interest Rate

The supply of money—the stock of money available in the economy at a particular time—is determined primarily by the Fed through its control over currency and over excess reserves in the banking system. The supply of money $S_m$ is depicted as a vertical line in Exhibit 2. A *vertical supply curve implies that the quantity of money supplied is independent of the interest rate.*

The intersection of the demand for money $D_m$ with the supply of money $S_m$ determines the equilibrium interest rate, $i$—the interest rate that equates the quantity of money demanded with the quantity supplied. At interest rates above the equilibrium level, the opportunity cost of holding money is higher, so the quantity of money people want to hold is less than the quantity supplied. At interest rates below the equilibrium level, the opportunity cost of holding money is lower, so the quantity of money people want to hold exceeds the quantity supplied.

If the Fed increases the money supply, the supply curve shifts to the right, as shown by the movement

from $S_m$ out to $S'_m$ in Exhibit 2. At interest rate $i$, the quantity supplied now exceeds the quantity demanded. Because of the increased supply of money, people are *able* to hold more money. But at interest rate $i$ they are *unwilling* to hold that much. The opportunity cost of doing so is too high. Because people are now holding more of their wealth as money than they would like, they exchange some money for other financial assets, such as bonds. As the demand for bonds increases, bond sellers can pay less interest yet still attract enough buyers. The interest rate falls until the quantity of money demanded just equals the quantity supplied. With the decline in the interest rate to $i'$ in Exhibit 2, the opportunity cost of holding money falls enough that the public is willing to hold the now-larger stock of money. Equilibrium moves from point $a$ to point $b$. *For a given money demand curve, an increase in the money supply drives down the interest rate, and a decrease in the money supply drives up the interest rate.*

Now that you have some idea how money demand and money supply determine the market interest rate, you are ready to see how money fits into our model of the economy. Specifically, let's see how changes in the money supply affect aggregate demand and equilibrium output.

> **"For a given money demand curve, an increase in the money supply drives down the interest rate, and a decrease in the money supply drives up the interest rate."**

## 15-2 MONEY AND AGGREGATE DEMAND IN THE SHORT RUN

*In the short run, money affects the economy through changes in the interest rate.* Monetary policy influences the market interest rate, which in turn affects investment, a component of aggregate demand. Let's work through the chain of causation.

### 15-2a Interest Rates and Investment

Suppose the Fed believes that the economy is producing less than its potential and decides to stimulate output and employment by increasing the money supply. Recall

> **"In the short run, money affects the economy through changes in the interest rate."**

from the previous chapter that the Fed's primary tool for increasing the money supply is open-market purchases of U.S. government securities. The three panels of Exhibit 3 trace the links between changes in the money supply and changes in aggregate demand. We begin with equilibrium interest rate $i$, which is determined in panel (a) by the intersection of the money demand curve $D_m$ with the money supply curve $S_m$. Suppose the Fed purchases U.S. government bonds and thereby increases the money supply, as shown by a rightward shift of the money supply curve from $S_m$ to $S'_m$. After the increase in the supply of money, people are holding more money than they would prefer at interest rate $i$, so they try to exchange one form of wealth, money, for other financial assets. Exchanging dollars for financial assets has no direct effect on aggregate demand, but it does reduce the market interest rate. At the lower interest rate $i'$, the quantity of money demanded equals the quantity supplied.

A decline in the interest rate to $i'$, other things constant, reduces the opportunity cost of financing new

*Exhibit 3*

**Effects of an Increase in the Money Supply on Interest Rates, Investment, and Aggregate Demand**

In panel (a), an increase in the money supply forces the interest rate down to $i'$. With the cost of borrowing lower, the amount invested increases from $I$ to $I'$, as shown in panel (b). This sets off the spending multiplier process, so the aggregate output demanded at price level $P$ increases from $Y$ to $Y'$. The increase is shown by the shift of the aggregate demand curve to the right in panel (c).

plants and equipment, thereby making new investment more profitable. Likewise, a lower interest rate reduces the cost of financing a new house. So a decline in the interest rate increases the quantity of investment demanded. Panel (b) shows the demand for investment $D_I$ first introduced several chapters back. When the interest rate falls from $i$ to $i'$, the quantity of investment demanded increases from $I$ to $I'$.

If the spending multiplier exceeds 1.0, this increase in investment could lead to a greater increase in aggregate demand, reflected in panel (c) by a rightward shift of the aggregate demand curve from $AD$ to $AD'$. At the given price level $P$, real GDP increases from $Y$ to $Y'$. The sequence of events can be summarized as follows:

$$M \uparrow \rightarrow i \downarrow \rightarrow I \uparrow \rightarrow AD \uparrow \rightarrow Y \uparrow$$

An increase in the money supply, $M$, reduces the interest rate, $i$. The lower interest rate stimulates investment, $I$, which increases aggregate demand from $AD$ to $AD'$. At a given price level, real GDP demanded increases from $Y$ to $Y'$. The entire sequence is also traced out in each panel by the movement from point $a$ to point $b$.

Now let's consider the effect of a Fed-orchestrated *increase* in interest rates. In Exhibit 3 such a policy could be traced by moving from point $b$ to point $a$ in each panel, but we'll dispense with a blow-by-blow discussion of the graphs. Suppose the Federal Reserve decides to reduce the money supply to cool down an overheated economy. A decrease in the money supply would increase the interest rate. At the higher interest rate, businesses find it more costly to finance plants and equipment, and households find it more costly to finance new homes. Hence, a higher interest rate reduces the amount invested. The resulting decline in investment leads to a decline in aggregate demand.

As long as the interest rate is sensitive to changes in the money supply, and as long as investment is sensitive to changes in the interest rate, changes in the money supply affect investment. The extent

to which a given change in investment affects aggregate demand depends on the size of the spending multiplier.

## 15-2b Adding the Short-Run Aggregate Supply Curve

Even after tracing the effect of a change in the money supply on aggregate demand, we still have only half the story. To determine the effects of monetary policy on the equilibrium real GDP in the economy, we need the supply side. An aggregate supply curve helps show how a given shift of the aggregate demand curve affects real GDP and the price level. In the short run, the aggregate supply curve slopes upward, so the quantity supplied increases only if the price level increases. *For a given shift of the aggregate demand curve, the steeper the short-run aggregate supply curve, the smaller the increase in real GDP and the larger the increase in the price level.*

Suppose the economy is producing at point $a$ in Exhibit 4, where the aggregate demand curve $AD$

*Exhibit 4*

**Expansionary Monetary Policy to Close a Recessionary Gap**

At point *a*, the economy is producing less than its potential in the short run, resulting in a recessionary gap of $0.2 trillion. If the Federal Reserve increases the money supply by just the right amount, the aggregate demand curve shifts rightward from *AD* to *AD'*. A short-run and long-run equilibrium is established at point *b*, with the price level at 110 and output at the potential level of $17.0 trillion.

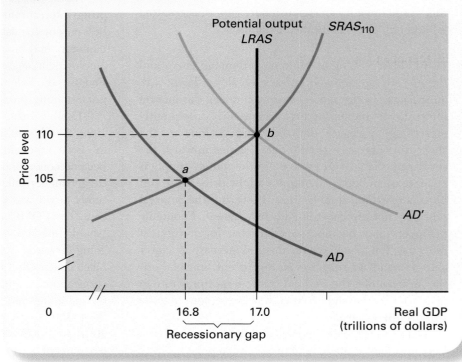

intersects the short-run aggregate supply curve $SRAS_{110}$, yielding a short-run equilibrium output of $16.8 trillion and a price level of 105. As you can see, the actual price level of 105 is below the expected price level of 110, and the short-run equilibrium output of $16.8 trillion is below the economy's potential of $17.0 trillion, yielding a recessionary gap of $0.2 trillion.

At point $a$, real wages are higher than had been negotiated and many people are looking for jobs. The Fed can wait to see whether the economy recovers on its own. Market forces could cause employers and workers to renegotiate lower nominal wages. This would lower production costs, pushing the short-run aggregate supply curve rightward, thus closing the recessionary gap. But if Fed officials are impatient with natural market forces, they could try to close the gap using an expansionary monetary policy. For example, during 2007 and 2008, the Fed aggressively cut the federal funds rate from 5.25 percent to between 0 and 0.25 percent to stimulate aggregate demand. If the Fed lowers that rate by just the right amount, this stimulates investment, thus increasing the aggregate demand curve enough to achieve a new equilibrium at point $b$, where the economy produces its potential output. Given all the connections in the chain of causality between changes in the money supply and changes in equilibrium output, however, it would actually be quite remarkable for the Fed to execute monetary policy so precisely. If the Fed overshot the mark and stimulated aggregate demand too much, this would open up an expansionary gap, thus creating inflationary pressure in the economy.

**TO REVIEW:** As long as the money demand curve and the investment demand curve each slope downward, an increase in the money supply reduces the market interest rate, increasing investment and consequently increasing aggregate demand. And as long as the short-run aggregate supply curve slopes upward, the short-run effect of an increase in the money supply is an increase in both real output and the price level. But here is one final qualification: Lowering the interest rate may not always stimulate investment. Economic prospects may become so glum that lower interest rates may fail to achieve the desired increase in aggregate demand. In response to the recent financial crisis, for example, the Fed cut the federal funds rate to near zero by the end of 2008, but investment in 2009 still dropped sharply.

That's the theory of monetary policy in the short run. Let's next look at the federal funds rate in practice.

## 15-2c Recent History of the Federal Funds Rate

At 2:15 P.M. on December 16, 2008, immediately following a regular meeting, the Federal Open Market Committee (FOMC) announced that it would lower its target for the federal funds rate to between 0 and 0.25 percent, the tenth reduction in 15 months. As you know by now, the federal funds rate is the interest rate banks charge one another for overnight lending of reserves at the Fed. Because lowering the rate reduces the cost of covering any reserve shortfall, banks are more willing to lend to the public. To execute this monetary policy, the FOMC authorized the New York Fed to make open-market purchases to increase bank reserves until the federal funds rate fell to the target level.

For four decades, the Fed has reflected its monetary policy in this interest rate. (For a few years, the Fed targeted money aggregates, but more on that later.) There are many interest rates in the economy—for credit cards, new cars, mortgages, home equity loans, personal loans, business loans, and more. Why focus on such an obscure rate? First, by changing bank reserves through open-market operations, the Fed has a direct lever on the federal funds rate, so the Fed's grip on this rate is tighter than on any other market rate. Second, the federal funds rate serves as a benchmark for determining other short-term interest rates in the economy. For example, after the Fed announces a rate change, major banks around the country usually change by the same amount their prime interest rate—the interest rate banks charge their best corporate customers. The federal funds rate affects monetary and financial conditions, which in turn affect employment, aggregate output, and the price level. The Fed uses the federal funds rate to pursue its twin goals of price stability and maximum employment.

Exhibit 5 shows the federal funds rate since early 1999. As a lesson in monetary policy, let's walk through the Fed's rationale. In the summer of 1999, the FOMC became concerned that robust economic growth would trigger higher inflation. In a series of steps, the federal funds target was raised from 4.75 percent to 6.5 percent. The FOMC announced at the time that the moves "should markedly diminish the risk of rising inflation going forward." Some critics argued that the Fed's rate hikes contributed to the 2001 recession. In 2001, concerns about waning consumer confidence, weaker capital spending, and the 9/11 terrorist attacks prompted the FOMC to reverse course. Between the beginning of 2001 and mid-2003, the FOMC cut the rate from 6.5 percent to 1.0 percent, reflecting at the time the

*Exhibit 5*

**Recent Ups and Downs in the Federal Funds Rate**

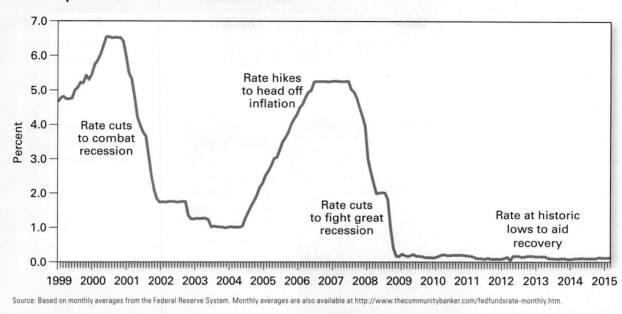

Source: Based on monthly averages from the Federal Reserve System. Monthly averages are also available at http://www.thecommunitybanker.com/fedfundsrate-monthly.htm.

most concentrated monetary stimulus on record. The rate remained at 1.0 percent for a year. Some economists criticized the Fed for keeping rates too low too long. They charged that this "easy money" policy overstimulated the housing sector, encouraging some people to buy homes they couldn't afford. These home purchases, critics argued, inflated the bubble in housing prices and sowed the seeds for mortgage defaults that hit years later.

Anyway, after leaving the rate at 1.0 percent for a year, the FOMC began worrying again about inflationary pressure. Between June 2004 and June 2006, the target federal funds rate was increased from 1.0 percent to 5.25 percent in 17 steps. The FOMC then hit the pause button, leaving the rate at 5.25 percent for more than a year. This takes us up to September 2007, when troubles in the housing sector, a rising mortgage default rate, and a softening economy prompted the first in a series of federal funds rate cuts. After 10 cuts over 15 months, the target rate in December 2008 stood between 0 and 0.25 percent, the lowest in history. As you can see from Exhibit 5, the rate remained at a record low for years.

With the primary tool of monetary policy already at the bottom of its range, was the Fed out of ammunition in fighting the Great Recession? Another policy tool that the Fed relied upon more after 2008 is the way it communicates with the public, particularly its intentions about future policy.

## 15-3 MONEY AND AGGREGATE DEMAND IN THE LONG RUN

When we looked at the impact of money on the economy in the short run, we found that money influences aggregate demand and equilibrium output through its effect on the interest rate. Here we look at the long-run effects of changes in the money supply on the economy. *The long-run view of money is more direct: if the central bank supplies more money to the economy, sooner or later people will spend more. But because the long-run aggregate supply curve is fixed at the economy's potential output, this greater spending simply increases the price level.* In short, more money is chasing the same output. Here are the details.

### 15-3a The Equation of Exchange

Every transaction in the economy involves a two-way swap: The buyer exchanges money for goods and the seller exchanges goods for money. One way of expressing this relationship among key variables in the economy is the **equation of exchange**, first

> **equation of exchange** The quantity of money, *M*, multiplied by its velocity, *V*, equals nominal GDP, which is the product of the price level, *P*, and real GDP, *Y*; or $M \times V = P \times Y$

developed by classical economists. Although this equation can be arranged in different ways, depending on the emphasis, the basic version is

$$M \times V = P \times Y$$

where $M$ is the quantity of money in the economy; $V$ is the **velocity of money**, or the average number of times per year each dollar is used to purchase final goods and services; $P$ is the average price level; and $Y$ is real GDP. The equation of exchange says that the quantity of money in circulation, $M$, multiplied by $V$, the number of times that money changes hands, equals the average price level, $P$, times real output, $Y$. The price level, $P$, times real output, $Y$, equals the economy's nominal income and output, or nominal GDP.

By rearranging the equation of exchange, we find that velocity equals nominal GDP divided by the money stock, or

$$V = \frac{P \times Y}{M}$$

For example, nominal GDP in 2015 was about 18.2 trillion, and the money stock as measured by M1 averaged about $3.0 trillion. The velocity of money indicates how often each dollar is used on average to pay for final goods and services during the year. So in 2015, velocity was $18.2 trillion divided by $3.0 trillion, or 6.1. Given GDP and the money supply, each dollar in circulation must have been spent 6.1 times on average to pay for final goods and services. There is no other way these market transactions could have occurred. The value of velocity is implied by the values of the other variables. Incidentally, velocity measures spending only on final goods and services—not on intermediate products, secondhand goods, financial assets, dollar transactions abroad, or illegal activity,

Just like "Miles per Gallon (MPG) = Gallons Used/Miles Driven" is an identity, so is $M \times V = P \times Y$. Both are true by definition.

© Thinkstock/First Light

even though such spending also occurs. So velocity underestimates how hard the money supply works during the year.

The equation of exchange says that total spending ($M \times V$) always equals total receipts ($P \times Y$), as was the case in our circular-flow analysis. As described so far, however, the equation of exchange is simply an *identity*—a relationship expressed in such a way that it is true by definition. Another example of an identity would be a relationship equating miles per gallon to the distance driven divided by the gasoline required.

## 15-3b The Quantity Theory of Money

If velocity is relatively stable over time, or at least predictable, the equation of exchange turns from an identity into a theory—the quantity theory of money. The **quantity theory of money** states that if the velocity of money is stable, or at least predictable, then the equation of exchange can be used to predict the effects of changes in the money supply on *nominal* GDP, $P \times Y$. For example, if $M$ increases by 5 percent and $V$ remains constant, then $P \times Y$, or nominal GDP, must also increase by 5 percent. For a while, some economists believed they could use the equation of exchange to predict nominal output in the short run. Now, if at all, it's used primarily as a rough guide in the long run.

So an increase in the money supply results in more spending in the long run, meaning a higher nominal GDP. How is this increase in $P \times Y$ divided between changes in the price level and changes in real GDP? The answer does not lie in the quantity theory, for that theory is stated only in terms of nominal GDP. The answer lies in the shape of the aggregate supply curve.

The long-run aggregate supply curve is vertical at the economy's potential level of output. With real output, $Y$, fixed and the velocity of money, $V$, relatively stable, a change in the stock of money translates directly into a change in the price level. Exhibit 6 shows the effect of an increase in the money supply in the long run.

**velocity of money** The average number of times per year each dollar is used to purchase final goods and services

**quantity theory of money** If the velocity of money is stable, or at least predictable, changes in the money supply have predictable effects on nominal GDP

## Exhibit 6

### In the Long Run, an Increase in the Money Supply Results in a Higher Price Level, or Inflation

The quantity theory of money predicts that if velocity is stable, then an increase in the money supply in the long run results in a higher price level, or inflation. Because the long-run aggregate supply curve is fixed, increases in the money supply affect only the price level, not real output.

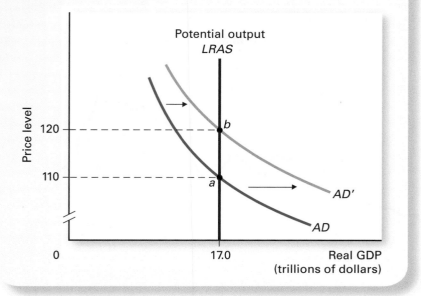

An increase in the money supply causes a rightward shift of the aggregate demand curve, which increases the price level but leaves output unchanged at potential GDP. So the economy's potential output level is not affected by changes in the money supply. *In the long run, increases in the money supply, with velocity stable or at least not decreasing, result only in higher prices.* For example, an examination of 73 inflation periods across major economies since 1960 concludes that important triggers to inflation were expansionary monetary policies.[1]

**TO REVIEW:** If velocity is stable, or at least predictable, the quantity theory of money says that changes in the money supply will, in the long run, result in predictable effects on the economy's price level. Velocity's

1. John Boschen and Charles Weise, "What Starts Inflation: Evidence from OECD Countries," *Journal of Money, Credit and Banking*, 35 (June 2003): 323–349.

stability and predictability are key to the quantity theory of money. Let's consider some factors that might influence velocity.

## 15-3c What Determines the Velocity of Money?

Velocity depends in part on the customs and conventions of commerce. In colonial times, money could be tied up in transit for days as a courier on horseback carried a payment from a merchant in Boston to one in Baltimore. Today, the electronic transmission of funds occurs in an instant, so the same stock of money can move around much more quickly to finance many more transactions. *The velocity of money has also increased because of a variety of commercial innovations that facilitate exchange.* For example, a wider use of charge accounts and credit cards has reduced the need for shoppers to carry cash. Likewise, automatic teller machines have made cash more accessible at more times and in more places. What's more, debit cards are used at a growing number of retail outlets and consumers can get cash back on debit transactions, so people need less "walking-around" money.

Another factor affecting velocity depends on how stable money is as a store of value. *The better money serves as a store of value, the more money people hold, so the lower its velocity.* For example, the introduction of interest-bearing checking accounts made money a better store of value, so people were more willing to hold money in checking accounts; this financial innovation reduced velocity. On the other hand, when inflation increases, money turns out to be a poorer store of value. People become reluctant to hold money and try to exchange it for some asset that retains its value better. This reduction in people's

Cliff Lipson/CBS/Getty Images

> **"The better money serves as a store of value, the more money people hold, so the lower its velocity."**

willingness to hold money during periods of high inflation increases the velocity of money. During hyperinflations, workers usually get paid daily, boosting velocity even more. Thus, *velocity increases with a rise in the inflation rate, other things constant.* Money becomes a hot potato—nobody wants to hold it for long.

Again, the usefulness of the quantity theory in predicting changes in the price level in the long run hinges on how stable and predictable the velocity of money is over time.

## 15-3d How Stable Is Velocity?

Exhibit 7 graphs velocity since 1960, measured both as nominal GDP divided by M1 in panel (a) and as nominal GDP divided by M2 in panel (b). Between 1960 and 1980, M1 velocity increased steadily and in that sense could be considered at least predictable. M1 velocity bounced around during the 1980s. But in the early 1990s, more and more banks began offering money market funds that included limited check-writing privileges, or what is considered M2. Deposits shifted from M1 to M2, which increased the velocity of M1. Also, as already noted, more people used debit cards which increased the velocity of M1

because people carried less cash (plus they could easily get cash back on debit-card transactions). M1 velocity increased from about 6.0 in 1993 to 10.5 in

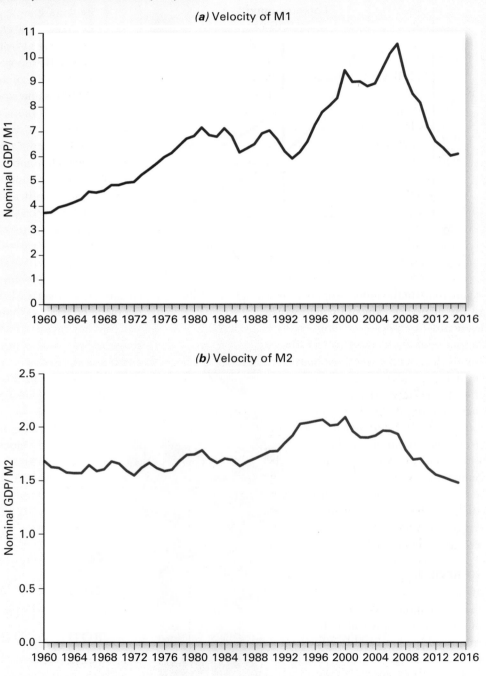

### Exhibit 7

**The Velocity of Money**

M1 velocity fluctuated so much during the 1980s that M1 growth was abandoned as a short-run policy target. M2 velocity appears more stable than M1 velocity, but both are now considered by the Fed as too unpredictable for short-run policy use.

*(a)* Velocity of M1

*(b)* Velocity of M2

Sources: *Economic Report of the President*, February 2015, and the Federal Reserve Board. Velocity in 2015 was estimated by the author based on nominal GDP and the money supply projections as of May 2015.

2007. M1 velocity has dropped since the 2007–2009 recession. Because of extremely low interest rates, the opportunity cost of holding wealth in the form of money declined, so the quantity of money demanded increased. Also, because of anxiety about the economy, people hoarded more cash, all of which slowed velocity to 6.1 by 2015. M2 velocity appears slightly more stable, as you can see by comparing the two panels in Exhibit 7.

For a few years, the Fed focused on changes in the money supply as a target for monetary policy in the short run. Because M1 velocity became so unstable during the 1980s, the Fed in 1987 switched from targeting M1 to targeting M2. But when M2 velocity became volatile in the early 1990s, the Fed announced that money aggregates, including M2, would no longer be considered reliable guides for monetary policy in the short run. *Since 1993, the equation of exchange has been considered only a rough guide linking changes in the money supply to inflation in the long run.*

What is the long-run relationship between increases in the money supply and inflation? Since the Federal Reserve System was established in 1913, the United States has suffered three episodes of high inflation, and each was preceded and accompanied by sharp increases in the money supply. These occurred from 1913 to 1920, 1939 to 1948, and 1967 to 1980. There is abundant evidence linking money growth with inflation in the long run.

## 15-4 TARGETS FOR MONETARY POLICY

In the short run, monetary policy affects the economy largely by influencing interest rates. In the long run, changes in the money supply affect the price level, though with an uncertain and variable lag. Should monetary authorities focus on the interest rates in the short run or the supply of money in the long run? As we will see, the Fed lacks the tools to focus on both at the same time.

### 15-4a Contrasting Policies

To demonstrate the effects of different policies, we begin with the money market in equilibrium at point e in Exhibit 8.

The interest rate is i and the money stock is M, values the monetary authorities find appropriate. Suppose there is an increase in the demand for money in the economy, perhaps because of an increase in nominal GDP. The money demand curve shifts to the right, from $D_m$ to $D'_m$.

When confronted with an increase in the demand for money, monetary authorities can choose to do nothing, thereby allowing the interest rate to rise, or they can increase the money supply enough to hold the interest rate constant. If monetary authorities do nothing, the quantity of money in the economy remains at M, but the interest rate rises because the greater demand for money increases the equilibrium combination from point e up to point e'. Alternatively, monetary authorities can try to keep the interest rate at its initial level by increasing the supply of money from $S_m$ to $S'_m$. In terms of possible combinations of the money stock and the interest rate, monetary authorities must choose from points lying along the new money demand curve, $D'_m$.

A growing economy usually needs a growing money supply to pay for the increase in aggregate output. If monetary authorities maintain a constant growth in the money supply, and if velocity remains stable, the interest rate fluctuates unless the growth in the supply of money

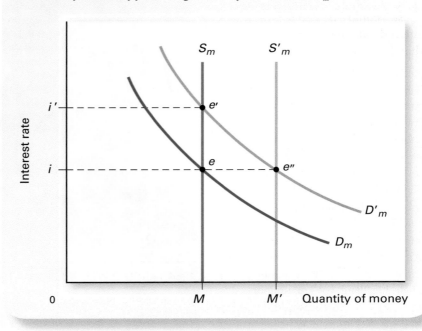

### Exhibit 8

**Targeting Interest Rates Versus Targeting the Money Supply**

An increase in the price level or in real GDP, with velocity stable, shifts rightward the money demand curve from $D_m$ to $D'_m$. If the Federal Reserve holds the money supply at $S_m$, the interest rate rises from i (at point e) to i' (at point e'). Alternatively, the Fed could try to hold the interest rate constant by increasing the money supply to $S'_m$. The Fed may choose any point along the money demand curve $D'_m$.

each period just happens to match the growth in the demand for money (as in the movement from *e* to *e″* in Exhibit 8). Alternatively, monetary authorities could try to adjust the money supply each period by the amount needed to keep the interest rate stable. With this latter approach, changes in the money supply would have to offset any changes in the demand for money. This essentially is what the Fed does when it holds the federal funds target constant, as from late 2008 well into 2015.

Interest rate fluctuations could be harmful if they create undesirable fluctuations in investment. For interest rates to remain stable during economic expansions, the money supply would have to grow at the same rate as the demand for money. Likewise, for interest rates to remain stable during economic contractions, the money supply would have to shrink at the same rate as the demand for money. Hence, for monetary authorities to maintain the interest rate at some specified level, the money supply must increase during economic expansions and decrease during contractions. But an increase in the money supply during an expansion would increase aggregate demand even more, and a decrease in the money supply during a contraction would reduce aggregate demand even more. *Such changes in the money supply would thus tend to worsen fluctuations in economic activity, thereby adding more instability to the economy.* With this in mind, let's review monetary policy over the years.

## 15-4b Targets before 1982

Between World War II and October 1979, the Fed attempted to stabilize interest rates. Stable interest rates were viewed as a prerequisite for an attractive investment environment and, thus, for a stable economy. Milton Friedman, a Nobel Prize winner, argued that this exclusive attention to interest rates made monetary policy a source of instability in the economy because changes in the money supply reinforced fluctuations in the economy. He argued that the Fed should pay less attention to interest rates and instead should focus on a steady and predictable growth in the money supply. The debate raged during the 1970s, and Friedman won some important converts. Amid growing concern about a rising inflation rate, the Fed, under a new chairman, Paul Volcker, announced in October 1979 that it would deemphasize interest rates and would instead target specific money aggregates. Not surprisingly, interest rates became much more volatile.

But many observers believe that a sharp reduction in money growth in the latter half of 1981 caused the recession of 1982. Inflation declined rapidly, but unemployment climbed to 10 percent. People were worried. As you might expect, the Fed was widely criticized. Farmers, politicians, and businesspeople denounced Volcker. Emotions ran high. Volcker was reportedly even given Secret Service protection. In October 1982, three years after the focus on interest rates was dropped, Volcker announced that the Fed would again pay some attention to interest rates.

## 15-4c Targets after 1982

The Fed is always feeling its way, looking for signs about the direction of the economy. The rapid pace of financial innovations and deregulation during the 1980s made the definition and measurement of the money supply more difficult. Alan Greenspan, who became the Fed chairman in 1987, said that, in the short run, changes in the money supply "are not linked closely enough with those of nominal income to justify a single-minded focus on the money supply."[2] In 1993, he testified in Congress that the Fed would no longer target money aggregates, such as M1 and M2, as a guide to monetary policy. As we've seen, the Fed in recent years has targeted the federal funds rate. *No central bank in a major economy now makes significant use of money aggregates to guide policy in the short run. Still, most policy makers also agree that in the long run, changes in the money supply influence the price level and inflation.*

While monetary targets are important, also significant is what Fed officials have to say. For example, they might announce that they are following a problem closely and are prepared to stabilize financial markets as needed. Such reassurance is sometimes all that's required to calm market jitters.

## 15-4d Other Fed Responses to the Financial Crisis

As we have seen, the Fed shapes monetary policy in a variety of other ways, as it did during

Former Fed Chairman Alan Greenspan helped shift the focus of the Fed from money aggregates (M1 and M2) to the federal funds rate.

Brooks Kraft/Corbis News/Corbis

2. Quoted in "Greenspan Asks That Fed Be Allowed to Pay Interest," *Wall Street Journal*, 11 March 1992.

and after the Great Recession of 2007–2009. To get a flavor of what the Fed has been up to, let's take a look at some of its responses.

## Bailing Out AIG

In September 2008, as the global financial crisis was spreading, the Fed teamed up with the U.S. Treasury with a $182.5 billion package to rescue the insurance giant AIG from failure. At the time, the company was so interconnected with other financial entities that regulators believed they could not risk another bankruptcy, particularly after the panic created by the failure of Lehman Brothers. The Fed purchased some of AIG's troubled assets, taking them off AIG's balance sheet. The Fed and the Treasury also lent AIG enough money to keep the company running. AIG survived, and by June 2012 it had paid back the Fed with interest.

Some critics charged that AIG and some other large financial institutions should not have been bailed out because they helped cause the financial crisis. The Fed chairman at the time, Ben Bernanke, said that the Fed tried to protect U.S. workers and consumers, groups that would have been hurt the most by a collapse of the financial system. He also noted that the Fed's investments that seemed like bailouts actually paid off well enough that the Fed sent $80 billion in "profit" to the U.S. Treasury in 2010 and $77 billion in 2011, record amounts to that point and nearly double what was sent in 2009. We should also note that a share of AIG stock, which was selling for as much as $1,400 before the financial crisis, plunged to just $10 by early 2009, so shareholders lost nearly all their investment. Not much of a bailout for them.

## Reducing the Risk of "Too Big to Fail"

Large financial institutions like AIG have dealings with thousands of other financial entities, so if one of these giants fails, as Lehman Brothers did in September 2008, that entails much collateral damage on the wider economy. With tougher supervisory oversight and greater capital requirements, the Fed and other regulators are trying to reduce the chances that a big financial institution will fail. For example, the Fed helped conduct a **stress test** of the 19 largest banks to determine which ones needed additional financial capital to weather a bad economy. Many banks had to raise billions more in capital.

> **❝No central bank in a major economy now makes significant use of money aggregates to guide policy in the short run.❞**

The Dodd-Frank Act gave the Fed and the FDIC expanded oversight of large financial institutions, including for the first time those that are not depository institutions. Over the years, nonbank financial intermediaries such as mortgage companies, insurance companies, brokerage firms, money market mutual funds, and hedge funds came to represent a larger share of all lending in the economy, but because they did not rely on customer deposits, they had been out of the Fed's scope and control. The Dodd-Frank Act brought this so-called **shadow banking system** under the Fed's regulatory control.

Again, the objective of regulations is to reduce the probability that a large financial institution will collapse. But if one of these financial giants should get into serious trouble, the approach going forward is to let it fail through an orderly liquidation of the firm's assets. To that end, the Fed and the FDIC have set out rules for so-called *living wills*, which requires each large financial institution, even one that appears in great shape, to prepare a blueprint for how it should be taken apart in the event of bankruptcy.

## Quantitative Easing

The Fed typically changes the federal funds rate by buying or selling short-term government securities. But with that interest rate already at rock bottom by late 2008, the Fed was looking for other ways to help the economy. The Fed's answer was to buy long-term assets, such as government bonds and mortgage-backed securities. Doing so did not reduce short-term rates, which could not go lower, but it did bring down long-term rates, making investments more attractive. Purchasing mortgage-backed securities supported the mortgage and housing markets and helped stabilize financial markets more generally.

Through a variety of aggressive purchases since late 2008, the Fed added over $3 trillion in assets to its balance sheet. These asset

**stress test** Bank regulators assessed the soundness of large banks to determine which ones needed more financial capital to weather a bad economy

**shadow banking system** Financial institutions, such as mortgage companies and brokerage firms, that do not rely on customer deposits to make loans purchases, called **quantitative easing**, directly lowered long-term interest rates, and indirectly raised bank reserves. Bank funds on deposit with the Fed increased by more than $2.5 trillion.

What are the risks of quantitative easing? The Fed could lose money on its purchases if these assets are sold back for less. Because the tool is unconventional and not well tested, nobody knows how much quantitative easing is too much. And too much money creation could trigger inflation, which is discussed next.

All these actions could be summed up as the *Fed trying to do whatever it takes to comply with its statutory mandate of price stability with maximum employment*. Fed officials did not want a repeat of the Great Depression, when they dropped the ball by not supplying the liquidity the financial system needed. As a result, some 10,000 banks failed during the Great Depression, versus about 500 since the onset of the Great Recession.

## 15-4e What about Inflation?

At press conferences, the head of the Fed has reminded the public that the Fed's twin statutory mandates are price stability and maximum employment. In terms of price stability, the Fed seeks a target rate of 2 percent. Why not zero percent? According to the Fed, that would mean the economy at times would experience deflation—something the Fed wants to avoid. In terms of maximum employment, the Fed would like to see the minimum sustainable unemployment rate get down to a range between 5.0 percent and 5.2 percent. Why not lower? The Fed believes a rate much below that would tighten labor markets too much, risking higher inflation. (Each quarter, FOMC participants estimate the minimum sustainable unemployment rate, so that target changes over time.)

Because of asset purchases by the Fed, total assets on its balance sheet expanded from about $0.9 trillion in the summer of 2007, before the financial crisis, to about $4.5 trillion in the summer of 2015, with quantitative easing the reason for the jump. Some critics feared that buying all those assets would sooner or later lead to inflation. Why hasn't it, at least not as of 2015? Well, most of the funds that the Fed created to buy these assets ended up as idle bank reserves on account with the Fed. Remember that bank reserves are not part of the money supply. Banks were lending less because (1) the demand for loans was down, (2) lending standards had tightened with Dodd-Frank, (3) reducing the opportunity cost of excess reserves banks were now earning

**quantitative easing**
Fed purchases of long-term assets to stabilize financial markets, reduce long-term interest rates, and improve the investment environment

interest on their reserves at the Fed, and (4) the financial crisis made banks more wary of lending. In the summer of 2015, banks had over $2.6 trillion on deposit with the Fed; this was up from just $13 billion in the summer of 2007, before the trouble started. Thus, between 2007 and 2015, bank reserves at the Fed increased 200-fold.

The money supply as measured by M1 did increase by 117 percent, between 2007 and 2015, a period when real GDP grew by a total of only 11 percent. Doesn't that sound like a recipe for inflation? Not if the velocity of M1 slowed down considerably, which it did. The lower interest rate reduced the opportunity cost of holding cash, so people held more of it. And the uncertain economic times increased the demand for cash, with some people even hoarding it. All this slowed the velocity of M1, which fell from 10.5 in 2007 to 6.1 in 2015, a drop of 42 percent. The drop in velocity meant that the increase in the money supply did not increase nominal spending that much and thus did not result in much inflation. Between 2007 and 2015, the CPI increased an average of just 1.8 percent per year.

As noted earlier, the equation of exchange is an identity, meaning it is true by definition. Its usefulness as the quantity theory depends on velocity's stability or at least its predictability. Recent history shows that velocity has been neither stable nor predictable, so the quantity theory is of little use, particularly in the short run. Still, decades of research around the world suggest a link in the long run between sharp increases in the money supply and higher inflation. Between 2007 and 2013 the price level increased by a total of only 13 percent. Between 2007 and 2015, the CPI increased an average of only 1.8 percent per year.

As noted earlier, the equation of exchange is an identify and will hold by definition. The usefulness as the quantity theory depends on velocity's stability or at least its predictability. In Exhibit 7, recent history shows that velocity has been neither stable nor predictable, so the quantity theory does not help much, particularly in the short run. Still, decades of research around the world suggest a link in the long run between sharp increases in the money supply and subsequent inflation. Even if the quantity theory is not a useful in predicting nominal GDP, the equation of exchange, as an identity, still helps us think more clearly about macroeconomic variables.

Perhaps by the time you read this, the Fed will have begun to unwind long-term asset purchases made during and after the financial crisis. It will have to do so in a way that does not destabilize the economy. Remember that as the Fed sells these long term assets, this will reduce bank reserves in the system. If it sells its assets too quickly, the Fed must be mindful of the possibility of deflation, which is bad news and can be self-reinforcing. But as long as trillions of dollars sit in excess reserves at the Fed, inflation remains a risk. If banks start tapping their huge accumulation of excess reserves to make loans, the money supply will grow quickly. Unless velocity continues to drop, this growth in the money supply could trigger inflation. That's why the Fed officials have made it clear that once the recovery picks up speed, they will begin selling assets to reduce bank reserves. But Fed officials have little experience with winding down assets of this magnitude.

## 15-4f International Considerations

As national economies grow more interdependent, the Fed has become more sensitive to the global implications of its action. What happens in the United States often affects markets overseas and vice versa. The Fed has tried to soothe troubled world markets in a variety of ways. When Mexico faced financial difficulties in 1982 and again in 1994, Fed officials helped arrange loans to prevent a financial crisis. A worldwide financial panic in the fall of 1998 because of defaults on Russian bonds prompted the Fed to lower the federal funds rate to supply more liquidity here and abroad. And a worldwide shortage of credit in 2007–2009 caused by mortgage defaults in the United States prompted the Fed to supply additional liquidity to the banking system to ensure the orderly functioning of financial markets.

Central banks around the world have also begun coordinating their activities, particularly during economic turmoil. For example, in October 2008, during the global financial crisis, six major central banks reduced interest rates in a joint effort to restore financial stability to world markets. Chairman Bernanke said he was in frequent contact with other central bankers, including Mario Draghi, head of the European Central Bank. (Incidentally, Draghi, like Bernanke, earned a Ph.D. in economics from MIT.)

Although not the main focus of monetary policy, international considerations are of growing importance to the Fed, particularly because of recent fiscal instability in the eurozone.

## 15-5 FINAL WORD

This chapter has described two ways of viewing the effects of money on the economy's performance, but we should not overstate the differences. In the model that focuses on the short run, an increase in the money supply means that people are holding more money than they would like at the prevailing interest rate, so they exchange one form of wealth, money, for other financial assets, such as corporate or government bonds. This greater demand for other financial assets has no direct effect on aggregate demand, but it does reduce the interest rate, and thereby stimulates investment. The higher investment increases aggregate demand. The effect of this increase in demand on real output and the price level depends on the shape of the short-run aggregate supply curve.

In the model that focuses on the long run, changes in the money supply act more directly on the price level. If velocity is relatively stable or at least predictable, then a change in the money supply has a predictable effect on the price level in the long run. As long as velocity is not declining, an increase in the money supply means that people eventually spend more, increasing aggregate demand. But because long-run aggregate supply is fixed at the economy's potential output, increased aggregate demand leads simply to a higher price level, or to inflation, in the long run. Since 2007 the velocity of money has declined, so the increase in the money supply since then has not fueled much inflation, at least not as of 2015.

# STUDY TOOLS 15

# CHAPTER 15 PROBLEMS

*Your instructor can access the answers to these problems online at http://cengagebrain.com.*

## 15-1 Explain how the demand and supply of money determine the market interest rate

1. *(Money Demand)* Suppose that you never carry cash. Your paycheck of $1,000 per month is deposited directly into your checking account, and you spend your money at a constant rate so that at the end of each month your checking account balance is zero.
   a. What is your average money balance during the pay period?
   b. How would each of the following changes affect your average monthly balance?
      i. You are paid $500 twice monthly rather than $1,000 each month.
      ii. You are uncertain about your total spending each month.
      iii. You spend a lot at the beginning of the month (e.g., for rent) and little at the end of the month.
      iv. Your monthly income increases.

2. *(Market Interest Rate)* With a diagram, show how the supply of money and the demand for money determine the rate of interest? Explain the shapes of the supply curve and the demand curve.

## 15-2 Outline the steps between an increase in the money supply and an increase in equilibrium output

3. *(Money and Aggregate Demand)* Would each of the following increase, decrease, or have no impact on the ability of open-market operations to affect aggregate demand? Explain your answer.
   a. Investment demand becomes less sensitive to changes in the interest rate.
   b. The marginal propensity to consume rises.
   c. The money multiplier rises.
   d. Banks decide to hold additional excess reserves.
   e. The demand for money becomes more sensitive to changes in the interest rate.

4. *(Monetary Policy and Aggregate Supply)* Assume that the economy is initially in long-run equilibrium. Using an AD–AS diagram, illustrate and explain the short-run and long-run impacts of an increase in the money supply.

5. *(Monetary Policy and an Expansionary Gap)* Suppose the Fed wishes to use monetary policy to close an expansionary gap.
   a. Should the Fed increase or decrease the money supply?
   b. If the Fed uses open-market operations, should it buy or sell government securities?
   c. Determine whether each of the following increases, decreases, or remains unchanged in the short run: the market interest rate, the quantity of money demanded,

investment spending, aggregate demand, potential output, the price level, and equilibrium real GDP.

## 15-3 Describe the relevance of velocity's stability on monetary policy

6. *(Equation of Exchange)* Calculate the velocity of money if real GDP is 3,000 units, the average price level is $4 per unit, and the quantity of money in the economy is $1,500. What happens to velocity if the average price level drops to $3 per unit? What happens to velocity if the average price level remains at $4 per unit but the money supply rises to $2,000? What happens to velocity if the average price level falls to $2 per unit, the money supply is $2,000, and real GDP is 4,000 units?

7. *(Quantity Theory of Money)* What basic assumption about the velocity of money transforms the equation of exchange into the quantity theory of money? Also:
   a. According to the quantity theory, what will happen to nominal GDP if the money supply increases by 5 percent and velocity does not change?
   b. What will happen to nominal GDP if, instead, the money supply decreases by 8 percent and velocity does not change?
   c. What will happen to nominal GDP if, instead, the money supply increases by 5 percent and velocity decreases by 5 percent?
   d. What happens to the price level in the short run in each of these three situations?

## 15-4 Summarize the specific policies the Fed pursued during and after the Great Recession

8. *(Great Recession)* How did the Fed try to bring the economy back during and after the Great Recession? What specific policies did it pursue.

9. *(Money Supply Versus Interest Rate Targets)* Assume that the economy's real GDP is growing.
   a. What will happen to money demand over time?
   b. If the Fed leaves the money supply unchanged, what will happen to the interest rate over time?
   c. If the Fed changes the money supply to match the change in money demand, what will happen to the interest rate over time?
   d. What would be the effect of the policy described in part (c) on the economy's stability over the business cycle?

10. *(Quantitative Easing)* What's the difference between ordinary open-market purchases and quantitative easing?

11. *(Quantitative Easing)* Because of quantitative easing, the Fed purchased more than two trillion dollars of financial assets. Why did the Fed do this? How are these purchases reflected on the Fed's balance sheet? And why hasn't this increased the rate of inflation, at least not as of May 2015?

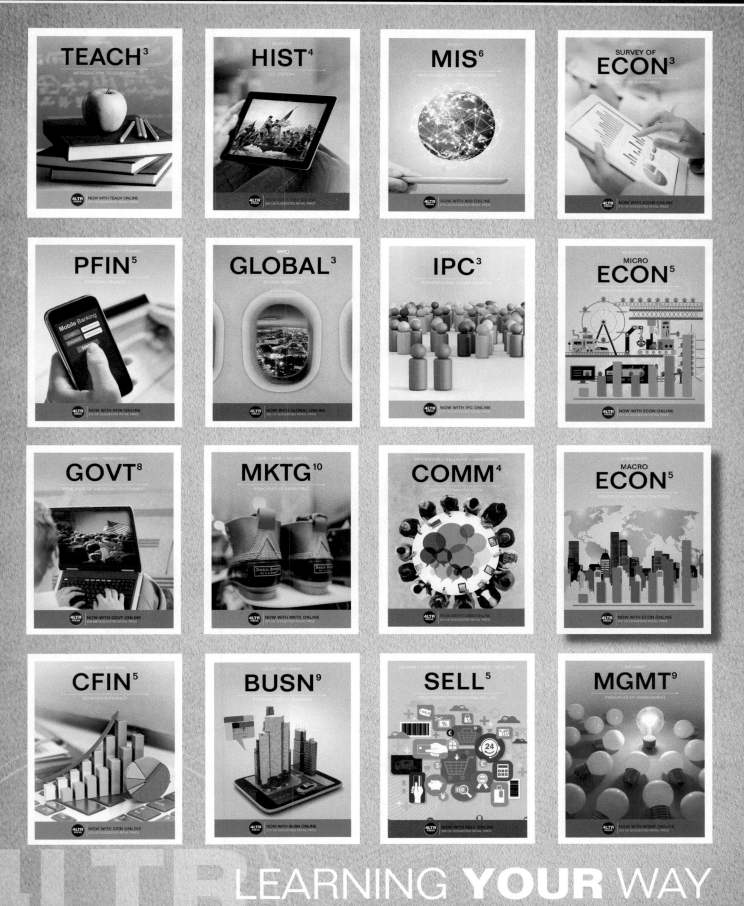

# 16 | Macro Policy Debate: Active or Passive?

## LEARNING OUTCOMES

After studying this chapter, you will be able to...

**16-1** Outline the difference between active policy and passive policy, and explain how the two approaches differ in their assumptions about how well the economy works on its own

**16-2** Describe how expectations can influence the effectiveness of discretionary policy

**16-3** Summarize why some economists prefer that policy be shaped by predictable rules rather than by the discretion of policy makers

**16-4** Explain the shape of the short-run Phillips curve and the long-run Phillips curve

After finishing this chapter go to **PAGE 302** for **STUDY TOOLS**

**Topics discussed in Chapter 16 include:**

- Active versus passive approach
- Self-correcting mechanisms
- Problem of Lags
- Rational expectations
- Policy rules and policy credibility
- The time-inconsistency problem
- Short-run and long-run Phillips curves
- Natural rate hypothesis

© iStockphoto.com/PeskyMonkey

- Does the economy work fairly well on its own, or does it require active government intervention?

- Does government intervention do more harm than good?

- If people expect government to intervene when the economy falters, does this expectation affect people's behavior?

- Does this expectation affect government behavior?

- Is there a relationship between unemployment and inflation in the short run and in the long run?

*Answers to these and other questions are provided in this chapter, which discusses the appropriate role of government in economic stabilization.*

You have studied both fiscal and monetary policy, and are now in a position to consider the overall impact of public policy on the U.S. economy. This chapter distinguishes between two general approaches: the active approach and the passive approach. The active approach views the economy as relatively unstable and unable to recover from shocks when they occur. According to the active approach, economic fluctuations arise primarily from the private sector, particularly investment, and natural market forces may not help much or may be too slow once the economy gets off track. To move the economy to its potential output, the active approach calls for government intervention and discretionary policy.

> **"Does the economy work fairly well on its own, or does it require active government intervention?"**

The passive approach, on the other hand, views the economy as relatively stable and able to recover from shocks when they do occur. When the economy derails, natural market forces and automatic stabilizers nudge it back on track in a timely manner. According to the passive approach, not only is active discretionary policy unnecessary, but such activism may do more harm than good.

In this chapter, we consider the pros and cons of *active* intervention in the economy versus *passive* reliance on natural market forces and automatic stabilizers. We also examine the role that expectations play in stabilization policy. You will learn why unanticipated stabilization policies have more impact on employment and output than do anticipated ones. Finally, the chapter explores the trade-off between unemployment and inflation.

## 16-1 ACTIVE POLICY VERSUS PASSIVE POLICY

According to the *active approach,* discretionary fiscal or monetary policy can reduce the costs of an unstable economy, such as higher unemployment. According to the *passive approach,* discretionary policy may contribute to the instability of the economy and is therefore part of the problem, not part of the solution. The two approaches differ in their assumptions about the effectiveness of natural market forces compared with government intervention.

### 16-1a Closing a Recessionary Gap

Perhaps the best way to describe each approach is by examining a particular macroeconomic problem. Suppose the economy is in short-run equilibrium at point *a* in panel (a) of Exhibit 1, with real GDP at $16.8 trillion, which is below the economy's potential of $17.0 trillion. The recessionary gap of $0.2 trillion drives unemployment above its natural rate (the rate when the economy

*Exhibit 1*

## Closing a Recessionary Gap

At point *a* in both panels, the economy is in short-run equilibrium, with unemployment exceeding its natural rate. According to the passive approach, shown in panel (a), high unemployment eventually causes wages to fall, reducing the cost of doing business. The decline in costs shifts the short-run aggregate supply curve rightward from $SRAS_{110}$ to $SRAS_{100}$, moving the economy to its potential output at point *b*. In panel (b), the government employs an active approach to shift the aggregate demand curve from *AD* to *AD'*. If the active policy works perfectly, the economy moves to its potential output at point *c*.

**(a)** *The passive approach*

**(b)** *The active approach*

produces potential GDP). This gap could result from lower-than-expected aggregate demand. What should public officials do?

## Passive Approach

Those who subscribe to the passive approach, as did their classical predecessors, have more faith in the *self-correcting forces* of the economy than do those who favor

Tony Garcia/SuperStock

the active approach. In what sense is the economy self-correcting? According to the passive approach, wages and prices are flexible enough to adjust within a reasonable period to labor shortages or surpluses. High unemployment causes wages to fall, which reduces production costs, which in turn shifts the short-run aggregate supply curve rightward in panel (a) of Exhibit 1. (Money wages need not actually fall; money wage increases need only lag behind price increases, so that real wages fall. Or perhaps nonwage compensation is reduced, such as health care benefits.) The short-run aggregate supply curve, within a reasonable period, shifts from $SRAS_{110}$ to $SRAS_{100}$, moving the economy to its potential output at point *b*.

*According to the passive approach, the economy is stable enough, gravitating in a reasonable time toward potential GDP. Automatic stabilizers also help move the economy toward potential GDP. Consequently, advocates of passive policy see little reason for discretionary policy.* The passive approach is to let natural market forces and automatic stabilizers close the recessionary gap. So the prescription of passive policy is to do nothing beyond relying on the automatic stabilizers already built into taxes, transfers, and government purchases.

> **"Advocates of passive policy see little reason for discretionary policy."**

## Active Approach

Advocates of an active approach, on the other hand, believe that prices and wages are not that flexible, particularly in the downward direction. They think that when adverse supply shocks or sagging demand push unemployment above its natural rate, market forces may be too slow to respond. The longer market forces take to reduce unemployment to the natural rate, the greater the output lost and the greater the economic and psychological cost to those unemployed. *Because advocates of an active policy associate a high cost with the passive approach, they favor an active stabilization policy to stimulate aggregate demand.*

## Active Response to the Great Recession

A decision by public officials to intervene in the economy to achieve potential output—that is, a decision to use discretionary policy—reflects an active approach. In panel (b) of Exhibit 1, we begin at the same point *a* as in panel (a). At point *a*, short-run equilibrium output is below potential output, so the economy is experiencing a recessionary gap. Through discretionary monetary policy, discretionary fiscal policy, or some of both, as occurred in 2008 and 2009, active policy attempts to increase aggregate demand from *AD* to *AD′*, moving equilibrium from point *a* to point *c*, thus closing the recessionary gap.

During the Great Recession, policy makers tried to revive a troubled economy using both fiscal and monetary policy. President Barack Obama's $831 billion stimulus plan, the largest on record, was approved by Congress in February 2009 and was aimed at counteracting the sharp drop in output and employment triggered by the financial crisis. As noted in the previous chapter, the Fed had by that time already cut its target interest rate a record amount. This combination of fiscal and monetary policy was the most concentrated attempt to boost aggregate demand ever. One possible cost of using discretionary policy to stimulate aggregate demand is an increase in the price level, or inflation. But inflation has not been a problem in recent years. A larger cost of fiscal stimulus was an increase in the federal budget deficit, which rocketed from $459 billion in 2008 to $1.4 trillion in 2009. The deficit exceeded $1 trillion in each of the next three years.

## 16-1b Closing an Expansionary Gap

Let's consider the situation in which the short-run equilibrium output exceeds the economy's potential. Suppose the actual price level of 115 exceeds the expected price level of 110, resulting in an expansionary gap of $0.2 trillion, as shown in Exhibit 2. The passive approach argues that natural market forces prompt workers and firms to negotiate higher wages at their next opportunity. These higher nominal wages increase production costs, shifting the short-run supply curve leftward, from $SRAS_{110}$ to $SRAS_{120}$, as shown in panel (a). Consequently, the price level increases and output decreases to the economy's potential. So the natural adjustment process results in a higher price level, or inflation.

An active approach sees discretionary policy as a way to reach potential output without increasing the price level. Advocates of an active policy believe that if aggregate demand can be reduced from *AD″* to *AD′*, as shown in panel (b) of Exhibit 2, the equilibrium point will move down along the initial aggregate supply curve from *d* to *c*. *Whereas the passive approach relies on natural market forces and automatic stabilizers to close an expansionary gap through a decrease in the short-run aggregate supply curve, the active approach relies on just the right discretionary policy to close the gap through a decrease of the aggregate demand curve.*

In the long run, the passive approach results in a higher price level and the active approach results in a lower price level. Thus, the correct discretionary policy

> **"Because advocates of an active policy associate a high cost with the passive approach, they favor an active stabilization policy to stimulate aggregate demand."**

*Exhibit 2*

## Closing an Expansionary Gap

At point *d* in both panels, the economy is in short-run equilibrium, producing $17.2 trillion, which exceeds the economy's potential output. Unemployment is below its natural rate. In the passive approach reflected in panel (a), the government makes no change in policy, so natural market forces eventually bring about a higher negotiated wage, increasing firm costs and shifting the short-run supply curve leftward to $SRAS_{120}$. The new equilibrium at point *e* results in a higher price level and lower output and employment. An active policy reduces aggregate demand, shifting the equilibrium in panel (b) from point *d* to point *c*, thus closing the expansionary gap without increasing the price level.

can relieve the inflationary pressure associated with an expansionary gap. Whenever the Fed attempts to cool down an overheated economy by increasing its target interest rate, as it did in 17 steps between mid-2004 and mid-2006, it employs an active monetary policy to close an expansionary gap. The Fed tried to orchestrate a so-called *soft landing* to gently slow the rate of growth before that growth triggered unacceptably high inflation. We should note that heading off higher inflation is one thing, but policy makers are reluctant to take action that would actually reduce the price level—that is, create deflation. For example, in October 2014, the Bank of Japan announced a massive stimulus program to prevent deflation.[1] Once deflation takes hold, it can be self-reinforcing, as has been the case in Japan in recent years.

## 16-1c Problems with Active Policy

The timely adoption and implementation of an active policy is not easy. One problem is identifying the economy's potential output and the natural rate of unemployment.

1. Jacob Schlesinger, Eleanor Warnock, and Takashi Nakamichi, "Bank of Japan Announces Massive Stimulus Move," *Wall Street Journal*, 31 Oct. 2014.

Suppose the natural rate of unemployment is 5 percent, but policy makers mistakenly believe it's 4 percent. As they pursue their elusive goal of 4 percent, they push aggregate output beyond its potential, fueling higher prices in the long run but with no permanent reduction in unemployment. Recall that when output exceeds the economy's potential, this opens up an expansionary gap, causing a leftward shift of the short-run aggregate supply curve until the economy returns to its potential output at a higher price level.

Even if policy makers can accurately estimate the economy's potential output and the natural rate of unemployment, formulating an effective policy requires detailed knowledge of current and future economic conditions. To craft an effective strategy, policy makers must first be able to forecast what aggregate demand and aggregate supply would be without active intervention. In other words, they must be able to predict what would happen with a passive approach. Second, they must have the tools needed to achieve the desired result relatively quickly. Third, they must be able to predict the effects of an active policy on the economy's key performance measures. Fourth, fiscal and monetary policy makers must work together, or at least not work at cross-purposes. Congress and the president pursue fiscal policy while the Fed pursues monetary policy; these groups usually fail to coordinate their efforts. If an active policy requires coordination, the policy may not work as desired. In early 1995, for example, Congress was considering an expansionary tax cut while the Fed was pursuing a contractionary monetary policy. Fifth, policy makers must be able to implement the appropriate policy, even when this involves short-term political costs. For example, during inflationary times, the optimal policy may call for a tax increase, a reduction in government spending, or a tighter monetary policy—steps that are unpopular because they could increase unemployment. Finally, policy makers must be able to deal with a variety of timing lags. As we see next, these lags complicate the execution of an active policy.

## 16-1d The Problem of Lags

So far, we have ignored the time required to implement policy. That is, we have assumed that the desired policy is selected and implemented instantaneously. We have also assumed that, once implemented, the policy works as advertised—again, in no time. Actually, there may be long, sometimes unpredictable, lags at several stages in the process. These lags reduce the effectiveness and increase the uncertainty of active policies.

### Recognition Lag

First, is a **recognition lag**—the time it takes to identify a problem and determine how serious it is. For example, time is required to accumulate evidence that the economy is indeed performing below its potential. Even if initial data look troubling, many are usually revised later. For example, the government releases three estimates of quarterly GDP growth coming a month apart—an *advanced* estimate, a *preliminary* estimate, and a *final* estimate. What's more, these estimates are often revised years later. For example, in the third quarter of 2012, GDP growth estimates were revised all the way back to the first quarter of 2009. Therefore, policy makers sometimes wait for more proof before responding to what may turn out to be a false alarm. Because a recession is not identified as such until more than 6 months after it begins and because the average recession since 1945 has lasted only about 11 months, a typical recession is nearly over before officially recognized as a recession. What's more, the average lag between a recession's end and the official announcement that it has ended is about 15 months. So for a year or more after a recession ends, policy makers don't know for sure that it has ended. For example, the Great Recession ended in June 2009, but the announcement that the recession had ended did not come until September 2010.

### Decision-Making Lag

Even after enough evidence accumulates, policy makers often need time to decide what to do, so there is a **decision-making lag**. In the case of discretionary fiscal policy, Congress and the president must agree on an appropriate course of action. Fiscal policy usually takes months to develop and approve; it could take more than a year. On the other hand, the Fed can implement monetary policy more quickly and does not even have to wait for regular meetings. For example, as the economy weakened in 2008, the Fed announced interest rate cuts twice between regular FOMC meetings. So the decision-making lag is shorter for monetary policy than for fiscal policy.

### Implementation Lag

Once a decision has been made, the new policy must be introduced, which usually involves an **implementation lag**. Again, monetary policy has the advantage: After a policy has been adopted, the Fed can immediately begin buying or selling bonds to influence bank reserves and thereby change the federal funds rate. The implementation lag is longer for fiscal policy. If tax rates change, new tax forms must be printed and distributed advising employers of changes in tax withholding. If government spending changes, the appropriate government agencies must get involved.

The implementation of fiscal policy can take more than a year. For example, in February 1983, the nation's unemployment rate reached 10.3 percent. The following month, Congress approved $9 billion to create what supporters claimed would be hundreds of thousands of

Comstock/Jupiter Images

**recognition lag** The time needed to identify a macroeconomic problem and assess its seriousness

**decision-making lag** The time needed to decide what to do once a macroeconomic problem has been identified

**implementation lag** The time needed to introduce a change in monetary or fiscal policy new jobs. Fifteen months later, only $3.1 billion had been spent and only 35,000 new jobs had been created, according to a U.S. General Accounting Office study. By that time, the economy was already recovering on its own, lowering the unemployment rate from 10.3 percent to 7.1 percent and adding 6.2 million new jobs. So this public spending program was implemented only after the economy had bottomed out and began recovering. Likewise, in spring 1993, President Clinton proposed a $16 billion stimulus package to boost what appeared to be a sluggish recovery. The measure was defeated because it would have increased an already large federal deficit, yet the economy still added 5.6 million jobs over the next two years anyway. As a final example of an implementation lag, in early 2009, President Obama proposed what turned out to be a $831 billion program of tax cuts and spending increases to stimulate an economy reeling from the global financial crisis and the recession. Although Congress passed the measure relatively quickly, it took years to fully implement parts of the program. President Obama later acknowledged that many of the spending projects were not as "shovel-ready" as he had believed.

## Effectiveness Lag

Once a policy has been implemented, there is an **effectiveness lag** before the full impact of the policy registers on the economy. With monetary policy, the lag between a change in the federal funds rate and the change in aggregate demand and output can take from months to a year or more. Fiscal policy, once enacted, usually requires 3 to 6 months to take effect and between 9 and 18 months to register its full effect. Because of the effectiveness lag, the economy may turn around on its own before the policy registers its full impact. A fiscal stimulus may end up merely adding more inflationary pressure and more federal debt to a recovering economy.

## Lags Reduce Effectiveness of Active Policy

All these lags make active policy difficult to execute. The more variable the lags, the harder it is to predict when a particular policy will take hold and what the state of the economy will be at that time. To advocates of passive policy, these lags are reason enough to avoid active discretionary

**effectiveness lag** The time needed for changes in monetary or fiscal policy to affect the economy

policy. *Advocates of a passive approach argue that an active stabilization policy imposes troubling fluctuations in the price level and real GDP because it often takes hold only after market forces have already returned the economy to its potential output level.*

Talk in the media about "jump-starting" the economy reflects the active approach, which views the economy as a sputtering engine that can be fixed by an expert mechanic. The passive approach views the economy as more like a super-tanker on automatic pilot. The policy question then becomes whether to trust that automatic pilot (the self-correcting tendencies of the economy) or to try to override the mechanism with active discretionary policies.

## 16-1e A Review of Policy Perspectives

The active and passive approaches reflect different views about the stability and resiliency of the economy and the ability of Congress or the Fed to implement appropriate discretionary policies. As we have seen, advocates of an active approach think that the natural adjustments of wages and prices can be painfully slow, particularly when unemployment is high. Prolonged high unemployment means that much output must be sacrificed, and the unemployed must suffer personal hardship during the slow adjustment period. If high unemployment lasts a long time, labor skills may grow rusty, and some people may drop out of the labor force. Therefore, prolonged unemployment may cause the economy's potential GDP to fall and the natural rate of unemployment to rise.

Thus, active policy advocates see a high cost of not using discretionary policy. Despite the lags involved, they prefer action—through discretionary fiscal policy, discretionary monetary policy, or some combination of the two—to inaction. Passive policy advocates, on the other hand, believe that uncertain lags and ignorance about how the economy works undermine active policy. Rather than pursue a misguided activist policy, passivists prefer to rely more on the economy's natural ability to correct itself just using automatic stabilizers.

## 16-1f Active Policies, Passive Policies, and Presidential Politics

Consider the active and passive policies reflected in U.S. presidential politics. During the third quarter of 1990, after the longest peacetime economic expansion to that point of the 20th century, the U.S. economy slipped into a recession, triggered by Iraq's invasion of oil-rich Kuwait. Because of what at the time was considered a large federal deficit, policy makers were reluctant to pursue discretionary fiscal measures to revive the economy. That was left to the Fed. The recession lasted only eight months, but the unemployment rate continued to edge up in what was sarcastically called a "jobless recovery."

That sluggish recovery was the economic backdrop for the presidential election of 1992 between Republican President George H. W. Bush and Democratic challenger Bill Clinton. Because monetary policy did not seem to be providing enough of a kick, was more fiscal stimulus needed? With the federal budget deficit in 1992 already approaching $300 billion, a record amount to that point, would a higher deficit do more harm than good?[2]

Bush's biggest liabilities during the campaign were the slow recovery and high federal deficits; these were Clinton's biggest assets. Clinton argued that (1) Bush had not done enough to revive the economy; (2) Bush could not be trusted because he broke a 1988 campaign pledge of "no new taxes" by signing a tax increase in 1990 to help cut federal deficits; and (3) Bush and his predecessor, Ronald Reagan, were responsible for the sizable federal deficits. Clinton promised to raise tax rates on the rich and cut them for the middle class. He also promised to create jobs through government spending programs that would "invest in America."

Bush tried to remind voters that the economy was growing again, so the recession was over. But that was a hard sell with unemployment averaging 7.6 percent during the six months leading up to the election (remember that the unemployment rate is a lagging indicator of economic activity). Clinton saw a stronger role for government, and Bush saw a stronger role for the private sector. Clinton's approach was more active and Bush's more passive. In the end, high unemployment rates during the campaign made people more willing to gamble on Clinton. Apparently, during troubled times, an active policy has more voter appeal than a passive one. Ironically, the economy at the time was stronger than described by the media and by challenger Clinton ("It's the economy, stupid" was Clinton's rallying cry). When the campaign dust settled, real GDP in the election year of 1992 grew by 3.6 percent. This would turn out to exceed the average annual growth rate of 3.3 percent during Clinton's first term. As a more recent comparison, not once between 2005 and 2015 did the U.S. economy grow as much as 3.6 percent a year.

George W. Bush was not about to make the same mistake as his father. Shortly after taking office in 2001, he proposed the first of three tax cuts to stimulate an economy in recession. This fiscal policy of tax cuts coincided with an aggressive monetary policy of federal funds rate cuts. This one-two punch was the greatest stimulus of aggregate demand to that point since World War II. Although the recession was over by the end of 2001, the unemployment rate continued to rise to a peak of 6.3 percent in June 2003 (again, the unemployment rate is a trailing economic indicator). Then, as if on cue, during the final 12 months before the election of 2004, the economy added 2 million jobs. Despite an unpopular war in Iraq, the additional jobs helped Bush get reelected.

The 2008 presidential election was like no other. President Bush was presiding over two unpopular wars and an economy sinking fast because of the financial crisis. But Bush was not on the ballot. Republican John McCain faced Democrat Barack Obama. Days after the financial crisis of September 2008, the two candidates issued a joint statement supporting TARP, the federal program to invest billions in ailing financial institutions and the most significant legislative action prior to the November election. So there was no policy difference between the two candidates on that big policy measure.

But the candidates differed on other issues. For example, McCain favored extending all the Bush tax cuts, which were set to expire. Obama said he would extend the Bush tax cuts only for those making less than $250,000 a year. Obama proposed broad health insurance mandates with more government regulations. McCain favored tax incentives to increase health coverage, saying he preferred "choices" to "mandates." Obama proposed creating millions of new jobs by investing in "green energy" programs. Not McCain. A presidential poll taken a month before the election found that those whose top concern was the economy preferred Obama over McCain by 2 to 1.[3] When the economy is in trouble, voters seem to support a more active approach.

That's what they got with President Obama, whose active fiscal approach was joined by the most active monetary policy in history. Despite all that firepower, the recovery was modest through 2015. Supporters of the active approach argued that the tepid recovery was evidence of just how bad off things were to begin with. Critics of the active approach argued that the added taxes, public spending, and regulations created uncertainty about private enterprise and blunted incentives to work and to create jobs.

2. David Wessel, "Wanted: Fiscal Stimulus Without Higher Taxes," *Wall Street Journal*, 5 October 1992.

3. "Obama, McCain Lay Out Contrasts Before Undecided Voters," *CNN*, 8 October 2008.

# 16-2 THE ROLE OF EXPECTATIONS

The effectiveness of a particular government policy depends in part on what people expect. As we saw in an earlier chapter, the short-run aggregate supply curve is drawn for a given expected price level reflected in long-term wage contracts. If workers and firms expect continued inflation, their wage agreements reflect these inflationary expectations. One approach in macroeconomics, called **rational expectations**, argues that people form expectations on the basis of all available information, including information about the probable future actions of policy makers. Thus, aggregate supply depends on what sort of macroeconomic course policy makers are expected to pursue. For example, if people were to observe policy makers using discretionary policy to stimulate aggregate demand every time output falls below potential, people would come to anticipate the effects of this policy on the price level and output. Robert Lucas, of the University of Chicago, won the 1995 Nobel Prize in Economics for his studies of rational expectations. We consider the role of expectations in the context of monetary policy, but fiscal policy would have a similar effect.

## 16-2a Discretionary Policy and Inflation Expectations

Monetary authorities must testify before Congress regularly to offer an assessment of the economy. As noted in the previous chapter, the Fed also announces, after each meeting of the FOMC, any changes in its interest rate targets and the likely direction, or "bias," of future changes. The Fed head also holds a press conference after half of the meetings to be more transparent about FOMC policy. And Fed officials often deliver speeches around the country. Those interested in the economy sift through all this material to discover the likely path of monetary policy.

Let's examine the relationship between Fed policy pronouncements, Fed actions, and equilibrium output. Suppose the economy is producing potential output such that unemployment is at its natural rate. At the beginning of the year, firms and employees must negotiate wage agreements. While negotiations are under way, the Fed announces that throughout the year, monetary policy will aim at sustaining potential output while keeping the price level stable. This policy seems appropriate because unemployment is already at the natural rate. Workers and firms understand that the

**rational expectations**
A school of thought that argues people form expectations based on all available information, including the likely future actions of government policy makers

Fed's stable price policy appears optimal under the circumstances because an expansionary monetary policy would likely lead only to higher inflation in the long run. Until the year is under way and monetary policy is actually implemented, however, the public can't know for sure what the Fed will do.

As long as wage increases do not exceed the growth in labor productivity, the Fed's plan of a stable price level should work. Alternatively, workers could try to negotiate a higher wage growth, but that would ultimately lead to inflation. Suppose workers and firms believe the Fed's pronouncements and reach wage settlements based on a constant price level. If the Fed follows through as promised, the price level should turn out as expected. Output remains at the economy's potential, and unemployment remains at the natural rate. The situation is depicted in Exhibit 3. The short-run aggregate supply curve, $SRAS_{110}$, is based on wage contracts reflecting an expected price level of 110. If the Fed follows the announced course, the aggregate demand curve will be

### Exhibit 3

**Short-Run Effects of an Unexpected Expansionary Policy**

At point *a*, workers and firms expect a price level of 110; supply curve $SRAS_{110}$ reflects that expectation. But an unexpected expansionary policy shifts the aggregate demand curve out to $AD'$. Output in the short run (at point *b*) exceeds its potential. In the long run, costs increase, shifting $SRAS$ leftward until the economy produces its potential output at point *c* (the resulting supply curve is not shown). The short-run effect of an unexpected expansion is greater output, but the long-run effect is just a higher price level, or inflation.

AD and equilibrium will be at point *a*, where the price level is as expected and the economy is producing $17.0 trillion, the potential output.

Suppose, however, that after workers and firms have agreed on nominal wages—that is, after the short-run aggregate supply curve has been determined—public officials become dissatisfied with the unemployment rate. Perhaps election-year concerns about unemployment, a false alarm about a recession, or overestimating potential output convince the Fed to act. An expansionary monetary policy increases the aggregate demand curve from *AD*, the level anticipated by firms and employees, to *AD′*. This unexpected policy stimulates output and employment in the short run to equilibrium point *b*. Output increases to $17.2 trillion, and the price level increases to 115. This temporary boost in output and reduction in unemployment may last long enough to help public officials get reelected.

So the price level is now higher than workers expected, and their agreed-on wage buys less in real terms than workers bargained for. At their earliest opportunity, workers will negotiate higher wages. These higher wage agreements will eventually cause the short-run aggregate supply curve in Exhibit 3 to shift leftward, intersecting *AD′* at point *c*, the economy's potential output (to reduce clutter, the shifted short-run aggregate supply curve is not shown). So output once again returns to the economy's potential GDP, but in the process the price level rises to 122.

Thus, the unexpected expansionary policy causes a short-run pop in output and employment. But in the long run, the increase in the aggregate demand curve yields only inflation. The **time-inconsistency problem** arises when policy makers have an incentive to announce one policy to shape expectations but then to pursue a different policy once those expectations have been formed and acted on.

## 16-2b Anticipating Policy

Suppose policy makers become alarmed by the high inflation. The next time around, the Fed once again announces a monetary policy aimed at producing potential output while keeping the price level stable at 122. Based on their previous experience, however, workers and firms have learned that the Fed is willing to accept higher inflation in exchange for a temporary boost in output. Workers may be fooled once by the Fed's actions, but they won't be fooled again. Thus, they and their employers take the Fed's announcement with a grain of salt. Workers, in particular, do not want to get caught again with their real wages down should the Fed implement a stimulative monetary policy. Workers and firms expect the Fed's actions will increase the price level. The bottom line is that workers and firms negotiate a high wage increase.

*Exhibit 4*

**Short-Run Effects of a More Expansionary Policy Than Announced**

The Fed announces it plans to keep prices stable at 122. Workers and firms, however, expect monetary policy to be expansionary. The short-run aggregate supply curve, SRAS₁₃₂, reflects their expectations. If the Fed follows the announced stable-price policy, short-run output at point *d* is less than the economy's potential output of $17.0 trillion. To keep the economy at its potential, the Fed must stimulate aggregate demand as much as workers and firms expect (shown by point *e*), but this is inflationary.

In effect, workers and firms are betting the Fed will pursue an expansionary policy regardless of pronouncements to the contrary. The short-run aggregate supply curve reflecting these higher wage agreements is depicted by $SRAS_{132}$ in Exhibit 4, where 132 is the expected price level. Note that *AD′* would result if the Fed followed its announced policy; that demand curve intersects the potential output line at point *c*, where the price level is 122. But *AD″* is the aggregate demand that workers and firms expect based on an expansionary monetary policy. They have agreed to wage settlements that will produce the economy's potential output if the Fed behaves as *expected*, not as *announced*. Thus, a price level of 132 is based on rational expectations. In effect, workers and firms expect the expansionary monetary policy to shift aggregate demand from *AD′* to *AD″*.

**time-inconsistency problem** When policy makers have an incentive to announce one policy to influence expectations but then pursue a different policy once those expectations have been formed and acted on

Monetary authorities must now decide whether to stick with their announced plan of a stable price level or follow a more expansionary monetary policy. If they pursue the constant-price-level policy, aggregate demand turns out to be $AD'$ and short-run equilibrium occurs at point $d$. Short-run output falls below the economy's potential, resulting in unemployment exceeding the natural rate. If monetary authorities want to keep output at its potential, they have only one alternative—to match public expectations. Monetary authorities will likely pursue an expansionary monetary policy, an action that increases inflation and reinforces public skepticism of policy announcements. This expansionary policy results in an aggregate demand of $AD''$, leading to equilibrium at point $e$, where the price level is 132 and output equals the economy's potential.

Thus, workers and firms enter negotiations realizing that the Fed has an incentive to pursue an expansionary monetary policy. So workers and firms agree to higher wage increases, and the Fed follows with an expansionary policy, one that results in more inflation. Once workers and firms come to expect an expansionary monetary policy and the resulting inflation, such a policy does not spur even a temporary increase in output beyond the economy's potential. *Economists of the rational expectations school believe that if the economy is already producing its potential, an expansionary policy, if fully anticipated, has no effect on output or employment, not even in the short run. Only unanticipated expansionary policy can temporarily push output beyond its potential.*

## 16-2c Policy Credibility

If the economy is already producing its potential, an unexpected expansionary policy would increase output and employment temporarily. The costs, however, include not only inflation in the long term but also a loss of credibility in Fed pronouncements the next time around.

**cold turkey** The announcement and execution of tough measures to reduce high inflation

> "Economists of the rational expectations school believe that if the economy is already producing its potential, an expansionary policy, if fully anticipated, has no effect on output or employment, not even in the short run."

Is there any way out of this? For the Fed to pursue a policy consistent with a constant price level, its announcements must somehow be *credible,* or believable. Workers and firms must believe that when the time comes to make a hard decision, the Fed will follow through as promised. Perhaps the Fed could offer some sort of guarantee to convince people it will stay the course—for example, the Fed chairman could promise to resign if the Fed does not follow the announced policy. Ironically, policy makers are often more credible and therefore more effective if they have some of their discretion taken away. In this case, a hard-and-fast rule could be substituted for a policy maker's discretion. We examine policy rules in the next section.

Consider the problems facing central banks in countries that have experienced hyperinflation. For an anti-inflation policy to succeed at the least possible cost in forgone output, the public must believe central bankers. How can central bankers in an economy ripped by hyperinflation establish credibility? Some economists believe that the most efficient anti-inflation policy is **cold turkey**: announcing and executing tough measures to stop inflation, such as halting the growth in the money supply. For example, in 1985, the annual rate of inflation in Bolivia was running at 20,000 percent when the new government announced a stern policy. The restrictive measures worked, and inflation was stopped within a month, with little loss in output. Around the world, credible anti-inflation policies have been successful.[4] However, drastic measures sometimes involve costs. For example, some economists argue that the Fed's dramatic efforts to curb high U.S. inflation in the early 1980s triggered what was then the worst recession since the Great Depression. Some say that the Fed's pronouncements were simply not credible and therefore resulted in a recession.

Much depends on the Fed's time horizon. If policy makers take the long view, they will not risk their long-term policy effectiveness for a temporary reduction in unemployment. If Fed officials realize that their

4. For a discussion about how four hyperinflations in the 1920s ended, see Thomas Sargent, "The Ends of Four Big Inflations" in *Inflation: Causes and Consequences*, edited by Robert Hall (University of Chicago Press, 1982): 41–98.

credibility is hard to develop but easy to undermine, they will be reluctant to pursue policies that ultimately just increase inflation. As Fed Chairman Bernanke noted during his press briefing after an FMOC meeting,

> I guess the question is, does it make sense to actively seek a higher inflation rate in order to achieve a slightly [faster] reduction in the unemployment rate? The view of the Committee is that that would be very reckless. We have—we, the Federal Reserve, have spent 30 years building up credibility for low and stable inflation, which has proved extremely valuable in that we've been be able to take strong accommodative actions in the last four or five years to support the economy without leading to an unanchoring of inflation expectations or a destabilization of inflation. To risk that asset for what I think would be quite tentative and perhaps doubtful gains on the real side would be, I think, an unwise thing to do.[5]

Often Congress tries to pressure the Fed to stimulate the economy. By law, the Fed must "promote effectively the goals of maximum employment, stable prices, and moderate long-term interest rates." The law lets the Fed decide how best to do this. The Fed does not rely on congressional appropriations, so Congress can't threaten to withhold funds. Thus, although the U.S. president appoints the Board of Governors, and the Senate must approve these appointments, the Fed operates somewhat independently.

## 16-3  POLICY RULES VERSUS DISCRETION

Again, the active approach views the economy as unstable and in need of discretionary policy to cut cyclical unemployment when it arises. The passive approach views the economy as stable enough that discretionary policy is not only unnecessary but may actually worsen economic fluctuations. In place of discretionary policy, the passive approach often calls for predetermined rules to guide policy makers. In the context of fiscal policy, these rules take the form of

5. "Transcript of Chairman Bernanke's Press Conference," 25 April 2012, p. 8 at http://www.federalreserve.gov/monetarypolicy/fomccalendars.htm.

automatic stabilizers, such as unemployment insurance, a progressive income tax, and transfer payments, all of which aim to dampen economic fluctuations. In the context of monetary policy, passive rules might be the decision to allow the money supply to grow at a predetermined rate, to maintain interest rates at some predetermined level, or to keep inflation below a certain rate. For example, as noted in the previous case study, the European Central Bank announced a rule that it would not lower its target interest rate if inflation exceeded 2.0 percent a year. Most central banks have committed to achieving low **inflation targets**, usually specifying a particular rate for the next year or two. Advocates of inflation targets say such targets encourage workers, firms, and investors to plan on a low and stable inflation rate. Opponents of inflation targets worry that the Fed would pay less attention to jobs and economic growth. In this section, we examine the arguments for policy rules versus discretion mostly in the context of monetary policy, the policy focus in recent decades.

### 16-3a Limitations on Discretion

The rationale for the passive approach rather than the use of active discretion arises from different views of how the economy works. One view holds that *the economy is so complex and economic aggregates interact in such obscure ways and with such varied lags that policy makers cannot possibly comprehend all that is going on well enough to pursue an active monetary or fiscal policy.* For example, if the Fed adopts a discretionary policy that is based on a misreading of the current economy or a faulty understanding of the lag structure, the Fed may be lowering the federal funds rate when a more appropriate course would be to leave the rate unchanged or even to raise it. As a case in point, during a meeting of the FOMC, one member lamented the difficulty of figuring out what was going on with the economy, noting, "As a lesson for the future, I'd like to remind us all that as recently as two meetings ago we couldn't see the strength that was unfolding in the second half [of the year].... It wasn't in our forecast; it wasn't in the other

© Constantine Pankin/Shutterstock.com

**inflation target**
Commitment of central bankers to keep inflation at or below a certain rate for the next year or two

forecasts; and it wasn't in the anecdotal reports. We were standing right on top of it and we couldn't see it. That's just an important lesson to remember going forward."[6]

A comparison of economic forecasters and weather forecasters may shed light on the position of those who advocate the passive approach. Suppose you are in charge of the heating and cooling system at a major shopping mall. You realize that weather forecasts are unreliable, particularly in the early spring, when days can be warm or cold. Each day you must guess what the temperature will be and, based on that guess, decide whether to fire up the heater, turn on the air conditioner, or leave them both off. Because the mall is huge, you must start the system long before you know for sure what the weather will be. Once the system is turned on, it can't be turned off until much later in the day.

Suppose you guess the day will be cold, so you turn on the heat. If the day turns out to be cold, your policy is correct and the mall temperature will be just right. But if the day turns out to be warm, the heating system will make the mall unbearable. You would have been better off with nothing. In contrast, if you turn on the air conditioning system expecting a warm day but the day turns out to be cold, the mall will be freezing. The lesson is that if you are unable to predict the weather, you should use neither system. Similarly, if policy makers cannot predict the course of the economy, they should not try to fine-tune monetary or fiscal policy. Complicating the prediction problem is the fact that policy officials are not sure about the lags involved with discretionary policy. The situation is comparable to your not knowing how long the system actually takes to come on once you flip the switch.

This analogy applies only if the cost of doing nothing—using neither heat nor air conditioning—is relatively low. In the early spring, you can assume that there is little risk of weather so cold that water pipes freeze or so hot that walls sweat. A similar assumption in the passive view is that the economy is fairly stable and periods of prolonged unemployment are unlikely. In such an economy, the costs of *not* intervening are relatively low. In contrast, advocates of active policy believe that wide and prolonged swings in the economy (analogous to wide and prolonged swings in the outside temperature) make doing nothing risky.

## 16-3b Rules and Rational Expectations

Another group of economists also advocates the passive approach, but not because they believe the economy is too complex. Proponents of the rational expectations approach, discussed earlier, claim that people have a pretty good idea of how the economy works and what to expect from government policy makers. For example, people know enough about monetary policies pursued in the past to forecast, with reasonable accuracy, future policies and their effects on the economy. Some individual forecasts are too high and some too low, but on average, forecasts turn out to be about right. *To the extent that monetary policy is fully anticipated by workers and firms, it has no effect on the level of output; it affects only the price level.* Thus, only unexpected changes in policy can bring about short-run changes in output.

> **"To the extent that monetary policy is fully anticipated by workers and firms, it has no effect on the level of output; it affects only the price level."**

In the long run, changes in the money supply affect only inflation, not potential output, so followers of the rational expectations theory believe that the Fed should avoid discretionary monetary policy. Instead, the Fed should follow a predictable monetary rule. A monetary rule would reduce policy surprises and keep output near the natural rate. *Whereas some economists favor rules over discretion because of ignorance about the lag structure of the economy, rational expectations theorists advocate a predictable rule to avoid surprises, because surprises result in unnecessary departures from potential output.* For example, broad legislation to stimulate the economy, bail out the banks and automakers, and regulate financial institutions extensively were said to create uncertainty in the economy about what might be next. And this uncertainty discouraged some firms from hiring and kept some consumers from spending. Stanford economist John Taylor has argued that "we have plenty of evidence that rules-based monetary policies work and unpredictable discretionary policies don't."[7]

Despite support by some economists for explicit rules rather than discretion, central bankers have been reluctant to follow hard-and-fast rules about the course

6. FOMC board member Thomas Melzer, in a transcript of the 22 December 1992 meeting of the Federal Open Market Committee, p. 14. Meeting transcripts are published after a five-year lag and are available at http://www.federalreserve.gov/monetarypolicy/fomc_historical.htm.

7. John Taylor, "The Dangers of an Interventionist Fed," *Wall Street Journal*, 28 March 2012.

of future policy. Discretion has been used more than explicit rules since the early 1980s, though policy has become more predictable because the Fed now announces the probable trend of future target rate changes. As Fed Chairman Paul Volcker argued more than three decades ago:

> The appeal of a simple rule is obvious. It would simplify our job at the Federal Reserve, make monetary policy easy to understand, and facilitate monitoring of our performance. And if the rule worked, it would reduce uncertainty....But unfortunately, I know of no rule that can be relied on with sufficient consistency in our complex and constantly evolving economy.[8]

Volcker's successor, Alan Greenspan, expressed similar sentiment:

> The Federal Reserve, should, some conclude, attempt to be more formal in its operations by tying its actions solely to the prescriptions of a formal policy rule. That any approach along these lines would lead to an improvement in economic performance, however, is highly doubtful.[9]

Ben Bernanke, who succeeded Greenspan in 2006, viewed the matter mostly as a nonissue:

> [T]he argument that monetary policy should adhere mechanically to a strict rule, made by some economists in the past, has fallen out of favor in recent years. Today most monetary economists use the term "rule" more loosely to describe a general policy strategy, one that may include substantial scope for policymaker discretion and judgment.[10]

Nor did Janet Yellen, who succeeded Bernanke in 2014, want to have her hands tied by any rule:

> It would be a grave mistake for the Fed to commit to conduct monetary policy according to a mathematical rule....It is utterly necessary for us to provide more monetary-policy accommodation than those simple rules would have suggested.[11]

Former Fed Chairman Ben Bernanke felt that monetary policy should allow for discretion by the policy maker and not adhere to strict rules.

© Albert H. Teich/Shutterstock.com

The Fed has been around for more than a century, and during that time there has been an ongoing tension between rules and discretion. For example, the Fed had to learn how to slow the high inflation of the 1970s and early 1980s. The Fed experimented briefly with targeting the money supply, then targeting interest rates. More recently the Fed began targeting the inflation rate and has tried to influence long-term interest rates by purchasing mortgage backed securities. Thus, from time to time, Fed officials have used discretion to change the rules as circumstances changed, but once a new rule was adopted, such as inflation-rate targeting, that rule is followed until circumstances warrant a new rule.[12]

So far, we have looked at active stabilization policy, which focuses on shifts of the aggregate demand curve, and passive stabilization policy, which relies more on automatic stabilizers and natural shifts of the short-run aggregate supply curve. In the final section, we focus on an additional model, the Phillips curve, to shed more light on the relationship between aggregate demand and aggregate supply in the short and long runs.

## 16-4  THE PHILLIPS CURVE

At one time, policy makers thought they faced a long-run trade-off between inflation and unemployment. This view was suggested by the research of New Zealand economist A. W. Phillips, who in 1958 published an article that examined the historical relation between inflation and unemployment in the United Kingdom.[13] Based on about 100 years of evidence, his data traced an inverse relationship between the unemployment rate and the rate of change in nominal wages (serving as a measure of inflation). This relationship implied that the opportunity cost of reducing unemployment was higher inflation, and the opportunity cost of reducing inflation was higher unemployment.

8. Paul Volcker, before the Committee on Banking, Finance, and Urban Affairs, U.S. House of Representatives, August 1983.

9. Alan Greenspan, "Monetary Policy Under Uncertainty," Remarks at a symposium sponsored by the Federal Reserve Bank of Kansas City, Jackson Hole, Wyoming, 29 August 2003, which can be found at http://www.federalreserve.gov/boarddocs/speeches/2003/20030829/default.htm.

10. Ben Bernanke, "The Logic of Monetary Policy," Remarks Before the National Economists Club, Washington, D.C., 2 December 2004, which can be found at http://www.federalreserve.gov/boarddocs/Speeches/2004/20041202/default.htm.

11. As quoted in Pedro Nicolaci da Costa and Ben Leubsdorf, "Yellen Balks at Proposal to Tie Rate to Formula," *Wall Street Journal*, 16 July 2014.

12. Benjamin M. Friedman, "Rules Versus Discretion at the Federal Reserve: On to the Second Century," *Journal of Macroeconomics*, 34 (September 2012): 608–615.

13. A. W. Phillips, "Relation between Unemployment and the Rate of Change in Money Wage Rates in the United Kingdom, 1861–1957," *Economica*, 25 (November 1958): 283–299.

## 16-4a The Phillips Framework

The possible options with respect to unemployment and inflation are illustrated by the hypothetical **Phillips curve** in Exhibit 5. The unemployment rate is measured along the horizontal axis and the inflation rate along the vertical axis. Let's begin at point *a*, which depicts one possible combination of unemployment and inflation. Fiscal or monetary policy could be used to stimulate output and thereby reduce unemployment, moving the economy from point *a* to point *b*. Notice, however, that the reduction in unemployment comes at the cost of higher inflation. A reduction in unemployment with no change in inflation would be represented by point *c*. But as you can see, this alternative is not available.

Most policy makers of the 1960s came to believe that they faced a stable, long-run trade-off between unemployment and inflation. The Phillips curve was based on an era when inflation was low and the primary disturbances in the economy were shocks to aggregate demand. The effect of changes in aggregate demand can be traced as movements along a given short-run aggregate supply curve. If aggregate demand increases, the price level rises but unemployment falls. If aggregate demand decreases, the price level falls but unemployment rises. With appropriate demand-management tools, policy makers believed they could choose any point along the Phillips curve. The 1970s proved this view wrong in two ways. First, some of the biggest disturbances were adverse *supply* shocks, such as those created by OPEC oil embargoes and worldwide crop failures. These shocks shifted the aggregate supply curve leftward. A reduction of the aggregate supply curve led to both higher inflation *and* higher unemployment. Stagflation was at odds with the Phillips curve. Second, economists learned that when short-run output exceeds potential, an expansionary gap opens. As this gap closes by a leftward shift of the short-run aggregate supply curve, greater inflation *and* higher unemployment result—again, an outcome inconsistent with a Phillips curve.

The increases in both inflation and unemployment caused by a decrease in aggregate supply can be represented by an outcome such as point *d* in Exhibit 5. By the end of the 1970s, increases in both inflation and unemployment suggested either that the Phillips curve had shifted

**Phillips curve** A curve showing possible combinations of the inflation rate and the unemployment rate

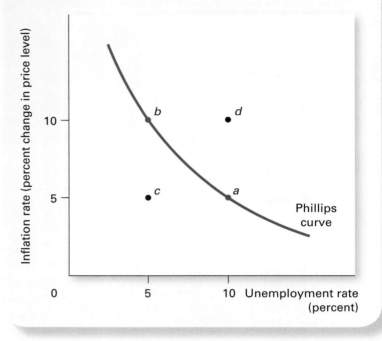

*Exhibit 5*

### Hypothetical Phillips Curve

The Phillips curve shows an inverse relation between unemployment and inflation. Points *a* and *b* lie on the Phillips curve and represent alternative combinations of inflation and unemployment that are attainable as long as the curve itself does not shift. Points *c* and *d* are off the curve.

outward or that it no longer described economic reality. The dilemma called for a reexamination of the Phillips curve, and this led to a distinction between the short-run Phillips curve and the long-run Phillips curve.

## 16-4b The Short-Run Phillips Curve

To discuss the underpinnings of the Phillips curve, we must return to the short-run aggregate supply curve. Suppose the price level this year is reflected by a price index of, say, 100, and that people expect prices to be about 3 percent higher next year. So the price level expected next year is 103. Workers and firms therefore negotiate wage contracts based on that expectation. As the short-run aggregate supply curve in Exhibit 6(a) indicates, if *AD* is the aggregate demand curve and the price level is 103, as expected, output equals the economy's potential, shown here to be $17.0 trillion. Recall that when the economy produces its potential, unemployment is at the natural rate.

The short-run relationship between inflation and unemployment is presented in Exhibit 6(b) under the assumption that people expect inflation to be 3 percent.

## Exhibit 6

### Aggregate Supply Curves and Phillips Curves in the Short Run and the Long Run

If people expect a price level of 103, which is 3 percent higher than the current level, and if *AD* turns out to be the aggregate demand curve, then the actual price level is 103 and output is at its potential. Point *a* in both panels represents this situation. Unemployment is the natural rate, assumed to be 5 percent in panel (b). If aggregate demand turns out to be greater than expected (*AD'* instead of *AD*), the economy in the short run is at point *b* in panel (a), where the price level of 105 exceeds expectations and output exceeds its potential. The resulting higher inflation and lower unemployment are shown as point *b* in panel (b). If aggregate demand turns out to be less than expected (*AD"* instead of *AD*), short-run equilibrium is at point *c* in panel (a), where the price level of 101 is lower than expected and output falls short of potential. Lower inflation and higher unemployment are shown as point *c* in panel (b). In panel (b), points *a*, *b*, and *c* trace a short-run Phillips curve. In the long run, the actual price level equals the expected price level. Output is at the potential level, $17.0 trillion, in panel (a). Unemployment is at the natural rate, 5 percent, in panel (b). Points *a*, *d*, and *e* depict long-run points in each panel. In panel (a) these points trace potential output, or long-run aggregate supply (*LRAS*). In panel (b), these points trace a long-run Phillips curve.

**(a)** *Short-run aggregate supply curve*

**(b)** *Short-run and long-run Phillips curves*

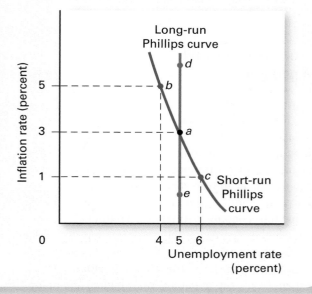

Unemployment is measured along the horizontal axis and inflation along the vertical axis. Panel (a) shows that when inflation is 3 percent, the economy produces its potential. Unemployment is at the natural rate, assumed in panel (b) to be 5 percent. The combination of 3 percent inflation and 5 percent unemployment is reflected by point *a* in panel (b), which corresponds to point *a* in panel (a).

What if aggregate demand turns out to be greater than expected, as indicated by *AD'*? In the short run, the greater demand results in point *b*, with a price level of 105 and output of $17.1 trillion. Because the price level exceeds that reflected in wage contracts, inflation also exceeds expectations. Specifically, inflation turns out to be 5 percent, not 3 percent. Because output exceeds potential, unemployment falls below the natural rate to 4 percent. The new combination of unemployment and inflation is depicted by point *b* in panel (b), which corresponds to point *b* in panel (a).

What if aggregate demand turns out to be lower than expected, as indicated by *AD"*? In the short run, the lower demand results in point *c*, where the price level of 101 is less than expected and output of $16.9 trillion is below potential. Inflation of 1 percent is less than the expected 3 percent, and unemployment of 6 percent exceeds the natural rate. This combination is reflected by point *c* in panel (b), which corresponds to point *c* in panel (a).

Note that the short-run aggregate supply curve in panel (a) can be used to develop the inverse relationship between inflation and unemployment shown in panel (b), called a **short-run Phillips curve**. This curve is created by the intersection of alternative aggregate demand curves along a given short-run aggregate supply curve. *The*

**short-run Phillips curve** Based on an expected inflation rate, a curve that reflects an inverse relationship between the inflation rate and the unemployment rate short-run Phillips curve is based on labor contracts that reflect a given expected price level, which implies a given expected rate of inflation. The short-run Phillips curve in panel (b) is based on an expected inflation of 3 percent. If inflation turns out as expected, unemployment equals the natural rate. If inflation exceeds expectations, unemployment in the short run falls below the natural rate. If inflation is less than expected, unemployment in the short run exceeds the natural rate.

## 16-4c The Long-Run Phillips Curve

If inflation exceeds expectations, output exceeds the economy's potential in the short run but not in the long run. Labor shortages and shrinking real wages prompt higher wage agreements. The short-run aggregate supply curve shifts leftward until it passes through point *d* in panel (a) of Exhibit 6, returning the economy to its potential output. The unexpectedly higher aggregate demand curve has no lasting effect on output or un-employment. Point *d* corresponds to a higher price level, and thus higher inflation. Closing the expansionary gap generates both higher unemployment and higher in-flation, a combination depicted by point *d* in panel (b). Note that whereas points *a*, *b*, and *c* are on the same short-run Phillips curve, point *d* is not.

To trace the long-run effects of a lower-than-expected price level, let's return to point *c* in panel (a), where the actual price level is below the expected level, so output is below its potential. If workers and firms negotiate lower money wages (or if the growth in nominal wages trails inflation), the short-run aggregate supply curve could shift rightward until it passes through point *e*, where the economy returns once again to its potential output. Both inflation and unemployment fall, as reflected by point *e* in panel (b).

**long-run Phillips curve**
A vertical line drawn at the economy's natural rate of unemployment that traces equilibrium points that can occur when workers and employers have the time to adjust fully to any unexpected change in aggregate demand

**natural rate hypothesis**
The natural rate of unemployment is largely independent of the stimulus provided by monetary or fiscal policy

> "When workers and employers adjust fully to any unexpected change in aggregate demand, the long-run Phillips curve is a vertical line drawn at the economy's natural rate of unemployment."

Note that points *a*, *d*, and *e* in panel (a) depict long-run equilibrium points; the expected price level equals the actual price level. At those same points in panel (b), expected inflation equals actual inflation, so unemployment equals the natural rate. We can connect points *a*, *d*, and *e* in the right panel to form the **long-run Phillips curve**. *When workers and employers adjust fully to any unexpected change in aggregate demand, the long-run Phillips curve is a vertical line drawn at the economy's natural rate of unemployment.* As long as prices and wages are flexible enough, the rate of unemployment, in the long run, is independent of the rate of inflation. *Thus, according to proponents of this type of analysis, policy makers cannot, in the long run, choose between unemployment and inflation. They can choose only among alternative rates of inflation.*

## 16-4d The Natural Rate Hypothesis

The natural rate of unemployment occurs at the economy's potential output, discussed extensively already. An important idea that emerged from this reexamination of the Phillips curve is the **natural rate hypothesis**, which states that in the long run, the economy tends toward the natural rate of unemployment. This natural rate is largely independent of any *aggregate demand* stimulus provided by monetary or fiscal policy. Policy makers may be able to push output beyond its potential temporarily, but only if the policy surprises the public. The natural rate hypothesis implies that *the policy that results in low inflation is generally the optimal policy in the long run.* As noted earlier, the Fed believed that the natural rate of unemployment in 2015 was in the range of 5.0 percent to 5.2 percent. As noted already, each quarter those who participate in FOMC meetings estimate the natural rate, or sustainable rate, of unemployment.

## 16-4e Evidence of the Phillips Curve

What has been the actual relationship between unemployment and inflation in the United States? In Exhibit 7, each year since 1960 is represented by

## Exhibit 7

### Six Short-Run Phillips Curves Since 1960

Each curve represents the U.S. unemployment-inflation combination for a given period, with colored points showing the years associated with each colored curve. Shifts of the short-run Phillips curve reflect changes in inflation expectations. Curves closer to the origin reflect lower expected inflation.

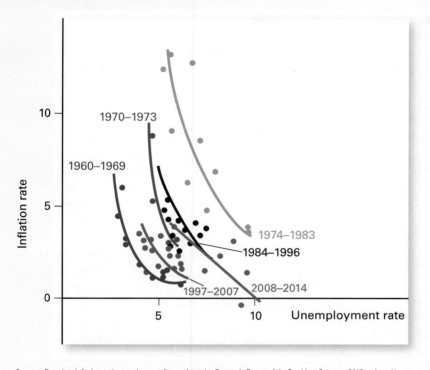

Sources: Based on inflation and unemployment figures from the *Economic Report of the President,* February 2015, at http://www.whitehouse.gov/administration/eop/cea/economic-report-of-the-President and the U.S. Bureau of Labor Statistics at http://www.bls.gov/.

a point, with the unemployment rate measured along the horizontal axis and the inflation rate measured along the vertical axis. Superimposed on these points are short-run Phillips curves showing patterns of unemployment and inflation during what appears to be six distinct periods since 1960. Remember, each short-run Phillips curve is drawn for a given *expected inflation rate*. An increase in inflationary expectations shifts the short-run Phillips curve up and to the right, away from the origin.

The clearest trade-off between unemployment and inflation occurred between 1960 and 1969; the blue points for those years fit neatly along the blue curve. In the early part of the decade, inflation was low but unemployment relatively high; as the 1960s progressed, unemployment declined but inflation increased. Inflation during the decade averaged only 2.5 percent, and unemployment averaged 4.8 percent.

The short-run Phillips curve shifted away from the origin for the period from 1970 to 1973 (in maroon), when inflation and unemployment each climbed to an average of 5.2 percent. In 1974, sharp increases by OPEC in oil prices and crop failures around the world reduced aggregate supply, which sparked another outward shift of the Phillips curve. During the 1974–1983 period (in orange), inflation averaged 8.2 percent and unemployment 7.5 percent. After the Fed reduced inflationary expectations in the early 1980s, the short-run Phillips curve shifted inward. Average inflation for 1984–1996 (in black) fell to 3.7 percent and average unemployment fell to 6.1 percent. Data for 1997 to 2007 (in green) indicate a lower short-run Phillips curve, with average inflation of 2.5 percent and average unemployment of 5.0 percent. Finally, data for 2008 to 2014 (in red) suggest that the short-run Phillips curve may have shifted out, with inflation averaging 1.8 percent and unemployment averaging 7.9 percent. Thus, the Phillips curve shifted rightward between the 1960s and the early 1980s. Then the curve shifted back in stages between 1984 and 2007. But since 2008, the curve has shifted out again because of higher unemployment in the wake of the Great Recession. Also during the early years of most recent period, higher energy prices boosted expectations for higher inflation.[14]

## 16-5 FINAL WORD

This chapter examined the implications of active and passive policy. The important question is whether the economy is stable and self-correcting when it gets off track, or whether it is, instead, unstable and in need

14. Olivier Coiban and Yurly Gorodnichenko, "Is The Phillips Curve Alive and Well After All? Inflation Expectations and the Missing Disinflation," *American Economic Journal: Macroeconomics* (forthcoming). For more evidence on the Phillips curve, see Robert J. Gordon, "The Phillips Curve is Alive and Well: Inflation and the NAIRU During the Slow Recovery," NBER Working Paper No. 19390 (August 2013).

of active government intervention. Advocates of active policy believe that the Fed or Congress or both should reduce economic fluctuations by stimulating aggregate demand when output falls below its potential level and by dampening aggregate demand when output exceeds its potential level. Advocates of active policy argue that government attempts to reduce the ups and downs of the business cycle may not be perfect but are still better than nothing. Some activists also believe that a long stretch of high unemployment may be self-reinforcing, because some unemployed workers lose valuable job skills and grow to accept unemployment as a way of life, as may have happened in Europe.

Advocates of passive policy, on the other hand, believe that discretionary policy may worsen cyclical swings in the economy, leading to higher inflation in the long run with no permanent increase in potential output and no permanent reduction in the unemployment rate. Worse still, repeated efforts to stimulate the economy through fiscal policy have resulted in a huge federal debt, creating uncertainty and instability. Because of all this, this group of economists favors passive rules for monetary policy and automatic stabilizers for fiscal policy.

The active-passive debate in this chapter has focused primarily on monetary policy because discretionary fiscal policy has been hampered by large federal deficits that ballooned the national debt. But the Great Recession of 2007–2009 was so severe that most fiscal policy makers decided to worry later about deficits and debt.

# STUDY TOOLS 16

## READY TO STUDY? IN THE BOOK, YOU CAN:

☐ Work the Problems at the end of the chapter.

☐ Rip out the chapter review card for a handy summary of the chapter and key terms.

## ONLINE AT CENGAGEBRAIN.COM YOU CAN:

☐ Collect StudyBits while you read and study the chapter.

☐ Quiz yourself on key concepts.

☐ Prepare for tests with chapter flash cards as well as flash cards that you create.

☐ Watch videos to explore economics further.

# CHAPTER 16 PROBLEMS

*Your instructor can access the answers to these problems online at http://cengagebrain.com.*

## 16-1 Outline the difference between active policy and passive policy and explain how the two approaches differ in their assumptions about how well the economy works on its own

1. *(Active Versus Passive Policy)* Discuss the role each of the following plays in the debate between the active and passive approaches:
   a. The speed of adjustment of the nominal wage
   b. The speed of adjustment of expectations about inflation
   c. The existence of lags in policy creation and implementation
   d. Variability in the natural rate of unemployment over time

2. *(Problems with Active Policy)* Use an *AD–AS* diagram to illustrate and explain the short-run and long-run effects on the economy of the following situation: Both the natural rate of unemployment and the actual rate of unemployment are 5 percent. However, the government believes that the natural rate of unemployment is 6 percent and that the economy is overheating. Therefore, it introduces a policy to reduce aggregate demand.

## 16-2 Describe how expectations can influence the effectiveness of discretionary policy

3. *(Rational Expectations)* Using an *AD–AS* diagram, illustrate the short-run effects on prices, output, and employment of an increase in the money supply that is correctly anticipated by the public. Assume that the economy is initially at potential output.

## 16-3 Summarize why some economists prefer that policy be shaped by predictable rules rather than by the discretion of policy makers

4. *(Policy Lags)* What lag in discretionary policy is described in each of the following statements? Why do long lags make discretionary policy less effective?
   a. The time from when the government determines that the economy is in recession until a tax cut is approved to reduce unemployment

   b. The time from when the money supply is increased until the resulting effect on the economy is felt
   c. The time from the start of a recession until the government identifies the existence and severity of the recession
   d. The time from when the Fed decides to reduce the money supply until the money supply actually declines

## 16-4 Explain the shape of the short-run Phillips curve and the long-run Phillips curve

5. *(Long-Run Phillips Curve)* Suppose the economy is at point *d* on the long-run Phillips curve shown in the accompanying exhibit. If that inflation rate is unacceptably high, how can policy makers get the inflation rate down? Would rational expectations help or hinder their efforts?

**Phillips Curves in the Short Run and Long Run**

# 17 | International Trade

Rafael Ramirez/istockphoto

## LEARNING OUTCOMES

After studying this chapter, you will be able to...

**17-1** Outline the gains from trade, and explain why countries might still decide to trade even if no country had a comparative advantage

**17-2** Explain how trade restrictions harm an economy, and why they persist

**17-3** Identify international efforts to reduce trade barriers

**17-4** Summarize five arguments often used to justify trade restrictions, and describe some unintended consequences of protecting certain industries from international competition

### After finishing this chapter go to PAGE 322 for STUDY TOOLS

**Topics discussed in Chapter 17 include:**

- Gains from trade
- Absolute and comparative advantage revisited
- Tariffs and quotas
- Cost of trade restrictions
- Free trade agreements
- World Trade Organization, or WTO
- Common markets
- Arguments for trade restrictions

- If the United States is such a rich and productive country, why do we import so many goods and services?
- Why don't we produce everything ourselves?
- How can the U.S. economy grow if we import more goods and services?

- And why do some U.S. producers try to block imports?

*Answers to these and other questions are addressed in this chapter.*

The world is a giant shopping mall, and Americans are big spenders. For example, the U.S. population is less than 5 percent of the world's population, but Americans buy 38 percent of the diamond jewelry sold around the world. Americans also buy Japanese cars, French wine, European vacations, Chinese products galore, and millions of other goods and services from around the globe. Foreigners buy U.S. products too—grain, aircraft, movies, software, trips to New York City, and millions of other goods and services. For example, California grows 80 percent of the world's almond supply.

**"Why don't we produce everything ourselves?"**

In this chapter, we examine the gains from international trade and the effects of trade restrictions on the allocation of resources. The analysis is based on the familiar tools of demand and supply.

## 17-1 THE GAINS FROM TRADE

A Virginia family that sits down to a dinner of Kansas prime rib, Idaho potatoes, and California string beans, with Georgia peach cobbler for dessert, is benefiting from interstate trade. You already understand why the residents of one state trade with those of another. Back in Chapter 2, you learned about the gains arising from specialization and trade. You may recall how you and your roommate could maximize output when you each specialized. The law of comparative advantage says that the individual with the lowest opportunity cost of producing a particular good should specialize in that good. Just as individuals benefit from specialization and trade, so do states and, indeed, nations. To reap the gains that arise from specialization, countries engage in international trade. *Each*

**"Each country specializes in making goods with the lowest opportunity cost."**

*country specializes in making goods with the lowest opportunity cost.*

### 17-1a A Profile of Exports and Imports

Just as some states are more involved in interstate trade than others, some nations are more involved in international trade than others. For example, exports account for about one-quarter of the gross domestic product (GDP) in Canada and the United Kingdom; about one-third of GDP in Germany, Sweden, and Switzerland; and about half of GDP in the Netherlands. Despite the perception that Japan has a huge export sector, exports make up only about one-sixth of its GDP.

#### U.S. Exports

*U.S. exports of goods and services amounted to $2.3 trillion in 2014, or 13 percent of GDP.* The left panel of Exhibit 1 shows the composition by major category in 2014.

## Exhibit 1
### Composition of U.S. Exports and Imports in 2014

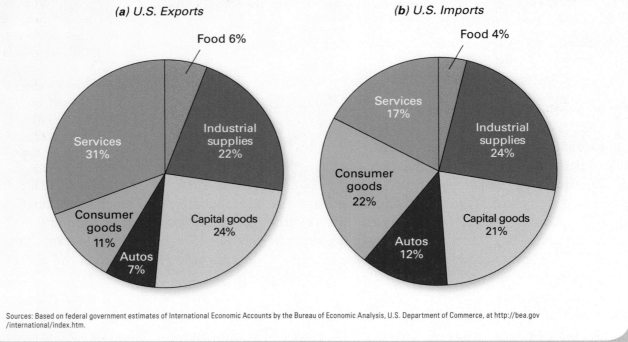

(a) U.S. Exports

Food 6%

Services 31%

Industrial supplies 22%

Consumer goods 11%

Capital goods 24%

Autos 7%

(b) U.S. Imports

Food 4%

Services 17%

Industrial supplies 24%

Consumer goods 22%

Capital goods 21%

Autos 12%

Sources: Based on federal government estimates of International Economic Accounts by the Bureau of Economic Analysis, U.S. Department of Commerce, at http://bea.gov/international/index.htm.

The largest category is services, which accounted for 31 percent of U.S. exports. U.S. service exports include transportation, insurance, banking, education, consulting, and tourism. Capital goods ranked second at 24 percent of the total, with aircraft the largest export industry (Boeing is the top U.S. exporter). The third most important are industrial supplies, at 22 percent of exports, with chemicals and plastics at the top of this list. Capital goods and industrial supplies, which help foreign producers make stuff, together accounted for nearly half of U.S. exports. Consumer goods (except food and autos, which appear separately) accounted for only 11 percent of exports (pharmaceuticals tops this group). Consumer goods also include entertainment products, such as movies and recorded music.

## U.S. Imports

*U.S. imports of goods and services totaled $2.8 trillion in 2014, or 16 percent relative to GDP.* The right panel of Exhibit 1 shows the composition of U.S. imports. The biggest category, at 24 percent, is industrial supplies, with petroleum products accounting for most of that. Although consumer goods accounted for only 11 percent of U.S. exports, they were 22 percent of U.S. imports, with pharmaceuticals the largest item. Ranked third is

capital goods, at 21 percent, with computers the largest item. Note that services, which accounted for 31 percent of U.S. exports, were only 17 percent of U.S. imports.

## Trading Partners

World trade totaled about $21 trillion in 2014, or 20 percent relative to world output of $105 trillion that year. To give you some feel for America's trading partners, here were the top 10 destinations for U.S. exports of goods and services for 2014 in order of importance: Canada, Mexico, China, the United Kingdom, Japan, Germany, Brazil, South Korea, France, and India. The top 10 sources of U.S. imports in order of importance were China, Canada, Mexico, Japan, Germany, the United Kingdom, South Korea, France, India, and Saudi Arabia.

## 17-1b Production Possibilities without Trade

The rationale behind most international trade is obvious. For example, the United States produces little coffee because, except for Hawaii, our climate is not suited to growing coffee beans. More revealing, however, are the gains from trade where the comparative advantage is not so obvious. Suppose

## Exhibit 2

### Production Possibilities Schedules for the United States and Izodia

| (a) The United States | | | | | | |
|---|---|---|---|---|---|---|
| Production Possibilities with 100 Million Workers (millions of units per day) | | | | | | |
| | $U_1$ | $U_2$ | $U_3$ | $U_4$ | $U_5$ | $U_6$ |
| Food | 600 | 480 | 360 | 240 | 120 | 0 |
| Clothing | 0 | 60 | 120 | 180 | 240 | 300 |

| (b) Izodia | | | | | | |
|---|---|---|---|---|---|---|
| Production Possibilities with 200 Million Workers (millions of units per day) | | | | | | |
| | $I_1$ | $I_2$ | $I_3$ | $I_4$ | $I_5$ | $I_6$ |
| Food | 200 | 160 | 120 | 80 | 40 | 0 |
| Clothing | 0 | 80 | 160 | 240 | 320 | 400 |

that just two goods—food and clothing—are produced and consumed and that there are only two countries in the world—the United States, with a labor force of 100 million workers, and the mythical country of Izodia, with 200 million workers. The conclusions derived from this simple model have general relevance for international trade.

Exhibit 2 presents production possibilities tables for each country, based on the size of the labor force and the productivity of workers in each country. The exhibit assumes that each country has a given technology and that labor is efficiently employed. If no trade occurs between countries, Exhibit 2 also represents each country's *consumption possibilities* table. The production numbers imply that each worker in the United States can produce either 6 units of food or 3 units of clothing per day. If all 100 million U.S. workers produce food, they make 600 million units per day, as shown in column $U_1$ in panel (a). If all U.S. workers make clothing, they produce 300 million units per day, as shown in column $U_6$. The columns in between show some workers making food and some making clothing. Because a U.S. worker can produce either 6 units of food or 3 units

of clothing, *the opportunity cost of 1 more unit of clothing is 2 units of food.*

Suppose Izodian workers are less educated, work with less capital, and farm less fertile soil than U.S. workers, so each Izodian worker can produce only 1 unit of food or 2 units of clothing per day. If all 200 million Izodian workers specialize in food, they can make 200 million units per day, as shown in column $I_1$ in panel (b) of Exhibit 2. If they all make clothing, total output is 400 million units per day, as shown in column $I_6$. Some intermediate production possibilities are also listed in the exhibit. Because an Izodian worker can produce either 1 unit of food or 2 units of clothing, *the opportunity cost of 1 more unit of clothing is ½ unit of food.*

We can convert the data in Exhibit 2 to a production possibilities frontier for each country, as shown in Exhibit 3. In each diagram, the amount of food produced is measured on the vertical axis and the amount of clothing on the horizontal axis. U.S. combinations are shown in the left panel by $U_1$, $U_2$, and so on. Izodian combinations

## Exhibit 3

### Production Possibilities Frontiers for the United States and Izodia Without Trade (millions of units per day)

Panel (a) shows the U.S. production possibilities frontier; its slope indicates that the opportunity cost of an additional unit of clothing is 2 units of food. Panel (b) shows production possibilities for Izodia; an additional unit of clothing costs 1/2 unit of food. Clothing has a lower opportunity cost in Izodia.

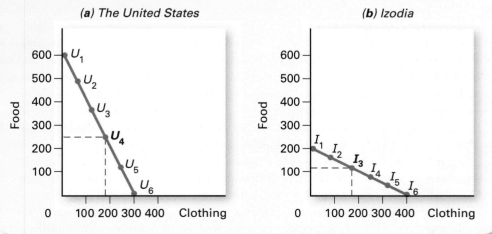

are shown in the right panel by $I_1$, $I_2$, and so on. Because we assume for simplicity that resources are perfectly adaptable to the production of either good, each production possibilities curve is a straight line. The slope of this line differs between countries because the opportunity cost of production differs between countries. The slope equals the opportunity cost of clothing—the amount of food a country must give up to produce another unit of clothing. The U.S. slope is $-2$, and the Izodian slope is $-\frac{1}{2}$. The U.S. slope is steeper because its opportunity cost of producing clothing is greater.

Exhibit 3 illustrates possible combinations of food and clothing that residents of each country can produce and consume if all resources are efficiently employed and there is no trade between the two countries. **Autarky** is the situation of national self-sufficiency, in which there is no economic interaction with foreign producers or consumers. Suppose that U.S. producers maximize profit and U.S. consumers maximize utility with the combination of 240 million units of food and 180 million units of clothing—combination $U_4$. This is called *autarky equilibrium.* Suppose also that Izodians are in autarky equilibrium, identified as combination $I_3$, with 120 million units of food and 160 million units of clothing.

## 17-1c Consumption Possibilities Based on Comparative Advantage

In our example, each U.S. worker can produce more clothing and more food per day than can each Izodian worker, so Americans have an *absolute advantage* in the production of both goods. Recall from Chapter 2 that having an absolute advantage means being able to produce something using fewer resources than other producers require. Should the U.S. economy remain in autarky—that is, self-sufficient in both food and clothing—or could there be gains from specialization and trade?

As long as the opportunity cost of production differs between the two countries, there are gains from specialization and trade. *According to the law of comparative advantage, each country should specialize in producing the good with the lower opportunity cost.* The opportunity cost of producing 1 more unit of clothing is 2 units of food in the United States compared with $\frac{1}{2}$ unit of food in Izodia. Because the opportunity cost of producing clothing is lower in Izodia, both countries will gain if

**autarky** National self-sufficiency; no economic interaction with foreigners

**terms of trade** How much of one good exchanges for a unit of another good

> "According to the law of comparative advantage, each country should specialize in producing the good with the lower opportunity cost."

Izodia specializes in clothing and exports some to the United States, and the United States specializes in food and exports some to Izodia.

Before countries can trade, however, they must agree on how much of one good exchanges for another—that is, they must agree on the **terms of trade**. As long as Americans can get more than $\frac{1}{2}$ a unit of clothing for each unit of food produced, and as long as Izodians can get more than $\frac{1}{2}$ a unit of food for each unit of clothing produced, both countries will be better off specializing. After all, in autarky it costs Americans $\frac{1}{2}$ unit of clothing to produce another unit of food, and it costs Izodians $\frac{1}{2}$ unit of food to produce another unit of clothing, so neither country would want to trade unless they can improve on that.

Suppose that market forces shape the terms of trade so that 1 unit of clothing exchanges for 1 unit of food. To produce another unit of clothing themselves, Americans would have to sacrifice 2 units of food. Likewise, to produce another unit of food themselves, Izodians would have to sacrifice 2 units of clothing.

Exhibit 4 shows that with 1 unit of food trading for 1 unit of clothing, Americans and Izodians can consume anywhere along their blue consumption possibilities frontiers. *The consumption possibilities frontier* shows a nation's possible combinations of goods available as a result of specialization and trade. (Note that the U.S. consumption possibilities curve does not extend to the right of 400 million units of clothing, because Izodia could produce no more than that.) The amount each country actually consumes depends on the relative preferences for food and clothing. Suppose Americans select combination $U$ in panel (a) and Izodians select point $I$ in panel (b).

Without trade, the United States produces and consumes 240 million units of food and 180 million units of clothing. With trade, Americans specialize to

## Exhibit 4

**Production (and Consumption) Possibilities Frontiers With Trade (millions of units per day)**

If Izodia and the United States can specialize and trade at the rate of 1 unit of clothing for 1 unit of food, both can benefit as shown by the blue lines. By trading with Izodia, the U.S. can produce only food and still consume combination *U*, which has more food and more clothing than *U₄*. Likewise, Izodia can attain preferred combination *I* by producing only clothing, then trading some clothing for U.S. food.

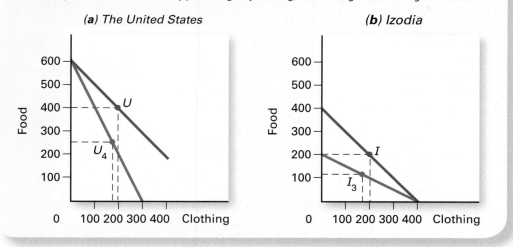

**(a)** *The United States*          **(b)** *Izodia*

produce 600 million units of food; they eat 400 million units and exchange the rest for 200 million units of Izodian clothing. This consumption combination is reflected by point *U*. Through exchange, Americans increase their consumption of both food and clothing.

Without trade, Izodians produce and consume 120 million units of food and 160 million units of clothing. With trade, Izodians specialize to produce 400 million units of clothing; they wear 200 million and exchange the rest for 200 million units of U.S. food. This consumption combination is shown by point *I*. Through trade, Izodians, like Americans, are able to increase their consumption of both goods. How is this possible?

Because Americans are more efficient in the production of food and Izodians more efficient in the production of clothing, total output increases when each specializes. Without specialization and trade, world production is 360 million units of food and 340 million units of clothing. With specialization and trade, food increases to 600 million units and clothing to 400 million units. Thus, both countries increase consumption with trade. *Although*

> **"Remember that comparative advantage, not absolute advantage, creates gains from specialization and trade."**

*the United States has an absolute advantage in both goods, differences in the opportunity cost of production between the two nations ensure that specialization and trade result in mutual gains.* Remember that comparative advantage, not absolute advantage, creates gains from specialization and trade. The only constraint on trade is that, for each good, *world production must equal world consumption.*

We simplified trade relations in our example to highlight the gains from specialization and trade. We assumed that each country would completely specialize in producing a particular good, that resources were equally adaptable to the production of either good, that the costs of transporting goods from one country to another were inconsequential, and that there were no problems in arriving at the terms of trade. The world is not that simple. For example, we don't expect a country to produce just one good. Regardless, there is broad evidence that specialization based on the law of comparative advantage still leads to gains from trade. For example, after examining the productivity of 17 crops on 1.6 million parcels of land in 55 countries around the world, researchers found strong evidence that international trade arises from comparative advantage.[1]

## 17-1d Reasons for International Specialization

Countries trade with one another—or, more precisely, people, firms, and governments in one country trade with those in another—because each

1. Arnaud Costinot and David Donaldson, "Ricardo's Theory of Comparative Advantage: Old Idea, New Evidence," *American Economic Review,* 102 (May 2012): 453–458.

side expects to gain from trade. How do we know what each country should produce and what each should trade?

## Differences in Resource Endowments

Differences in resource endowments often create differences in the opportunity cost of production across countries. Some countries are blessed with an abundance of fertile land and favorable growing seasons. The United States, for example, has been called the "breadbasket of the world" because of its rich farmland ideal for growing wheat and corn. Coffee grows best in the climate and elevation of Colombia, Brazil, and Vietnam. Honduras has the ideal climate for bananas. Thus, the United States exports wheat and corn and imports coffee and bananas. Seasonal differences across countries also encourage trade. For example, in the winter, Americans import fruit from Chile, and Canadians travel to Florida for sun and fun. In the summer, Americans export fruit to Chile, and Americans travel to Canada for camping and hiking.

Resources are often concentrated in particular countries: crude oil in Saudi Arabia, fertile soil in the United States, copper ore in Chile, rough diamonds in South Africa. The United States grows abundant supplies of oil seeds such as soybeans and sunflowers, but does not yet extract enough crude oil to satisfy domestic demand. Thus, the United States exports oil seeds and imports crude oil. More generally, *countries export products they can produce more cheaply in return for products that are unavailable domestically or are cheaper elsewhere.*

Exhibit 5 shows, for 12 key resources, U.S. production as a percentage of U.S. consumption. If production falls short of consumption, this means the United States imports the difference. For example, because America grows coffee only in Hawaii, U.S. production is only 1 percent of U.S. consumption, so nearly all coffee is imported. The exhibit also shows that U.S. production falls short of U.S. consumption for crude oil and natural gas, and for metals such as zinc, copper, and aluminum. If U.S. production exceeds U.S. consumption, the United States exports the difference. For example, U.S.–grown cotton amounts to 502 percent of U.S. cotton consumption, so most U.S.-grown cotton is exported. U.S. production also exceeds U.S. consumption for other crops, including wheat, oil seeds (soybeans, sunflower seeds, cottonseeds), and coarse grains (corn, barley, oats). In short, when it comes to basic resources, the United States is a net importer of crude oil, natural gas, and metals and a net exporter of coal and farm crops.

*Exhibit 5*

**U.S. Production as a Percentage of U.S. Consumption for Various Resources**

If U.S. production is less than 100 percent of U.S. consumption, then imports make up the difference. If U.S. production exceeds U.S. consumption, then the amount by which production exceeds 100 percent of consumption is exported.

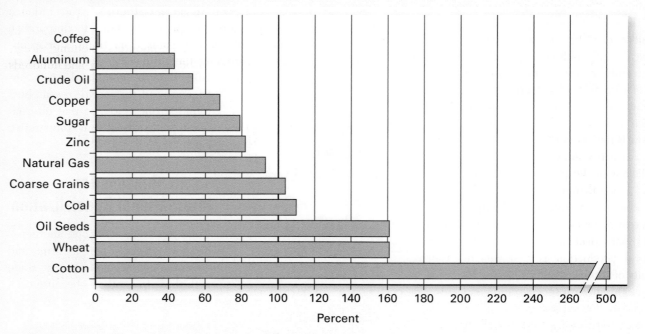

Source: Based on annual figures selected from *The Economist Pocket World in Figures: 2015 Edition* (Profile Books, 2014).

## Economies of Scale

If production is subject to *economies of scale*—that is, if the long-run average cost of production falls as a firm expands its scale of operation—countries can gain from trade if each nation specializes. Such specialization allows firms in each nation to produce more of a particular good, which reduces average costs. For example, one country can make computer chips that are sold in many countries, and another country can make cars that are sold in many countries. The primary reason for establishing the single integrated market of the European Union was to offer producers there a large, open market of now more than 500 million consumers. Producers could thereby achieve economies of scale. Firms and countries producing at the lowest opportunity costs are most competitive in international markets. For example, most of the world's buttons and zippers come from the same Chinese city. Another Chinese city is the source of most of the world's socks.

## Differences in Tastes

Even if all countries had identical resource endowments and combined those resources with equal efficiency, each country would still gain from trade as long as tastes differed across countries. Consumption patterns differ across countries and some of this results from differences in tastes. For example, the Czechs and Irish drink three times as much beer per capita as do the Swiss and Swedes. The French drink three times as much wine as do Australians. The Danes eat twice as much pork as do Americans. Americans eat twice as much chicken as do Hungarians. Americans like chicken, but not all of it. The United States is the world's leading exporter of chicken feet, and China is the world's leading importer (Tyson Foods alone ships

about three billion chicken feet to China each year). Residents of West Africa prefer the dark bony meat of a chicken, such as backs and necks, so chicken farmers there sell these parts locally and ship chicken breasts abroad, where they are valued more.[2] Soft drinks are four times more popular in the United States than in Europe. The English like tea; Americans, coffee. Algeria has an ideal climate for growing grapes (vineyards there date back to Roman times). But Algeria's population is 99 percent Muslim, a religion that forbids alcohol consumption. Thus, Algeria exports wine.

## More Variety

Yet another reason for trade is to increase the *variety* of goods and services available. People prefer having a choice of products, and international trade helps broaden that choice.[3] International trade expands your selection of automobiles, computers, clothing, drugs, wine, cheese, ethnic foods, music, movies, and hundreds of other items.

## 17-2 TRADE RESTRICTIONS AND WELFARE LOSS

Despite the benefits of international trade, nearly all countries at one time or another erect trade barriers, which benefit some domestic producers but harm other domestic producers and all domestic consumers. In this section, we consider the effects of trade barriers and why they are imposed.

2. Drew Hinshaw, "As KFC Goes to Africa, It Lacks Only One Thing: Chickens," *Wall Street Journal*, 8 February 2013.

3. Marc Melitz and Daniel Trefler, "Gains from Trade When Firms Matter," *Journal of Economic Perspectives*, 26 (Spring 2012): 91–118.

## Exhibit 6

### Consumer Surplus and Producer Surplus

Consumer surplus, shown by the blue triangle, indicates the net benefits consumers reap from buying 60 pounds of apples at $1.00 per pound. Some consumers would have been willing to pay $3.00 or more per pound for the first few pounds. Consumer surplus measures the difference between the maximum sum of money consumers would pay for 60 pounds of apples and the actual sum they pay. Producer surplus, shown by the gold triangle, indicates the net benefits producers reap from selling 60 pounds at $1.00 per pound. Some producers would have supplied apples for %0.50 per pound or less. Producer surplus measures the difference between the actual sum of money producers receive for 60 pounds of apples and the minimum amount they would accept for this amount.

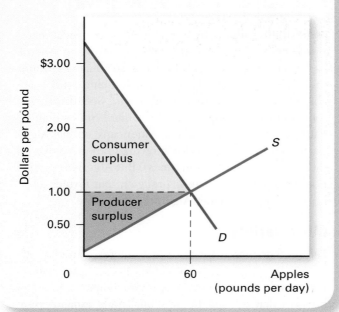

## 17-2a Consumer Surplus and Producer Surplus From Market Exchange

Before we explore the net effects of world trade on social welfare, let's develop a framework showing the benefits that consumers and producers get from market exchange. Consider the hypothetical market for apples shown in Exhibit 6. The height of the demand curve shows what consumers are willing and able to pay for each additional pound of apples. In effect, the height of the demand curve shows the *marginal benefit* consumers expect from each pound of apples. For example, the demand curve indicates that some consumers in this market are willing to pay $3.00 or

**world price** The price at which a good is traded on the world market; determined by the world demand and world supply for the good

more per pound for the first few pounds of apples. But every consumer gets to buy apples at the market-clearing price, which here is $1.00 per pound. Most consumers thus get a bonus, or a surplus, from market exchange.

The blue-shaded triangle below the demand curve and above the market price reflects the *consumer surplus* in this market, which is the difference between the most that consumers would pay for 60 pounds of apples per day and the actual amount they do pay. We all enjoy a consumer surplus from most products we buy.

Producers usually derive a similar surplus. The height of the supply curve shows what producers are willing and able to accept for each additional pound of apples. That is, the height of the supply curve shows the expected *marginal cost* from producing each additional pound. For example, the supply curve indicates that some producers face a marginal cost of $0.50 or less per pound for supplying the first few pounds. But every producer gets to sell apples for the market-clearing price of $1.00 per pound. The gold-shaded triangle above the supply curve and below the market price reflects the *producer surplus*, which is the difference between the actual amount that producers receive for 60 pounds and what they would accept to supply that amount.

The point is that market exchange usually generates a surplus, or a bonus, for both consumers and producers. In the balance of this chapter, we look at the gains from international trade and how trade restrictions affect consumer and producer surplus.

## 17-2b Tariffs

A *tariff*, a term first introduced in Chapter 3, is a tax on imports. (Tariffs can apply to exports, too, but we will focus on import tariffs.) A tariff can be either *specific*, such as a tariff of $5 per barrel of oil, or *ad valorem*, such as 10 percent on the import price of jeans. Consider the effects of a specific tariff on a particular good. In Exhibit 7, *D* is the U.S. demand for sugar and *S* is the supply of sugar from U.S. growers (there are about 10,000 U.S. sugarcane growers). Suppose that the world price of sugar is $0.10 per pound. The **world price** is determined by the world supply and demand for a product. It is the price at which any supplier can sell output on the world market and at which any demander can purchase output on the world market.

With free trade, any U.S. consumers could buy any amount desired at the world price of $0.10 per pound, so the quantity demanded is 70 million pounds per month, of which U.S. producers supply 20 million pounds and importers supply 50 million pounds. Because U.S. buyers can purchase sugar at the world price, U.S. producers can't charge more than that. Now suppose that a specific tariff of $0.05 is imposed on each pound of imported sugar, raising the U.S. price from $0.10 to $0.15 per pound. U.S. producers can therefore raise their own price to

$0.15 per pound without losing business to imports. At the higher price, the quantity supplied by U.S. producers increases to 30 million pounds, but the quantity demanded by U.S. consumers declines to 60 million pounds. Because quantity demanded has declined and quantity supplied by U.S. producers has increased, U.S. imports fall from 50 million to 30 million pounds per month.

Because the U.S. price is higher after the tariff, U.S. consumers are worse off. Their loss in consumer surplus is identified in Exhibit 7 by the combination of the blue- and pink-shaded areas. Because both the U.S. price and the quantity supplied by U.S. producers have increased, their total revenue increases by the areas *a* plus *b* plus *f*. But only area *a* represents an increase in producer surplus. Revenue represented by the areas *b* plus *f* merely offsets the higher marginal cost U.S. producers face in expanding sugar output from 20 million to 30 million pounds per month. Area *b* represents part of the net welfare loss to the domestic economy because those 10 million pounds could have been imported for $0.10 per pound rather than produced domestically at a higher marginal cost.

Government revenue from the tariff is identified by area *c*, which equals the tariff of $0.05 per pound multiplied by the 30 million pounds imported, for tariff revenue of $1.5 million per month. Tariff revenue is a loss to consumers, but because the tariff goes to the government, it can be used to lower taxes or to increase public services, so it's not a loss to the U.S. economy. Area *d* shows a loss in consumer surplus because less sugar is consumed at the higher price. This loss is not redistributed to anyone else, so area *d* reflects part of the net welfare loss of the tariff. Therefore, areas *b* and *d* show the domestic economy's net welfare loss of the tariff; *the two triangles measure a loss in consumer surplus that is not offset by a gain to anyone in the domestic economy.*

In summary: Of the total loss in U.S. consumer surplus (areas

## Exhibit 7
### Effect of a Tariff

At a world price of $0.10 per pound, U.S. consumers demand 70 million pounds of sugar per month, and U.S. producers supply 20 million pounds per month; the difference is imported. After the imposition of a $0.05 per pound tariff, the U.S. price rises to $0.15 per pound. U.S. producers supply 30 million pounds, and U.S. consumers cut back to 60 million pounds. At the higher U.S. price, consumers are worse off; their loss of consumer surplus is the sum of areas *a, b, c,* and *d*. The net welfare loss to the U.S. economy consists of areas *b* and *d*.

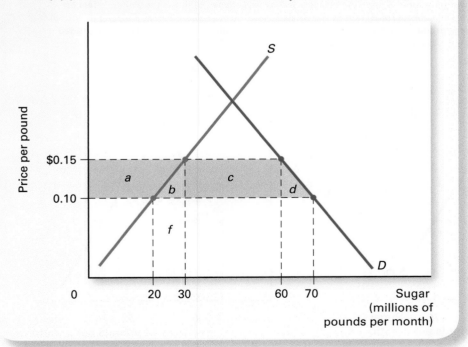

*a*, *b*, *c*, and *d*) resulting from the tariff, area *a* goes to U.S producers, area *c* becomes government revenue, but areas *b* and *d* are net losses in domestic social welfare.

## 17-2c Import Quotas

An *import quota* is a legal limit on the amount of a commodity that can be imported. Quotas usually target imports from certain countries. For example, a quota may limit furniture from China or shoes from Brazil. To have an impact on the domestic market, a quota must be less than what would be imported with free trade. Consider a quota on the U.S. market for sugar. In panel (a) of Exhibit 8, *D* is the U.S. demand curve and *S* is the supply curve of U.S. sugar producers. Suppose again that the world price of sugar is $0.10 per pound. With free trade, that price would prevail in the U.S. market as well, and a total of 70 million pounds would be demanded per month. U.S. producers would supply 20 million pounds and importers, 50 million pounds. With a quota of 50 million pounds or more per month, the U.S. price would

remain the same as the world price of $0.10 per pound, and the U.S. quantity would be 70 million pounds per month. In short, a quota of at least 50 million pounds would not raise the U.S. price above the world price because 50 million pounds were imported without a quota. A more stringent quota, however, would cut imports, which, as we'll see, would raise the U.S. price.

Suppose U.S. trade officials impose an import quota of 30 million pounds per month. As long as the U.S. price is at or above the world price of $0.10 per pound, foreign producers will supply 30 million pounds. So at prices at or above $0.10 per pound, the total supply of sugar to the U.S. market is found by adding 30 million pounds of imported sugar to the amount supplied by U.S. producers. U.S. and foreign producers would never sell in the U.S. market for less than $0.10 per pound because they can always get that price on the world market. Thus, the supply curve that sums domestic production and imports is horizontal at the world price of $0.10 per pound and remains so until the quantity supplied reaches 50 million pounds.

### Exhibit 8

**Effect of a Quota**

In panel (a), *D* is the U.S. demand curve and *S* is the supply curve of U.S. producers. If the government establishes a sugar quota of 30 million pounds per month, the supply curve combining U.S. production and imports becomes horizontal at the world price of $0.10 per pound and remains horizontal until the quantity supplied reaches 50 million pounds. For higher prices, the new supply curve equals the horizontal sum of the U.S. supply curve, *S*, plus the quota of 30 million pounds. The new U.S. price, $0.15 per pound, is determined by the intersection of the new supply curve, *S'*, with the U.S. demand curve, *D*. Panel (b) shows the welfare effect of the quota. As a result of the higher U.S. price, consumer surplus is cut by the shaded area. The blue-shaded areas illustrate the loss in consumer surplus that is captured by domestic producers and by those who are permitted to fulfill the quota, and the pink-shaded triangles illustrate the net welfare cost of the quota on the U.S. economy.

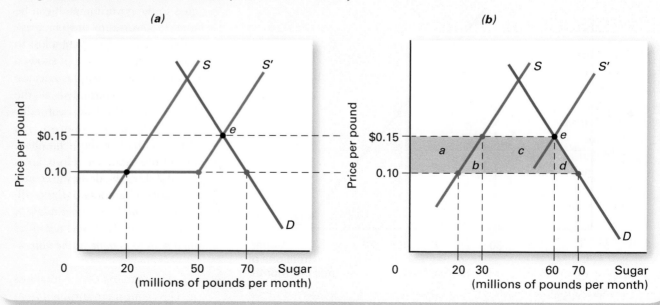

**(a)**

**(b)**

Again, for prices above $0.10 per pound, the new supply curve, $S'$, adds horizontally the 30-million-pound quota to $S$, the supply curve of U.S. producers. The U.S. price is found where this new supply curve, $S'$, intersects the domestic demand curve, which in Exhibit 8 occurs at point $e$. *By limiting imports, the quota raises the domestic price of sugar above the world price and reduces quantity below the free trade level.* (Note that to compare more easily the effects of tariffs and quotas, this quota is designed to yield the same equilibrium price and quantity as the tariff examined earlier.)

Panel (b) of Exhibit 8 shows the distribution and efficiency effects of the quota. As a result of the quota, U.S. consumer surplus declines by the combined blue and pink areas. Area $a$ becomes U.S. producer surplus and thus involves no loss of U.S. welfare. Area $c$ shows the increased economic profit to those permitted by the quota to sell Americans 30 million pounds for $0.15 per pound, or $0.05 above the world price. If foreign exporters rather than U.S. importers reap this profit, area $c$ reflects a net loss in U.S. welfare.

Area $b$ shows a welfare loss to the U.S. economy, because sugar could have been purchased abroad for $0.10 per pound, and the U.S. resources employed to increase sugar production could instead have been used more efficiently producing other goods. Area $d$ is also a welfare loss because it reflects a reduction in consumer surplus with no offsetting gain to anyone. Thus, areas $b$ and $d$ in panel (b) of Exhibit 8 measure the minimum U.S. welfare loss from the quota. If the profit from quota rights (area $c$) accrues to foreign producers, this increases the U.S. welfare loss.

### 17-2d  Quotas in Practice

The United States has granted quotas to specific countries. These countries, in turn, distribute these quota rights to their exporters through a variety of means. *By rewarding domestic and foreign producers with higher prices, the quota system creates two groups intent on securing and perpetuating these quotas.* Lobbyists for foreign producers work the halls of Congress, seeking the right to export to the United States. This strong support from producers, coupled with a lack of opposition from consumers (who remain rationally ignorant for the most part), has resulted in quotas that have lasted decades. For example, sugar quotas have been around more than 50 years. For the past three

> **"Tariffs and quotas are only two of many devices used to restrict foreign trade."**

decades, U.S. sugar prices have ranged from 50 to 100 percent above the world price, costing American consumers billions.[4] Sugar growers, who account for only 1 percent of U.S. farm sales, accounted for 17 percent of political contributions from agriculture.[5] Sugar growers even reversed a North American Free Trade Agreement provision that would have allowed tariff-free sugar imports from Mexico.

Some economists have argued that if quotas are to be used, the United States should auction them off to foreign producers, thereby capturing at least some of the difference between the world price and the U.S. price. Auctioning off quotas would not only increase federal revenue at a time when it's desperately needed, but an auction would reduce the profitability of getting quota rights, which would reduce pressure on Washington to perpetuate them. American consumers are not the only victims of sugar quotas. Thousands of poor farmers around the world miss out on an opportunity to earn a living by growing sugar cane for export to America.

### 17-2e  Tariffs and Quotas Compared

Consider the similarities and differences between a tariff and a quota. Because both have identical effects on the price in our example, they both lead to the same change in quantity demanded. In both cases, U.S. consumers suffer the same loss of consumer surplus, and U.S. producers reap the same gain of producer surplus. The primary difference is that the revenue from the tariff goes to the U.S. government, whereas the revenue from the quota goes to whoever secures the right to sell foreign goods in the U.S. market. *If quota rights accrue to foreigners, then the domestic economy is worse off with a quota than with a tariff.* But even if quota rights go to domestic importers, quotas, like tariffs, still increase the domestic price, restrict quantity, and thereby reduce consumer surplus and economic welfare. Quotas and tariffs can also raise production costs. For example, U.S. candy manufacturers face higher production costs

4. Burleigh Leonard, "U.S. Sugar Policy: Sweet Deal for a Few, Sour for Most," *Wall Street Journal*, 2 November 2014.

5. Michael Schroeder, "Sugar Growers Hold Up Push for Free Trade," *Wall Street Journal*, 3 February 2004.

because of sugar quotas, making them less competitive on world markets. Finally, and most importantly, *quotas and tariffs encourage foreign governments to retaliate with quotas and tariffs of their own, thus shrinking U.S. export markets, so the welfare loss is greater than shown in Exhibits 7 and 8.*

## 17-2f Other Trade Restrictions

Besides tariffs and quotas, a variety of other measures limit free trade. A country may provide *export subsidies* to encourage exports and *low-interest loans* to foreign buyers. Some countries impose *domestic content requirements* specifying that a certain portion of a final good must be produced domestically. Other requirements masquerading as health, safety, or technical standards often discriminate against foreign goods. For example, Nigeria protects chicken growers by banning chicken imports (which is why KFCs there added fish to the menu). To gain access to Chinese markets, foreign producers must transfer their technological know-how to a Chinese partner, so it can be made available throughout China.[6] European countries once prohibited beef from hormone-fed cattle, a measure aimed at U.S. beef. Purity laws in Germany bar many non-German beers. Until the European Community adopted uniform standards, differing technical requirements forced manufacturers to offer as many as seven different versions of the same TV for that market. Sometimes exporters will voluntarily limit exports, as when Japanese automakers agreed to cut exports to the United States. The point is that *tariffs and quotas are only two of many devices used to restrict foreign trade.*

Recent research on the cost of protectionism indicates that international trade barriers slow the introduction of new goods and better technologies. So, rather than simply raising domestic prices, trade restrictions slow economic progress.

**bilateral agreement**
Trade agreement between two countries

**multilateral agreement**
Trade agreement among more than two countries

**General Agreement on Tariffs and Trade (GATT)** An international tariff-reduction treaty adopted in 1947 that resulted in a series of negotiated "rounds" aimed at freer trade; the Uruguay Round created GATT's successor, the World Trade Organization (WTO)

**dumping** Selling a product abroad for less than charged in the home market or for less than the cost of production

6. Thomas J. Holmes, Ellen R. McGrattan, and Edward C. Prescott, "Quid Pro Quo: Technology Capital Transfers for Market Access in China," *Review of Economic Studies*, 82 (July 2015): 1154–1193.

## 17-3 EFFORTS TO REDUCE TRADE BARRIERS

Although some groups in the economy have a special interest in restricting trade, the trend has been toward freer trade. In this section, we examine international efforts to lower trade barriers. A nation sometimes negotiates a trade agreements with another nation, in what is know as a **bilateral agreement**. For example, the United States has negotiated bilateral open-skies agreements to deregulate airline competition on international routes, agreements that have generated at least $4 billion a year in gains to travelers. And travelers would gain another $4 billion a year if agreements were reached with other countries where Americans travel frequently.[7]

### 17-3a Freer Trade by Multilateral Agreement

Mindful of how high tariffs cut world trade during the Great Depression, the United States, after World War II, invited its trading partners to negotiate lower tariffs and other trade barriers. A **multilateral agreement** is one reached among more than two countries. The result was the **General Agreement on Tariffs and Trade (GATT)**, an international trade treaty adopted in 1947 by 23 countries, including the United States. Each GATT member agreed to (1) reduce tariffs through multinational negotiations, (2) reduce import quotas, and (3) treat all members equally with respect to trade.

Trade barriers have been reduced through trade negotiations, or "trade rounds," under the auspices of GATT. Trade rounds offer a package approach rather than an issue-by-issue approach to trade negotiations. Concessions that are necessary but otherwise difficult to defend in domestic political terms can be made more acceptable in the context of a larger package that also contains politically and economically attractive benefits. Most early GATT trade rounds were aimed at reducing tariffs. The Kennedy Round in the mid-1960s included new provisions against **dumping**, which is selling a commodity abroad for less than is charged in the home market or less than the cost of production. The Tokyo Round of the 1970s was a more sweeping attempt to extend and improve the system.

The most recently completed round was launched in Uruguay in September 1986 and ratified by 123 participating countries in 1994. The number of signing

7. Clifford Winston and Jia Yan, "Open Skies: Estimating Travelers' Benefits From Free Trade in Airline Service," *American Economic Journal: Economic Policy*, 7 (May 2015): 370–414.

countries now exceeds 150. This so-called **Uruguay Round**, the most comprehensive of the eight postwar multilateral trade negotiations, included 550 pages of tariff reductions on 85 percent of world trade. As a result of the Uruguay Round, average tariffs fell from 6 percent to 4 percent of the value of imports (when GATT began in 1947, average tariffs averaged 40 percent). The Uruguay Round also created the World Trade Organization to succeed GATT.

## 17-3b World Trade Organization

The **World Trade Organization (WTO)** provides the legal and institutional foundation for world trade. Although GATT was a multilateral agreement with no institutional foundation, the WTO is a permanent institution in Geneva, Switzerland. A staff of about 600 economists and lawyers helps shape policy and resolves trade disputes among member countries. Although GATT involved only merchandise trade, the WTO also covers services and trade-related aspects of intellectual property, such as books, movies, and computer programs. The WTO will eventually phase out quotas, but tariffs will remain legal.

Although GATT relied on voluntary cooperation, the WTO settles disputes in a way that is faster, more automatic, and less susceptible to blockage than the GATT system was. The WTO resolved more trade disputes in its first decade than GATT did in nearly 50 years. Since 2000, developing countries have filed 60 percent of the disputes.

## 17-3c Common Markets

Some countries looked to the success of the U.S. economy, which is essentially a free trade zone across 50 states, and have tried to develop free trade zones of their own. The largest and best known is the European Union, which began in 1958 with a half dozen countries and by 2015 had expanded to 28 countries and over 500 million people. The idea was to create a barrier-free European market like the United States in which goods, services, people, and capital are free to flow to their highest-valued use. As of 2015, 19 members of the European Union had also adopted a common currency, the *euro*, which replaced national currencies in 2002. The European Union is an example of a **common market**, which consists of a group of countries with few or no trade restrictions with one another.

> **"**Free trade areas are springing up around the world.**"**

The United States, Canada, and Mexico introduced a free trade pact in 1994 called the North American Free Trade Agreement, or NAFTA. Through NAFTA, Mexico hopes to attract more U.S. investment by guaranteeing companies that locate there duty-free access to U.S. markets, which is where over two-thirds of Mexico's exports go. Mexico's 117 million people represent an attractive export market for U.S. producers, and Mexico's oil reserves could ease U.S. energy problems. The United States would also like to support Mexico's efforts to become more market oriented, as is reflected, for example, by Mexico's privatization of its phone system and banks. Creating job opportunities in Mexico also reduces pressure for Mexicans to cross the U.S. border illegally to find work. After more than a decade of NAFTA, agricultural exports to Mexico have doubled, as has overall trade among the three nations, but Americans still buy much more from Mexicans and Canadians than the other way around.

Free trade areas are springing up around the world. The United States signed a free trade agreement with five Central American countries and the Dominican Republic, called CAFTA-DR. Ten Latin American countries form Mercosur. And in 2015, the United States was negotiating the Trans-Pacific Partnership with 11 other nations in the Pacific, including China. Together, these countries represent up to 40 percent of world output. Elsewhere in the world, the Association of Southeast Asian Nations, or ASEAN, consists of 10 member countries. And South Africa and its four neighboring countries form the Southern African Customs Union. Regional trade agreements require an exception to WTO rules because bloc members can make special deals among themselves and thus discriminate against outsiders. Under WTO's requirements, any trade concession granted to one country must usually be granted to *all other* WTO members.

Incidentally, economic initiatives such as the European Union binds nations together economically so they are less likely to go to war

Protesters of the WTO and its policies are often concerned with how free trade policies will impact domestic jobs and wages.

David Grossman/Alamy

would be more efficient simply to transfer money from domestic consumers to domestic producers. But such a bald payoff would be politically unpopular. Arguments for trade restrictions avoid mention of transfers to domestic producers and instead cite loftier goals. As we shall now see, none of these goals makes a strong case for restrictions, but some make a little more sense than others.

> **"Trade restrictions are often little more than handouts for the domestic industries they protect."**

### 17-4a National Defense Argument

Some industries claim they need protection from import competition because their output is vital for national defense. Products such as strategic metals and military hardware are often insulated from foreign competition by trade restrictions. Thus, national defense considerations outweigh concerns about efficiency and equity. How valid is this argument? Trade restrictions may shelter the defense industry, but other means, such as government subsidies, might be more efficient. Or the government could stockpile basic military hardware so that maintaining an ongoing productive capacity would become less critical. Still, technological change could make certain weapons obsolete. Because most industries can play some role in national defense, instituting trade restrictions on this basis can get out of hand. For example, many decades ago U.S. wool producers secured trade protection at a time when some military uniforms were still made of wool.

The national defense argument has also been used to discourage foreign ownership of U.S. companies in some industries. For example, in 2005 a Chinese state-owned company was prevented from buying Unocal Oil. And in 2010, the Congressional Steel Caucus tried to block a Chinese attempt to buy a Mississippi steel plant, saying that such a deal "threatens American jobs and our national security."[8]

8. Yjun Zhang, "China Steel Group Accuses U.S. Lawmakers of Protectionism," *Wall Street Journal*, 5 July 2010.

against each other. War with countries that are trading partners would involve more economic loss than war with other countries. That's yet another benefit of freer trade.

Still, economic integration is not a perfect solution, as evidenced by recent financial problems in the eurozone, which arose because unsustainable government deficits in some member countries such as Greece and Spain reduced confidence in the common currency. Member countries became much more vulnerable to fiscal problems of other member countries.

## 17-4 ARGUMENTS FOR TRADE RESTRICTIONS

Trade restrictions are often little more than handouts for the domestic industries they protect. Given the loss in social welfare that results from these restrictions, it

## 17-4b Infant Industry Argument

The infant industry argument was formulated as a rationale for protecting emerging domestic industries from foreign competition. In industries where a firm's average cost of production falls as output expands, new firms may need protection from imports until these firms grow enough to become competitive. Trade restrictions let new firms achieve the economies of scale necessary to compete with mature foreign producers.

But how do we identify industries that merit protection, and when do they become old enough to look after themselves? Protection often fosters inefficiencies. The immediate cost of such restrictions is the net welfare loss from higher domestic prices. These costs may become permanent if the industry never realizes the expected economies of scale and thus never becomes competitive. As with the national defense argument, policy makers should be careful in adopting trade restrictions based on the infant industry argument. Here again, temporary production subsidies may be more efficient than import restrictions.

## 17-4c Antidumping Argument

As we have noted already, *dumping* is selling a product abroad for less than in the home market or less than the cost of production. Exporters may be able to sell the good for less overseas because of export subsidies, or firms may simply find it profitable to sell for less in foreign markets where consumers are more sensitive to prices. But why shouldn't U.S. consumers pay as little as possible? If dumping is *persistent,* the increase in consumer surplus would more than offset losses to domestic producers. *There is no good reason why consumers should not be allowed to buy imports for a persistently lower price.*

An alternative form of dumping, termed *predatory dumping,* is the *temporary* sale abroad at prices below cost to eliminate competitors in that target market. Once the competition is gone, so the story goes, the exporting firm can raise the price in the foreign market. The trouble with this argument is that if dumpers try to take advantage of their monopoly position by sharply increasing the price, then other firms, either domestic or foreign, could enter the market and sell for less. There are few documented cases of predatory dumping.

Sometimes dumping may be *sporadic,* as firms occasionally try to unload excess inventories. Retailers hold periodic "sales" for the same reason. Sporadic dumping can be unsettling for domestic producers, but the economic impact is not a matter of great public concern.

Regardless, all dumping is prohibited in the United States by the Trade Agreements Act of 1979, which calls for the imposition of tariffs when a good is sold for less in the United States than in its home market or less than the cost of production. In addition, WTO rules allow for offsetting tariffs when products are sold for "less than fair value" and when there is "material injury" to domestic producers. For example, U.S. producers of lumber and beer frequently accuse their Canadian counterparts of dumping.

## 17-4d Jobs and Income Argument

One rationale for trade restrictions that is commonly heard in the United States, and is voiced by WTO protesters, is that they protect U.S. jobs and wage levels. Using trade restrictions to protect domestic jobs is a strategy that dates back centuries. One problem with such a policy is that other countries usually retaliate by restricting *their* imports to save *their* jobs, so international trade is reduced, jobs are lost in export industries, and potential gains from trade fail to materialize. That happened big time during the Great Depression, as high tariffs choked trade and jobs.

Wages in other countries, especially developing countries, are often a fraction of wages in the United States. For example, including benefits, General Motors (GM) workers in Michigan earn about $50 per hour versus $7 for GM workers in Mexico, $4.50 in China, and $1 in India. (The minimum wage in Mexico is less than $1 per hour.) Looking simply at differences in wages, however, narrows the focus too much. Wages represent just one component of the total production cost and may not necessarily be the most important. Employers are interested in the labor cost per unit of output, which

While cheap labor in other countries may reduce the price of imports, it does not tell the whole story.

depends on both the wage and labor productivity. Wages are high in the United States partly because U.S. labor productivity remains the highest in the world. High productivity can be traced to better education and training and to the abundant computers, machines, and other physical capital that make workers more productive. U.S. workers also benefit greatly from better management and a relatively stable business climate.

But what about the lower wages in many developing countries? Low wages are often linked to workers' lack of education and training, to the meager physical capital available to each worker, and to a business climate that is less stable and hence less attractive for producers. For example, the total value of manufacturing output is about the same in the United States as in China, but Americans produce that output with only about 10 percent of the manufacturing workforce that's employed in China.[9] What's more, advances in technology are making differences in labor costs across countries less relevant. One example is, as noted earlier, that in the original iPad, manufacturing labor accounted for only $33 of its $499 retail price, and the final assembly in China accounted for just $8 of that $33.[10]

Once multinational firms build plants and provide technological know-how in developing countries, U.S. workers lose some of their competitive edge, and their relatively high wages could price some U.S. products out of the world market. This has already happened in the consumer electronics and toy industries. China makes 80 percent of the toys sold in the United States. Some U.S. toy sellers, such as the makers of Etch A Sketch, would no longer exist had they not outsourced manufacturing to China. Overall, competition from Chinese imports between 1999 and 2011 cost the U.S. economy about 2 million jobs, according to one estimate.[11]

Domestic producers do not like to compete with foreign producers whose costs are lower, so they often push for trade restrictions. Labor unions protested the Trans-Pacific Partnership on those grounds. According to one report, "Unions see the pact as one of the biggest threats to organized labor and the U.S. middle class since the North American Free Trade Agreement took effect in 1994."[12] But if restrictions negate any cost advantage a foreign producer might have, the law of comparative advantage becomes inoperative and domestic consumers are denied access to the lower-priced goods.

9. "Manufacturing and Innovation: Back to Making Stuff," *The Economist*, 21 April 2012.

10. "The Third Industrial Revolution," *The Economist*, 21 April 2012.

11. Daron Acemoglu et al. "Import Competition and the Great U.S. Employment Sag of the 2000s," NBER Working Paper No. 20395 (August 2014).

12. Melanie Trottman, "Unions Flex Muscle to Fight Pacific Trade Pace," *Wall Street Journal*, 10 June 2015.

Over time, as labor productivity in developing countries increases, wage differentials among countries will narrow, much as they narrowed between the northern and southern United States during the last century. As technology and capital spread, U.S. workers, particularly unskilled workers, cannot expect to maintain wage levels that are far above comparable workers in other countries. So far, research and development has kept U.S. producers on the cutting edge of technological developments, but staying ahead in the technological race is a constant battle. As a sign of the times about how competition could squeeze down the wage gap across countries, the Volkswagen factory in Tennessee pays workers only about half of what GM pays in Michigan, yet in 2011, many thousands of job seekers applied for the 2,000 openings at the Tennessee factory.

## 17-4e Declining Industries Argument

Where an established domestic industry is in jeopardy of closing because of lower-priced imports, could there be a rationale for *temporary* import restrictions? After all, domestic producers employ many industry-specific resources—both specialized labor and specialized machines. This human and physical capital is worth less in its best alternative use. If the extinction of the domestic industry is forestalled through trade restrictions, specialized workers can retire voluntarily or can gradually pursue more promising careers. Specialized machines can be allowed to wear out naturally.

Thus, in the case of declining domestic industries, trade protection can help lessen shocks to the economy and can allow for an orderly transition to a new industrial mix. But the protection offered should not be so generous as to encourage continued investment in the industry. Protection should be of specific duration and should be phased out over that period.

The clothing industry is an example of a declining U.S. industry. The 22,000 U.S. jobs saved as a result of one trade restriction paid an average of less than $30,000 per year. But a Congressional Budget Office study estimated that the higher domestic clothing prices resulting from trade restrictions meant that U.S. consumers paid two to three times more than apparel workers earned. Trade restrictions in the U.S. clothing and textile industry started phasing out in 2005 under the Uruguay Round of trade agreements.

Free trade may displace some U.S. jobs through imports, but it also creates U.S. jobs through exports. When Americans celebrate a ribbon-cutting ceremony for a new software company, nobody credits free trade for those jobs, but when a steel plant closes here, everyone talks about how those jobs went overseas. What's more, many foreign companies have built plants in the United States and employ U.S. workers. For example, a dozen foreign television manufacturers and all major Japanese automakers now operate plants in the United States.

The number employed in the United States has nearly doubled in the last four decades. To recognize this job growth is not to deny the problems facing workers displaced by imports. Some displaced workers, particularly those in steel and other unionized, blue-collar industries, are not likely to find jobs that pay nearly as well as the ones they lost. As with infant industries, however, the problems posed by declining industries need not require trade restrictions. To support the affected industry, the government could offer wage subsidies or special tax breaks that decline over time. The government has also funded programs to retrain affected workers for jobs that are in greater demand.

## 17-4f Problems with Trade Protection

Trade restrictions raise a number of problems in addition to those already mentioned. First, protecting one stage of production usually requires protecting downstream stages of production as well. Protecting the U.S. textile industry from foreign competition, for example, raised the cost of cloth to U.S. apparel makers, reducing *their* competitiveness. Thus, when the government protected domestic textile manufacturers, the domestic garment industry also needed protection. Second, the cost of protection includes not only the welfare loss from the higher domestic price but also the cost of the resources used by domestic producer groups to secure the favored protection. The cost of *rent seeking*—lobbying fees, propaganda, and legal actions—can sometimes equal or exceed the direct welfare loss from restrictions. The third problem with trade restrictions is the transaction costs of enforcing the myriad quotas, tariffs, and other trade restrictions. These often lead to smuggling and black markets. The fourth problem is that economies insulated from foreign competition become less innovative and less efficient. On the other hand, competing in the export market increases a firm's efficiency and productivity.[13] The final and biggest problem with imposing trade restrictions is that other countries usually retaliate, thus shrinking the gains from trade.

Retaliation can set off still greater trade restrictions, leading to an outright trade war.

## 17-5 FINAL WORD

International trade arises from voluntary exchange among buyers and sellers pursuing their self-interest. Since 1950 world output has risen eightfold, while world trade has increased twentyfold. World trade offers many advantages to the trading countries: access to markets around the world, lower costs through economies of scale, a wider choice of products, the opportunity to utilize abundant resources, better access to information about markets and technology, improved quality honed by competitive pressure, reduced likelihood of war, and, most importantly, lower prices for consumers. Recent research suggests that access to higher quality goods may be one of the most significant gains from international trade, especially in developing countries such as India.[14]

This kiosk is the gateway to New York City's garment district, which continues to be severely affected by low-price competition from overseas markets.

13. David Atkin, Amit K. Khandelwal, and Adam Osman, "Exporting and Firm Performance: Evidence from a Randomized Trial," NBER Working Paper No. 20690 (November 2014); and Jan De Loecker, "Detecting Learning by Exporting," American Economic Journal: Microeconomics, 5 (August 2014): 1–21.

14. Gloria Sheu, "Price, Quality, and Variety: Measuring the Gains from Trade in Differentiated Products," *American Economic Journal: Applied Economics*, 6 (October 2014): 66–89.

Comparative advantage, specialization, and trade allow people to use their scarce resources efficiently to satisfy their unlimited wants.

Despite the clear gains from free trade, restrictions on international trade date back centuries, and pressure on public officials to impose trade restrictions continues today. Domestic producers (and their resource suppliers) benefit from trade restrictions in their markets because they can charge domestic consumers more. Trade restrictions insulate domestic producers from the rigors of global competition, in the process stifling innovation and leaving protected industries vulnerable to technological change from abroad. With trade quotas, the winners also include those who have secured the right to import goods at the world prices and sell them at the domestic prices. Consumers, who must pay higher prices for protected goods, suffer from trade restrictions, as do the domestic producers who import resources. Other losers include U.S. exporters, who face higher trade barriers as their foreign counterparts retaliate with their own trade restrictions.

Producers have a laser-like focus on trade legislation, but consumers remain largely oblivious. Consumers purchase thousands of different goods and thus have no special interest in the effects of trade policy on any particular good. Congress tends to support the group that makes the most noise, so trade restrictions often persist, despite the clear and widespread gains from freer trade.

## STUDY TOOLS 17

### READY TO STUDY? IN THE BOOK, YOU CAN:

☐ Work the Problems at the end of the chapter.

☐ Rip out the chapter review card for a handy summary of the chapter and key terms.

### ONLINE AT CENGAGEBRAIN.COM YOU CAN:

☐ Collect StudyBits while you read and study the chapter.

☐ Quiz yourself on key concepts.

☐ Prepare for tests with chapter flash cards as well as flash cards that you create.

☐ Watch videos to explore economics further.

# CHAPTER 17 PROBLEMS

*Your instructor can access the answers to these problems online at http://cengagebrain.com.*

## 17-1 Outline the gains from trade, and explain why countries might still decide to trade even if no country had a comparative advantage

1. *(Trade Without Comparative Advantage)* Even if neither country had a comparative advantage, why might these countries still experience gains from trade?

2. *(Comparative Advantage)* Suppose that each U.S. worker can produce 8 units of food or 2 units of clothing daily. In Fredonia, which has the same number of workers, each worker can produce 7 units of food or 1 unit of clothing daily. Why does the United States have an absolute advantage in both goods? Which country enjoys a comparative advantage in food? Why?

3. *(Comparative Advantage)* The consumption possibilities frontiers shown by the blue lines in the following exhibit assume terms of trade of 1 unit of clothing for 1 unit of food. What would the consumption possibilities frontiers look like if the terms of trade were 1 unit of clothing for 2 units of food?

**Production (and Consumption) Possibility Frontiers with Trade (millions of units per day)**

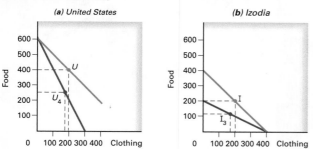

4. *(Reasons for International Specialization)* What determines which goods a country should produce and export?

## 17-2 Explain how trade restrictions harm an economy, and why they persist

5. *(Import Quotas)* How low must a quota be to have an impact on trade? Using a demand-and-supply diagram, illustrate and explain the net welfare loss from imposing such a quota. Under what circumstances would the net welfare loss from an import quota exceed the net welfare loss from an equivalent tariff (one that results in the same price and import level as the quota)?

6. *(Trade Restrictions)* Suppose that the world price for steel is below the U.S. domestic price, but the government requires that all steel used in the United States be domestically produced.
   a. Use a diagram like the one that follows to show the gains and losses from such a policy.
   b. How could you estimate the net welfare loss (deadweight loss) from such a diagram?
   c. What response to such a policy would you expect from industries (like automobile producers) that use U.S. steel?
   d. What government revenues are generated by this policy?

**Effect of a Tariff**

**Effect of a Quota**

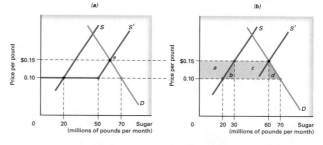

7. *(Trade Restrictions)* The previous three graphs show net losses to the economy of a country that imposes tariffs or quotas on imported sugar. What kinds of gains and losses would occur in the economies of countries that export sugar?

## 17-3 Identify international efforts to reduce trade barriers

8. *(The World Trade Organization)* What is the World Trade Organization (WTO) and how does it help foster multilateral trade? (Check the WTO Website at http://www.wto.org/.)

## 17-4 Summarize five arguments often used to justify trade restrictions, and describe some unintended consequences of protecting certain industries from international competition

9. *(Arguments for Trade Restrictions)* Explain the national defense, declining industries, and infant industry arguments for protecting a domestic industry from international competition.

10. *(Arguments for Trade Restrictions)* Firms hurt by lower priced imports typically argue that restricting trade will save U.S. jobs. What's wrong with this argument? Are there ever any reasons to support such trade restrictions?

# 18 | International Finance

Paul Maguire/Shutterstock.com

## LEARNING OUTCOMES

After studying this chapter, you will be able to...

18-1 Summarize the major accounts in the balance of trade, and explain how they balance out

18-2 Describe how the foreign exchange rate is determined using demand and supply curves and explain the shapes of the curves

18-3 Describe the purchasing power parity theory

18-4 Trace the evolution of exchange rate regimes from the gold standard to the current system

After finishing this chapter go to **PAGE 337** for **STUDY TOOLS**

**Topics discussed in Chapter 18 include**

- Balance of payments
- Trade deficits and surpluses
- Foreign exchange markets
- Arbitrageurs and speculators
- Purchasing power parity
- Flexible exchange rates
- Fixed exchange rates
- International monetary system
- Bretton Woods agreement
- Managed float

I f Starbucks wants to buy 1,000 espresso machines from the German manufacturer Krups, it will be quoted a price in euros. Suppose the machines cost a total of €1 million (euros). How much is that in dollars? The dollar cost will depend on the exchange rate. When trade takes place across international borders, two currencies are usually involved. Supporting the flows of goods and services are flows of currencies that fund international transactions. The exchange rate between currencies—the price of one in terms of the other—is how the price of a product in one country translates into the price facing a buyer in another country. Cross-border trade therefore depends on the exchange rate.

> **"Why does a nation try to influence the exchange value of its currency?"**

## 18-1 BALANCE OF PAYMENTS

A country's gross domestic product, or GDP, measures the economy's income and output during a given period, usually quarterly and yearly. To account for dealings abroad, countries must also keep track of international transactions. A country's *balance of payments*, as introduced in Chapter 3, summarizes all economic transactions during a given period between residents of that country and residents of other countries. *Residents* include people, firms, organizations, and governments.

### 18-1a International Economic Transactions

The balance of payments measures economic transactions between a country and the rest of the world, whether these transactions involve goods and services, real and financial assets, or transfer payments. The balance of payments measures a *flow* of transactions during a particular period. Some transactions do not involve actual payments. For example, if *Time* magazine ships a new printing press to its Australian subsidiary, no payment is made, yet an economic transaction involving another country has occurred. Similarly, if CARE sends food to Africa or the Pentagon provides military assistance to the Middle East, these transactions must be captured in the balance of payments. So remember, although we speak of the *balance of payments*, a more descriptive phrase would be the *balance-of-economic transactions*.

Balance-of-payments accounts are maintained according to the principles of *double-entry bookkeeping*. Some entries are called *credits*, and others are called

> **"If merchandise exports exceed merchandise imports, the trade balance is in *surplus*. If merchandise imports exceed merchandise exports, the trade balance is in *deficit*."**

*debits.* As you will see, the balance of payments consists of several individual accounts. An individual account may not balance, but a deficit in one or more accounts must be offset by a net surplus in the other accounts. Because total credits must equal total debits, there is a *balance* of payments—hence, the name. During a given period, such as a year, the inflow of receipts from the rest of the world, which are entered as credits, must equal the outflow of payments to the rest of the world, which are entered as debits.

The first of two major categories in the balance of payments is the current account. The current account records *current* flows of funds into and out of the country, including imports and exports of goods and services, net income earned by U.S. residents from foreign assets, and net transfer payments from abroad. These are discussed in turn.

> **"The current account records *current* flows of funds into and out of the country, including imports and exports of goods and services, net income earned by U.S. residents from foreign assets, and net transfer payments from abroad."**

## 18-1b The Merchandise Trade Balance

The *merchandise trade balance,* a term introduced in Chapter 3, equals the value of merchandise exports minus the value of merchandise imports. The merchandise account reflects trade in goods, or tangible products (stuff you can put in a box), like French wine or U.S. computers, and is often referred to simply as the *trade balance.* Revenue from U.S. merchandise exports is a credit in the U.S. balance-of-payments account because U.S. residents get *paid* for the exported goods. Spending on U.S. merchandise imports is a debit in the balance-of-payments account because U.S. residents *pay* foreigners for imported goods.

If merchandise exports exceed merchandise imports, the trade balance is in *surplus.* If merchandise imports exceed merchandise exports, the trade balance is in *deficit.* The merchandise trade balance, which is reported monthly, influences foreign exchange markets, the stock market, and other financial markets. The trade balance depends on a variety of factors, including the relative strength and competitiveness of the domestic economy compared with other economies and the relative value of the domestic currency compared with other currencies. Strong economies with growing incomes tend to buy more of everything, including imports.

U.S. merchandise trade since 1960 is depicted in Exhibit 1, where exports, the blue line, and imports, the red line, are expressed as a percentage of GDP. During the 1960s, exports exceeded imports, and the resulting trade surpluses are shaded blue. Since 1976, imports have exceeded exports, and the resulting trade deficits are shaded pink. Trade deficits as a percentage of GDP increased from 1.3 percent in 1991 to a peak of 6.3 percent in 2006. The Great Recession of 2007–2009 slowed U.S. imports more than U.S. exports, so by 2009 the trade deficit relative to GDP fell to 3.6 percent, the lowest in more than a decade. Since then, merchandise imports increased more than merchandise exports, so the U.S. trade deficit rose to $735.8 billion in 2014, or 4.2 percent relative to GDP that year.

Because per capita income in the United States ranks among the highest in the world, the United States imports more goods from each of the world's major economies than it exports to them. Exhibit 2 shows the U.S. merchandise trade deficit with major economies or regions of the world in 2014. The $343 billion trade deficit with China was by far the largest, more than double that of the combined 28 countries of the European Union. The Chinese spent $125 billion on U.S. goods in 2014, but sold $468 billion to Americans, or about $3,900 per U.S. household. So China sold America nearly four times more than it bought from America. Chances are, most of the utensils in your kitchen are from China; most toys are also Chinese made. China alone accounted for nearly half the U.S. merchandise trade deficit in 2014. The United States has a trade surplus with only a few major economies.

## 18-1c Balance on Goods and Services

The merchandise trade balance focuses on the flow of goods, but services are also traded internationally. *Services* are intangibles, such as transportation, insurance,

## Exhibit 1

### U.S. Imports Have Topped Exports Since 1976, but Both Dropped During the Great Recession

Note that since 1980, merchandise exports have remained in the range of about 5 percent to 10 percent of GDP. But merchandise imports have trended up from about 9 percent in 1980 to about 15 percent in 2008, before dropping off to 11 percent in 2009, the year following the financial crisis. Imports were back up to about 14 percent relative to GDP by 2011 and have remained there.

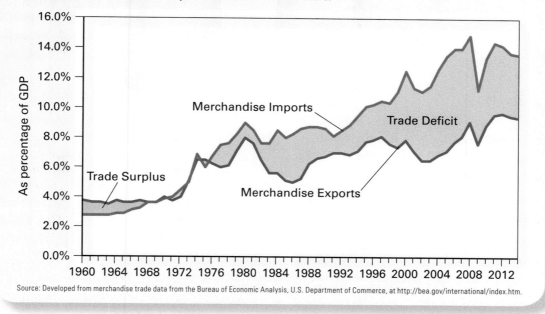

Source: Developed from merchandise trade data from the Bureau of Economic Analysis, U.S. Department of Commerce, at http://bea.gov/international/index.htm.

banking, education, consulting, and tourism. Services are often called "invisibles" because they are not tangible. The value of U.S. service exports, as when an Irish tourist visits New York City, is listed as a credit in the U.S. balance-of-payments account because U.S. residents get paid for these services. The value of U.S. service imports, like computer programming outsourced to India, is listed as a debit in the balance-of-payments account because U.S. residents must pay for the imported services.

Because the United States exports more services than it imports, services have been in surplus for the last three decades. In 2014, the surplus in the services account totaled $231.1 billion. The **balance on goods and services** is the export value of goods and services minus the import value of goods and services, or *net exports*, a component of GDP. Because deficits in the merchandise trade account dominated surpluses in the services account, net exports of goods and services have been in deficit for decades. That deficit in 2014 totaled $504.7 billion.

### 18-1d  Net Investment Income

U.S. residents earn investment income, such as interest and dividends, from foreign assets. This investment

income flows to the United States and is a credit in the balance-of-payments account. On the other side, foreigners earn investment income on their U.S. assets, and this payment flows out of the United States. This outflow is a debit in the balance-of-payments account. **Net investment income from abroad** is U.S. investment earnings from foreign assets minus foreigners' earnings from their U.S. assets. This figure bounces around from year to year between a positive and a negative number. In 2014, net investment income from foreign holdings totaled $217.9 billion.

### 18-1e  Unilateral Transfers and the Current Account Balance

Unilateral transfers consist of government transfers to foreign residents, foreign aid, money workers send to families abroad, personal gifts to friends and relatives abroad,

**balance on goods and services** The portion of a country's balance-of-payments account that measures the value of a country's exports of goods and services minus the value of its imports of goods and services

**net investment income from abroad** Investment earnings by U.S. residents from their foreign assets minus investment earnings by foreigners from their assets in the United States

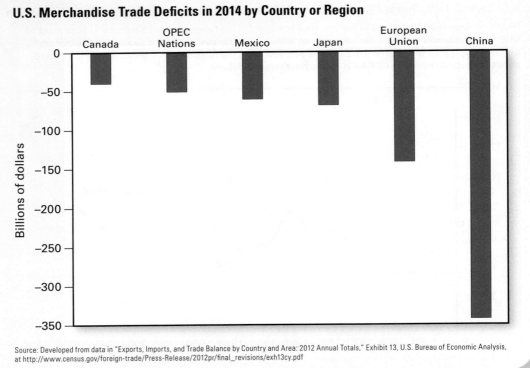

*Exhibit 2*

**U.S. Merchandise Trade Deficits in 2014 by Country or Region**

Source: Developed from data in "Exports, Imports, and Trade Balance by Country and Area: 2012 Annual Totals," Exhibit 13, U.S. Bureau of Economic Analysis, at http://www.census.gov/foreign-trade/Press-Release/2012pr/final_revisions/exh13cy.pdf

contributions of foreign charities, and the like. Money sent out of the country is a debit in the balance-of-payments account. For example, immigrants in the United States often send money to families back home. **Net unilateral transfers abroad** equal the unilateral transfers received from abroad by U.S. residents minus unilateral transfers sent abroad by U.S. residents. U.S. net unilateral transfers have been negative since World War II, except for 1991, when the U.S. government received sizable transfers from foreign governments to help pay their share of the Persian Gulf War. In 2014, net unilateral transfers were a negative $123.8 billion, with private transfers accounting for most of that (government grants and transfer payments made up the rest). Net unilateral transfers abroad averaged about $1,000 per U.S. household.

The United States places few restrictions on money sent out of the country. Other countries, particularly developing countries, strictly limit the amount that may be sent abroad. More generally, many developing countries, such as China, restrict the convertibility of their currency into other currencies.

When we add net unilateral transfers to net exports of goods and services and net income from assets owned abroad, we get the **balance on current account**, which is reported quarterly. Thus, *the current account includes all international transactions in currently produced goods and services, net income from foreign assets, and net unilateral transfers.* It can be negative, reflecting a current account deficit; positive, reflecting a current account surplus; or zero. In 2014, the current account deficit was $410.6 billion.

## 18-1f The Financial Account

The current account records international transactions in goods, services, asset income, and unilateral transfers. The **financial account** records international purchases of assets, including financial assets, such as stocks, bonds, and bank balances, and real assets such as land, housing, factories, and other physical assets. For example, U.S.

**net unilateral transfers abroad** The unilateral transfers (gifts and grants) received from abroad by U.S. residents minus the unilateral transfers U.S. residents send abroad

**balance on current account** The portion of the balance-of-payments account that measures a country's balance on goods and services, net investment income from abroad, plus net unilateral transfers abroad

**financial account** The record of a country's international transactions involving purchases and sales of financial and real assets residents purchase foreign securities to earn a higher return and to diversify their investments. Money flows out when Americans buy foreign assets or build factories overseas. Money flows in when foreigners buy U.S. assets or build factories here. The international purchase or sale of assets is recorded in the financial account.

Between 1917 and 1982, the United States ran a financial account deficit, meaning that U.S. residents purchased more foreign assets than foreigners purchased U.S. assets. The net income from these foreign assets improved our current account balance. But in 1983, for the first time in 65 years, foreigners bought more U.S. assets than U.S. residents purchased abroad. Since 1983, foreigners have continued to buy more U.S. assets most years than the other way around, meaning there has usually been a surplus in the financial account. This is not as bad as it sounds, because foreign purchases of assets in the United States add to America's productive capacity and promote employment and labor productivity here. But any income from these assets flows to their foreign owners, not to Americans. Remember, the investment income from these assets shows up in the current account. Foreigners find America an attractive place to invest because U.S. capital markets are the deepest and most liquid in the world. In 2014, the financial account surplus was $141.6 billion.

## 18-1g Trade Deficits and Surpluses

Nations, like households, operate under a budget constraint. Spending cannot exceed income plus cash on hand and borrowed funds. We have distinguished between *current* transactions, which include exports, imports, asset income, and unilateral transfers, and *financial* transactions, which reflect net purchases of foreign real and financial assets. Any surplus or deficit in one account must be offset by deficits or surpluses in other balance-of-payments accounts.

Exhibit 3 presents the U.S. balance-of-payments statement for 2014. All transactions requiring payments from foreigners to U.S. residents are entered as credits, indicated by a plus sign (+), because they result in an inflow of funds from foreign residents to U.S. residents. All transactions requiring payments to foreigners from U.S. residents are entered as debits, indicated by a minus

> **"Money flows out when Americans buy foreign assets or build factories overseas. Money flows in when foreigners buy U.S. assets or build factories here."**

sign (−), because they result in an outflow of funds from U.S. residents to foreign residents. As you can see, a surplus in the financial account of $141.6 billion was more than offset by a current account deficit of $410.6 billion. A *statistical discrepancy* is required to balance the payments, and that come to $269.0 billion in 2014. Think of the statistical discrepancy as the official "fudge factor" that (1) measures the error in the balance of payments and (2) satisfies the double-entry bookkeeping requirement that total debits must equal total credits. The statistical discrepancy was large in 2014, because the global financial crisis created unusual gyrations that continued to affect international accounts.

*Foreign exchange* is the currency of another country needed to carry out international transactions. A country runs a deficit in its current account when the amount of foreign exchange received from exports, from foreign assets, and from unilateral transfers falls short of the

*Exhibit 3*

### U.S. Balance of Payments for 2014 (billions of dollars)

| Current Account | |
|---|---|
| 1. Merchandise exports | +1,635.1 |
| 2. Merchandise imports | −2,370.9 |
| 3. Merchandise trade balance (1 + 2) | −735.8 |
| 4. Service exports | +709.4 |
| 5. Service imports | −478.3 |
| 6. Goods and services balance (3 + 4 + 5) | −504.7 |
| 7. Net investment income from abroad | +217.9 |
| 8. Net unilateral transfers | −123.8 |
| 9. Current account balance (6 + 7 + 8) | −410.6 |
| **Financial Account** | |
| 10. Change in U.S. owned assets abroad | −820.5 |
| 11. Change in foreign-owned assets in United States | +962.1 |
| 12. Financial account balance (10 + 11) | +141.6 |
| 13. Statistical discrepancy | +269.0 |
| **TOTAL (9 + 12 + 13)** | **0.0** |

Source: Computed from estimates by the Bureau of Economic Analysis, U.S. Department of Commerce at http://bea.gov/international/index.htm.

amount needed to pay for imports, pay foreign holders of U.S. assets, and make unilateral transfers. If the current account is in deficit, the necessary foreign exchange must come from a net inflow in the financial account. Such an inflow in the financial account could stem from borrowing from foreigners, selling domestic stocks and bonds to foreigners, selling a steel plant in Pittsburgh or a ski lodge in Aspen to foreigners, and so forth.

If a country runs a current account surplus, the foreign exchange received from exports, from foreign assets, and from unilateral transfers from abroad exceeds the amount needed to pay for imports, to pay foreign holders of U.S. assets, and to make unilateral transfers abroad. If the current account is in surplus, this excess foreign exchange results in a net outflow in the financial account through lending abroad, buying foreign stocks and bonds, buying a shoe plant in Italy or a villa on the French Riviera, and so forth.

When all transactions are considered, accounts must balance. The statistical discrepancy ensures that, in the aggregate, accounts sum to zero. A deficit in a particular account should not necessarily be viewed as a source of concern, nor should a surplus be a source of satisfaction. The deficit in the U.S. current account in recent years has usually been offset by a financial account surplus. As a result, foreigners have been acquiring more claims on U.S. assets.

## 18-2 FOREIGN EXCHANGE RATES AND MARKETS

Now that you have some idea about international flows, we can take a closer look at the forces that determine the underlying value of the currencies involved. Let's begin by looking at exchange rates and the market for foreign exchange.

### 18-2a Foreign Exchange

Foreign exchange, recall, is foreign money needed to carry out international transactions. The **exchange rate** is the cost measured in one country's currency of one unit of another country's currency. Exchange rates are determined by the interaction of the households, firms, private financial institutions, governments, and central banks that buy and sell foreign exchange. The exchange rate fluctuates to equate the quantity of foreign exchange

**exchange rate** The cost, measured in one country's currency, of one unit of another country's currency

demanded with the quantity supplied. Typically, foreign exchange is made up of bank deposits denominated in the foreign currency. When foreign travel is involved, foreign exchange often consists of foreign paper money.

The foreign exchange market incorporates all the arrangements used to buy and sell foreign exchange. This market is not so much a physical place as a network of telephones and computers connecting financial centers all over the world. Perhaps you have seen pictures of foreign exchange traders in New York, Frankfurt, London, or Tokyo in front of computer screens amid a tangle of phone lines. The foreign exchange market is like an all-night diner—it never closes. A trading center is always open somewhere in the world.

We will consider the market for the euro in terms of the dollar. But first, a little more about the euro. For decades the nations of Western Europe tried to increase their economic cooperation and trade. These countries believed they would be more productive and more

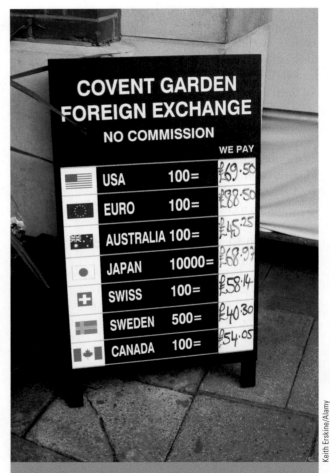

**This sign in London lists the prices of different foreign currencies in British Pounds. These prices can change daily or even several times a day!**

Keith Erskine/Alamy

competitive with the United States if they acted less like many separate economies and more like the 50 United States, with a single set of trade regulations and a single currency. Imagine the hassle involved if each of the 50 states had its own currency.

In 2002, euro notes and coins entered circulation in the 12 European countries adopting the common currency. The big advantage of a common currency is that Europeans no longer have to change money every time they cross a border or trade with another country in the group. Again, the inspiration for this is the United States, arguably the most successful economy in world history.

So the euro is the common currency of the *eurozone,* as the now 19-country region is usually called. The cost, or exchange rate, of the euro in terms of the dollar is the number of dollars required to purchase one euro. An increase in the number of dollars needed to purchase a euro indicates weakening, or **depreciation**, of the dollar. A decrease in the number of dollars needed to purchase a euro indicates strengthening, or **appreciation**, of the dollar. Put another way, a decrease in the number of euros needed to purchase a dollar is a depreciation of the dollar, and an increase in the number of euros needed to purchase a dollar is an appreciation of the dollar.

Because the exchange rate is usually a market price, it is determined by demand and supply: The equilibrium price is the one that equates quantity demanded with quantity supplied. To simplify the analysis, suppose that the United States and the eurozone make up the entire world, so the demand and supply for euros in international finance is the demand and supply for foreign exchange from the U.S. perspective.

## 18-2b The Demand for Foreign Exchange

Whenever U.S. residents need euros, they must buy them in the foreign exchange market, which could include your local bank, paying for them with dollars. Exhibit 4 depicts a market for foreign exchange—in this case, euros. The horizontal axis shows the quantity

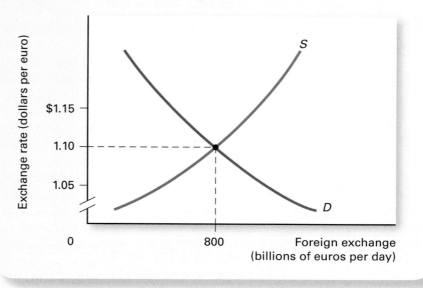

*Exhibit 4*

**The Foreign Exchange Market**

The fewer dollars needed to purchase one unit of foreign exchange, the lower the price of foreign goods and the greater the quantity of foreign goods demanded. Thus, the demand curve for foreign exchange slopes downward. An increase in the exchange rate makes U.S. products cheaper for foreigners. This implies an increase in the quantity of foreign exchange supplied. The supply curve of foreign exchange slopes upward.

of foreign exchange, measured here in billions of euros per day. The vertical axis shows the price per unit of foreign exchange, measured here in dollars per euro. The demand curve *D* for foreign exchange shows the inverse relationship between the dollar price of the euro and the quantity of euros demanded. Assumed constant along the demand curve are the incomes and preferences of U.S. consumers, expected inflation in the United States and in the eurozone, the euro price of goods in the eurozone, and interest rates in the United States and in the eurozone. U.S. residents have many reasons for demanding foreign exchange, but in the aggregate, the lower the dollar price of foreign exchange, other things constant, the greater the quantity of foreign exchange demanded.

A drop in the dollar price of foreign exchange, in this case the euro, means that fewer dollars are needed to purchase each euro, so the dollar prices of eurozone products (like German cars, Italian shoes, tickets to the

**currency depreciation**
With respect to the dollar, an increase in the number of dollars needed to purchase one unit of foreign exchange in a flexible rate system

**currency appreciation**
With respect to the dollar, a decrease in the number of dollars needed to purchase one unit of foreign exchange in a flexible rate system

Louvre, and eurozone securities) become cheaper. The cheaper it is to buy euros, the lower the dollar price of eurozone products to U.S. residents, so the greater the quantity of euros demanded by U.S. residents, other things remain constant. For example, a cheap enough euro might persuade you to tour Rome, climb the Austrian Alps, wander the museumsw of Paris, or crawl the pubs of Dublin.

> **"The cheaper it is to buy euros, the lower the dollar price of eurozone products to U.S. residents, so the greater the quantity of euros demanded by U.S. residents, other things remain constant."**

## 18-2c The Supply of Foreign Exchange

The supply of foreign exchange is generated by the desire of foreign residents to acquire dollars—that is, to exchange euros for dollars. Eurozone residents want dollars to buy U.S. goods and services, acquire U.S. assets, make loans in dollars, or send dollars to their U.S. friends and relatives. Euros are supplied in the foreign exchange market to acquire the dollars people want. An increase in the dollar-per-euro exchange rate, other things constant, makes U.S. products cheaper for eurozone residents because foreign residents need fewer euros to get the same number of dollars. For example, suppose a Dell computer sells for $1,155. If the exchange rate is $1.05 per euro, that computer costs 1,100 euros; if the exchange rate is $1.10 per euro, it costs only 1,050 euros. The number of Dell computers demanded in the eurozone increases as the dollar-per-euro exchange rate increases, other things constant, so more euros will be supplied on the foreign exchange market to buy dollars.

The positive relationship between the dollar-per-euro exchange rate and the quantity of euros supplied on the foreign exchange market is expressed in Exhibit 4 by the upward-sloping supply curve for foreign exchange

(again, euros in our example). The supply curve assumes that other things remain constant, including eurozone incomes and tastes, expectations about inflation in the eurozone and in the United States, and interest rates in the eurozone and in the United States.

## 18-2d The Foreign Exchange Rate

Exhibit 4 brings together the demand and supply for foreign exchange to determine the exchange rate. At a rate of $1.10 per euro, the quantity of euros demanded equals the quantity supplied—in our example, 800 billion euros per day. Once achieved, this equilibrium rate will hold until a change occurs in one of the factors that affect supply or demand. If the exchange rate is allowed to adjust freely, or to *float*, in response to market forces, the market will clear continually, as the quantities of foreign exchange demanded and supplied are equated.

What if the initial equilibrium is upset by a change in one of the underlying forces that affect demand or supply? For example, suppose higher U.S. incomes increase American demand for all normal goods, including those from the eurozone. This shifts the U.S. demand curve for foreign exchange to the right, as Americans buy more Italian marble, Dutch chocolate, German automobiles, Parisian vacations, and eurozone securities.

This increased demand for euros is shown in Exhibit 5 by a rightward shift of the demand curve for foreign exchange. The demand increase from $D$ to $D'$ leads to an increase in the exchange rate per euro from $1.10 to $1.12. Thus, the euro increases in value, or appreciates, while the dollar falls in value, or depreciates. An increase in U.S. income should not

> **"An increase in the dollar-per-euro exchange rate, other things constant, makes U.S. products cheaper for foreigners because foreign residents need fewer euros to get the same number of dollars."**

If the exchange rate is allowed to adjust freely, or to float, in response to market forces, the market will clear continually, as the quantities of foreign exchange demanded and supplied are equated.

Don Farrall/Getty Images

*Exhibit 5*

**Effect on the Foreign Exchange Market of an Increased Demand for Euros**

The intersection of the demand curve for foreign exchange, *D*, and the supply curve for foreign exchange, *S*, determines the exchange rate. At an exchange rate of $1.10 per euro, the quantity of euros demanded equals the quantity supplied. An increase in the demand for euros from *D* to *D′* increases the exchange rate from $1.10 to $1.12 per euro.

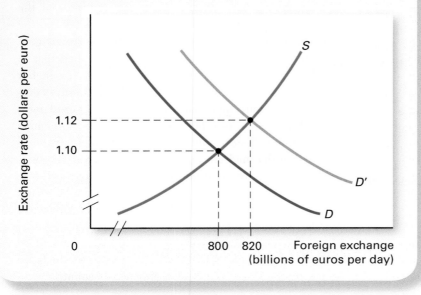

affect the euro supply curve, though it does increase the *quantity of euros supplied*. The higher exchange value of the euro prompts those in the eurozone to buy more American products and assets, which are now cheaper in terms of the euro.

**TO REVIEW:** Any increase in the demand for foreign exchange or any decrease in its supply, other things constant, increases the number of dollars required to purchase one unit of foreign exchange, which is a depreciation of the dollar. On the other hand, any decrease in the demand for foreign exchange or any increase in its supply, other things constant, reduces the number of dollars required to purchase one unit of foreign exchange, which is an appreciation of the dollar.

## 18-3 OTHER FACTORS INFLUENCING FOREIGN EXCHANGE MARKETS

So far, the market for foreign exchange has been presented just like any other market: Demand and supply come together to determine the equilibrium exchange rate, or price of foreign exchange. Simple enough, but the market for foreign exchange is complicated by the types of actors in this market and by the types of regulations and restrictions involved. In this section, we look at how these other factors shape this market.

### 18-3a Arbitrageurs and Speculators

Exchange rates between two currencies are nearly identical at any given time in markets around the world. For example, the dollar price of a euro is usually the same in New York, Frankfurt, Tokyo, London, Zurich, Hong Kong, Istanbul, and other financial centers. **Arbitrageurs**—dealers who take advantage of tiny differences in exchange rates across markets by buying low and selling high—ensure this equality. For example, if one euro

> **arbitrageur** Someone who takes advantage of tiny differences in the exchange rate across markets by simultaneously purchasing currency in one market and selling it in another market

costs $1.09 in New York but $1.10 in Frankfurt, an arbitrageur could buy, say, $1,000,000 worth of euros in New York and at the same time sell them in Frankfurt for $1,009,174, thereby earning $9,174 minus the transaction costs of the trades.

Because an arbitrageur buys and sells simultaneously, little risk is involved. In our example, the arbitrageur increased the demand for euros in New York and increased the supply of euros in Frankfurt. These actions increased the dollar price of euros in New York and decreased it in Frankfurt, thereby squeezing down the difference in exchange rates. Note that arbitrage opportunities are short lived; most are available for less than a second. High speed computers act on such opportunities instantly.[1] Exchange rates may still change because of market forces, but they tend to change in all markets simultaneously.

The demand and supply of foreign exchange arises from many sources—from importers and exporters, investors in foreign assets, central banks, tourists, arbitrageurs, and speculators. **Speculators** buy or sell foreign exchange in hopes of profiting by trading the currency at a more favorable exchange rate later. By taking risks, speculators aim to profit from market fluctuations—they try to buy low and sell high. In contrast, arbitrageurs take less risk, because they *simultaneously* buy currency in one market and sell it in another.

Finally, people in countries suffering from economic and political turmoil, such as occurred in Russia, Indonesia, the Philippines, and Zimbabwe, may buy *hard* currency as a hedge against the depreciation and instability of their own currencies. The dollar has long been accepted as an international medium of exchange. It is also the currency of choice in the world markets for oil and illegal drugs. But the euro eventually may challenge that dominance, in part because the largest euro denomination, the 500-euro note, is worth more than five times the largest U.S. denomination, the $100 note. So it would be about five times easier to smuggle euro notes than U.S. notes of equal value. Still, fiscal problems in some eurozone nations such as Greece and Spain have taken some of the shine off the euro.

**speculator** Someone who buys or sells foreign exchange in hopes of profiting from fluctuations in the exchange rate over time

**purchasing power parity theory** The idea that the exchange rate between two countries will adjust in the long run to equalize the cost of a basket of internationally traded goods

1. Takatoshi Ito et al. "Free Lunch: Arbitrage Opportunities in the Foreign Exchange Markets," NBER Working Paper No. 18541 (November 2012).

## 18-3b Purchasing Power Parity

As long as trade across borders is unrestricted and as long as exchange rates are allowed to adjust freely, the **purchasing power parity (PPP) theory** predicts that the exchange rate between two currencies will adjust in the long run to equalize the cost across countries of an internationally traded basket of goods. *A given basket of internationally traded goods should therefore sell for about the same around the world (except for differences reflecting transportation costs and the like).* Suppose a basket of internationally traded goods that sells for $11,000 in the United States sells for €10,000 in the eurozone. According to the purchasing power parity theory, the equilibrium exchange rate should be $1.10 per euro. If this were not the case—if the exchange rate were, say, $1.05 per euro—then you could exchange $10,500 for €10,000, with which you buy the basket of commodities in the eurozone. You could then sell that basket of goods in the States for $11,000, yielding you a profit of $500 minus any transaction costs. Selling dollars and buying euros will also drive up the dollar price of euros.

> **"A given basket of internationally traded goods should sell for about the same around the world."**

The purchasing power parity theory is more of a long-run predictor than a day-to-day indicator of the relationship between changes in the price level and the exchange rate. For example, a country's currency generally appreciates when inflation is lower than that of other countries and depreciates when inflation is higher compared to other countries. Likewise, a country's currency generally appreciates when its real interest rates are higher than in other countries, because foreigners are more willing to buy and hold investments denominated in that high-interest currency. As a case in point, the dollar appreciated during the first half of the 1980s, when real U.S. interest rates were relatively high, and depreciated during 2002 to 2004, when real U.S. interest rates were relatively low.

Because of trade barriers, central bank intervention in exchange markets, and the fact that many products are not traded or are not comparable across countries, the purchasing power parity theory usually does not explain exchange rates at a particular point in time that well. For example, if you went shopping in Switzerland tomorrow, you would soon notice a dollar does not buy as much there as it does in the United States.

## 18-3c Flexible Exchange Rates

For the most part, we have been discussing **flexible exchange rates**, which are determined by demand and supply. Flexible, or *floating,* exchange rates adjust continually to the myriad forces that buffet foreign exchange markets. Consider how the exchange rate is linked to the balance-of-payments accounts. Debit entries in the current or financial accounts increase the demand for foreign exchange, resulting in a depreciation of the dollar. Credit entries in these accounts increase the supply of foreign exchange, resulting in an appreciation of the dollar.

## 18-3d Fixed Exchange Rates

When exchange rates are flexible, governments usually have little direct role in foreign exchange markets. But if governments try to set exchange rates, active and ongoing central bank intervention is often necessary to establish and maintain these **fixed exchange rates**. Suppose the European Central Bank selects what it thinks is an appropriate rate of exchange between the dollar and the euro. It attempts to *fix,* or to *peg,* the exchange rate within a narrow band around the particular value selected. If the euro threatens to climb above the maximum acceptable exchange rate, monetary authorities must sell euros and buy dollars, thereby keeping the dollar price of the euro down. Conversely, if the euro threatens to drop below the minimum acceptable exchange rate, monetary authorities must sell dollars and buy euros. This increased demand for the euro will keep its value up relative to the dollar. Through such intervention in the foreign exchange market, monetary authorities try to stabilize the exchange rate, keeping it within the specified band.

If monetary officials must keep selling foreign exchange to keep the value of their domestic currency from falling, they risk running out of foreign exchange reserves. Faced with this threat, the government has several options for eliminating the exchange rate disequilibrium. First, the pegged exchange rate can be increased, meaning that foreign currency costs more dollars. This is a **devaluation** of the dollar. (A decrease in the pegged exchange rate is called a **revaluation**.) Second, the government can reduce the domestic demand for foreign exchange directly by imposing restrictions on imports or on financial outflows. Many developing countries do

this. Third, the government can adopt policies to slow the domestic economy, increase interest rates, or reduce inflation relative to that of the country's trading partners, thereby indirectly decreasing the demand for foreign exchange and increasing the supply of foreign exchange. Several Asian economies, such as South Korea and Indonesia, pursued such policies to stabilize their currencies. Finally, the government can allow the disequilibrium to persist and ration the available foreign reserves through some form of foreign exchange control.

This concludes our introduction to the theories of international finance. Let's examine international finance in practice.

## 18-4 INTERNATIONAL MONETARY SYSTEM

From 1879 to 1914, the international monetary system operated under a **gold standard**, whereby the major currencies were convertible into gold at a fixed rate. For example, the U.S. dollar could be redeemed at the U.S. Treasury for one-twentieth of an ounce of gold. The British pound could be redeemed at the British Exchequer, or treasury, for one-fourth of an ounce of gold. Because each British pound could buy five times as much gold as each dollar, one British pound exchanged for $5.

The gold standard provided a predictable exchange rate, one that did not vary as long as currencies could be redeemed for gold at the official rate. But the money supply in each country was determined in part by the flow of gold among countries, so each country's monetary policy was influenced by the supply of gold. A balance-of-payments deficit resulted in a loss of gold, which theoretically caused a country's money supply to shrink. A balance-of-payments surplus resulted in an influx of gold, which theoretically caused a country's money supply to expand. The supply of money throughout the

**flexible exchange rate**
Rate determined in foreign exchange markets by the forces of demand and supply without government intervention

**fixed exchange rate**
Rate of exchange between currencies pegged within a narrow range and maintained by the central bank's ongoing purchases and sales of currencies

**currency devaluation**
An increase in the official pegged price of foreign exchange in terms of the domestic currency

**currency revaluation**
A reduction in the official pegged price of foreign exchange in terms of the domestic currency

**gold standard** An arrangement whereby the currencies of most countries were convertible into gold at a fixed rate world also depended on the vagaries of gold discoveries. When gold production did not keep pace with the growth in economic activity, the price level dropped. When gold production exceeded the growth in economic activity, the price level rose. For example, gold discoveries in Alaska and South Africa in the late 1890s expanded the U.S. money supply, leading to inflation.

## 18-4a The Bretton Woods Agreement

During World War I, many countries could no longer convert their currencies into gold, and the gold standard eventually collapsed, disrupting international trade during the 1920s and 1930s. Once an Allied victory in World War II appeared certain, the Allies met in Bretton Woods, New Hampshire, in July 1944 to formulate a new international monetary system. Because the United States had a strong economy and was not ravaged by the war, the dollar was selected as the key reserve currency in the new international monetary system. All exchange rates were fixed in terms of the dollar, and the United States, which held most of the world's gold reserves, stood ready to convert foreign holdings of dollars into gold at a rate of $35 per ounce. Even though the rate that dollars could be exchanged for gold was fixed by the Bretton Woods agreement, *other* countries could adjust *their* exchange rates relative to the U.S. dollar if they found a chronic disequilibrium in their balance of payments—that is, if a country faced a large and persistent deficit or surplus. In short, America's promise to redeem foreign holdings of U.S. dollars for a fixed amount of gold anchored the international monetary system.

**International Monetary Fund** An international organization that establishes rules for maintaining the international monetary system and makes loans to countries with temporary balance-of-payments problems

Under the Bretton Woods agreement, U.S. dollars could be traded in for gold at a price of $35 per ounce.

© istockphoto.com/mathieukor

The Bretton Woods agreement also created the **International Monetary Fund (IMF)** to set rules for maintaining the international monetary system, to standardize financial reporting for international trade, and to make loans to countries with temporary balance-of-payments problems. The IMF lends a revolving fund of about $400 billion to economies in need of reserves. Headquartered in Washington, D.C., the IMF has about 190 member countries and a staff of 2,600 drawn from around the world (half the staff are economists).

## 18-4b Demise of the Bretton Woods System

During the latter part of the 1960s, inflation increased in the United States more than in other countries. Because of U.S. inflation, the dollar had become *overvalued* at the official exchange rate, meaning that the gold value of the dollar exceeded the exchange value of the dollar. In 1971, U.S. merchandise imports exceeded merchandise exports for the first time since World War II. Foreigners exchanged dollars for gold. To stem this gold outflow, the United States stopped exchanging gold for dollars, but this just made the dollar less attractive. In December 1971, the world's 10 richest countries met in Washington and devalued the dollar by 8 percent. They hoped this would put the dollar on firmer footing and would save the "dollar standard." With prices rising at different rates around the world, however, an international monetary system based on fixed exchange rates was doomed.

When the U.S. trade deficit tripled in 1972, it became clear that the dollar was still overvalued. In early 1973, the dollar was devalued another 10 percent, but this did not quiet foreign exchange markets. The dollar, for three decades the anchor of the international monetary system, suddenly looked vulnerable, and speculators began betting that the dollar would fall even more, so they sold dollars. Dollars were exchanged for German marks because the mark appeared to be the most stable currency. Bundesbank, Germany's central bank, tried to defend the dollar's official exchange rate by selling marks and buying dollars. Why didn't Germany want the mark to appreciate? Appreciation would make German goods more expensive abroad and foreign goods cheaper in Germany, thereby reducing German exports and increasing German imports. So the mark's appreciation would reduce German output and employment. But after selling $10 billion worth of marks to buy dollars, the Bundesbank gave up defending the dollar. As soon as the value of the dollar was allowed to float against the mark, the Bretton Woods system, already on shaky ground, collapsed.

## 18-4c The Current System: Managed Float

The Bretton Woods system has been replaced by a **managed float system**, which combines features of a freely floating exchange rate with sporadic intervention by central banks as a way of moderating exchange rate fluctuations among the world's major currencies. Most small countries, particularly developing countries, still peg their currencies to one of the major currencies (such as the U.S. dollar) or to a "basket" of major currencies. What's more, in developing countries, private international borrowing and lending are severely restricted; some governments allow residents to purchase foreign exchange only for certain purposes. In some countries, different exchange rates apply to different categories of transactions.

> **"An ideal exchange rate system is one that would foster international trade, lower inflation, and promote a more stable world economy."**

Critics of flexible exchange rates argue that they are inflationary, because they free monetary authorities to pursue expansionary policies; furthermore, flexible exchange rates have often been volatile. This volatility creates uncertainty and risk for importers and exporters, increasing the transaction costs of international trade. Furthermore, exchange rate volatility can lead to wrenching changes in the competitiveness of a country's export sector. These changes cause swings in employment, resulting in louder calls for import restrictions. For example, the exchange rate between the Japanese yen and the U.S. dollar has been relatively unstable, particularly because of international speculation.

Policy makers are always on the lookout for a system that will perform better than the current managed float system, with its fluctuating currency values. *Their ideal is a system that will foster international trade, lower inflation, and promote a more stable world economy.* International finance ministers have acknowledged that the world must find an international standard and establish greater exchange rate stability.

## 18-5 FINAL WORD

The United States is very much a part of the world economy, not only as one of the largest exporter nations but also as the largest importer nation. Although the dollar remains the unit of transaction in many international settlements—OPEC, for example, still prices crude oil in dollars—gyrations of exchange rates have made those involved in international finance wary of putting all their eggs in one basket. The international monetary system is now going through a difficult period as it gropes for a new source of stability more than four decades after the collapse of the Bretton Woods agreement.

**managed float system**
An exchange rate system that combines features of freely floating rates with sporadic intervention by central banks

## STUDY TOOLS 18

### READY TO STUDY? IN THE BOOK, YOU CAN:

☐ Work the Problems at the end of the chapter.

☐ Rip out the chapter review card for a handy summary of the chapter and key terms.

### ONLINE AT CENGAGEBRAIN.COM YOU CAN:

☐ Collect StudyBits while you read and study the chapter.

☐ Quiz yourself on key concepts.

☐ Prepare for tests with chapter flash cards as well as flash cards that you create.

☐ Watch videos to explore economics further.

# CHAPTER 18 PROBLEMS

*Your instructor can access the answers to these problems online at http://cengagebrain.com.*

## 18-1 Summarize the major accounts in the balance of trade, and explain how they balance out

1. *(Balance of Payments)* The following are hypothetical data for the U.S. balance of payments. Use the data to calculate each of the following:
   a. Merchandise trade balance
   b. Balance on goods and services
   c. Balance on current account
   d. Financial account balance
   e. Statistical discrepancy

   |  | Billions of Dollars |
   |---|---|
   | Merchandise exports | 350.0 |
   | Merchandise imports | 2,425.0 |
   | Service exports | 2,145 |
   | Service imports | 170 |
   | Net income and net transfers | 221.5 |
   | Change in U.S.-owned assets abroad | 245.0 |
   | Change in foreign-owned assets in U.S. | 100.0 |

2. *(Balance of Payments)* Explain where in the U.S. balance of payments an entry would be recorded for each of the following:
   a. A Hong Kong financier buys some U.S. corporate stock.
   b. A U.S. tourist in Paris buys some perfume to take home.
   c. A Japanese company sells machinery to a pineapple company in Hawaii.
   d. U.S. farmers gave food to starving children in Ethiopia.
   e. The U.S. Treasury sells a bond to a Saudi Arabian prince.
   f. A U.S. tourist flies to France on Air France.
   g. A U.S. company sells insurance to a foreign firm.

## 18-2 Describe how the foreign exchange rate is determined using demand and supply curves and explain the shapes of the curves

3. *(Determining the Exchange Rate)* Use these data to answer the following questions about the market for British pounds:

| Pound Price (in $) | Quantity Demanded (of pounds) | Quantity Supplied (of pounds) |
|---|---|---|
| $4.00 | 50 | 100 |
| 3.00 | 75 | 75 |
| 2.00 | 100 | 50 |

   a. Draw the demand and supply curves for pounds, and determine the equilibrium exchange rate (dollars per pound).
   b. Suppose that the supply of pounds doubles. Draw the new supply curve.
   c. What is the new equilibrium exchange rate?
   d. Has the dollar appreciated or depreciated?
   e. What happens to U.S. imports of British goods?

## 18-3 Describe the purchasing power parity theory

4. *(Purchasing Power Parity Theory)* What is the purchasing power parity theory. Is it a short-run or a long-run theory. Why may it not always work?

## 18-4 Trace the evolution of exchange rate regimes from the gold standard to the current system

5. *(Exchange Rate Regimes)* Briefly trace the exchange rate regimes beginning with the gold standard up to our current system.

6. *(Exchange Rates)* Discuss the differences between a flexible exchange rate and a fixed exchange rate. What measures can the government take to maintain fixed exchange rates?

7. *(The Current System: Managed Float)* What is a managed float? What are the disadvantages of freely floating exchange rates that led countries to the managed float system?

YOUR
FEEDBACK
MATTERS.

ww.cengage.com/4ltrpress

# 19 | Economic Development

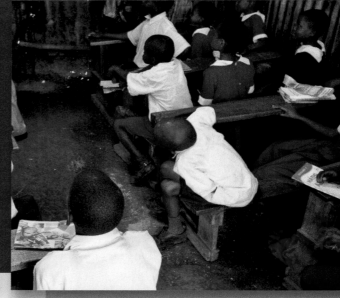

dbimages/Alamy

## LEARNING OUTCOMES

After studying this chapter, you will be able to...

**19-1** Besides income, identify ways that low-income economies differ from high-income economies

**19-2** Describe the factors that help make workers in high-income economies more productive than workers in other economies

**19-3** Explain how trade restrictions can slow economic development in poorer countries

**19-4** Outline some unintended consequences of foreign aid on economic development

After finishing this chapter go to **PAGE 358** for **STUDY TOOLS**

**Topics discussed in Chapter 19 include**

- Developing countries
- The key to development
- Privatization
- The poorest billion
- Foreign trade and development
- Foreign aid and development
- Import substitution vs. export promotion
- Economic convergence

- Why are some countries so poor while others are so rich?

- What determines the wealth of nations?

- Why do families in low-income countries have more children than those in higher-income countries?

- And how might programs that send subsidized food and used clothing to poor countries have the unintended consequence of retarding economic development there?

People around the world face the day under quite different circumstances. Even during a national recession, most Americans rise from a comfortable bed in a nice home, select the day's clothing from a wardrobe, choose from a variety of breakfast foods, and ride to school or to work in one of the family's personal automobiles. But some of the world's 7.4 billion people have little housing, clothing, or food. They have no automobile and no formal job. Their health is poor, as is their education. Many cannot read or write. The World Health Organization (WHO) estimates that a billion people need eyeglasses but can't afford them.

> **"Why are some countries so poor while others are so rich?"**

In this chapter, we sort out rich nations from poor ones and try to explain the difference. We discuss sources of economic development, weigh the pros and cons of foreign aid, and see whether poorer countries are closing the income gap with richer ones.

## 19-1 WORLDS APART

Differences in economic vitality among countries are huge. Countries are classified in a variety of ways based on their economic development. The yardstick most often used to compare living standards across nations is the amount an economy produces per capita, or *output per capita*. The World Bank, an economic development institution affiliated with the United Nations (UN), classifies economies based on income per capita. The measure begins with *gross national income (GNI)*, which is the market value of all goods and services produced by resources supplied by the countries' residents and firms, regardless of the location of the resources. For example, U.S. GNI includes profit earned by an American factory in Great Britain but excludes profits earned by a Japanese factory in Kentucky.

GNI measures both the value of output produced and the income that output generates. The World Bank estimates the GNI per capita, then adjusts figures across countries based on the purchasing power of that income in each country. Using this measure, the World Bank sorts countries around the world into three major groups: *high-income economies*, *middle-income economies*, and *low-income economies*.

Data on world population and world output are summarized in Exhibit 1. High-income economies in 2014 made up only 18 percent of the world's population, but accounted for 52 percent of world output. So high-income economies, *with less than one fifth of the world's population, produced more than half of the world's output*. Middle-income economies made up 70 percent of the world's population, but accounted for 46 percent of world output. And low-income countries made up 12 percent of the world's population, but account for just 2 percent of world output.

### 19-1a Developing and Industrial Economies

The low- and middle-income economies are usually referred to as **developing countries**. Most high-income economies are also referred to as **industrial market countries**. So low- and middle-income economies, what are called developing countries, made up 82 percent of the world's

**developing countries** Low-income and middle-income economies; most are also known as emerging market economies

**industrial market countries** Economically advanced capitalist countries of Europe, North America, Australia, New Zealand, and Japan; also known as developed countries and high-income economies

Exhibit 1

**Share of World Population and World Output From High-, Middle-, and Low-Income Economies as of 2014**

**(a)** Share of world population from high-, middle-, and low-income economies

**(b)** Share of world output from high-, middle-, and low-income economies

Source: Based on population and output estimated from the World Bank's *World Development Indicators: 2015*, Table 1. Find the World Bank at http://data.worldbank.org/products/wdi.

population in 2014 but produced only 48 percent of the output. Compared to industrial market countries, developing countries usually have higher rates of illiteracy, higher unemployment, faster population growth, and exports consisting mostly of agricultural products and raw materials. Most developing countries are also known as emerging market economies.

On average, nearly half of the labor force in developing countries works in agriculture versus only about 3 percent in industrial market countries. Because farming methods are sometimes primitive in developing countries, farm productivity is low and some households barely subsist. For example, over half the labor force in India works in agriculture, but that sector accounts for less than one-fifth of the nation's output.[1] Industrial market countries, or *developed countries,* are primarily the economically advanced capitalist countries of Europe, North America, Australia, New Zealand, and Japan. They were the first to experience long-term economic growth during the 19th century.

Exhibit 2 presents income per capita in 2014 for a sample of high-, middle-, and low-income economies. Because most countries in the sample have large populations, together they account for about 55 percent of the world's population. Countries are listed from top to bottom in descending order based on income per capita. Again,

figures have been adjusted to reflect the actual purchasing power of the local currency in its respective economy. The bars in the chart are color-coded, with high-income economies in blue, middle-income economies in orange, low-income economies in red, and the world average in green. Per capita income in the United States, the exhibit's top-ranked country, was more than 4 times that of China, a middle-income economy. But per capita in China, in turn, was more than 8 times that of Ethiopia and 18 times that of the Democratic Republic of the Congo, both poor African nations. Residents of China likely feel poor relative to Americans, but they appear well off compared to residents of the poorest nations. U.S per capita income was 36 times that of Ethiopia, and 78 times that of the Congo, one of the poorest nations on Earth. Thus, there is a tremendous range of per capita income around the world. World per capita income in 2014 was $16,100, as shown by the green bar.

Exhibit 2 looks at income per capita, but neither income nor population is always measured accurately, especially in the poorest countries. Some economists have looked for other ways of measuring an economy, such as how lit up a country is at night. Consumption of most goods and services at night requires light. As personal income rises, so does consumption and night lights, which can be measured by satellite from outer space. This night-light measure is useful when other data are of poor quality, as with many African economies, or when data are simply not available, as in Somalia, Liberia, and North Korea.[2]

## 19-1b Health and Nutrition

Different stages of development among countries are reflected in a number of ways besides per capita income. For example, many people in developing countries suffer from poor health as a result of malnutrition and disease.

1. U.S. International Trade Commission, *Effect of Tariffs and Nontariff Measures on U.S. Agricultural Exports,* Investigation No. 332-504, USITC Publication 4107 (November 2009).

2. J. Vernon Henderson, Adam Storeygard, and David Weil, "Measuring Economic Growth from Outer Space," *American Economic Review,* 102 (April 2012): 994–1028.

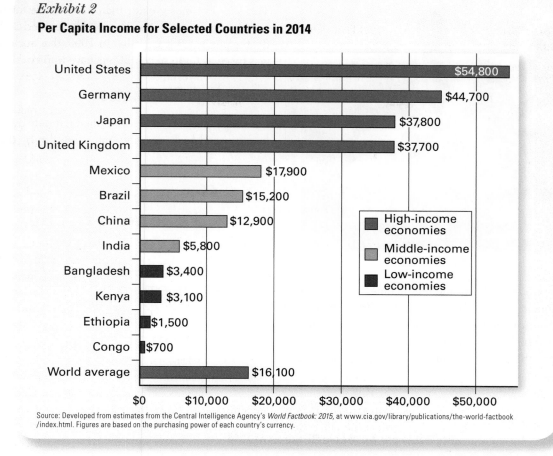

**Exhibit 2**

**Per Capita Income for Selected Countries in 2014**

| Country | Income |
|---|---|
| United States | $54,800 |
| Germany | $44,700 |
| Japan | $37,800 |
| United Kingdom | $37,700 |
| Mexico | $17,900 |
| Brazil | $15,200 |
| China | $12,900 |
| India | $5,800 |
| Bangladesh | $3,400 |
| Kenya | $3,100 |
| Ethiopia | $1,500 |
| Congo | $700 |
| World average | $16,100 |

Legend: High-income economies; Middle-income economies; Low-income economies

Source: Developed from estimates from the Central Intelligence Agency's *World Factbook: 2015,* at www.cia.gov/library/publications/the-world-factbook /index.html. Figures are based on the purchasing power of each country's currency.

HIV/AIDS is devastating some developing countries, particularly those in sub-Saharan Africa. In 2013, about 25 percent of people ages 15 to 49 in Swaziland, Botswana, and Lesotho had HIV/AIDS, compared to less than 1 percent in the United States.[3] The 20 countries with the highest incidence of HIV/AIDS were in Africa. Another health scourge in Africa is the tsetse fly. Harmful to humans and lethal to livestock, this fly has slowed the domestication of animals and reduced the use of plows, all of which has retarded economic development in Africa.[4] In sub-Saharan Africa, life expectancy at birth averaged 53 years versus 80 years in high-income economies, 69 years in middle-income economies, and 58 years in all low-income economies. Poor health has other bad consequences for the individual and the economy. For example, research shows that a higher rate of HIV/AIDS cuts the general level of education in the country. Even those not infected are less willing to invest in their own education.[5]

3. *World Development Indicators: 2015,* World Bank, Table 3 at http://data.worldbank .org/products/wdi.

4. Marcella Alsan, "The Effects of the TseTse Fly on African Development," *American Economic Review,* 105 (January 2015): 382–410.

5. Jane Fortson, "Mortality Risk and Human Capital Investment: The Impact of HIV/AIDS in Sub-Saharan Africa," *Review of Economics and Statistics,* 93 (February 2011): 1–15.

## Malnutrition

Those in the poorest countries consume only half the calories of those in high-income countries. Even if an infant survives the first year, malnutrition can turn normal childhood diseases, such as measles, into life-threatening events. The WHO cites malnutrition as the biggest single threat to the world's public health. Malnutrition is a primary or contributing factor in more than half of the deaths of children under the age of 5 in low-income countries. Diseases that are well controlled in the industrial countries—malaria, whooping cough, polio, dysentery, typhoid, and cholera—can become epidemics in poor countries. About a billion people on Earth don't have enough to eat.

## Infant Mortality

Health differences among countries are reflected in mortality rates among infants less than one year old. These rates are much greater in low-income countries than in high-income countries. Rates for our representative sample of high-, medium-, and low-income economies appear in Exhibit 3. Again, high-income

Cases of HIV and AIDS, as well as outbreaks of diseases like Ebola are much more common in many less developed nations.

in 2014 averaged 53.6 infant deaths per 1,000 live births. This was 13 times greater than the 4.1 rate for the four high-income economies. The world averaged 35.6 infant deaths per 1,000 live births. In 1990, the world average was twice as high, so conditions have improved.

### 19-1c  High Birth Rates

Developing countries are identified not only by their low incomes and high mortality rates but also by their high

economies are blue bars, middle-income are orange bars, low-income are red bars, and the world average is the green bar. Among the dozen countries shown, infant mortality was highest in the sub-Saharan African nation of the Congo. Rates for the four low-income economies

> ❝The birth rate is one of the clearest ways of distinguishing between industrial and developing countries.❞

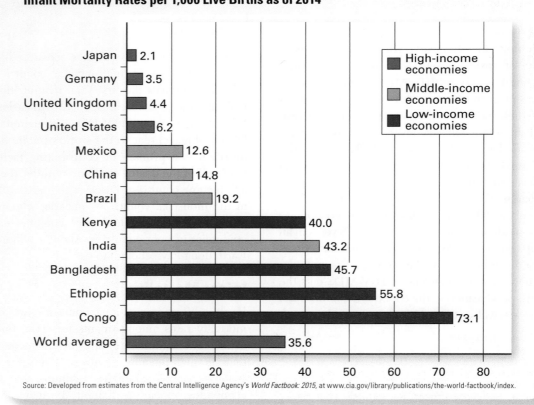

*Exhibit 3*

**Infant Mortality Rates per 1,000 Live Births as of 2014**

| Country | Rate |
|---|---|
| Japan | 2.1 |
| Germany | 3.5 |
| United Kingdom | 4.4 |
| United States | 6.2 |
| Mexico | 12.6 |
| China | 14.8 |
| Brazil | 19.2 |
| Kenya | 40.0 |
| India | 43.2 |
| Bangladesh | 45.7 |
| Ethiopia | 55.8 |
| Congo | 73.1 |
| World average | 35.6 |

Legend:
- High-income economies
- Middle-income economies
- Low-income economies

Source: Developed from estimates from the Central Intelligence Agency's *World Factbook: 2015,* at www.cia.gov/library/publications/the-world-factbook/index.

100 years ago, and it is one of the most developed Latin American nations today. The growth of education in Japan during the 19th century contributed to a ready acceptance of technology and thus to Japan's remarkable economic growth in the 20th century.

Education is valued more in some economies than in others. For example, many teachers in Mexico are allowed to sell their tenured positions or pass them on to their children.[6] And in India, about one-quarter of teachers in rural public schools were absent on any given day.[7]

## 19-2c Inefficient Use of Labor

Another feature of developing countries is that they use labor less efficiently than do industrial nations. Unemployment and underemployment reflect inefficient uses of labor. *Underemployment* occurs when skilled workers are employed in low-skill jobs or when people are working less than they would like— for example, a worker seeking full-time employment may find only a part-time job. *Unemployment* occurs when those willing and able to work can't find jobs.

Unemployment is measured primarily in urban areas, because in rural areas farm work is usually an outlet for labor even if many workers are underemployed there. The unemployment rate in developing nations on average is about 10 percent to 15 percent of the urban labor force. Unemployment among young workers—those aged 15 to 24—is typically twice that of older workers. In developing nations, about 30 percent of the combined urban and rural workforce is either unemployed or underemployed. In Zimbabwe, most people are unemployed; it's no surprise why Zimbabwe is so poor.

In some developing countries, the average farm is as small as two acres. Productivity is also low because few other inputs, such as capital and fertilizer, are used. *Although more than half the labor force in developing countries works in agriculture, only about one-third of output in these countries stems from agriculture.* In the United States, farmers account for only 2 percent of the labor force, but because of modern equipment one farmer can work hundreds or even thousands of acres (the average U.S. farm is about 500 acres). U.S. farmers, though only one-fiftieth of the labor force, grow enough to feed a nation and to lead the world in exports of grain, oil seeds, and cotton. The average value added per U.S.

Susan Liebold/Alamy

farm worker is about 75 times that of farm workers in low- and middle-income countries.

Low productivity obviously results in low income, but low income can, in turn, affect worker productivity. Low income means less saving and less saving means less investment in human and physical capital. Low income can also mean poor nutrition during the formative years, which can retard mental and physical development. These difficult beginnings may be aggravated by poor diet and insufficient health care in later life, making workers poorly suited for regular employment. Poverty can result in less saving, less education, less capital formation, a poor diet, and little health care—all of which can reduce a worker's productivity. Thus, *low income and low productivity may reinforce each other in a cycle of poverty.*

> **"Low income and low productivity may reinforce each other in a cycle of poverty."**

## 19-2d Natural Resources

Some countries are rich in natural resources. The difference is most striking when we compare countries with oil reserves and those without. The Middle East countries of Bahrain, Kuwait, Qatar, Saudi Arabia, and the United Arab Emirates are classified as high-income economies because they are lucky enough to be sitting atop huge oil reserves. But oil-rich countries are the exception. Many developing countries, such as Chad and Ethiopia, have

6. "Why Are Mexico's Teachers Wielding Axes?" *The Economist*, 28 April 2013.

7. Karthik Muralidharan et al. "The Fiscal Cost of Weak Governance: Evidence from Teacher Absences in India," NBER Working Paper No. 20299 (July 2014).

Penka Todorova Vitkova/Shutterstock

little in the way of natural resources. Most developing countries without oil reserves are in trouble whenever oil prices rise. Since oil must be imported, higher oil prices drain oil-poor countries of precious foreign exchange.

Oil-rich countries also show us that an abundant supply of a natural resource is not in itself enough to create a modern industrial economy. On the other hand, Japan has one of the most developed economies in the world, yet has no oil reserves and little in the way of natural resources. Connecticut is consistently the most productive of the United States as measured by per capita income, but the state has few natural resources (its main natural resource is gravel). In fact, many researchers believe that reliance on resource wealth can be something of a curse for a nation.

### 19-2e Financial Institutions

Another requirement for development is an adequate and trusted system of financial institutions. An important source of funds for investment is the savings of households and firms. People in some developing countries have little confidence in their currency because their governments finance a large fraction of public outlays by printing money. This practice results in high inflation and sometimes very high inflation, or hyperinflation, as has occurred recently in Zimbabwe, where annual inflation was just about incalculable. High and unpredictable inflation discourages saving and hurts development.

Developing countries have special problems because banks are often viewed with suspicion. At the first sign of trouble, many depositors withdraw their funds. Because banks cannot rely on a continuous supply of deposits, they cannot make loans for extended periods. If financial institutions fail to serve as intermediaries between savers

and borrowers, the lack of funds for investment becomes an obstacle to growth. During the global financial crisis of 2008, banks in industrial market countries also suffered from depositors' sagging confidence. One measure of banking presence is the credit provided by banks as a percent of that nation's total output. This measure is more than five times greater in high-income countries than in low-income countries.

### 19-2f Capital Infrastructure

Production and exchange depend on a reliable infrastructure of transportation, communication, sanitation, and electricity. Roads, bridges, airports, harbors, and other transportation facilities are vital to commercial activity. Reliable mail service, telephone communications, Internet connections, clean water, and electricity are also essential for advanced production techniques. Imagine how difficult it would be to run even a personal computer if the supply of electricity and access to the Internet were unavailable or continually interrupted, as is often the case in many developing countries.

Some developing countries have serious deficiencies in their physical infrastructures. As just one measure, Exhibit 5 shows the number of mobile telephones per 100 people in 2013 for the 12 countries examined earlier. The high-income countries averaged about twice as many mobile phones per 100 people as the low-income countries. Brazil, the top rated in this category, had 135 mobile phones per 100 people. Bottom-ranked Ethiopia had just 27 mobile phones per 100 people. The world average was 93 mobile phones per 100 people. More Indians have access to mobile phones than to toilets (only about half the population has access to toilets). Incidentally, mobile phones in poor countries create opportunities to deliver education to those without access to schools. In an experiment in the African nation of Niger, those who took lessons on mobile phones tested quite well and retained what they learned.[8]

Phone lines help knit together an economy's communications network. Countries without reliable phone service have difficulty not only communicating but also reaping the benefits of other technology advances, such as the Internet. Exhibit 6 shows Internet users as a percent of the population in 2013 for our sample of countries. There is an unmistakable digital divide between high-income and low-income economies. In the four high-income economies, an average 86 percent of the population used

8. Jenny C. Aker, Christopher Ksoll, and Travis J. Lybbert, "Can Mobile Phones Improve Learning? Evidence from a Field Experiment in Niger," American Economic Journal: Applied Economics, 4 (October 2012): 94–120.

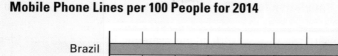

*Exhibit 5*

## Mobile Phone Lines per 100 People for 2014

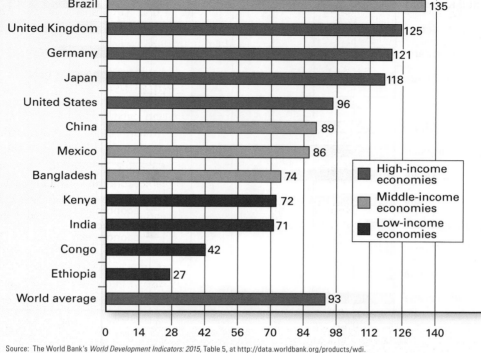

| Country | Value |
|---|---|
| Brazil | 135 |
| United Kingdom | 125 |
| Germany | 121 |
| Japan | 118 |
| United States | 96 |
| China | 89 |
| Mexico | 86 |
| Bangladesh | 74 |
| Kenya | 72 |
| India | 71 |
| Congo | 42 |
| Ethiopia | 27 |
| World average | 93 |

Legend:
- High-income economies
- Middle-income economies
- Low-income economies

Source: The World Bank's *World Development Indicators: 2015*, Table 5, at http://data.worldbank.org/products/wdi.

the Internet. In the four low-income economies, just 12 percent used the Internet on average. Even in India, which has a reputation as computer savvy, what with all the online support centers and software companies we read about, only 15 percent of the population were Internet users. Worldwide, 38 percent of the population used the Internet in 2013.

## 19-2g Entrepreneurship

An economy can have abundant supplies of labor, capital, and natural resources, but without entrepreneurship, the other resources will not necessarily be combined efficiently to produce goods and services. Unless a country has entrepreneurs who are able to bring together resources and take the risk of profit or loss, development may never get off the ground. Many developing countries were once under colonial rule, a system of government that offered the local population fewer opportunities to develop entrepreneurial skills. One sign of entrepreneurship is a willingness to become self-employed. Immigrants to the United States from developing countries are less likely to become self-employed

here than are immigrants to the United States from industrial economies.[9]

One source of entrepreneurial experience for developing countries comes from McDonald's and other international franchises. For example, by providing management training, McDonald's stimulates entrepreneurship directly through its franchises and indirectly by showing competitors how a business is run. Such franchises also demonstrate to customers what they should come to expect in the way of service, cleanliness, quality, and the like.[10]

Franchise operators often face obstacles. For example, chicken farmers in Ghana were not up to KFC's standards for quality, so the franchise operators there tried to import chicken. But because Ghana's currency was weak, imported chicken was too expensive. Needless to say, KFC is having a hard time in Ghana.[11]

9. Ruth Owaifo Oyelere and Willie Belton, "Coming to America: Does Having a Developed Home Country Matter for Self-Employment in the United States?" *American Economic Review*, 102 (May 2012): 538–542.

10. Adrian Tschoegli, "McDonald's—Much Maligned, But an Engine of Economic Development," *Global Economy Journal*, 7 (October 2007): 1–18.

11. Drew Hinshaw, "As KFC Goes to Africa, It Lacks Only One Thing: Chickens," Wall Street Journal, 8 February 2013.

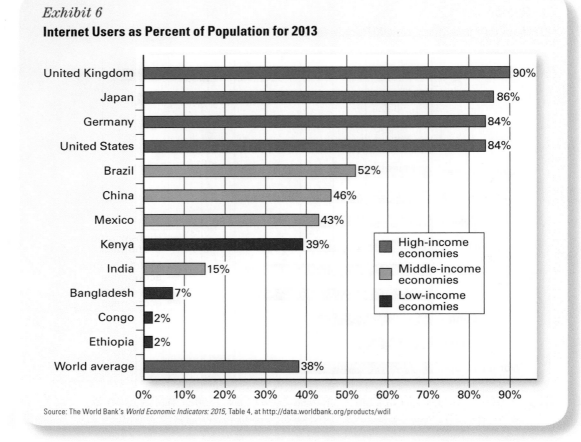

## Exhibit 6
### Internet Users as Percent of Population for 2013

| Country | Percent |
|---|---|
| United Kingdom | 90% |
| Japan | 86% |
| Germany | 84% |
| United States | 84% |
| Brazil | 52% |
| China | 46% |
| Mexico | 43% |
| Kenya | 39% |
| India | 15% |
| Bangladesh | 7% |
| Congo | 2% |
| Ethiopia | 2% |
| World average | 38% |

Legend:
- High-income economies
- Middle-income economies
- Low-income economies

Source: The World Bank's *World Economic Indicators: 2015,* Table 4, at http://data.worldbank.org/products/wdil

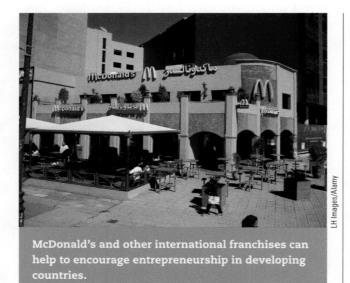

**McDonald's and other international franchises can help to encourage entrepreneurship in developing countries.**

LH Images/Alamy

Government officials sometimes decide that entrepreneurs are unable to generate the kind of economic growth the country needs. State enterprises are therefore created to do what government believes the free market cannot do. But state-owned enterprises may have objectives other than producing goods efficiently—objectives that could include providing jobs for friends and relatives of government officials. Also, with most state enterprises, there is little or no competition.

## 19-2h Rules of the Game

Finally, in addition to human capital, natural resources, financial institutions, capital infrastructure, and entrepreneurship, a successful economy needs reliable *rules of the game*. Perhaps the most elusive ingredients for development are the formal and informal institutions that promote production and exchange: the laws, customs, conventions, and other institutional elements that sustain an economy. A stable political environment with well-defined property rights is important. Little private-sector investment will occur if potential investors believe their capital might be appropriated by government, destroyed by civil unrest, blown up by terrorists, or stolen by thieves. For example, because of frequent ambushes and hijackings, many truckers have abandoned roads through Congo, South Sudan,

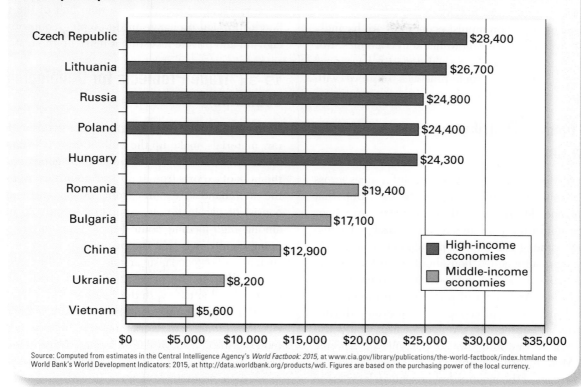

### Exhibit 7
**GDP per Capita for Transitional Economies in 2013**

| Country | GDP per Capita |
|---|---|
| Czech Republic | $28,400 |
| Lithuania | $26,700 |
| Russia | $24,800 |
| Poland | $24,400 |
| Hungary | $24,300 |
| Romania | $19,400 |
| Bulgaria | $17,100 |
| China | $12,900 |
| Ukraine | $8,200 |
| Vietnam | $5,600 |

Legend:
■ High-income economies
■ Middle-income economies

Source: Computed from estimates in the Central Intelligence Agency's *World Factbook: 2015*, at www.cia.gov/library/publications/the-world-factbook/index.htmland the World Bank's World Development Indicators: 2015, at http://data.worldbank.org/products/wdi. Figures are based on the purchasing power of the local currency.

and the Central African Republic, thereby reducing commercial opportunities for trade there.[12]

Under capitalism, the rules of the game include private ownership of most resources and the coordination of economic activity by the price signals generated by market forces. Market coordination answers the questions of what to produce, how to produce it, and for whom to produce it. Under socialism, the rules of the game include government ownership of most resources and the allocation of resources through central plans. For example, countries such as Cuba and North Korea carefully limit the private ownership of resources like land and capital. More generally, personal freedom is limited in centrally planned economies (e.g., in North Korea, people need a government permit just to travel outside their own town).[13]

Although there is no universally accepted theory of economic development, around the world markets have been replacing central plans in many once-socialist countries. **Privatization** is the process of turning government enterprises into private enterprises in these transitional economies. Privatization is the opposite of *nationalization* (what the U.S. government did with airport security after 9/11, taking it away from airlines and federalizing it). For example, Russian privatization began in 1992 with the sale of municipally owned shops. Exhibit 7 presents, for 10 transitional economies, the gross domestic product (GDP) per capita in 2014 based on the purchasing power of the domestic currency. Notice the differences across these economies, with GDP per capita in the Czech Republic five times that of Vietnam. The Czech Republic, Lithuania, Russia, Poland, and Hungary, identified with blue bars, have joined the ranks of high-income economies. The other five are middle-income economies, and are identified with orange bars. Some of these transitional economies still have aspects of central planning. For example, banks in Vietnam are more likely to lend to businesses that are

**privatization** The process of turning government enterprises into private enterprises

12. Nicholas Bariyo, "Africa's Sugar Ambitions Turn Sour," *Wall Street Journal*, 20 October 2014.

13. Peter Wonacott, "The Mystery of North Korean Fans," *Wall Street Journal*, 26 June 2010.

politically connected than to businesses that are the most profitable. Thus, the most profitable Vietnamese firms tend to avoid banks and rely instead on reinvested earnings and informal loans.[14]

But many once-communist economies are having a hard time with the transition to market economies. For example, manufacturers in Kazakhstan still have poor management practices. Such practices improve with greater privatization and more competition.[15]

## 19-2i Income Distribution Within Countries

Thus far the focus has been on income differences across countries, and these differences can be vast. But what about income differences within a country? Are poor countries uniformly poor or are there sizable income differences among that nation's population? One way to measure inequality across households is to look at the share of national income going to the poorest fifth of the population. As a point of reference, in the unlikely event that income in an economy were evenly distributed across all households, the poorest fifth would also receive exactly one-fifth, or 20 percent, of national income. More realistically, the poorest fifth receives less than 20 percent of the income, but how much less? Is the percent of income going to the poorest fifth higher for low-income countries than for high-income countries? In other words, is income more evenly distributed within poor countries than within rich countries? Not necessarily. Among our 12 nations, the poorest fifth of the population got an average of 7.7 percent of the income in the high-income countries, 5.8 percent in middle-income countries, and 7.2 percent in low-income countries. So, at least in this sample, income was less evenly distributed among middle-income countries than in high- or low-income countries.

# 19-3 INTERNATIONAL TRADE AND DEVELOPMENT

Developing countries need to trade with developed countries to acquire the capital and technology that will increase labor productivity on the farm, in the factory,

in the office, and in the home. To import capital and technology, developing countries must first acquire the funds, or foreign exchange, needed to pay for imports. Exports usually generate more than half of the annual flow of foreign exchange in developing countries. Foreign aid and private investment make up the rest.

## 19-3a Trade Problems for Developing Countries

Primary products, such as agricultural goods and other raw materials, make up the bulk of exports from developing countries, just as manufactured goods make up the bulk of exports from industrial countries. About half the merchandise exports from low-income countries consist of raw materials, compared to only 20 percent among high-income countries. A problem for developing countries is that the prices of primary products, such as coffee, cocoa, sugar, and rubber, fluctuate more widely than do the prices of finished goods, because crop yields fluctuate with the weather.

When developing countries experience trade deficits, they often try to restrict imports. Because imported food is critical to survival, developing countries are more likely to cut imports of capital goods—the very items needed to promote long-term growth and productivity. Thus, many developing countries cannot afford the

Ammit Jack/Shutterstock.com

14. Edmund J. Malesky and Markus Taussig, "Where Is Credit Due? Legal Institutions, Connections, and the Efficiency of Bank Lending in Vietnam," *Journal of Law, Economics, and Organization*, 25 (October 2009): 525–578.

15. Nicholas Bloom, Helena Schweiger, and John Van Reenen, "The Land That Lean Manufacturing Forgot? Management Practices in Transition Countries," *Economics of Transition*, 20 (October 2012): 593–635.

modern machinery that will help workers there become more productive. Developing countries must also confront industrial countries' trade restrictions, such as tariffs and quotas, which often discriminate against primary products. For example, the United States strictly limits sugar imports and has done so for more than half a century. Such restrictions are one reason the Doha Round of trade agreements stalled.

## 19-3b Migration and the Brain Drain

Migration plays an important role in the economies of developing countries. A major source of foreign exchange in some countries is the money sent home by migrants who find jobs in industrial countries. Migrant workers around the world sent home about $440 billion in 2014, and that's expected to top $500 billion by 2016, according to the World Bank. For example, migrants from Mexico send home about a third of their U.S. earnings.[16] Thus migration provides a valuable safety valve for poor countries, and remittances can account for 10 percent of all income in poor countries.[17] There is evidence that migrant remittances help family members back home get more education or even start a business. But there is a downside. Often the best and the brightest professionals, such as doctors, nurses, and engineers, migrate to developed countries. For example, every year thousands of nurses migrate from countries such as Kenya and the Philippines to the United States, where half the world's nurses are employed. The financial attraction is powerful: A nurse in the Philippines would start there at less than $8,000 a year, compared with $36,000 in the United States.

So the upside of the brain drain for the poor country is the money sent home by overseas workers. What's more, recent research suggests some benefits to the country of origin when trained professionals move abroad. For example, some Indians who have migrated to the United States to work in computer technology have helped nurture India's software industry.[18] Still, a nation is usually hurt when its best and brightest leave for opportunities elsewhere. Some African countries are demanding compensation for the cost of educating the doctors and nurses who then move to high-income economies.

16. Dean Yang, "Migrant Remittances," *Journal of Economic Perspectives*, 25 (Summer 2011): 133.

17. Julian di Giovanni, Andrei Levchenko, and Francesc Ortega, "A Global View of Cross-Border Migration," *Journal of the European Economic Association*, 13 (February 2015): 168–202.

18. Frederic Docquier and Hillel Rapoport, "Globalization, Brain Drain, and Development," *Journal of Economic Literature*, 50 (September 2012): 681–730.

## 19-3c Import Substitution Versus Export Promotion

An economy's progress usually involves moving up the production chain from agriculture and raw material to manufacturing then to services. If a country is fortunate, this transformation occurs gradually through natural market forces. For example, in 1850 most U.S. jobs were in agriculture. Now most U.S. jobs are in the service sector. Sometimes governments try to speed up the evolution. Many developing countries, including Argentina and India, pursued a strategy called **import substitution**, whereby domestic manufacturers made products that until then had been imported. To insulate domestic manufacturers from foreign competition, the government imposed stiff tariffs and quotas. This development strategy became popular for several reasons. First, demand already existed for these products, so the "what to produce" question was easily answered. Second, import substitution provided infant industries with a protected market. Finally, import substitution was popular with those who supplied resources to the favored domestic industries.

Like all trade protection, however, import substitution erased the gains from specialization and comparative advantage among countries. Often the developing country replaced low-cost foreign goods with high-cost domestic versions of those same goods. And domestic producers, shielded from foreign competition, often supplied inferior products and usually failed to become efficient. Worse still, other countries often retaliated with their own trade restrictions.

Critics of import substitution claim that export promotion is a surer path to economic development. **Export promotion** concentrates on producing for the export market. This development strategy begins with relatively simple products, such as textiles. As a developing country builds its technological and educational base—that is, as the developing economy learns by doing—producers can then make more complex products for export. Economists favor export promotion over import substitution because the emphasis is on comparative advantage and trade expansion rather than on trade restriction. Export promotion also forces producers to grow more efficient in order to compete on world markets. Research shows that

**import substitution** A development strategy that emphasizes domestic manufacturing of products that had been imported

**export promotion** A development strategy that concentrates on producing for the export market facing global competition boosts domestic efficiency. What's more, export promotion requires less government intervention in the market than does import substitution.

Of the two approaches, export promotion has been more successful around the world. For example, the newly industrialized countries of East Asia have successfully pursued export promotion, while Argentina, India, and Peru have failed with their import-substitution approach. In 1965, the newly industrialized economies of Hong Kong, South Korea, Singapore, and Taiwan had an average income only 20 percent that of high-income countries. Now these four are themselves high-income countries. Most Latin American nations, which for decades had favored import substitution, are now pursuing free trade agreements with each other and with the United States. Even India is dismantling trade barriers, with an emphasis on importing high-technology capital goods. One slogan of Indian trade officials is "Microchips, yes! Potato chips, no!"

### 19-3d Trade Liberalization and Special Interests

Although most people would benefit from freer international trade, some would be worse off. Consequently, governments in developing countries often face difficulty pursuing policies conducive to development. Often the gains from economic development are widespread, but the beneficiaries, such as consumers, do not recognize their potential gains. On the other hand, the losers tend to be concentrated, such as producers in an industry that had been sheltered from foreign competition, and they know quite well the source of their losses. So the government often lacks the political will and support to remove impediments to development, because the potential losers fight reforms that might harm their livelihood while the potential winners remain largely unaware of what's at stake. What's more, consumers have difficulty organizing even if they become aware of what's going on. A recent study by the World Bank suggests a strong link in Africa between governments that cater to special-interest groups and low rates of economic growth.

Nonetheless, many developing countries have been opening their borders to freer trade. People around the world have been exposed to information about the opportunities and products available on world markets. So consumers want the goods and firms want the technology and capital that are available abroad. Both groups want government to ease trade restrictions.

> "Studies by the World Bank and others have underscored the successes of countries which have adopted trade liberalization policies."

Studies by the World Bank and others have underscored the successes of countries which have adopted trade liberalization policies.

## 19-4 FOREIGN AID AND ECONOMIC DEVELOPMENT

We have already seen that because most poor countries do not generate enough savings to fund an adequate level of investment, these countries often rely on foreign financing. Private international borrowing and lending are heavily restricted by the governments of developing countries. Governments may allow residents to purchase foreign exchange only for certain purposes. In some developing countries, different exchange rates apply to different categories of transactions. Thus, the local currency is not easily convertible into other currencies. Some developing countries also require foreign investors to find a local partner who must be granted controlling interest. All these restrictions discourage foreign investment. In this section, we will look primarily at foreign aid and its link to economic development.

> "Most poor countries do not generate enough savings to fund an adequate level of investment."

## 19-4a Foreign Aid

**Foreign aid** is any international transfer made on especially favorable terms for the purposes of promoting economic development. Foreign aid includes grants, which need not be repaid, and loans extended on more favorable repayment terms than the recipient could normally secure. Such loans have lower interest rates, longer repayment periods, or grace periods during which repayments are reduced or even waived (similar to some student loans). Foreign aid can take the form of money, capital goods, technical assistance, food, and so forth.

> **"Foreign aid can take the form of money, capital goods, technical assistance, food, and so forth."**

Some foreign aid is granted by a specific country, such as the United States, to another specific country, such as the Philippines. Country-to-country aid is called *bilateral* assistance. Other foreign aid goes through international bodies such as the World Bank. Assistance provided by organizations that use funds from a number of countries is called *multilateral*. For example, the World Bank provides loans and grants to support activities that are viewed as prerequisites for development, such as health and education programs or basic development projects like dams, roads, and communications networks. And the International Monetary Fund extends loans to countries that have trouble with their balance of payments.

During the last four decades, the United States has provided the developing world with over $400 billion in aid. Most U.S. aid has been coordinated by the United States Agency for International Development (USAID), which is part of the U.S. Department of State. This agency focuses on health, education, and agriculture, providing both technical assistance and loans. USAID emphasizes long-range plans to meet the basic needs of the poor and to promote self-sufficiency. Foreign aid is a controversial, though relatively small, part of the federal budget. Since 1993, official U.S. aid has been less than 0.2 percent of U.S. GDP, compared to an average of 0.3 percent from 21 other industrialized nations.

## 19-4b Does Foreign Aid Promote Economic Development?

In general, foreign aid provides additional purchasing power and thus the possibility of increased investment, capital imports, and consumption. But it remains unclear whether foreign aid *supplements* domestic saving, thus increasing investment, or simply *substitutes* for domestic saving, thereby increasing consumption rather than investment. What is clear is that foreign aid often becomes a source of discretionary funds that benefit not the poor but their leaders. Historically, more than 90 percent of the funds distributed by USAID have gone to governments, whose leaders assume responsibility for distributing these funds. One goal of foreign aid seems to be to keep a friendly government in power.[19]

Much bilateral funding is tied to purchases of goods and services from the donor nation, and such programs can sometimes be counterproductive—they have unintended consequences. For example, in the 1950s, the United States began the Food for Peace program,

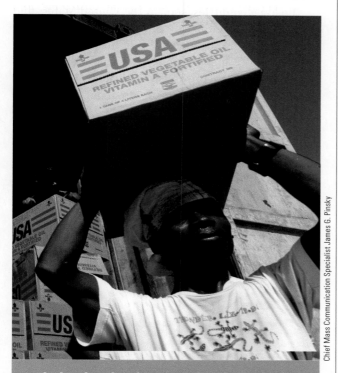

In the last four decades, USAID has donated more than $400 billion in aid to developing countries.

Chief Mass Communication Specialist James G. Pinsky

19. Michael Faye and Paul Niehaus, "Political Aid Cycles," *American Economic Review*, 102 (December 2012): 3516–3530.

**foreign aid** An international transfer made on especially favorable terms for the purpose of promoting economic development

> **"It remains unclear whether foreign aid *supplements* domestic saving, thus increasing investment, or simply *substitutes* for domestic saving, thereby increasing consumption rather than investment."**

which helped supply U.S. farm products abroad, but some recipient governments turned around and sold that food to finance poorly conceived projects. Worse yet, the availability of low-priced food from abroad drove down farm prices in the developing countries, hurting poor farmers there. The same holds for clothing. Used clothing donated to thrift shops and charitable organizations in industrialized countries typically winds up for sale in Africa, where the low price discourages local production of clothing.[20] Before used clothing swamped the continent, Africa had a textile industry, but no more. Textiles are often the first rung on the ladder to developing a broader manufacturing base.

Foreign aid may have temporarily raised the standard of living in some developing countries, but it has not necessarily increased their ability to become self-supporting at that higher standard of living. Many countries that receive aid are doing less of what they had done well. Their agricultural sectors have suffered. For example, though we should be careful when drawing conclusions about causality, per capita food production in Africa has fallen since 1960. Outside aid has often insulated public officials from their own incompetence and from the fundamental troubles of their own economies. There is also evidence that food aid increases the incidence and

**convergence** A theory predicting that the standard of living in economies around the world will grow more similar over time, with poorer countries eventually catching up with richer ones

duration of civil conflicts in a country.[21] Most countries today that have achieved industrial status did so without foreign aid. Development success typically takes time and involves gradual movements toward freer markets.

In some cases, foreign aid has helped corrupt governments stay in power. Because of disappointment with the results of government aid, the trend is toward channeling funds through private nonprofit agencies such as CARE. More than half of foreign aid now flows through private channels. The privatization of foreign aid follows a larger trend toward privatization in transitional economies around the world.

## 19-4c Do Economies Converge?

If given enough time, will poor countries eventually catch up with rich ones? The **convergence** theory argues that developing countries can grow faster than advanced ones and should eventually close the gap. Here's why: It is easier to copy existing technology than to develop new technologies. Countries that are technologically backward can grow faster by adopting existing technology. But economies already using the latest technology must come up with a steady stream of breakthroughs to grow faster. For example, it's infinitely easier to buy a smartphone than to invent one.

Leading countries, such as the United States, find growth limited by the rate of creation of new knowledge and better technology. But follower countries can grow more quickly by, for example, adding computers where they previously had none. Until 1995, the United States, which made up about five percent of the world's population at the time, accounted for most of the world's computer purchases by households. But by 2000, most computers were bought by non-U.S. households.

What's the evidence on convergence? Between 1993 and 2012, growth in real GDP for developing countries averaged 5.4 percent per year, more than double the averaged for industrial countries.[22] National economies have been converging for decades, closing half the gap in the last 35 years. In 1990, 43 percent of the population in developing countries subsisted

---

20. Garth Frazer, "Used-Clothing Donations and Apparel Production in Africa," *Economic Journal*, 118 (October 2008): 1764–1784.

21. Nathan Nunn and Nancy Qian, "US Food Aid and Civil Conflict," *American Economic Review*, 104 (June 2014): 1630-1666; and Benjamin Crost, Joseph Felter, and Patrick Johnston, "Aid Under Fire: Development Projects and Civil Conflicts," *American Economic Review*, 104 (June 2014): 1833–1856.

22. Anusha Chari and Peter Blair Henry, "Learning from Doers: Developing Country Lessons for Advanced Economic Growth," *American Economic Review*, 104 (May 2014): 260–265.

on less than $1 a day. By 2010, after adjusting for inflation, that share had fallen to 21 percent.[23] Some formerly poor countries have become advanced economies. As noted already, the newly industrialized Asian economies of Hong Kong, Singapore, South Korea, and Taiwan, by adopting the latest technology and investing in human resources, have closed the gap with the world leaders. These *Asian Tigers* have graduated from developing economies to industrial market economies. More generally, there does appear to be convergence in manufacturing productivity across a large group of developed and developing countries.[24] Even Africa has been doing better. Living standards in Sub-Saharan Africa have been rising by an average of 3.5 percent per year over the last two decades.[25] Still as many as a billion people seem trapped in poor economies.

> **"It is easier to copy existing technology than to develop new technologies. Countries that are technologically backward can grow faster by adopting existing technology."**

One reason per capita consumption has not grown faster in the poorest economies is that birthrates there are double those in richer countries, so poor economies must produce still more just to keep up with a growing population. Another reason why convergence is slow for the poorest parts of the world is the vast difference in the quality of human capital across countries. Although technology is indeed portable, the knowledge, skill, and training needed to take advantage of that technology are not. Common heritage seems to facilitate adoption of technology across nations. For example, some recent research finds that the closer the genetic distance between populations across nations—that is, the shorter the time since they shared common ancestors—the lower the barriers to technology adoption across nations.[26]

Countries with a high level of human capital can make up for other shortcomings. For example, much of the capital stock in Japan and Germany was destroyed during World War II. But the two countries retained enough of their well-educated and highly skilled labor force to rejoin elite industrial market economies in little more than a generation. But some countries, such as those in Africa, simply lack the human capital needed to identify and absorb new technology. As noted already, such poor economies tend to have low education levels and low literacy rates. What's more, some countries lack the stable macroeconomic environment and the established institutions needed to nurture economic growth, such as reliable banks. Many developing countries have serious deficiencies in their infrastructures, lacking, for example, the steady source of electricity to power new technologies. In Northern Nigeria, near the Sahara, most villages have no electricity. Some of the poorest nations

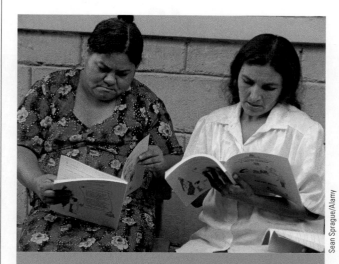

Sean Sprague/Alamy

**Low educational levels and literacy rates hinder economic growth in poor countries such as South Sudan, where the literacy rate is 27%. Literacy programs like this one in South Sudan are a good investments in the country's human capital.**

23. Nicola Gennaioli et al. "Growth in Regions," *Journal of Economic Growth*, 19 (September 2014): 259–303.

24. See Dani Rodrik, "Unconditional Convergence," in Manufacturing, *Quarterly Journal of Economics*, 128 (February 2013): 165–204.

25. Alwyn Young, "The African Growth Miracle," *Journal of Political Economy*, 120 (August 2012): 696–739.

26. Enrico Spolaore and Romain Wacziarg, "How Deep Are the Roots of Economic Development," *Journal of Economic Literature*, 51 (June 2013): 325–369.

have been ravaged by civil war for years. And simply communicating can be challenging in some developing countries. Among Nigeria's 180 million population, for example, more than 500 languages are spoken by 250 distinct ethnic groups.

Even in the United States, with it's common language, currency, and free flow of resources across state borders, large differences in productivity across states still exist. Researchers argue that not much convergence has occurred among U.S. states since 1975.[27]

One final reason that convergence may take a long time is that the roots of economic development go back centuries. For example, researchers find that regions using the most advanced technologies in the year 1000 B.C. tended to remain the users of the most advanced technologies in 1500 A.D., and continue to do so today.[28]

27. Chi-Young Choi and Xiaojun Wang, "Discontinuity of Output Convergence Within the United States: Why Has the Course Changed," *Economic Inquiry*, 53 (January 2015): 49–71.

28. Diego Comin, William Easterly, and Efick Gong, "Was the Wealth of Nations Determined in 1000 B.C.?" *American Economic Journal: Macroeconomics*, 2 (August 2010): 65–97.

## 19-5 FINAL WORD

Because no single theory of economic development has become widely accepted, this chapter has been more descriptive than theoretical. We can readily identify the features that distinguish developing from industrial economies. Education is key to development, both because of its direct effect on productivity and because those who are more educated tend to be more receptive to new ideas. A physical infrastructure of transportation and communication systems and utilities is needed to link economic participants. And trusted financial institutions link savers and borrowers. A country needs entrepreneurs with the vision to move the economy forward. Finally, the most elusive ingredients are the laws, manners, customs and ways of doing business that nurture economic development. Economic history is largely a story of economies that have failed to produce a set of economic rules of the game that lead to sustained economic growth. However, some transitional economies and some newly emerging industrial countries in Asia show that economic development continues to be achievable.

# STUDY TOOLS 19

## READY TO STUDY? IN THE BOOK, YOU CAN:

☐ Work the Problems at the end of the chapter.

☐ Rip out the chapter review card for a handy summary of the chapter and key terms.

## ONLINE AT CENGAGEBRAIN.COM YOU CAN:

☐ Collect StudyBits while you read and study the chapter.

☐ Quiz yourself on key concepts.

☐ Prepare for tests with chapter flash cards as well as flash cards that you create.

☐ Watch videos to explore economics further.

# CHAPTER 19 PROBLEMS

*Your instructor can access the answers to these problems online at http://cengagebrain.com.*

## 19-1 Besides income, identify ways that low-income economies differ from high-income economies

1. *(Worlds Apart)* Per capita income most recently was about 160 times greater in the United States than in the Democratic Republic of the Congo. Suppose per capita income grows an average of 3 percent per year in the richer country and 6 percent per year in the poorer country. Assuming such growth rates continue indefinitely into the future, how many years would it take before per capita income in the Congo exceeds that of the United States? (To simplify the math, suppose at the outset per capita income is $160,000 in the richer country and $1,000 in the poorer country.)

## 19-2 Describe the factors that make workers in high-income economies more productive than workers in other economies

2. *(Why Incomes Differ)* What factors help workers in high-income economies become more productive than those in other economies?

3. *(Import Substitution Versus Export Promotion)* Explain why domestic producers who supply a good that competes with imports would prefer an import-substitution approach to trade policy rather than an export-promotion approach. Which policy would domestic consumers prefer and why?

## 19-3 Explain how trade restrictions can slow economic development in poorer countries

4. *(International Trade and Development)* From the perspective of citizens in a developing country, what are some of the benefits and drawbacks of international trade?

## 19-4 Outline some unintended consequences of foreign aid on economic development

5. *(Foreign Aid and Economic Development)* Foreign aid, if it is to be successful in enhancing economic development, must lead to a more productive economy. Describe some of the problems in achieving such an objective through foreign aid.

6. *(In-Kind Aid)* What has been an unintended consequences of richer countries giving food and clothing to poorer countries?

# INDEX

# F

# G

# I

Nondurable goods, 43, 97
Nonexclusive goods, 49
Nonincome determinants of consumption, 156–159
Nonrivals in consumption, 48–49
Normal goods, 60
Normative economic statement, 11–12
North American Free Trade Agreement (NAFTA), 317
Not-for-profit organizations, 46
Nutrition, 342–344

# O

Obama, President Barack, 131, 191, 215, 243, 291
    stimulus spending, 201, 202, 203, 287, 290
Off-the-books production, 102
One child policy, 158
OPEC (Organization of Petroleum Exporting Countries), 87, 145, 186
Open-market operations, 236–237, 260, 262
Open-market purchases, 260
Open-market sales, 260
Opportunity costs, 25–27
    ideal money, 229
    increasing, law of, 32
    of money, 268–269
    and the Production Possibilities Frontier (PPF), 34
Opportunity lost, 25
Organization of Petroleum Exporting Countries (OPEC), 87, 145, 186
Origin, 17
Other-things-constant assumption, 11
Outlays, 101, 207, 214
    governments', 215
Output, 78–79
    aggregate, 82
    equilibrium, 292
    natural rate of, 174
    per capita, 145, 341
    potential, 174–176
Owners equity, 254

# P

Partnerships, 44–45
Passive discretionary policy, 285–291
    active, compared with, 290–291, 295–296
    expansionary gap, 287–288
    recessionary gap, 286
Payroll taxes, 51
    regressive taxation, 52
Pecuniary, defined, 228
Permanent income, 198–199
Personal consumption expenditures, 97
Per-worker production function, 138–139
Phillips, A.W., 297
Phillips Curve, 297–301

Phone lines, 348–349
Physical capital, 4, 97, 138, 346
Political business cycles, 198
Pollution and GDP, 104
Positive economic statement, 11–12
Positive relation, 19, 20
Positive slope, 21–22
Potential output, 174–176, 177
    expansionary gap, 178–180
    recessionary gap, 180–181
    tracing, 181–182
Poverty rates, 346
PPF (Production Possibilities Frontier), 31–34, 136–137
Predatory dumping, 319
Presidential politics, 290–291
Presidential role in budget, 208
Price ceilings, 71–72
Price changes
    accounting for, 105–109
    demand, 60–61
    income effect of, 58–59
    substitution effect of, 58
    supply of goods, 64
    surplus or shortage, 66
Price expectations, changes in, 60–61
Price floors, 70–71
Price index, 82, 89, 105, 108
    consumer price index, 106–108
Price levels, 79, 90, 157
    and aggregate expenditures, 166–168
    and aggregate output, 82
    and aggregate supply, 175
    expected, 174
    and inflation, 126–127
Primary discount rates, 261
Prime borrowers, 241
Prison economics, 230–231
Private goods, 48
Private property rights, 35
Privatization, 351
Producer cooperatives, 46
Producer surplus, 312
Production, 137
    households, 46–48
    United States, 310
    without trade, 306–308
    world, 309
Production function, 138–139
Production possibilities, 30–34
Production Possibilities Frontier (PPF), 31–34, 136–137
Productivity, 137–138
    and development, 346–352
    financial institutions, 348
    and growth, 135–141

TARP (Troubled Asset Relief Program), 89, 200, 242–243
Tastes, 61–62, 311
Taxes, 51–53
    cuts, as stimulation, 197
    and fiscal policy, 191
    household production, 47
    increases in, 78, 214–215
    net, 161–162
Tax incidence, 51
Taylor, John, 296
Technology
    change in, 139–140
    and education, 346–347
    and household productivity, 47–48
    and the Production Possibilities Frontier (PPF), 33, 137
    research and development, 147–149
    and supply changes, 63–64
    and unemployment, 146–147
Terms of trade, 308
Theory, role of, 9–10, 77
Thrift institutions, 234
Thrifts, 234
Time, 8
    as constraint, 26
    as resource, 4
Time deposits, 250
Time horizon, 194
Time-inconsistency problem, 293
Time-series graph, 17
Token money, 231
Tokyo Round, 316
Too big to fail, 243, 245
    reducing risk of, 279
Trade. *See* International trade
Trade Agreements Act of 1979, 319
Trade balance, 326, 329–330
Trade deficits, 213–214, 326, 327
    international finance, 329–330
Trade liberalization, 354
Trade restrictions, 54
    dumping, 319
    and welfare loss, 311–316
Trade rounds, 316–317
Trading partners, 306
Transaction costs, 43, 65
    household production, 47
    of variable inflation, 128–129
Transfer payments, 43, 49, 161
Transitional economies, 36–37
Trillion dollar deficits, 215
Troubled Asset Relief Program (TARP), 89, 200, 242–243
Truman, President Harry, 114
Twin deficits, 213–214

# U

Unattainable combinations, 31
Uncontrollable budget items, 209
Underemployment, 124, 347
Underground economy, 102–103, 124
Unemployment, 113–122, 347
    compensation, 122–123
    cyclical, 121
    duration of, 116–117
    by education level, 117
    and fiscal policy, 197–198
    frictional, 120–121
    and inflation, 297–301
    international comparisons of, 119–120
    natural rate hypothesis, 300
    natural rate of, 174–175, 177, 186–187, 197–198
    by occupation, 118–119
    over time, 116
    rate of, 114–115
    rates, problems with, 124
    regional, 118–119
    structural, 121–122
    and technology, 146–147
Unemployment benefits, 122–123, 199
Unemployment insurance, 196
United Nations (UN), 341
Unit of account, 228–229
Units of measurement, 20
Unplanned inventory buildups, 164
Unrelated goods, 61
Unrelated variables, 19
Uruguay Round, 317
U.S. Agency for International Development (USAID), 355
U.S. Bureau of Economic Analysis, 96, 108
U.S. Bureau of Engraving and Printing, 249–250
U.S. Bureau of Labor Statistics, 108, 114, 145
U.S. Commerce Department, 104
U.S. Comptroller of the Currency, 253
U.S. Department of State, 355
U.S. economy, 84–91
    fluctuations in, 78–80
U.S. General Accounting Office, 290
U.S. Internal Revenue Service, 52
U.S. Mint, 250
U.S. Treasury Department, 213, 214, 234, 243, 250
Utility, 42
U-6 unemployment rate, 124

# V

Value added, 99
Value judgments, 12
Value of money, 229, 232–234
Variable inflation, 128–129

## KEY CONCEPTS

**1-1 Explain the economic problem of scarce resources and unlimited wants.** The problem is that, although your wants, or desires are virtually unlimited, the resources available to satisfy these wants are scarce. Because resources are scarce, you must choose from among your many wants, and whenever you choose, you must forgo satisfying some other wants. Without scarcity, there would be no economic problem and no need for prices.

### The Simple Circular-Flow Model for Households and Firms

Households earn income by supplying resources to resource markets, as shown in the lower portion of the model. Firms demand these resources to produce goods and services, which they supply to product markets, as shown in the upper portion of the model. Households spend their income to demand these goods and services. This spending flows through product markets as revenue to firms.

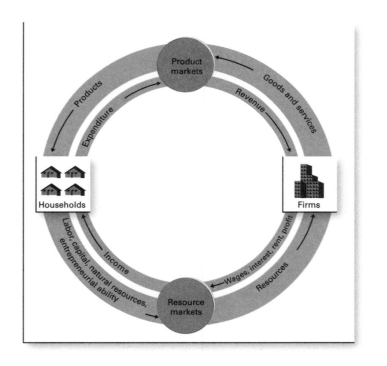

**1-2 Describe the forces that shape economic choices.** An economy results from the choices that millions of individuals make in attempting to satisfy their unlimited wants. A key economic assumption is that individuals, in making choices, rationally select alternatives they perceive to be in their best interests. Economic choice is based on a comparison of the expected marginal benefit and the expected marginal cost of the action under consideration.

**1-3 Explain the relationship between economic theory and economic reality.** An economic theory is a simplification of economic reality that is used to make predictions about the real world. A theory, or model, captures the important elements of the problem under study but need not spell out every detail and interrelation. You might think of economic theory as a streamlined version of economic reality.

## KEY TERMS

**economics** The study of how people use their scarce resources to satisfy their unlimited wants

**resources** The inputs, or factors of production, used to produce the goods and services that people want; resources consist of labor, capital, natural resources, and entrepreneurial ability

**labor** The physical and mental effort used to produce goods and services

**capital** The buildings, equipment, and human skills used to produce goods and services

**natural resources** All gifts of nature used to produce goods and services; includes renewable and exhaustible resources

**entrepreneurial ability** The imagination required to develop a new product or process, the skill needed to organize production, and the willingness to take the risk of profit or loss

**entrepreneur** A profit-seeking decision maker who starts with an idea, organizes an enterprise to bring that idea to life, and assumes the risk of the operation

**wages** Payment to resource owners for their labor

**interest** Payment to resource owners for the use of their capital

**rent** Payment to resource owners for the use of their natural resources

**profit** Reward for entrepreneurial ability; sales revenue minus resource cost

**good** A tangible product used to satisfy human wants

**service** An activity, or intangible product, used to satisfy human wants

**scarcity** Occurs when the amount people desire exceeds the amount available at a zero price

**market** A set of arrangements by which buyers and sellers carry out exchange at mutually agreeable terms

**product market** A market in which a good or service is bought and sold

**resource market** A market in which a resource is bought and sold

**circular-flow model** A diagram that traces the flow of resources, products, income, and revenue among economic decision makers

**rational self-interest** Each individual tries to maximize the expected benefit achieved with a given cost or to minimize the expected cost of achieving a given benefit

**marginal** Incremental, additional, or extra; used to describe a change in an economic variable

**microeconomics** The study of the economic behavior in particular markets, such as that for computers or unskilled labor

**macroeconomics** The study of the economic behavior of entire economies, as measured, for example, by total production and employment

**economic fluctuations** The rise and fall of economic activity relative to the long-term growth trend of the economy; also called business cycles

**economic theory, or economic model** A simplification of reality used to make predictions about cause and effect in the real world

**variable** A measure, such as price or quantity, that can take on different values at different times

**other-things-constant assumption** The assumption, when focusing on the relation among key economic variables, that other variables remain unchanged; in Latin, *ceteris paribus*

**behavioral assumption** An assumption that describes the expected behavior of economic decision makers—what motivates them

**hypothesis** A theory about how key variables relate

**positive economic statement** A statement that can be proved or disproved by reference to facts

**normative economic statement** A statement that reflects an opinion, which cannot be proved or disproved by reference to the facts

**association-is-causation fallacy** The incorrect idea that if two variables are associated in time, one must necessarily cause the other

**fallacy of composition** The incorrect belief that what is true for the individual, or part, must necessarily be true for the group, or the whole

**secondary effects** Unintended consequences of economic actions that may develop slowly over time as people react to events

**The Scientific Method: Step-by-Step**
The steps of the scientific method are designed to develop and test hypotheses about how the world works. The objective is a theory that predicts outcomes more accurately than the best alternative theory. A hypothesis is rejected if it does not predict as accurately as the best alternative. A rejected hypothesis can be modified in light of the test results.

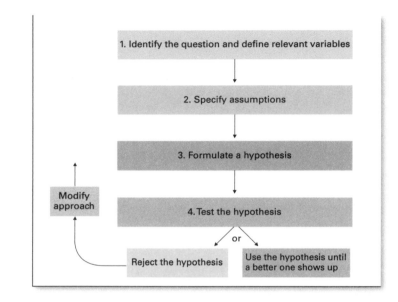

**1-4 Identify some pitfalls of economic analysis.** Economic analysis, like other forms of scientific inquiry, is subject to common mistakes in reasoning that can lead to faulty conclusions. Three sources of confusion are the fallacy that association is causation, the fallacy of composition, and the mistake of ignoring secondary effects.

**1-5 Describe several reasons to study economics.** The economics profession thrives because its models usually do a better job of making economic sense out of a confusing world than do alternative approaches. Studies show that economics majors earn more than most and they experience no pay difference based on gender.

# APPENDIX TERMS

**origin** on a graph depicting two-dimensional space, the zero point

**horizontal axis** line on a graph that begins at the origin and goes to the right and left; sometimes called the *x* axis

**vertical axis** line on a graph that begins at the origin and goes up and down; sometimes called the *y* axis

**graph** a picture showing how variables relate in two-dimensional space; one variable is measured along the horizontal axis and the other along the vertical axis

**dependent variable** a variable whose value depends on that of the independent variable

**independent variable** a variable whose value determines that of the dependent variable

**positive relation (direct relation)** occurs when two variables increase or decrease together; the two variables move in the same direction

**negative relation (inverse relation)** occurs when two variables move in opposite directions; when one increases, the other decreases

**slope of a line** a measure of how much the vertical variable changes for a given increase in the horizontal variable; the vertical change between two points divided by the horizontal increase

**tangent** a straight line that touches a curve at a point but does not cut or cross the curve; used to measure the slope of a curve at a point

## KEY CONCEPTS

**2-1  Describe the relationship between choice and opportunity cost.** Resources are scarce, but human wants are unlimited. Because you cannot satisfy all your wants, you must choose, and whenever you choose, you must forgo some option. Choice involves an opportunity cost. The opportunity cost of the selected option is the value of the best alternative forgone.

**2-2  Explain how comparative advantage, specialization, and exchange affect economic outcomes (output).** The law of comparative advantage says that the individual, firm, region, or country with the lowest opportunity cost of producing a particular good should specialize in that good. Specialization according to the law of comparative advantage promotes the most efficient use of resources. The specialization of labor increases efficiency by (a) taking advantage of individual preferences and natural abilities, (b) allowing each worker to develop expertise and experience at a particular task, (c) reducing the need to shift between different tasks, and (d) allowing for the introduction of more specialized machines and large-scale production techniques.

**2-3  Outline how economies function as production systems.** The production possibilities frontier, or PPF, shows the productive capabilities of an economy when all resources are used efficiently. The frontier's bowed-out shape reflects the law of increasing opportunity cost, which arises because some resources are not perfectly adaptable to the production of different goods. Over time, the frontier can shift in or out as a result of changes in the availability of resources, in technology, or in the rules of the game. The frontier demonstrates several economic concepts, including efficiency, scarcity, opportunity cost, the law of increasing opportunity cost, economic growth, and the need for choice.

**The Economy's Production Possibilities Frontier**

If the economy uses its available resources and its technology and know-how efficiently in producing consumer goods and capital goods, that economy is on its production

### The Economy's Production Possibilities Frontier

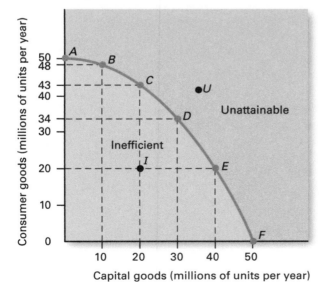

## KEY TERMS

**opportunity cost**  The value of the best alternative forgone when an item or activity is chosen

**sunk cost**  A cost that has already been incurred, cannot be recovered, and thus is irrelevant for present and future economic decisions

**law of comparative advantage**  The individual, firm, region, or country with the lowest opportunity cost of producing a particular good should specialize in that good

**absolute advantage**  The ability to make something using fewer resources than other producers use

**comparative advantage**  The ability to make something at a lower opportunity cost than other producers face

**barter**  The direct exchange of one product for another without using money

**division of labor**  Breaking down the production of a good into separate tasks

**specialization of labor**  Focusing work effort on a particular product or a single task

**production possibilities frontier (PPF)**  A curve showing alternative combinations of goods that can be produced when available resources are used efficiently; a boundary line between inefficient and unattainable combinations

**efficiency**  The condition that exists when there is no way resources can be reallocated to increase the production of one good without decreasing the production of another; getting the most from available resources

**law of increasing opportunity cost**  To produce more of one good, a successively larger amount of the other good must be sacrificed

**economic growth**  An increase in the economy's ability to produce goods and services; reflected by an outward shift of the economy's production possibilities frontier

**economic system**  The set of mechanisms and institutions that resolve the what, how, and for whom questions

**pure capitalism** An economic system characterized by the private ownership of resources and the use of prices to coordinate economic activity in unregulated markets

**private property rights** An owner's right to use, rent, or sell resources or property

**pure command system** An economic system characterized by the public ownership of resources and centralized planning

**mixed system** An economic system characterized by the private ownership of some resources and the public ownership of other resources; some markets are regulated by government

possibilities frontier, *AF*. The *PPF* is bowed out to reflect the law of increasing opportunity cost: additional units of capital goods require the economy to sacrifice more and more units of consumer goods. Note that more consumer goods must be given up in moving from *E* to *F* than in moving from *A* to *B*, although in each case the gain in capital goods is 10 million units. Points inside the *PPF*, such as *I*, represent inefficient use of resources. Points outside the *PPF*, such as *U*, represent unattainable combinations.

### Shifts of the Economy's Production Possibilities Frontier

When the resources available to an economy change, the *PPF* shifts. If more resources become available or if technology and know-how improve, the *PPF* shifts outward, as in panel (a), indicating that more output can be produced. A decrease in available resources causes the *PPF* to shift inward, as in panel (b). Panel (c) shows a change affecting consumer goods production. More consumer goods can now be produced at any given level of capital goods. Panel (d) shows a change affecting capital goods production.

## Shifts of the Economy's Production Possibilities Frontier

**(a)** Increase in available resources, better technology, more know-how, or improvement in the rules of the game

**(b)** Decrease in available resources or greater uncertainty in the rules of the game

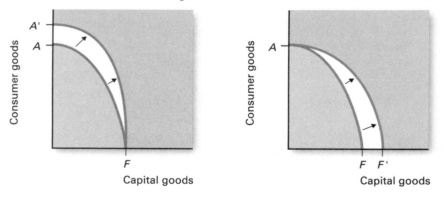

**(c)** Change in resources, technology, know-how, or rules that benefits consumer goods

**(d)** Change in resources, technology, know-how, or rules that benefits capital goods

**2-4 Describe different economic systems and the decision-making rules that define them.** All economic systems, regardless of their decision-making processes, must answer three basic questions: What is to be produced? How is it to be produced? And for whom is it to be produced? Economies answer the questions differently, depending on who owns the resources and how economic activity is coordinated. Economies can be directed by market forces, by the central plans of government, or, in most cases, by a mix of the two.

## KEY CONCEPTS

**3-1 Describe the major sources of income and expenditures for households.** Households play the starring role in a market economy. Their demand for goods and services determines what gets produced and their supplies of labor, capital, natural resources, and entrepreneurial ability produce that output. As demanders of goods and services and suppliers of resources, households make all kinds of choices in an attempt to maximize utility.

### Where U.S. Personal Income Comes From and Where It Goes

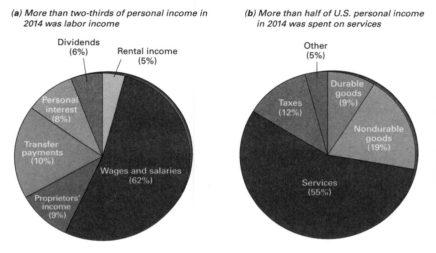

**(a)** *More than two-thirds of personal income in 2014 was labor income*

Dividends (6%)
Rental income (5%)
Personal interest (8%)
Transfer payments (10%)
Wages and salaries (62%)
Proprietors' income (9%)

**(b)** *More than half of U.S. personal income in 2014 was spent on services*

Other (5%)
Durable goods (9%)
Taxes (12%)
Nondurable goods (19%)
Services (55%)

**3-2 Outline the evolution of production over the centuries from the household to the modern corporation.** Household members once did everything for themselves. Over time, however, the efficiency arising from comparative advantage resulted in greater specialization. Firms are economic units formed by entrepreneurs who combine labor, capital, and natural resources to produce goods and services in an attempt to maximize profit. For-profit firms organize in one of three ways: as a sole proprietorship, as a partnership, or as a corporation. Not-for-profit organizations engage in activities that often have a social purpose, while cooperatives are groups that organize with the goal of minimizing costs.

### Percent Distribution by Type of Firm Based on Number of Firms and Firm Sales

**(a)** *Most firms are sole proprietorships*

Corporations (19%)
Partnerships (10%)
Sole proprietorships (71%)

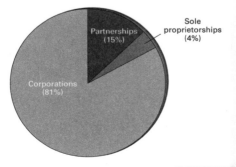

**(b)** *Corporations account for most sales*

Partnerships (15%)
Sole proprietorships (4%)
Corporations (81%)

## KEY TERMS

**utility** The satisfaction received from consumption; sense of well-being

**transfer payments** Cash or in-kind benefits given to individuals by the government

**Industrial Revolution** Development of large-scale factory production that began in Great Britain around 1750 and spread to the rest of Europe, North America, and Australia

**firms** Economic units formed by profit-seeking entrepreneurs who employ resources to produce goods and services for sale

**sole proprietorship** A firm with a single owner who has the right to all profits but who also bears unlimited liability for the firm's losses and debts

**partnership** A firm with multiple owners who share the profits and bear unlimited liability for the firm's losses and debts

**corporation** A legal entity owned by stockholders whose liability is limited to the value of their stock ownership

**cooperative** An organization consisting of people who pool their resources to buy and sell more efficiently than they could individually

**not-for-profit organizations** Groups that do not pursue profit as a goal; they engage in charitable, educational, humanitarian, cultural, professional, or other activities, often with a social purpose

**Information Revolution** Technological change spawned by the microchip and the Internet that enhanced the acquisition, analysis, and transmission of information

**market failure** A condition that arises when the unregulated operation of markets yields socially undesirable results

**antitrust laws** Prohibitions against price fixing and other anticompetitive practices

**monopoly** A sole supplier of a product with no close substitutes

**natural monopoly** One firm that can supply the entire market at a lower per-unit cost than could two or more firms

**private good** A good, such as pizza, that is both rival in consumption and exclusive

# CHAPTER REVIEW 3

**public good** A good that, once produced, is available for all to consume, regardless of who pays and who doesn't; such a good is nonrival and nonexclusive, such as a safer community

**externality** A cost or a benefit that affects neither the buyer nor seller, but instead affects people not involved in the market transaction

**fiscal policy** The use of government purchases, transfer payments, taxes, and borrowing to influence economy-wide variables such as inflation, employment, and economic growth

**monetary policy** Regulation of the money supply to influence economy-wide variables such as inflation, employment, and economic growth

**ability-to-pay tax principle** Those with a greater ability to pay, such as those earning higher incomes or those owning more property, should pay more taxes

**benefits-received tax principle** Those who get more benefits from the government program should pay more taxes

**tax incidence** The distribution of tax burden among taxpayers; who ultimately pays the tax

**proportional taxation** The tax as a percentage of income remains constant as income increases; also called a flat tax

**progressive taxation** The tax as a percentage of income increases as income increases

**marginal tax rate** The percentage of each additional dollar of income that goes to the tax

**regressive taxation** The tax as a percentage of income decreases as income increases

**merchandise trade balance** The value during a given period of a country's exported goods minus the value of its imported goods

**balance of payments** A record of all economic transactions during a given period between residents of one country and residents of the rest of the world

**foreign exchange** Foreign money needed to carry out international transactions

**tariff** A tax on imports

**quota** A legal limit on the quantity of a particular product that can be imported or exported

## 3-3 Summarize the seven roles of government in an economy.

Governments attempt to improve society's overall welfare by intervening in cases of market failure. Beneficial government interventions in markets include (1) establishing and enforcing the rules of the game, (2) promoting competition, (3) regulating natural monopolies, (4) providing public goods, (5) dealing with externalities, (6) more equally distributing income, and (7) pursuing full employment, price stability, and economic growth.

### Redistribution Has Grown and Defense Has Declined as Share of Federal Outlays: 1960–2016

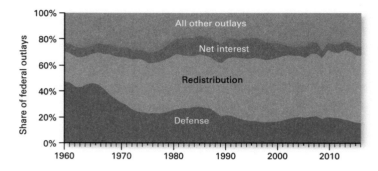

### Composition of Federal Revenue Between 1960 and 2016

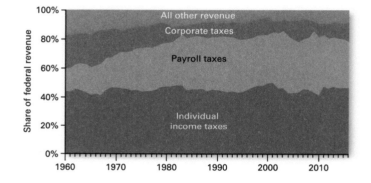

### Top Marginal Rate on Federal Personal Income Tax Since 1913

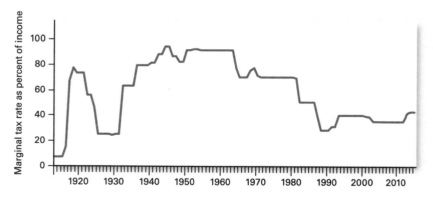

## 3-4 Explain why countries trade with each other and why they sometimes act to restrict that trade.
The rest of the world affects what U.S. households consume and what U.S. firms produce. U.S. households and firms are consumers and suppliers of manufactured goods and raw materials from and to foreign economies, and these transactions impact U.S. prices, wages, and profits. Although consumers gain from comparative advantage, nearly all countries impose trade restrictions to protect domestic industries from foreign competition.

## KEY CONCEPTS

**4-1 Explain why a demand curve slopes downward.** Demand is a relationship between the price of a product and the quantity consumers are willing and able to buy per period, other things constant. According to the law of demand, quantity demanded varies negatively, or inversely, with the price. A demand curve slopes downward because a price decrease makes consumers (a) more willing to substitute this good for other goods and (b) more able to buy the good because the lower price increases real income.

**4-2 Identify five things which could shift a demand curve to the right or left.** A change in any of the following could shift a demand curve right or left: (1) money income, (2) prices of other goods, (3) consumer expectations, (4) the number or composition of consumers in the market, and (5) consumer tastes.

**4-3 Explain why a supply curve usually slopes upward.** Supply is a relationship between the price of a good and the quantity producers are willing and able to sell per period, other things constant. The supply curve slopes upward because higher prices make producers (a) more willing to supply this good rather than supply other goods that use the same resources and (b) more able to cover the higher marginal cost associated with greater output rates.

**4-4 Identify five things which could shift a supply curve to the right or left.** A change in any of the following could shift a supply curve right or left: (1) the state of technology and know-how, (2) the prices of resources used to produce the good, (3) the prices of other goods that could be produced with these resources, (4) supplier expectations, and (5) the number of producers in the market.

**4-5 Explain why surpluses push prices down while shortages drive prices up.** A surplus means there are more goods supplied at that price than demanded. Suppliers lower the price to sell these surplus goods. A shortage means there are more goods demanded than supplied. Consumers bid up the price to buy these goods.

### The Market Demand Curve for Pizza

The market demand curve *D* shows the quantity of pizza demanded, at various prices, by all consumers. Price and quantity demanded are inversely related other things constant, reflecting the law of demand.

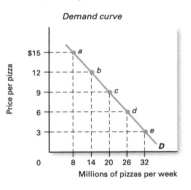

### The Market Supply Curve for Pizza

The Market supply curve *S* shows the quantities of pizza supplied, at various prices, by all pizza makers. Price and quantity supplied are directly related.

## KEY TERMS

**demand** A relation between the price of a good and the quantity that consumers are willing and able to buy per period, other things constant

**law of demand** The quantity of a good that consumers are willing and able to buy per period relates inversely, or negatively, to the price, other things constant

**substitution effect of a price change** When the price of a good falls, that good becomes cheaper compared to other goods so consumers tend to substitute that good for other goods

**money income** The number of dollars a person receives per period, such as $400 per week

**real income** Income measured by the goods and services it can buy; real income changes when the price changes

**income effect of a price change** A fall in the price of a good increases consumers' real income, making consumers more able to purchase goods; for a normal good, the quantity demanded increases

**demand curve** A curve showing the relation between the price of a good and the quantity consumers are willing and able to buy per period, other things constant

**quantity demanded** The amount of a good consumers are willing and able to buy per period at a particular price, as reflected by a point on a demand curve

**individual demand** The relation between the price of a good and the quantity purchased per period by an individual consumer, other things constant

**market demand** The relation between the price of a good and the quantity purchased per period by all consumers in the market, other things constant; sum of the individual demands in the market

**normal good** A good, such as new clothes, for which demand increases, or shifts rightward, as consumer income rises

**inferior good** A good, such as used clothes, for which demand decreases, or shifts leftward, as consumer income rises

**substitutes** Goods, such as tacos and pizza, that relate in such a way that an increase in the price of one shifts the demand for the other rightward

# CHAPTER REVIEW 4

**complements** Goods, such as Pepsi and pizza, that relate in such a way that an increase in the price of one shifts the demand for the other leftward

**tastes** Consumer preferences; likes and dislikes in consumption; assumed to remain constant along a given demand curve

**movement along a demand curve** A change in quantity demanded resulting from a change in the price of the good, other things constant

**shift of a demand curve** Movement of a demand curve right or left resulting from a change in one of the determinants of demand other than the price of the good

**supply** A relation between the price of a good and the quantity that producers are willing and able to sell per period, other things constant

**law of supply** The amount of a good that producers are willing and able to sell per period is usually directly related to its price, other things constant

**supply curve** A curve showing the relation between price of a good and the quantity producers are willing and able to sell per period, other things constant

**quantity supplied** The amount offered for sale per period at a particular price, as reflected by a point on a supply curve

**individual supply** The relation between the price of a good and the quantity an individual producer is willing and able to sell per period, other things constant

**market supply** The relation between the price of a good and the quantity all producers are willing and able to sell per period, other things constant

**movement along a supply curve** Change in quantity supplied resulting from a change in the price of the good, other things constant

**shift of a supply curve** Movement of a supply curve left or right resulting from a change in one of the determinants of supply other than the price of the good

**transaction costs** The costs of time and information required to carry out market exchange

**surplus** At a given price, the amount by which quantity supplied exceeds quantity demanded; a surplus usually forces the price down

**shortage** At a given price, the amount by which quantity demanded exceeds quantity supplied; a shortage usually forces the price up

**equilibrium** The condition that exists in a market when the plans of buyers match those of sellers, so quantity demanded equals quantity supplied and the market clears

## 4-6 Predict the impact of a change in demand or supply on the equilibrium price and quantity.
Market equilibrium, once established, will continue unless there is a change in a determinant that shapes demand or supply. The diagrams below demonstrate the impact of a shift of demand (upper panel) and a shift of supply (lower panel) on equilibrium price and quantity.

### Effects of an Increase in Market Demand

An increase in demand is shown by a shift of the demand curve rightward from *D* to *D'*. Both price and quantity are higher following the rightward shift of the demand curve.

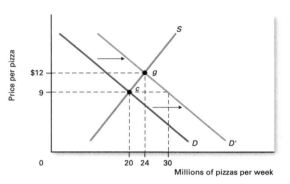

### Effects of an Increase in Market Supply

An increase in supply is shown by a shift of the supply curve rightward, from *S* to *S'*. At the new equilibrium, quantity is greater and the price is lower than before the increase in supply.

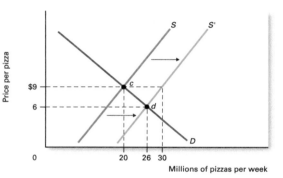

## 4-7 Describe the result of a government-set price floor and price ceiling on a market.
If the floor price is set above the market clearing price, quantity supplied exceeds quantity demanded, creating a surplus. If the ceiling price is set below the market clearing price, quantity demand exceeds that quantity supplied, creating a shortage.

**disequilibrium** The condition that exists in a market when the plans of buyers do not match those of sellers; a temporary mismatch between quantity supplied and quantity demanded as the market seeks equilibrium

**price floor** A minimum legal price below which a product cannot be sold; to have an

impact, a price floor must be set above the equilibrium price

**price ceiling** A maximum legal price above which a product cannot be sold; to have an impact, a price ceiling must be set below the equilibrium price

## KEY CONCEPTS

**5-1 Explain what's special about a national economy compared to regional, state, or local economies.** The national economy has its own currency, its own system of government, its own laws, regulations, customs, manners, and ways of doing business within its borders and across borders. Regional, state, and local economies operate within the larger, national economy.

**5-2 Describe the phases of the business cycle.** The economy fluctuates between two phases: periods of expansion and periods of contraction. See the figures below for details. No two business cycles are the same. Before 1945, expansions averaged 29 months and contractions 21 months. Since 1945, expansions have averaged 57 months and contractions 11 months. Despite the Great Depression and later recessions, the economy's output has grown more than fifteenfold since 1929 and jobs have grown faster than the population.

### Hypothetical Business Cycles

Business cycles reflect movements of economic activity around a trend line that shows long-term growth. An expansion (shaded in blue) begins when the economy starts to grow and continues until the economy reaches a peak. After an expansion has peaked, a contraction (shaded in pink) begins and continues until the economy reaches a trough.

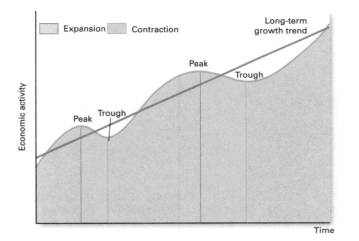

### Annual Percentage Change in U.S. Real GDP Since 1929

Years of declining real GDP are shown as red bars and years of growth as blue bars. Note that the year-to-year swings in output became less pronounced after World War II.

## KEY TERMS

**economy** The structure of economic activity in a community, a region, a country, a group of countries, or the world

**gross domestic product (GDP)** The market value of all final goods and services produced in the nation during a particular period, usually a year

**gross world product** The market value of all final goods and services produced in the world during a given period, usually a year

**flow variable** A measure of something per period of time, such as your spending per week

**stock variable** A measure of something at a point in time, such as the amount of money you have with you right now

**mercantilism** The incorrect theory that a nation's economic objective should be to accumulate precious metals in the public treasury; this theory prompted trade barriers, which cut imports, but other countries retaliated, reducing trade and the gains from specialization

**expansion** A period during which the economy grows as reflected by rising output, employment, income, and other aggregate measures

**contraction** A period during which the economy declines as reflected by falling output, employment, income, and other aggregate measures

**depression** A severe and prolonged reduction in economic activity, as occurred during the 1930s

**recession** A period of decline in economic activity lasting more than a few months, as reflected by falling output, employment, income, and other aggregate measures

**inflation** An increase in the economy's average price level

**leading economic indicators** Variables that predict or lead to a recession or recovery; examples include consumer confidence, stock market prices, business investment, and big-ticket purchases, such as automobiles and homes

**coincident economic indicators** Variables that reflect peaks and troughs in economic activity as they occur; examples include employment, personal income, and industrial production

**lagging economic indicators** Variables that follow, or trail, changes in overall economic activity; examples include the interest rate, the unemployment rate, and the average duration of unemployment

**aggregate output** A composite measure of all final goods and services produced in an economy during a given period; real GDP

**aggregate demand** The relationship between the economy's price level and aggregate output demanded, with other things constant

**price level** A composite measure reflecting the prices of all goods and services in the economy relative to prices in a base year

**real gross domestic product (real GDP)** The economy's aggregate output measured in dollars of constant purchasing power

**aggregate demand curve** A curve representing the relationship between the economy's price level and real GDP demanded per period, with other things constant

**aggregate supply curve** A curve representing the relationship between the economy's price level and real GDP supplied per period, with other things constant

**federal budget deficit** A flow variable measuring the amount by which federal government outlays exceed federal government revenues in a particular period, usually a year

**demand-side economics** Macroeconomic policy that focuses on shifting the aggregate demand curve as a way of promoting full employment and price stability

**stagflation** A contraction, or stagnation, of a nation's output accompanied by inflation in the price level

**supply-side economics** Macroeconomic policy that focuses on a rightward shift of the aggregate supply curve through tax cuts or other changes to increase production incentives

**federal debt** A stock variable that measures the net accumulation of annual federal deficits

**real GDP per capita** Real GDP divided by the population; the best measure of an economy's standard of living

**5-3 Explain the shapes of the aggregate demand curve and the aggregate supply curve, and how they interact to determine real GDP and the price level for a nation.** The aggregate demand curve slopes downward, reflecting a negative, or inverse, relationship between the price level and real GDP demanded. The aggregate supply curve slopes upward, reflecting a positive, or direct, relationship between the price level and real GDP supplied. The intersection of the two curves determines the economy's real GDP and price level. See the figures below.

### U.S. Aggregate Demand Curve

The quantity of aggregate output demanded is inversely related to the price level, other things constant. This inverse relationship is reflected by the aggregate demand curve AD.

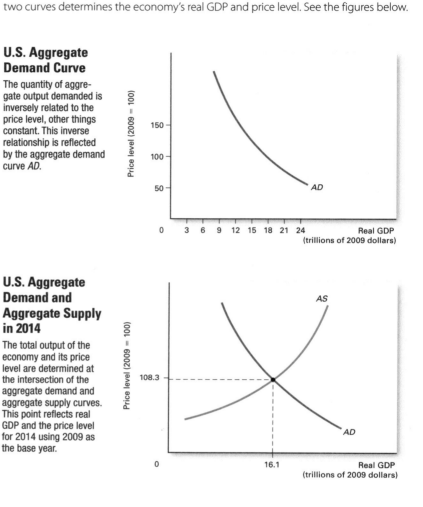

### U.S. Aggregate Demand and Aggregate Supply in 2014

The total output of the economy and its price level are determined at the intersection of the aggregate demand and aggregate supply curves. This point reflects real GDP and the price level for 2014 using 2009 as the base year.

**5-4 Identify the five eras of the U.S economy, and describe briefly what went on during each.** 1) The Great Depression and Before: The Great Depression and earlier depressions prompted John Maynard Keynes to argue that the economy is unstable, largely because business investment is erratic. Keynes did not believe that contractions were self-correcting. 2) The Age of Keynes: His demand-side policies of increased government spending and decreased taxes dominated macroeconomic thinking between World War II and the late 1960s.

(3) Stagflation: During the 1970s, higher oil prices and global crop failures reduced aggregate supply. The result was stagflation, the troublesome combination of declining real GDP and rising inflation. 4) Somewhat Normal Times of 1980 until 2007: Output and employment also grew nicely during this era. The expanding economy increased federal revenues enough to create a federal budget surplus by the end of the 1990s. But after the longest expansion on record, the economy experienced an eight-month recession in 2001. The economy started growing again, and that expansion lasted until the end of 2007.

5) The Great Recession of 2007 to 2009 and Beyond: After peaking in December 2007, the economy entered a recession because of falling home prices and rising foreclosure rates. The collapse of a Wall Street bank in September 2008 panicked financial markets around the world, cutting investment and consumption. Job losses during this Great Recession were the highest since the Great Depression. Massive federal programs aimed at stabilizing the economy resulted in gigantic federal deficits. Economic growth returned in the second half of 2009, but the unemployment rate remained stubbornly high for years.

## KEY CONCEPTS

**6-1 Describe the two ways of computing GDP and explain why they are equivalent.** Gross domestic product, or GDP, measures the market value of all final goods and services produced during the year by resources located in the United States, regardless of who owns those resources. The expenditure approach to GDP adds up the market value of all final goods and services produced in the economy during the year. The income approach to GDP adds up all the income generated as a result of that production.

**6-2 Trace through the circular-flow model, explaining each of the 10 steps along the way.** The circular-flow model summarizes the flow of income and spending through the economy. Saving, net taxes, and imports leak from the circular flow. These leakages equal the injections into the circular flow from investment, government purchases, and exports. See the figure below, which traces the 10 steps along the way.

### Circular Flow of Income and Expenditure

The circular-flow model captures important relationships in the economy. The bottom half depicts the income arising from production. At juncture (1), GDP equals aggregate income. Taxes leak from the flow at (2), but transfer payments enter the flow at (3). Taxes minus transfers equal net taxes, *NT*. Aggregate income minus net taxes equals disposable income, *DI*, which flows to households at juncture (4). The top half of the model shows the flow of expenditure. At (5), households either spend disposable income or save it. Consumption enters the spending flow directly. Saving leaks from the spending flow into financial markets, where it is channeled to borrowers. At (6), investment enters the spending flow. At (7), government purchases enter the spending flow. At (8), imports leak from the spending flow, and at (9), exports enter the spending flow. Consumption plus investment plus government purchases plus net exports add up to the aggregate expenditure on GDP received by firms at (10).

## KEY TERMS

**expenditure approach to GDP** Calculating GDP by adding up spending on all final goods and services produced in the nation during the year

**income approach to GDP** Calculating GDP by adding up all earnings from resources used to produce output in the nation during the year

**final goods and services** Goods and services sold to final, or end, users

**intermediate goods and services** Goods and services purchased by firms for further reprocessing and resale

**double counting** The mistake of including both the value of intermediate products and the value of final products in calculating gross domestic product; counting the same production more than once

**consumption** Household purchases of final goods and services, except for new residences, which count as investment

**investment** The purchase of new plants, new software, new equipment, new buildings, and new residences, plus net additions to inventories

**physical capital** Manufactured items used to produce goods and services; includes new plants and new equipment

**residential construction** Building new homes or dwelling places

**inventories** Producers' stocks of finished and in-process goods

**government purchases** Spending for goods and services by all levels of government; government outlays minus transfer payments

**net exports** The value of a country's exports minus the value of its imports

**aggregate expenditure** Total spending on final goods and services in an economy during a given period, usually a year; the sum of consumption, investment, government purchases, and net exports

**aggregate income** All earnings of resource suppliers in an economy during a given period, usually a year

**value added** At each stage of production, the selling price of a product minus the cost of intermediate goods purchased from other firms

**disposable income (DI)** The income households have available to spend or to save after paying taxes and receiving transfer payments

**net taxes (NT)** Taxes minus transfer payments

**financial markets** Banks and other financial institutions that facilitate the flow of funds from savers to borrowers

**injection** Any spending other than by households or any income other than from resource earnings; includes investment, government purchases, exports, and transfer payments

**leakage** Any diversion of income from the domestic spending stream; includes saving, taxes, and imports

**underground economy** Market transactions that go unreported either because they are illegal or because people involved want to evade taxes

**depreciation** The value of capital stock used up to produce GDP or that becomes obsolete during the year

**net domestic product** Gross domestic product minus depreciation

**nominal GDP** GDP based on prices prevailing at the time of production

**base year** The year with which other years are compared when constructing an index; the index equals 100 in the base year

**price index** A number that shows the average price of products; changes in a price index over time show changes in the economy's average price level

**consumer price index, or CPI** A measure of inflation based on the cost of a fixed market basket of goods and services

**GDP price index** A comprehensive inflation measure of all goods and services included in the gross domestic product

**chain-weighted system** An inflation measure that adjusts the weights from year to year in calculating a price index, thereby reducing the bias caused by a fixed-price weighting system

**6-3    Identify the limitations of the national income accounting system.** GDP reflects market production in a given period, usually a year. Most household production and the underground economy are not captured by GDP. Improvements in the quality and variety of products also are often missed in GDP. In other ways GDP may overstate production. GDP fails to subtract for the depreciation of the capital stock or for the depletion of natural resources and fails to account for any negative externalities arising from production.

**6-4    Define a price index and explain why is it useful.** Nominal GDP in a particular year values output based on market prices when the output was produced. To determine real GDP, nominal GDP must be adjusted for price changes. The consumer price index, or CPI, tracks prices for a market basket of goods and services over time. The GDP price index tracks price changes for all output. No adjustment for price changes is perfect, but current approaches offer a reasonably good estimate of real GDP both at a point in time and over time.

### U.S. Gross Domestic Product in Nominal Dollars and Chained (2009) Dollars Since 1929

Real GDP, the red line, shows the value of output measured in chained (2009) dollars. The blue line measures GDP in nominal dollars, of each year shown. The two lines intersect in 2009, when real GDP equaled nominal GDP. Year-to-year changes in nominal-dollar GDP reflect changes in both real GDP and in the price level. Year-to-year changes in chained-dollar GDP reflect changes in real GDP only. Nominal-dollar GDP grows faster than chained-dollar GDP. Prior to 2009, nominal-dollar prices are less than chained-dollar prices, so nominal-dollar GDP is less than chained-dollar GDP.

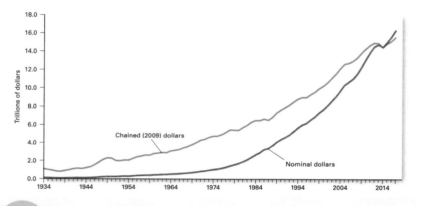

## CHAPTER EQUATIONS

### Aggregate Expenditure

$$C + I + G + (X - M) = \text{Aggregate expenditure} = \text{GDP}$$
$$C = \text{Consumption}$$
$$I = \text{Investment}$$
$$G = \text{Government purchases}$$
$$(X - M) = \text{Net exports} = \text{Exports} - \text{Imports}$$

### Aggregate Income

$$\text{GDP} = \text{Aggregate income} = DI + NT$$

### Disposable Income

$$DI = C + S$$
$$C + I + G + (X - M) = DI + NT$$
$$C + I + G + (X - M) = C + S + NT$$
$$I + G + X = S + NT + M$$

### GDP Price Index

$$\text{GDP price index} = \frac{\text{Nominal GDP}}{\text{Real GDP}} \times 100$$

## KEY CONCEPTS

**7-1 Describe what the unemployment rate measures, and summarize four sources of unemployment.** The unemployment rate is the number of people looking for work divided by the number in the labor force. The unemployment rate masks differences among particular groups and across regions. The rate is lowest among white adults and highest among black teenagers.

There are four sources of unemployment. Frictional unemployment arises because employers and qualified job seekers need time to find one another. Seasonal unemployment stems from the effects of weather and the seasons on certain industries, such as construction and agriculture. Structural unemployment arises because changes in tastes, technology, taxes, and competition reduce the demand for certain skills and increase the demand for other skills. And cyclical unemployment results from fluctuations in economic activity caused by the business cycle. Policy makers and economists are less concerned with frictional and seasonal unemployment. Full employment occurs when cyclical unemployment is zero.

**The Adult Population Sums the Employed, the Unemployed, and Those Not in the Labor Force: February 2015 (in millions)**

The labor force, depicted by the left circle, consists of those employed plus those unemployed. Those not working, depicted by the right circle, consists of those not in the labor force and those unemployed. The adult population sums the employed, the unemployed, and those not in the labor force.

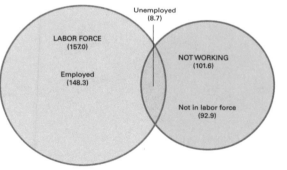

**7-2 Outline the pros and cons of unemployment insurance.** Unemployment often creates both an economic and a psychological hardship. For some, this burden is reduced by an employed spouse and by unemployment insurance. Unemployment insurance provides a safety net for some and that's good, but it may also reduce incentives to find work, as is the case in Europe, and that's an unintended consequence. Research suggests that those collecting unemployment insurance remain unemployed longer than those who don't.

**7-3 Define inflation and describe the two sources of inflation.** Inflation is a sustained rise in the average price level. An increase in aggregate demand can cause demand-pull inflation. A decrease in aggregate supply can cause cost-push inflation. Prior to World War II, both inflation and deflation were common, but since then the price level has increased virtually every year.

**7-4 Explain how unanticipated inflation harms some individuals and harms the economy as a whole.** Anticipated inflation causes fewer distortions in the economy than unanticipated inflation. Unanticipated inflation arbitrarily creates winners and losers, and forces people to spend more time and energy coping with the effects of inflation. The negative effects of high and variable inflation on productivity can be observed most dramatically in countries that have experienced hyperinflation, such as Zimbabwe.

## KEY TERMS

**labor force** Those 16 years of age and older who are either working or looking for work

**unemployment rate** The number unemployed as a percentage of the labor force

**discouraged workers** Those who drop out of the labor force in frustration because they can't find work

**labor force participation rate** The labor force as a percentage of the adult population

**long-term unemployed** Those looking for work for 27 weeks or longer

**frictional unemployment** Unemployment that occurs because job seekers and employers need time to find each other

**seasonal unemployment** Unemployment caused by seasonal changes in the demand for certain kinds of labor

**structural unemployment** Unemployment because (1) the skills demanded by employers do not match those of the unemployed, or (2) the unemployed do not live where the jobs are

**cyclical unemployment** Unemployment that fluctuates with the business cycle, increasing during recessions and decreasing during expansions

**full employment** Employment level when there is no cyclical unemployment

**unemployment benefits** Cash transfers to those who lose their jobs and actively seek employment

**underemployment** Workers are overqualified for their jobs or work fewer hours than they would prefer

**hyperinflation** A very high rate of inflation

**deflation** A sustained decrease in the price level

**disinflation** A reduction in the rate of inflation

**demand-pull inflation** A sustained rise in the price level caused by a rightward shift of the aggregate demand curve

**cost-push inflation** A sustained rise in the price level caused by a leftward shift of the aggregate supply curve

**interest** The dollar amount paid by borrowers to lenders

**interest rate** Interest per year as a percentage of the amount loaned

**nominal interest rate** The interest rate expressed in dollars of current value (that is, not adjusted for inflation) as a percentage of the amount loaned; the interest rate specified on the loan agreement

**real interest rate** The interest rate expressed in dollars of constant purchasing power as a percentage of the amount loaned; the nominal interest rate minus the inflation rate

**COLA** Cost-of-living adjustment; an increase in wage or transfer payments tied to increases in the price level

## Inflation Caused by Shifts of Aggregate Demand and Aggregate Supply Curves

Panel (a) illustrates demand-pull inflation. An outward shift of the aggregate demand to *AD'* "pulls" the price level up from *P* to *P'*. Panel (b) shows cost-push inflation. A decrease of aggregate supply to *AS'* "pushes" the price level up from *P* to *P'*.

(a) Demand-pull inflation: inflation caused by an increase of aggregate demand

(b) Cost-push inflation: inflation caused by a decrease of aggregate supply

## Consumer Price Index Since 1913

Panel (a) shows that, despite fluctuations, the price level, as measured by the consumer price index, was lower in 1940 than in 1920. The price level began rising in the 1940s. Panel (b) shows the annual rate of change in the price level.

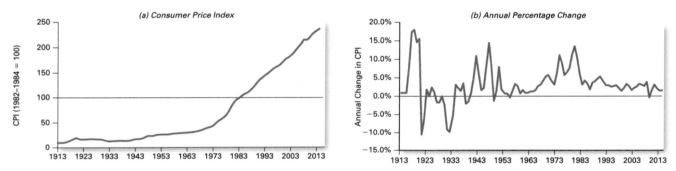

(a) Consumer Price Index

(b) Annual Percentage Change

## The Market for Loanable Funds

The upward-sloping supply curve, *S*, shows that more loanable funds are supplied at higher interest rates. The downward-sloping demand curve, *D*, shows that the quantity of loanable funds demanded is greater at lower interest rates. The two curves intersect to determine the market interest rate, *i*.

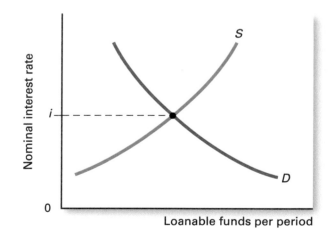

## KEY CONCEPTS

**8-1 Describe how we measure labor productivity, and explain why is it important for a nation's standard of living.** If the population is continually increasing, an economy must produce more goods and services simply to maintain its standard of living, as measured by output per capita. If output grows faster than the population, the standard of living rises.

The per-worker production function shows the relationship between the amount of capital per worker in the economy and the output per worker. As capital per worker increases, so does output per worker but at a decreasing rate. Technological change, increased know-how, and improvements in the rules of the game shift the per-worker production function upward.

### Economic Growth Shown by Shifts Outward of the Production Possibilities Frontier

An economy that produces more capital goods will grow more, as reflected by a shift outward of the production possibilities frontier. More capital goods are produced in panel (b) than in panel (a), so the PPF shifts out more in panel (b).

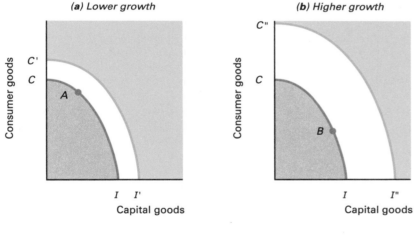

**(a) Lower growth**

**(b) Higher growth**

### Per-Worker Production Function

The per-worker production function, *PF*, shows a direct relationship between the amount of capital per worker, *k*, and the output per worker, *y*. The bowed shape of *PF* reflects the law of diminishing marginal returns from capital, which holds that as more capital is added to a given number of workers, output per worker increases but at a diminishing rate and eventually could turn negative.

## KEY TERMS

**production** A process that transforms resources into goods and services

**productivity** The ratio of a specific measure of output, such as real GDP, to a specific measure of input, such as labor; in this case productivity measures real GDP per hour of labor

**labor productivity** Output per unit of labor; measured as real GDP divided by the hours of labor employed to produce that output

**per-worker production function** The relationship between the amount of capital per worker in the economy and average output per worker

**capital deepening** An increase in the amount of capital per worker; one source of rising labor productivity

**rules of the game** The laws, customs, manners, conventions, and other institutional elements that determine transaction costs and thereby affect people's incentive to undertake production and exchange

**social capital** The shared values and trust that promote cooperation in the economy

**industrial market countries** The economically advanced capitalist countries of Western Europe, North America, Australia, New Zealand, and Japan, plus the newly industrialized Asian economies of Taiwan, South Korea, Hong Kong, and Singapore

**developing countries** Countries with a lower living standard because of less human and physical capital per worker

**basic research** The search for knowledge without regard to how that knowledge will be used

**applied research** Research that seeks answers to particular questions or to apply scientific discoveries to develop specific products

**industrial policy** The view that government—using taxes, subsidies, and regulations—should nurture the industries and technologies of the future, thereby giving these domestic industries an advantage over foreign competition

## 8-2 Summarize the history of U.S. labor productivity changes since World War II, and explain why these changes matter.

Since 1870, U.S. labor productivity growth has averaged 2.1 percent per year. The quality of labor and capital is much more important than the quantity of these resources. Between 1947 and 1973, labor productivity was strong, averaging 2.8 percent. (See the bar chart on the lower right portion of this page.) Labor productivity growth slowed between 1973 and 1982, in part because of spikes in energy prices and implementation of costly but necessary environmental and workplace regulations. After 1982 productivity growth picked up, especially between 1995 and 2005, due primarily to information technology. But since 2005, productivity growth has slowed down perhaps because of uncertainty created by the Great Recession. Labor productivity growth is key to a higher standard of living, as reflected by per capita income and output.

Among the seven major industrial market economies, the United States has experienced the second highest growth rate in real GDP per capita over the last two decades and most recently produced the highest real GDP per capita.

## 8-3 Evaluate the evidence that technological change increases the unemployment rate.

Technological change sometimes costs jobs in the short run when workers fail to adjust. Over time, however, most displaced workers find other jobs, sometimes in new industries created by technological change. There is no evidence that, in the long run, technological change increases unemployment in the economy.

Some governments use industrial policy in an effort to nurture the industries and technologies of the future, giving domestic industries an advantage over foreign competitors. But critics are wary of the government's ability to pick the winning technologies of the future.

### U.S. GDP Per Capita in 2014 Was Highest of G-7 Economies and Four Times China's

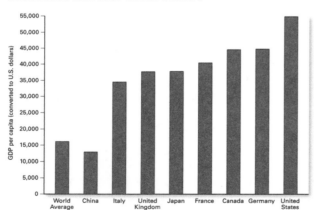

### Impact of a Technological Breakthrough on the Per-Worker Production Function

A technological breakthrough increases output per worker at each level of capital per worker. Better technology makes workers more productive. This is shown by a rotation upward in the per-worker production function from $PF$ to $PF'$. An improvement in know-how or the rules of the game would have a similar effect.

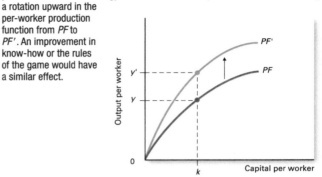

### Long-Term Trend in U.S. Labor Productivity Growth: Annual Average by Decade

Annual productivity growth, measured as the growth in real output per work hour, is averaged by decade. For the entire period since 1870, labor productivity grew an average of 2.1 percent per year. Note the big dip during the Great Depression of the 1930s and the big bounce back during World War II. Productivity growth slowed during the 1970s and 1980s but recovered slightly during the 1990s and 2000s.

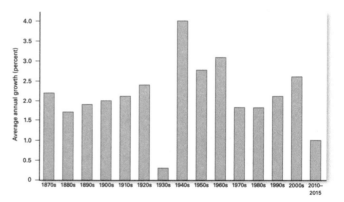

### U.S. Labor Productivity Growth Since 1947

The growth in labor productivity declined from an average of 2.8 percent per year between 1947 and 1973 to only 0.9 percent between 1973 and 1982. A jump in the price of oil contributed to three recessions during that stretch, and new environmental and workplace regulations, though necessary and beneficial, slowed down productivity growth temporarily. The information revolution powered by the computer chip and the Internet has boosted productivity between 1982 and 2005.

## KEY CONCEPTS

### 9-1 Explain what a consumption function illustrates and interpret its slope.
The most predictable and most useful relationship in macroeconomics is between consumption and income. The more people have available to spend, the more they spend on consumption, other things constant. The consumption function shows the link between consumption and income in the economy. The slope of the consumption function reflects the marginal propensity to consume, which is the change in consumption divided by the change in income. The slope of the saving function reflects the marginal propensity to save, which is the change in saving divided by the change in income.

### The Consumption Function

The consumption function, *C*, shows the relationship between consumption and disposable income, other things constant.

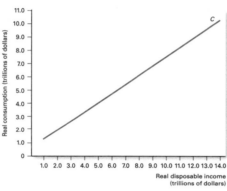

### The Marginal Propensity to Consume and the Consumption Function

The slope of the consumption function equals the marginal propensity to consume. For the straight-line consumption function, the slope is the same at all levels of income and is given by the change in consumption divided by the change in disposable income that causes it. Thus, the marginal propensity to consume equals $\Delta C/\Delta DI$, or $0.4/0.5 = 4/5$.

$$MPC = \frac{\Delta C}{\Delta DI} = \frac{0.4}{0.5} = \frac{4}{5}$$

### 9-2 Describe what can shift the consumption function up or down.
Changes in certain variables, such as household wealth, the price level, interest rates, and consumer expectations, can shift the consumption function up or down. Where people are in their "life-cycle" also influences their spending habits.

### Shifts of the Consumption Function

A downward shift of the consumption function, such as from *C* to *C'*, can be caused by a decrease in net wealth, an increase in the price level, an unfavorable change in consumer expectations, or an increase in the interest rate. An upward shift, such as from *C* to *C''*, can be caused by an increase in net wealth, a decrease in the price level, a favorable change in expectations, or a decrease in the interest rate.

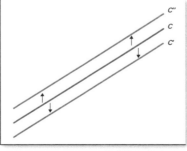

## KEY TERMS

**consumption function** The relationship in the economy between consumption and income, other things constant

**marginal propensity to consume (MPC)** The fraction of a change in income that is spent on consumption; the change in consumption divided by the change in income that caused it

**marginal propensity to save (MPS)** The fraction of a change in income that is saved; the change in saving divided by the change in income that caused it

**net wealth** The value of assets minus liabilities

**life-cycle model of consumption and saving** Young people borrow, middle agers pay off debts and save, and older people draw down their savings; on average, net savings over a lifetime is usually little or nothing

**aggregate expenditure line** A relationship tracing, for a given price level, spending at each level of income, or real GDP; the total of $C + I + G + (X - M)$ at each level of income, or real GDP

**income-expenditure model** A relationship that shows how much people plan to spend at each income level; this model identifies, for a given price level, where the amount people plan to spend equals the amount produced in the economy

**simple spending multiplier** The ratio of a change in real GDP demanded to the initial change in spending that brought it about; the numerical value of the simple spending multiplier is $1/(1 - MPC)$; called "simple" because only consumption varies with income

## CHAPTER EQUATION

$$MPC + MPS = 1$$

**9-3 Explain why investment varies more than consumption from year to year.** Investment depends on the market interest rate and on business expectations. Investment fluctuates from year to year but averaged about one-sixth of GDP during the last decade. Consumption is more stable because people still need to eat, pay their electricity bills and buy gas even if the economy slows down. But businesses do not have to invest nearly as much if their profit expectations sour.

**9-4 Describe how the aggregate expenditure line determines the quantity of aggregate output demanded.** The aggregate expenditure line indicates, for a given price level, spending plans at each income level. At a given price level, real GDP demanded is found where the amount that people plan to spend equals the amount produced.

### Deriving the Real GDP Demanded for a Given Price Level

Real GDP demanded for a given price level is found where aggregate expenditure equals aggregate output—that is, where spending equals the amount produced, or real GDP. This occurs at point *e*, where the aggregate expenditure line intersects the 45-degree line.

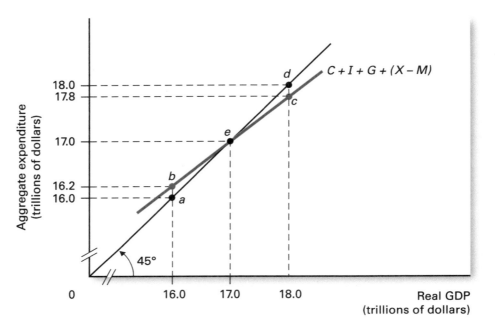

**9-5 Determine the simple spending multiplier and explain its relevance.** The spending multiplier indicates the multiple by which a change in the amount people plan to spend changes real GDP demanded. The simple spending multiplier developed in this chapter is $1/(1 - MPC)$. The larger the MPC, the more is spent and the less is saved, so the larger the simple spending multiplier. This multiplier is called "simple" because only consumption changes with changes in income.

**9-6 Summarize the relationship between the aggregate expenditure line and the aggregate demand curve.** A higher price level causes a downward shift of the aggregate expenditure line, leading to a lower real GDP demanded. A lower price level causes an upward shift of the aggregate expenditure line, increasing real GDP demanded. By tracing the impact of price changes on real GDP demanded, we can derive an aggregate demand curve.The aggregate expenditure line and the aggregate demand curve portray real output from different perspectives. The aggregate expenditure line shows, for a given price level, how much people plan to spend at each income level. Real GDP demanded is found where spending equals income, or real GDP. The aggregate demand curve shows, for various price levels, the quantities of real GDP demanded. At a given price level, a change in spending plans shifts the aggregate demand curve.

## KEY CONCEPTS

### 10-1 Explain what determines the shape and position of the short-run aggregate supply curve.
Short-run aggregate supply is based on resource demand and supply decisions that reflect the expected price level. If the price level turns out as expected, the economy produces its potential output. If the price level exceeds expectations, short-run output exceeds the economy's potential, creating an expansionary gap. If the price level is below expectations, short-run output falls short of the economy's potential, creating a recessionary gap.

### Short-Run Aggregate Supply Curve

The short-run aggregate supply curve is based on a given expected price level, in this case, 110. Point *a* shows that if the actual price level equals the expected price level of 110, firms supply potential output. If the actual price level exceeds 110, quantity supplied exceeds potential. If the actual price level is below 110, quantity supplied is less than potential. Output levels that fall short of the economy's potential are shaded pink; output levels that exceed the economy's potential are shaded blue.

### 10-2 Describe the market forces that push the economy toward its potential output in the long run.
Output can exceed the economy's potential in the short run, but in the long run, higher nominal wages will be negotiated at the earliest opportunity. This increases the cost of production, shifting the short-run aggregate supply curve leftward along the aggregate demand curve until the economy produces its potential output.

### Long-Run Adjustment When the Price Level Exceeds Expectations

If the expected price level is 110, the short-run aggregate supply curve is $SRAS_{110}$. If the actual price level turns out as expected, the quantity supplied is the potential output of $17.0 trillion. But here the price level ends up higher than expected, and output exceeds potential, as shown by the short-run equilibrium at point *b*. The amount by which actual output exceeds the economy's potential output is called the expansionary gap. In the long run, price-level expectations and nominal wages will be revised upward. Costs will rise and

the short-run aggregate supply curve will shift leftward to $SRAS_{120}$. Eventually, the economy will move to long-run equilibrium at point *c*, thus closing the expansionary gap.

### Long-Run Adjustment When the Price Level Is Below Expectations

When the actual price level is below expectations, as indicated by the intersection of the aggregate demand curve AD'' with the short-run aggregate supply curve $SRAS_{110}$, short-run equilibrium occurs at point *d*. Production below the economy's potential opens a recessionary gap of $0.2 trillion. If prices and wages are flexible enough in the long run, nominal wages will be renegotiated lower. As resource costs fall, the short-run aggregate supply curve eventually shifts rightward to $SRAS_{100}$ and the economy moves to long-run equilibrium at point *e*, with output increasing to the potential level of $17.0 trillion.

## KEY TERMS

**nominal wage** The wage measured in dollars of the year in question; the dollar amount on a paycheck

**real wage** The wage measured in dollars of constant purchasing power; the wage measured in terms of the quantity of goods and services it buys

**potential output** The economy's maximum sustainable output, given the supply of resources, technology and know-how, and rules of the game; the output level when there are no surprises about the price level

**natural rate of unemployment** The unemployment rate when the economy produces its potential output

**short run** In macroeconomics, a period during which some resource prices, especially those for labor, remain fixed by explicit or implicit agreements

**short-run aggregate supply (SRAS) curve** A curve that shows a direct relationship between the actual price level and real GDP supplied in the short run, other things constant, including the expected price level

**short-run equilibrium** The price level and real GDP that result when the aggregate demand curve intersects the short-run aggregate supply curve

**expansionary gap** The amount by which actual output in the short run exceeds the economy's potential output

**long run** In macroeconomics, a period during which wage contracts and resource price agreements can be renegotiated; there are no surprises about the economy's actual price level

**long-run equilibrium** The price level and real GDP that occur when (1) the actual price level equals the expected price level, (2) real GDP supplied equals potential output, and (3) real GDP supplied equals real GDP demanded

**recessionary gap** The amount by which actual output in the short run falls short of the economy's potential output

**long-run aggregate supply (LRAS) curve** A vertical line at the economy's potential output; aggregate supply when there are no surprises about the price level and all resource contracts can be renegotiated

**coordination failure** A situation in which workers and employers fail to achieve an outcome that all would prefer

**supply shocks** Unexpected events that affect aggregate supply, sometimes only temporarily

**beneficial supply shocks** Unexpected events that increase aggregate supply, sometimes only temporarily

**adverse supply shocks** Unexpected events that reduce aggregate supply, sometimes only temporarily

**hysteresis** The theory that the natural rate of unemployment depends in part on the recent history of unemployment; a long period of high unemployment can increase the natural rate of unemployment

## Long-Run Aggregate Supply Curve

In the long run, when the actual price level equals the expected price level, the economy produces its potential. In the long run, $17.0 trillion in real GDP is supplied regardless of the actual price level. As long as wages and prices are flexible enough, the economy's potential GDP is consistent with any price level. Thus, shifts of the aggregate demand curve, in the long run, do not affect potential output. The long-run aggregate supply curve, *LRAS*, is a vertical line at potential GDP.

### 10-3 Explain why shifts of the aggregate demand curve change the price level in the long run but do not change potential output. 
If output in the short run is less than the economy's potential and if wages and prices are flexible enough, lower nominal wages will reduce production costs in the long run. These lower costs shift the short-run aggregate supply curve rightward along the aggregate demand curve until the economy produces its potential output.

Evidence suggests that when output exceeds the economy's potential, nominal wages and the price level increase. But there is less evidence that nominal wages and the price level fall when output is below the economy's potential. Wages appear to be "sticky" in the downward direction. What usually closes a recessionary gap is an increase in aggregate demand. If the economy is already producing it's potential output, a shift of the aggregate demand curve can change the price level in the long run but will not change potential output.

### 10-4 Summarize what can shift an economy's potential output in the long run. 
The long-run aggregate supply curve, or the economy's potential output, depends on the amount and quality of resources available, the state of technology, and formal and informal institutions, such as patent laws and business practices, that shape production incentives. Increases in resource availability, improvements in technology, or institutional changes that provide more attractive production incentives increase aggregate supply and potential output.

Supply shocks are unexpected, often temporary changes in aggregate supply. Beneficial supply shocks increase output, sometimes only temporarily. Adverse supply shocks reduce output and increase the price level, a combination called stagflation. Adverse supply shocks may be temporary.

Sometimes, the natural rate of unemployment can depend in part on the recent history of unemployment. A long period of high unemployment may increase the natural rate of unemployment. This effect is known as hysteresis.

### Effect of a Gradual Increase in Resources on Aggregate Supply

A gradual growth in the supply of resources increases the potential GDP—in this case, from $17.0 trillion to $17.5 trillion. The long-run aggregate supply curve shifts to the right.

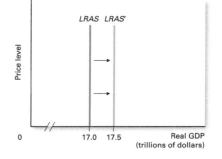

### Effects of a Beneficial Supply Shock on Aggregate Supply

A beneficial supply shock that has a lasting effect, such as a breakthrough in technology, permanently shifts both the short-run and the long-run aggregate supply curves to the right. A beneficial supply shock lowers the price level and increases output, as reflected by the change in equilibrium from point *a* to point *b*. A temporary beneficial supply shock shifts the aggregate supply curves only temporarily.

### Effects of an Adverse Supply Shock on Aggregate Supply

Given the aggregate demand curve, an adverse supply shock, such as a drought, shifts the short-run and long-run aggregate supply curves to the left, increasing the price level and reducing real GDP, a movement called stagflation. This change is shown by the move in equilibrium from point *a* to point *c*. If the shock is just temporary, the shift of the aggregate supply curves will be temporary.

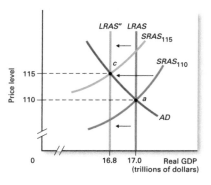

## KEY CONCEPTS

### 11-1 Describe the discretionary fiscal policies to close a recessionary gap and an expansionary gap.
The tools of fiscal policy are automatic stabilizers and discretionary fiscal measures. Automatic stabilizers, such as the federal income tax, once implemented, operate year after year without congressional action. Discretionary fiscal policy results from specific legislation about government spending, taxation, and transfers. If that legislation becomes permanent, then discretionary fiscal policies often become automatic stabilizers.

An expansionary fiscal policy can close a recessionary gap by increasing government purchases, reducing net taxes, or both. Because the short-run aggregate supply curve slopes upward, an increase in aggregate demand raises both output and the price level in the short run. A contractionary fiscal policy can close an expansionary gap by reducing government purchases, increasing net taxes, or both. Fiscal policy that reduces aggregate demand to close an expansionary gap reduces both output and the price level.

### Discretionary Fiscal Policy to Close a Recessionary Gap

The aggregate demand curve $AD$ and the short-run aggregate supply curve, $SRAS_{110}$, intersect at point $e''$. Output falls short of the economy's potential. The resulting recessionary gap could be closed by discretionary fiscal policy that increases aggregate demand by just the right amount. An increase in government purchases, a decrease in net taxes, or some combination could shift aggregate demand out to $AD^*$, moving the economy out to its potential output at $e^*$.

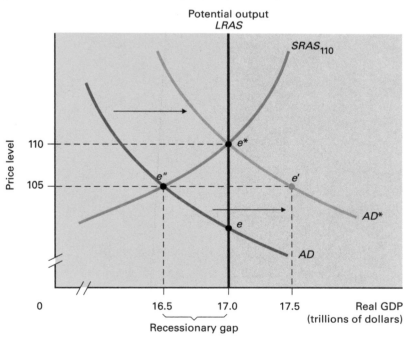

## KEY TERMS

**automatic stabilizers** Structural features of government spending and taxation that reduce fluctuations in disposable income, and thus consumption, over the business cycle

**discretionary fiscal policy** The deliberate manipulation of government purchases, taxation, and transfer payments to promote macroeconomic goals, such as full employment, price stability, and economic growth

**expansionary fiscal policy** An increase in government purchases, decrease in net taxes, or some combination of the two aimed at increasing aggregate demand enough to reduce unemployment and return the economy to its potential output; fiscal policy used to close a recessionary gap

**contractionary fiscal policy** A decrease in government purchases, increase in net taxes, or some combination of the two aimed at reducing aggregate demand enough to return the economy to potential output without worsening inflation; fiscal policy used to close an expansionary gap

**classical economists** A group of 18th- and 19th-century economists who believed that economic downturns corrected themselves through natural market forces

**Employment Act of 1946** Law that assigned to the federal government the responsibility for promoting full employment and price stability

**political business cycles** Economic fluctuations that occur when discretionary policy is manipulated for political gain

**permanent income** Income that individuals expect to receive on average over the long term

**American Recovery and Reinvestment Act** At an estimated cost of $831 billion, the largest stimulus measure in U.S history; enacted in February 2009

# CHAPTER EQUATIONS

$$\Delta \text{ Real GDP Demanded} =$$
$$\Delta G \times \frac{1}{1 - MPC}$$

$$\Delta \text{ Real GDP Demanded} =$$
$$(-MPC \times \Delta NT) \times \frac{1}{1 - MPC}$$

$$\Delta \text{ Real GDP Demanded} =$$
$$\Delta NT \times \frac{-MPC}{1 - MPC}$$

## Discretionary Fiscal Policy to Close an Expansionary Gap

The aggregate demand curve $AD'$ and the short-run aggregate supply curve, $SRAS_{110}$, intersect at point $e'$, resulting in an expansionary gap of $0.5 trillion. Discretionary fiscal policy aimed at reducing aggregate demand by just the right amount could close this gap without inflation. An increase in net taxes, a decrease in government purchases, or some combination could shift the aggregate demand curve back to $AD^*$ and move the economy back to potential output at point $e^*$.

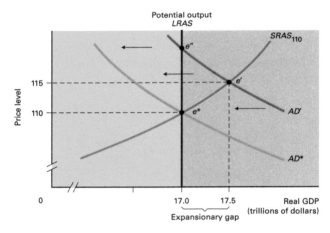

## 11-2 Summarize fiscal policy from the Great Depression to stagflation.
Fiscal policy from the Great Depression to the 1970s focused primarily on the demand side, not the supply side. This has been described as the Golden Age of Keynesian economics, when policymakers believed they could tweak taxes and government spending to fine tune the economy.

## 11-3 Identify some reasons why discretionary fiscal policy may not work very well.
The problems of the 1970s, however, resulted more from a decline of aggregate supply than from a decline of aggregate demand, so demand-side remedies seemed less effective. A more fundamental problem is that discretionary fiscal policy usually requires knowledge about aggregate supply, aggregate demand, potential output, and the natural rate of unemployment, but policymakers usually lack that information. Without such knowledge, fiscal policy can be too little, too much, or too late. The inflationary consequences of overshooting the mark are described in the final exhibit.

## 11-4 Summarize fiscal policy during the 1980s and 1990s. When and why did the federal budget show a surplus?
The tax cuts of the early 1980s aimed to increase aggregate supply. But government spending grew faster than tax revenue, creating budget deficits that stimulated aggregate demand. These huge deficits discouraged additional discretionary fiscal policy, but success in erasing deficits in the late 1990s spawned renewed interest in discretionary fiscal policy, as reflected by President Bush's tax cuts in the face of the 2001 recession.

## 11-5 Summarize fiscal policy during and after the Great Recession.
After peaking in December 2007, the economy turned down, as consumers, firms, and financial markets were spooked by falling home prices and rising foreclosure rates.

Job losses increased sharply after the financial crisis of September 2008. Government officials first tried to calm financial markets with TARP, then tried to stimulate the economy with the largest fiscal program in history. The economy lost 8.7 million jobs between December 2007 and December 2009. Those jobs returned by 2014, but economic growth during the recovery was still among the weakest on record.

## When Discretionary Fiscal Policy Overshoots Potential Output

If public officials underestimate the natural rate of unemployment, they may attempt to stimulate aggregate demand even if the economy is already producing its potential output, as at point $a$. This expansionary policy yields a short-run equilibrium at point $b$, where the price level and output are higher and unemployment is lower, so the policy appears to succeed. But the resulting expansionary gap will, in the long run, reduce the short-run aggregate supply curve from $SRAS_{110}$ to $SRAS_{120}$, eventually reducing output to its potential level of $17.0 trillion while increasing the price level to 120. Thus, attempts to increase production beyond potential GDP lead only to inflation in the long run.

## KEY CONCEPTS

**12-1 Summarize how federal spending priorities have changed since the 1960s.** The federal budget is a plan of outlays and revenues for a specified period, usually a year. As you can see from the figure below, national defense accounted for about half of all federal outlays in 1960. That share declined to only 15 percent in 2016. The share going to Social Security and Medicare, programs that aid the elderly, more than doubled between 1960 and 2016. In general, since 1960 national defense spending has declined and redistribution has increased.

**Defense's Share of Federal Outlays Declined Since 1960 and Redistribution Increased**

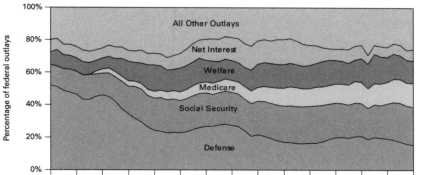

**12-2 Explain why the federal budget has been in deficit in most years since the Great Depression.** The federal budget has been in deficit for all but 14 years since 1929, when the Great Depression began. The most obvious reason why federal deficits have persisted it that, unlike budgeters in 49 states, federal officials are not required to balance the budget. Elected officials maximize their chances of getting elected and reelected by supporting spending programs but failing to raise the needed taxes. That's because voters like spending programs but hate taxes. Individual members of Congress push their favorite spending programs with little regard for the overall budget. All this results in deficits in most years, as shown by the figure below.

**The Great Recession of 2007–2009 Cut Federal Revenues and Increased Federal Outlays, Resulting in Huge Deficits**

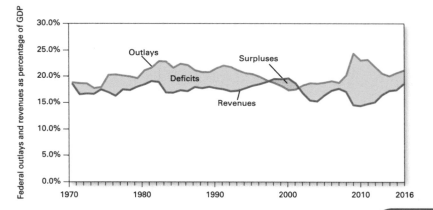

## KEY TERMS

**federal budget** A plan for federal government outlays and revenues for a specified period, usually a year

**budget resolution** A congressional agreement about total outlays, spending by major category, and expected revenues; it guides spending and revenue decisions by the many congressional committees and subcommittees

**continuing resolutions** Budget agreements that allow agencies, in the absence of an approved budget, to spend at the rate of the previous year's budget

**entitlement programs** Guaranteed benefits for those who qualify for government transfer programs such as Social Security and Medicare

**annually balanced budget** Budget philosophy prior to the Great Depression; aimed at matching annual revenues with outlays, except during times of war

**cyclically balanced budget** A budget philosophy calling for budget deficits during recessions to be financed by budget surpluses during expansions

**functional finance** A budget philosophy using fiscal policy to achieve the economy's potential GDP, rather than balancing budgets either annually or over the business cycle

**crowding out** The displacement of interest-sensitive private investment that occurs when higher government deficits drive up market interest rates

**crowding in** The potential for government spending to stimulate private investment in an otherwise dead economy

**sequestration** Automatic cuts to certain categories of federal spending enacted in 2011 to reduce the growth of federal spending from 2012 to 2021

**national debt** The net accumulation of federal budget deficits

**debt ceiling** A limit on the total amount of money the federal government can legally borrow

## Government Outlays as a Percentage of GDP in 1997 and 2016

Government outlays relative to gross domestic product (GDP) increased in seven of the 10 industrial economies between 1997 and 2016. The 10-country average increased slightly from 42 percent to 43 percent. In the United States, the percentage increased from 36 to 38.

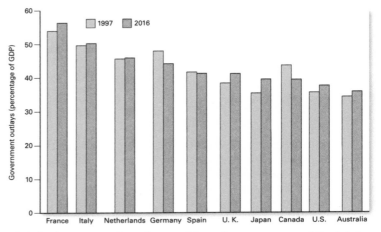

**12-3 Outline what has happened to the federal debt in recent decades and how it compares with debt levels in other countries.** The federal or national debt is a stock variable measuring the net accumulation of past deficits, the amount owed by the federal government. Most recently the U.S. federal debt measured relative to GDP was somewhat above the average for major industrial countries and was relatively high compared to U.S. historical levels stretching back to 1940. The recession of 2009–2010 and policy responses to it pushed the federal deficit above $1 trillion through 2012 and sharply increased the national debt.

### Federal Debt Held by the Public as Percent of GDP Spiked Because of World War II and the Great Recession

The huge cost of World War II rocketed federal debt from 44 percent of GDP in 1940 to over 100 percent by 1946. During the next few decades, GDP grew faster than federal debt so by 1980, federal debt had dropped to only 26 percent of GDP. But high deficits in recent years increased federal debt to 75 percent relative to GDP by 2016. That's double the percentage in 2007 and the highest since the early 1950s.

### Relative to GDP, U.S. Net Public Debt Is Above Average for Major Economies in 2016

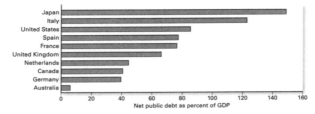

**12-4 Describe how a giant federal debt could have a negative impact on the economy.** The Great Recession and policy responses to it rocketed the federal deficit above $1 trillion for several years, substantially increasing the size of the national debt. Federal deficits of one generation can affect the standard of living of the next generation, as a larger share of the budget goes toward servicing the debt. One sign of possible problems in the United States was the downgrading of the nation's credit rating in 2011. For the first time in 70 years U.S. federal debt was rated as more risky. Research suggests that a high federal debt slows the economy, and the slowdown can last for years. To head off a fiscal crisis, policy makers must cut federal spending, raise taxes, or some combination of the two.

### Interest Payments on Federal Debt Held by the Public as Percent of Federal Outlays Peaked in 1996

After remaining relatively constant during the 1960s and 1970s, interest payments as a share of federal outlays climbed during the 1980s and early 1990s because of growing deficits and higher interest rates. After peaking in 1996 at 15.4 percent of outlays, interest payments declined first because of budget surpluses and later because of record-low interest rates.

## KEY CONCEPTS

### 13-1 Identify three functions of money and six qualities of the ideal money.
Money fulfills three important functions: a medium of exchange, a unit of account, and a store of value (see the definitions given at left). As a store of value, money has not performed well during the last half century. As the chart below indicates, U.S. money has lost about 88 percent of its value since 1960.

The ideal money is durable, portable, divisible, of uniform quality, involves a low opportunity cost of production, and has a stable value. See the table below for details.

### Six Properties of Ideal Money

| Quality | Rationale | Good Examples | Bad Examples |
|---|---|---|---|
| 1. Durable | Money should not wear out quickly | Paper money; coins; sea shells | Strawberries; seafood |
| 2. Portable | Money should be easy to carry, even relatively large sums | Diamonds; paper money | Lead bars; corn |
| 3. Divisible | Market exchange is easier if denominations support a range of possible prices | Honey; paper money and coins | Cattle; diamonds |
| 4. Uniform Quality | If money is not of uniform quality, people will hoard the best and spend the rest, reducing the quality in circulation | Salt bricks; paper money; coins | Diamonds |
| 5. Low Opportunity Cost | The fewer resources tied up in creating money, the more available for other uses | Iron coins; paper money | Gold coins; diamonds; corn |
| 6. Stable Value | People are more willing to accept and hold money if they believe it will keep its value over time | Anything whose supply can be limited by the issuing authority, such as paper money | Farm crops |

### Purchasing Power of $1.00 Measured in 1982–1984 Constant Dollars
An increase in the price level over time reduces what $1.00 buys. Since 1960 the price level has risen every year except 2009, so the purchasing power of $1.00 (measured in 1982–1984 constant dollars) has fallen from $3.38 in 1960 to $0.42 in 2015.

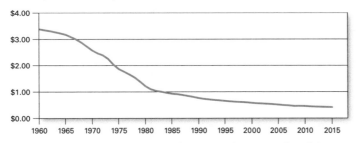

### 13-2 Explain what is meant by a fractional reserve banking system.
Banks can make loans based on customer deposits. These loans, in effect, become money. The banks has created a deposit for the borrower. Thus, the total claims against the bank now consist of the claims of people who deposited their money in the bank and the claims by borrowers for whom the bank has created deposits. Because these claims against the bank exceed the amount initially on deposit, we have a fractional reserve banking system, one in which bank reserves account for just a fraction of funds on deposit with the bank (i.e., from regular depositors and from borrowers).

## KEY TERMS

**double coincidence of wants** Two traders are willing to exchange their products directly

**money** Anything that is generally accepted in exchange for goods and services

**medium of exchange** Anything that facilitates trade by being generally accepted by all parties in payment for goods or services

**commodity money** Anything that serves both as money and as a commodity; money that has intrinsic value such as gold or silver coins

**unit of account** A common unit for measuring the value of each good or service

**store of value** Anything that retains its purchasing power over time

**token money** Money whose face value exceeds its cost of production

**check** A written order instructing the bank to pay someone from an amount deposited

**fractional reserve banking system** Bank reserves amount to only a fraction of funds on deposit with the bank

**bank notes** Originally, pieces of paper promising a specific amount of gold or silver to anyone who presented them to issuing banks for redemption; today, Federal Reserve notes are mere paper money

**fiat money** Money not redeemable for any commodity; its status as money is conferred initially by government decree but eventually by common experience

**legal tender** Currency that constitutes a valid and legal offer of payment of debt

**financial intermediaries** Institutions such as banks, mortgage companies, and finance companies, that serve as go-betweens by borrowing from people who have saved to make loans to others

**depository institutions** Commercial banks and thrift institutions; financial institutions that accept deposits from the public

**commercial banks** Depository institutions that historically made short-term loans, primarily to businesses

**thrift institutions, or thrifts** Savings banks and credit unions; depository institutions that historically lent money to households

**Federal Reserve System, or the Fed** The central bank and monetary authority of the United States

**reserves** Funds that banks use to satisfy the cash demands of their customers and the reserve requirements of the Fed; reserves consist of cash held by banks plus deposits at the Fed

**Federal Open Market Committee** The 12-member group that makes decisions about open-market operations—purchases and sales of U.S. government securities by the Fed that affect the money supply and interest rates; consists of the seven Board governors plus five of the 12 presidents of the Reserve banks

**open-market operations** Purchases and sales of government securities by the Fed in an effort to influence the money supply

**money market mutual fund** A collection of short-term interest-earning assets purchased with funds collected from many shareholders

**bank branches** A bank's additional offices that carry out banking operations

**bank holding company** A corporation that owns banks

**subprime mortgage** Mortgage for a borrower with a not-so-good credit rating

**mortgage-backed security** A claim on payments made on the many mortgages bundled into this financial instrument

**Troubled Asset Relief Program, or TARP** Government program that invested in financial institutions and automakers to help stabilize financial markets

**too big to fail** A financial institution had become so large and so interconnected with other financial institutions that its failure would be a disaster for the wider economy; its collapse had to be prevented even if that required a bailout

**Dodd-Frank Wall Street Reform and Consumer Protection Act** Sweeping regulatory changes in 2010 aimed at preventing another financial crisis

**13-3 Describe the Fed, summarize its two mandated objectives, and outline some of its other goals.** The Federal Reserve System, or the Fed, was established in 1913 to regulate the banking system and issue the nation's currency. After a third of the nation's banks failed during the Great Depression, the Fed's powers were increased and centralized. The Fed's two mandated objectives are price stability and maximum employment. Stable prices promote greater certainty, making it easier to plan, and help savers retain their spending power over time. Maximum employment means that jobs are easier to find so more people have more money to spend. Some other Fed goals are economic growth, interest rate stability, financial market stability, and exchange rate stability.

### The Twelve Federal Reserve Districts

The map shows by color the area covered by each of the 12 Federal Reserve districts. Black dots note the locations of the Federal Reserve bank in each district. Identified with a white star is the Board of Governors headquarters in Washington, DC.

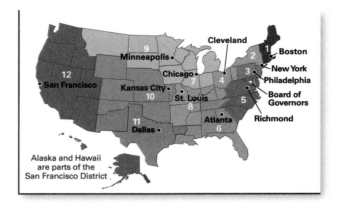

### Organization Chart of the Federal Reserve System

Members of the Board of Governors are appointed by the president and confirmed by the Senate. The seven board members also belong to the 12-member Federal Open Market Committee, which advises the board. The Board of Governors controls the Reserve banks in each of the 12 districts, which in turn control the U.S. banking system.

**13-4 Describe subprime mortgages and the role they played in the financial crisis of 2008.** Subprime mortgages are loans to home-buyers with not-so-good credit ratings. Prior to the financial crisis of 2008, hundreds of subprime mortgages would be bundled together and sold as a mortgage-backed security. The feeling at the time was that housing prices would continue to rise, so if any of these risky borrowers were to default on their mortgage, the house itself would become valuable collateral to pay off the loan. But when housing prices began to slide, holders of mortgage backed securities lost a bundle, and the entire financial system became unglued. Credit dried up. The government first tried to stabilize markets by investing in financial institutions. Later, the Dodd-Frank Act of 2010, the most sweeping reform of financial markets since the Great Depression, authorized regulators to write and interpret hundreds of new financial rules. Banks are back to being more tightly regulated about the kinds of assets they can own and trade.

## KEY CONCEPTS

**14-1 Explain why using a debit card is like using cash, but using a credit card is not.** When you use a debit card, you tap directly into your checking account, paying with electronic money—part of M1 (see the bar chart below for the distinctions between M1 and M2). Debit cards get their name because they debit, or draw down, your checking account immediately. In contrast, credit cards offer a convenient way to get a loan from the card issuer. If you buy an airline ticket with a credit card, the card issuer lends you the money to pay for the ticket. You don't need money until you repay the credit card issuer. The credit card has not eliminated your use of money, merely delayed it.

The money supply is narrowly defined as M1, which consists of currency held by the nonbanking public plus checkable deposits and traveler's checks. A broader money aggregate, M2, includes M1 plus savings deposits, small-denomination time deposits, money market mutual funds, and other near-monies. While used effectively as a medium of exchange in some cases, Bitcoin is not yet seen as a safe store of value and is not counted a party of M1 or M2.

**Two Measures of the Money Supply (Week of May 4, 2015)**

**14-2 Explain why a bank is in a better position to lend your savings than you are.** Banks are unlike other financial intermediaries because they can turn a borrower's IOU into money—they can create money. Banks are better able than you to evaluate loan applications and diversify portfolios of assets to reduce the risk to any one saver. In acquiring portfolios of assets, banks try to maximize profit while maintaining enough liquidity to satisfy depositors' requests for money. Assets that earn the bank more interest are usually less liquid.

## KEY TERMS

**checkable deposits** Bank deposits that allow the account owner to write checks to third parties; debit cards can also access these deposits and transmit them electronically

**money aggregates** Measures of the economy's money supply

**M1** The narrow measure of the money supply, consisting of currency and coins held by the nonbanking public, checkable deposits, and traveler's checks

**savings deposits** Bank deposits that earn interest but have no specific maturity date

**time deposits** Bank deposits that earn a fixed interest rate if held for the specified period, which can range from several months to several years; also called certificates of deposit

**M2** A money aggregate consisting of M1 plus savings deposits, small-denomination time deposits, money market mutual funds, and other near-monies

**debit card** Cards that tap directly into the depositor's bank account to fund purchases; also called check cards

**asymmetric information** A situation in which one side of the market has more reliable information than the other side

**net worth** Assets minus liabilities; also called owners' equity

**balance sheet** A financial statement at a given point in time showing assets on one side and liabilities and net worth on the other side; because assets must equal liabilities plus net worth, the two sides of the statement must balance, hence the name

**asset** Anything of value that is owned

**liability** Anything that is owed to other people or institutions

**required reserves** The dollar amount of reserves a bank is obligated by regulation to hold as cash in the bank's vault or on account at the Fed

**required reserve ratio** The ratio of reserves to deposits that banks are obligated by regulation to hold

**excess reserves** Bank reserves exceeding required reserves

**liquidity** A measure of the ease with which an asset can be converted into money without a significant loss of value

**federal funds market** A market for overnight lending and borrowing of reserves among banks; the interbank market for reserves on account at the Fed

**federal funds rate** The interest rate charged in the federal funds market; the interest rate banks charge one another for overnight borrowing; the Fed's target interest rate

**money multiplier** The multiple by which the money supply changes as a result of a change in fresh reserves in the banking system

**simple money multiplier** The reciprocal of the required reserve ratio, or 1/r; the maximum multiple of fresh reserves by which the money supply can increase

**open-market purchase** The purchase of U.S. government bonds by the Fed to increase the money supply

**open-market sale** The sale of U.S. government bonds by the Fed to reduce the money supply

**discount rate** The interest rate the Fed charges banks that borrow reserves

## CHAPTER EQUATIONS

Assets = Liabilities + Net worth

**Simple Money Multiplier**

$$\Delta \text{ money supply} =$$

$$\Delta \text{ fresh reserves} \times 1/r$$

**14-3 Describe how banks create money.** Banks are able to create money by making loans. When a bank makes a loan, it creates a deposit for the borrower based on excess reserves. Any single bank can expand the money supply by the amount of its excess reserves. For the banking system as a whole, however, the maximum expansion of the money supply equals a multiple of fresh bank reserves. The simple money multiplier is the reciprocal of the reserve ratio, or 1/r. This multiplier is reduced to the extent that (a) banks allow excess reserves to remain idle, (b) borrowers sit on their proceeds, and (c) the public withdraws cash from the banking system and holds it.

**14-4 Summarize the Fed's tools of monetary policy.** The key to changes in the money supply is the Fed's impact on excess reserves in the banking system. To increase excess reserves and thus increase the money supply, the Fed can buy U.S. government bonds, reduce the discount rate, or lower the reserve requirement. To reduce excess reserves and thus reduce the money supply, the Fed can sell U.S. government bonds, increase the discount rate, or increase the reserve requirement. The Fed's most important tool by far is the buying or selling of U.S. bonds.

The Fed was quite active during the financial crisis of 2008, pursuing several efforts to stabilize financial markets and unfreeze the flow of credit. Fed actions included extending discount loans to banks, offering interest on bank reserves at the Fed, helping AIG stay in business, and spending more than $1 trillion buying mortgage-backed securities to stabilize banks and keep mortgage rates low.

## NOTES

## KEY CONCEPTS

**15-1 Explain how the demand and supply of money determine the market interest rate.** The opportunity cost of holding money is the higher interest forgone by not holding other financial assets instead. Along a given money demand curve, the quantity of money demanded relates inversely to the interest rate. The demand for money curve shifts rightward as a result of an increase in the price level, an increase in real GDP, or an increase in both.

### Demand for Money

The money demand curve, $D_m$, slopes downward. As the interest rate falls, other things constant, so does the opportunity cost of holding money; the quantity of money demanded increases.

### Effect of an Increase in the Money Supply

Because the money supply is determined by the Federal Reserve, it can be represented by a vertical line. At point *a*, the intersection of the money supply, $S_m$, and the money demand, $D_m$, determines the market interest rate, *i*. Following an increase in the money supply to $S'_m$, the quantity of money supplied exceeds the quantity demanded at the original interest rate, *i*. The new equilibrium occurs at point *b*.

**15-2 Outline the steps between an increase in the money supply and an increase in equilibrium output.** The Fed determines the supply of money, which is assumed to be independent of the interest rate. The intersection of the supply and demand curves for money determines the market interest rate. In the short run, an increase in the supply of money reduces the interest rate, which increases investment. This boosts aggregate demand, which increases real output and the price level. The figures below trace the steps between an increase in the money supply and an increase in aggregate demand. To figure out the effects of this on real output and the price level, simply sketch in an aggregate supply in the right-hand figure.

### Effects of an Increase in the Money Supply on Interest Rates, Investment, and Aggregate Demand

In panel (a), an increase in the money supply forces the interest rate down to *i'*. With the cost of borrowing lower, the amount invested increases from *I* to *I'*, as shown in panel (b). This sets off the spending multiplier process, so the aggregate output demanded at price level *P* increases from *Y* to *Y'*. The increase is shown by the shift of the aggregate demand curve to the right in panel (c).

## KEY TERMS

**demand for money** The relationship between the interest rate and how much money people choose to hold

**equation of exchange** The quantity of money, *M*, multiplied by its velocity, *V*, equals nominal GDP, which is the product of the price level, *P*, and real GDP, *Y*; or $M \times V = P \times Y$

**velocity of money** The average number of times per year each dollar is used to purchase final goods and services

**quantity theory of money** If the velocity of money is stable, or at least predictable, changes in the money supply have predictable effects on nominal GDP

**stress test** Bank regulators assessed the soundness of large banks to determine which ones needed more financial capital to weather a bad economy

**shadow banking system** Financial institutions, such as mortgage companies and brokerage firms, that do not rely on customer deposits to make loans

**quantitative easing** Fed purchases of long-term assets to stabilize financial markets, reduce long-term interest rates, and improve the investment environment

## CHAPTER EQUATIONS

**Effects of an Increase in the Money Supply**

$$M \uparrow \rightarrow i \downarrow \rightarrow I \uparrow \rightarrow AD \uparrow \rightarrow Y \uparrow$$

**Equation of Exchange**

$$M \times V = P \times Y$$

**Velocity**

$$V = \frac{P \times Y}{M}$$

**Total Spending** $= M \times V$

**Total Receipts** $= P \times Y$

## Expansionary Monetary Policy to Close a Recessionary Gap

At point *a*, the economy is producing less than its potential in the short run, resulting in a recessionary gap of $0.2 trillion. If the Federal Reserve increases the money supply by just the right amount, the aggregate demand curve shifts rightward from *AD* to *AD'*. A short-run and long-run equilibrium is established at point *b*, with the price level at 110 and output at the potential level of $17.0 trillion.

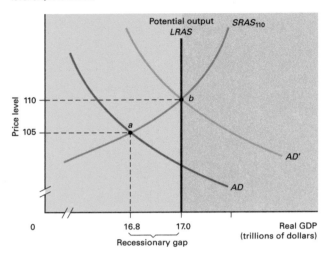

## 15-3 Describe the relevance of velocity's stability on monetary policy.
The long-run approach focuses on the role of money through the equation of exchange, which states that the quantity of money, *M*, multiplied by velocity, *V*, the average number of times each dollar gets spent on final goods and services, equals the price level, *P*, multiplied by real output, *Y*. So $M \times V = P \times Y$. Because the aggregate supply curve in the long run is a vertical line at the economy's potential output, a change in the money supply affects the price level in the long run but not real output. See the accompanying graph.

### In the Long Run, an Increase in the Money Supply Results in a Higher Price Level, or Inflation

The quantity theory of money predicts that if velocity is stable, then an increase in the money supply in the long run results in a higher price level, or inflation. Because the long-run aggregate supply curve is fixed, increases in the money supply affect only the price level, not real output.

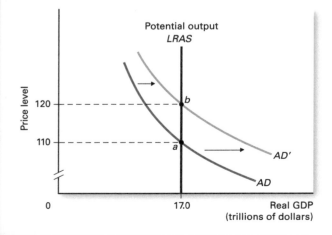

## The Velocity of Money

M1 velocity fluctuated so much during the 1980s that M1 growth was abandoned as a short-run policy target. M2 velocity appears more stable than M1 velocity, but both are now considered by the Fed as too unpredictable for short-run policy use.

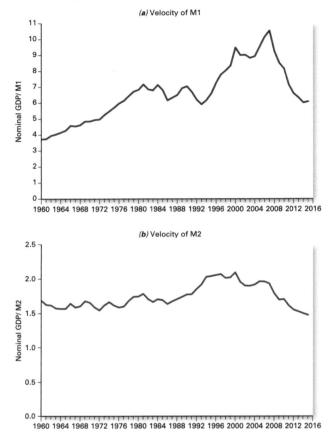

## 15-4 Summarize the specific policies the Fed pursued during and after the Great Recession.
Between World War II and October 1979, the Fed tried to maintain stable interest rates as a way of promoting a stable investment environment. During the 1980s and early 1990s, the Fed paid more attention to growth in money aggregates, first M1 and then M2. But the velocity of M1 and M2 became so unstable that the Fed shifted focus back to interest rates, particularly the federal funds rate. To pursue its mandated goals of price stability and maximum employment, the Fed uses open-market operations to adjust the federal funds rate, raising the rate to prevent higher inflation and lowering the rate to stimulate employment.

As a result of the financial crisis of September 2008, the Fed broadened its scope of action to include offering interest on bank reserves at the Fed, bailing out a huge financial institution, increasing discount loans to banks, investing more than $1 trillion in mortgage-backed securities to keep mortgage rates low, helping financial regulators perform stress tests on the nation's largest banks, introducing measures to help reduce the probability that a giant financial institution will fail, and reducing the impact of such a failure should one occur. The Fed's actions during the crisis suggest that it would try to do whatever was required to ensure the survival of the banking system and the economy.

## KEY CONCEPTS

### 16-1 Outline the difference between active policy and passive policy, and explain how the two approaches differ in their assumptions about how well the economy works on its own.

Advocates of active policy view the private sector—particularly fluctuations in investment—as the primary source of economic instability in the economy. Activists argue that achieving potential output through natural market forces can be slow and painful, so the Fed or Congress should stimulate aggregate demand when actual output falls below potential.

Advocates of passive policy argue that the economy has enough natural resiliency to return to potential output within a reasonable period if upset by some shock. They point to the variable and uncertain lags associated with discretionary policy as reason enough to steer clear of active intervention.

### Closing a Recessionary Gap

At point *a* in both panels, the economy is in short-run equilibrium, with unemployment exceeding its natural rate. According to the passive approach, shown in panel (a), high unemployment eventually causes wages to fall, reducing the cost of doing business. The decline in costs shifts the short-run aggregate supply curve rightward from $SRAS_{110}$ to $SRAS_{100}$, moving the economy to its potential output at point *b*. In panel (b), the government employs an active approach to shift the aggregate demand curve from *AD* to *AD'*. If the active policy works perfectly, the economy moves to its potential output at point *c*.

### Closing an Expansionary Gap

At point *d* in both panels, the economy is in short-run equilibrium, producing $17.2 trillion, which exceeds the economy's potential output. Unemployment is below its natural rate. In the passive approach reflected in panel (a), the government makes no change in policy, so natural market forces eventually bring about a higher negotiated wage, increasing firm costs and shifting the short-run supply curve leftward to $SRAS_{120}$. The new equilibrium at point *e* results in a higher price level and lower output and employment. An active policy reduces aggregate demand, shifting the equilibrium in panel (b) from point *d* to point *c*, thus closing the expansionary gap without increasing the price level.

## KEY TERMS

**recognition lag** The time needed to identify a macroeconomic problem and assess its seriousness

**decision-making lag** The time needed to decide what to do once a macroeconomic problem has been identified

**implementation lag** The time needed to introduce a change in monetary or fiscal policy

**effectiveness lag** The time needed for changes in monetary or fiscal policy to affect the economy

**rational expectations** A school of thought that argues people form expectations based on all available information, including the likely future actions of government policy makers

**time-inconsistency problem** When policy makers have an incentive to announce one policy to influence expectations but then pursue a different policy once those expectations have been formed and acted on

**cold turkey** The announcement and execution of tough measures to reduce high inflation

**inflation target** Commitment of central bankers to keep inflation at or below a certain rate for the next year or two

**Phillips curve** A curve showing possible combinations of the inflation rate and the unemployment rate

**short-run Phillips curve** Based on an expected inflation rate, a curve that reflects an inverse relationship between the inflation rate and the unemployment rate

**long-run Phillips curve** A vertical line drawn at the economy's natural rate of unemployment that traces equilibrium points that can occur when workers and employers have the time to adjust fully to any unexpected change in aggregate demand

**natural rate hypothesis** The natural rate of unemployment is largely independent of the stimulus provided by monetary or fiscal policy

**16-2 Describe how expectations can influence the effectiveness of discretionary policy.** The effect of particular government policies on the economy depends on what people come to expect. The theory of rational expectations holds that people form expectations based on all available information, including past behavior by public officials. According to the rational expectations school, government policies are mostly anticipated by the public, and therefore have less effect than unexpected policies.

**16-3 Summarize why some economists prefer that policy be shaped by predictable rules rather than by the discretion of policy makers.** The active approach views the economy as unstable and in need of discretionary policy to eliminate excess unemployment. The passive approach, however, suggests that discretionary policy is not necessary and may even be harmful. The passive approach suggests that the government should follow clear and predictable policies and avoid discretionary intervention to stimulate or dampen aggregate demand. According to the passive approach, a lack of knowledge about how the economy works and uncertainty about lags make discretionary policy risky. Passive policies are reflected in automatic fiscal stabilizers and in explicit monetary rules, such as keeping inflation below a certain rate.

**16-4 Explain the shape of the short-run Phillips curve and the long-run Phillips curve.** At one time, public officials thought they faced a stable trade-off between higher unemployment and higher inflation. More recent research suggests that if there is a trade-off, it exists only in the short run, not in the long run. The hypothetical Phillips curve illustrates the relationship between inflation and unemployment. Expansionary fiscal or monetary policies may stimulate output and employment in the short run. But if the economy is already at or near its potential output, these expansionary policies, in the long run, result only in more inflation. And federal deficits from expansionary fiscal policy can create a huge federal debt, which itself can create uncertainty and instability.

## Hypothetical Phillips Curve

The Phillips curve shows an inverse relation between unemployment and inflation. Points *a* and *b* lie on the Phillips curve and represent alternative combinations of inflation and unemployment that are attainable as long as the curve itself does not shift. Points *c* and *d* are off the curve.

## Aggregate Supply Curves and Phillips Curves in the Short Run and the Long Run

If people expect a price level of 103, which is 3 percent higher than the current level, and if *AD* turns out to be the aggregate demand curve, then the actual price level is 103 and output is at its potential. Point *a* in both panels represents this situation. Unemployment is the natural rate, assumed to be 5 percent in panel (b). If aggregate demand turns out to be greater than expected (*AD′* instead of *AD*), the economy in the short run is at point *b* in panel (a), where the price level of 105 exceeds expectations and output exceeds its potential. The resulting higher inflation and lower unemployment are shown as point *b* in panel (b). If aggregate demand turns out to be less than expected (*AD″* instead of *AD*), short-run equilibrium is at point *c* in panel (a), where the price level of 101 is lower than expected and output falls short of potential. Lower inflation and higher unemployment are shown as point *c* in panel (b). In panel (b), points *a*, *b*, and *c* trace a short-run Phillips curve. In the long run, the actual price level equals the expected price level. Output is at the potential level, $17.0 trillion, in panel (a). Unemployment is at the natural rate, 5 percent, in panel (b). Points *a*, *d*, and *e* depict long-run points in each panel. In panel (a) these points trace potential output, or long-run aggregate supply (LRAS). In panel (b), these points trace a long-run Phillips curve.

(a) Short-run aggregate supply curve

(b) Short-run and long-run Phillips curves

## KEY CONCEPTS

**17-1 Outline the gains from trade, and explain why countries might still decide to trade even if no country has a comparative advantage.** The law of comparative advantage says that the individual with the lowest opportunity cost of producing a particular good should specialize in that good. Just as individuals benefit from specialization and exchange, so do states and, indeed, nations. To reap the gains that arise from specialization, countries engage in international trade. Each country specializes in making goods with the lowest opportunity cost. Before countries can trade, however, they must agree on how much of one good exchanges for another (i.e., the terms of trade).

### Composition of U.S. Exports and Imports in 2014

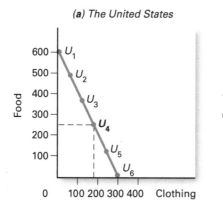

**(a)** U.S. Exports

Food 6%
Services 31%
Industrial supplies 22%
Consumer goods 11%
Capital goods 24%
Autos 7%

**(b)** U.S. Imports

Food 4%
Services 17%
Industrial supplies 24%
Consumer goods 22%
Capital goods 21%
Autos 12%

### Production Possibilities Frontiers for the United States and Izodia Without Trade (millions of units per day)

Panel (a) shows the U.S. production possibilities frontier; its slope indicates that the opportunity cost of an additional unit of clothing is 2 units of food. Panel (b) shows production possibilities for Izodia; an additional unit of clothing costs 1/2 unit of food. Clothing has a lower opportunity cost in Izodia.

**(a)** The United States

**(b)** Izodia

## KEY TERMS

**autarky**  National self-sufficiency; no economic interaction with foreigners

**terms of trade**  How much of one good exchanges for a unit of another good

**world price**  The price at which a good is traded on the world market; determined by the world demand and world supply for the good

**bilateral agreement**  Trade agreement between two countries

**multilateral agreement**  Trade agreement among more than two countries

**General Agreement on Tariffs and Trade (GATT)**  An international tariff-reduction treaty adopted in 1947 that resulted in a series of negotiated "rounds" aimed at freer trade; the Uruguay Round created GATT's successor, the World Trade Organization (WTO)

**dumping**  Selling a product abroad for less than charged in the home market or for less than the cost of production

**Uruguay Round**  The final multilateral trade negotiation under GATT; this 1994 agreement cut tariffs, formed the World Trade Organization (WTO), and will eventually eliminate quotas

**World Trade Organization (WTO)**  The legal and institutional foundation of the multilateral trading system that succeeded GATT in 1995

**common market**  Group of countries that have few of no trade restrictions with one another

## Production (and Consumption) Possibilities Frontiers With Trade (millions of units per day)

If Izodia and the United States can specialize and trade at the rate of 1 unit of clothing for 1 unit of food, both can benefit as shown by the blue lines. By trading with Izodia, the U.S. can produce only food and still consume combination $U$, which has more food and more clothing than $U_4$. Likewise, Izodia can attain preferred combination $I$ by producing only clothing, then trading some clothing for U.S. food.

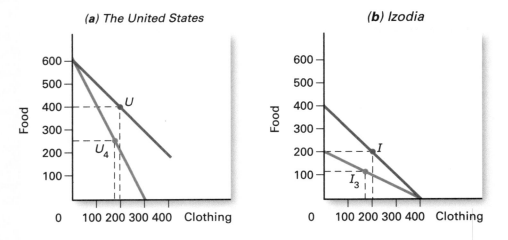

*(a) The United States*   *(b) Izodia*

Countries export products they can produce more cheaply in return for products that are unavailable domestically or are cheaper elsewhere. If production is subject to economies of scale (i.e., if the long-run average cost of production falls as a firm expands its scale of operation), countries can gain from trade if each nation specializes. Consumption patterns differ across countries, and some of this results from differences in tastes, a situation that allows countries to gain from trade.

## U.S. Production as a Percentage of U.S. Consumption for Various Resources

If U.S. production is less than 100 percent of U.S. consumption, then imports make up the difference. If U.S. production exceeds U.S. consumption, then the amount by which production exceeds 100 percent of consumption is exported.

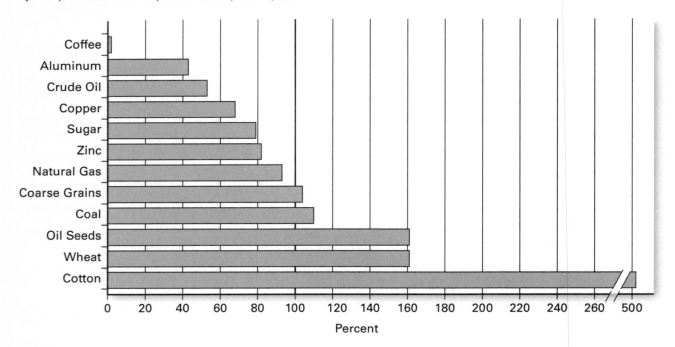

## 17-2 Explain how trade restrictions harm an economy, and why they persist. Market exchange usually generates a surplus, or a bonus, for both consumers and producers. Governments try to regulate surpluses by imposing tariffs (either specific or *ad valorem*) and import quotas, granting export subsidies, or extending low-interest loans to foreign buyers. Loss in U.S. consumer surplus resulting from tariffs is divided three ways: a portion goes to domestic producers; a portion becomes government revenue; and the last portion represents net losses in domestic social welfare. Welfare loss occurs when consumers must pay a higher price for products that could have been imported and sold at a lower price.

### Consumer Surplus and Producer Surplus

Consumer surplus, shown by the blue triangle, indicates the net benefits consumers reap from buying 60 pounds of apples at $1.00 per pound. Some consumers would have been willing to pay $3.00 or more per pound for the first few pounds. Consumer surplus measures the difference between the maximum sum of money consumers would pay for 60 pounds of apples and the actual sum they pay. Producer surplus, shown by the gold triangle, indicates the net benefits producers reap from selling 60 pounds at $1.00 per pound. Some producers would have supplied apples for %0.50 per pound or less. Producer surplus measures the difference between the actual sum of money producers receive for 60 pounds of apples and the minimum amount they would accept for this amount.

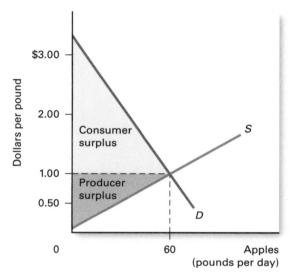

### Effect of a Tariff

At a world price of $0.10 per pound, U.S. consumers demand 70 million pounds of sugar per month, and U.S. producers supply 20 million pounds per month; the difference is imported. After the imposition of a $0.05 per pound tariff, the U.S. price rises to $0.15 per pound. U.S. producers supply 30 million pounds, and U.S. consumers cut back to 60 million pounds. At the higher U.S. price, consumers are worse off; their loss of consumer surplus is the sum of areas *a, b, c,* and *d*. The net welfare loss to the U.S. economy consists of areas *b* and *d*.

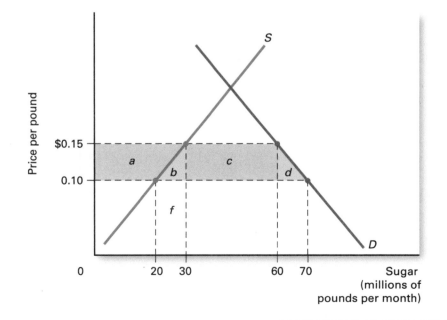

## Effect of a Quota

In panel (a), *D* is the U.S. demand curve and *S* is the supply curve of U.S. producers. If the government establishes a sugar quota of 30 million pounds per month, the supply curve combining U.S. production and imports becomes horizontal at the world price of $0.10 per pound and remains horizontal until the quantity supplied reaches 50 million pounds. For higher prices, the new supply curve equals the horizontal sum of the U.S. supply curve, *S*, plus the quota of 30 million pounds. The new U.S. price, $0.15 per pound, is determined by the intersection of the new supply curve, *S'*, with the U.S. demand curve, *D*. Panel (b) shows the welfare effect of the quota. As a result of the higher U.S. price, consumer surplus is cut by the shaded area. The blue-shaded areas illustrate the loss in consumer surplus that is captured by domestic producers and by those who are permitted to fulfill the quota, and the pink-shaded triangles illustrate the net welfare cost of the quota on the U.S. economy.

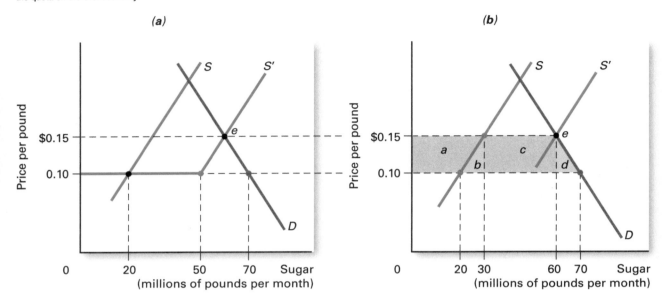

**(a)**       **(b)**

**17-3 Identify international efforts to reduce trade barriers.** Trade restrictions impose a variety of strains on the economy besides the higher costs to consumers, so countries have worked to create free trade agreements and common markets to reduce or eliminate trade barriers. The General Agreement on Tariffs and Trade (GATT) was an international treaty ratified in 1947 to reduce trade barriers. Subsequent negotiations lowered tariffs and reduced trade restrictions. The Uruguay Round, ratified in 1994, lowered tariffs, phased out quotas, and created the World Trade Organization (WTO) as the successor to GATT.

**17-4 Summarize five arguments often used to justify trade restrictions, and describe some unintended consequences of protecting certain industries from international competition.** Arguments used by producer groups to support trade restrictions include promoting national defense, nurturing infant industries, preventing foreign producers from dumping goods in domestic markets, protecting domestic jobs, and allowing declining industries time to wind down and exit the market.

Trade restrictions impose a variety of strains on the economy besides the higher costs to consumers. These include (1) the need to protect downstream stages of production as well, (2) expenditures made by favored domestic industries to seek and perpetuate trade protection, (3) costs incurred by the government to enforce trade restrictions, (4) the inefficiency and lack of innovation that result when an industry is insulated from foreign competition, and (5), most important, the trade restrictions imposed by other countries in retaliation.

## KEY CONCEPTS

**18-1 Summarize the major accounts in the balance of trade, and explain how they balance out.** The balance of payments reflects all economic transactions between one country and the rest of the world. The current account measures flows from (a) goods; (b) services, including consulting and tourism; (c) income from holdings of foreign assets; and (d) unilateral transfers, or public and private transfer payments to and from foreign residents. The financial account measures international transactions in real and financial assets.

### U.S. Balance of Payments for 2014 (billions of dollars)

| Current Account | |
| --- | --- |
| 1. Merchandise exports | +1,635.1 |
| 2. Merchandise imports | −2,370.9 |
| 3. Merchandise trade balance (1 + 2) | −735.8 |
| 4. Service exports | +709.4 |
| 5. Service imports | −478.3 |
| 6. Goods and services balance (3 + 4 + 5) | −504.7 |
| 7. Net investment income from abroad | +217.9 |
| 8. Net unilateral transfers | −123.8 |
| 9. Current account balance (6 + 7 + 8) | −410.6 |
| **Financial Account** | |
| 10. Change in U.S. owned assets abroad | −820.5 |
| 11. Change in foreign-owned assets in United States | +962.1 |
| 12. Financial account balance (10 + 11) | +141.6 |
| 13. Statistical discrepancy | +269.0 |
| **TOTAL (9 + 12 + 13)** | **0.0** |

Source: Computed from estimates by the Bureau of Economic Analysis, U.S. Department of Commerce at http://bea.gov/international/index.htm.

## KEY TERMS

**balance on goods and services** The portion of a country's balance-of-payments account that measures the value of a country's exports of goods and services minus the value of its imports of goods and services

**net investment income from abroad** Investment earnings by U.S. residents from their foreign assets minus investment earnings by foreigners from their assets in the United States

**net unilateral transfers abroad** The unilateral transfers (gifts and grants) received from abroad by U.S. residents minus the unilateral transfers U.S. residents send abroad

**balance on current account** The portion of the balance-of-payments account that measures a country's balance on goods and services, net investment income from abroad, plus net unilateral transfers abroad

**financial account** The record of a country's international transactions involving purchases and sales of financial and real assets

**exchange rate** The cost, measured in one country's currency, of one unit of another country's currency

**currency depreciation** With respect to the dollar, an increase in the number of dollars needed to purchase one unit of foreign exchange in a flexible rate system

### U.S. Imports Have Topped Exports Since 1976, but Both Dropped During the Great Recession

Note that since 1980, merchandise exports have remained in the range of about 5 percent to 10 percent of GDP. But merchandise imports have trended up from about 9 percent in 1980 to about 15 percent in 2008, before dropping off to 11 percent in 2009, the year following the financial crisis. Imports were back up to 14 percent relative to GDP by 2011 and have remained there.

Source: Developed from merchandise trade data from the Bureau of Economic Analysis, U.S. Department of Commerce, at http://bea.gov/international/index.htm.

### U.S. Merchandise Trade Deficits in 2014 by Country or Region

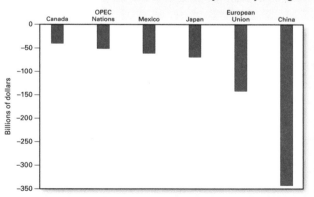

Source: Developed from data in "Exports, Imports, and Trade Balance by Country and Area: 2012 Annual Totals," Exhibit 13, U.S. Bureau of Economic Analysis, at http://www.census.gov /foreign-trade/Press-Release/2012pr/final_revisions/exh13cy.pdf

**currency appreciation** With respect to the dollar, a decrease in the number of dollars needed to purchase one unit of foreign exchange in a flexible rate system

**arbitrageur** Someone who takes advantage of tiny differences in the exchange rate across markets by simultaneously purchasing currency in one market and selling it in another market

**speculator** Someone who buys or sells foreign exchange in hopes of profiting from fluctuations in the exchange rate over time

**purchasing power parity theory** The idea that the exchange rate between two countries will adjust in the long run to equalize the cost of a basket of internationally traded goods

**flexible exchange rate** Rate determined in foreign exchange markets by the forces of demand and supply without government intervention

**fixed exchange rate** Rate of exchange between currencies pegged within a narrow range and maintained by the central bank's ongoing purchases and sales of currencies

**currency devaluation** An increase in the official pegged price of foreign exchange in terms of the domestic currency

**currency revaluation** A reduction in the official pegged price of foreign exchange in terms of the domestic currency

**gold standard** An arrangement whereby the currencies of most countries were convertible into gold at a fixed rate

**International Monetary Fund** An international organization that establishes rules for maintaining the international monetary system and makes loans to countries with temporary balance-of-payments problems

**managed float system** An exchange rate system that combines features of freely floating rates with sporadic intervention by central banks

## 18-2 Describe how the foreign exchange rate is determined using demand and supply curves and explain the shapes of the curves.

Because the exchange rate is usually a market price, it is determined by demand and supply. The equilibrium exchange rate is one that equates quantity demanded with quantity supplied (see the diagrams below).

### The Foreign Exchange Market

The fewer dollars needed to purchase one unit of foreign exchange, the lower the price of foreign goods and the greater the quantity of foreign goods demanded. Thus, the demand curve for foreign exchange slopes downward. An increase in the exchange rate makes U.S. products cheaper for foreigners. This implies an increase in the quantity of foreign exchange supplied. The supply curve of foreign exchange slopes upward.

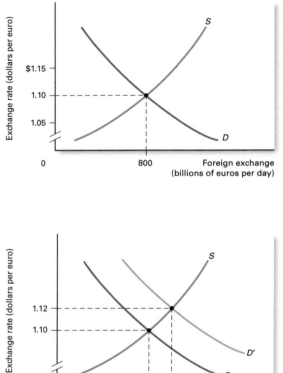

### Effect on the Foreign Exchange Market of an Increased Demand for Euros

The intersection of the demand curve for foreign exchange, *D*, and the supply curve for foreign exchange, *S*, determines the exchange rate. At an exchange rate of $1.10 per euro, the quantity of euros demanded equals the quantity supplied. An increase in the demand for euros from *D* to *D'* increases the exchange rate from $1.10 to $1.12 per euro.

## 18-3 Describe the purchasing power parity theory.
According to the theory of purchasing power parity (PPP), the exchange rate between two countries will adjust in the long run to equalize the cost of a basket of internationally traded goods. A given basket of internationally traded goods should, therefore, sell for about the same around the world (except for differences reflecting transportation costs and the like).

## 18-4 Trace the evolution of exchange rate regimes from the gold standard to the current system.
From 1879 to 1914, the international financial system operated under a gold standard, whereby the major currencies of the world were convertible into gold at a fixed rate. During World War I, many countries could no longer convert their currencies into gold, so the gold standard eventually collapsed, disrupting international trade during the 1930s and 1940s. From 1945 to 1973 fixed exchange rates were in effect, and since 1973 a managed float has been in effect, a system that combines features of freely fluctuating rates with sporadic market intervention by central banks.

## KEY CONCEPTS

**19-1 Besides income, identify ways that low-income economies differ from high-income economies.** The most common measure of comparison of standards of living between different countries is output per capita. Developing countries are distinguished by low output per capita, poor health and nutrition, high fertility rates, and poor education.

### Share of World Population and World Output From High-, Middle-, and Low-Income Economies as of 2014

**(a)** Share of world population from high-, middle-, and low-income economies

High (18%)
Low (12%)
Middle (70%)

**(b)** Share of world output from high-, middle-, and low-income economies

Low (2%)
High (52%)
Middle (46%)

### Per Capita Income for Selected Countries in 2014

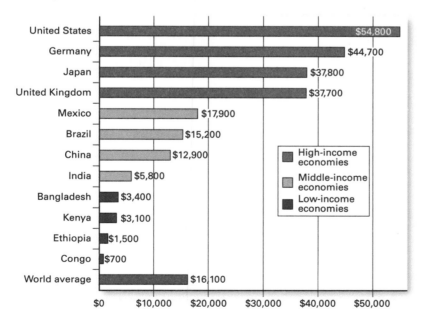

| Country | Per Capita Income |
| --- | --- |
| United States | $54,800 |
| Germany | $44,700 |
| Japan | $37,800 |
| United Kingdom | $37,700 |
| Mexico | $17,900 |
| Brazil | $15,200 |
| China | $12,900 |
| India | $5,800 |
| Bangladesh | $3,400 |
| Kenya | $3,100 |
| Ethiopia | $1,500 |
| Congo | $700 |
| World average | $16,100 |

Legend:
- High-income economies
- Middle-income economies
- Low-income economies

## KEY TERMS

**developing countries** Low-income and middle-income economies; most are also known as emerging market economies

**industrial market countries** Economically advanced capitalist countries of Europe, North America, Australia, New Zealand, and Japan; also known as developed countries and high-income economies

**privatization** The process of turning government enterprises into private enterprises

**import substitution** A development strategy that emphasizes domestic manufacturing of products that had been imported

**export promotion** A development strategy that concentrates on producing for the export market

**foreign aid** An international transfer made on especially favorable terms for the purpose of promoting economic development

**convergence** A theory predicting that the standard of living in economies around the world will grow more similar over time, with poorer countries eventually catching up with richer ones

**19-2 Describe the factors that help make workers in high-income economies more productive than workers in other economies.** Labor productivity, measured in terms of output per worker, is by definition low in low-income countries, as it depends on the quality of the labor and other inputs that combine with labor, such as capital and natural resources. The key to a rising standard of living is increased productivity. To foster productivity, developing nations must stimulate investment, support education and training programs, provide sufficient infrastructure, and foster supportive rules of the game.

**19-3 Explain how trade restrictions can slow economic development in poorer countries.** Developing countries need to trade with developed countries to acquire the capital and technology that will increase labor productivity. Exports usually generate more than half of the annual flow of foreign exchange in developing countries. Foreign aid and private investment make up the rest. Developing countries often use either import substitution or export promotion strategies to improve production. With import substitution, domestic manufacturers make products that had previously been imported and the government supports them with tariffs and quotas. Export promotion concentrates on producing for the export market. Export promotion has proven generally more successful.

**19-4 Outline some unintended consequences of foreign aid on economic development.** Foreign aid has been a mixed blessing for most developing countries. In some cases, that aid has helped countries build the roads, bridges, schools, and other capital infrastructure necessary for development. In other cases, foreign aid has simply increased consumption and insulated government from painful but necessary reforms. Worse still, subsidized food from abroad has undermined domestic agriculture, hurting poor farmers. And subsidized clothing from abroad has undermined the textile industries in poor countries.

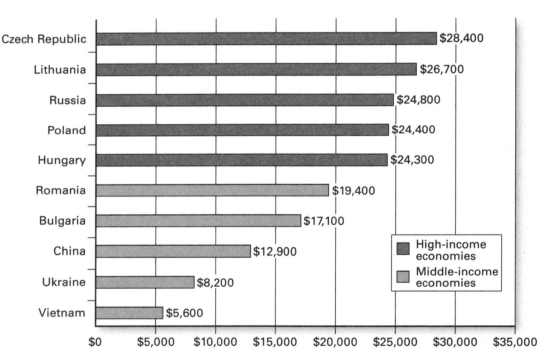

**GDP per Capita for Transitional Economies in 2013**

| Country | GDP per Capita |
|---|---|
| Czech Republic | $28,400 |
| Lithuania | $26,700 |
| Russia | $24,800 |
| Poland | $24,400 |
| Hungary | $24,300 |
| Romania | $19,400 |
| Bulgaria | $17,100 |
| China | $12,900 |
| Ukraine | $8,200 |
| Vietnam | $5,600 |

Legend:
- High-income economies
- Middle-income economies

# Everyday Number Sense
## Mental Math and Visual Models

# TEACHER BOOK

TERC

Mary Jane Schmitt, Myriam Steinback,
Tricia Donovan, Martha Merson

Key Curriculum Press
Innovators in Mathematics Education

TERC, Technical Education Research Centers, Inc.
2067 Massachusetts Avenue
Cambridge, Massachusetts 02140

**Key College Publishing and Key Curriculum Press:**
Development Editor: Erika Shaffer
Production Director: McKinley Williams
Production Project Manager: Ken Wischmeyer
Project Manager: Susan Yates
Consultant: Donna Curry
Text Designer: Laura Murray Productions
Proofreader: Publication Services
Photo Researcher: Laura Murray Productions
Art and Design Coordinator: Jensen Barnes
Cover and Logo Design: Kavitha Becker, Marilyn Perry
Cover Photo Credit: Jensen Barnes
Printer: Alonzo Printing

Editorial Director: Richard J. Bonacci
Vice President/General Manager: Mike Simpson
Publisher: Steven Rasmussen

**EMPower Research and Development Team**
Principal Investigator: Myriam Steinback
Co-Principal Investigator: Mary Jane Schmitt
Research Associate: Martha Merson
Curriculum Developers: Donna Curry, Tricia Donovan

**Technical Team**
Production and Design Coordinator: Valerie Martin
Project Assistant and Graphic Designer: Juania Ashley
Copyeditor: Jill Pellarin

**Evaluation Team**
Brett Consulting Group:
   Belle Brett
   Marilyn Matzko

EMPower™ was developed at TERC in Cambridge, Massachusetts. This material is based upon work supported by the National Science Foundation under award number ESI-9911410 and by the Education Research Collaborative at TERC. Any opinions, findings, and conclusions or recommendations expressed in this publication are those of the authors and do not necessarily reflect the views of the National Science Foundation.

TERC is a not-for-profit education research and development organization dedicated to improving mathematics, science, and technology teaching and learning.

Key Curriculum Press
1150 65th Street
Emeryville, CA 94608
510-595-7000
editorial@keycollege.com
www.keypress.com

Printed in the United States of America
10 9 8 7 6 5 4 3 2 1    08 07 06 05

ISBN 1-55953-727-2

# EMPower Teacher Participants

## Arizona

Gila River Indian Community 21st Century
   Community Learning Center, Gila River
Andrea Parrella

## Illinois

Adult Education Center, Rock Valley College,
   Rockford
Phyllis Flanagan, Melinda Harrison

Comprehensive Community Solutions, Inc.,
   YouthBuild, Rockford
Ryan Boyce

Township High School District 214
   Community Education, Arlington Heights
Kathy Conrad

## Maine

Bailey Evening School, Bath
Pam Bessey

Gardiner Adult and Community Education Program
Diann Bailey

Windham Adult Education, Windham
Eva Giles

## Massachusetts

Action for Boston Community Development, Inc.,
   LearningWorks, Boston
Kelly Qualman

Adult Learning Center at Middlesex Community
   College, Bedford
Roberta Froelich

Brockton Adult Learning Center, Brockton
Marilyn Moses

Community Learning Center, Cambridge
Nellie Dedmon, Sylvia Lotspeich Greene,
   Linda Huntington

Dimock Commuity Health Center, Roxbury
Martha Gray

Harvard Bridge to Learning and Literacy,
   Cambridge
Judy Hikes, Carol Kolenik

Holyoke Adult Learning Opportunities (HALO)
   Center, Holyoke
Kelly Martin, Glenn Yarnell

Hyde Square Task Force, Jamaica Plain
Nora O'Connor

Jewish Vocational Services, Boston
Susan Arase, Terry Lerner, Jeff Snyder

Lowell Adult Education Program, Lowell
Barbara Goodridge

Mount Wachusett Community College, Gardner
Patricia Vorfeld

Notre Dame Education Center, South Boston
Esther D. Leonelli

Pioneer Valley Adult Education Center,
   Northampton
Olu Odusina

Project Place, Boston
Sharon Carey, Maia Hendrickson

Quinsigamond Community College Adult Basic
   Education Program, Worcester
Cathy Coleman

Read/Write/Now, Springfield
Lee E. Boone, Susanne Campagna, Michelle Faith
   Brown, Lucille Fandel

Somerville Center for Adult Learning Experiences
   (SCALE), Somerville
Tom Glannon

X-Cel Adult Education, Dorchester
Don Sands

# EMPower Teacher Participants (continued)

**New Jersey**

New Brunswick Public Schools—Adult Learning Center, New Brunswick
Jacqueline Arkoe, Phyllis Boulanger, Sue Helfand, Karen C. Pickering

**New York**

Adult Learning Center, La Guardia Community College, Long Island City
Norma Andrade, Mark Trushkowsky

BEGIN Managed Programs, New York
Charles Brover, Solange Farina, Santiago Perez, Elizabeth Reddin

Borough of Manhattan Community College/CUNY Adult Basic Education Program, Center for Continuing Education and Workforce Development, New York
Elliot Fink, Mark Lance

City University of New York, Continuing Education, New York
Lisa Simon

Lehman Adult Learning Center, Bronx
Deidre Freeman

SafeSpace-LifeSkills, New York
Jonna Rao

The Adult Learning Center, College of Staten Island, Staten Island
Karen Johnsen

**Pennsylvania**

Lancaster-Lebanon Intermediate Unit 13/Career Link, Lancaster
Margaret Giordano, Barbara Tyndall

**Rhode Island**

Dorcas Place, Parent Literacy Center, Providence
Shannon Dolan, Jerelyn Thomas

**Tennessee**

Hawkins County Adult Education Program, Rogersville
Lisa Mullins

## Acknowledgments

Many friends and family members supported the teachers' and EMPower's efforts. Thank you, Denise Deagan, Judith Diamond, Cara Dimattia, Ellen McDevitt, Sandy Strunk, and the board of the Adult Numeracy Network. Roberta Froelich, Brad Hamilton, Michael Hanish, David Hayes, Judy Hikes, Alisa Izumi, Esther D. Leonelli, Myra Love, Lambrina Mileva, Luz Rivas, Johanna Schmitt, Rachael Stark, Jonathan Steinback, and Sean Sutherland all made unique and timely contributions to the project.

We appreciate the encouragement and advice from John (Spud) Bradley, EMPower's program officer, and Gerhard Salinger of the National Science Foundation.

We are indebted to every adult student who participated in the piloting of EMPower. Their honest feedback and suggestions for what worked and what did not work were invaluable. We could not have completed the curriculum without them or their teachers.

# Contents

# Introduction to the EMPower Curriculum

## Background

*Extending Mathematical Power* (EMPower) integrates recent mathematics education reform into the field of education for adults and out-of-school youth. EMPower was designed especially for those students who return for a second chance at education by enrolling in remedial and adult basic education programs, high school equivalency programs, and developmental programs at community colleges. However, the curriculum is appropriate for a variety of other settings as well, such as high schools, workplaces, and parent and paraprofessional education programs. EMPower builds interest and competency in mathematical problem solving and communication.

Over the course of four years (2000–2004), a collaboration of teachers and researchers with expertise in adult numeracy education and K–12 mathematics reform developed and piloted eight contextualized curriculum units. These units are organized around four central topics: number and operation sense; patterns, functions, and relations; geometry and measurement; and data and graphs. The EMPower program serves as a model for a cohesive mathematics curriculum that offers content consistent with the *Principles and Standards for School Mathematics* (NCTM, 2000), as well as frameworks that are adult-focused, such as the *Equipped for the Future Content Standards* (Stein, 2000), the *Massachusetts ABE Curriculum Frameworks for Mathematics and Numeracy* (Massachusetts Department of Education, 2001), and the Adult Numeracy Network's *Framework for Adult Numeracy Standards* (Curry, Schmitt & Waldron, 1996). The curriculum fosters a pedagogy of learning for understanding; it embeds teacher support and is transformative, yet realistic, for multi-level classrooms.

EMPower challenges students and teachers to consistently extend their ideas of what it means to do math. The curriculum focuses on mathematical reasoning, communication, and problem solving with a variety of approaches and strategies, not just rote memorization and symbol manipulation. The program fosters a learning community in which students are encouraged to expand their understanding of mathematics through open-ended investigations, working collaboratively, sharing ideas, and discovering multiple ways for solving problems. The goal of EMPower is to help people build experience managing the mathematical demands of various life situations, such as finances and commerce, interpretation of news stories, and leisure activities, and to connect those experiences to mathematical principles.

## A Focus on Mathematical Content

The EMPower curriculum supports students' and teachers' growth by directing attention to significant mathematical understandings.

## EMPower emphasizes:

- Data analysis, geometry and measurement, algebra, and numbers and operations at all student levels.

- Reliance on benchmark numbers—such as powers and multiples of 10, common fractions, and their decimal and percent equivalents—for making mental calculations.

- Early use of calculators to support computation.

- Development of reasoning on proportion and parts of quantities before consideration of formal operations with rational numbers.

- Making decisions about data where students generate, as well as interpret, graphical representations.

- Geometry and measurement based on opportunities to see and touch in developing an understanding of spatial relationships and formulas.

- Leading with patterns and relationships in contextual situations and the representations of these situations with diagrams, tables, graphs, verbal rules, and symbolic notation to develop algebraic competence.

# A Focus on Pedagogy

Mathematics is meaningful within a social context. While mathematical truths are universal, the meaning and relevance of numbers changes according to the setting and culture. Therefore, the EMPower pedagogy is focused on sets of connected activities that require communication and discourse.

EMPower asks students to

- Work collaboratively with others on open-ended investigations;

- Share strategies orally and in writing; and

- Justify answers in multiple ways.

Key features of curriculum activities provide

- Clear mathematical goals;

- Contexts that are engaging and useful for young people and adults;

- Opportunities to strengthen mathematical language and communication skills;

- Various ways of entering and solving problems; and

- Puzzles that draw students into problems and motivate them to seek a solution.

# Overview of EMPower Units
## *Features of the Teacher Book*

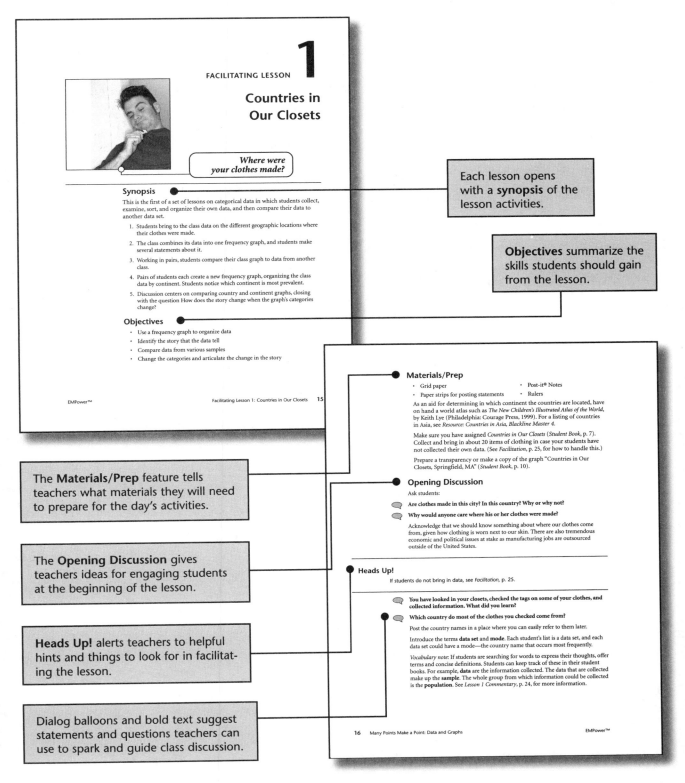

FACILITATING LESSON

**1**

## Countries in Our Closets

*Where were your clothes made?*

### Synopsis

This is the first of a set of lessons on categorical data in which students collect, examine, sort, and organize their own data, and then compare their data to another data set.

1. Students bring to the class data on the different geographic locations where their clothes were made.
2. The class combines its data into one frequency graph, and students make several statements about it.
3. Working in pairs, students compare their class graph to data from another class.
4. Pairs of students each create a new frequency graph, organizing the class data by continent. Students notice which continent is most prevalent.
5. Discussion centers on comparing country and continent graphs, closing with the question How does the story change when the graph's categories change?

### Objectives

- Use a frequency graph to organize data
- Identify the story that the data tell
- Compare data from various samples
- Change the categories and articulate the change in the story

EMPower™    Facilitating Lesson 1: Countries in Our Closets    **15**

> Each lesson opens with a **synopsis** of the lesson activities.

> **Objectives** summarize the skills students should gain from the lesson.

### Materials/Prep

- Grid paper
- Paper strips for posting statements
- Post-it® Notes
- Rulers

As an aid for determining in which continent the countries are located, have on hand a world atlas such as *The New Children's Illustrated Atlas of the World*, by Keith Lye (Philadelphia: Courage Press, 1999). For a listing of countries in Asia, see *Resource: Countries in Asia, Blackline Master 4*.

Make sure you have assigned *Countries in Our Closets* (*Student Book*, p. 7). Collect and bring in about 20 items of clothing in case your students have not collected their own data. (See *Facilitation*, p. 25, for how to handle this.)

Prepare a transparency or make a copy of the graph "Countries in Our Closets, Springfield, MA" (*Student Book*, p. 10).

### Opening Discussion

Ask students:

💬 **Are clothes made in this city? In this country? Why or why not?**

💬 **Why would anyone care where his or her clothes were made?**

Acknowledge that we should know something about where our clothes come from, given how clothing is worn next to our skin. There are also tremendous economic and political issues at stake as manufacturing jobs are outsourced outside of the United States.

### Heads Up!

If students do not bring in data, see *Facilitation*, p. 25.

💬 **You have looked in your closets, checked the tags on some of your clothes, and collected information. What did you learn?**

💬 **Which country do most of the clothes you checked come from?**

Post the country names in a place where you can easily refer to them later.

Introduce the terms **data set** and **mode**. Each student's list is a data set, and each data set could have a mode—the country name that occurs most frequently.

*Vocabulary note*: If students are searching for words to express their thoughts, offer terms and concise definitions. Students can keep track of these in their student books. For example, **data** are the information collected. The data that are collected make up the **sample**. The whole group from which information could be collected is the **population**. See *Lesson 1 Commentary*, p. 24, for more information.

**16**    Many Points Make a Point: Data and Graphs    EMPower™

> The **Materials/Prep** feature tells teachers what materials they will need to prepare for the day's activities.

> The **Opening Discussion** gives teachers ideas for engaging students at the beginning of the lesson.

> **Heads Up!** alerts teachers to helpful hints and things to look for in facilitating the lesson.

> Dialog balloons and bold text suggest statements and questions teachers can use to spark and guide class discussion.

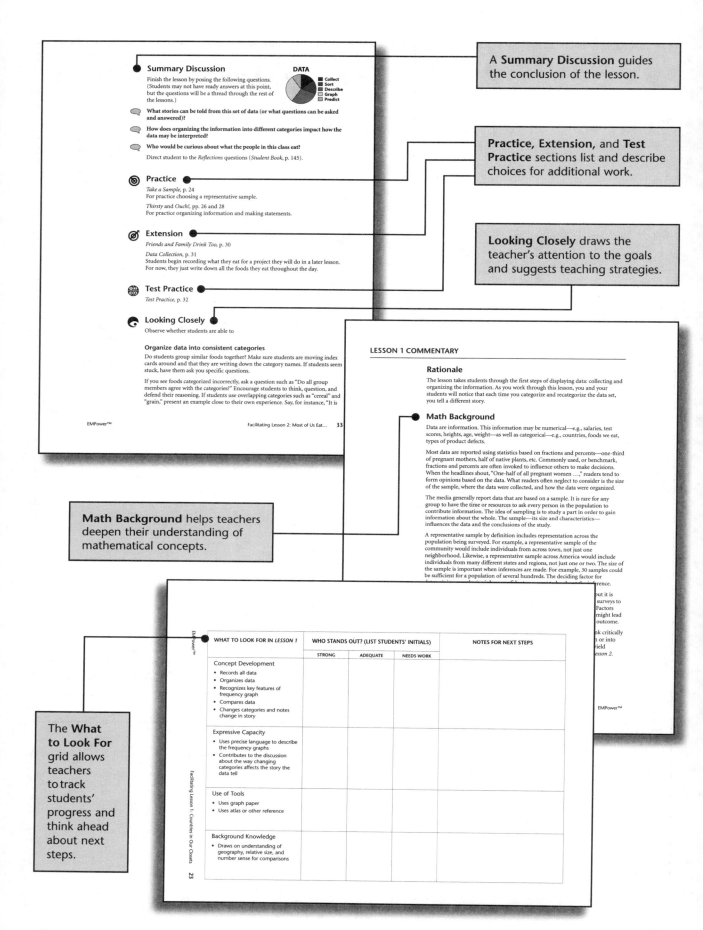

A **Summary Discussion** guides the conclusion of the lesson.

### Summary Discussion

Finish the lesson by posing the following questions. (Students may not have ready answers at this point, but the questions will be a thread through the rest of the lessons.)

**DATA**
- Collect
- Sort
- Describe
- Graph
- Predict

💬 **What stories can be told from this set of data (or what questions can be asked and answered)?**

💬 **How does organizing the information into different categories impact how the data may be interpreted?**

💬 **Who would be curious about what the people in this class eat?**

Direct student to the *Reflections* questions (*Student Book*, p. 145).

**Practice, Extension,** and **Test Practice** sections list and describe choices for additional work.

### 🎯 Practice

*Take a Sample*, p. 24
For practice choosing a representative sample.

*Thirsty* and *Ouch!*, pp. 26 and 28
For practice organizing information and making statements.

### 🎯 Extension

*Friends and Family Drink Too*, p. 30

*Data Collection*, p. 31
Students begin recording what they eat for a project they will do in a later lesson. For now, they just write down all the foods they eat throughout the day.

**Looking Closely** draws the teacher's attention to the goals and suggests teaching strategies.

### Test Practice

*Test Practice*, p. 32

### 🌀 Looking Closely

Observe whether students are able to

**Organize data into consistent categories**

Do students group similar foods together? Make sure students are moving index cards around and that they are writing down the category names. If students seem stuck, have them ask you specific questions.

If you see foods categorized incorrectly, ask a question such as "Do all group members agree with the categories?" Encourage students to think, question, and defend their reasoning. If students use overlapping categories such as "cereal" and "grain," present an example close to their own experience. Say, for instance, "It is

## LESSON 1 COMMENTARY

### Rationale

The lesson takes students through the first steps of displaying data: collecting and organizing the information. As you work through this lesson, you and your students will notice that each time you categorize and recategorize the data set, you tell a different story.

### ● Math Background

Data are information. This information may be numerical—e.g., salaries, test scores, heights, age, weight—as well as categorical—e.g., countries, foods we eat, types of product defects.

Most data are reported using statistics based on fractions and percents—one-third of pregnant mothers, half of native plants, etc. Commonly used, or benchmark, fractions and percents are often invoked to influence others to make decisions. When the headlines shout, "One-half of all pregnant women …," readers tend to form opinions based on the data. What readers often neglect to consider is the size of the sample, where the data were collected, and how the data were organized.

The media generally report data that are based on a sample. It is rare for any group to have the time or resources to ask every person in the population to contribute information. The idea of sampling is to study a part in order to gain information about the whole. The sample—its size and characteristics—influences the data and the conclusions of the study.

A representative sample by definition includes representation across the population being surveyed. For example, a representative sample of the community would include individuals from across town, not just one neighborhood. Likewise, a representative sample across America would include individuals from many different states and regions, not just one or two. The size of the sample is important when inferences are made. For example, 30 samples could be sufficient for a population of several hundreds. The deciding factor for [...] ference.

[...] ut it is [...] surveys to [...] Factors [...] might lead [...] outcome.

[...] nk critically [...] n or into [...] ield [...] *esson 2.*

EMPower™

**Math Background** helps teachers deepen their understanding of mathematical concepts.

The **What to Look For** grid allows teachers to track students' progress and think ahead about next steps.

| WHAT TO LOOK FOR IN *LESSON 1* | WHO STANDS OUT? (LIST STUDENTS' INITIALS) | | | NOTES FOR NEXT STEPS |
|---|---|---|---|---|
| | STRONG | ADEQUATE | NEEDS WORK | |
| **Concept Development**<br>• Records all data<br>• Organizes data<br>• Recognizes key features of frequency graph<br>• Compares data<br>• Changes categories and notes change in story | | | | |
| **Expressive Capacity**<br>• Uses precise language to describe the frequency graphs<br>• Contributes to the discussion about the way changing categories affects the story the data tell | | | | |
| **Use of Tools**<br>• Uses graph paper<br>• Uses atlas or other reference | | | | |
| **Background Knowledge**<br>• Draws on understanding of geography, relative size, and number sense for comparisons | | | | |

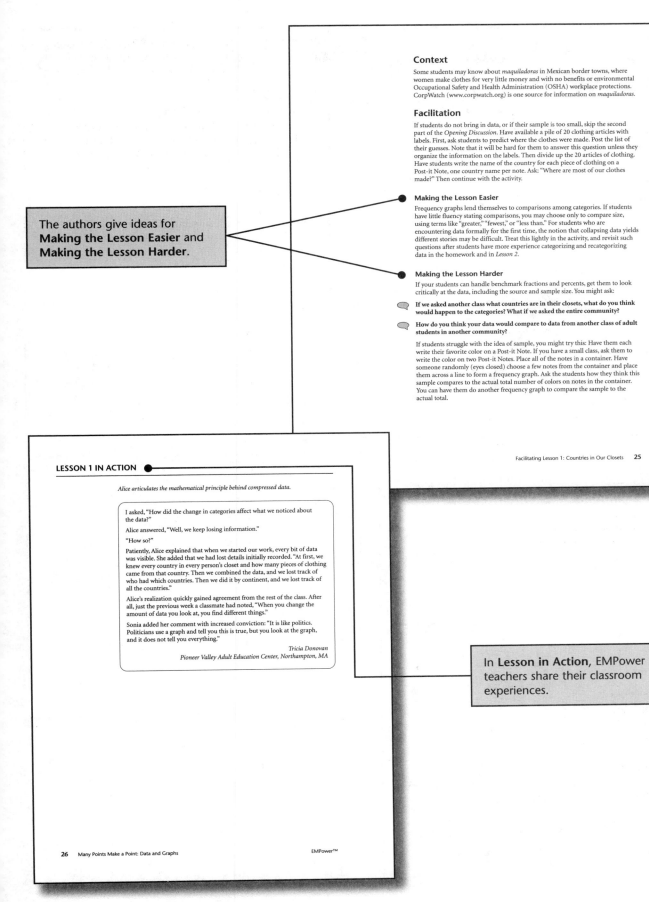

### Context

Some students may know about *maquiladoras* in Mexican border towns, where women make clothes for very little money and with no benefits or environmental Occupational Safety and Health Administration (OSHA) workplace protections. CorpWatch (www.corpwatch.org) is one source for information on *maquiladoras*.

### Facilitation

If students do not bring in data, or if their sample is too small, skip the second part of the *Opening Discussion*. Have available a pile of 20 clothing articles with labels. First, ask students to predict where the clothes were made. Post the list of their guesses. Note that it will be hard for them to answer this question unless they organize the information on the labels. Then divide up the 20 articles of clothing. Have students write the name of the country for each piece of clothing on a Post-it Note, one country name per note. Ask: "Where are most of our clothes made?" Then continue with the activity.

### Making the Lesson Easier

Frequency graphs lend themselves to comparisons among categories. If students have little fluency stating comparisons, you may choose only to compare size, using terms like "greater," "fewest," or "less than." For students who are encountering data formally for the first time, the notion that collapsing data yields different stories may be difficult. Treat this lightly in the activity, and revisit such questions after students have more experience categorizing and recategorizing data in the homework and in *Lesson 2*.

### Making the Lesson Harder

If your students can handle benchmark fractions and percents, get them to look critically at the data, including the source and sample size. You might ask:

💬 **If we asked another class what countries are in their closets, what do you think would happen to the categories? What if we asked the entire community?**

💬 **How do you think your data would compare to data from another class of adult students in another community?**

If students struggle with the idea of sample, you might try this: Have them each write their favorite color on a Post-it Note. If you have a small class, ask them to write the color on two Post-it Notes. Place all of the notes in a container. Have someone randomly (eyes closed) choose a few notes from the container and place them across a line to form a frequency graph. Ask the students how they think this sample compares to the actual total number of colors on notes in the container. You can have them do another frequency graph to compare the sample to the actual total.

The authors give ideas for **Making the Lesson Easier** and **Making the Lesson Harder**.

---

## LESSON 1 IN ACTION ●

*Alice articulates the mathematical principle behind compressed data.*

> I asked, "How did the change in categories affect what we noticed about the data?"
>
> Alice answered, "Well, we keep losing information."
>
> "How so?"
>
> Patiently, Alice explained that when we started our work, every bit of data was visible. She added that we had lost details initially recorded. "At first, we knew every country in every person's closet and how many pieces of clothing came from that country. Then we combined the data, and we lost track of who had which countries. Then we did it by continent, and we lost track of all the countries."
>
> Alice's realization quickly gained agreement from the rest of the class. After all, just the previous week a classmate had noted, "When you change the amount of data you look at, you find different things."
>
> Sonia added her comment with increased conviction: "It is like politics. Politicians use a graph and tell you this is true, but you look at the graph, and it does not tell you everything."
>
> *Tricia Donovan*
> *Pioneer Valley Adult Education Center, Northampton, MA*

In **Lesson in Action**, EMPower teachers share their classroom experiences.

# Overview of EMPower Units
## *Features of the Student Book*

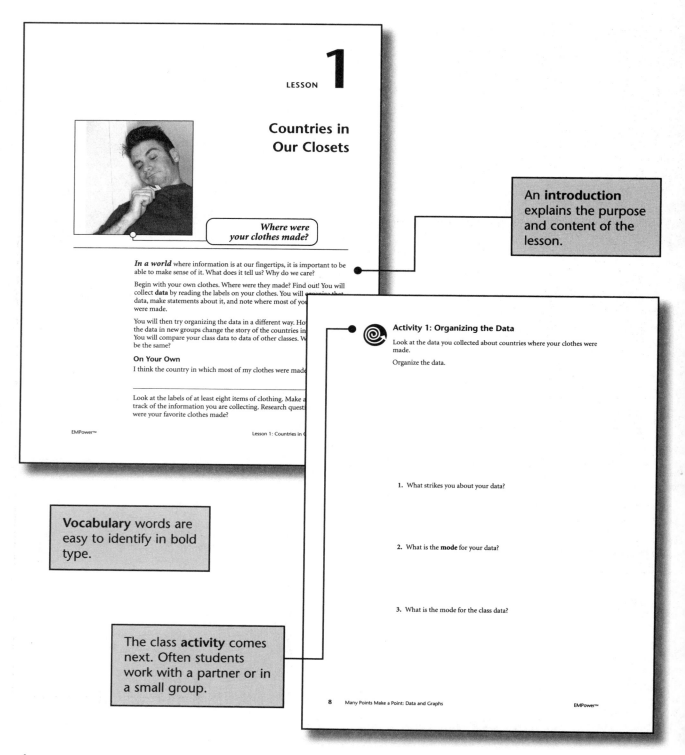

LESSON **1**

### Countries in Our Closets

*Where were your clothes made?*

*In a world* where information is at our fingertips, it is important to be able to make sense of it. What does it tell us? Why do we care?

Begin with your own clothes. Where were they made? Find out! You will collect **data** by reading the labels on your clothes. You will organize that data, make statements about it, and note where most of your ~~clothes~~ were made.

You will then try organizing the data in a different way. How ~~does~~ the data in new groups change the story of the countries in ~~?~~ You will compare your class data to data of other classes. W~~ill it~~ be the same?

**On Your Own**

I think the country in which most of my clothes were made

Look at the labels of at least eight items of clothing. Make a ~~?~~ track of the information you are collecting. Research questi~~on~~ were your favorite clothes made?

EMPower™                    Lesson 1: Countries in ~~?~~

An **introduction** explains the purpose and content of the lesson.

@ **Activity 1: Organizing the Data**

Look at the data you collected about countries where your clothes were made.

Organize the data.

1. What strikes you about your data?

2. What is the **mode** for your data?

3. What is the mode for the class data?

**Vocabulary** words are easy to identify in bold type.

The class **activity** comes next. Often students work with a partner or in a small group.

8    Many Points Make a Point: Data and Graphs                    EMPower™

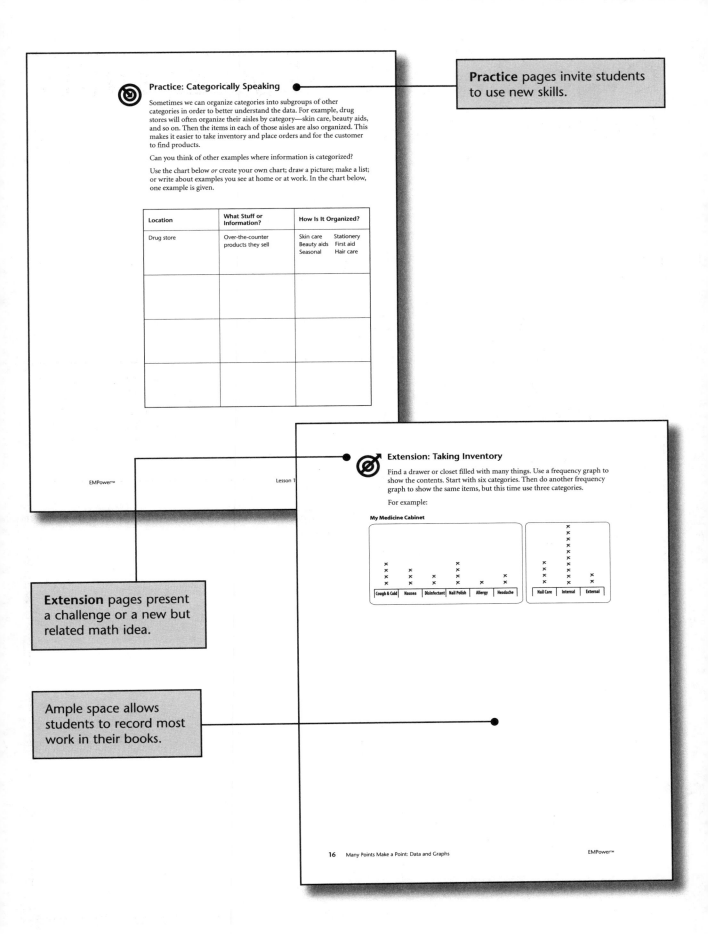

**Practice pages invite students to use new skills.**

### Practice: Categorically Speaking

Sometimes we can organize categories into subgroups of other categories in order to better understand the data. For example, drug stores will often organize their aisles by category—skin care, beauty aids, and so on. Then the items in each of those aisles are also organized. This makes it easier to take inventory and place orders and for the customer to find products.

Can you think of other examples where information is categorized?

Use the chart below *or* create your own chart; draw a picture; make a list; or write about examples you see at home or at work. In the chart below, one example is given.

| Location | What Stuff or Information? | How Is It Organized? |
|----------|---------------------------|----------------------|
| Drug store | Over-the-counter products they sell | Skin care    Stationery<br>Beauty aids   First aid<br>Seasonal    Hair care |
|  |  |  |
|  |  |  |
|  |  |  |

EMPower™                                        Lesson 1

### Extension: Taking Inventory

Find a drawer or closet filled with many things. Use a frequency graph to show the contents. Start with six categories. Then do another frequency graph to show the same items, but this time use three categories.

For example:

**My Medicine Cabinet**

| Cough & Cold | Nausea | Disinfectant | Nail Polish | Allergy | Headache |
|---|---|---|---|---|---|

| Nail Care | Internal | External |
|---|---|---|

**Extension pages present a challenge or a new but related math idea.**

**Ample space allows students to record most work in their books.**

16    Many Points Make a Point: Data and Graphs                                        EMPower™

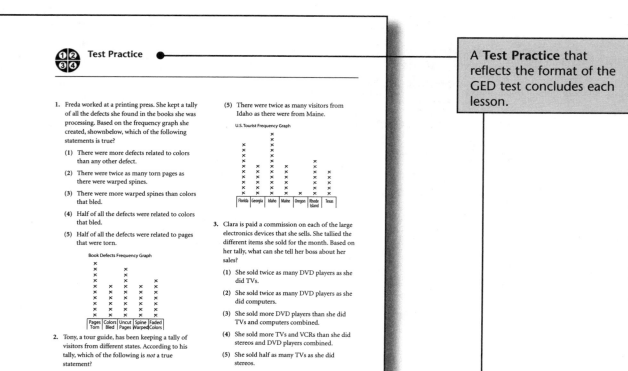

### Test Practice

1. Freda worked at a printing press. She kept a tally of all the defects she found in the books she was processing. Based on the frequency graph she created, shownbelow, which of the following statements is true?

   (1) There were more defects related to colors than any other defect.

   (2) There were twice as many torn pages as there were warped spines.

   (3) There were more warped spines than colors that bled.

   (4) Half of all the defects were related to colors that bled.

   (5) Half of all the defects were related to pages that were torn.

   Book Defects Frequency Graph

2. Tony, a tour guide, has been keeping a tally of visitors from different states. According to his tally, which of the following is *not* a true statement?

   (1) The fewest number of visitors came from Oregon.

   (2) There were as many visitors from Maine as there were from Georgia.

   (3) There were as many visitors from Georgia as there were from Oregon and Texas.

   (4) There were twice as many visitors from Florida as there were from Rhode Island.

   (5) There were twice as many visitors from Idaho as there were from Maine.

   U.S. Tourist Frequency Graph

3. Clara is paid a commission on each of the large electronics devices that she sells. She tallied the different items she sold for the month. Based on her tally, what can she tell her boss about her sales?

   (1) She sold twice as many DVD players as she did TVs.

   (2) She sold twice as many DVD players as she did computers.

   (3) She sold more DVD players than she did TVs and computers combined.

   (4) She sold more TVs and VCRs than she did stereos and DVD players combined.

   (5) She sold half as many TVs as she did stereos.

   Home Media Frequency Graph

4. Bronson, a forest ranger in the Green Mountains, kept track of the different animals that were reportedly seen in one of the campgrounds during the month of May. Based on his tally, which of the following statements could he tell the media?

   (1) There were twice as many wolves reportedly seen as bears.

   (2) Half of all the reported sightings were wolves.

   (3) There were more bears than wolves reportedly seen.

   (4) There were twice as many moose reportedly seen than there were black bears.

   (5) One-quarter of all reported sightings were brown bears.

   North American Wildlife Frequency Graph

5. According to Global Exchange, some workers in China who make clothing for Disney are paid as little as $0.16 per hour. At this wage, what amount would a worker make for a 40-hour workweek?

   (1) $64.00

   (2) $6.40

   (3) $6.00

   (4) $80.00

   (5) $0.60

6. In 2003 the U.S. Department of Labor (DOL) issued new regulations for overtime pay. The DOL estimated that under the new regulations 1.3 million low-wage workers would become eligible for overtime pay, unless their wages were raised to $425 per week. The DOL estimated that 24.8 percent of those workers were Hispanic and 16.6 percent were African American. What percent were neither Hispanic nor African American?

# Changing the Culture

The authors have created this curriculum to follow the National Council of Teachers of Mathematics (NCTM) Principles and Standards; however, teachers who use EMPower face the challenge of transforming the prevailing culture of their math classrooms. EMPower pilot teachers offer some ideas for facilitating this transition:

- Set the stage. As a class, set ground rules. Explicitly state that this is a space for everyone to learn. As one teacher said, "We are in this together. Share, even if you do not think you are right. Whatever you add will be helpful. It lets us see how you are looking at things."

- Group your students. Match students whose learning styles and background knowledge complement each other. Ask questions, such as How did it go to work together? How did everyone contribute?

- Allow wait time. Studies have shown that teachers often wait less than three seconds before asking another question. Students need more time to think.

- Sit down. Watch students before interrupting to help them. Listen for logic and evidence of understanding. Follow the thread of students' thinking to uncover unconventional approaches. During discussions with the whole group, hand over the chalk.

- Review written work. Look beyond right and wrong answers to learn everything you can about what a student knows. Determine what seems solid and easy, as well as patterns in errors. If students are scattered, suggest ways they can organize their work; this is likely to lead to more efficient problem solving and clearer communication.

- Question. Hearing the right answer is not necessarily a cue to move on. Question students at this point too. Specific questions are included in the lesson facilitation.

## Unit Sequences and Connections

The sequence in which the EMPower units can be used effectively with your class will depend on the backgrounds and interests of students. The units are not numbered, so teachers can order them according to their class needs; however, the authors suggest specific unit arrangements that will support students' progression through certain concepts.

The authors do not recommend sequencing the units according to the traditional basic math model that begins with whole numbers and follows with fractions, decimals, and percents; data and graphs; algebra; and then geometry. Instead, they suggest you integrate the five units that focus on numbers with the units on geometry, data, and algebra. The authors found that this integration of topics helped to motivate the adult students in their pilot classes.

Although the units were not specifically designed to build on one another, there are clear connections between some of the units in the series. *Over, Around, and Within: Geometry and Measurement* provides a nice introduction to the program because it focuses on small whole numbers. *Everyday Number Sense: Mental Math and Visual Models* could follow to further develop whole number mental math skills and visual models. *Using Benchmarks: Fractions, Decimals, and Percents* provides the necessary groundwork with fractions, decimals, and percents to describe approximate relationships between data sets in *Many Points Make a Point: Data and Graphs*. And

*Split It Up: More Fractions, Decimals, and Percents* continues to expand students' repertoire of familiar fractions, decimals, and percents. *Seeking Patterns, Building Rules: Algebraic Thinking* builds upon the tools and relationships used in *Keeping Things in Proportion: Reasoning with Ratios*; finally, *Operations Sense: Even More Fractions, Decimals, and Percents* introduces more complex fractions and operations in geometric, graphic, and algebraic contexts. The following diagram demonstrates this integrated sequence:

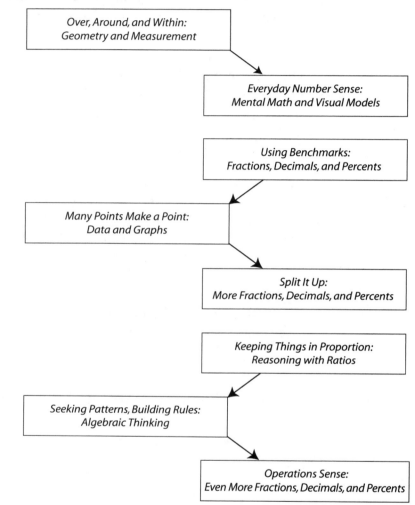

## Unit Descriptions

*Over, Around, and Within: Geometry and Measurement*
Students explore the features and measures of basic shapes. Perimeter and area of two-dimensional shapes and volume of rectangular solids provide the focus.

*Everyday Number Sense: Mental Math and Visual Models*
Students solve problems and compute with whole numbers using mental math strategies with benchmarks of 1, 10, 100, and 1,000. Number lines, arrays, and diagrams support their conceptual understanding of number relationships and the four operations.

*Using Benchmarks: Fractions, Decimals, and Percents*
Students use the fractions ½, ¼, ¾, and ¹⁄₁₀; the decimals 0.1, 0.5, 0.25, and 0.75; and the percents 50%, 25%, 75%, 100%, and the multiples of 10% as benchmarks to describe and compare all part-whole relationships.

*Many Points Make a Point: Data and Graphs*
Students collect, organize, and represent data using frequency, bar, and circle graphs. They use line graphs to describe change over time. They use benchmark fractions and the three measures of central tendency—mode, median, and mean—to describe sets of data.

*Split It Up: More Fractions, Decimals, and Percents*
Building on their command of common benchmark fractions, students add thirds, eighths, and hundredths and their decimal and percent equivalents to their repertoire of part-whole relationships.

*Keeping Things in Proportion: Reasoning with Ratios*
Students use various tools—objects, diagrams, tables, graphs, and equations—to understand proportional and nonproportional relationships.

*Seeking Patterns, Building Rules: Algebraic Thinking*
Students use a variety of representational tools—diagrams, words, tables, graphs, and equations—to understand linear patterns and functions. They connect the rate of change with the slope of a line and compare linear with nonlinear relationships. They also gain facility with and comprehension of basic algebraic notation.

*Operation Sense: Even More Fractions, Decimals, and Percents*
Students extend their understanding of the four operations with whole numbers as they puzzle over questions such as "How is it possible that two fractions multiplied might yield a smaller amount than either fraction?" and "What does it mean to divide one-half by six?"

## Frequently Asked Questions

*Q: I have classes that are widely multi-level. Can this work?*

**A:** Many teachers see a wide range of levels within the group as an obstacle. Turn the range of levels to your advantage. Focus on students' representations (words, graphs, equations, sketches). This gives everyone the chance to see that answers emerge in several ways. Slowing down deepens understanding and avoids facile responses. Having calculators available can even the playing field. Implement the suggestions in *Making the Lesson Easier* and *Making the Lesson Harder* of each lesson facilitation in the *Lesson Commentary* sections.

*Q: How do I deal with erratic attendance patterns?*

**A:** Uneven attendance can be disruptive. Students who miss class may feel disoriented; however, the lessons spiral back to the most important concepts. When the curriculum circles back, students will have a chance to revisit concepts and get a toehold.

*Q: What do I do if I run out of time, and there is no way to finish a lesson?*

**A:** Each activity is important, but reviewing it is equally important. It is better to cut the activity short so there is time to talk with students about what they noticed. Maximize the time by selecting a student or group whose work you feel will add to the class's understanding to report their findings. Be conscious of when you are letting an activity go on too long because the energy is high. Fun is good, but be sure important learning is happening. If you like to give time in class to reviewing homework, and you want to hear from everyone in discussions, you will run out of time. Schedule a catch-up session every three or four lessons.

*Q: How do I respond to comments such as "Can't we go back to the old way?"*

**A:** Change is unsettling, especially for students who are accustomed to math classes where their job is to work silently on a worksheet solving problems by following a straightforward example. Be clear about the reasons why you have chosen to de-emphasize some of the traditional ways of teaching in favor of this approach. Ultimately, you may need to agree to some changes to accommodate students' input. Meanwhile, stick with the curriculum. Reiterate for students what they have accomplished. When there is an "Aha!" moment, point it out.

*Q: My own math background is not strong. Will I be able to teach this curriculum?*

**A:** Yes! Most teachers tend to teach the way they were taught. Adopting a different stance requires support, and the more types of support, the better. This curriculum offers support in a few ways. The *Teacher Book* for each unit lists open-ended questions designed to keep the math on track. In the *Lesson Commentary* sections, the *Math Background* helps teachers deepen their understanding of a concept. In addition, the *Lesson in Action* sections provide examples of student work with comments that illuminate the underlying mathematics.

The best support often comes from a colleague. If no one at your site is currently teaching EMPower, join the Adult Numeracy Network, http://shell04.theworld.com/std/anpn, and attend your regional NCTM conference. Look for others who are integrating the NCTM Principles and Standards through the use of a curriculum such as *The Investigations in Number, Data, and Space Curriculum* (Russell et al., 1998); *Connected Mathematics* (Lappan et al., 1998); or *Interactive Mathematics Program* (Fendel et al., 1997).

# Unit Introduction
## *Everyday Number Sense: Mental Math and Visual Models*

### Major Themes

#### The Importance of Adults Bringing Their Understanding into the Classroom

The ways in which adults manage the mathematical demands of their everyday and work lives do not always look like the ways they were taught in school. Observations of adults at work and in consumer situations uncover a surprising assortment of non-textbook methods. Highly numerate adults use flexible, accurate, and efficient strategies for manipulating numbers and quantities in real-world problem-solving. Such strategies can support insight into higher mathematics as well.

Many adults have invented or amassed a set of strategies that circumvent the tedium of the historically taught procedures (algorithms), yet may think those are not the school-approved or "real" ways. It is important that adults be encouraged to bring their own good math sense to bear in various situations. These may include a mix of finger counting, mental math, estimation, calculator use, and paper-and-pencil methods.

This unit strives to make the most of the strategies adults bring to the table and makes explicit the understandings adults hold about numbers so that new ideas can be built on this foundation.

#### Developing Number Sense

To have sense about numbers means to understand how numerical quantities are constructed and how they relate to one another.

Numerate adults are flexible about numbers. They are able to break apart numbers in different ways. For example, they might see 36 as six more than 30, four less than 40, or more than half of 50. They use numbers such as 10, 100, and 1,000 as benchmarks with which to reason. Moreover, they can compare numbers to one another in an absolute way (how much more is 3,000 than 200?) as well as in a relative way (3,000 is how many times as great as 200?).

To support the development of this useable and supple appreciation of numbers, the lessons in the unit encourage students to look for patterns and generalizations. For example, mental math practices require students to generalize about patterns of multiplying by powers of 10 or to examine a multiplication table for patterns. Students are repeatedly asked to deconstruct numbers in various ways, such as in the activity "Number of the Day," where they express the number 48 in as many ways as they can.

## Developing Operation Sense

Most of the lessons in *Everyday Number Sense: Mental Math and Visual Models* are not about teaching or even reviewing the usual algorithms for the four operations. Rather, learners share and strengthen their own trustworthy strategies, which may include sequential doubling, halving, multiplying by multiples of 10, and using the commutative, associative, and distributive properties.

A common question in any math class is, "What should I do: add, subtract, multiply or divide?" This puzzle may stem from several factors: Students may have difficulty moving between text and print; sketchy place value and mental math or estimating skills (so that they are not sure of the magnitude of the answer); or lack of a true understanding of addition, subtraction, multiplication, and division. We agree with the NCTM statement that learners need to "understand meanings of operations and how they relate to one another" (NCTM, 2000, p. 34).

Deep understanding comes when a person has a sense for the various models for an operation. It is not enough, for example, to conceive of subtraction as taking away one amount from another. The "take away" model works for having an amount of money, spending some, and figuring out what you have left. However, nothing is taken away when you compare the amount of money you have in the bank with the amount you wish you had. A concept of subtraction as difference or comparison is helpful in such a case. One major idea expounded here is learning operations not in isolation, but in relation to one another: addition as it relates to multiplication, division as it relates to subtraction, and multiplication as it relates to division. The order of operations is stressed, as is the commutativity of addition and multiplication.

Knowing how operations relate to one another gives a person a wider range of ways to approach solving a problem. Some people see addition in a problem such as, "How much do four apples cost at 50 cents each?" Some see multiplication. The connection between multiplication and repeated addition is why both methods work.

In *Everyday Number Sense*, lessons focus on helping students both develop various understandings for the operations and make connections between them.

## The Importance of Mental Math

When a group of adults were asked to keep track of how they used math in a 24-hour period, most (85%) of the math they did was in their heads or by arriving at good estimations (Northcote & McIntosh, 1999). These researchers also found that estimates were sufficient for approximately 60% of all calculations, and exact answers necessary only 40% of the time.

In this unit, mental math always remains the focus. Students are encouraged to solve problems by grouping, visualizing, and decomposing numbers. Calculators are available for those who want to check their work, but only after mental math strategies have been experienced and shared.

Estimation is treated as a first step in problem-solving. Precision or accuracy can be as easily achieved by rounding and adjusting as it can by lengthy calculations on paper. Furthermore, students recognize that estimating or rounding (and adjusting) can help them determine a solution that is accurate enough for many circumstances. Estimations are particularly useful for gauging the accuracy of calculator-generated solutions, and it is vital for students to know how and when to use a calculator. A numerate person has all of these strategies at his or her disposal.

## The Importance of Visual Models

To ably communicate mathematically and to flexibly approach problems, adults need visualization and expressive skills. They need to "see" the problem, and they need to know how to express it and their solution processes not only in words and with notation, but with pictures as well.

A recurring question for students here is "How do you know?" To answer this question and to make the workings of mathematics visible, we count on visual representations, such as number lines, arrays (where objects are arranged in rows and columns), diagrams, words, and equations. The lessons extend opportunities to develop multiple ways to solve problems. Having multiple ways to approach a problem is a key in distinguishing adults who are comfortable doing math from those who are not. Only by perceiving more than one way can the problem-solver then choose the most efficient method.

The lessons also encourage multiple ways to perform calculations. Students are encouraged to visualize and decompose numbers (to see 14 as 10 + 4, for instance) in order to facilitate multi-digit operations and lay the groundwork for algebra. The unit clues students into the simplicity and elegance of the base-10 number system (by applying the pattern of multiplying by powers of 10 or adding and subtracting by multiples of 10's and 1's, for instance). The emphasis is on observing and understanding patterns rather than learning short-cuts by rote.

Throughout these lessons, students work with equations, diagramming tools, and words, so they will be equally at home with a word problem or a graphic representation of a situation.

## Frequently Asked Questions

**Q:** *What happens if some people don't know their multiplication tables? Shouldn't those be taught first?*

**A:** In most classes, there can be a wide range of automaticity with one-digit addition, subtraction, and multiplication facts. Some students have never learned to recite their tables automatically. But adults who have never memorized 6 x 7 = 42, or even 6 + 7 = 13, buy things, earn money, and pay bills, and in doing so, do a lot of math. You don't have to know your multiplication tables to do some interesting math, but it certainly helps. Memorization is one strategy; however, for learners late to memorizing the tables, this is not always the most effective strategy. Noticing patterns and using known facts may be more advantageous.

In each lesson, there is at least one *Mental Math Practice* that focuses on using patterns to get a good grasp on number facts. These practices are designed to build number fact facility.

**Q:** *Shouldn't calculators come later?*

**A:** Knowing how to use a calculator well is a basic skill for all adults. The calculator will even the playing field in your class. Students with strong conceptual skills will be able to punch in numbers, arrive at answers more quickly, and therefore participate more actively in class. The calculator is one more strategy for learners who are extending their comfort with math into new ground. Having the calculator at hand frees their thinking for problem-solving and communicating their reasoning. For some students, using a calculator, particularly the scientific calculator, will be a first. Finally, to those who fear that the calculator will be a substitute for strong mathematical thinking and computation, to use this tool well, good mental math and estimation skills are essential. To ensure the accuracy, efficiency, and flexibility that are the basis for strong number sense, the unit stresses mental math and visualization, supported by the calculator.

**Q:** *Why are the traditional algorithms de-emphasized?*

**A:** One of the hallmarks of people who work with numbers in their daily lives is that their calculations tend to be quite accurate. Good numeracy requires making sense with numbers, and that good sense is often suspended when a person loses his or her inner compass and applies school-taught algorithms that were never quite understood.

So most of the lessons in *Everyday Number Sense* are not about teaching or even reviewing the usual algorithms. Rather, learners share and strengthen their own trustworthy strategies that go beyond the historically taught paper-and-pencil algorithms.

**Q:** *What is the hallmark of a numerate adult?*

**A:** One of the goals for adults revisiting arithmetic is to become computationally fluent with whole numbers. The notion of computational fluency, as discussed by Susan Jo Russell (1999), entails making error-free calculations (accuracy); approaching the calculation in a variety of ways (flexibility); and selecting a less tedious method from among the variety of possibilities (efficiency).

Competency in reaching these objectives is a process, and abilities to do so lie along a continuum. The more numerate a person is, the richer the host of skills and understandings he or she brings to problem-solving. Take, for instance, the simple "naked number" problem: 23 x 13. A numerate adult has the following options:

- Enter the numbers into a calculator and achieve precise results.

- Use a pencil-and-paper procedure to achieve precise results.

- Decompose the numbers mentally to achieve precise results (23 x 10 = 230 + 23 x 3 = 230 + 69 = 299).

- Round quantities to estimate an answer (20 x 10 = 200; the answer must be greater than 200).

- Picture 23 on a number line with that interval repeated 13 times.

- Picture an array with 23 rows and 13 columns.

- Picture 13 groups of 23 objects.

- Envision a situation represented by the numbers, such as, "I have to make 13 payments of $23 each, so that is a year plus one month or 23 x 12 +23."

- Recognize the inverse situation; for example, in a division problem, take the total of 299 and divide it by 23 to yield an answer of 13.

## Unit Goals

By the end of this unit, students should be able to

- Solve problems mentally with estimates and exact answers;

- Represent operations (×, ÷, +, −) using objects, pictures, arrays, and number lines to explain and support reasoning;

- Select appropriate operation(s) to represent problem situations (e.g., when is it appropriate to multiply and when to divide?) and write expressions in mathematical notation;

- Explain and develop strategies for rounding, adjusting, and using benchmark numbers (10's and 100's) to solve problems;

- Use the scientific calculator.

## The Flow of the Unit

There are twelve lessons with embedded ongoing assessments as well as three separate assessment sessions in the opening, midpoint, and closing sessions (see *Assessments*, pp. xxvi–xxvii, for more detail). Each lesson has one or more activities or investigations. Allowing time for opening and summary discussions (including time for student reflections) and assuming a thoughtful pace, most lessons will exceed an hour. Students' literacy levels will affect how long each lesson takes.

In *Lessons 1* and *2*, students

- Use mental math strategies to estimate totals;

- Mentally calculate by rounding and adjusting;

- Use mathematics notation to describe mental math strategies.

In *Lessons 3–5*, students

- Use the number line as a thinking tool;

- Locate numbers on the number line and determine the distance (difference) between the numbers. In *Lesson 5*, the number line is extended to include negative numbers;

- Record mental math and number line actions with equations.

In *Lessons 6* and *7*, students

- Examine and identify the composition of numbers in terms of 10's, 100's and 1,000's;

- Use mathematical notation, including parentheses, to show how they solve a problem;

- Identify and use patterns when multiplying and dividing by 10, 100, and 1,000.

In *Lessons 8* and *9*, students

- Represent expressions using arrays and/or groups arranged to correspond with numbers and operations;

- Identify and find equivalent expressions;

- Record problem-solving strategies using equations and pictures.

In *Lessons 10–12*, students

- Focus on two models of division and making sense of remainders;

- Solve division problems involving splitting an amount into equal parts;

- Work with direct measurements and scale to find the number of groups of a given size in a total;

- Establish the relation between division and multiplication;

- Identify factors of numbers such as 48 and 72;

- Find remainders and express them using fractions, decimals, and whole numbers.

## Assessments

*Everyday Number Sense: Mental Math and Visual Models* opens and closes with assessment. In both cases, the *Teacher Book* provides multiple ways to gauge what students know. There are also tools for ongoing assessment. These components are described below.

### Opening the Unit: Everyday Numbers

This session provides an opportunity to welcome students to the unit and to surface students' everyday use of whole numbers and strategies for working with them. The purpose of the opening session is to introduce students to the content of the unit and to give you information about their understanding. It is not designed as a teaching lesson, so refrain from using the session as an opportunity to teach all the concepts. The 12 lessons are designed to help students solidify their grasp of the content.

The components of the opening session are as follows:

*Where Is the Math in Your Life?*: Students share personal experiences using math and reflect upon how they did the math—in their heads, with a calculator, or with paper and pencil.

*Number of the Day*: Students write as many expressions as they can for a given number.

*Initial Assessment*: There are three tasks—Mental Math Challenge, Picturing the Math, and Four Problems. Before students attempt the problems in Tasks 2 and 3, they read through the problems together, self-assessing how confident they are about solving each one.

### Midpoint Activity: What Math Means to Me

This activity serves as an assessment of students' perceptions of mathematics. Each person makes a collage to communicate "What math means to me." Students interpret one another's collages.

### Closing the Unit: Computer Lab

The closing session is an opportunity for students to synthesize and reflect upon what they have learned.

*Computer Lab Project*: When they reach *Closing the Unit: Computer Lab*, students are equipped to make a plan for outfitting a computer lab with a $10,000 budget. They present their plan, choices, and problem-solving strategies to the class.

*Final Assessment*: Mirroring the *Initial Assessment*, the *Final Assessment* has three tasks and again asks students to self-assess their confidence levels before they do the problems in Tasks 2 and 3.

## Ongoing Assessment

Much of the work students do will take place in small groups or pairs. This work must be evaluated to determine the extent to which students are comfortable with the main ideas and to diagnose difficulties, as well as provide more challenging work, if needed. *The Looking Closely* section of each lesson focuses teachers' attention on the lesson's objectives and the corresponding observable behavior. As students gain skills, teachers will want to track their progress and communicate observations to them. Each lesson has a chart called *What to Look For in Lesson X* with four dimensions for assessing students' progress:

*Number Development*: grasp of major concepts and skills.

*Expressive Capacity*: ability to describe, reason aloud, and explain to others. This is easiest to observe in written work, a record with strong evidence of understanding and misconceptions or errors. However, a student's oral remarks are often a more accurate reflection of what he or she knows.

*Notation Use*: ability to accurately encode mathematical thinking in symbolic notation.

*Use of Tools*: encompasses the ability to use calculators, number lines, and diagrams to communicate, verify answers, and enrich understanding.

Bearing in mind these dimensions of assessment will help you formulate "next steps" for teaching.

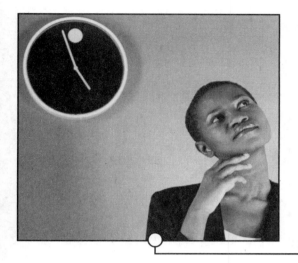

# Facilitating
# Opening the Unit:
# Everyday Numbers

*Where is math in your everyday life?*

## Synopsis

This session is designed to welcome students to the unit by asking them to reflect upon and share their uses of math in daily life. It is also an opportunity to assess how fluently and flexibly they work with whole numbers, including how they use **mental math** and connect **mathematical notation** with **visual models** and problem situations.

1. Students reflect upon occasions when they have used math recently, how they did the math (in their heads, with calculators, or with paper and pencils), and whether the answer was exact or an estimate.

2. The class works on "Number of the Day," writing numerical **expressions** for "360."

3. Students complete an *Initial Assessment* of mental math and ways they connect symbolic expressions, situations, and visual models.

## Objectives

- Share personal experiences using math
- Demonstrate mental math skills
- Demonstrate fluency with visual models and symbolic expressions

## Materials/Prep

- Overhead projector (optional)
- Markers
- Newsprint
- Photocopies of *Initial Assessment*, p. 169, one per student

Make transparencies of *Number of the Day* (*Blackline Master 1*) and *Mental Math Challenges* (*Blackline Masters 2–4*).

## Heads Up!

If an overhead projector is not available, prepare newsprints of the three blackline masters.

## Opening Discussion

Tell students that you are interested in gathering information about where and how they use math in their everyday lives. You also want to know how they do calculations and connect different ways of describing and picturing the math. Today is a day to show how many ways they know to work with numbers.

 ## Activity 1: Where Is the Math in Your Life?

Refer students to *Activity 1: Where Is the Math in Your Life?* (*Student Book*, p. 2).

Say:

 **How do you use math in your daily lives? Take a few minutes to think of all the times during the past month or so that you used numbers and did some math. Make a list, filling in the first column with at least five examples. Do not count the math you do in school. List the math you do in your everyday life.**

After everyone has made his or her list, begin a class list on the board with students' reported uses. For each reported use, ask:

 **How did you do the math? Did you do it in your head? Did you use a paper and pencil? Did you use a calculator?**

 **Did you find an exact answer or did you get an estimate?**

The board might look something like this as you record offerings:

| Where We Used Math | Head/Paper/ Calculator? | Exact/ Estimate |
| --- | --- | --- |
| Figuring a 25% discount | H | Estimate |
| Figured out how many hours I worked | P | Exact |
| Saw if I had enough money for shopping | H | Estimate |
| Figured my bank balance | C | Exact |
| Paid bills | H | Exact |
| Made a cake | H | Exact |

Ask students to mark each of their own entries in their books with "H," "P," or "C" and to note whether they got an exact or estimated answer.

Then ask:

 **What do you notice about our list?**

Students might say

"We did a lot of the math in our heads."

"We didn't always need the exact answer."

"It's about money and time."

Conclude the opening by saying that this unit, *Everyday Number Sense: Mental Math and Visual Models,* is designed to give everyone a chance to work with numbers in a variety of ways. It should help everyone get better at using math in daily life, and that will include improving mental math skills. Sometimes students will estimate; sometimes they will be asked to calculate an exact answer.

## ⊚ Activity 2: Number of the Day

Refer students to *Activity 2: Number of the Day*, p. 3. You might want to start with an example, explaining that if the number of the day were 12, there would be many ways you could arrive at that number, using different operations. For instance, you might write "6 + 6" or "3 x 4."

Say:

 **Today's number is 360. Let's see how many different numerical expressions you can write that have the answer 360.**

When everyone is clear about the directions, allow individuals about 10 minutes to generate expressions. Encourage students to use each of the four operations at least once, as well as any other mathematical notation they know.

Pull the class together and ask for suggestions, writing responses on a transparency of *Number of the Day* (*Blackline Master 1*) or on a piece of newsprint.

The responses might include

| | |
|---|---|
| 100 + 100 + 100 + 60 | 400 − 40 |
| 3(100) + 60 | 4 × 100 − 40 |
| 12(30) | 40(10) − 40 |
| 36(10) | 720 ÷ 2 |

When several expressions have been offered, ask whether there are any that are questionable. You want to see whether students detect any incorrect expressions. It is not necessary to point them out yourself, but take note of any incorrect responses.

Save the transparency or newsprint for comparison with the one created in the final lesson. You will want to see whether students become more flexible in the ways they break up numbers.

##  Activity 3: Initial Assessment

Distribute a copy of the *Initial Assessment* to everyone.

Explain that there are three tasks:

Task 1: Mental Math Challenge

Task 2: Picturing the Math

Task 3: Four Problems

### Facilitating Task 1

Tell students:

**I am going to show and read some problems. Your challenge is to do the math in your head and then write down the answer. Do not use paper and pencils or calculators!**

Starting with *Mental Math Challenge* (*Blackline Master 2*), cover up the problems with a paper, revealing each problem one at a time and reading it aloud. For each problem, allow a few moments for students to think about and write the answer. This is not a timed test, but move along at a good pace. You are trying to see how fluent students are with the numbers. Continue with the next two *Mental Math Challenges* (*Blackline Masters 3* and *4.*).

### Facilitating Tasks 2 and 3

Before students attempt the problems in Tasks 2 and 3, read through the problems together, asking them to self-assess how confident they are about solving the problems. They should check off "can do," "don't know how," or "not sure" without doing the problem. Keep the momentum going, reading each problem together, and then moving on to the next one.

The *Initial Assessment* is a flexible tool. Some teachers proceed either to assign the problems students feel most confident about or to ask students to try them all. Establish a time limit, and collect the packets to analyze later. Students' work on the problems will provide a point of comparison for assessing progress with the *Final Assessment*.

See the *Initial Assessment Checklist*, p. 175, for instructional decisions.

## Summary Discussion

Ask students to comment on the assessment session by writing in the *Reflections* section of their books, p. 185.

 **What did you find out about your strong points?**

 **What challenged you?**

Explain that the goal of this unit is to prepare students so they can solve any of these problems and others. They will use the methods they already know and explore new ways to look at problems.

Introduce the unit goals by reading together *Everyday Number Sense: Mental Math and Visual Models Unit Goals* (*Student Book*, p. 4). Ask students to add any of their own goals.

## Looking Closely

Observe whether students are able to

### Share personal experiences using math

Do students come up with examples of their math use? Don't be surprised if an initial reaction is, "I never use math!" There are studies documenting adults' under-reporting of math in their lives. Probe if necessary. Ask students whether they shopped or paid bills, made any decisions with numbers, or figured out anything to do with time, such as how much longer it would be until the bus came or work was over. Did they ever have to measure anything?

### Demonstrate mental math skills

To what extent are students able to handle the mental math challenge? Do they exhibit some automaticity with basic facts? Do they have strategies or tricks that they count on? The amounts in the *Mental Math Challenge* are presented in dollars and cents to make the numbers very real. If the *Mental Math Challenge* is a struggle, that is a good indication that the unit will be quite appropriate. As you complete each lesson, make sure to assign the *Mental Math Practices*, which are designed to develop skills at doing math in one's head.

### Demonstrate fluency with visual models and symbolic expressions

How complex are the symbolic expressions students create for *Activity 2: Number of the Day* (*Student Book*, p. 3)? This activity is challenging for students and is an excellent assessment tool, appropriate at every level. The expressions each student writes will demonstrate which operations he or she is comfortable doing. As you proceed through the unit, you should expect students to generate more complex expressions.

Are students able to create or interpret visual models for the word problem? Are they able to use a number line to show the math? Again, if these are challenging, the necessary skills will be developed in these lessons.

| WHAT TO LOOK FOR IN OPENING THE UNIT | WHO STANDS OUT? (LIST STUDENTS' INITIALS) | | | NOTES FOR NEXT STEPS |
|---|---|---|---|---|
| | STRONG | ADEQUATE | NEEDS WORK | |
| **Number Development**<br>• Knows basic number facts<br>• Is fluent with the four basic operations<br>• Uses mental math strategies<br>• Can break apart numbers efficiently | | | | |
| **Expressive Capacity**<br>• Explains how a picture connects to symbolic notation | | | | |
| **Notation Use**<br>• Rewrites a number using various notations<br>• Connects symbolic notation to the meaning of a contextual situation | | | | |
| **Use of Tools**<br>• Makes good use of a number line<br>• Uses a calculator | | | | |

## Rationale

By knowing students' strengths and weaknesses before starting a unit of study, you can make wise instructional decisions. You can help students recognize a need to learn some things and affirm what they already know.

## Math Background

The mathematics in these assessment activities involve whole numbers (or dollars and cents) and the four basic operations. Students are asked to apply representational skills and use basic number facts. The decision to emphasize mental math is based on two premises. First, many of the calculations numerate adults perform in their everyday lives tend to be done with mental math, either to arrive at good estimations or to check the reasonableness of electronically computed results. For example, when paying for a $2.59 coffee and a 79¢ donut with a $10 bill, one might estimate the change to be a little more than $6 because, if one starts with $2.59, the 79¢ brings the total to somewhere just short of $3.50. The customer would expect to get six dollars and coins back from the cashier.

There is another reason why mental math is a focus of this unit on whole number and dollar and cents calculations. By stressing the need to be thoughtful about the many ways to break up or combine numbers, the underlying algebraic properties of arithmetic are brought to the fore. The distributive, commutative, and associative properties come into play as one reasons more precisely that
$2.59 + $0.79 = $[(2.60 − 0.01) + (0.80 − 0.01)] = $[(2.60 + 0.80) − (0.01 + 0.01)] = $3.40 − $0.02. = $3.38.

## Context

The session is launched from students' everyday math use. As they report on meeting the mathematical demands of daily life, they share strategies.

## Facilitation

Note who has mental math skills and visualization skills. Be aware that some students will require more time than others. Also, note who is relying on algorithms (applied correctly or incorrectly), as these students will be challenged in the unit to learn new ways of seeing problems. They may need to be reminded of the purposes of visualizing math problems: to represent them in a variety of ways that are helpful when problems are confusing; and to solve them mentally when pencil and paper or calculator are not handy.

### Making the Lesson Easier

Work through the problems as a class. Get a sense of individuals' knowledge by the level of participation in various activities.

### Making the Lesson Harder

Try some larger or "messier" numbers in the various problems.

FACILITATING LESSON

# Close Enough with Mental Math

> **When do you do math in your head?**

## Synopsis

Students draw upon their prior knowledge from everyday shopping experiences as they estimate the total cost of several items. Then they apply rounding to several situations, relying upon mental math to arrive at reasonable answers.

1. The class practices **rounding** when finding **approximate,** or "ballpark," totals.

2. Student pairs create wish lists of items for a community center area or for themselves, using mental math as they round to make estimates.

3. Student pairs review each other's work, and the class hears about strategies used.

4. The class summarizes strategies used to estimate totals.

## Objectives

- Use mental math strategies to estimate totals

## Materials/Prep

- Copies of a catalog (e.g., Sears, LL Bean, JC Penney), one per student pair
- Markers
- Newsprint
- Post-it® Notes (a few for each student or student pair)
- Transparencies

Make a transparency of *Six Problems (Blackline Master 5)* for *Activity 1,* or write the six problems on newsprint or the board. (You will show only one problem at a time.)

# Opening Discussion

Get students thinking about a familiar situation involving some mental math estimation by posing the following scenario:

 **A friend and I go out for a night on the town. We see a movie and have dinner. The movie costs $9.50 per ticket. Dinner for the two of us is $43.50. About how much will our evening out cost each of us?**

Ask students to make their estimates in their heads without using pencils and paper.

When students share estimates, ask them how they arrived at their answers, recording what they say in writing on the board or on an overhead transparency. Expect some students to raise the idea of rounding numbers. If the following points do not come up, bring them up yourself:

- $9.50 is about $10.
- $43.50 is about $44; half of $44 is $22.
- $22 and $10 is $32.
- It will cost each of us about $32.

Or

- $9.50 is about $10.
- Two tickets are about $20.
- Dinner is almost $44.
- $44 and $20 is $64, and half of that is $32.

Stress estimation:

 **Rather than getting exact answers, today we will make estimates that are close enough, or, as they say, "in the ballpark."**

## Activity 1: About How Much?

Explain that for each of the six problems you will show, students will select the closest answer from among three choices.

Show the first problem in *Six Problems (Blackline Master 5)*, giving students only a short time to find the closest answer; they should not have enough time to find the exact answer.

Ask for volunteers to explain how they found the closest answer. Record students' strategies.

If the following issues are not shared, raise them yourself:

- Round up each number.
- $1.95 is close to $2, and $3.95 is close to $4.
- $2 + $4 is $6.
- Add the dollars ($1 + $3 is $4), and then round the cents up to $1, and add another $2.

Repeat the process for the rest of the problems.

End the activity by saying:

 **How do the ballpark estimates you made in these six problems relate to estimates you make in your daily life?**

Ask for specific examples. Then proceed to *Activity 2*.

 ## Activity 2: Wish List

Refer students to *Activity 2*: *Wish List* (*Student Book*, p. 7).

Review the directions:

- Using a catalog and working in pairs, students shop for items for a community center, themselves, or their families.
- They are responsible for buying at least five different items from the catalog.
- Each pair has a spending limit of $500 (or another limit that makes sense in relation to the prices in the catalog).
- Student pairs will report an estimate of the total cost of their items and then find the actual total cost.

Distribute the catalog.

Decide spending limits and assignments (e.g., library, garden, after-school program, themselves, their children's new rooms, etc.).

Spending limits will depend on the cost of the items in each catalog. To maintain students' focus on estimation and rounding, choose a spending limit that enables them to purchase five or more different items.

Emphasize mental math—although pairs should try to stay within their budget, they do not need to count every penny but should instead make close estimates.

Once student pairs have chosen and recorded their items, they write about how they made their estimates, using what you recorded in *Activity 1* as a model for the process.

As students finish up, they share their lists and strategies with another pair of students. If many students finish up at about the same time, distribute newsprint for posting lists. Students read each other's wish lists. They place Post-it Notes on one another's work with any questions or comments they have. Finally, they figure out if their partner pair was a bit over or under the spending limit—and by how much.

Ask each student pair:

 **How did you keep track of all the prices to make sure you were close to your spending limit?**

**Once you made your choices, how did you find out whether you were over or under your spending limit? Are you satisfied with your estimate?**

Listen to students' descriptions and name strategies you recognize—rounding, grouping by 10's, grouping by 100's, etc.

## Summary Discussion

Ask students to share how they made their estimates in today's activities:

**Everyday Numbers**

Mental Math / Visual Models

3(4 + 2)

 **What estimating methods did you use?**

 **How would you teach someone how to estimate? What would you say?**

Then summarize with some general statements that you have heard students make about estimates and mental math. For example:

 **Round numbers to the nearest dollar—you do not need to work with cents.**

 **Tens are easy to work with, so it is helpful to combine numbers to make 10's or to round to a multiple of $10.**

 **It can be easy to find the answers in your head but it helps to use a pencil and paper to keep track of the subtotals.**

Refer students to *Reflections* (*Student Book,* p. 185), where they describe their favorite way of estimating a total for a number of items or explain what is difficult for them when trying to estimate a total.

## Practice

*Nearest Dollar*, p. 8
Students practice rounding to the nearest dollar.

*Nearest 10*, p. 9
Students practice rounding to the nearest $10.

*Closest Answer*, p. 10
For practice estimating answers to addition and subtraction problems.

*It's about . . .*, p. 11
For estimating totals by rounding and using mental math strategies.

 ## Mental Math Practice

*How Much Money Is in the Jar?* p. 12
For practice finding friendly combinations that make $1.

*Bigger Jars of Money*, p. 13
Further practice finding friendly combinations that make $10.

**Extension**

*Big Bucks Estimates*, p. 14
For work on estimating with larger numbers.

 **Test Practice**

*Test Practice*, p. 15

 **Looking Closely**

Observe whether students are able to

### Use mental math strategies to estimate totals

Can students round money amounts to the nearest dollar? Students struggling with this would benefit from working on *Practice: Nearest Dollar* (*Student Book,* p. 8) and *Practice: Nearest 10* (*Student Book,* p. 9).

Ask students to write down all number combinations that equal 10 if they are not familiar with them. As they do this, encourage them to organize their number pairs so they can keep track of which they have already done and which are missing. *Mental Math Practices: How Money Much Is in the Jar?* (*Student Book,* p. 12) and *Bigger Jars of Money* (*Student Book,* p. 13) provide practice.

What strategies do students use for estimating? Help students find an approach that makes sense given the numbers they are working with. For instance, if prices end with $0.99, they should round up to the nearest dollar. If they are working with larger amounts, they might round to the nearest $10.

When choosing items from a catalog, are students able to get started and keep track of their selections? Help them organize with one of these first steps:

- Start with one item. If needed, round its price to the nearest dollar or $10. Then subtract the cost of the item from the spending limit. How much is left to spend?

- Start with two items. Round their prices and find out about how much they cost together. Are you past the spending limit yet? If so, exchange at least one item for a cheaper one. If not, choose another item.

| WHAT TO LOOK FOR IN *LESSON 1* | WHO STANDS OUT? (LIST STUDENTS' INITIALS) | | | NOTES FOR NEXT STEPS |
|---|---|---|---|---|
| | STRONG | ADEQUATE | NEEDS WORK | |
| **Number Development**<br>• Knows number combinations for 1 and 10<br>• Combines more than two amounts and gives a ballpark estimate of the total | | | | |
| **Expressive Capacity**<br>• Articulates mental math strategies for estimating<br>• Explains rounding for ballpark estimates | | | | |
| **Notation Use**<br>• Uses appropriate addition (+) and equality (=) symbols to represent a sum and total | | | | |
| **Use of Tools**<br>• Uses rounding correctly | | | | |

## Rationale

Numeracy skills in day-to-day life often do not require exact answers. Those who can estimate and know when an answer is "close enough," or "in the ballpark," will feel more at ease in the grocery store, on job sites, taking tests, and in other such situations. Making ballpark estimates requires an understanding of rounding. For example, if something costs $1.29, do you round to $2 or to $1? By asking students to make estimates in their heads, you enable them to think through the numbers and develop a practical real-life skill that numerate adults need.

## Math Background

Estimation skills are among the most important skills in arithmetic. Knowing when an answer is in the ballpark involves having a good idea of what the numbers are individually, combined, separated, or grouped. So, for example, seeing 29 as 1 less than 30 or 4 more than 25 is important for different reasons and different problems (e.g., $29 + 17 \approx 30 + 20$; $29 + 74 \approx 25 + 75$). By practicing estimation, students will gain flexibility in their thinking and problem solving, both critical to attaining fluency with computation.

## Context

Money is often the everyday context in which people estimate. This lesson has several scenarios that enable students to think through and arrive at ballpark estimates in familiar situations involving money.

## Facilitation

### Making the Lesson Easier

To solidify the idea of ballpark estimates, pose problems such as these:

> The real cost is $19.74. Jamal estimates the cost to be $20. Is he in the ballpark? Karen estimates it will be about $15. Is she in the ballpark?

> The real cost is $1,100. Jamal estimates the cost to be $1,500. Is he in the ballpark? Karen estimates the total to be $1,000. Is she in the ballpark?

Explain that ballpark estimates are context dependent. How high the actual cost is and how tight money is are key factors.

For *Activity 2*, set a low spending limit and select catalogs with prices that are easy to round. Where appropriate, suggest students select no more than three or four items for their wish lists.

*Mental Math Practices: How Much Money Is in the Jar?* (*Student Book*, p. 12) and *Bigger Jars of Money* (*Student Book*, p. 13) will help students with combinations, and *Nearest Dollar* (*Student Book*, p. 8) will give them practice rounding.

## Making the Lesson Harder

Set a high spending limit for each area and ask students to mentally calculate the exact amount of their planned purchases. Tell them to explain in writing how they know they are within the limit.

Introduce estimation with units of measure other than dollars and cents, such as lengths in inches and feet or weights in pounds and ounces.

# LESSON 1 IN ACTION

*In this class, the teacher found a way to help her students think about why mental math may be useful.*

Students continuously stated, "Why would I do this in my head? It's much easier if I write it down"; "This seems more complicated to me than just writing it down"; or, "I don't do it this way." Only two out of seven students said they used estimation when they shopped. Someone said, "I just throw the stuff in, and if I don't have enough money, then I don't." Another student said, "I just get what I need, and if I don't have enough money—oh well. 'I'm poor', I tell them, 'so just put these items back.'"

At the end of class, I shared a problem I had done in my head recently while driving: The Festival bought 75 bales of hay for $1.50 each. Five were destroyed during the event, leaving 70 bales. We planned on selling those to someone for 75¢ each. How much money would we get?

Students asked me why I didn't use a pencil and paper to figure out the answer. I said, "I really couldn't do that while I was driving."

"Well, why didn't you just wait?" one student wondered.

I replied, "Sometimes you get to thinking about a problem, and you want to solve it right then and there. That's what's so great about mental math: You can!"

*Tricia Donovan*
*Pioneer Valley Adult Education Center, Northampton, MA*

# Mental Math in the Checkout Line

> *Do you have enough money to cover the cost of your purchases?*

## Synopsis

Students first estimate grocery prices by rounding amounts and then adjust the estimated totals using mental math to find exact totals.

1. The class shares strategies for determining totals in a few scenarios you pose. You model a way to record the steps in reasoning.

2. Student pairs work on four problems and share strategies.

3. The class focuses on using notation to describe strategies.

4. Volunteers share what they learned today, and the whole class works on one last problem.

## Objectives

- Mentally compute by rounding and then adjusting
- Use mathematical notation to describe mental math processes

## Materials/Prep

- Markers
- Newsprint
- Transparencies

# Opening Discussion

Write the following items in no particular order on the board:

4 cans of tomato paste @ $0.49 each

1 box of spaghetti for $1.59

1 jar of sauce for $3.74

1 loaf of bread for $2.29

Set the scenario:

 **Suppose you were in a grocery store and had $10 to pay for seven items. Would you have enough money? Answer the question using mental math instead of a calculator or pencil and paper.**

Ask:

 **How did you come up with an estimate?**

**How did you come up with an exact answer?**

If no one has an exact answer, present strategies for rounding and adjusting. (See *Lesson Commentary*, p. 27, for ways students might either estimate or mentally calculate an exact answer.)

Ask who uses mental math and how they do it.

 **Who does this sort of mental math at the store? Why?**

**On what other occasions is mental math useful?**

For each example students give, inquire:

**How close does your estimate need to be?**

Ask for specifics. For instance, if you have only $10 to spend at the grocery store, you need to make sure your purchases do not exceed that amount, so you might round all the items up to avoid going over your limit. On the other hand, if you want just a ballpark figure for the cost of gas for a trip, you might only need to know whether it would be *about* $10, $50, or $100.

---

## Heads Up!

Students might insist that using paper and pencil and the traditional algorithm is easier. Remind them that mental math can be useful in real life as well as test situations and that with practice they will find it more efficient than using pencil and paper. Encourage them to look for opportunities to use mental math in the next week.

---

Discuss with the class when and why it would be useful to be able to figure out the cost of items using mental math. If the following ideas do not arise, raise them yourself:

- Knowing whether you are being charged correctly
- Figuring out whether you have enough money to buy something additional
- Knowing whether you are being given the correct amount of change
- Knowing whether your department at work can afford a purchase

Tell the class that today they will work on honing their mental math skills so they will be able to figure out exact totals in their heads.

 **This will involve rounding and adjusting. You will round to figure out about how much something costs and then adjust to figure out the precise total.**

Post the words "rounding" and "adjusting" with definitions and examples.

##  Activity 1: Math in Line

Allow time for students to practice rounding and adjusting amounts to find precise answers.

Refer students to *Student Book,* p. 18, and read the story in the first problem together:

 **On the way home from work yesterday, I stopped at the store and bought two items. One cost $1.89 and the other cost $3.15. While I was waiting at the checkout line, I reached into my wallet and realized I only had a five-dollar bill. Did I have enough money for my purchases? How do you know?**

**Do the math in your heads—no pencils and paper!**

One possible response is: "$1.89 is a bit under $2, and $3.15 is a bit more than $3, so I might have enough, but I'm not sure and I need to check."

On a transparency or newsprint, record students' approaches, using a combination of words and numbers and following students' language:

- $1.89 is 11¢ less than $2 ($2 is rounded amount).
- $3.15 is 15¢ more than $3 ($3 is rounded amount).
- $2 + $3 = $5 (estimated total).
- That's 11¢ less than $2.00 and 15¢ more than $3.00, so that's 15¢ − 11¢ = 4¢ more than $5.00 (now adjusting).
- You did not have enough money! You are 4¢ short.

Summarize by recording:

$1.89 + $3.15 = ($2 + $3) + (15¢ − 11¢) = $5 + 4¢ = $5.04

Then ask:

**If the cost of one of the items remained the same, what could the cost of the other item be so that $5 would be enough money to pay for both?**

Expect many possible responses. For example, $1.89 and $1.00, $1.89 and $3.11, $3.15 and $1.50, or $3.15 and $1.85. Ask a few students to explain their reasoning.

Next, mention a price just over a whole dollar amount; such prices often include tax (base prices often being just under a whole dollar amount). Ask :

 **Suppose you are buying two rolls of tape that cost $2.05 each, including tax, and you give the cashier a $5 bill. How much change would you get back?**

Share solutions for finding the change due. Prompt for a variety of responses, including counting up and subtracting from a dollar:

 **Did anyone count up? How?**

**Did anyone use the fact that $5 – $4 is $1? What did you do?**

Pair students. Refer them to Problems 2–5, *Activity 1: Math in Line* (*Student Book*, p. 18). Partners take turns explaining their strategies and answers, as you did on the posted newsprint.

Tell students:

**Work with a partner. Solve the problems and compare your strategies.**

Remind students that they can record intermediate steps.

When everyone has completed the activity, call the group together to share various solution strategies. Prompt for those that involve rounding, adjusting, and breaking apart dollars and cents. If someone mentions multiplying (likely with Problem 4), connect it with addition strategies.

## Heads Up!

Keep the focus on students' strategies.

As a final step, you might have a volunteer "cashier" use the calculator to confirm the other solution methods, but only if students are able to stay focused on the mental math.

Process problems with questions such as these:

 **To find the exact cost, did anyone round up? How did you adjust the price?**

**Did anyone figure out the dollars and cents separately? How? When?**

**To find how much change was owed, did anyone count up from the total cost? What did you do?**

**How could you find the change by counting down from the total cash available? What would you do?**

**Did anyone find the answer a different way?**

## Activity 2: Rounding and Adjusting

To prepare for the activity, check students' rounding skills. Write on the board:

$1.95          $0.39          $18.99          $5.10          $6.75

Ask volunteers, one at a time:

**How would you round each of these amounts?**

Record answers and look for consensus on the rounded figures.

Ask:

**By how much did you change each amount to round it?**

Probable answers respective to the amounts listed above are by 5¢, 1¢, 1¢, 10¢, and 25¢.

Pose one more question before starting the activity:

**So, if you bought two (or three or four) items at $1.95, about how much would the total cost be?**

**By how much would your estimate differ from the real cost?**

Students should see that if the estimate differs from the actual cost by 5¢ for one item, then it will differ by 10¢ for two items, 15¢ for three items, and so on.

Pair up students. Review directions for *Activity 2: Rounding and Adjusting* (*Student Book*, p. 21). To model the activity, do the first problem together as a class.

Allow about 15 minutes for students to work on these problems. Then ask:

**How did you round the amounts?**

**How did you figure out how much to adjust by to find the exact amounts?**

Strategies that involve separating dollars and cents to see the difference between the actual and the rounded amount and adding or multiplying that difference for the number of items should be shared.

## Summary Discussion

Ask students to share ideas on what they learned or practiced today that will be helpful in everyday life.

Then pose a final everyday shopping problem (involving nontaxable items) designed to engage everyone in reflecting on the strategies they learned in the lesson:

**Everyday Numbers**

**Mental Math**

**Visual Models**

**3(4 + 2)**

**You are on the way to a friend's house for dinner, and you want to buy some flowers. You have $10 to spend. You see some beautiful sunflowers for $2.97 each. How many could you buy and still have enough left over for a drink that costs 89¢?**

As students share their strategies for finding the solution, make sure these ideas are raised:

- You can round $2.97 to $3 to help you find the answer.
- The total amount you can spend on flowers will be about $9, because you need about $1 for the drink.
- You will be able to buy three flowers because they will cost a little under $9, leaving enough money for the drink.

Invite students to take a few moments to capture their thoughts about today's lesson in *Reflections* (*Student Book,* p. 185).

 ## Practice

*Using Math Notation,* p. 22
Provides practice using parentheses and other appropriate mathematical notation.

*Adjustments,* p. 23
For practice rounding and adjusting using money.

*Exactly,* p. 24
For practice estimating, finding the exact answer, and determining the exact change due.

*Closer to $50 or $60?* p. 25
For practice estimating using rounding and adjusting.

 ## Mental Math Practice

*Fast Actions with 10 or 100,* p. 26
For practice adding or subtracting 10 or 100 mentally.

*Fast Actions with 9 or 90,* p. 27
For practice adding or subtracting 9 or 90 mentally.

 ## Extension

*Weekly Totals,* p. 28
For practice rounding and adjusting in different contexts: hours and minutes, and miles.

 ## Test Practice

*Test Practice,* p. 30

# Looking Closely

Observe whether students are able to

## Mentally compute by rounding and then adjusting

Can students keep track of the difference between rounded and actual amounts? Students might jot down intermediate steps to help them keep track. If the actual price is $1.95 and they round to $2, they can note that they need to account for the 5¢ difference.

Do students know when to adjust by adding and when to adjust by subtracting? Work through this concept with them by referring to everyday shopping situations: If your total purchase is $3.97, how much less than $4 is it? How can you figure out your change?

Do students rely on number sense and knowledge of basic facts? Help students relate problems to everyday shopping situations they face, adjusting numbers to simplify if needed. Try to engage students in using their own number sense to solve computation problems; even if they choose to use traditional paper-and-pencil strategies, they should have some exposure to other approaches. Over time, as they build number sense, they may come to value and rely more upon mental strategies. *Mental Math Practices* are designed to give practice with building number sense.

## Use mathematical notation to describe mental math processes

In addition to spoken explanations, can students describe their solution process using appropriate notation? As they explain their strategies, model these using notation, as shown in the examples in the *Opening Discussion* and in *Activity 1*.

Be explicit about an actual amount being more or less than an estimated amount to help students see how to make adjustments. For example, in *Activity 2*, to figure out the cost of five items at $6.98 each, $6.98 is rounded to $7, and then a 2¢ adjustment must be made for each item:

$7 x 5 = $35

2¢ x 5 = 10¢ (and this is 10¢ too much)

So,

$35 − 10¢ = $34.90

More formally, this might be recorded as follows:

$5(\$6.98) = 5(\$7) - 5(\$0.02) = \$35.00 - \$0.10 = \$34.90$

| WHAT TO LOOK FOR IN *LESSON 2* | WHO STANDS OUT? (LIST STUDENTS' INITIALS) | | | NOTES FOR NEXT STEPS |
| --- | --- | --- | --- | --- |
| | STRONG | ADEQUATE | NEEDS WORK | |
| **Number Development**<br>• Rounds to the nearest dollar<br>• Adjusts up or down<br>• Computes by rounding and then adjusting | | | | |
| **Expressive Capacity**<br>• Explains mental math strategies for adjusting<br>• Distinguishes between adjusting for more than or less than the rounded estimates | | | | |
| **Notation Use**<br>• Uses appropriate math notation to describe mental processes | | | | |
| **Use of Tools**<br>• Uses rounding efficiently | | | | |

## Rationale

When making estimates of sums, the ability to round and adjust numbers is critical. Often you only need an estimate, for example, to make sure that the amount of money you have is enough to cover the items you want to purchase. However, at times it is necessary to find an exact amount. Students have opportunities to do both of these in this lesson.

## Math Background

The difference between an estimate and an exact amount is such that an adjustment is necessary. If $10.11 is rounded to $10, and $19.99 is rounded to $20, $30 would be a good estimate of their sum. To figure out the exact amount, however, an adjustment is needed: 11¢ short (rounding $10.11 to $10) and 1¢ over (rounding $19.99 to $20), so 10¢ short, total. The exact amount, then, is $30.10. To use this process implies that we know that $19.99 + 1¢ = $20 *and* that $20 − 1¢ = $19.99, and $20 − $19.99 = 1¢.

More generally, one of the big ideas in mathematics is that if $a + b = c$, then $c − b = a$ or $c − a = b$.

One way to keep track of the adjustments is to notate as follows:

| Rounded | Adjusted by |
|---------|-------------|
| $20... | −1¢ |
| $10... | +11¢ |
| $30... | −1¢ + 11¢ = 10¢ |

## Context Background

Most people are familiar with various prices that end in 90-something cents. When this topic arises in the lesson, it may be worth digressing to talk about why items are priced this way—sometimes to keep a price under a whole dollar amount, for example, so it seems less expensive.

## Facilitation

Bear in mind that this lesson works on listening skills as well as problem-solving skills. In order to record problem solvers' steps, it is necessary to listen carefully and ask clarifying questions. Model using notation where needed.

If necessary, ask students whether they know how to write "a dollar and two cents." If some students confuse $1.02 and $1.20, give them a couple of other dollars-and-cents amounts to write, such as $5.01 and $5.10, $7.05 and $7.50, and $0.03 and $0.30.

To support the development of faster mental math, assign *Mental Math Practices: Fast Actions with 10 or 100* (*Student Book,* p. 26) and *Fast Actions with 9 or 90* (*Student Book,* p. 27).

## Making the Lesson Easier

Ask students to find the total of only two items.

Use labeled diagrams, real objects, or coins to help those students who struggle to understand what is meant by rounding and adjusting.

## Making the Lesson Harder

Solve problems involving amounts *not* close to a whole dollar, such as $3.79 and $15.44. Ask students to use appropriate mathematical notation to describe their solution processes.

Ask students to work on *Extension: Weekly Totals* (*Student Book,* p. XXX), where the units involve hours and minutes, and miles in decimals.

Suggest that students pose their own problems. Their partners could solve these and then pairs could verify the answer together.

*One teacher found a way to bring students' math reasoning outside of the classroom into the class.*

I asked a group of my GED math students to tell me how much it would cost if I bought four shirts for $7.98 each. They were told they could figure it out any way they wanted, except they could not use paper and pencil. I watched as they used their fingers in the air or "wrote" on the desk. Most were able to multiply and get the right answer. When I asked *how* they got their answers, all agreed that they needed to multiply $7.98 by four.

I then asked whether when they were in a store and had to figure out the same problem, they would have done it the same way. All agreed they probably would *not* solve it the same way in "real life." Some said they would have multiplied four by seven and four by one, added the products, and then subtracted eight cents from that total. Others said they would have rounded $7.98 to $8.00, multiplied that number by four, and then subtracted $0.08 from the product. I then asked why no one admitted to solving the problem that way in class. The response was that this was math class so they needed to "do it out."

*Marilyn Moses*
*Brockton Adult Learning Center, Brockton, MA*

# Traveling with Numbers

> *Have you ever driven across the United States?*

## Synopsis

Students work together to locate numbers on a **number line** and begin to use the number line as a thinking tool.

1. The class estimates the number of pages in a large book. Students place their estimates on a number line and compare their estimates to the actual number of pages.

2. Student pairs track an imaginary trip across the United States along Interstate 90 (I-90) using a number line.

3. Pairs round the distances to the nearest 10 or 100, add them, and use a calculator or mental math to check the totals.

4. The class summarizes by stating how they know one number is bigger than another and listing what they consider when comparing numbers.

## Objectives

- Locate, order, and operate with numbers on a number line
- Round numbers to the nearest 10 and 100

## Materials/Prep

- A book with more than 1,000 pages (but less than 3,000), such as a large city's Yellow Pages, a dictionary, or a bible
- Colored markers
- Meter stick
- Post-it Notes
- Large U.S. wall map (optional)

Make a three-meter-long number line marked from 0 to 3,000 in increments of 100 and labeled at the 0, 1,000, 2,000, and 3,000 marks.  Cash register tape works well for this. Use the meter stick markings as a guide. Each meter will stand for 1,000, each decimeter for 100.

## Opening Discussion

Display a large book with more than 1,000 pages for all to see.

Ask:

 **How good are you at estimating large amounts? Take a look at this book (don't open it), and guess how many pages it has. I'll give you one hint: It's a number somewhere between 0 and 3,000.**

Ask each student to write a best estimate on a Post-it Note. You want to have 10–20 numbers to use. If the class is small, ask each person to write down two or three guesses.

When everyone has made one or more estimates, draw attention to the 0–3,000 number line, posted for all to see.

Ask:

 **What do you notice about this number line?**

Then ask more specific questions:

**If this mark stands for 0 and this one for 1,000, what is the value of each of these smaller parts?** (100)

**How many 100's make up 1,000? 2,000?**

Ask for volunteers to carefully place their Post-it Notes on the number line. You might organize the postings by asking:

**Who guessed 500 or less?** (Establish where the 500 mark is.)

**Where is a number that is more than 500, but less than 1,000 indicated on the line?** (Continue in groupings of 500.)

Encourage students to consult with and help each other. Then ask:

 **What is the highest estimate? The lowest?**

 **Whose estimates are almost the same?**

Post the actual number of pages in the book on the number line, distinguishing this number from the estimates. Ask:

 **Which estimate was the closest to the actual number of pages? How far off was it? How can you show that difference using the number line?**

 **How can you figure out how far off your estimate was?**

Ask for a few examples of how people figured this out, and point out that the distance between any two numbers is the **difference**.

Summarize by asking:

 **What helped you place your estimate on the number line?** (For example, "First, I look at the largest part of the number and then decide whether it is more than half of the number line.")

Keep the number line posted.

## ◉ Activity 1: How Many Miles to Boston?

Display the U.S. map on the wall, if possible.

**Have you ever driven across the United States? How far do you think that is?**

**Look at the map in your *Student Book* that shows Interstate Highway 90. If you started in the west and traveled east, in which cities would you start and end?**

**What are some states you would pass through?**

After students offer guesses, refer pairs to *Activity 1: How Many Miles to Boston?* (*Student Book,* p. 32). After they have worked on the activity, draw the class together to share responses.

First, concentrate on the questions which have to do with the map (Problems 1–3). If there is disagreement about the longest and shortest distances across states or the midpoint, allow discussion.

Second, focus on the number line (Problem 4). Ask for a demonstration of the 300-mile jumps on the posted number line.

To emphasize the jumps of 300 on the number line (in Problem 1, 300 miles each day), ask:

**How far have you traveled by day 2? By day 4?**

## Activity 2: Planning Where to Stay

Refer students to *Activity 2: Planning Where to Stay* (*Student Book*, p. 34).

To decide on places to stay, students should be mentally counting up by 300. They might count by 3's to get the first digit of each new number (300, 600, 900, 1,200, and so on).

There are various plans that are reasonable because none of the cities or towns are exactly 300 miles apart.

Ask students to find a partner to share plans. How were their plans the same? How were they different?

## Activity 3: Rounding Distances

Refer students to *Activity 3: Rounding Distances* (*Student Book*, p. 34).

Note that the distances across each state (in miles) are listed in the chart. Students must round those distances to friendlier numbers.

First, they will round to the nearest 10. Do the first few problems together, always asking:

 **Between which two 10's is the number?**

 **To which 10 is it closer?**

Ask students to use the number line as a tool to demonstrate or test proximity.

Do the same for rounding to 100's, asking:

 **Between which two 100's is the number?**

 **To which 100 is it closer?**

Finally, compare the sums of the different roundings.

## Summary Discussion

Ask students:

**How did you know that one number was bigger than another?**

**What do you look at when you are comparing numbers?**

If the following ideas do not arise, prompt for them:

- More digits means a bigger number (unless there is a decimal point in the number, as with money).
- To compare numbers, look at the number of places and the digits.
- Compare digits starting with the number with the largest value—for example, 100's first, then 10's, then 1's.

Focus on the number line. Ask:

 **What do you notice about the numbers going to the right? To the left?**

 **What do you notice about the spaces between the numbers?**

 **Where else do you see number lines in everyday life?**

End by asking students to write in the *Reflections* section (*Student Book*, p. 185).

##  Practice

*High and Not So High Peaks*, p. 39
For practice ordering large numbers.

*Checks—Say It in Words*, p. 41
For practice going from words to numbers.

*More Check Writing*, p. 43
For practice going from numbers to words.

*Filing*, p. 45
For practice ordering numbers.

*More Filing*, p. 46
For more practice ordering numbers.

##  Mental Math Practice

*Doubles*, p. 47
For practice seeing patterns multiplying by two.

*Triples*, p. 48
For practice seeing patterns multiplying by three.

##  Test Practice

*Test Practice*, p. 49

##  Looking Closely

Observe whether students are able to

### Locate, order, and operate with numbers on a number line

How well are students able to use the number line as a thinking tool? Are they able to determine the value of unlabeled markings? To deepen their facility with number lines, ask students to create number lines of their own.

Do students accurately locate and order their estimates on the number line, using cues from the markings? If not, labeling the markings with their number values could be helpful.

For students having trouble ordering numbers, assign the three practices which present other contexts: *High and Not So High Peaks* (*Student Book*, p. 39); *Filing* (*Student Book*, p. 45); and *More Filing* (*Student Book*, p. 46).

Do students connect mathematical operations to the work on the number line? For example, when asked how far off from the actual number their estimates were, do they connect the distance between any two numbers to the difference, the result of subtraction? Or do they see how traveling up by 300 in consecutive jumps is analogous to both repeated addition and multiplication? Do they see the connection to division? In other words, do students understand that finding the number of 300-mile jumps across the country (3,112 miles) is the same as dividing 3,112 by 300?

## Round numbers to the nearest 10 and 100

The activities in this lesson call upon a sense of estimation. At this point, how solid are students' rounding skills?

Emphasize rounding as an activity on the number line, rather than a rote procedure (e.g., if the number ends in five or more…). When rounding to 10 ask, "Between which two 10's is the number? To which is it closer?" Do the same when rounding to the nearest 100.

| WHAT TO LOOK FOR IN *LESSON 3* | WHO STANDS OUT? (LIST STUDENTS' INITIALS) | | | NOTES FOR NEXT STEPS |
|---|---|---|---|---|
| | STRONG | ADEQUATE | NEEDS WORK | |
| **Number Development**<br>• Connects numbers to corresponding points on a number line<br>• Connects distance between two points as the difference between any two numbers<br>• Rounds numbers appropriately<br>• Counts by 3 (300) | | | | |
| **Expressive Capacity**<br>• Explains how to round numbers to the nearest 10 and to the nearest 100<br>• Explains reasons for number placement on a number line | | | | |
| **Notation Use**<br>• Uses a number line to locate, order, and compute | | | | |
| **Use of Tools**<br>• Identifies state abbreviations<br>• Uses knowledge of U.S. geography | | | | |

## Rationale

Both elements of the subtitle of the unit, *Mental Math and Visual Models*, become the foci of this lesson. The visual model of the number line can support the development of mental math ability by providing a different way to see the numbers and their relationships to one another.

## Math Background

The number line is a visual model that can be used as a thinking tool. Connecting numbers to points is a powerful idea and grounds understanding of graphs and analog instruments (e.g., thermometers, scales on maps, and rulers). A number line allows one to see the relative values of numbers and also illuminates operations on numbers.

Rounding draws attention to the markings on a number line. For example, students are asked to consider the placement of 1,170 on a number line extending from 0–3,000, marked in increments of 100. The corresponding point should be closer to 1,200 than to 1,100.

Adding and subtracting can be viewed as jumping up and down the number line. Differences between numbers connect to the distance between points. Multiplication is visually represented by jumps of equivalent size (repeated addition), and division can be seen as counting the number of times a particular distance can be found in another distance.

*Lesson 4* will further develop the number line as a time line, and *Lesson 5* will ask students to extend their thinking to numbers below zero.

## Context

*Lessons 1* and *2* rely on students' familiarity with dollars and cents. This lesson focuses on non-money contexts, such as the number of pages in a book, distances traveling across the United States, and filing. The main activities create a social studies context for students as they examine the states from west to east across the country.

## Facilitation

Students who already have a handle on paper-and-pencil methods may not at first see the value of using number lines. If this is the case, emphasize the many applications of the number line, such as graphs and measurement tools. Number lines are used often in algebra courses.

Comparing the number line work with paper-and-pencil procedures offers students the chance to see the math in different ways.

## Making the Lesson Easier

Work together as a class, and check students' work often if using the U.S. map is too much of a challenge.

## Making the Lesson Harder

Incorporate numbers with fractions or decimals when rounding or working with the number line. For example, ask where the number 297.6 would fall on the 0–3,000 number line and what 297.6 rounded to the nearest 100 would be.

*A teacher commented on her students' engagement with the lesson and offered her own adaptations.*

We are using the number lines. The students totally understand the concept and are thrilled to be using it. However, when it came time to solve the problems, they wanted to do it the "old way" (with paper and pencil). I encouraged them to keep on showing their thinking on the number line. Then they had a substitute teacher who tried to show them another traditional algorithm. The students held firm and told her I wouldn't let that happen.

In *Practice: High and Not So High Peaks,* I added the task of rounding off to the nearest hundred. It was interesting because the first mountain's height was 48 feet. I had those who finished early figure the average height of the mountain peaks; their own goals were to learn more about averages.

The students loved doing the practices with file drawers. They saw real-life applications—not only for filing, but also for putting other things in order, for example, nuts and bolts in a hardware store.

*Michelle Brown*
*Read, Write, Now, Springfield, MA*

# Traveling in Time

How long ago was that?

## Synopsis

Students place dates of birth and historical events on number lines. Using the number lines and mental math, they add and subtract using 10's and 1's to calculate people's ages and calculate how long ago their birthdays occurred. Students record their strategies both on the number line, a tool that makes mental math strategies visible, and by writing **equations**.

1. Working as a group and then in pairs, students figure out different time spans and explain their strategies. They use the number line as a tool for computing and for showing their problem-solving methods and record their strategies using equations.

2. Students share what they learned about using number lines in order to solve problems.

## Objectives

- Use a number line to compute and to explain mental math strategies
- Use counting up and down by 10's and 1's to solve addition and subtraction problems
- Record mental math and number-line actions using equations

# Materials/Prep

- Colored markers
- Newsprint
- Rulers

For the *Opening Discussion,* gather and bring to class assorted items that have number lines—a thermometer, rulers, yardsticks, meter sticks, pictures of gauges, etc.

For *Activity 1,* make a current timeline from machine tape or long strips of paper, marked from 1850–2020, to post in the front of the classroom.

For *Activity 2,* make one copy of *U.S. Historical Events* (*Blackline Master 6*) for each group of three students. Cut each copy into a set of six cards and place them in an envelope.

# Opening Discussion

Review what students remember about the number lines used in *Lesson 3.* Distribute items that use number lines (thermometers, barometers, tape measures, yard sticks, rulers, meter sticks, beakers, timelines, etc.) to pairs of students.

Say to students:

 **Describe the number line in your object. What does it measure?**

 **Compare the objects, highlighting what they are designed to measure, the numbers listed, and the values of the marked intervals.**

Conclude by saying:

 **Today we will use number lines to explain how we find the difference between two numbers in our heads.**

#  Activity 1: Birthday Numbers

Start with the following scenario to introduce the first problem in *Activity 1: Birthday Numbers,* p. 52:

 **A friend of mine just celebrated her 36th birthday. I was trying to figure out in my head when she was born. In what year was my friend born? How do you know?**

Invite students to share their strategies for solving the problem. Someone may be 36 years old and know the answer immediately. However, try to bring out the mental calculations students used.

# Heads Up!

The following examples are written for the year 2005. Adjust the lesson to the current year and follow the same method.

Starting with the first volunteer, write on the board the mental steps he or she used to determine the birth year for the 36-year-old. Use the number line to demonstrate the steps, explaining the student's process as you write. For instance:

> **You started at this year (2005 or the current year, 20XX). You went back 5 years (or X years) to the year 2000, a round number. Then you went back 30 years to 1970, and then you went back one more year to 1969. Adding 5 and 30 and 1, you get 36 years.**

> **Did anyone solve the problem a different way?**

Listen to examples, tracking students' reasoning on the number line. If student examples are not forthcoming, offer one of your own.

Once you record the number-line jumps and written steps for a few strategies on the timeline, begin to describe the steps, using mathematical notation. For instance, for the example above, you might write and talk through the problem as follows:

$$2005 - 5 = 2000$$
$$2000 - 30 = 1970$$
$$1970 - 1 = 1969$$
$$2005 - 5 - 30 - 1 = 1969$$

Ask students to write both the number-line jumps and an equation in their books as they complete the problems on the page.

Take time for students to share number-line strategies and equations for each problem.

Name the methods you see students using—counting back by 10's, or multiples of 10's; adding on by 1's and 10's; or finding a benchmark date, such as 2000, and working from there. Summarize briefly:

> **All these strategies help us find the difference between two dates and how far apart different birth dates are from the current year, 2005 (or 20XX).**

> **The equations show—in writing—how we add and subtract mentally. Though it might take more steps to calculate in our heads than with paper and pencil, what are some of the advantages of calculating mentally?**

# Activity 2: How Long Ago?

Distribute one envelope of cards cut from *U.S. Historical Events* (*Blackline Master 6*) to each group. Tell students:

 **History sometimes seems like a jumble of dates and events. We often wonder, "When did that war happen?" or "Did that event happen recently or long ago?"**

**You have a set of cards depicting important events in U.S. history. With books closed, please arrange the cards in the order in which you think the events happened, starting with the one farthest back in time and working up to the most recent one.**

**Then look at your book to find the date of each event. Write the dates on your cards and rearrange them, if necessary.**

After students have arranged the cards, review the directions for *Activity 2: How Long Ago?* (*Student Book,* p. 54). Ask students to answer the questions, and as you circulate, notice who is working with 10's and 1's comfortably. Always ask:

**How would you find the answer in your head without using pencil and paper?**

**What is another way you could do the problem?**

Notice how students determine missing numbers. Do they count spaces accurately? Do they see the patterns of increments? Notice how they use the number line. Do they mark off 10's and 1's accurately? Do they use multiples of 10? The more fluent the students become, the more likely they will be able to work with larger increments of numbers, preferring to go down by 50 rather than 10, for instance. Encourage this efficiency and connect it with five 10's jumps on the number line when sharing strategies with the class.

If no one chunks time into larger intervals, ask them how they could do that.

Ask students to share their methods by putting their number lines and equations on chart paper. Post these for the class to see.

Choose some examples and ask:

**How did you know what the missing numbers were here?**

**What other numbers did you put on the number line? How did you decide where to place them?**

Compare methods students used. Then focus on their solutions, asking:

**Who first counted up? Who counted back?**

**How did you know how many years ago this event happened?**

**Who counted by 10's?**

**Who used multiples of 10, such as 20, 30, 40, and so on?**

**Did you do the problem first in your head or on the number line?**

**How do you know that the event happened less than 100 years ago (or 50 years ago, 25 years ago, etc.)?**

Highlight various strategies. For example,

 **From the Civil War date, you counted up from 1860 to 1870 to 1880 to 1890 to 1900, then from 1900 to 2000, and then from 2000 to 2005; you counted 10 + 10 + 10 + 10 + 100 + 5.**

 **You knew the event happened more than 100 years ago because it happened in the 1800's, and it is now the 2000's.**

If students subtract in some other way (traditional algorithm, for example), make sure they also show what they did on the number line.

Because student pairs will only choose two or three events, you may want to assign them the rest for homework as extra practice.

## Summary Discussion

Ask students to turn to a partner and share one new idea they learned today.

End this conversation by asking students what they learned about comparing two amounts:

 **Think about all the problems you worked on today in which you found the difference between dates (and times). What did you learn that helped you solve those problems?**

If the following points are not raised, bring them up yourself:

- A number line can help you understand and solve problems.

- Counting up or down by 10's can help you solve an addition or subtraction problem more easily.

- There is more than one way to solve problems; sometimes adding on is easier and other times counting back is easier.

- Any time you have two or more quantities that are different in number or size, you can use a number line to compare them.

Suggest that students record vocabulary definitions (*Student Book*, p. 183) and respond to the reflection question (*Student Book*, pp. 186–187). An example: Suppose a friend said, "We number every customer file in our office. So far I have numbered 237 files in the main file drawer. It will hold 575. How many more customer files can I fit in that drawer?" Explain how you would answer your friend by using mental math.

##  Practice

*Use Up the Space—Plan Well*, p. 60
To practice marking even increments on number lines.

*On the Number Line*, p. 61
For more practice locating numbers on the number line and using them to solve problems.

## Mental Math Practice

*Count Up and Down by 10's,* p. 62
For skip counting practice.

*By What Did I Count?* p. 63
For more practice with skip counting.

## Extension

*Life Line,* p. 64
For practice making a number line with personal life events.

## Test Practice

*Test Practice,* p. 65

## Looking Closely

Observe whether students are better able to

### Use a number line to compute and to explain mental math strategies

Emphasize that a number line helps one think about the meaning of the problem, rather than only the question "Do I add or subtract the two numbers?"

Do students understand equal intervals? Make the connection between equal-sized spaces and the number of years each space represents. If students are unsure about how to label amounts between marked intervals, ask where the halfway mark is and what number that would be.

Are students able to set up the number line? Help them move from smallest number on the left to largest on the right; choose a starting point appropriate to the problem; recognize when they need to label each number; label the jumps (for instance, +10, + 3); and then use those labels to arrive at the solution of the problem, as well as to write their equations.

Help students get started if they seem confused. For example, for *Problem 3* in *Activity 1*, tell students to start with the year 1919. If they add 10, what number do they have? How many more numbers must they add to get to the year 1999? to 2000? to 2005?

If students use the number line but only write the starting and ending numbers and do not indicate any moves other than the jump, ask, "How do you know how many years that is?" Help them by starting the count yourself.

## Use counting up and down by 10's and 1's to solve addition and subtraction problems

Are students counting by 10's and multiples of 10? Encourage them by repeatedly asking them to do so in each problem.

Draw students' attention to the year 2000, and ask them why that year is a good reference point. Encourage them to move first to a number that ends in zero, so, for example, if they are finding how many years have passed since President Kennedy's assassination (1963), they can move seven on the number line to reach 1970 and continue to add years from that date.

As needed, simplify numbers so students can easily count up or back by 10's or multiples of 10. If the numbers are too easy, adjust them so students will be challenged, starting with dates such as 1919 or 1957.

## Record mental math and number line actions using equations

Are students writing equations that accurately reflect their mental strategies and movements on the number line? Model writing number sentences and equations for the jumps they make on the number line.

How flexible are students with notation? Can they move between an addition statement and a subtraction statement and connect the two? If more than one operation per line is too confusing, advise students to limit their equations to one step and operation at a time.

Are they able to judge the accuracy of an equation? When students write their equations, suggest they check back with the moves on the number line to confirm that what they have written reflects the moves they made.

| WHAT TO LOOK FOR IN *LESSON 4* | WHO STANDS OUT? (LIST STUDENTS' INITIALS) | | | NOTES FOR NEXT STEPS |
| --- | --- | --- | --- | --- |
| | STRONG | ADEQUATE | NEEDS WORK | |
| **Number Development**<br>• Distinguishes between counting forward (addition) and counting back (subtraction)<br>• Counts forward and back using 1's and 10's<br>• Adds the jumps on the number line to get the answer<br>• Computes with mental math | | | | |
| **Expressive Capacity**<br>• Explains reasoning using appropriate mathematical language | | | | |
| **Notation Use**<br>• Writes number sentences (equations) that reflect the jumps on the number line | | | | |
| **Use of Tools**<br>• Uses the number line to support reasoning | | | | |

## Rationale

Time and time intervals play an important role in our lives. Dates provide landmarks that we use as reference points. For example, the number of days, months, or years since we no longer had to wear braces, lived at home, went on our last vacation, or got our first cell phone. There are many ways that people count these time intervals, and some claim they cannot do this without a paper and pencil. Using mental math strategies, accompanied by a visual tool (number line) to show the strategies, people can find these intervals and explain their reasoning to others.

Timelines are used to show the sequence of historical events by displaying the dates of those events as marks on the line. Number lines are sequential; the numbers increase to the right of 0 and decrease to the left of 0. Sometimes the lines include marks for every number; other times, for example, for every 10, 25, 50, or 100 intervals. Sometimes the lines include 0; other times they do not. The better able students are to count by 10's and multiples of 10, the better they will be able to travel along the number line.

The ability to calculate differences or to compare amounts mentally empowers people to make decisions more efficiently. Some may not possess the strategy of counting by 10's or multiples of 10 to reach quick solutions to problems. This lesson encourages students to build up to or down from numbers in increments of 10 or multiples of 10 to develop and refine their number sense and, thereby, their facility with numbers. The use and construction of number lines paves the way for reading and constructing graphs. This topic is developed in EMPower's data and algebra books.

## Math Background

These problems about number comparisons call for either subtraction or addition to solve them:

- I'm 54, Rachel is 27, how much older am I?
- Sally lives on 53rd Street and I live on 120th Street; how far apart do we live?
- How long ago did the Wright Brothers fly their first plane?

The problems above represent two models for subtraction: (1) how much larger one number is than another (the age example) and (2) the distance between two numbers (the address and airplane examples). In each one, subtraction solves the problem. So does addition. Traditionally, school books teach these as $54 - 27$ or $120 - 53$. However, when people solve these mentally, they often use addition. Using the age problem as an example, people may count on:

"27 to 30 is 3, to 54 is 24, and 3 and 24 is 27."

Or they count on and adjust:

"27 to 57 is 30, but I've gone too far, so it's 3 less, or 27."

And when subtracting, people sometimes explain the problem as follows:

"54 minus 4 is 50, minus 20 is 30, minus another 3 is 27, so that's 4 and 20 and 3, or 27."

Or they may picture the traditional vertical algorithm and borrowing:

$$\begin{array}{r} {}^{4}\!\!\not{5}{}^{1}\!4 \\ -27 \\ \hline 27 \end{array}$$

Here is another way to notate this:

$$\begin{array}{r} 40 \\ -20 \\ \hline 20 \end{array} \qquad \begin{array}{r} 14 \\ -7 \\ \hline 7 \end{array} \qquad 20 + 7 = 27$$

All of these strategies get to the solution, in this case 27. The focus in this lesson is on counting forward or back and using the number line to help show the moves.

Using groups of 10's, 5's and 1's to count is one of the first efficient methods that students acquire for totaling or comparing numbers. In this lesson, you may notice that some students count only by 1's. The number line can encourage different strategies, such as counting on, adding on, and counting back.

The following is one way you might introduce those categories in class.

💬 **I drew a number line to show when Prohibition started.**

**1919**

💬 **I went from 1919 to '20, '20 to '30, and then what?**

As students answer, for instance, '30 to '40, and '40 to '50, add these to your number line, and indicate the number above each jump, like this:

💬 This way is called "count on or add up to a multiple of 10."

💬 What if you started with the larger number and counted back? I started at '05, then went to '04, '03, '02, '01, '00, then '90 then '80... then what?

As students tell you the rest (for instance, '70, '60, '50, ...'20, '19), ask them to help you label the numbers, and write

$1 + 1 + 1 + 1 + 1 + 10 + 10 + 10 + 10 + 10 + 10 + 10 + 10 + 1 = 86$ years

or

$5 + 80 + 1 = 86$ years.

💬 This way is called "subtract/count down to a multiple of 10."

Working with 10's and 1's reinforces the place value system we use for numbers. As students become more proficient, however, expect that they will count by multiples of 10—by 20's, 50's, or 100's.

## Context

Most of the historical dates in this lesson center on 20th century U.S. history. If students in the class are from other countries, ask for important dates in their own countries' histories, locate them on the timeline, and do some math with those dates.

## Facilitation

Acknowledge students' interest in, and history with, traditional algorithms, but remind them that mental math is extremely useful in daily life and will also strengthen their ability to select the correct answers on tests. Often on tests, they are asked to solve a problem more than one way; they can use their algorithm for their second way.

Some students will need to label the number lines in more detail than others. Encourage them to do that, and then move them to bigger intervals. That is, when finding the number of years between 1939 and 2005, some will mark only 1939, 1940, and 2005, and note their jumps, although others will need to mark more numbers between those dates.

### Making the Lesson Easier

Together, mark off 1's on at least part of the number line.

Practice counting by 10's , starting at a number between decade numbers—at 1933 or 1987, for example.

Refer students to *Mental Math Practices: Count Up and Down by 10's* (*Student Book*, p. 62) and *What Did I Count By?* (*Student Book*, p. 63), where they practice counting back and subtracting.

Consider working only from events with easy dates such as 1920, women getting the vote; 1935, The Great Depression; or 1945, the end of World War II.

Find historical events that are closer to the current date or, as a jumping-off point for comparing numbers on a number line, have students work from their birth dates (in the 1900's), rather than the current date.

Ask:

 **How many years ago were you born?**

## Making the Lesson Harder

Choose dates farther back in time, thus using 100's as well as 10's and 1's: Simon Bolivar, South America's "George Washington," declares Venezuela's independence from Spain (1810); the United States Declaration of Independence (1776); Discovery of Photosynthesis (1779); the Discovery of Bacteria (1683); Queen Elizabeth I ascends the throne in England, and Shakespeare is actively writing (1558); Christopher Columbus's arrival in the Western Hemisphere (1492); Joan of Arc leads the French army to victory over the invading English (1429); and the Norman Conquest of Britain (1066).

# LESSON 4 IN ACTION

*This teacher opened the session by connecting the context to students' lives. Here are the observer's notes from that session.*

The teacher opened by saying, "I know we have some people from Haiti here, so I want to congratulate them on the 200th anniversary of their country's independence. For the rest of you who aren't from Haiti, when was that?"

Silence.

The teacher wrote "2004"on the board and asked again, "If Haiti won it's independence 200 years ago, when was that?"

Mabel, an ESOL student, replied, "Nineteen thousand."

The teacher wrote "19,000" on the board and asked, "Is this what you mean?"

Immediately, Mabel answered, "No, nineteen hundred."

"Hmm. . . Is that exact or an estimate?" asked the teacher, as she wrote "1900" to the right of the two numbers, 2004 and 2000.

"It looks like a pretty good estimate to me," declared Carol, who sat one seat over from Mabel.

"Yes, but what would it be exactly?"

Silence.

The observer asked, "What date would be 100 years ago from the year 2000?"

The students responded with a chorus of "1900."

The teacher drew a line connecting 1900 and 2000, saying, "So, one hundred years ago from the year 2000 would be 1900."

"So, what would be 100 years ago from 2004?" the observer asked.

Finally, Mable announced, "1904."

The teacher wrote "1904" on the board. "That would be exactly 100 years ago from this year. What would be 200 years ago?"

Several students called out, "1804," which the teacher wrote on the board.

The teacher then provided the historical date 1776 and asked how many years ago that had been. When no one replied, she explained, " You need to know this date for citizenship tests and for the GED. The United States won its independence in 1776. How many years ago was that?"

*continued on next page*

*continued from previous page*

Students forwarded several guesses, and the teacher posted these as if they were answers for a multiple-choice question. She wrote on the board:

The United States won its independence in 1776.
How many years ago was that?
1. 300
2. 229
3. 228
4. 3,580
5. Not enough information

The teacher asked for a show of hands as to which answer students thought was right. Everyone chose 228.

"How can we check that to see if it's right?" she inquired.

"Add them," came the reply from several students.

The teacher set up the problem, and a student performed the calculations. They were all correct.

*Esther Leonelli, observed by Tricia Donovan*
*Notre Dame Education Center, Boston, MA*

FACILITATING LESSON 5

# Extending the Line

*What do you wear when the temperature drops below zero?*

## Synopsis

This lesson introduces negative numbers (integers) on an extended number line, which continues to be employed as a problem-solving tool.

1. The class shares knowledge about negative numbers and reviews use of the number line. You show how the number line extends below zero.

2. Pairs construct an extended number line to track checking account actions.

3. Pairs find differences between world-record high and low temperatures using a picture of a thermometer's number line.

4. The class summarizes, sharing what they know about finding the difference between any two numbers.

## Objectives

- Locate **negative** and **positive numbers** on the number line
- Determine the difference between two numbers

## Materials/Prep

- Calculators
- 11″ × 14″ paper
- Colored pencils (including red and black) or markers
- Rulers
- Nondigital outdoor thermometer(s)

Prepare some large blank number lines and post them at the front of the class.

Post a world map with the various cities mentioned in *Activity 2* (*Student Book*, p. 69) located and labeled.

Construct a number line with zero in the center, and mark some positive and negative numbers on the line.

## Opening Discussion

To prepare students for today's lesson, review number line conventions and how numbers on the line are compared, referring back to *Lessons 3* and *4*:

- Numbers increase to the right.
- Numbers decrease to the left.
- Intervals are evenly spaced.
- Make jumps from one number to the next, count the spaces covered, and label the jumps.
- Add up the numbers on the jumps to find the total difference between two numbers.

Survey the class about previous experience with negative numbers.

If no one raises the following points, raise them yourself:

- Negative numbers are located to the left of the zero on a number line and below zero on a thermometer.
- When they are recorded, they are preceded by a minus sign (−).
- They represent amounts less than zero.

## Heads Up!

*See Lesson Commentary: Math Background, p. 62, for ways to address misconceptions.*

Post a class definition of negative numbers, and solicit some examples of negative numbers occurring—a business operating in the red, budget deficits, overdrawn bank accounts, feet below sea level, etc. Add to the class vocabulary list a definition for positive numbers.

# Activity 1: In the Red

Pair students. Distribute an 11″ × 14″ sheet of paper, a red pencil, a black pencil, and a ruler to each pair. Refer them to *Activity 1: In the Red* (*Student Book,* p. 68). Make sure everyone understands what a bounced check is and what the terms "in the red" and "in the black" mean.

As students show George's balance for each date on the number line, ask questions that emphasize the negative amounts. For example:

 **How did you know it was –$75? What does a negative amount of money mean?**

**Is George's balance on January 27 enough for him to pay his $650 car loan?**

Reach agreement on George's final balance.

If it has not come up in the discussion, mention that zero is neither a positive nor a negative number. If George has a balance of $0, he is neither in the red nor in the black.

# Activity 2: Record Highs, Record Lows

Begin a discussion about number lines and temperature by saying something such as this:

**In today's newspaper, the weather report says, "high 60°F to 65°F, low 52°F to 57°F." Those temperatures represent a range of temperatures that we can expect.**

**By the end of the day, though, there will be a high and a low.**

Discuss the term **range**. You might use as an example the range of ages in the class. Note:

- The range in everyday language describes highest to lowest or lowest to highest (such as, 18-years-old to 60-years-old).

- The range can be described by a single number that represents the difference between these two values (a range of 42 years).

Post a class definition of the term "range" as described by students in their own words.

Continue:

**Depending on where you live, temperatures may dip into negative numbers. What is the coldest temperature you have ever known?**

Draw a line on the board. Ask a volunteer to set up the number line so all suggested temperatures can be posted on it. Watch for correct placement and notation of negative numbers. If no one mentions a temperature below zero, mention one or two yourself.

Ask:

**What is the warmest temperature you have ever known?**

Ask volunteers to place their temperatures on the number line on the board and to initial them.

## Heads Up!

The activity refers to Fahrenheit temperatures. Be sure to ask whether temperatures mentioned are Fahrenheit or Celsius, and make sure students distinguish between the two. For background information on both, see *Lesson Commentary*, p. 62.

---

Refer students to *Activity 2: Record Highs, Record Lows* (*Student Book*, p. 59). After they complete Part 1 on the thermometer, ask students to find partners for Part 2.

As you circulate, observe how students mark the thermometers and number lines. Ask:

 **What is similar about marking temperatures on a thermometer and on a number line? What is different?**

Make sure the fact that negative numbers on a thermometer appear *below* zero, and negative numbers on a number line appear *above* zero is understood, and the connection is made between these numbers and the horizontal number line.

Question how students arrived at the difference between the highest and lowest recorded temperatures. Push for number-line explanations.

---

## Heads Up!

Focus students' attention on marking jumps using 10's and 1's, as they did in *Lesson 4*. Remind them to total only the numbers recorded above the jumps.

---

Because different pairs have likely chosen different temperatures to compare, ask students to share their methods. End by asking them what they noticed about finding the difference between two numbers (as in Problem 14).

## Summary Discussion

Expand students' awareness of the use of negative numbers by posing a question with a different context:

**What do you now know about finding the difference between any two numbers?**

You want students to use mental math to find an answer and then to show the class their reasoning on a number line.

Refer students to *Reflections* (*Student Book*, p. 185), where they write about what they know about negative numbers and finding the difference between any two numbers.

## Practice

*Planting Zones*, p. 72
For practice finding ranges and differences on the number line.

*What's the Range?* p. 74
For practice finding differences between numbers using a variety of visual models.

*Ordering Numbers*, p. 75
For practice ordering positive and negative numbers.

## Mental Math Practice

*Count Up and Down by 10's*, p. 76
For practice skip-counting by 10 along the extended number line (positive and negative regions).

## Extension

*Sorry, Account Overdrawn*, p. 77
To challenge reasoning about numbers and applying number-line strategies to a money situation.

*Below Sea Level*, p. 78
For a challenge finding differences between large numbers.

## Test Practice

*Test Practice*, p. 79

## Looking Closely

Observe whether students are able to

### Locate positive and negative numbers on the number line

Most students are comfortable counting up, moving to the right on a number line; however, counting down, or "backward" to the left, can pose some problems, especially when negative numbers are involved.

First make sure students can easily count forward and backward with positive numbers. Then help them see the symmetry in the number line. Draw attention to the zero as the pivotal point that separates positive numbers from negative numbers. Zero itself is neither postive nor negative. It may be helpful to mark positive numbers in black and negative numbers in red.

Examination of thermometers and elevation markers may help students focus on the "up-ness" and "down-ness" of the positive and negative numbers, but they should see the connection to the horizontal representation, where going left is similar to going down, and going right is analogous to going up.

## Determine the difference between two numbers

Although students have been working on the difference between two numbers in *Lesson 4*, in this lesson they encounter negative numbers for the first time. Locating them on a number line is intended to help them see the difference as the distance between any two numbers, including negative numbers. If they have difficulty with this at first, use smaller numbers. For example, ask them to find the difference between 8 and –6. If students think about the difference in terms of the distance model, they will be able to see 8 to the right of zero and 6 to the left, which totals 14 altogether.

When they are comfortable with small numbers and have begun working with larger numbers, remind them to think in terms of the distance between the two. Examples that use money seem to be helpful, as most people are familiar with gains and losses.

Two issues may arise for students as they seek to determine a range. They may think of the range as the listing of high and low values and not the interval between them, and they may think that a range of negative numbers is negative.

To help students see the interval, mark it off and label it "range." Then apply counting techniques within the established range. Ask questions such as, "How many spaces (numbers) does the range cover?"

Explain that whether the numbers are located above or below zero—that is, whether they are positive or negative—is irrelevant when determining the range. One needs to know how many intervals, or spaces, are between the highest and lowest numbers that mark the boundaries of the range. Students can mark the spaces off and count the total, as discussed in *Lesson 4*.

| WHAT TO LOOK FOR IN *LESSON 5* | WHO STANDS OUT? (LIST STUDENTS' INITIALS) | | | NOTES FOR NEXT STEPS |
| --- | --- | --- | --- | --- |
| | STRONG | ADEQUATE | NEEDS WORK | |
| **Number Development**<br>• Recognizes and locates negative numbers on a number line<br>• Distinguishes between negative and positive numbers<br>• Finds the difference between any two numbers on the extended number line | | | | |
| **Expressive Capacity**<br>• Explains reasoning using language<br>• Explains reasoning using equations | | | | |
| **Notation Use**<br>• Correctly writes negative numbers<br>• Writes equations that reflect the difference between any two numbers | | | | |
| **Use of Tools**<br>• Uses visual tools and models to support reasoning | | | | |

## Rationale

Negative numbers are interesting to adults returning to school. Particularly in this time of budget deficits, personal debt, and growing awareness of natural phenomena, familiarity with a number line expands students' ability to follow or participate in public discourse on these topics.

## Math Background

The focus in this lesson is on locating positive and negative integers on the number line. Finding differences between any two points and moving up and down the number line to record changes continues that focus. Thus the mathematics in the lesson anticipates, but does not cover, formal operations with integers.

The introduction of negative numbers challenges what people know about positive numbers. For example, that the number –500 is less than –50 can present a challenge, given that +500 is larger than +50. Further confounding understanding is the fact that when talking about debt, –$500 actually indicates *more* debt than –$50, and –45°F is colder than –25°F. Help students reframe the ideas—the person with a checking balance of –$500 has *less* money available than the person with –$50; when the temperature is –45°F, there is *less* heat in the air (and a thermometer measures "heat" not "cold") than when it is –25°F. These language issues can lead to deep confusion about relative sizes or amounts and need to be addressed when they arise.

Locating negative numbers on a number line and understanding the convention that as one moves farther to the left, the numbers get smaller and smaller are essential to understanding how to work with negative numbers. In addition, the distance model of subtraction between two numbers is helpful, because when finding the difference between two numbers—say, 107 and –125—locating and then seeing the space between the two numbers is what makes the answer, 232, reasonable.

## Context

Most everyone is familiar with rising and dropping temperatures. You might use this opportunity to introduce the Celsius and Fahrenheit scales, both derived from the temperatures at which water freezes and boils and both invented in the 1700's.

Note that the coldest theoretical temperature is believed to be "absolute zero," or –273.15°C, the temperature at which it is theorized that molecular action would cease.

## Facilitation

This is not a lesson about operating with negative numbers; it is designed only to demonstrate that the number line can be extended to the left and include negative numbers, or numbers less than zero.

## Making the Lesson Easier

Build number lines together as a class.

Work with familiar numbers (multiples of 10 or 5). Avoid pinpointing the exact differences at first. Concentrate on weather change scenarios, such as those where the temperature was 10°F and then dropped to −20°F. (How many degrees did it drop?)

Encourage students to do the *Mental Math Practice* (*Student Book*, p. 76).

Use real thermometers and have students demonstrate on those, counting up or down by 10's. Then work with number lines or mental strategies. Assign *Practice: Record Highs, Record Lows* (*Student Book*, p. 69) only when students are comfortable with these easier numbers.

## Making the Lesson Harder

This lesson could be a good lead-in to addition and subtraction with integers.

*Activity 1* provides a banking analogy for addition. Track George's transactions in *Activity 1* by recording the deposits (addition of positive amounts) and withdrawals (addition of negative amounts) with mathematical notation. For example,

"George had $100 in the bank. He paid the gas bill of $175," would be recorded as

$$\$100 + (-\$175) = -\$75.$$

"George deposited his $950 paycheck," would be shown as

$$(-\$75) + \$950 = \$875.$$

"George paid his rent of $725," would be notated as

$$\$875 + (-\$725) = \$150.$$

"George paid off his credit card: $450," would be recorded as

$$\$150 + (-\$450) = -\$300.$$

"George made a transfer from savings to checking: $800," would be recorded as

$$-\$300 + (+\$800) = \$500.$$

*Activity 2* provides an analogy for the model of subtraction as the difference (or distance) between two numbers.

For example, the absolute value of the difference between 121°F and − 29°F would be written as

$$121°F - (-29°F) = 150°F.$$

*The following dialogue illustrates how one class began the discussion on negative numbers and worked on* Activity 2.

---

**Teacher:** "When have you heard of negative numbers?"

**Student 1:** "Paying bills. Money not coming in, but going out."

**Student 2:** "Four numbers in a PIN code."

**Teacher:** "States have hard times right now. There are huge budget what? (Silence) Starts with a 'd.'"

**Student 1:** "Deficit."

**Student 2:** "What's that mean?"

**Student 1:** "Loss, debt."

**Teacher:** "How about temperatures?"

**Student:** "Below zero, −10°F, when it freezes."

The class looked at a sample number line from −9°F to 9°F.

**Teacher:** "Which temperature is higher or warmer? −1 or −9? Let me see whether you have it right: Is −9 more than −1?"

Students seemed to grasp that −9°F is less, that is, a lower temperature. The class did three more problems together. In one, a student at the board read, "Start at 25. Go down 30." He ended up at −10°F, then changed his mind and chose −5°F. Once he showed the jumps above the number line, everyone agreed with his answer.

Using one more example, the students created a number line with increments by 100's to show a company that made $500 but spent $600 on labor and supplies.

The class read over the information about high and low temperatures worldwide, but, as I did, initially assumed the questions would ask about the differences among highs and lows rather than among high temperatures worldwide. Several students started their number lines with zero in the middle. This meant that the extreme highs and lows were squished together at one end. Lynn had the most trouble getting started. Her classmate tried to explain her own number line, where the increments were listed by 25°F increments. Lynn wondered how to determine where to place Africa's high temperature of 136°F. She seemed puzzled by how Una had known to number up to 150°F, and she asked, "Is there another way to do it?" Una started to explain again, but I called Lynn's attention to another classmate's work. I noticed Alex began with a list of the high temperatures from highest to lowest. Then he numbered his line in increments of 10. He was able to explain what he did to Lynn. His strategy seemed more accessible, and it was easier to see where to place 136°F.

*continued on next page*

---

*continued form previous page*

Alex knew to subtract 59°F from 136°F to find the range of high temperatures. I asked him to show the difference on the number line. He counted back from 136°F ("6°F + 10°F, 20°F, 30°F, 40°F, 50°F, 60°F, 70°F. That's 76°F + 1°F, 77°F"). Would it work the same way if you started from 59°F? He tried it and it worked.

*Martha Merson, Observer*
*Community Learning Center, Cambridge, MA*

# Take Your Winnings

> *What is the largest amount you have ever won?*

## Synopsis

In this lesson, students examine and record the make-up of whole numbers. In the context of lottery winnings, they think about how a number is composed in terms of 1's, 10's, 100's, and 1,000's. Then they play a game of concentration, matching equivalent amounts.

Mental math remains the focus when calculators are introduced. Savvy students can "beat the calculator" in arriving at an answer by examining the change in place values.

1. The class relates concrete experiences with $10, $100, and $1,000 bills to math operations and notation.

2. Student pairs use the context of a lottery to consider the make-up of large amounts of money in terms of 1,000's, 100's, and 10's. They use notation with **parentheses** to record their various solutions.

3. In pairs, students play a game of concentration, matching amounts written in **expanded notation**.

4. Individuals predict calculator operations by deconstructing numbers.

5. The class summarizes what they notice when they examine the composition of a number.

## Heads Up!

*Activity 1* is situated in a lottery context. If gambling is a sensitive issue in your class, rework the problems with the total representing a shared bonus or gift.

# Objectives

- Examine and identify the composition of a number in terms of 10's, 100's, and 1,000's
- Use parentheses in expanded notation
- Mentally add or subtract multiples of 10, 100, and 1,000 and then check mental math with a calculator

# Materials/Prep

- Calculators
- Play money or slips of paper marked in denominations of $1, $10, $100 and $1,000 (Monopoly™ money works well

Make copies of *Concentration Cards* (*Blackline Masters 7* and *8*), one per student pair. Cut each into a set of 12 cards, and clip each set together or place in an envelope.

# Opening Discussion

Tell students that today they will work more with tens, hundreds, and thousands. They will need to think about the make-up of large amounts of money.

As an introduction, pose the following questions:

 **If you had $1,000 in $100 bills, how many $100 bills would you have?**

**How do you know?**

Ask a volunteer to demonstrate the solution using play money or slips of paper marked in appropriate denominations. Then ask someone to describe that solution process with numbers and math symbols.

Students might write

$100 + $100 + ⋯ + $100 = $1,000

or

10 x $100 = $1,000

or

$1,000 ÷ $100 = 10.

Make explicit the connection between the concrete task in the money demonstration and the symbolic math notation.

Then ask:

**If you had $1,000 in $10 bills, how many $10 bills would you have?**

**How do you know?**

Again ask for a demonstration of the solution both in paper money and symbolically.

Students might write

$100 \times \$10 = \$1,000$

or

$\$1,000 \div \$10 = 100$.

##  Activity 1: How Do You Take Your Winnings?

Ask a volunteer to read the story aloud at the beginning of *Activity 1: How Do You Take Your Winnings?* (*Student Book*, p. 82). When everyone is clear about the directions, encourage student pairs to talk with one another to reach agreement on the ways each woman (Andrea, Barbara, and Carla) will receive her winnings.

Observe who is doing mental calculations, who is using pencil and paper, and who is counting out money. Ask those who finish early to seek an alternative solution method. For those who are having difficulty, offer the play money as a way to work out the problem.

When everyone has finished the first problem, ask for volunteers to explain their solutions for the three different distributions of $3,843. Ask:

**Who wants to share how they solved this problem?**

**Who solved it differently?**

**How can you be sure your answer is right?**

Write all offerings on the board. If there is disagreement, ask for verification with play money.

Correct solutions are as follows:

**Andrea receives three $1,000 bills** and the rest ($843) in various denominations. There are many ways to combine the rest. They might be:

- three $1,000 bills, eight $100 bills, four $10 bills, and three $1 bills, or
- three $1,000 bills, 84 $10 bills, and three $1 bills, or
- three $1,000 bills, seven $100 bills, 14 $10 bills and three $1 bills.

**Barbara receives 38 $100 bills** and the rest ($43) in various denominations.

**Carla receives 384 $10 bills** with three $1 bills for the remainder.

Use this activity as an opportunity to introduce the convention of **parentheses** in notation. Establish the practice that from now on the class will write three $1,000 bills and eight $100 bills and four $10 bills and three $1 bills as

$3(\$1,000) + 8(\$100) + 4(\$10) + 3(\$1)$.

Have pairs continue with Problems 2 and 3, asking students now to use parentheses in the notation. In other words, "3($1,000)" will be a way to write "three $1,000 bills." Post offerings for Problems 2 and 3 on the board and reach agreement on possible ways each woman might receive her money.

Say:

 **We have looked at various ways that an amount of money can be given; now we are going to think about a different situation.**

Post these questions or share them on a transparency one at a time:

 **Suppose Dora won the lottery and asked for her winnings in $10 bills. The clerk gave her 28($10) + 5($1). What were her winnings?** ($285)

 **Suppose Emilia won the lottery. The clerk gave her 36($100) + 5($10). What were her winnings?** ($3,650)

Conclude this activity by pushing for some generalizations about the relationship between 1,000's, 100's, and 10's.

Ask:

 **What patterns have you noticed about the make-up of a number?**

Students might offers statements such as these:

- "Three thousand, four hundred can be read as thirty-four hundred."
- "One thousand is the same as 10 hundreds."
- "One thousand is the same as 100 tens."

If no one mentions that a number such as 3,000 is the same as 30 hundreds or 300 tens [$3(1,000) = 30(100) = 300(10)$], ask people to fill in the missing amounts in number sentences such as these: $3(1,000) = ?(100) = ?(10)$. Then ask students again what patterns they notice, especially with the zeroes.

##  Activity 2: Concentration

Distribute one set of *Concentration Cards* (*Blackline Masters 7* and *8*) to each pair of students.

Ask for a volunteer to read the directions for *Activity 2: Concentration* (*Student Book*, p. 83). When everyone understands the directions and the goal of winning the most money, ask pairs to play the game, reminding them to replace the cards if there is not a match. Pairs that finish quickly might play the game a few more times.

After everyone has played the game successfully at least once, bring the class together and ask some students to write equations on the board that describe their matched pairs, using parentheses in their notation.

Some possible equations are listed here:

$5(\$1,000) + 2(\$100) = 52(\$100)$

$\$5,200 = 520(\$10)$

$50(\$10) + 2(\$1) = 5(\$100) + 2(\$1)$

$\$502 = 502(\$1)$

$2(\$1,000) + 5(\$100) = 25(\$100)$

$\$2,500 = 20(\$100) + 50(\$10)$

Conclude by asking:

 **Who won the most money? How much was that?**

**How do you know?**

## Activity 3: Mystery Numbers

This activity presents a game in which students figure out the amount that has been added or subtracted to change one number into another on the calculator screen. The goal is to investigate the effects of adding and subtracting **multiples of 10, 100, and 1,000**. The activity should go quickly, but it will afford another opportunity to concentrate on deconstructing numbers. Students will need to pay attention to place value.

Make sure everyone has a calculator.

On the board, write a three- or four-digit number as the starting number. Ask students to clear their screens and enter that number in their calculators. Now secretly add 100 to the number and write the result as the end number.

Set up the board like this:

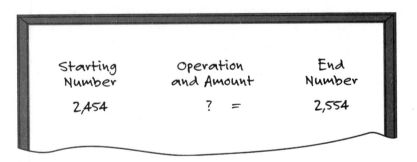

| Starting Number | Operation and Amount | End Number |
|---|---|---|
| 2,454 | ? = | 2,554 |

Ask:

 **What could you do to the starting number to arrive at the end number? Do this in your head.**

**How do you know?**

Take all suggestions and ask students to verify accuracy, using the calculator to check the operation with the number of the proposed answer and then pressing the "=" key to arrive at the result.

Do another problem, this time secretly adding or subtracting a multiple of 10, 100, or 1,000 to a starting number to get the end number. Students first arrive at the operation and amount using mental math and then verify their answers with calculators.

For example: You write "6,753" and students enter in their calculators "6,753." You secretly subtract 300 and write down "6,453"for the end number. Students again use mental math to find the answer and calculators to check its accuracy.

| Starting Number | Operation and Amount | Ending Number |
|---|---|---|
| 6,753 | ? = | 6,453 |

Next, ask students to suggest some starting numbers. Proceed with each number as you did with the previous problems, and give students the end number. For example:

$$7,541 - 40 = 7,501$$

## Heads Up!

Be prepared for issues about calculator use to arise. For example, students may note that there are no commas on the calculator and that the decimal point is not a comma. Or they may need to be reminded that after the operation and amount are entered, it is important to press the "=" key. See *Look closely*, p. 74, for more about issues that have come up in classes when introducing the calulator.

Direct individuals to complete *Activity 3: Mystery Numbers* (Student Book, p. 84).

When everyone is done, compare and verify solutions and summarize by asking:

 **What did you look at to make your decisions about the operation and amount?**

 **What makes it so easy to do these problems in your head?**

Students should notice which digit changed, the value of the digit in that place, and whether there was an increase or decrease. In each case, they should see that adding or subtracting a multiple of 10, 100, or 1,000 made the math easy to do mentally.

When you review this activity, call attention to "wrap-around" numbers, those that change in more than one column as you add or subtract. Ask students to share their strategies for solving these, and illustrate their comments with a number line. Provide a few more examples if these problems interest students (for example, 526 − 80; 739 + 70).

Conclude by asking:

 **When you found the mystery numbers, were you faster than the calculator?**

## Summary Discussion

Give students time to write in the *Reflections* section (*Student Book*, p. 185) what they want to remember from today's lesson about the make-up of whole numbers and especially about any shortcuts they used. Then ask for volunteers to share what they have written.

 ## Practice

*True or False?* p. 85
For practice interpreting equivalent amounts written in expanded notation.

*More Mystery Numbers,* p. 86
For practice mentally adding or subtracting multiples of 10, 100, or 1,000 to a given amount and then checking the answer with a calculator.

*Calculating With Money,* p. 87
For practice entering dollars and cents into the calculator. Students will need to be careful with decimal points and zeroes.

*College Registration,* p. 88
For practice thinking about and calculating with 100's in context.

 ## Mental Math Practice

*Double Trouble,* p. 89
For practice doubling or halving amounts quickly.

 ## Test Practice

*Test Practice,* p. 91

 ## Looking Closely

Observe whether students are able to

### Examine and identify the composition of a number in terms of 10's, 100's, and 1,000's

Are students developing confidence and flexibility as they consider the various ways to take the lottery winnings? Allow time for them to make confident connections between the concrete play money and the written amounts.

Are students noticing number patterns? For example, do they see that when $3(\$1{,}000) = 30(\$100) = 300(\$10)$, the total amount of zeroes remains the same? Make sure there is explicit discussion about such patterns. For more practice, assign *True or False?* (*Student Book*, p. 85).

Finally, are students able to read a number such as 6,500 as "six thousand, five hundred," as well as "sixty-five hundred," and thus see the connection between $6(1{,}000) + 500$ and $65(100)$?

### Use parentheses in expanded notation

Do students appropriate the use of parentheses as a convenient grouping convention? Do they understand $4(\$1{,}000)$ to mean "four 1,000's?" The use of parentheses in *Lesson 6* anticipates the interpretation of $4(\$1{,}000)$ as $4 \times \$1{,}000$, but it is not necesary to point out the multiplication meaning in this lesson. However, if someone brings it up, verify that this is so.

### Mentally add or subtract multiples of 10, 100, and 1,000 and then check mental math with a calculator

Are students readily able to identify the addition or subtraction of multiples of 10, 100, or 1,000? See *Lesson 6 in Action*, p. 78, for how one teacher took time to list examples of multiples before starting *Mystery Numbers.*

In the *Mystery Numbers* activity, also assess the students' comfort with calculators. If you think they might benefit from more calculator practice, assign the practices *More Mystery Numbers* (*Student Book*, p. 86) and *Calculating With Money* (*Student Book*, p. 87), where their attention is focused on the zeroes and decimal points. When dealing with dollars and cents, several dilemmas often arise:

When adding \$3 and 7¢, punching in "3 + 7" does not lead to a reasonable answer. One needs either to convert all numbers to dollars (\$3 + \$0.07 or \$3.00 + \$0.07) or to cents (300¢ + 7¢).

The calculator leaves out some (unnecessary) zeroes. For example, 3 + .50 = appears as 3.5 on the calculator. On the other hand, the calculator will often append zeroes (.70 + .10 = 0.8). The interpretation of \$0.8 as 80¢ can be puzzling.

Commas are not the same as zeroes. In fact, there are no commas on a calculator.

Be aware that if students come from other countries, decimals and commas may have been used very differently than they are in the United States. For example, in South America, a comma indicates a separation between the whole and the decimal fraction, whereas the point marks off the thousands and millions. In other words, the comma and the decimal point have opposite meanings than they do in the United States.

| WHAT TO LOOK FOR IN *LESSON 6* | WHO STANDS OUT? (LIST STUDENTS' INITIALS) | | | NOTES FOR NEXT STEPS |
|---|---|---|---|---|
| | STRONG | ADEQUATE | NEEDS WORK | |
| **Number Development**<br>• Identifies the make-up of a whole number in terms of 10's, 100's, and 1,000's<br>• Starting with any number, adds or subtracts a multiple of 10, 100, or 1,000 mentally | | | | |
| **Expressive Capacity**<br>• Explains the connection between concrete money and math symbols<br>• Explains the pattern occuring in number sentences such as $3(1,000) = 30(100) = 300(10)$ | | | | |
| **Notation Use**<br>• Uses parentheses appropriately as a grouping convention<br>• Accurately interprets and generates expanded notation | | | | |
| **Use of Tools**<br>• Uses the calculator to add and subtract whole numbers<br>• Uses the calculator in conjunction with mental math | | | | |

## Rationale

Adults' familiarity with denominations of money provides a basis for developing a deepened awareness of the composition of numbers in the base-10 system. This familiarity also is a foundation for an intuitive understanding of an expanded notation for a number, place value, and ease with mental calculations.

## Math Background

This lesson develops three important mathematical ideas.

### Noticing patterns in the composition of base-10 numbers provides a basis for more powerful mental math calculations.

The lottery activity requires students to go beyond identifying the place value of the digits in a four-digit number. Although it is important to be able to note the place value of each digit (the usual treatment of place value in basic math books), this excercise is designed to go a step further. By calculating how many $1,000, $100, and $10 bills they can derive from a certain amount of money, students not only attend to place value but at the same time develop connections between 10's, 100's, and 1,000's. Knowing that there are 10 hundreds in 1,000, 100 tens in 1,000, and 10 tens in 100 is important and provides a basis for later work, such as mentally multiplying and dividing by 10's, 100's, 1,000's, and their multiples.

### It is important to increase the repertoire of notation conventions and connect the conventions to concrete experiences.

Parentheses are introduced in this lesson as a way to group and separate amounts. Their connection to multiplication, e.g., that $2 \times 30 = 2(30)$, and their use as a way to impose order, e.g., $3(4 + 5) = 3(9)$, will be explored in the next lesson.

The lesson also treats expanded notation more broadly than merely writing a number to show the value of each place, e.g., $679 = 6(100) + 7(10) + 9(1)$. Although students should be familiar with what is traditionally understood as expanded notation, they are asked to think about alternative and equivalent expansions of the number, such as $67(10) + 9(1)$.

Knowing equivalent expressions for a quantity is important, but it is essential that students connect the expressions and demonstrate understanding along the way with concrete representations. Play money is useful here.

### The calculator is a tool that can be used in tandem with mental calculations.

This lesson focuses on the calculator as a way to check against reasonable mental calculations. Dissonance caused by answers that vary when both a calculator and mental math are used presents an opportunity to bring in concrete examples as the arbiter.

## Context

Money launches the lesson with the lottery context of the first activity, but students are also encouraged to leave context for awhile as they attend to number patterns that support mental math computation.

## Facilitation

### Making the Lesson Harder

Introduce larger numbers that involve 10,000's, 100,000's and 1,000,000's.

Introduce non-whole numbers (dollars and cents).

### Making the Lesson Easier

Slow down and keep examples concrete. It is more important to focus on the concept of the make-up of a number than alternative notation.

*In one class, the teacher took the time to solidify the multiples of 10, 100, and 1,000 as a prelude to the* Mystery Numbers *activity.*

Today we worked on *Activity 3: Mystery Numbers*. We started off with the question "What is a multiple?" and then made lists of multiples of 10, 100, and 1,000. I put all answers on the board, whether they were correct or not. If we weren't sure, we put the answer up with a question mark. Then I asked the students whether they could make any observations, which I recorded on the board, for example, "There are a lot of zeroes" and "All numbers that are multiples of 100 have at least two zeroes." We used these statements to reconsider our numbers with question marks and move them to the correct columns. I gave the students time to copy these notes from the board.

Then I put a box on the board with a number in it and asked whether it was a multiple of a certain number. For example, I'd write "30" and ask, "Is this a multiple of 100? How do you know?" I gave different students a chance to come to the board and put numbers in the box.

Finally, we started working on mystery addition and subtraction, on the board only. I encouraged students to use their calculators to figure how to get from the beginning number to the end number. First, we would decide whether to add or subtract; then we would decide how much we needed to add or subtract.

*Jonna Rao*
*SafeSpace, New York City, NY*

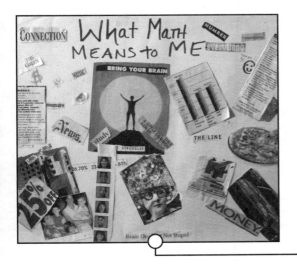

# Facilitating Midpoint Activity: What Math Means to Me

> *How are we feeling about math these days?*

## Synopsis

This session involves a different kind of assessment. So far, the focus of the unit has been on math and its uses. Here, however, the emphasis is on affective aspects of math; students have the opportunity to share how they feel about math. They create and display pictorial collages communicating what math means to them. Each student interprets and writes about a peer's collage, answering the question "What is the person who made the collage trying to communicate?"

## Objectives

- Describe and share personal feelings and perspectives about math
- Interpret another's perspective

## Materials/Prep

- Glue sticks or tape
- Magazines and newspapers. Before the class, ask students to bring in some old copies of their favorite magazines that they will not mind cutting up.
- Markers
- Newsprint or large paper, one piece per student
- Scissors

# Heads Up!

This session is not included in the *Student Book*. Facilitation notes for making the collage and interpretation are included here.

 ## Activity 1: What Math Means to Me

Explain that in this session, you want students to be creative and visual as they express what math means to them, using pictures. Tell the students they will create a poster that effectively communicates this idea.

Distribute magazines, newsprint, markers, and glue or tape, and ask students to look through the magazines, find pictures to cut out, and make a collage of *What Math Means to Me*. They can use the markers to write words or phrases on their collages.

Say:

 **Be creative. Give free rein to your imagination as you express your opinions and feelings.**

When everyone is done, display the posters on the walls.

### Interpreting Another Student's Collage

Now ask each student to choose someone else's poster to interpret. Explain that each interpreter is to consider three questions:

1. How does the student who created the collage feel about mathematics?
2. With what numbers, operations, and math is that student familiar?
3. What activities does he or she associate with math?

Display these questions on the board.

Everyone then writes a poem, dialogue, list, prose, or other literary form to express *What Math Means to Me*, as if he or she were the person who created the collage.

After everyone has written, ask for volunteers to stand by the collages they have studied and present their interpretations aloud.

## Summary Discussion

Close by asking for general comments on what students learned about themselves today. Ask:

 **What did we learn about one another?**

 **Were there any surprises?**

## Looking Closely

Observe whether students are able to

### Describe and share their personal feelings and perspectives about math

Consider the following questions as students share their perspectives. What are you learning about your students? What question(s) do you, as the teacher, want to ask each student after studying his or her collage? How might a student's collage help you teach that student math?

### Interpret others' perspectives

How well do students put themselves in another's position? Are they using the data on the collage rather than projecting their own feelings?

# Rationale

Most math assessments, whether professionally published or locally designed, focus solely on math thinking and require computation, problem solving, or demonstration of understanding of concepts. The collage activity involves a different kind of assessment. By highlighting students' affective disposition toward and associations with mathematics, you will gain a lot of information. Often teachers attribute negative attitudes to adults in basic math classes, but you will likely find a rich combination of feelings—that math is challenging, useful, and fun, as well as that it is difficult or taxing. See *Midpoint Activity in Action*, pp. 83–84, for examples from one class.

Math, usually referred to as a cold subject, is actually quite a hot topic. The interplay of cognition and emotion is the subject of a long-term study conducted by Jeff Evans, "Adults Mathematical Thinking and Emotions: A Study of Adult Numerate Practices" (2000). Evans' central point is that "affect and emotion [are] inseparable from thinking, including mathematical thinking." Emotion does not necessarily interfere with mathematical thinking; rather "emotion [is seen] in terms of charges of feeling attached to ideas and thus related to the cognitive."

Strong negative emotions associated with math are often referred to as math anxiety, phobia, or panic. Whatever one calls it, we are referring to an emotion that blocks a person's reasoning ability when that person is confronted with a mathematical situation. Some excellent resources of interest in this area are listed in *Sources and Resources*, p. 235.

Although emotions, both negative and positive, have undoubtedly arisen in class before today, the collage activity is a chance for students to air and talk about them explicitly. It should give you, the teacher, a better read on what students are feeling at this point in the unit. As you proceed, keep in mind that the researchers who study math anxiety say that among the causes are the traditional ways math has been taught in school with an emphasis on abstraction, individualism, and speed, and the persistent myth that there is one right method to do math and one right order in which to learn it. This unit—and the EMPower series as a whole— try to provide an alternative approach for adults who return to study "the basics" by emphasizing meaning-making, multiple methods, connections to real-life situations and collaboration as central to mathematical activity.

*Students in a multi-level employment and training GED programs assembled collages to convey "What Math Means to Me." Here are examples of their work.*

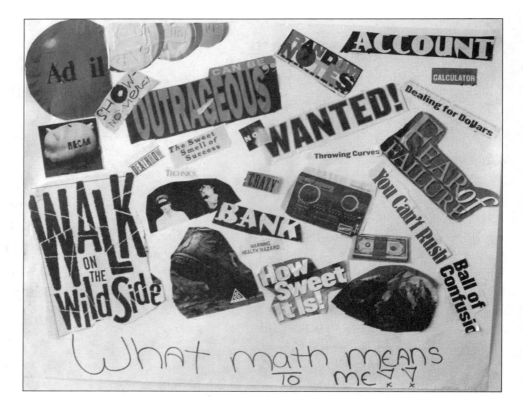

*Tricia Donovan*
*Franklin Hampshire Employment and Training Program, Greenfield, MA*

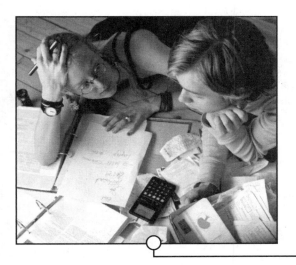

# Patterns and Order

> *Which is faster—
> mental math or
> calculator?*

## Synopsis

Students identify patterns when multiplying and dividing by 10, 100, and 1,000 and then test their mental math skills against the calculator. Using mental math and the calculator, they begin to explore the importance of **order of operations**.

1.  The class agrees upon patterns that occur when multiplying and dividing by 10, 100, and 1,000.

2.  Working in pairs, students test whether they can solve multiplication and division problems faster using mental math or with calculators.

3.  Students solve equations involving the numbers 3, 4, and 5 and addition and multiplication and compare their results with those of the calculator.

4.  Students use parentheses to impose an order of operations in various equations.

5.  The class summarizes findings.

## Objectives

*   Identify and use patterns when multiplying and dividing by 10, 100, and 1,000

*   Use order of operations to solve problems

## Materials/Prep

- Calculators—one per student

Prepare an overhead transparency of *Patterns with 10, 100, and 1,000* (*Blackline Master 9*) or copy the numbers on the board.

## Heads Up!

This lesson develops two ideas: (1) multiplication and division patterns with powers of 10 (10, 100, and 1,000) and (2) the importance of order when two operations are involved. You may wish to break the lesson into two sessions.

## Opening Discussion

Start by saying:

 **In math, noticing and making use of patterns is important. Some people have said mathematics is the study of patterns.**

 **Let's look at some of the patterns from the previous lesson, where people took their winnings in different ways.**

What are the different ways people could take their cash lottery winnings for $5,000?

Ask volunteers to write solutions on the board. If necessary, prompt by asking for how many $1,000 bills, $100 bills, $10 bills, or $1 bills there could be. If no one uses parentheses as notation, ask whether someone could rewrite any of the answers with parentheses.

Focus on 5($1,000), 50($100), 500($10), and 5,000($1) by circling them. Next, ask:

 **What about $900?** [9($100), 90($10), or 900($1)]

Ask:

 **Do you see any patterns in the numbers here? What do you notice?**

Students might say:

"There are always the same number of zeroes."

"It always means multiplication."

"You just count the number of zeroes at the end."

If it does not come up in the discussion, connect the notation with parentheses to multiplication, pointing out that, e.g., 3(1,000) is one way to write 3 x 1,000.

Display *Patterns with 10, 100, and 1,000* (*Blackline Master 9*) or copy the numbers on the board. Ask individuals to try the multiplication problems, first doing all the multiplications by 10, using patterns whenever they can; then the multiplications by 100; and finally all the multiplications by 1,000.

When students are done, ask pairs to check answers with one another, and then ask for responses to the question:

 **What is the rule or pattern you notice?**

Make the connection between multiplication and division. Ask:

 **How could knowing these patterns in multiplication help with a division problem, such as 70 ÷ 10? How do you know?**

Make sure the relationship between multiplication and division is explicit. Ask:

 **If you know that 261 x 10 = 2,610, then what is 2,610 ÷ 10?**

Ask for a few more examples of connecting division to the multiplication problems.

##  Activity 1: Mental Math or Calculator?

Introduce the activity by asking:

 **Mental math or calculator—which is faster?**

Refer students to *Activity 1: Mental Math or Calculator?* (*Student Book,* p. 94). Pair students and go over the directions.

After students finish the first 10 problems, they will write some of the things they notice about multiplying and dividing by 10, 100, and 1,000. Bring the class together to share.

Students may give examples such as these:

> "Multiplying by 10 or 100 is easy because I just add one or two zeroes."
> "Dividing a number that ends in zero by 10 is easy—I just take out the last zero."

Ask for explanations.

Anticipate that the issue of order may arise as a result of the use of a calculator. Although order does not make a difference for multiplication (e.g., 90 x 10 = 10 x 90), it does for division (e.g., 300 ÷ 10 does not give the same result as 10 ÷ 300).

Reinforce the importance of estimation for arriving at reasonable answers.

##  Activity 2: 3,4,5

Refer students to *Activity 2: 3, 4, 5* (*Student Book,* p. 96).

Review the directions for *Part 1*.

**Use the numbers 3, 4, and 5 and two operations, addition and multiplication. Write as many *number sentences* as you can. Use each number and operation exactly once in each sentence.**

Ask students to work on this individually at first.

 **Now check your number sentences with the calculator.**

Then ask:

 **Which answers are different? What did the calculator do differently?**

Record some sentences that resulted in different responses.

For example, 3 + 4 x 5 = 23 if the operations are performed with the calculator, but if done left to right, 3 + 4 x 5 = 35.

After a few examples, establish that the calculator always does the multiplication first.

Post the rule "Multiply first and then add" in students' words.

Next, students work on *Part 2, Student Book*, p. 97. They complete each part in Problem 3 the way a calculator would and write the order of operations the calculator used. Ask students not to work on Problem 4 just yet.

---

## Heads Up!

Use of GED or scientific calculators is assumed.

---

Verify answers with the whole class and then ask:

 **What answers would you get if you did the operations left to right?**

Post answers. Note that three of the answers would be different from the ones obtained with a calculator.

 **How would you write these three number sentences if you wanted the answer to match your left-to-right order?**

If no one mentions parentheses, introduce them. Draw parentheses around the addition where appropriate, and explain that when there are parentheses, they indicate that you perform the operations inside of the parentheses first. For example, 1 + 9 x 5 would be written as (1 + 9) x 5 if left-to-right order were wanted.

Now direct students to do Problem 4, using parentheses to ensure left-to-right order.

Ask students to generate three or four more examples done the calculator way and the left-to-right way with parentheses.

For example, 12 + 9 x 2 = 12 + 18 = 30 if done with the calculator, but if the intent were left to right, would be written and entered as (12 + 9) x 2 = 21 x 2 = 42.

Add:

 **Order matters! In mathematics, parentheses help us communicate order. If there are no parentheses, then the order of operations is to multiply first and then add.**

 **What happens if we work with division and subtraction? What did you find in Problem 5?**

The problem is similar to the ones with multiplication and addition. Push for the rule "Divide first and then subtract."

Students will have opportunities to pursue this further in *Practice: Just Like the Calculator* (*Student Book*, p. 98).

## Summary Discussion

Ask students:

 **What are some of the things you need to be aware of when you use a calculator?**

 **How does estimation help when using a calculator?**

Establish that although the calculator can help you find an answer, you may not catch a mistake made by pressing keys if you do not first have an estimate in mind.

Recap the order of operations:

 **When a problem includes multiplication, division, addition, and subtraction, but no parentheses, what is the order of operations?**

Refer students to *Reflections* (*Student Book*, p. 185), where they can write down some of these ideas.

##  Practice

*Just like the Calculator*, p. 98
For more practice with order of operations.

*More or Less?* p. 99
For practice making estimates.

## Mental Math Practice

*Multiply and Divide with 10, 100, or 1,000*, p. 100
For practice computing mentally with powers of 10.

## Extension

*The Answer Is 24*, p. 101
For practice with writing word problems and checking equations with the calculator.

*Wrong Number!* p. 103
For practice using mental math to solve problems.

## Test Practice

*Test Practice*, p. 104

## Looking Closely

Observe whether students are able to

### Identify and use patterns when multiplying and dividing by 10, 100, and 1,000

Do students use the strategies they have learned in the unit to make reasonable estimates? Realizing that they can solve the problems faster using mental math than by entering the numbers on the calculator should give them confidence.

Do students use the calculator correctly, finding the appropriate keys and reading the display? Review calculator use with those students who need the help or with the whole group.

As needed, review related material or sheets from previous lessons on rounding and making mental estimates.

### Use order of operations to solve problems

Do students adjust to the convention of order of operations? Watch students as they begin a problem. Do they take a second to scan the equation, looking for multiplication and division signs? Encourage students to make notes on or around an equation. Colored markers or different colored pencils or pens might help students highlight the operations and put in parentheses as reminders.

Help students articulate the difference between working an equation left to right and following the order of operations.

| WHAT TO LOOK FOR IN *LESSON 7* | WHO STANDS OUT? (LIST STUDENTS' INITIALS) | | | NOTES FOR NEXT STEPS |
|---|---|---|---|---|
| | STRONG | ADEQUATE | NEEDS WORK | |
| **Number Development**<br>• Multiplies and divides efficiently with powers of 10<br>• Distinguishes between working an equation left to right and following order of operations<br>• Estimates or solves problems using mental math strategies | | | | |
| **Expressive Capacity**<br>• Explains reasoning using appropriate mathematical language | | | | |
| **Notation Use**<br>• Uses parentheses to indicate order of operations | | | | |
| **Use of Tools**<br>• Uses the calculator to get or check answers | | | | |

## Rationale

Sound mental math computational skills depend on the ability to see patterns. One of the most useable patterns is the one that occurs when multiplying by powers of 10.

Because the lesson centers on calculator use, it introduces some conventions about order of operation. Although there are mnemonic devices for remembering the order (Please Excuse My Dear Aunt Sally, PEMDAS, etc.), the multiple experiences solving equations in a left-to-right manner and comparing them with the same equations solved by the calculator will help students see the importance of order of operation.

## Math Background

### Patterns with Powers of 10

Multiplication and division by 10 and powers of 10 involve zeroes. How many zeroes should be added or removed? It is important to have an idea of the magnitude of the result so that the answer makes sense. For example, 760 x 10 should be a large number because it can be thought of as 100 groups of 760—for example, 100 baskets, each filled with 760 cherries. That's a lot of cherries!

760 x 10 = 7,600

760 x 100 = 76,000

Similarly, 8,700 ÷ 10 can be solved using the fact that 100 = 10 x 10, so 8,700 ÷ 10 = 870, and 870 ÷ 10 = 87.

Although a calculator will yield the answers, it is likely just as fast, if not faster, to solve these problems using mental math. In all cases, the reasonableness of the solution is important.

### Order of Operations

As in reading, where commas indicate a pause and periods mean "stop," in mathematics, the operations in a string of numbers also have meaning, indicating order. Establishing order of operations determines universal reading and solving of equations: Parentheses take precedence—anything inside of them is to be done or solved first; then exponents; after that multiplication and division; and last, addition and subtraction. For example, 62 + 8 x 5 is *not* solved left to right, but instead, by doing the multiplication first—8 x 5 = 40—followed by the addition— 62 + 40 = 102.

On the other hand, (62 + 8) x 5 is solved by adding the amounts inside the parentheses first (62 + 8 = 70) and then multiplying (70 x 5 = 350).

The two equations communicate different stories.

# Facilitation

For those who question the need to use the order of operations, it will help to discuss other sequential activities and what happens when steps are done out of order—for instance, drying clothes before washing them. Students might also relate this mathematical convention to grammatical conventions they automatically follow, such as placing the verb after the subject of the sentence unless it is a question. English speakers do not put the verb first, saying, "Go I"; the convention is that the noun comes first: "I go."

## Making the Lesson Easier

Stretch out the activities over a number of days. After doing one activity, choose a related practice and do that with the class.

Encourage students to do the *Mental Math Practice* (*Student Book*, p. 100) before they work on any of the other practices in this lesson.

## Making the Lesson Harder

Use numbers that do not end in 0, and ask students to divide by 10, 100, or 1,000. This will yield answers with decimals.

Use dollars and cents. The inclusion of the decimal point requires more careful use and interpretation of the calculator. Refer students to the extensions, *The Answer Is 24* (*Student Book*, p. 101) and *Wrong Number!* (*Student Book*, p. 103).

# LESSON 7 IN ACTION

*Two teachers wrote the following about* Activity 2: 3, 4, 5.

> The group really enjoyed generating the number sentences for *3, 4, 5*. For most of them, using two operations in one number sentence was a big hit. At the point when we looked at which equations got different answers, the class started to diverge into two groups: a few who got it quickly and the rest who didn't.
>
> Those who got it were excited. One woman wrote in her journal:
>
> "Today is one of my best days. I actually look forward to [class] because I get to learn something new like using the parentheses. I was actually having fun doing it because I never knew it was so interesting. I got to like it. I also learned how to use the scientific calculator."
>
> *Deidre Freeman*
> *Lehman College, Bronx, NY*

> All were engaged and attentive for most of the lesson period. Everyone learned something and felt successful. Ted said he had figured out how to use the function keys. Elana, a younger student, exclaimed as she checked her *3, 4, 5* problems on the calculator, "I know what's going on; you're trying to trick us. I see what I did wrong." (I had to urge her to refrain from spilling the beans to the other learners before they had a chance to see for themselves.)
>
> Nora asked the key question: "Why are we getting different answers?" Nora's question led to a grand discussion of "Elana's Rule" that multiplication should always come first. Jay, a young and restless learner, said he did not think the rule would hold in all cases, so we tried each suggested number sentence to see whether her rule would work to get the same number as shown on the calculator. Lo and behold, it did! Everyone was convinced and, I think, surprised and pleased. Here was a fact, a "truth" they could hold: Do the multiplication first.
>
> Jay was enthusiastic when it came time for everyone to write two or three of their own number sentences on the board. "We get to write the problems— all right!" Fred provided a great challenge to the class with his example — $(2 \times 3) + 4 \times 2$. Most people, including Ted, thought the answer was 16, though at least one person said 20. The "20" answer indicated that they had forgotten to do the multiplication first the second time around. Those who answered 16 acknowledged that they, for some reason, multiplied 6 by 2 before adding 4. When we worked it out by rewriting the sentences after each step, they all saw immediately what the answer was. Ted noted that, "I tricked everyone" (himself included).
>
> *Tricia Donovan*
> *Pioneer Adult Education Center, Northampton, MA*

# Picture This

*How many are there?*
*How do you know?*

## Synopsis

Students explore ways to visualize and represent numbers and operations with arrangements of objects in arrays (rows and columns) and equal groups. This lesson is the first of two lessons that focus on totaling and breaking apart groups of items while making connections among visual representations, mathematical expressions and equations, and word problems.

1. The class discusses ways to total items without individually counting each object. They record ideas using words and equations and by marking off arrays.

2. Individuals find at least two ways to record the total number of items in pictured groups, and then student pairs match equations with arrays.

3. Student pairs arrange collections of objects for ease in counting and write equations that reflect their arrangements.

4. Student pairs solve the *Garden Pathway* problem, and the whole class reviews the problem.

5. The class summarizes what they learned about showing equations and writing equations. Then they discuss using math to find totals in their daily lives.

## Objectives

- Write expressions to reflect regular arrangements of objects in groups and arrays

- Represent expressions using arrays and/or equal groups arranged to correspond with numbers and operations

- Identify **equivalent expressions**

## Materials/Prep

- Colored markers
- Newsprint
- Small objects, such as paper clips, pennies or chips, enough so that each student or pair of students can have between 30 and 60

Make an overhead transparency or an enlarged copy of *Windows* (*Blackline Master 10*).

Take note of arrays around your classroom, for example, the arrangement of floor or ceiling tiles, desks, or windowpanes. Bring to class some items that come in arrays, for instance, egg cartons, six-pack containers, flats of garden plants, or booklets of stamps. These may be empty, as long as it is clear how many items they would contain. You could also take photographs and/or cut out magazine pictures showing things in rows and columns.

## Opening Discussion

Set up the lesson by saying:

 **We have discussed different ways we calculate with numbers—mentally, with a number line, or with a calculator. Today we focus on a way of using math to describe an arrangement of objects. In this lesson, you will concentrate on visualizing the operations of multiplication and addition or subtraction.**

Post and say aloud the definition for **arrays**:

**Arrays show items arranged in rows and columns.**

Show or sketch actual arrangements of 6 × 2 and 3 × 4 arrays.

Direct students to look around the class for examples of other arrays. Ask:

**How many items are in this array? In this one?**

 **How did you count them?**

There are many ways to count. Students will likely say, "I counted one by one"; "I counted one row and then multiplied by the number of rows"; or "I skip counted by 4's." Ask whether they might have counted the number differently if they looked at the array differently, vertically instead of horizontally, for instance.

Display *Windows* (*Blackline Master 10*) and say:

**I know someone who *thinks* in arrays! She washes windows for a living and charges $5 a window. She needs to make quick estimates for her customers, so she never counts one by one. When she looks at a building like this, how many windows does she see?**

Give students a moment to talk to a partner. As volunteers share approaches, record their ideas with equations. If someone says, "I counted by 3's," ask for details—what he or she said or thought when counting each group. Demonstrate on the board how the person saw the numbers in the array, and record the numbers as well as any explanation of mental arithmetic.

3, 6, 9, 12, and 12 more is 24

3 x 4 is 12, 12 + 12 is 24

2 times 4 is 8
8 x 3 equals 24

If someone explains, "I just knew that three 4's equal 12, so I added 12 and 12," post a copy of the picture and record:

- 3 x 4 = 12 (Box the first set of windows and label the sides with the numbers 3 and 4.)
- 12 + 12 = 24 (Box the second set of windows and label it "12.")

If the question "I saw 4 x 3—is that the same?" arises, take the opportunity to rotate the array pictured and ask, "Has the total changed?" You may wish to try a few more array examples to emphasize that 6 x 2 = 2 x 6, and these are equivalent because their total is equal.

Encourage a variety of approaches by asking questions such as these:

> **Did anyone count by 4's?**

> **Did anyone use only addition? What did you do?**

> **Did anyone use only multiplication? What did you do?**

> **Did anyone multiply different numbers together or multiply numbers in a different order?**

> **Did anyone use addition *and* multiplication?**

As you record equations, ask whether anyone is familiar with other ways to record. For instance, if you record "3 x 4 = 12," ask whether anyone knows another way to show multiplication. Occasionally, vary your own recording to help students learn the different notation, in particular, "dot"—(3 • 4)—and parentheses—3(4).

# Activity 1: Pictures and Numbers

Refer students to *Activity 1: Pictures and Numbers* (*Student Book*, p. 106).

## Part 1

Students find totals without counting each individual item; instead they focus on groups of things.

They record at least two ways to find the total and mark the chosen pictures with different colored markers to show how they saw the numbers. Each student does this for two sets of objects.

Students who finish early can try the other *Part 1* items or find a partner and proceed to *Part 2*.

To review, summarize each problem separately and ask students to demonstrate how they saw the numbers.

 **In the faces problem, I noticed you counted in different ways and wrote different equations. Some people counted by 1's, some people added 10's, and others multiplied 10 by 10.**

 **How are those ways alike? How are they different?**

 **Is the same true for the chocolates problem, where some people added and multiplied and some people counted?**

As connections are made between the expressions, take this opportunity to define **equivalent expressions**—those that result in the same total.

Then focus on the counting:

 **Each way you counted involves multiplying some number a certain number of times.**

 **With counting by 3's, 6's, 10's, etc., and repeated addition, you say or think, for instance, of all the 3's up to the total of 18. Multiplication is shorthand for that.**

## Part 2

Continue with *Part 2*, where the pictures are grids of squares and less literal.

First take suggestions for mathematical expressions, writing students' offerings on the board.

Probe:

 **Where did you see the 10 multiplied by 13? Where did you see the one multiplied by 13?**

 **How does seeing the problem that way help you find the answer to the multiplication problem 11 x 13?**

Have volunteers show the rest of the class how they matched the remaining expressions and arrays.

Bring into the discussion ideas about pulling apart numbers to make multiplying easier and "seeing" expressions in different formats that can be connected visually as well as by notation.

When you discuss the equation $10 \times 10 + 1 \times 13 + 3 \times 10$, highlight the $10 \times 10$ block, and introduce the raised **exponent** as another shorthand way to record an instance when a number is multiplied by itself ($10^2$). Numbers that can be drawn in arrays where the rows and columns are equal are called "**square numbers.**" In this case, the exponent 2 tells you that two 10's are multiplied by one another. Ask:

 **Why do you think they are called "square numbers"?**

**What other square numbers can you think of? How would you write equations for them using an exponent? How would you write equations for them *without* using an exponent?**

##  Activity 2: Counting Smart

Refer students to *Activity 2: Counting Smart* (*Student Book*, p. 110) and review the directions for *Part 1*. Give each pair a small handful of paper clips, pennies, or chips (about 30 to 60).

As students work, ask them how they are deciding on their arrangements and supporting the arrangements by recording the expressions. Ask students who are done quickly to create an arrangement that involves two operations.

Student pairs that finish early look at another pair's arrangement and explain with an equation how they found the total without counting each item. Pairs then compare their equations, noting how they are alike and different.

Call the class together to share some of the ways they grouped the paper clips or tiles. Find one pair who made arrays and ask them to make their sketch on the board. Ask:

 **How many rows did you use? What did you do with the extra items that didn't make up a full row?**

**Who has another way to write an expression for this arrangement?**

**Did anyone put the paper clips or tiles in groups of the same size? What size groups did you use? Why?**

**Which was easier for you to count? Why?**

In the sharing, highlight equivalent expressions and equivalent equations. If equations or expressions are incorrect, show how *you* see what the student's equation represents pictorially.

Move students to *Part 2 (Student Book*, p. 111), where students draw pictures to match mathematical expressions. Pairs of students select two expressions to draw, and those pairs who finish quickly might draw a picture for all four expressions.

Students share and compare their pictures, checking to see that the pictures correspond to the expressions.

See *Lesson 8 in Action*, p. 106, for ways students in pilot classes created pictures.

By the end of *Activity 2*, students will have used objects to create arrangements which they then wrote as mathematical expressions and have drawn pictures to represent expressions.

 ## Activity 3: Garden Pathway

Refer students to *Activity 3: Garden Pathway* (*Student Book*, p. 112).

When everyone is clear about the directions, allow time for individuals to create at least two ways to show the number of tiles mathematically. Then bring the class together to share expressions.

There are several ways that students might write the expression for 96 tiles. Some might see the double rows of two 10's on the sides and the corners with four tiles each:

$20 + 20 + 20 + 20 + 4 + 4 + 4 + 4$

$4(20) + 4(4)$

$4(2 \times 10) + 4 \times 4$

Some students may section off each corner with a side:

$4(24)$

Some may focus on the inside and outside borders:

$[4(10) + 4] + [4(12) + 4]$

And some students may figure out the number of tiles to cover the area, and subtract those that cover the garden:

$14(14) - 10(10)$

$14^2 - 10^2$

If no one brings up the subtractive method, say:

 **I saw this as $14(14) - 10(10)$. What did I see?**

During the review, insist that students demonstrate to one another how they came to their expressions.

Conclude by having them evaluate each expression, using the rules of order to verify that each expression equals 96.

## Summary Discussion

Refer students to *Reflections* (*Student Book*, p. 185).

After students have written their responses, take statements from volunteers.

# Practice

*Cartons of Eggs*, p. 113
For practice writing equations to match arrays.

*Expressions, Arrays, and Stories*, p. 114
For practice connecting arrays with various expressions and relating stories to each array.

*How Do You See It?* p. 115
For practice writing equations and finding totals without counting.

*Stone Paths*, p. 117
For practice with rectangular arrays.

# Mental Math Practice

*Square Numbers*, p. XXX
For practice squaring numbers and using exponential notation.

# Extension

*Missing Rolls of Film*, p. 120
For a challenge counting objects in a three-dimensional arrangement.

*Seeing Squarely*, p. 122
For practice visualizing arrangements for expressions that include exponents.

# Test Practice

*Test Practice*, p. 123

# Looking Closely

Observe whether students are able to

### Write equations to reflect regular arrangements of objects in groups and arrays

Can students find the total number of objects in such an arrangement without counting (e.g., by adding or multiplying)?

Can students explain their approaches with reference to arithmetic and record their approaches using equations? Encourage them to explain their thinking using words such as "multiply" or "add." Say, for example, "You knew that there were three rows and each row had six squares. What did you do to find that there were 18 squares in all?"

Help students become familiar with the appropriate arithmetic terms: "So, you knew that three 6's are 18—you multiplied 3 by 6 and got 18."

Refer students to equations you (or others) recorded for the class and, as needed, model correct recording yourself. Some students may be familiar with different ways of recording operations and equations. For this lesson, encourage them to record in ways that are comfortable—as long as they are correct—but also point out alternative notation, e.g., $3 \times 4 = 3(4) = 3 \cdot 4$.

Ask those students who struggle to explain how they are counting the objects or to count aloud for you so you can repeat or record for them what they said. With a pencil, mark off the sets of objects to reflect how students are seeing them.

Do students notice commutative relationships among operations—in other words, that three rows of four is the same as four rows of three?

### Represent equations using arrays and/or equal groups arranged to correspond with numbers and operations

Do students recognize that arranging objects into equal groups makes it possible to find the total without counting each object?

Ask students to arrange the items into groups of a particular size (say, four or five items to a group) and then to find the total number of items without counting each item one by one. If needed, work with students to add or skip-count to find the total: "Okay, we have four groups of five items. So, this first group has five items; how many items are in these two groups together? How many are in three groups?"

Are students able to find a total number in an array by multiplication? As above, ask students to model the number with objects in groups of 10, and ask them to find the total by counting by 10's.

### Identify equivalent expressions

Are students able to verify that equations are equivalent or nonequivalent by demonstrating with visual models? Take time to connect the visual models with the mathematical symbols.

Are they able to use rules of order to evaluate an expression? Return to *Lesson 7*, where order of operations was a main focus.

| WHAT TO LOOK FOR IN *LESSON 8* | WHO STANDS OUT? (LIST STUDENTS' INITIALS) | | | NOTES FOR NEXT STEPS |
|---|---|---|---|---|
| | STRONG | ADEQUATE | NEEDS WORK | |
| **Number Development**<br>• Accurately and flexibly interprets the mathematical operations of visual arrangements<br>• Connects features of an *a* by *b* array to multiplication, *a* x *b* | | | | |
| **Expressive Capacity**<br>• Explains reasoning using appropriate mathematical language | | | | |
| **Notation Use**<br>• Correctly interprets and uses the exponent when squaring a number<br>• Uses parentheses to indicate order of operations | | | | |
| **Use of Tools**<br>• Uses the calculator to find or check answers | | | | |

## Rationale

Arrays provide a clear picture of multiplication and open the way for visualizing multi-operational equations. The lesson provides plenty of opportunity to practice multiplication facts, but the emphasis is on the conceptual understanding of multiplication.

This lesson also helps to build flexibility with breaking apart and putting together numbers, an essential skill throughout mathematics.

## Math Background

Arrays lend themselves to a discussion of commutativity; one can rotate the array to see the rows and columns change, but the total remains the same. Arrays are generally more useful than groups for quick totaling because arrays show at a glance that they contain equal numbers of items; groups do not.

Some students may be comfortable with commutativity in addition and multiplication. They may take it for granted that 40 + 7 is the same as 7 + 40, or that 3 x 5 is the same as 5 x 3. Others may be less certain and may benefit from a visual approach. For instance, suppose students are explaining how they know how many squares are in the following array:

One student may see this as five rows of three—5 x 3, others may see it as three rows of five and write "3 x 5." With repeated experiences such as these, over time students will gain understanding of commutativity in multiplication and addition.

## Facilitation

The more time devoted to notation, the longer this lesson will take.

Some students take the direction to sketch literally. Recommend the use of sticks, X's, or dots as ways to sketch a representation of an arrangement.

To connect the lesson more firmly with daily life, take some time to examine objects and photographs of real arrays and discuss how students see the total in each.

## Making the Lesson Easier

Assign fewer sets in *Activity 1: Pictures and Numbers* (*Student Book*, p. 106) and limit selection to the simpler arrangements. Distribute fewer paper clips to student pairs.

## Making the Lesson Harder

Discuss square and prime numbers with students. Assign *Extension: Seeing Squarely* (*Student Book*, p. 122) as a challenge.

# LESSON 8 IN ACTION

*Pilot teachers commented on the value of connecting expressions with visual representations.*

When drawing out the situations for a number sentence, it was interesting to find that students see multiplication as addition. Having to illustrate a situation made them really think about what it meant. Once I suggested that they try to think a little differently, they began to change their illustrations. This has such potential really to bring so many big ideas of multiplication to the surface.

*Phyllis Flanagan*
*Adult Education Center, Rock Valley College, Rockford, Illinois*

This lesson worked fairly well as an introduction to seeing and discussing multiplication. Students were immediately engaged in counting the numbers of things in each photo. The discussion went well, but there are such huge gaps in how people approach this problem (from counting one by one to counting by groups, and *not* often by multiplication). Making the pictures for the equations was equally as engaging, though the frustration level was higher. Again, multiplication was definitely seen as addition.

One student began to see that three groups of three was also one group of nine. That was big to me, but the concept was a slippery one for awhile and I'm not so sure that he solidly understands it.

*Deidre Freeman*
*Lehman College, New York*

FACILITATING LESSON **9**

# What's the Story?

> *What math do you see in this picture?*

---

## Synopsis

This lesson draws attention to the various ways people successfully represent and solve word problems. Students explain possible solution paths to solve a problem and represent contextual situations with pictures and mathematical expressions. Individuals compare their solutions for *The Rose Problem*, using pictures and math symbols to support their reasoning.

1.  Partners complete two possible solution paths for contextual problems, and students demonstrate their mathematical reasoning with arrangements of objects and mathematical expressions.

2.  Individuals solve *The Rose Problem* and then share their own solution paths, using pictures and mathematical expresssions to explain and confirm their reasoning.

3.  To summarize, volunteers share insights about the lesson.

## Objectives

*   Represent word problems with pictures and mathematical equations
*   Record problem-solving strategies with equations and pictures

## Materials/Prep

- Grid paper
- Paper clips, chips, or pennies

Set up your board so that equations, diagrams, and word problems can be situated next to each other.

| Equations | Diagrams | Word Problems |

## Opening Discussion

Introduce word problems as the focus of today's lesson:

 **Who has worked on word problems in math? About what do word problems usually ask?**

Record a list of word problem topics. Note that word problems often talk about amounts or quantities, such as miles, dollars, inches, etc.

Explain:

 **There are often many paths you can take to solve a word problem. What is important is that you see the problem clearly. Pictures can help you see the math relationships. Today, think about how the word problem connects to a picture and the mathematical symbols.**

Point out the headings on the board: equations, diagrams, and word problems. Tell students to use each of these forms as they do the activities.

##  Activity 1: What's the Story?

There are two points to this activity. First, there are often various ways to enter a problem, and second, pictures and math symbols are ways to see the structure of the problem.

Refer students to *Activity 1: What's the Story?* (*Student Book*, p. 126). Ask a volunteer to read the problem aloud. Then ask students to partner up. One partner will be Person A; the other, Person B.

 **Problems such as this one might be solved in different ways. In this activity, one of you will solve the problem starting out the way Person A did; the other will solve the problem starting out the way Person B did.**

Individuals work on the problem and then share with their partner the way they solved it as they continued the line of thinking for their role as Person A or Person B. Remind everyone to both draw a picture and write the math expressions and equations.

Bring the class together and focus first on Person A's thinking. Ask:

 **What would Person A's picture look like? What part of the picture would Person A look at first?**

 **What math would Person A do first? What would Person A's mathematical equation look like?**

Take all suggestions but insist upon continuing Person A's thinking. Because Person A thought first about the number of windows in each building, the drawing and mathematical equations should indicate that there are 34 windows in each building and that there would be four times as many in total. The picture and equations might look like these:

$4(10 + 12 + 12) = 4(34) = 136$

or

$4(3 \times 10 + 4) = 136$

or

$2 \times 12 + 10 = 34$

$4 \times 34 = 136$

Seek explicit connections between each of the pictures and each of the equations.

Next, review Person B's solution path. Because Person B focused on each floor first, the picture and mathematical equation should indicate a totaling of the windows, floor by floor, and then a sum of the three floor totals. The pictures and equations might look like these:

$4(12) = 48$ (total 1st floor windows)

$4(12) = 48$ (total 2nd floor windows)

$4(10) = 40$ (total 3rd floor windows)

$48 + 48 + 40 = 136$

or

$4 \times 12 + 4 \times 12 + 4 \times 10 = 136$

Conclude by asking:

 **What are the differences between Person A's and Person B's solutions?**

 **What is the same in both solutions?**

Continue with Problem 2, asking partners to take on the different roles, and then review, comparing Person A's and Person B's solution paths.

Say:

 **Person A started out by finding out how many children need T-shirts. What do you think he did?**

 **Did anyone else following Person A's thinking solve the problem differently?**

After students share equations and pictures, continue with Person B.

 **How did Person B start and then solve the problem?**

 **What equations and pictures did you use in solving the problem?**

See *Lesson 9 in Action*, p. 117, for one student's explanation.

## ⊚ Activity 2: The Rose Problem

Refer students to *Activity 2: The Rose Problem* (*Student Book*, p. 130). Ask for a volunteer to read the problem aloud.

Allow all individuals enough time to thoroughly think through the problem. Encourage students who finish early to think of another solution method or to start some of the practices or the extension.

When everyone has finished solving the problem, ask volunteers to come up to the board to explain their solution methods.

It is important that students follow and critique one another's reasoning and ask questions of the presenter if they do not understand the explanation.

Keep asking until all solution methods have been presented:

 **Did anyone do it another way?**

As we have seen in pilot classes, *The Rose Problem* has many solution methods. See *Lesson 9 in Action,* p. 117, for ways students have solved the problem.

## Summary Discussion

Direct students to turn to a partner and tell one thing they already knew from today's lesson and one thing they found challenging or new. Volunteers share their own challenges.

Wrap up by asking what students learned about ways to solve problems:

 **Think about how you made up and solved problems today. What did you learn that helped you to solve problems?**

Students might say, for example:

"Making a drawing can be helpful."

"There can be more than one way to start thinking about a problem."

"There can be more than one way to solve a problem. For instance, sometimes you can use multiplication or addition, sometimes both."

"Sometimes it helps to take numbers apart, to think of 12 as 10 + 2, for example."

Refer student to *Reflections* (*Student Book*, p. 185), where they write about what they learned today.

 # Practice

*Drawings and Equations*, p. 131
For practice using pictures and equations to solve word problems.

*Equations and Word Problems*, p. 132
For practice seeing the math and a story in an arrangement of objects.

*The Answer Is _____*, p. 133
For practice making up and solving word problems.

*One Day, I . . .* p. 134
For practice making up and solving real-world word problems.

 # Mental Math Practice

*Patterns in the Multiplication Table*, p. 135
For practice seeing the patterns in the multiplication table.

 # Test Practice

*Test Practice*, p. 136

# Looking Closely

Observe whether students are able to

### Represent word problems with pictures and mathematical equations

Do students see an accurate picture of the situation? Do they also see the mathematical structures in the problem and connect the two?

Talk through the story in the problem. Suggest the use of grid paper or paper clips to represent the problem. Ask specific questions, such as, "How could you show the 10 six-packs? What about the packs that are missing two cans each? Where are the packs that are missing four cans each?" Encourage students to explain their pictures using words such as "multiplied" or "added."

Review with students what numbers and operations they see within the picture—are they seeing a larger whole with part taken away or a smaller whole with a few added? How are they building into the problem what they see?

### Record problem-solving strategies with equations and pictures

Do students have ideas for how to begin solving the problems? Can they record their approaches with pictures? Can they record their approaches with equations?

If students' equations include numbers that are not transparent from the picture prompts, seek an explanation or draw what you see written in the equation.

Slow down the problem-solving process. The point of the lesson is to make confident connections between the three representations: pictures, equations, and word problems. Label numbers in the equations to relate the story problem to the mathematical symbols. Have students talk through their solution processes, and model correct recording yourself.

Challenge those who perform ably to write their equations in different forms and to think about advantages and disadvantages of each form.

Some students should be able to write problems for situations related to, but extending beyond, the arrays pictured.

| WHAT TO LOOK FOR IN *LESSON 9* | WHO STANDS OUT? (LIST STUDENTS' INITIALS) | | | NOTES FOR NEXT STEPS |
| --- | --- | --- | --- | --- |
| | STRONG | ADEQUATE | NEEDS WORK | |
| **Number Development**<br>• Accurately and flexibly interprets the mathematical structure of word problems with expressions and equations<br>• Accurately and flexibly interprets the mathematical structure of word problems with pictures | | | | |
| **Expressive Capacity**<br>• Explains reasoning using appropriate mathematical language<br>• Restates others' solution strategies | | | | |
| **Notation Use**<br>• Verifies equivalence or nonequivalence of expressions | | | | |
| **Use of Tools**<br>• Uses the calculator to get or check answers | | | | |

## Rationale

As in literacy, making meaning is crucial in numeracy. Visualizing, or comprehending, and recording with notation story/word problems are among the essential numeracy skills adults acquire in order to make meaning. What makes these skills important is their practical application in out-of-school life. In this lesson, students have an opportunity to carefully examine word problems by entering into other people's thinking. The emphasis on sharing strategies develops flexibility.

## Context

Visualizing mathematics problems, like visualizing scenes in books and poems, helps us understand them. The contexts used here vary, but the need to picture what is going on in each situation remains. Help students visualize what happens in a problem by dramatizing with real objects or by offering ways to picture a problem quickly and easily.

Some students may prefer to draw literal pictures of the situation. Accept this, but try to guide students to more efficient representations that will aid them when solving problems in other contexts. Using grid paper arrays, dots, X's and slash marks are all more efficient, albeit more abstract, ways to represent numbers of objects. For larger numbers, it can be helpful to make a box with the number in it and repeat the box however many times it is added or multiplied.

## Mathematics Background

Because students generate most of the equations, the math on which you focus will depend on what issues students raise. As students compare equations and solution strategies, use the opportunity to probe for whether expressions are equivalent. You can then ask questions that bring attention to some regularities that occur in mathematics.

For example, you might focus on the commutative property by asking:

💬 **Does $5(4) = 4(5)$? (yes) How can you show that? Does order matter when you multiply two other numbers? Can you give another example?**

💬 **How about with addition? Does $5 + 4 = 4 + 5$?** (yes)

💬 **How about with subtraction? Does $10 - 6 = 6 - 10$?** (no)

💬 **How about with division? Does $20 \div 5 = 5 \div 20$?** (no)

There may be opportunities to probe for understanding of the associative property by asking:

💬 **Is (12 + 12) + 10 = 12 + (12 + 10)?** (yes)

💬 **When you add three or more numbers, does it matter which pair you add first?**

💬 **How about when you multiply three numbers? Does (3 × 4) × 5 = 3 × (4 × 5)?** (yes)

💬 **Does (20 − 10) − 6 = 20 − (10 − 6)?** (no)

💬 **Does (20 ÷ 10) ÷ 2 = 20 ÷ (10 ÷ 2)** (no)

Knowing that addition and multiplication are commutative and associative, but division and subtraction are not, is important.

Another property is the distributive property of multiplication over addition. When doing *Activity 1: What's the Story?* (*Student Book*, p. 126), students will have the opportunity to compare Person A's solution with Person B's. Ask:

💬 **Is 3(12 + 12 + 10) the same as 3(12) + 3(12) + 3(10)?**

💬 **Why are the statements equivalent?**

Pictures or concrete examples can be used to verify responses.

The following general mathematical properties form the basis of this discussion.

- Commutative property of addition: $a + b = b + a$
- Commutative property of multiplication: $a \times b = b \times a$
- Associative property of addition: $(a + b) + c = a + (b + c)$
- Associative property of multiplication: $(a \times b) \times c = a \times (b \times c)$
- Distributive property of multiplication over addition, and multiplication over subtraction: $a(b + c) = ab + ac$ and $a(b − c = a(b − c) = ab − bc$

## Facilitation

Solution paths depend on the first step taken, which in turn depends on which piece of information in a problem you choose to focus. For example, is the focus on the total number of windows in one building? Or on the total of first floor windows, then second floor windows, and then third floor windows in four buildings? One way is not more valid than another, though one can be seen to employ less steps or less opportunities for error. As students begin solving and analyzing solutions for math problems, it is not appropriate to push for efficiency. Only when students consistently understand problems is it useful to raise such issues.

Awareness of multiple solutions to problems is crucial here and throughout the study of mathematics. Remain open to different ways of approaching each problem. What is important is that the steps taken make sense in context of the problem. Over time, by sharing and listening, everyone reaches his or her own conclusions about the best way to approach a problem.

Some students may notice that problems can be solved with a variety of operations. For instance, you can find how many cans are in three six-packs of soda with 3 x 6 or with 6 + 6 + 6. Encourage these kinds of observations. As students explain and compare different ways to solve a problem, they learn about relationships among operations.

Students also need to learn which operations are not appropriate or efficient. If you want to find how many cans are in three six-packs, you could use multiplication or repeated addition; subtraction is not appropriate. As students make up and solve their own word problems, they deepen their understanding of which kinds of situations are best solved using which kinds of operations. Again, encouraging students to explain what operations they are choosing to solve a problem helps them gain better understanding. If students have difficulty either creating or solving problems, ask a volunteer to share what she or he is doing so far. This can help trigger ideas.

## Making the Lesson Easier

Work on one problem at a time. Share results and then ask students to apply what they just learned to the next problem.

Use real objects that students can count and arrange. Have them copy the arrangements onto grid paper or in literal drawings. As needed, simplify the numbers so that students can easily draw pictures or model with objects to help them find solutions.

## Making the Lesson Harder

Suggest that students substitute larger numbers in problems or consider alternate ways to solve the problem. Push for proof of generalizations of the properties (e.g., commutative, associative).

*In one class, three solutions for* The Rose Problem *emerged during a lesson. Though unique in framing and/or solving the problem, each method reveals sound reasoning.*

"Erin bought some roses to resell. She paid $6.00 for every 12 roses she bought. Later, Erin was charging $6.00 for eight roses. She sold them all and made a profit of $12.00. How many roses did Erin buy and resell?"

### Miguel's Method

Miguel drew an arrangement of objects that focused attention on each dozen roses and used it to support his presentation.

If she sells 8, she covers the cost of a dozen and 4 free.

The 4 free ones give her $3 because eight gave her $6.

$3 + $3 + $3 + $3 = $12, so 4 dozen or 48 roses.

### Noreen's Method

Noreen started out by focusing on how much profit Erin made on each rose.

Bought 12 roses for $6 = 50¢ each

Sold 8 roses for $6 = 75¢ each

So Erin made 25¢ on each rose.

2 roses = 50¢

3 roses = 75¢

4 roses = $1

12 × 4 = 48

### Monique's Method

Monique also began by focusing on each rose.

6 ÷ 12 = $0.50   "I divided to find the cost of one."

6 ÷ 8 = $0.75   "I divided to find the selling price of one."

12 ÷ $0.25 = 48   "Each one is 25¢ profit, so divide to find how many of those in total."

*continued on next page*

*continued from previous page*

*The observer commented on students' reasoning and solution methods:*

Miguel relies on his commercial experience. As a businessperson, he figures that the first task is to cover expenses. He demonstrates with a picture that Erin covers her cost by selling eight roses, leaving her four on which to profit. He further reasons that if she sold eight for $6, then the four left, being half of eight roses, will yield sales of $3. The reasoning is elegant. Miguel then shows that she needs to repeat her sales four times to yield the $12 target profit. The result is she needs to sell four dozen, or 48, roses.

Noreen finds the unit profit and then builds until she figures out how many roses are needed to make $1 profit. She is able to abstract that four roses equal $1, so she needs 12 times that many to get her targeted profit. Thus she needs 48 roses. Noreen clearly sees that an increase in the number of roses is matched by an increase in profits. If need be, she could build all the way to 48 roses = $12.

Monique determines the unit profit and then looks to find the number of those 25¢ profits in $12. She uses her equation to answer the question: How many single rose profits are there in $12 of profit?

*Tricia Donovan, Observer*
*Notre Dame Education Center, Boston, MA*

*In another class, the observer commented on the back-and-forth discussion about* The Rose Problem. *She wrote the following:*

The students had brought the problem home, and each showed his or her way on the board. When I arrived, the students were having a lively discussion about the problem. They had asked the lady in the lobby who sells flowers how she would do the problem (she said it was hard). Christina and her two kids (6th and 7th grade) had worked on it.

**1. Carl went first**

$12/6 - 8/6 = x/12$

$4/6 \qquad = x/12$

$2/3 \qquad = x/12$

$2 \cdot 12 \qquad = 3x$

$24/3 \qquad = x$

$8x \qquad$ (corrected by Judy, the teacher, to $8 = x$)

*continued on next page*

*continued from previous page*

I was at an impasse. Carl's confident mastery of algebraic symbol transformation floored me. But his conclusion was not correct. What question should I have asked? I did ask, "So what does the '8' mean?" He replied, "The profit." I think now I would have asked, "Could you confirm this another way?"

Judy asked if someone else could show how to solve the problem.

### 2. Maria went next

She spoke as she wrote:

"Buy 12 for $6 and sell eight for $6 to make it back."     12 = $6

                                                            8 = $6

"You have four roses left that you can sell."     4     Sell 8 for $6 profit

"Buy another dozen."     12 = $6

                         8 = $6

"You have another four roses left that you can sell."     4

"You have to do this twice.

"So, that makes four dozen that you had to buy ... 48 roses."

### 3. Joe said, "I did it a little like that."

50¢     "12 for $6.00."

50¢     "8 for $6.00."

50¢     "4 for $2.00."

Judy said, "You're changing the prices." Joe lost his train of thought and went back to think about it.

### 4. Christina started next.

"12 roses @ 50¢ each is $6.00 (I divided 12 by 6 [sic])

"8 roses @ 75¢ each is $6.00 (I divided 8 by 6 [sic])

"She makes 25¢ a rose."

Christina made marks on the board:

/ / / / gives $1

/ / / / / / / / / / / / / / / / / / / / gives $5; 40 gives $10

"We want two more dollars . . . that is eight roses."

*Mary Jane Schmitt*
*Bridge to Learning and Literacy Program, Harvard University, Cambridge, MA*

*Sometimes starting with smaller numbers allows people to see the mathematical structure more clearly. An observer wrote this:*

"Discount T-shirts come in packs of three. Lana needs to get a T-shirt for each child in the preschool where she works. There are four classes of nine children each. How many packs does she need?"

Tamika seems stuck on the T-shirt problem as she starts to make a picture.

● ● ● ● ● ● ● ● ●

**Teacher:** "Hmmm, I see one class of nine kids, but can you show me the other kids in your picture?"

Tamika adds more dots to her sketch.

**Teacher:** "Okay, how can you show how many kids get T-shirts out of the first pack?"

Tamika circles three dots. She does this until she runs out of dots and then counts her circles. She arrives at the right answer, but I can see how this has become very abstract. It takes a lot of imagination to look at this picture and to see 36 nursery school kids in 12 packs of T-shirts.

When we review as a group, Sarita shares her array:

**Teacher:** "Can you show me the nine kids in each class? Sarita then draws a line through her array after every 3 x 3 grouping."

It was nice to have both models: 4 x 9 and 3 x 12. But I found these difficult to share on the board, as it takes some students quite a while to draw 36 dots. Perhaps if the teacher had some models already prepared or enlarged students' drawings on the photocopier, this would have run more smoothly.

*Martha Gray, observed by Martha Merson*
*Dimock Community Health Center, Roxbury, MA*

# 10

# Deal Me In

> *How much will it cost per month?*

## Synopsis

This is the first of three lessons that focus on aspects of division. In this lesson, students build their sense of division as an act of equally dealing or splitting amounts into groups, and they generate notation and verbal language to connect with the action. They share strategies for dividing amounts by 4, 8, 12, and 24.

As students play *The Payment Plan Game*, they practice and refine mental math strategies for dividing by 10 and 100.

1. Students divide a total number of items fairly into four piles, and the whole group lists several options for writing division notation and using verbal language.

2. Individuals estimate and find exact answers for problems that demand splitting the cost of a purchase or loan over different time periods: 4, 8, 12, and 24 months. They share their mental math methods.

3. Teams play a division game where they split the cost of purchases into 10 or 100 monthly payments.

4. Individuals reflect on skills they used today.

## Objectives

- Connect division to the act of splitting or dealing out an amount
- Match the verbal language and symbolic notation for division to a concrete model
- Apply mental math strategies for division to situations calling for splitting dollar amounts over 4, 8, 12, 24, 10, or 100 time periods

## Materials/Prep

- Calculators
- Manipulatives, countable objects that are convenient to give to students in sets of 100, such as paper clips, pennies, tiles or cubes, playing cards, or Post-it Notes

Make transparencies of *10-Month Payment Plan Game Score Sheet* (*Blackline Master 11*) and *100-Month Payment Plan Game Score Sheet* (*Blackline Master 12*) or reproduce on the board.

## Opening Discussion

Give partners a set of small manipulatives. Ask students to take 52 of these and make four equal piles. Observe the ways students split up the total, and then ask for different strategies for dealing out the 52 objects.

Students might say:

"We dealt them out one by one."

"We dealt them out 10 to a pile and then had 12 left, so we put three more in each pile."

"We dealt them out by two's until they were all gone."

"We knew 4 x 10 = 40 and 4 x 3 = 12, so 4 x 13 = 52."

Summarize:

 **What total number did you have at the start? And how many piles did you make?**

 **How many are in each pile?**

Connect the concrete model to symbolic notation and verbal language.

Elicit students' wording for this division by asking:

**What is another way to say, "Take 52 of something and make four equal piles" in your own words?**

Listen and record expressions such as these:

"Fifty-two split up equally equals 13."

"Fifty-two divided by four equals 13."

"Four divided into 52 is 13." (This is incorrect.)

"Fifty-two shared among four people is 13."

"Fifty-two broken into four equal parts is 13."

Ask:

**How could you write this problem in math notation? What could an equation look like that would describe what you just did?**

Some may see this as multiplication, others as division. Students should generate different forms for writing division, e.g., the division sign, ÷; $\overline{)}$ ; or the fraction bar. List the problem in every format:

- Fifty-two divided by 4 equals 13
- $52 \div 4 = 13$
- $4 \times 13 = 52$
- $4\overline{)52}$ with quotient $13$
- $\dfrac{52}{4} = 13$

If students have gone to school in other countries, they may have learned to write and do long division with the dividend preceding the divisor and will write the quotient below, rather than above, the box.

- $\dfrac{52 \;|\; 4}{13}$

Check to see whether students' ways of writing equations and verbal expressions are all correct. Some students may not realize that the order of the numbers in division problems is important. Say and post:

**Is 52 ÷ 4 the same as 4 ÷ 52? Why or why not?**

Check to be sure that students can give a visual example demonstrating that the two expressions have different meanings. If students insist they are the same or are unsure, explore the problem using money: $52 divided among four people as opposed to $4 divided among 52 people. Acknowledge that in multiplication the order of the numbers makes no difference (4 x 13 or 13 x 4), but in division the order influences the meaning and the answer.

Connect this concept to using the calculator. Ask student to verify that 52 ÷ 4 is different from 4 ÷ 52.

## Heads Up!

At this point, if you think students need practice on the various ways of expressing division, assign practices *Four Ways to Write Division* (*Student Book*, p. 143) and *Which Is Not the Same?* (*Student Book*, p. 144). Otherwise, proceed with the activities.

**Activity 1: Easy Payments**

## Heads Up!

The emphasis is on mental calculations. Encourage students who are confident about long division algorithms to break up numbers in a meaningful way using mental math. If they wish, they can use the algorithm to check their mental math.

Refer students to *Activity 1: Easy Payments* (*Student Book*, p. 140). Given an amount ($9,600), their task is to first estimate and then mentally calculate exact monthly payments for four different time frames: 4, 8, 12, and 24 months. Finally, they check their answers with a calculator and, if they wish, a paper-and-pencil method.

After individuals are done, ask each to partner up to compare answers and to share methods they used to do the mental calculations. Then bring the class together and reinforce the variety of useable methods:

**Who had a mental math method that worked?**

Spend time on the mental math methods. Ask individuals to come up to the board to explain and record their mental math strategies. Observe the ways students are breaking up the numbers or building on the previous answers. Some may choose to reason with multiplication, others with division. There are many valid ways to do this. For example, some might reason about splitting up the money this way:

**$9,600 in 4 monthly payments means $2,400 per month.**

$4(\$2,000) = \$8,000$;

$4(\$400) = \$1,600$;

$\$2,000 + \$400 = \$2,400$.

or

$\$8,000 \div 4 = \$2,000$;

$\$1,000 \div 4 = \$250$;

$\$400 \div 4 = \$100$;

$\$200 \div 4 = \$50$;

$\$2,000 + \$250 + \$100 + \$50 = \$2,400$.

or

$9,600 is close to $10,000;

$\$10,000 \div 4 = \$2,500$.

But there is $400 less, so I will take $100 away four times;

$4(\$2,500) - 4(\$100) = 4(\$2,400)$.

**$9,600 in 8 monthly payments means $1,200 per month.**

I took the $2,400 and cut it in half because there are twice as many monthly payments now.

or

$8(\$1,000) = \$8,000;$

$8(\$100) = \$800;$

$8(\$100) = \$800;$

$\$1,000 + \$100 + \$100 = \$1,200.$

**$9,600 in 12 monthly payments means $800 per month.**

I took the answer for four monthly payments ($2,400) and split each in three parts;

$\$2,400 \div 3 = \$800.$

or

$10(\$800) = \$8,000;$

$2(800) = \$1,600;$

so, there are twelve $800's.

or

I put $500 in each of the 12 piles, totaling $6,000;

I put $200 more in each, totaling $2,400;

then I took the $1,200 left and put $100 more in each pile;

$\$6,000 + \$2,400 + \$1,200 = \$9,600.$

**$9,600 in 24 monthly payments means $400 per month**

I see that 24 payments is twice as many as 12 payments, so I cut each of the $800 payments in half.

If $\$9,600 \div 12 = \$800$, then $\$9,600 \div 24 = \$400.$

or

$\$100 \times 24 = \$2,400;$

$\$200 \times 24 = \$4,800;$

$\$400 \times 24 = \$9,600.$

Make sure everyone attends to the presenters' reasoning. Encourage critique and questions if a presenter's explanation is unclear. If there are disagreements or questions about answers or methods, ask for justification with diagrams.

Then ask for generalizations:

 **Do you see any patterns here?**

Students might say:

> "When you double the number of parts, you halve the amount of the payments."
>
> "The more payments you have, the smaller the payment."
>
> "Fewer payments mean you pay more each time."

Someone might point out that in reality paying on time doesn't quite work this way because the longer someone takes to pay, the more interest is charged. This activity does not take interest into account.

Acknowledge any paper-and-pencil methods. Depending on where and when they went to school, students may have learned different algorithms. Ask them to show those.

 **Who has a paper-and-pencil method that works well?**

**When you used the calculator, what did you have to keep in mind?**

You are trying to elicit the idea that order made a difference when keying numbers in the calculator. Summarize by remarking on the variety of ways a number can be divided or split.

## Activity 2: The Payment Plan Game

Explain that in this activity, the class will practice mental math by playing *The Payment Plan Game*. Students will draw on what they know about multiplying by 10 and 100.

Form three teams. Refer everyone to *Activity 2: The Payment Plan Game* (*Student Book*, p. 142). Review game directions and the scoring system.

Post the following Score Sheet. You can make transparencies of *10-Month Payment Plan Game Score Sheet* (*Blackline Master 11*) and *100-Month Payment Plan Game Score Sheet* (*Blackline Master 12*) or reproduce them on the board. Refer to them when sharing directions.

| | Total Cost | Team's Answer | Challenge/Pass? | Score |
|---|---|---|---|---|
| **10-Month Payment Plan** | | | | |
| Team 1 | | | | |
| Team 2 | | | | |
| Team 3 | | | | |

## Heads Up!

During the game, you might record mental math processes off to the side of the board, so they can be erased when the final, correct estimate is established.

### The Payment Plan Game

One at a time, each team will be asked to figure out the cost of one monthly payment from a total cost that you provide. Teams try to get as close as they can to the right answer but may only use mental math. No one may use pencils and paper or a calculator.

The team, after conferring, will share its final answer, as well as the strategy or strategies used to find the answer.

Opposing teams have the right to challenge the answer but must also share their strategies.

After all teams have either challenged or accepted (passed) the original team's answer, you will provide the correct answer. Then points are assigned for the round.

As a class, set parameters for good estimates. Often students say that answers must be correct to the nearest dollar, although differences in opinion may arise about whether the answer must be "the closest without going over." Be flexible with the rules. If students begin to question rules or previously set parameters, revisit and reset them democratically. Issues such as re-challenges may also arise; reach consensus on these as well.

A practice round might go something like this:

- You write "$111" as the total cost.
- Team 1 confers.

- "Our team guesses that the answer must be about $11 a month."
- Team 2 passes, accepting $11 as a good estimate.
- Team 3 challenges, saying that the extra $1 could be split into 10 cents. Their answer is $11.10.

- You then reveal the answer of $11.10. Team 1 gets five points for a good estimate—being close to the right answer; Team 2 gets nothing; Team 3 gets 10 points for having an answer even closer to the correct amount than Team 1's estimate.

The board with scoring for this example would look like this:

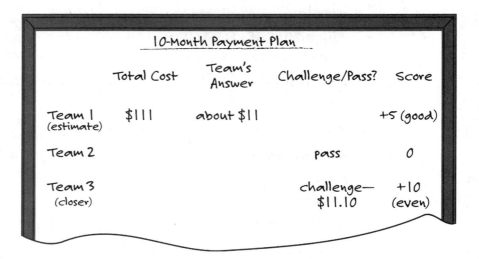

| | Total Cost | Team's Answer | Challenge/Pass? | Score |
|---|---|---|---|---|
| | 10-Month Payment Plan | | | |
| Team 1 (estimate) | $111 | about $11 | | +5 (good) |
| Team 2 | | | pass | 0 |
| Team 3 (closer) | | | challenge— $11.10 | +10 (even) |

Start the game by using the following totals for the 10-month payment plan rounds. Exact answers, to be revealed after every team has had a turn, are in parentheses:

Round 1:     $48 ($4.80)          $33 ($3.30)          $87 ($8.70)

Round 2:     $121 ($12.10)        $152 ($15.20)        $203 ($20.30)

Round 3:     $988 ($98.80)        $1,003 ($100.30)     $1,129 ($112.90)

---

## Heads Up!

It is important to use the numbers given because later rounds build from these.

---

As students share their thinking, name the concepts applied:

"Here you rounded the number to ___."

"So, you broke this number into two smaller amounts, ___ and ___, and then divided each by 10."

"In this case, you multiplied ___ by 10 and saw it was not enough, so you tried ___."

As the game progresses, remind teams that are struggling of methods used in past rounds by saying, for example:

 **A few rounds ago Team ___ solved the problem by rounding the number and then breaking it into two smaller amounts. How might that method help here?**

Present some *100-Month Payment Plan* rounds.

Use the following numbers for this part of the game.

| | | | |
|---|---|---|---|
| Round 1: | $480 ($4.80) | $330 ($3.30) | $870 ($8.70) |
| Round 2: | $1,210 ($12.10) | $1,520 ($15.20) | $2,030 ($20.30) |
| Round 3: | $9,880 ($98.80) | $10,030 ($100.30) | $11,290 ($112.90) |

Compare 100-month answers with those in the 10-month payment plan rounds. Promote consideration of place value by asking questions such as these:

 **Why are the answers the same in both the 10-month and 100-month rounds although the rounds' numbers are different?**

 **What is a rule you could use for dividing an amount by 10?**

 **What is a rule you could use for dividing an amount by 100?**

Post these rules.

## Summary Discussion

Ask students to answer the following questions and to provide examples or models:

 **What are some ways you can find a division answer if you have no paper and pencil or calculator?**

 **How do you know whether the exact answer would be a little less or a little more than an estimate?**

Listen carefully to get an idea of what students understand.

Close by asking students to write in *Reflections* (*Student Book*, p. 185), where they consider ways to respond to a division problem presented in a workplace.

Say:

 **In the *Reflections* section, grade yourself on your ability to use mental math to solve division problems. Do you need to improve? Do you see yourself getting better at this as you practice?**

# Practice

*Four Ways to Write Division*, p. 143
For practice writing division with various notation.

*Which Is Not the Same?* p. 144
For more practice with division notation.

*Those Monthly Payments*, p. 145
For practice comparing payment plans, indicating whether the monthly payments are greater, less than, or equal to each other.

*10's, 100's, and 1,000's*, p. 146
For more practice breaking numbers apart to multiply and divide mentally.

# Mental Math Practice

*Flowers by the Month*, p. 147
For more practice multiplying and dividing using number patterns.

# Test Practice

*Test Practice*, p. 148

# Looking Closely

Observe whether students are able to

### Connect division to the act of splitting or dealing out an amount

Use manipulatives to reinforce how the operation of division relates to the act of splitting into equal amounts. This is the most basic and important idea of the lesson.

To cement the connection between the payment plan problems and the "dealing" division model, use play money and month markers to represent the situations.

Spiral back to multiplication strategies. Though this lesson centers on ways to divide mentally, the contexts can also be used to reinforce multiplication strategies by asking students how much a yearly bill would be if each month they paid $X$ amount. In this way, they further practice breaking numbers apart, such as 12 into 10 and 2, in order to multiply. The fact that they cannot divide by 10 and then by 2 to divide by 12 raises some interesting questions. Explore these questions, only if they arise, with small totals.

## Match the verbal language and symbolic notation for division to a concrete model

Are students secure with the order in division notation? During the *Opening Discussion* session, emphasize the need for common understanding when someone writes or speaks about division. If, for instance, someone reads a problem as "12 divided into 3," it is commonly understood to mean $12\overline{\smash{)}3}$ or $3 \div 12$. If a student means to read the problem $12 \div 3$ and be understood, one might expect to hear "three divided into twelve" or "three into twelve" or "twelve divided by three," etc. Making the notation connections between expressions remains important as well. Which number belongs *inside* the box when writing out a division problem? Although such issues are less likely to arise when solving contextualized problems, students often encounter problems translating division expressions during testing situations.

Keep the meaning of the situation by restating the problems, emphasizing what is known: the total payment and the number of groups or the number of payments.

## Apply mental math strategies for division to situations calling for splitting dollar amounts over 4, 8, 12, 24, 10, or 100 time periods

Can students use what they know about multiplying by multiples of 10 and 100 to find a partial answer? Review mental math strategies for multiplication.

Do students draw on multiplication to solve problems and check their answers? Draw out silent class members with direct questions such as, "How did _____ use multiplication here?" or "How could you check _____'s work to see whether she is right?"

Do students see that breaking up numbers works along place value lines? Suggest approaches such as this:

> **The 10-month payment plan total is \$988. How much would you pay per month to pay back \$900? Eighty dollars? Eight dollars? How much would you pay per month to pay back \$988?**

Can students round and adjust appropriately? Rounding to a friendly number is the first step. Discuss the pros and cons of rounding with students, and make clear the difference between situations where a precise answer is necessary and those where an approximation will do. Another issue with rounding that may arise involves the question "Round to what?" Discuss in a case-by-case way with students whether they should round to the nearest multiple of 5, 10, or 100 and why.

To know whether to adjust by adding or subtracting, students must be aware of whether they rounded up or down and how that is likely to influence their answer. Talking through your reasoning may help. Also, reverting to smaller numbers as examples may help students visualize the situation. Working on rounding and estimating and holding off on adjusting until the first steps are solid may help some students feel more confident about tackling division mentally.

| WHAT TO LOOK FOR IN *LESSON 10* | WHO STANDS OUT? (LIST STUDENTS' INITIALS) | | | NOTES FOR NEXT STEPS |
|---|---|---|---|---|
| | STRONG | ADEQUATE | NEEDS WORK | |
| **Number Development**<br>• Applies mental math strategies for division<br>• Accurately divides using splitting or dealing out models | | | | |
| **Expressive Capacity**<br>• Explains mental math strategies for division<br>• Matches verbal language and symbolic notation for division to a concrete model | | | | |
| **Notation Use**<br>• Uses appropriate math notation to describe division<br>• Aware of order (e.g., that $30 \div 6$ is not the same as $6 \div 30$) | | | | |
| **Use of Tools**<br>• Uses concrete models and pictures to illustrate division problems | | | | |

## Rationale

Numerate adults use mental math skills all the time. Although the calculator is a very useful tool, as are paper-and–pencil algorithms, mental math strategies are the real basic skills for adults as they estimate and think on their feet in everyday life.

## Math Background

Division problems are often classified into two cognitive models. One model is referred to as *sharing* or *partitioning*. In the sharing model explored in this lesson, the number of groups is given, but the number of objects in the groups is unknown. For example, "I have six payments to make. How much will each payment be?" or "I am going to cut this 10-foot board into four pieces. How long will each piece be?" The action here is one of dividing, splitting, or partitioning a set into a predetermined number of equal groups. In the sharing model, one interprets $12 \div 4$ as 12 split into four equal groups of three.

●●● ●●● ●●● ●●●

The other model for division, referred to as *measurement* or *quotative*, will be explored in *Lesson 11*. In the measurement model, the amount in each group is given, and the task is to tell how many groups there are. For example, "How many $50 monthly payments would you need to make to pay off $2,000?" or "How many 18-inch segments could you cut from a five-foot long board?"

In the measurement model, $12 \div 4$ would be interpreted as counting how many 4's there are in 12. There are 3 groups of 4.

●●●● ●●●● ●●●●

Numerate adults tend to blur the distinctions between the two models of division. They easily call on one or the other way to make sense of a problem, but adults who struggle with division may benefit from explicitly dealing with one model at a time.

In this lesson, students break apart numbers. Essentially they are using the distributive property. This is not so different from the algorithm, but it keeps the sense of the value of the digits intact. Reasoning that $9,600 \div 8 = (8,000 + 1,600) \div 8 = (8,000 \div 8) + (1,600 \div 8) = 1,000 + 200$ is an application of the distributive property of division over addition.

## Context

Dealing is a very kinesthetic way to internalize the sharing model; making monthly payments is an experience we have all had.

# Facilitation

Team discourse needs to be developed in many cases. Students become so immersed in the game that they often call out responses without consulting teammates. One teacher addressed this problem by always asking the team, "Is that your *final* answer? Does everyone agree? Talk it over." After several instances of seeing the benefits of team discussion, students tend to make more of an effort to check with one another before announcing their answers.

## Making the Lesson Easier

If students are struggling, start with several problems where the number of payments is two or 10. Use less challenging numbers until they understand the concept.

When playing the game, stay with 10-month rounds longer, and start with numbers that do not need to be rounded, such as $50 or $150. Demonstrate with play money. Ask students whether their answers will be in 1's, 10's or 100's first, and then count out the money in that denomination. Practice "dealing" the money to the months (use Post-it Notes or markers to stand for the 10 months), saying:

**So, $1 a month would be $10 for the term of the payment plan. What would $2 (or $3 or $5) a month total?**

Review multiplying a number by 10 and 100.

## Making the Lesson Harder

*The Payment Plan Game* can be made more challenging by playing a round with 12 payments, including total amounts in dollars and cents.

Students can challenge each other by making up some payment plan scenarios that include interest.

# Lesson 10 in Action

*Notice how the teacher guides the discussion to include everyone and extends beyond the familiar into algebraic expressions and non-U.S. (in this case Haitian) methods of expressing division problems. Following is a copy of the blackboard at the end of the Opening Discussion.*

| Math Symbols | Words |
|---|---|
| $3 \overline{)6}$ | How many times does three go into six? <br> three divided into six <br> three fits into six <br> six divided by three |
| $12 \div 4$ | 12 divided by four |
| $\dfrac{18}{3}$ or 18/3 | 18 divided by 3 = 6 <br> How many times does three fit into 18? |

**Teacher:** "There is more than one way to say what we see; math has different ways to say or represent an idea, but we need to make sure we all understand each other, so if you have something different (than what was posted at first) written on your paper, please tell me. Did anybody say that differently?" (The two other ways are shared, and the teacher remarks that the third statement is similar to the first.)

**Observer:** "Could we start a statement with the number six?"

**Student:** "Six people divided into three piles or groups."

**Teacher:** "So you could say six divided by three."

They move on to the second expression. A student posts "twelve divided by four."

**Teacher:** "If we say it like Pam did, how might we say it?"

**Student:** "Four divided into 12."

**Teacher:** "How about this one (the third expression)? Anyone know the last one?"

**Student:** "I know it's not multiplication or addition."

**Student:** "It's not a fraction, is it?"

**Teacher:** "It is."

**Student:** "Is it division?" (Teacher nods). "Okay."

*continued on next page*

*continued from previous page*

Students post their replies and make corrections. A discussion ensues about the fraction form of division. Students report that it is "not familiar," "not outstanding like a daily routine."

**Teacher:** "It's more like algebra, like this. (She writes $x/y$ on the board.) Use the language to say what that says."

**Students:** "$x$ divided by $y$."

**Observer:** "Can anyone put the second one in fraction form? In a box?"

Students offer up the new notation, which is correctly written.

**Student:** "Doesn't it all come out the same way?"

**Teacher:** "Yes, no matter how you write it, it's the same problem."

The class then launches into a discussion of the Haitian way of writing, and they practice with the Haitian form being changed into the American form and vice versa.

(They write: $12 \left\lfloor \dfrac{4}{3} \right.$ in Haiti, $4\overline{\smash{)}12}^{\,3}$ in the United States.)

*Esther Leonelli*
*Notre Dame Education Center, Boston, MA*

---

*The following discussions took place during the* Payment Plan Game. *Playing by class rules can sometimes yield an answer that is mathematically troubling.*

**Teacher:** "Who can estimate what you would pay for each of 10 payments on a layaway for $48?"

**Student:** "Three dollars."

**Student:** "No, four dollars."

**Student:** "Three is too low."

**Teacher:** "How do you know?"

**Student:** "Well, three times 10 equals 30."

**Student:** "Ten by four is 40."

**Teacher:** "How far off are we?"

**Student:** "Ten by three is 30."

**Student:** "That's too low. You have some left over. It has to be four."

Everyone agrees the answer is four. The teacher suggests five, saying that it might actually be closer; but the students insist that the familiar game rule "closest without going over" should hold in this game. The teacher accepts their ruling.

*continued on next page*

*continued from previous page*

Later, when mentally dividing $988 into 10-month payments, students explained:

**Student**: "It's close to 1,000."

**Student**: "A hundred for 10 months; it will be 1,000."

**Student**: "Ninety will be 900."

**Teacher**: "Which is closer?"

Though the answer to her question was 100, the students were playing by the rule that the estimate had to be the closest without going over the target amount; however, they continued refining their answers.

**Student**: "Ninety-four is closer—940."

**Student**: "Ninety-eight times 10 is 980."

*Esther Leonelli*
*Notre Dame Adult Education Center, South Boston, MA*

One teacher wrote of students' initial reluctance to perform division using mental math.

The students seemed very engaged in the work today. There were still a couple who insisted the only right way to do the problems was by long division. I had said that if you do the math in your head, you are less likely to make a mistake. The ones who ignored the instructions and used long division usually got the problems wrong. When I started to repeat my statement, most of the class finished it for me because one of their classmates had proven what I had said. The new student, who was not to be won over without a battle, said, "I know my way is right because my daughter is in grade three, and I do her math homework and she always gets an A on it."

*Phyllis Flanagan*
*Rock Valley Community College, Rockford, IL*

# 11

# String It Along

> *How will this woman use division?*

## Synopsis

There are two meanings of 52 ÷ 4 (or more generally, $a \div b$). In the last lesson, students connected this notation to splitting 52 into four groups. Another way to understand division is to think of how many groups of a certain size are in a total. In other words, one can also interpret 52 ÷ 4 as "How many fours are in 52?" Using this second interpretation of division, students find how many of one measurement are in a larger one.

1. Use measuring containers to begin a discussion of how to handle the question: How many _____ in a _____?

2. Students work in pairs with pieces of string, equations, and numbers to explore "how many ___ in a ____" using **linear measurement**.

3. Pairs apply division knowledge to solve map scale problems.

4. The class discusses how division is used to find the number of groups of a given size in a total.

## Objectives

- Work with direct measurements and scale to find the number of groups of a given size in a total
- Use mathematical symbols to express the action of division
- Relate division to multiplication and identify **factors** of 48 and 72

## Materials/Prep

- Measuring containers: 2-oz. jigger (or 1/4-cup measure), 8-oz. paper or measuring cup, and a half-gallon jug or bottle full of some liquid
- String (approximately five yd. per group of three students)
- Envelopes
- Tape
- A variety of road maps or maps of the United States

For *Activity 1*, prepare two envelopes for every group of three students. Envelope A should have four strings: a 48″ long piece, and shorter pieces 3″, 4″, and 6″ long. Envelope B contains four strings: a 72″ long piece, and shorter pieces 6″, 9″, and 18″ long.

---

## Heads Up!

Precise measuring of strings is crucial.

---

## Opening Discussion

Open by saying:

 **We have used division to find equal shares. Today you will work with a model of division in which you find how many of various measures are in a total amount. We know the size of the groups but do not know how many groups there are.**

 **For instance, I have a 2-oz. measure. How could I figure out how many 2-oz. measures of water would fill this cup?**

Solicit ideas. If no one mentions physically pouring, suggest it. Take a cup of water and keep pouring out 2-oz. measures until the cup is empty. Write numbers on the board that correspond to what you do.

1 c. ÷ 2 oz. = 4 times

or

8 oz. ÷ 2 oz. = 4 times

Repeat the process, this time using the cup and the half-gallon containers. Ask:

 **How many of these cups are in the half-gallon?**

Again, if no one mentions pouring, using the numbers, or a number line, probe by asking:

 **How could you use the cup and the half-gallon jug to solve the problem?**

**If you knew the cup held eight ounces, how would that help you solve the problem?**

Start a number line and ask:

 **What would a diagram of this problem on the number line look like?**

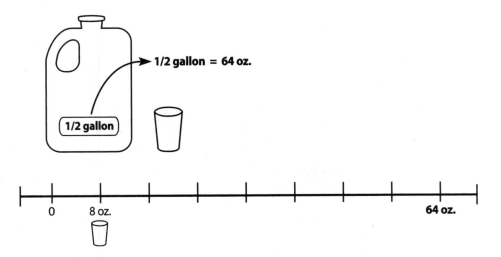

Mark the number line from 0 to 64 in increments of eight, as shown above.

Take a moment to re-read the problem emphasizing the language:

 **How many cups (8 oz.) in a half-gallon (64 oz.) jug?**

Write on the board:

$8 \overline{)\, 64}$

$64 \div 8$

## ⊚ Activity 1: String It Along

 **We just worked with cups and ounces, or liquid volumes. The next problems involve linear measurements.**

Connect the word "linear" with the word "line" to help students think of what linear means. Ask for some words for linear measurements, such as inches, feet, miles, centimeters, etc.

Form groups of three students and distribute Envelope A to each group. Say:

**Each group has a long piece of string and three short pieces of string. You will find how many of each of your short pieces could fit into your long piece. All you know is that the short strings are 3″, 4″, and 6″ long.**

**How long is the longest string?**

**How do you know?**

As students work, each member of a group with a different length of string, figuring out how many times their short pieces fit into the long piece, they may want to tape the longest string to a space on the wall.

Post on the board the question:

 **How many times does a _____ inch piece of string fit into a piece of string _____ inches long (the longest piece)?**

---

## Heads Up!

If someone posts a wrong number—something other than 12, 16, or 8—ask this student or another to check the results again.

---

Instruct groups to complete *Part 1* in *String It Along* (*Student Book*, p. 150). As you circulate, help with diagramming.

One or two students share their diagrams. Ask:

 **What does this diagram show you?**

Move on to writing math symbols. Ask for students to share the ways they wrote their problem in math symbols when using the 3″ string. Some may see this as a division problem, others as a multiplication (or even an addition or subtraction) problem. Students might write:

$$3'' \times 16'' = 48'' \qquad 4'' \times 12'' = 48'' \qquad 6'' \times 8'' = 48''$$

$$48'' \div 3'' = 16'' \qquad 48'' \div 4'' = 12'' \qquad 48'' \div 6'' = 8''$$

$$3''\overline{)48''} \qquad\qquad 4''\overline{)48''} \qquad\qquad 6''\overline{)48''}$$

In each case, ask students where they see the operation in the string situation.

 **Where do you see the multiplication?**

 **Where do you see the division?**

Ask students to generalize:

**As the size of the short strings gets longer, what happens to the number of times each fits into the long string? Why?**

Keep these equations on the board to refer to later.

Repeat the exercise, using Envelope B. After students see how many of each of the shorter strings physically fit in the longest, post all mathematical statements.

The board should be filled with statements such as these:

$$6'' \times 12'' = 72'' \qquad 9'' \times 8'' = 72'' \qquad 18'' \times 4'' = 72''$$

$$72'' \div 6'' = 12'' \qquad 72'' \div 9'' = 8'' \qquad 72'' \div 18'' = 4''$$

$$6'' \overline{)72''} \qquad\qquad 9'' \overline{)72''} \qquad\qquad 18'' \overline{)72''}$$

Conclude *String It Along* by introducing a question that leads to the definition of factors:

 **Look at the 48″ length. Would strings of any other size (cut in whole inches) fit neatly and exactly into the long one (besides the 3″, 4″, and 6″ strings)?**

Write down all suggestions, asking for verification. Possible whole number answers are 1″, 2″, 3″, 4″, 6″, 8″, 12″, 16″, 24″, and 48″.

Say:

 **In mathematics, whole numbers that divide evenly into a number are called the factors of that number. These are the factors of 48. Another way to say this is that the whole numbers which when multiplied together equal 48 are called the factors of 48.**

Ask:

 **What are the factors of 72?**

Write down all suggestions, asking for verification. Possible whole number answers are 1, 2, 3, 4, 6, 8, 9, 12, 18, 24, 36, and 72.

Ask:

 **Is 9 a factor or 48? Why or why not?**

## ◎ Activity 2: Scales on Maps

Now the context changes from string lengths to scales commonly found on maps. To make sure that everyone understands scale, ask:

 **How have you used scales on maps?**

Pass around a few road maps and, if you have a wall map, ask someone to find and read that scale as well. Students might share that they have approximated or exactly calculated distances using scales on maps. Start by saying:

 **When a scale reads "1 inch = 40 miles," how many miles would 5 inches represent?**

Suggest a few other amounts (6″, 10″, 20″), and ask students how they found the actual distance represented. Then ask:

 **If instead you knew that the distance between two places was 143 miles, how could you find how many inches that would be on your map?**

Ask:

 **Where and why did you use division in this problem?**

Refer students to *Activity 2: Scales on Maps* (*Student Book*, p. 152) and ask pairs to solve the problems, rounding where needed. When they are done and share their answers, ask:

 **What operation did you use to solve the problems?**

 **How are these problems like the string problems you did in *Activity 1*? How are they different?**

## Summary Discussion

Tell students:

 **Today you worked on two types of problems that used the measurement model of division. You found how many of the shorter strings fit in the longer string and how many inches or centimeters represented a distance given in miles on a scaled map.**

 **Many of you used division to solve these problems. What made them division problems?**

On the board write the following:

60 ÷ 5

Ask students to write two word problems and draw a sketch in the *Reflections* section (*Student Book*, p. 185) for the following:

1. Split 60 into five equal parts.

2. Find out how many fives are in 60.

Ask volunteers to share some examples of what they have written.

 **Practice**

*How Many Blanks in a Blank?* p. 154
For practice finding how many of one measure are in another.

*About How Many Times as Large?* p. 156
For practice finding out about how many times larger one amount is than another.

*Coin Rolling,* p. 157
For practice thinking with 5, 10, 25, and 50.

*Vacation Spots,* p. 159
For practice thinking about distance and time.

*Collecting Frequent Flyer Miles,* p. 160
For practice with larger numbers.

 ## Mental Math Practice

*Factors,* p. 161
For practice finding factors of some common numbers.

 ## Test Practice

*Test Practice,* p. 162

 ## Looking Closely

Observe whether students are able to

### Work with direct measurements and scale to find the number of groups of a given size in a total

Are students able to demonstrate the operations of division and multiplication using the measured strings? Are they able to "talk it out" as they do so? Make sure the words and actions are well connected. Help students see that the situation is one of dividing or measuring out a certain size group (length) within the larger total.

If students struggle with demonstrations, offer a diagram such as this:

Or use a number line:

Do students have experience with scales on maps? It might be helpful to examine some actual road maps.

## Use mathematical symbols to express the action of division

Do not insist on any one notation, but make sure all possibilities are shared. As students talk through how they solved the problem, model writing division in various ways:

- Horizontally, as in $8 \div 4 = 2$

- As a fraction, as in $\frac{8}{4} = 2$

- In the traditional way of writing division, as in $4 \overline{)\, 8}$

Also ask what the difference is between $8 \div 4$ and $4 \div 8$, and discuss this so students get a deeper understanding of division and how the order in which the numbers are written in a division problem matters. Be specific about the language: How many groups of four go into or make eight, as compared with how many groups of eight go into or make four? If students find it helpful, use objects to demonstrate the two situations.

## Relate division to multiplication and identify factors of 48 and 72

The numbers 48 and 72 used in *Activity 1* were chosen because they have many factors. This is meant to support the notion that multiplication can be used to solve division problems by finding the two numbers (the two factors) that multiplied together equal the total being divided.

| WHAT TO LOOK FOR IN *LESSON 11* | WHO STANDS OUT? (LIST STUDENTS' INITIALS) | | | NOTES FOR NEXT STEPS |
|---|---|---|---|---|
| | STRONG | ADEQUATE | NEEDS WORK | |
| **Number Development**<br>• Recognizes a problem about the number of groups of a given size in a total as a division problem<br>• Solves division problems efficiently using a variety of methods, including a physical demonstration<br>• Identifies factors of a number | | | | |
| **Expressive Capacity**<br>• Communicates about division problems and their solutions using appropriate language | | | | |
| **Notation Use**<br>• Uses division or multiplication symbols appropriately to express the mathematics in a problem<br>• Recognizes different symbols for division | | | | |
| **Use of Tools**<br>• Uses coins, string, and other objects to understand and demonstrate what a problem is asking and show its solution<br>• Uses a ruler to measure distances on a map | | | | |

## Rationale

Adults who can think flexibly about division can be more efficient in computing division problems. For example, $150 ÷ 75 is much easier to solve when you ask the question: How many $75's are in $150? It is more difficult to think about how much money is in 75 piles. Yet, many adults intuitively approach division using the model: How many *x*-sized groups are in the total given. Building on this intuition makes the repeated addition or subtraction in division apparent. The mathematical goal of this lesson is to cement a second meaning for the division operation.

## Math Background

Division problems are often interpreted using two models: *sharing* and *measurement*. In the sharing—or partitive—model discussed in *Lesson 10*, the number of groups is given, but the number of objects in the groups is unknown. For example, "We are sharing 52 objects among four people; how many objects does each person get?" This can be thought of as doling out one object at a time to each person in turn so that each person gets the same amount. We start out knowing we need four groups but do not know how many are in each group.

In the measurement—or quotative—model, the size of the groups is known, but the number of groups is not known. For example, "I need to order enough cars to transport 52 people for a field trip. A car holds four passengers. How many cars do I need?" In this case, the problem is to find how many groups of four will build to get to a total of 52. This model can also be seen as repeated subtraction or adding up.

Any decontextualized division problem may be approached either as a sharing or measurement model. For example, 10 ÷ 2 can be seen in each of these ways:

How do two people share $10? (sharing)

$$$$$         $$$$$

How many $2 piles are in $10? (measurement)

$$      $$      $$      $$      $$

As students understand the concept of division, they are more able to abstract the numbers and interchange the two models according to which is easier to visualize.

## Context

The premise for this lesson could be anything; some of the examples given here are liquid and linear measurements, coins in a roll, and distances on a scaled map.

This lesson is a jumping-off point for practice with maps and scale, ordering numbers, and multi-step problems, such as those that require students to find miles per hour and miles per gallon. The lesson could easily extend over multiple class sessions if all these possibilities are explored.

# Facilitation

## Making the Lesson Easier

Move from *Activity 1*: *String It Along* (*Student Book*, p. 150) to *Practice: Coin Rolling* (*Student Book*, p. 157).

## Making the Lesson Harder

In *Activity 2*, use actual numbers rather than rounded numbers. Compare results for rounded and actual numbers, and account for the difference.

Push for generalizations based on factors. If one factor is doubled, the other one is halved (6 x 8 is 6 x 2—or 12—multiplied by 1/2 of 8—or 4—or 12 x 4; likewise, 50 x 6 is the same as 100 x 3). Ask whether 40 ÷ 4 is the same as 4 ÷ 40 and why.

*Students try to make sense of cups and gallons and then lengths of string as the motivators for looking at division, multiplication, and factors.*

The teacher closed the cup-gallon demonstration, summing up, "We say this [amount] divided by this [amount], and our answer is how many *times* one goes into the other." She opened the string activity by saying, "I will give you a short and a long piece of string. You find how many times the short piece goes into the long one."

Student pairs determined how many times their short piece of string fit into the long piece and then posted their results on the board. The teacher taped the short pieces of string to the board and recorded the number of times each fit into the long piece posted above them.

The teacher wrote on the board:

"How many short pieces of ____ length are in this long piece?"

She had the students fill in their answers and then said, "So, we're supposed to write an equation. Let's do that together." Then she asked, "So what did you do?" A few students said, "We took the long piece." The teacher continued, "We started with this long piece of rope. What letter can we use to represent the long piece of rope?" The students chose "R," and the teacher wrote it under the posted data.

**Teacher**: "What did you do then?"

**Students**: "We found how many times it [the short rope] fit in [the long one]."

**Teacher** : "What are you doing there?"

**Students**: "Division."

**Michael**: "Adding—you're adding up the small pieces."

Esther did not hear Michael and so posted the division symbol after the "R" and then the length of the short rope, coming up with the following equation:

R ÷ 6″ = 8 times

Rope divided by a short length equals the number of times it fits in.

**Teacher** : "Okay. Write the equation you came up with on your sheet. Then see if you can figure out how long your piece was."

The students did this and then shared their equations and answers: "We said how many times does *x* go into 48, and we had the answer of six."

**Student**: "How long was the short piece? Eight inches because six times eight is 48."

*continued on next page*

*continued from previous page*

As students shared, it became clear that those who found an answer asked themselves the question, "What *multiplied by* six (or 24 or 16 or 12) equals 48?" Some even rewrote their equations after finding an answer by thinking about multiplication: $48 \div 6 = 8$ or $48 \div 16 = 3$, showing a deeper understanding of division and equations.

**Teacher**: "Why is this division, and how do you use multiplication?"

**Students**: "You have to make it equal" (referring to the equation).

**Teacher** : "How do you do that?"

**John**: "Multiply. You have the long piece, and you divide it by the short piece to find how many times it goes in. The whole piece divided by this (shows short piece)—find how many times it (shows short piece) goes in."

The teacher then made a diagram. She said, "Drawing pictures is a good way to solve a problem."

R = 48"

**Teacher** : "How would the picture change if we used 2" lengths?"

**Carol**: "It would make it longer." (I think Carol meant the small piece would fit into the longer one more times, but I'm not sure.)

**Teacher** : "But we know how long the long piece is; it's 48".

**Sandra**: "More pieces."

**John**: "You would draw more pieces."

The teacher shared the equation and changed the drawing, saying, "See how the picture changes?"

R = 48"

She then asked, "What happened to your answer as the little pieces got bigger?"

Everyone said, "Less," meaning the short piece went in fewer times.

**Teacher** : "What happens if the pieces get smaller?"

**Students**: "More."

*continued on next page*

*continued from previous page*

**Teacher:** "Let's generalize then. The smaller your piece, the more times it goes into the big one. The larger your piece, the fewer times. I have a vocabulary word for you: factors. When you have two numbers multiplied together to equal a number, they're called factors of that number. The factors of 48 are 2 and 24, 6 and 8, 12 and 4, and 16 and 3."

When I asked if those were all the factors, Michael, who is great with his times tables, suggested 1 and 48.

When asked what they were learning today, the students said, "Inches, ounces, feet, yards." Clearly the measurement context made an impression.

*Esther Leonelli, observed by Tricia Donovan*
*Notre Dame Education Center, Boston, MA*

# Making Do

> *What do I do with the leftovers?*

## Synopsis

Students refine their division skills by handling **remainders** with division in a sensible way.

1.  The class discusses past experiences with division when the results did not come out evenly.

2.  Student pairs look at various party favors and decide how to split them up sensibly among six children.

3.  Students describe remainders in words and with mathematical notation.

4.  Individuals apply these skills to another scenario that requires allocation of supplies and compare ways they handled the remainders.

5.  The class synthesizes what has been learned about division with remainders and writes a question or statement of understanding about remainders.

## Objectives

*   Deal with remainders in a sensible way, given the context of the problem
*   Write and understand remainders written as decimals, fractions, and whole numbers

## Materials/Prep

- Packs of gum (six pieces per pack) and Lifesavers™ or a similar type of candy that comes in rolls
- Small manipulatives, such as paper clips or chips
- Rope, string, or wire (something that comes in lengths that can be divided)

## Opening Discussion

Pose a question such as this:

 **Did you ever try to divide something that did not divide up evenly?**

Share several stories and then say:

 **In math, those leftovers are called "remainders."**

Connect the term "remainder" back to several of the students' stories. Post a definition.

## Activity 1: Party Favors

Refer students to *Activity 1: Party Favors* (*Student Book,* p. 164). Ask a volunteer to read the directions aloud, and when everyone is clear about the goal, have partners work together to complete the activity.

While they work, post on the board the three categories:

> E—evenly divided,      SL—split        CS—can't split
>   no leftovers        the leftovers      the leftovers

Bring the class together to share conclusions. Listen for and acknowledge disagreements, and encourage students to use pictures or objects to demonstrate their reasoning. All of the favors require dividing the total by six. Some of the favors can be easily redistributed in whole number amounts. For some, it makes sense to save the leftovers for another party. Other remainders can be split up and included in the party bags.

Ask first about the favors that divided up easily:

 **Which favors divided up evenly with nothing left over?**

Correct responses are the 30 stickers and the 60 marbles.

Next, ask about the favors where the leftovers could be split up:

 **Which favors had leftovers that you could split up?**

Correct responses are the 15 packs of Lifesavers and the 15 packs of gum; however, students may argue that there are no leftovers with the gum because the 90 sticks could be divided evenly among the bags.

Finally, ask about those favors where there were leftovers, but it didn't make sense to split them up:

 **Which favors had leftovers that you did not split up? Why?**

Correct responses are the 15 balloons, the 10 picture books, the 35 gummy bears, the 25 sparklers, the 15 quarters, and the five gift certificates. For instance, trying to cut a balloon into six pieces would be unrealistic. The gift certificates cannot be used at all for this party because there are only five, and ripping them into parts would make them unusable.

Encourage the use of demonstrations and pictures to support reasoning and solutions.

## Connecting Division with Remainders to Notation

When the class has agreed on the categories, connect division with remainders to symbolic notation, but make sure students relate their numbers back to real objects. Ask students to take turns coming to the board to write some division equations for each favor.

For those categorized as "E," expect:

$$30 \text{ stickers} \div 6 = 5 \text{ or } 6\overline{)30} \text{ or } 30/6 = 5$$

$$60 \text{ marbles} \div 6 = 10 \text{ or } 6\overline{)60} \text{ or } 60/6 = 10$$

Thoroughly talk through the examples of the packs of gum and Lifesavers. Have students do the division mentally and physically, opening the packs of gum and Lifesavers to deal out the pieces equally among the five goody bags. Then say:

 **You had 25 sparklers. You said each child received four and there was one left over. How could you write that in math language?**

For those favors categorized as "SL," there are several ways to express how much of each favor would be in each party bag:

15 packs of gum ÷ 6 = 2 3/6, or 2 1/2 packs for each bag (or 15 pieces per child).

Ask someone to use the calculator for the division. Connect 0.5 (five-tenths) with a half-pack of Lifesavers. Discuss whether or not student pairs' original answers on this support the calculator answer, how, and why.

15 packs of Lifesavers ÷ 6 = 2 1/2 packs each, or 2.5 packs

Listen for any of the three options: fractions, decimals, or writing "r" next to what is left to show that number is a remainder. Probe further, asking:

 **If we did not open up the packs of gum and divide out the pieces, if instead we kept the leftover packages whole, which way would you write that? Why?**

**Some people write remainders with a fraction bar. How would this look written as a fraction? When would you do that? Why?**

Make clear that the fraction 3/6 could be used to show either that they have three *out of* a total of six that they need or to show that they need to *divide* the three packs left into six piles. In either case, the children get two whole packs and part of another pack. Use labeled objects or diagrams to support the concepts—whole pack; half pack.

For those favors categorized as "CS," fractions and decimals do not make sense:

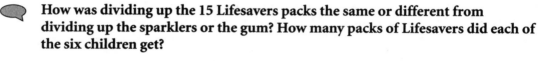

15 balloons ÷ 6 = 2 r3
(meaning two for each child with three leftovers to save for another time).

5 gift certificates ÷ 6 = 0 r5 (They cannot be divided by six because there are only five, and ripping them into parts would make them unusable.)

10 picture books ÷ 6 = 1 r4

25 sparklers ÷ 6 = 4 r1

Take time to put into words what the remainder means when notated as r___ .

Ask:

 **How was dividing up the 15 Lifesavers packs the same or different from dividing up the sparklers or the gum? How many packs of Lifesavers did each of the six children get?**

Pictures are absolutely necessary here to appreciate fully how remainders present themselves in different problem contexts.

 ## Activity 2: Making Do

Pair or group students. Assign *Activity 2: Making Do* (*Student Book,* p. 165). This problem is similar to the party favor scenario, but this time students must go one step further to divide up the supplies, deciding on a fraction or decimal to show the remainder.

Have partners compare ways they figured out and wrote their answers.

Review this activity with questions similar to those used for *Activity 1*:

 **Which items divided up evenly?**

**What did you do with those items that did not divide up evenly?**

**Which ways did you write the remainders? Why?**

Check students' decision-making processes. Regardless of whether you think so, in each case ask the class:

 **Does that way make sense?**

## Summary Discussion

Synthesize today's learning by asking:

 **What can happen when we divide up amounts of things?**

Expect statements such as these:

"Sometimes the items will divide up evenly."

"Sometimes there will be items left over because there are not enough to deal one out to everyone again."

"Sometimes you leave the remainders alone and do not divide them up further—like the sparklers."

"Sometimes you do divide up the remainders into parts of things—like a half pack of gum."

Ask students to write about remainders in *Reflections* (*Student Book*, p. 185). Reinforce the learning by asking:

 **How can you identify or write remainders in a division answer?**

##  Practice

*Interpreting Remainders*, p. 166
Asks students to do no division, but rather to say what the quotient represents and to restate the remainder in a different form.

*Pill Problems*, p. 167
For another context in which to think carefully about remainders.

*Meaningful Remainders*, p. 168
Provides practice matching reasonable ways to express the quotient.

##  Mental Math Practice

*Money in My Pocket*, p. 170
Provides a challenging experience with divisibility and remainders.

## Test Practice

*Test Practice*, p. 171

# Looking Closely

Observe whether students are able to

### Deal with remainders in a sensible way, given the context of the problem

Are students able to stay with the realistic meaning of the problem? Are they able to justify their decisions based on the context? That is the focus of the lesson, so take time for physical demonstrations.

### Write and understand remainders written as decimals, fractions, and whole numbers

Are students able to relate the different expressions of the remainders to the meaning of the problem? Spend time on breaking the answer apart. For example, in the equation 15 packs of gum ÷ 6 = 2 1/2, ask what the "2" means and what the "1/2" means. Is it two people, two packs, or two sticks? Is it a 1/2 pack or a 1/2 stick of gum? Students must be attentive to the context of the numbers.

Are students confused by fractions and decimals? The use of fractions in this lesson is limited to the fraction 1/2, which is relatively easy to demonstrate with visuals.

| WHAT TO LOOK FOR IN *LESSON 12* | WHO STANDS OUT? (LIST STUDENTS' INITIALS) | | | NOTES FOR NEXT STEPS |
|---|---|---|---|---|
| | STRONG | ADEQUATE | NEEDS WORK | |
| **Number Development**<br>• Sensibly interprets remainders in division | | | | |
| **Expressive Capacity**<br>• Justifies a particular expression of a remainder, given the situation | | | | |
| **Notation Use**<br>• Uses division or multiplication symbols appropriately to express the mathematics in a problem<br>• Can write the remainder as a fraction, decimal, or whole number | | | | |
| **Use of Tools**<br>• Uses coins, string, and other objects to understand and demonstrate what a given problem is asking and to show its solution<br>• Connects calculator answers with a decimal, such as 0.5, to the remainder | | | | |

## Rationale

Even the students most confident with division tend to look unsettled when they find they have an answer with a remainder, and this lesson seeks to raise awareness of the meaning of the remainder in a division problem. By laying out the three options for notating remainders and distilling the differences, students can make decisions on a case-by-case basis about how to treat remainders.

Several research studies have shown that students are often careless with remainders and offer nonsensical answers after doing the computation. Everyone should be helped to develop a deeper understanding of what quotients and remainders mean. Without this understanding, silly but common mistakes occur, such as, "11.5 buses are needed to take 322 children on a field trip, if 28 children can ride in each bus."

## Math Background

Most of the division in this lesson focuses on the partitioning, or splitting, model of division. When you split something up, what you do with the remainder is the central question. However, the issue of remainders is also central to questions in the form "How many ___ in a _____?"

Consider the question, "How many weeks are in a 30-day month?" One might answer "4" if one is thinking of full weeks, or "4 weeks and 2 days" to interpret the division $7\overline{)30}$ $\overset{4\ r2}{}$ . Another reasonable answer is 4 2/7 weeks, but somehow the answer in a nonterminating decimal, although mathematically correct, is contextually not very satisfactory (4.28572428451...). The context usually dictates the representation of the remainder.

## Facilitation

### Making the Lesson Easier

Spend most of the class time on the party favor scenario. Introduce students to the context and involve them in a multiplication and division review by asking students first to create a list of goodies for favor bags for five kids. Begin with the list on p. 164 (*Student Book*) and add to it.

Students should figure out how many of each party favor should be in each of the five goody bags. Then ask them, "How would you change the goody bags to keep things fair for six children?"

### Making the Lesson Harder

Increase the difficulty level and size of the numbers.

Give students a division problem such as 30 ÷ 4, and challenge them to write two different scenarios: one where the sensible answer is 7 r2 and one where the answer is 7 1/2.

# Facilitating Closing the Unit: Computer Lab

*How would you plan for your community?*

## Synopsis

Students draw upon their number skills as they work on a performance assessment planning project. Then they complete a written *Final Assessment*.

1. You introduce the *Computer Lab Project* to the class.

2. Student pairs complete four *Computer Lab Warm-Up* exercises.

3. Student pairs plan for the computer lab purchases and then write up a report to share with the class.

4. Individuals complete an assessment that mirrors the opening lesson's assessment activities and provides a direct before-and-after comparison of knowledge (optional).

5. The class reflects on what they have learned in the unit.

## Objectives

- Consolidate content taught in the unit
- Assess areas of strength and weakness

## Materials/Prep

- Calculators
- Markers
- Newsprint

For *Activity 1*, make copies of *E-Z Computer Mail Order Catalog* (*Blackline Master 13*) and *Computer Lab Scoring Rubric* (*Blackline Master 14*), one per student pair.

For *Activity 2*, make copies of *Final Assessment*, one per student. Make transparencies of *Mental Math Challenge* (*Blackline Masters 15–17*).

## Heads Up!

The closing will take two sessions.

## Opening Discussion

Explain that this final major activity in the unit presents a chance for students to show what they have learned. Working with a partner, students use mental math and estimation to figure prices for a computer lab and then use a calculator to make the final plan. They will make presentations to the whole class that will be scored. Then everyone will complete an individual final written assessment.

##  Activity 1: Computer Lab Project

Together, read aloud the scenario for *Activity 1: Computer Lab Project* (*Student Book*, p. 174).

Ask students to partner up. Distribute *E-Z Computer Mail Order Catalog* (*Blackline Master 13*), one per student pair.

Explain:

 **Before you start planning your lab, there are four activities to do first. These will help establish your mind set for planning. You can work on these activities in any order, but you may not use a calculator yet.**

Tell partners to read through the *Computer Lab Warm-Ups* (*Student Book*, pp. 174–178) and decide where they want to start. They will have about 20 minutes to work on these problems.

As they work, observe whether students are providing two solution methods when asked and whether they are using mental math. Encourage students to show their work or explain how they solved problems, so you can understand better how they are thinking.

After 20 minutes, bring the class together, and go over the answers and solutions.

Suggest to students that they reread the directions for the *Computer Lab* activity and begin their planning by reading through the list of necessary equipment and supplies. Remind students that they will present their final plans to the class next session. Distribute and read together *Computer Lab Project Scoring Rubric* (*Blackline Master 14*) by which the presentations will be judged.

Final plans are then copied onto chart paper for sharing with the class.

Each student pair presents their final plan to the class and explains how they made their choices. If they do not mention any estimates or calculations, encourage them to do so by asking questions such as these:

**What strategies did you use to figure out what you could buy?**

**How did estimation help you?**

**What helped you most to create a workable plan?**

**How did you keep track of all the prices to make sure you were close to, but not over, your spending limit?**

**Did you come up with any combinations of items that you wanted that were over your limit? What did you do?**

**What estimates did you make? How did you decide when to use the calculator and when to work in your head?**

**Once you made your choices, how did you find out whether you were over or under your spending limit?**

Other points to make that focus on the mathematical thinking include these:

Discuss when students multiplied and when they added, reinforcing the idea of using multiplication for repeated addition. Raise issues of commutativity and associativity by commenting:

**This pair of students added the items in this order, while this other pair added the items in a different order; did the order in which the pairs added make a difference in the total amount?**

**This pair entered "3" into the calculator first and then "699." What would happen if we entered "699" first and then "x 3"?**

If everyone says, "I just punched the numbers in the calculator," explore other ways they might have totaled amounts without using a calculator, as well as exactly how they entered numbers in the calculator in terms of keys and sequence.

Take this time to elicit from student pairs a few examples of equations that could represent all or a portion of the calculations. Assess skills with order of operations by having a few students insert parentheses on equations written on the board to indicate what operation would be done first by the calculator; or if the numbers are simple enough, have the class do the calculations using mental math and compare results with the calculator's.

For example, you might post 40 x 2 + 20 + 4 x 15 to represent the two surge protectors, one mouse, and four 25-packs of CD's that a group chooses to buy and then ask for parentheses or a comparison of calculation methods. You might suggest that you arrived at an answer by multiplying 40 x 22 and then adding 4 x 15; then ask, "What did I do wrong?"

Move the conversation to a broader topic by posing questions such as these:

 **How far apart were your estimated grand total and your actual grand total? Whose were the closest?**

 **Which plan seems to be the most reasonable? Why?**

 ## Activity 2: Final Assessment

The *Final Assessment* mirrors the *Initial Assessment* in the opening session. This is an opportunity for you and students to compare the quality of their work at the beginning and end of the unit.

Distribute a copy of the *Final Assessment* to everyone.

Explain that there are three tasks:

> Task 1: Mental Math Challenge
>
> Task 2: Picturing the Math
>
> Task 3: Four Problems

### Facilitating Task 1

Tell students:

 **I am going to show and read some problems. Your challenge is to do the math in your head and then write down the answers. Do not use pencils and paper or calculators!**

Starting with *Mental Math Challenge* (*Blackline Master 15*), cover up the problems with a paper, revealing each problem one at a time and reading it aloud. Allow a few moments for students to think about each problem and write the answer. This is not a timed test, but move along at a good pace. You are trying to see how fluent students are with the numbers. Continue with the next two *Mental Math Challenges* (*Blackline Masters 16* and *17*).

### Facilitating Tasks 2 and 3

Before students attempt the problems in Tasks 2 and 3, read through the problems together, asking students to self-assess how confident they are about solving the problems. They should check off "can do," "don't know how," or "not sure" without doing the problem. Keep the momentum going, reading each problem together and then moving on to the next one.

Then ask students to attempt the tasks. See the *Final Assessment Checklist*, p. 184, to evaluate work. Share these with students after you have reviewed their work. Consider scheduling individual conferences.

## Summary Discussion

Conclude by summarizing some statements about calculations that you heard students make today and in the last couple of classes that demonstrate all they have learned in the unit. Then ask students to add to these comments.

**Everyday Numbers**

Mental Math · Visual Models

3(4 + 2)

 ## Looking Closely

Observe whether students are able to

### Consolidate content taught in the unit

As students work on the activities, keep these questions in mind:

Are students demonstrating mastery of mental math and estimation, and flexibility with various solution methods?

Are they using visual models that match math symbols?

### Assess areas of strength and weakness

There are two guides for assessing student work.

For the *Computer Lab Project*, fill out a *Computer Lab Scoring Rubric* (*Blackline Master 14*) for each student pair. Use the *Final Assessment Checklist*, p. 184, for each individual student. Share these with students as a way to conclude the unit.

As you assess the various activity tasks, check for the following:

- Accuracy: Are totals and notation representation in equations accurate?
- Solution path choices: Are they appropriate and efficient?
- Flexibility: When asked for more than one solution method, does student represent multiple methods?
- Fluency: Did student work easily on each task or struggle with some? What blocked fluency?

# *Appendices*

**Name**                                        **Date**

# Everyday Number Sense: Mental Math and Visual Models

## INITIAL ASSESSMENT

### Task 1: Mental Math Challenge

After you see and hear each problem, do the math in your head and then write the answer here.

1. _____

2. _____

3. _____

4. _____

5. _____

6. _____

7. _____

8. _____

9. _____

10. _____

11. _____

12. _____

13. _____

14. _____

15. _____

16. _____

For Tasks 2 and 3, look at each problem and decide whether you can do it, don't know how to do it, or are not sure if you can. Check off the appropriate choice, and then complete the task if you can.

## Task 2. Picturing the Math

1. Tony and Marina each walk to the Learning Center for classes. Tony lives eight blocks from school. Marina lives 12 blocks from school.

   a. Draw a picture of how you see this situation.

   ____ Can do    ____ Don't know how    ____ Not sure

   b. Write a word problem for the situation. Then tell how you would solve it.

   ____ Can do    ____ Don't know how    ____ Not sure

**2.** Suppose the story read as follows:

Tony and Marina each walk to the Learning Center for classes. Tony lives eight blocks east of the school. Marina lives 12 blocks west of the school.

**a.** Describe or draw how that might look.

\_\_\_ Can do    \_\_\_ Don't know how    \_\_\_ Not sure

**b.** What changed from your drawing in Problem 1?

\_\_\_ Can do    \_\_\_ Don't know how    \_\_\_ Not sure

**3.** Write a number sentence to go with the picture:

\_\_\_ Can do    \_\_\_ Don't know how    \_\_\_ Not sure

**4.** Which picture is correct for 8 x 4 + 3? How do you know?

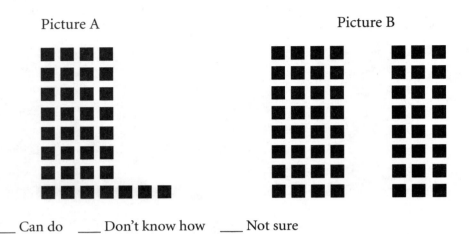

Picture A                      Picture B

___ Can do   ___ Don't know how   ___ Not sure

**5.** Make a picture for each of these expressions:

   **a.** 7(3) + 6               **b.** 7(3 + 6)

   ___ Can do   ___ Don't know how   ___ Not sure

**6.** Carl is 57 years old. His grandson is 39 years younger. Draw a number line showing how old Carl's grandson is.

___ Can do    ___ Don't know how    ___ Not sure

## Task 3: Four Problems

Show two different ways you could find the answer for each problem.

___ Can do    ___ Don't know how    ___ Not sure

| 1.  $382 + 49 + 118 =$ | 2.  $1,003 - 98 =$ |
|---|---|
| 3.  $78 \times 5 =$ | 4.  $689 \div 13 =$ |

# INITIAL ASSESSMENT CLASS TALLY

| Task | | Can Do | Don't Know How | Not Sure | Percent Who Can Do |
|------|------|--------|----------------|----------|--------------------|
| 1. | 1 | | | | |
| | 2 | | | | |
| | 3 | | | | |
| | 4 | | | | |
| | 5 | | | | |
| | 6 | | | | |
| | 7 | | | | |
| | 8 | | | | |
| | 9 | | | | |
| | 10 | | | | |
| | 11 | | | | |
| | 12 | | | | |
| | 13 | | | | |
| | 14 | | | | |
| | 15 | | | | |
| | 16 | | | | |
| 2. | 1a | | | | |
| | 1b | | | | |
| | 2a | | | | |
| | 2b | | | | |
| | 3 | | | | |
| | 4 | | | | |
| | 5 | | | | |
| | 6 | | | | |
| 3. | 1 | | | | |
| | 2 | | | | |
| | 3 | | | | |
| | 4 | | | | |

## Notes on Confidence Levels

# INITIAL ASSESSMENT CHECKLIST

Use a ✓, ✓+, or ✓– to assess how well students met each skill. When you give feedback to students, note areas in which they did well in addition to areas for improvement.

Use ✓ to show work that is mostly accurate; some details, additional work needed.

Use ✓+ to show work that is accurate, complete.

Use ✓– to show work that is inaccurate, incomplete.

Student's Name_____

| Task | Skills | Lesson Emphasized |
|---|---|---|
| **1. Mental Math Challenge** <br> 1 ____ <br> 2 ____ <br> 3 ____ <br> 4 ____ <br> 5 ____ <br> 6 ____ <br> 7 ____ <br> 8 ____ <br> 9 ____ <br> 10 ____ <br> 11 ____ <br> 12 ____ <br> 13 ____ <br> 14 ____ <br> 15 ____ <br> 16 ____ | Doubles and halves <br><br><br> Pairs numbers that add to 100 <br> Adds or subtracts a multiple of 10 or 100 from an amount <br> Multiplies by powers and multiples of 10 <br><br> Divides by powers and multiples of 10 <br><br> Estimates | 3, 6 <br><br><br> 2, 4, 5, 6 <br><br> 6, 7 <br><br> 7, 10 <br><br> All lessons |
| **2. Picturing the Math** <br> 1a ____ <br> 1b ____ <br> 2a ____ <br> 2b ____ <br> 3 ____ <br> 4 ____ <br> 5 ____ <br> 6 ____ | Connects diagrams, arrays, and number lines to word problems and mathematical expressions | 3, 4, 5, 8, 9, 10, 11, 12 |
| **3. Four Problems** <br> 1 ____ <br> 2 ____ <br> 3 ____ <br> 4 ____ | Knows various ways to add <br> Knows various ways to subtract <br> Knows various ways to multiply <br> Knows various ways to divide | 1, 2 <br> 3, 4, 5 <br> 6, 7, 8, 9 <br> 10, 11, 12 |

# OVERALL NOTES

## Strengths

_____

_____

_____

_____

_____

_____

_____

_____

## Areas for Improvement

_____

_____

_____

_____

_____

_____

_____

_____

_____

_____

**Name**                                          **Date**

# Everyday Number Sense: Mental Math and Visual Models

## FINAL ASSESSMENT

### Task 1: Mental Math Challenge

After you see and hear each problem, do the math in your head and then write the answer here.

1. _____

2. _____

3. _____

4. _____

5. _____

6. _____

7. _____

8. _____

9. _____

10. _____

11. _____

12. _____

13. _____

14. _____

15. _____

16. _____

For Tasks 2 and 3, look at each problem and decide whether you can do it, don't know how to do it, or are not sure if you can. Check off the appropriate choice, and then complete the task if you can.

## Task 2: Picturing the Math

1. John was born 25 years before his son Mark. John's father is 52 years older than Mark.

   a. Draw a picture of how you see this situation.

   ___ Can do    ___ Don't know how    ___ Not sure

   b. Write a word problem for the situation. Then tell how you would solve it.

   ___ Can do    ___ Don't know how    ___ Not sure

2. Suppose the story read as follows:

John was born 25 years before his son Mark, who was born in 2006. John's father is 52 years older than Mark.

a. Describe or draw how that situation might look.

___ Can do   ___ Don't know how   ___ Not sure

b. What changed from your drawing for Problem 1?

___ Can do   ___ Don't know how   ___ Not sure

3. Write a number sentence to go with this picture:

___ Can do    ___ Don't know how    ___ Not sure

4. Which picture is correct for 8 × 4 + 3? How do you know?

Picture A                              Picture B

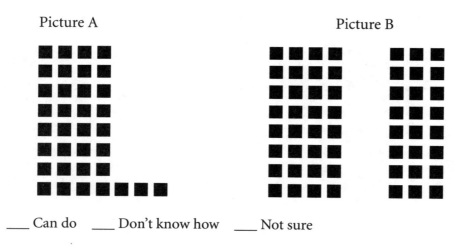

___ Can do    ___ Don't know how    ___ Not sure

**5.** Make a picture for each expression:

   **a.** $5(2) + 4$                   **b.** $5(2 + 4)$

   ___ Can do   ___ Don't know how   ___ Not sure

**6.** Carl lives in Boston, 200 miles north of New York. His mother lives in Washington, D.C., 175 miles south of New York. Draw a number line showing approximately how far Carl lives from his mother.

   ___ Can do   ___ Don't know how   ___ Not sure

## Task 3: Four Problems

Show two different ways you could find the answer for each problem.

___ Can do    ___ Don't know how    ___ Not sure.

| | |
|---|---|
| **1. 491 + 48 + 107 =** | **2. 2,005 – 97 =** |
| **3. 56 x 25 =** | **4. 736 ÷ 23 =** |

# FINAL ASSESSMENT CLASS TALLY

| Task | | Can Do | Don't Know How | Not Sure | Percent Who Can Do |
|------|------|--------|----------------|----------|--------------------|
| 1. | 1 | | | | |
| | 2 | | | | |
| | 3 | | | | |
| | 4 | | | | |
| | 5 | | | | |
| | 6 | | | | |
| | 7 | | | | |
| | 8 | | | | |
| | 9 | | | | |
| | 10 | | | | |
| | 11 | | | | |
| | 12 | | | | |
| | 13 | | | | |
| | 14 | | | | |
| | 15 | | | | |
| | 16 | | | | |
| 2. | 1a | | | | |
| | 1b | | | | |
| | 2a | | | | |
| | 2b | | | | |
| | 3 | | | | |
| | 4 | | | | |
| | 5a | | | | |
| | 5b | | | | |
| | 6 | | | | |
| 3. | 1 | | | | |
| | 2 | | | | |
| | 3 | | | | |
| | 4 | | | | |

## Notes on Confidence Levels

# FINAL ASSESSMENT CHECKLIST

Use a ✓, ✓+, or ✓− to assess how well students met each skill. When you give feedback to students, note areas in which they did well in addition to areas for improvement.

Use ✓ to show work that is mostly accurate; some details, additional work needed.

Use ✓+ to show work that is accurate, complete.

Use ✓− to show work that is inaccurate, incomplete.

Student's Name_____

| Task | Skills | Lesson Taught |
|------|--------|---------------|
| **1. Mental Math Challenge**<br>1 _____<br>2 _____<br>3 _____<br>4 _____<br>5 _____<br>6 _____<br>7 _____<br>8 _____<br>9 _____<br>10 _____<br>11 _____<br>12 _____<br>13 _____<br>14 _____<br>15 _____<br>16 _____ | Doubles and halves<br><br><br>Pairs numbers that add to 100<br>Adds or subtracts a multiple of 10 or 100 from an amount<br>Multiplies by powers and multiples of 10<br><br>Divides by powers and multiples of 10<br><br>Estimates | 3, 6<br><br><br>2, 4, 5, 6<br><br>6, 7<br><br>7, 10<br><br>All lessons |
| **2. Picturing the Math**<br>1a _____<br>1b _____<br>2a _____<br>2b _____<br>3 _____<br>4 _____<br>5 _____<br>6 _____ | Connects diagrams, arrays, and number lines to word problems and mathematical expressions | 3, 4, 5, 8, 9, 10, 11, 12 |
| **3. Four Problems**<br>1 _____<br>2 _____<br>3 _____<br>4 _____ | Knows various ways to add<br>Knows various ways to subtract<br>Knows various ways to multiply<br>Knows various ways to divide | 1, 2<br>3, 4, 5<br>6, 7, 8, 9<br>10, 11, 12 |

# OVERALL NOTES

## Strengths

_____

_____

_____

_____

_____

_____

_____

_____

## Areas for Improvement

_____

_____

_____

_____

_____

_____

_____

_____

_____

_____

# The number for today:

**1.** Double $10

**2.** Double $23

**3.** Halve $56

**4.** Double $1,500

**5.** Add 85¢ and 15¢

**6.** $1,500 − $20 =

**7.** $8,565 − $200 is

**8.** 10 times $25 is

**9.** 15 x $20 =

**10.** 22 x $100 =

**11.** How many $10 make $180?

**12.** $360 ÷ 4 =

## Yes or No?

If you have $10, do you have enough money to buy

**13.** Two books of stamps at $6.80 each?

**14.** Movie tickets for 4 children at $2.50 each?

**15.** 2 six-packs of soda at $1.99 each and 2 bags of chips at $1.49 each?

**16.** 7 tokens at $1.25 each and 4 transfers at 50¢ each?

1. $1.95 + $3.95

2. $12.75 + $3.19

3. $15.79 + $29.99

4. $11.88 + $18.00

5. $1.05 + $6.00 + $19.99

6. $4.00 + $8.95 + $5.75

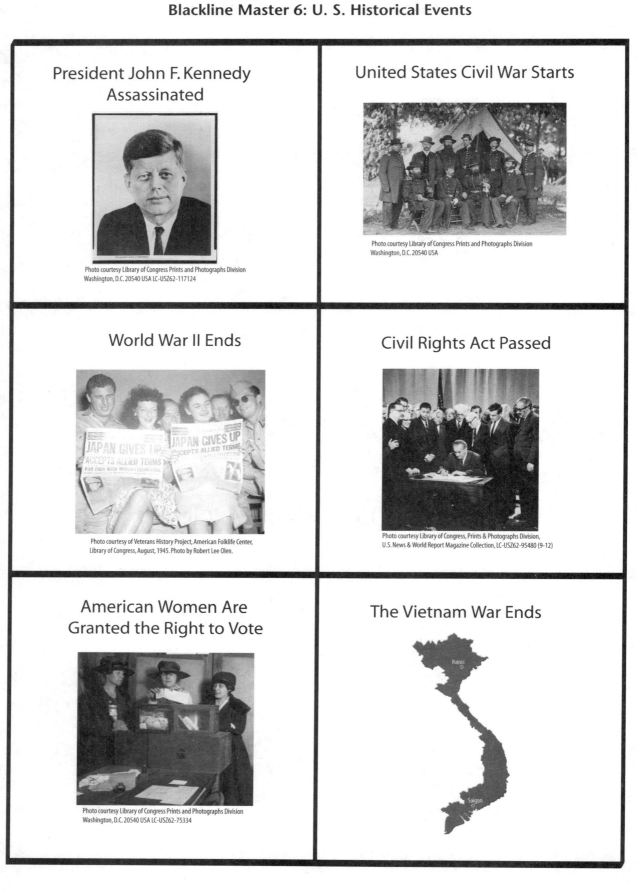

## President John F. Kennedy Assassinated

Photo courtesy Library of Congress Prints and Photographs Division
Washington, D.C. 20540 USA LC-USZ62-117124

## United States Civil War Starts

Photo courtesy Library of Congress Prints and Photographs Division
Washington, D.C. 20540 USA

## World War II Ends

Photo courtesy of Veterans History Project, American Folklife Center,
Library of Congress, August, 1945. Photo by Robert Lee Olen.

## Civil Rights Act Passed

Photo courtesy Library of Congress, Prints & Photographs Division,
U.S. News & World Report Magazine Collection, LC-USZ62-95480 (9-12)

## American Women Are Granted the Right to Vote

Photo courtesy Library of Congress Prints and Photographs Division
Washington, D.C. 20540 USA LC-USZ62-75334

## The Vietnam War Ends

# Blackline Master 7: Concentration Cards

5($100) + 2($1)

2($1,000) + 5($100)

50($10) + 2($1)

$5,200

5($1,000) + 2($100)

25($100)

$2,500

52($100)

502($1)

20($100) + 50($10)

52($10)

502

|  | Multiply by 10 | Multiply by 100 | Multiply by 1,000 |
| --- | --- | --- | --- |
| 7 |  |  |  |
| 19 |  |  |  |
| 24 |  |  |  |
| 261 |  |  |  |
| 501 |  |  |  |
| 2,500 |  |  |  |
| 2,505 |  |  |  |

# Ten-Month Payment Plan

| Total Cost | Team's Answer | Challenge/Pass? | Score |
|---|---|---|---|
| Team 1 | | | |
| Team 2 | | | |
| Team 3 | | | |

## One Hundred-Month Payment Plan

| Total Cost | Team's Answer | Challenge/Pass? | Score |
|---|---|---|---|
| Team 1 | | | |
| Team 2 | | | |
| Team 3 | | | |

# E-Z Computer Mail Order Catalog
*"For all of your computer needs"*

## Computers

(A) Desktop computer with CD-Rom Drive,
15" monitor (keyboard and mouse extra)
Super Savings!  **$699**

(B) Multimedia desktop computer with CD-RW Drive,
15" monitor with integrated speakers
Cutting Edge Performance!  **$999**

(C) Multimedia desktop computer Upgrade! Add a
17" flat panel monitor and CD burner!  **$1,399**

(D) Advanced Multimedia computer with CD/DVD-Rom Drive,
15" monitor, storage capacty of up to 4GB
Impressive Perfomance!  **$1,800**

(E) Upgrade to a 17" flat panel monitor
and CD/DVD burner!  **$2,000**

(F) Laptop computer with CD-Rom Drive,
15.4" screen  **$1,989**

(G) Laptop computer Upgrade! Add a
17" screen and CD/DVD burner!  **$2,275**

## Printers

(H) All-in-One Laser Printer
Up to 25 ppm!  **$1,299**

(I) Color Inkjet Printer
High Quality!  **$150**

(J) Color Inkjet Photo Printer, 2.5 LCD screen
Connect directly to your camera!  **$599**

## Digital Cameras

(K) Digital Camera 5.0 Megapixel, 6x optical zoom,
2.5" LCD screen  **$399**

(L) Digital Camcorder
Record directly to DVD!  **$1,400**

## Surge Protectors

(M) Essential 6-Outlet Surge Protector  **$18**

(N) 11-Outlet Surge Protector
with Phone and Coaxial Protection  **$40**

## Keyboard/Mouse

(O) USB QWERTY Keyboard  **$25**

(P) Cordless Ergonomic Keyboard  **$49**

(Q) USB Mouse  **$20**

(R) Optical Mouse—3 Button with scroll wheel  **$50**

(S) Expert Gaming Mouse—
Optical Trackball, 4 Button and scroll wheel  **$50**

## Ink Cartridges

(T) Laser Printer Ink Cartridges  **$90/each**

(U) Black Inkjet Printer Cartridges  **$24/each**

(V) Colot Inkjet Cartridges  **$25/each**

## Software

(W) Educational Software Package (for school practice)
Single copy (for one computer)  **$49**
For 15 computers  **$199**

(X) Game Software Package
Single copy (for one computer)  **$39**
For 15 computers  **$159**

(Y) Office Software (for creating office documents
like letters, reports, etc.)
Single copy  **$429**
Site license (110 computers)  **$2,500**

## Media

(Z) CD's (for storing information and documents)
25-pack  **$15/pack**

(AA) DVD's (for storing digital movies)
5-pack  **$10/pack**

## Paper

(BB) Standard Paper—500 sheets (1 ream)  **$5 per ream**

(CC) Bright White Paper—500 sheets (1 ream)  **$8 per rean**

# Blackline Master 14: Computer Lab Scoring Rubric

**Committee Members' Names:**

_____

_____

## Give 0–4 points for each area.

0 = not at all

1 = somewhat, but vague

2 = adequate

3 = well done

4 = exceeds expectations

_____ Selected equipment and supplies to meet the needs of the computer lab users

_____ Stayed within budget

_____ Used mental math to make reasonable cost estimates

_____ Used the calculator to arrive at exact costs

_____ Compared calculator results with estimated answers

_____ Clearly explained in words the reasoning behind the plan

_____ Clearly explained the plan with math notation and/or diagrams

_____ If an oral presentation to the class, answered questions from others fully

_____ Other _____

_____ **Total Points**

## Notes

_____

_____

_____

_____

_____

_____

**1.** Double $70

**2.** Double $45

**3.** Halve $38

**4.** Double $2,500

**5.** Add 65¢ and 35¢

**6.** $3,700 − $60 =

**7.** $9,770 – $400 is

**8.** 10 times $45 is

**9.** 15 x $30 =

**10.** 33 x $100 =

**11.** How many $10 make $270?

**12.** $480 ÷ 6 =

## Yes or No?

If you have $20, do you have enough money to buy

**13.** Two books of stamps at $13.60 each?

**14.** Movie tickets for 4 children at $4.50 each?

**15.** 4 six-packs of soda at $1.99 each and 4 bags of chips at $1.49 each?

**16.** 7 tokens at $2.50 each and 4 transfers at $1.00 each?

# Blackline Master 18: 0.5-cm Grid Paper

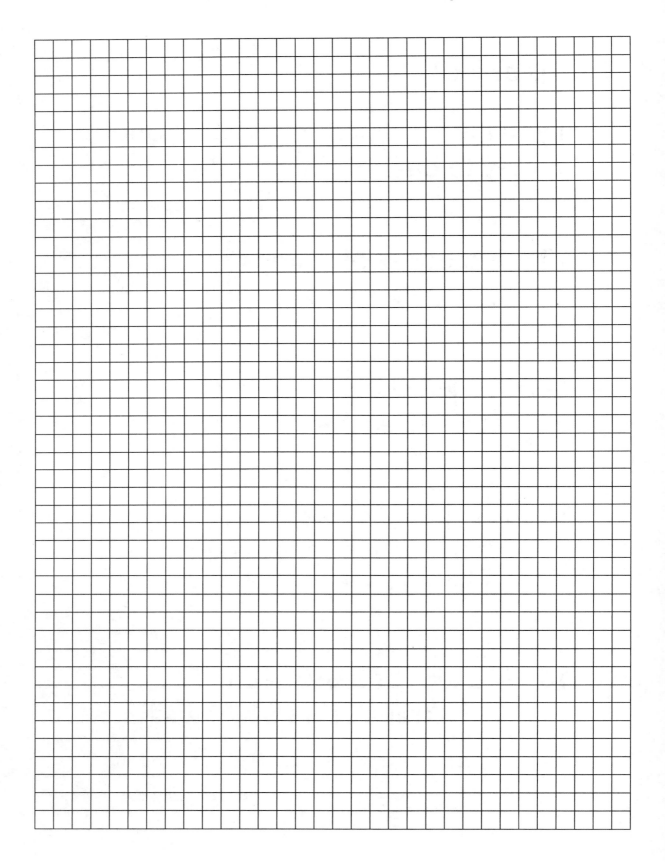

# Blackline Master 19: 0.5-Inch Grid Paper

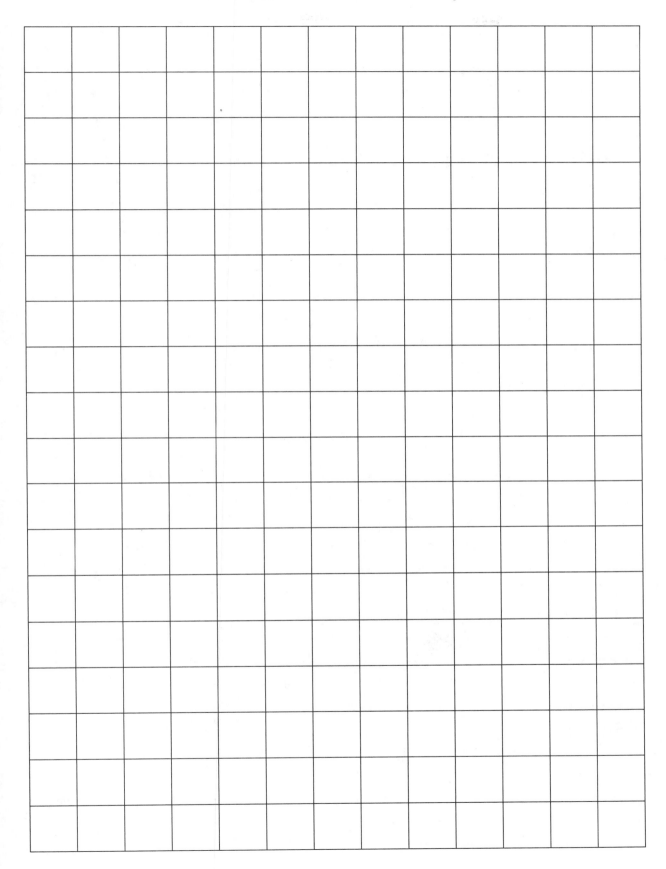

# Blackline Master 20: 0.25-Inch Grid Paper

# Blackline Master 21: Test Practice Answer Sheet

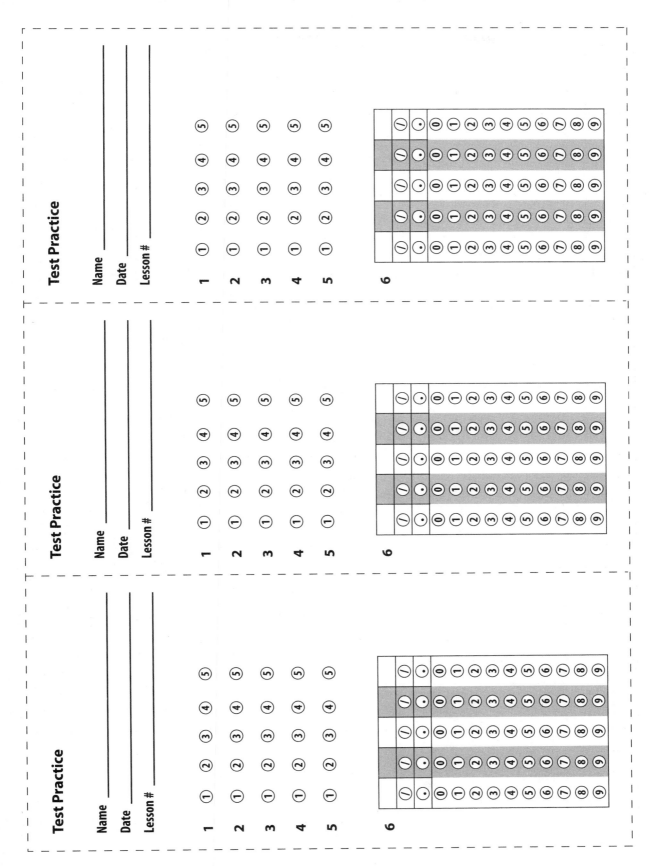

# *Glossary*

*Reminder:* Students generate their own definitions for terms as they arise in class, using language that makes sense to them. However, to help you guide the discussion, we include mathematical definitions for most of the terms.

Italicized terms are *not* included in the *Student Book* but are included in the *Teacher Book* as background information. The lesson number in which the term first appears is in parentheses following the term.

**10's place (2)**—in a number, the location of the digit with a value of 10. For example, in the number 593, 9 is in the 10's place and has a value of nine 10's, or 90.

**100's place (2)**—in a number, the location of the digit with a value of 100. For example, in the number 593, 5 is in the 100's place and has a value of five 100's, or 500.

**approximate (1)**—*adj.* not quite exact, but only slightly more or less in number or quantity. *v.* to make an estimate of something.

**array (8)**—an arrangement of objects in rows and columns. The following array has four rows and four columns, and 16 objects in all.

**difference (3)**—the amount by which one quantity is greater or smaller than another; the result of subtraction.

**equation (4)**—a mathematical statement that two expressions are of the same value.

**equivalent expressions (8)**—mathematical statements that have the same value.

**estimate (1)**—*n.* a number close to an exact amount. *v.* to make an approximate calculation of something.

*expanded notation (6)*—a way to write numbers to show the value of each digit. For example, $5,342 = 5(1,000) + 3(100) + 4(10) + 2(1) = 5,000 + 300 + 40 + 2$.

**exponent (8)**—a number placed to the upper right of a number or mathematical expression that indicates the number of times the number or expression is to be multiplied by itself. For example, in the equation $3^2=9$, 2 is the exponent.

**expression (Opening)**—a mathematical phrase that combines numbers and operations. More generally, a mathematical phrase that combines numbers, variables, and operations. For example, $3 + 6 \times 2$ or $500 - 75$.

**factor (11)**—one of two or more whole numbers that can be multiplied together to give a specified number. For example, 1, 2, 3, 4, 6, and 12 are the factors of 12 because $1 \times 12$, $2 \times 6$, and $3 \times 4 = 12$.

*linear measurement (11)*—a measurement of length, width, height, or distance. Some linear measurement units are inches, feet, yards, and miles.

*mathematical notation (Opening)*—the use of numerals, operations signs, and other mathematical symbols to write expressions and relationships.

**mental math (Opening)**—the process of performing mathematical calculations in one's head, whether partially or totally. The use of strategies which are less dependent on paper-and-pencil algorithms or calculators.

**multiples of 10, 100, and 1,000 (6)**—a number that can be divided exactly by 10, 100, or 1,000 respectively.

**negative numbers (5)**—numbers that are less than zero.

**number line (3)**—a line with equally spaced tick marks named by numbers. For example:

```
├──┼──┼──┼──┼──┼──┼──┼──┼──┼──┤
0  10 20 30 40 50 60 70 80 90 100
```

*number sentences (7)*—equations (or more generally, equations and inequalities).

**order of operations (7)**—rules for performing operations in mathematical expressions with more than one operation: First, do the operations within the parentheses; then, multiply or divide from left to right; then, add or subtract from left to right.

**parentheses (6)**—the symbols used to show which operation or operations should be done first. For example, $(20 - 4) \times 5 = 16 \times 5 = 80$.

**positive numbers (5)**—numbers that are greater than zero.

**range (5)**—the difference between the smallest and largest values in a set of data. For example, the range of the temperatures 32°F and 212°F is 180°F.

**remainder (12)**—the amount sometimes left over when one number is divided by another number.

**rounding (1)**—a type of estimation or approximation that makes it easier to work with numbers. For example, if you are counting clips and there are 148, you might round to 150, the nearest 10.

**square number (8)**—the number resulting from multiplying a whole number or integer by itself.

**sum (1)**—the total amount resulting when two or more numbers or quantities are added together.

***visual models* (*Opening*)**—pictures, diagrams, or concrete objects that make the mathematics in a situation visible. Examples of visual models for $3 \times 4 + 2$:

and

EMPower™

# Answer Key

## Opening the Unit: Everyday Numbers

### Activity 1: Where is the Math in Your Life?
Answers will depend on students' experiences.

### Activity 2: Number of the Day
Answers will vary.

### Activity 3: Initial Assessment

### Task 1: Mental Math Challenge

1. $20
2. $46
3. $28
4. $3,000
5. $1.00
6. $1,480
7. $8,365
8. $250
9. $300
10. $2,200
11. 18
12. $90
13. no
14. yes
15. yes
16. no

### Task 2: Picturing the Math

1. **a.** Answers will vary. Sample answer:

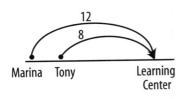

b. Answers will vary. Sample answer:
   How far does Marina live from Tony?
   $12 - 8 = 4$.

2. **a.**

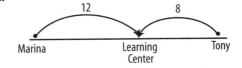

b. Answers will vary. Sample answer based on 1a and 2a: The distance between Tony's house and Marina's house increased.

3. Answers will vary. Sample answer: $3 \times 4 = 12$

4. Picture A

5. **a.** Answers will vary. Sample answer:

   XXX
   XXX
   XXX
   XXX
   XXX
   XXX
   XXX    XXXXXX

   **b.** Answers will vary. Sample answer:

   XXX  OOOOOO
   XXX  OOOOOO
   XXX  OOOOOO
   XXX  OOOOOO
   XXX  OOOOOO
   XXX  OOOOOO
   XXX  OOOOOO

6. Answers will vary. Sample answer:

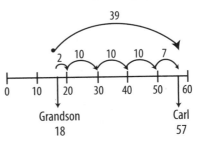

## Task 3: Four Problems

1. 549. Sample solution:
   $(380 + 50 + 120) + 2 - 1 - 2 = 550 - 1 = 549$

2. 905. Sample solution:
   $(1,000 - 100) = 900 + 3 + 2 = 905$

3. 390. Sample solution:
   $(70 + 8) \times 5 = (70 \times 5) + (8 \times 5) = 350 + 40 = 390$
   or
   $(80 \times 5) - (2 \times 5) = 400 - 10 = 390$

4. 53. Sample solution:
   $(650 + 39) \div 13 = (650 \div 13) + (39 \div 13) = 50 + 3 = 53$
   or
   $13 \times \underline{50} = 650$, $13 \times \underline{3} = 39$, so $13 \times \underline{53} = 689$

## Lesson 1: Close Enough with Mental Math

### Activity 1: About How Much?

1. c. $6
2. b. $16
3. c. $46
4. b. $30
5. b. $27
6. c. $19

### Activity 2: Wish List

1. Answers will vary.
2. Answers will vary.
3. Answers will vary.

### Practice: Nearest Dollar

1. $11
2. $1
3. $7
4. $0
5. $44
6. $30
7. $99
8. $610
9. $1,000

### Practice: Nearest Ten

1. $10
2. $80
3. $10
4. $0
5. $40
6. $40
7. $220
8. $600
9. $1,000

### Practice: Closest Answer

1. b. $50
2. c. 50
3. b. 75
4. b. 100
5. c. $45

### Practice: It's about . . .

1. a. 320
   b. 19 tables is about 20; $20 \times 8 = 160$; $160 \times 2 = 320$
   c. Above the actual amount because 19 was rounded up to 20.

2. a. $48 (or $50)
   b. Balloons are about $1 each; party favors are about $4.
      16 (8 children $\times$ 2 balloons) $\times$ 1 = $16;
      $4 \times 8 = $32$; $16 + $32 = $48$
   c. Above the actual amount because both the cost of the balloons and the favors were rounded up.

### Mental Math Practice: How Much Money Is in the Jar?

1. a. $6
   b. $5
2. $0.50 + 50¢ = $1; 60¢ + $0.40 = $1;
   $0.80 + $0.20 = $1; $0.75 + $0.25 = $1;
   $0.90 + $0.10 = $1
3. a. $4.50
   b. $5.00

### Mental Math Practice: Bigger Jars of Money

1. a. $50
   b. $600
2. $6.00 + $4.00 = $10.00; $7.50 + $2.50 = $10.00;
   $1.50 + $8.50 = $10.00; $3.50 + $6.50 = $10.00;
   $3.00 + $7.00 = $10.00
3. a. $45
   b. $450

## Extension: Big Bucks Estimates

1. a
2. $11 million + $9 million = $20 million + 14 million = $24 million + $2.5 million = a little more than $35 million
3. a
4. $879,000 is about $900,000. $154,000 is about $150,000. $53,000 is about $50,000, and $627,000 is about $600,000. So, $900,000 + 150,000 + $50,000 + $600,000 = $1,700,000.

## Test Practice

1. (2)
2. (5)
3. (5)
4. (2)
5. (1)
6. $88

## Lesson 2: Mental Math in the Checkout Line

### Activity 1: Math in Line

1. No, but almost enough. Explanations will vary. Sample explanation:
   The milk is about $2 and the cheese is about $3 for a total of about $5. Because the estimate is so close to the limit of $5, an exact answer is needed here.
2. a. Yes. Three loaves of bread at about $3 each is about $9.
   b. Answers will vary. Sample answer:
   She could round up to $3 for each loaf, but that is $0.02 more. 3 x 3 = $9 − $0.06 ($0.02 x 3) = $8.94.
3. a. $0.82
   b. Answers will vary. Sample answer:
   $5 − $4 (estimate) = $1. But each box cost $0.09 more than $2.00, so the actual cost is $4.18.
4. a. No. Each shirt cost about $7. $7 x 4 = $28, much more than $25.
   b. Answers will vary. Sample answer:
   He could round $6.95 to $7 and multiply that amount by 4 for a total of $28. Then he could subtract $0.05 four times because the estimate is $0.05 more than the actual amount. The total would be $28 − $0.20 = $27.80.

5. a. Olga had about $1.50 left in her wallet.
   b. The two books were $14, less $0.02; the two cards were $4.50. $14 + $4.50 = $18.50. $20 − $18.50 = $1.50 (and $0.02 from rounded amount for two books) for a total of $1.52.

### Activity 2: Rounding and Adjusting

1. b. $300
      $900
      −$5
      3($300) − 3($5) = $900 − $15 = $885
   c. $20
      $140
      −$0.50
      7($20) − 7($0.50) = $140 − $3.50 = $136.50
   d. $2
      $12
      +$0.10
      6($2) + 6($0.10) = $12 + $0.60 = $12.60
   e. $7
      $35
      −$0.02
      5($7) − 5($0.02) = $35 − $0.10 = $34.90
   f. $5
      $40
      −$0.03
      8($5) − 8($0.03) = $40 − $0.24 = $39.76
   g. $10
      $50
      + $0.25
      5($10) + 5($0.25) = $50 + $1.25 = $51.25

2. Answers will vary.

### Practice: Using Math Notation

2. 4($11) − 4($0.03)
3. 8($3) + 8($0.09)
4. 6($20) − 6($0.07)
5. Rounded down. Explanations will vary. Sample explanation:
   Because $0.02 had to be added to $3, the original amount was $3.02.
6. Rounded up. Explanations will vary. Sample explanation:
   Because $0.12 was subtracted from $32, the original amount was $31.88.

## Practice: Adjustments

1. **b.** 7 items at $1.05 each
    $1
    $7
    $0.05
    7 x $0.05
    7($1) + 7($0.05) = $7 + $0.35 = $7.35

   **c.** 2 items at $39 each
    $40
    $80
    $1
    2 x $1
    2($40) − 2($1) = $80 − $2 = $78

   **d.** 4 items at $2.19 each
    $2
    $8
    $0.19
    4 x $0.19
    4($2) + 4($0.19) = $8 + $0.76 = $8.76

   **e.** 5 items at $6.98 each
    $7
    $35
    $0.02
    5 x $0.02
    5($7) − 5($0.02) = $35 − $0.10 = $34.90

   **f.** 3 items at $9.97 each
    $10
    $30
    $0.03
    3 x $0.03
    3($10) − 3($0.03) = $30 − $0.09 = $29.91

2. Answers will vary.

## Practice: Exactly

1. Rachel bought two placemats for $4.07 each. She first made an estimate of $8 for her purchases and then adjusted by <u>adding 14¢</u> to get exactly <u>$8.14</u>.

2. Liu bought three pies for $5.98 each. He estimated they would cost $18 total and then adjusted by <u>subtracting 6¢</u> to get exactly <u>$17.94</u>.

3. Jon bought three cartons of milk for $2.95 each. He paid with a $10 bill. He first estimated his change by subtracting $9 from the $10 and then adjusted by <u>adding 15¢</u> to get exactly <u>$1.15</u>.

4. Ariel purchased seven packs of paper cups for $2.01 each. She paid with a $20 bill. She first estimated her change by thinking 7 x 2 = 14 and 20 − 14 = 6, and then she adjusted by <u>subtracting 7¢</u> to get exactly <u>$5.93</u>.

5. Answers will vary.

## Practice: Closer to $50 or $60?

1. Answers will vary. Sample answer: Troy may have left the radio price as $15 and then added $5 (for five cups) to get $20. Rounding $27.99 up to $30 would give an estimate of $50.

2. Answers will vary.

## Mental Math Practice: Fast Actions with 10 or 100

1. If you add $100 to $<u>5</u>68, you get $<u>668</u>.
2. If you add $10 to $2<u>8</u>3, you get $<u>293</u>.
3. If you add $100 to $<u>2</u>83, you get $<u>383</u>.
4. If you add $10 to $6<u>5</u>0, you get $<u>660</u>.
5. If you add $100 to $<u>6</u>50, you get $<u>750</u>.
6. If you add $10 to $3<u>9</u>6, you get $<u>406</u>.
7. If you add $100 to $<u>3</u>96, you get $<u>496</u>.
8. If you add $10 to $9<u>6</u>9, you get $<u>979</u>.
9. If you add $100 to $<u>9</u>69, you get $<u>1,069</u>.
10. 2
11. 7
12. 428

## Mental Math Practice: Fast Actions with 9 or 90

1. **a.** 75    **b.** 74
2. **a** 147    **b.** 146
3. **a.** 99    **b.** 98
4. **a.** 416    **b.** 415
5. **a.** 675    **b.** 674
6. **a.** 208    **b.** 207
7. Answers will vary. Sample answer: To add 9 to the number, first add 10 and then subtract 1.
8. **a.** 750    **b.** 740
9. **a.** 537    **b.** 527
10. **a.** 909    **b.** 899
11. **a.** 1,016    **b.** 1,006
12. Answers will vary. Sample answer: To add 90 to the number, first add 100 and then subtract 10.

## Extension: Weekly Totals

**1. a.** 28

   **b.** Answers will vary. Sample answer:
30 minutes or more is rounded to the next
hour, but less than 30 minutes is rounded
down. So, 5 hr. 15 min. is about 5 hr.;
3 hr. 45 min. is about 4 hr.; 7 hr. 10 min is
about 7 hr; and 5 hr. 15 min. is about 5 hr.
$5 + 7 + 4 + 7 + 5 = 28$ hours

**2. a.** 21 miles

   **b.** Answers will vary. Sample answer:
0.5 miles or more is rounded to the next
mile, but less than 0.5 miles is rounded
down. So, 3.1 mi. is about 3 mi.; 3.8 mi. is
about 4 mi.; 4.1 mi. is about 4 mi.; 2.7 mi.
is about 3 mi.
$3 + 4 + 3 + 4 + 3 + 4 = 21$ miles

## Test Practice

**1.** (4)

**2.** (2)

**3.** (3)

**4.** (2)

**5.** (4)

**6.** $7.12

## Lesson 3: Traveling with Numbers

### Activity 1: How Many Miles to Boston?

**1.** 13

**2.** Montana will probably take the longest time to
cross; Pennsylvania will probably take the
shortest time.

**3.** Somewhere in South Dakota. Minnesota is a
reasonable estimate as well.

**4. a.**

   **b.** 10–11 days

### Activity 2: Planning Where to Stay

**1.** Answers will vary. Sample answer:
Night 1—Post Falls, ID
Night 2—Butte, MT
Night 3—Sheridan, WY
Night 4—Box Elder, SD
Night 5—Hartford, SD

Night 6—La Cross, WI
Night 7—Chicago, IL
Night 8—Cleveland, OH
Night 9—Syracuse, NY
Night 10—Boston, MA

**2.** Answers will vary. Sample answer based on
sample answers for Problem 1:

**3.** Answers will vary. Sample answer based on
sample answer above: Yes, two nights in South
Dakota (depending on cities chosen, two nights
could be spent in Montana).

**4.** Hartford, SD (1,519 miles)

**5.** 10

**6.** Answers will vary.

### Activity 3: Rounding Distances

**1. a.** Washington: 300
     Idaho: 70
     Montana: 560
     Wyoming: 210
     South Dakota: 410
     Minnesota: 280
     Wisconsin: 190
     Illinois: 100
     Indiana: 160
     Ohio: 240
     Pennsylvania: 50
     New York: 390
     Massachusetts: 160

   **b.** Answers will vary. Sample answer:
If there were 5 miles or more in the 1's
place, I rounded up or I thought about the
10's on the number line and to which 10
the number was closer.

**2.** Answers will vary. Sample answer based on
sample rounding above:
$(280 + 70) + (100 + 300) + (410 + 190) + (210 + 390) + (160 + 240) + 50 + 160 + 560 = 3,120$

**3. a.** Washington: 300
     Idaho: 100
     Montana: 600
     Wyoming: 200

South Dakota: 400
Minnesota: 300
Wisconsin: 200
Illinois: 100
Indiana: 200
Ohio: 200
Pennsylvania: 0
New York: 400
Massachusetts: 200
Total estimate of miles: 3,200

**b.** Answers will vary.

## Practice: High and Not So High Peaks

**1. a.** Mt. David—48 ft.

 **b.** Bradbury Mountain—485 ft.

 **c.** Cadillac Mountain—1,532 ft.

 **d.** Mt. Apo—9,692 ft.

 **e.** Pico Duarte—10,417 ft.

 **f.** Mt. Etna—10,902 ft.

 **g.** Mt. Cook—12,349 ft.

 **h.** Kilimanjaro—19,340 ft.

**2.** Answers will vary. Sample answer:

**3.** Mt. David would be rounded to 0 ft.

**4.** Answers will vary.

## Practice: Checks—Say It in Words

**1. a.** Answers will vary, depending on how students rounded. Sample answer: $8,000 + $3,000 + $5,000 + $10,000 + $10,000 + $10,000 = $46,000

 **b.** $45,615

**2. a.** four thousand seven hundred nine and 00/100

 **b.** three thousand eighty-one and 00/100

 **c.** ten thousand one and 00/100

 **d.** ten thousand ten and 00/100

 **e.** ten thousand one hundred ans 00/100

## Practice: More Check Writing

**1. a.** $9,653.00

 **b.** $2,097.00

 **c.** $8,008.00

 **d.** $5,106.00

 **e.** $9,020.00

## Practice: Filing

**A.** 1998, 2992

**B.** 4107, 3002, 4080

**C.** 5555

**D.** 9777, 8989

## Practice: More Filing

**A.** 2110, 2992

**B.** 4459, 5551, 4397, 5555, 3878

**C.** 6632

**D.** None

## Mental Math Practice: Doubles

**1.** 0, 2, 4, 6, 8, 10, 12, 14, 16, 18, 20

**2.** 20, 40, 60, 80, 100, 120, 140, 160, 180, 200

**3.** 24, 42, 66, 88, 102, 124, 146, 168, 184, 206

**4.** 10, 30, 50, 70, 90, 110, 130, 150, 170, 190, 210

**5.** 32, 54, 76, 98, 112, 134, 156, 178, 192, 214

**6.** Answers will vary.

## Mental Math Practice: Triples

**1.** 0, 3, 6, 9, 12, 15, 18, 21, 24, 27, 30

**2.** 30, 60, 90, 120, 150, 180, 210, 240, 270, 300

**3.** 36, 63, 99, 132, 153, 186, 219, 252, 276, 309

**4.** 15, 45, 75, 105, 135, 165, 195, 225, 255, 285, 315

**5.** 48, 81, 114, 147, 168, 201, 234, 267, 288, 321

**6.** Answers will vary.

## Test Practice

**1.** (3)

**2.** (3)

**3.** (2)

**4.** (2)

**5.** (2)

**6.** 373

## Lesson 4: Traveling in Time

### Activity 1: Birthday Numbers

1. Answers will vary. Sample strategy:

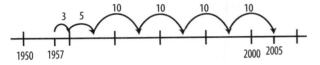

2. **a.** Answers will vary. Sample strategy:

   **b.** Answers will vary. Sample strategy:
   Go down or to the left 10 more (46) and
   2 more (48).

3. Answers will vary. Sample strategy:

4. Answers will vary.

### Activity 2: How Long Ago?

1. **a.**

   **b.** 145 years ago (based on year 2005)

   **c.** Answers will vary. Sample answer:
   100 + 10 + 10 + 10 + 10 + 5

2. **a.**

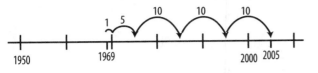

   **b.** 102 years ago (based on year 2005)

   **c.** Answers will vary. Sample answers:
   7 + 10 + 10 + 10 + 10 + 10 + 10 + 10 + 10
   + 10 + 5 = 102; or 100 + 2 = 102

3. **a.**

   **b.** 99 years ago (based on year 2005)

   **c.** Answers will vary. Sample answers:
   4 + 10 + 10 + 10 + 10 + 10 + 10 + 10 + 10
   + 10 + 5 = 99; or 100 − 1 = 99

4. **a.**

   **b.** 87 years ago (based on year 2005)

   **c.** Answers will vary. Sample answer:
   2 + 10 + 10 + 10 + 10 + 10 + 10 + 10 + 10
   + 5 = 87

5. **a.**

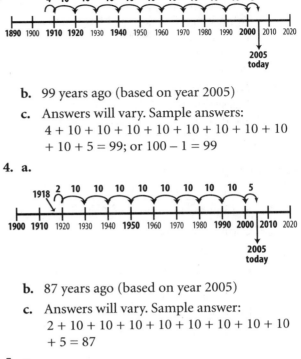

   **b.** 85 years ago (based on year 2005)

   **c.** Answers will vary. Sample answers:
   10 + 10 + 10 + 10 + 10 + 10 + 10 + 10 + 5
   = 85; or 80 + 5 = 85

6. **a.**

   **b.** 76 years ago (based on year 2005)

   **c.** Answers will vary. Sample answer:
   1 + 10 + 10 + 10 + 10 + 10 + 10 + 10
   + 5 = 76

**7. a.**

**b.** 70 years ago (based on year 2005)

**c.** Answers will vary. Sample answers:
5 + 10 + 10 + 10 + 10 + 10 + 10 + 5 = 70;
or 5 + 60 + 5 = 70

**8. a.**

**b.** 60 years ago (based on year 2005)

**c.** Answers will vary. Sample answer:
5 + 50 + 5 = 60

**9. a.**

**b.** 48 years ago (based on year 2005)

**c.** Answers will vary. Sample answer:
3 + 40 + 5 = 48

**10. a.**

**b.** 42 years ago (based on year 2005)

**c.** Answers will vary. Sample answers:
40 + 2 = 42; or 7 + 30 + 5 = 42

**11. a.**

**b.** 37 years ago (based on year 2005)

**c.** Answers will vary. Sample answer:
2 + 30 + 5 = 37

**12. a.**

**b.** 30 years ago (based on year 2005)

**c.** Answers will vary.
Sample answers: 10 + 10 + 10 = 30;
or 5 + 10 + 10 + 5 = 30

**Practice: Use Up the Space—Plan Well**

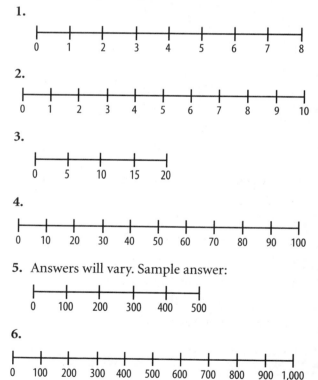

**1.**

**2.**

**3.**

**4.**

**5.** Answers will vary. Sample answer:

**6.**

## Practice: On the Number Line

**1.** Josey: 33; Tim: 52; Tia: 40; Anna: 74

**2.** 34 miles between Susan's home and Francisco's.

## Mental Math Practice: Count Up and Down by 10's

| 27 | 365 | 619 | 315 | 203 |
|-----|-----|-----|-----|-----|
| 37 | 375 | 629 | 305 | 193 |
| 47 | 385 | 639 | 295 | 183 |
| 57 | 395 | 649 | 285 | 173 |
| 67 | 405 | 659 | 275 | 163 |
| 77 | 415 | 669 | 265 | 153 |
| 87 | 425 | 679 | 255 | 143 |
| 97 | 435 | 689 | 245 | 133 |
| 107 | 445 | 699 | 235 | 123 |
| 117 | 455 | 709 | 225 | 113 |
| 127 | 465 | 719 | 215 | 103 |
| 137 | 475 | 729 | 205 | 93 |
| 147 | 485 | 739 | 195 | 83 |
| 157 | 495 | 749 | 185 | 73 |
| 167 | 505 | 759 | 175 | 63 |

## Mental Math Practice: By What Did I Count?

**1.** 83; counted by 10's

**2.** 100; counted by 30's

**3.** 414; counted by 100's

**4.** 230; counted back by 10's

**5.** 297; counted back by 40's

**6.** 996; counted back by 10's

**7.** 906; counted back by 100's

## Extension: Life Line

**1.** Answers will vary.

**2.** Answers will vary.

**3. a.** Answers will vary.

   **b.** Answers will vary.

## Test Practice

**1.** (2)

**2.** (3)

**3.** (4)

**4.** (4)

**5.** (2)

**6.** 115

## Lesson 5: Extending the Line

### Activity 1: In the Red

**1.** Balance: −$75

**2.** Balance: $875

**3.** Balance: $150

**4.** Balance: −$300

**5.** Balance $500

**6.** No, he only had $500 in his checking account.

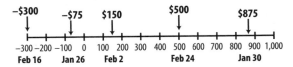

### Activity 2: Record Highs, Record Lows

**Part 1**

**1.** Answers will vary. Sample answer of 58°F shown on thermometer.

**2.** See thermometer.

**3.** See thermometer.

**4.** Answers will vary. Sample answer of 109°F shown on thermometer.

**5.** Answers will vary. Sample answer of −12°F shown on thermometer.

**6.** Answers will vary. Sample answer based on samples above: 121°F. From 0°F to 109°F = 109°F; from 0°F to −12°F is 12°F. 109°F + 12°F = 121°F.

**7.** Answers will vary.

**Part 2**

**8.** 136°F

**9.** −129°F

**10.**

11. c

12. 265°F; 136°F + 129°F = 265°F

13. Answers will vary. Sample answer: The difference in temperatures between Death Valley 134°F, and Northrice, Greenland –87°F, is 221°F. 134°F + 87°F = 221°F

14. Answers will vary. Sample answer: When you compare temperatures below 0°F with temperatures above 0°F, you add the two temperatures. When you compare the difference between two temperatures that are either both above 0°F or below 0°F, you subtract to find the difference.

## Practice: Planting Zones

1.

2. 50°F (–30°F compared to 20°F)

3. No, the temperature went down to –45°F which is below the average minimum temperature.

4. Yes, the temperature dropped down to about –5°F, which is still above the average minimum temperature.

## Practice: What's the Range?

1. 175°F

2. 182 kwh

3. 16″

## Practice: Ordering Numbers

1.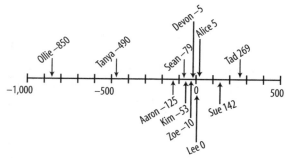

2. $1,850

3. **a.** Ollie: –$850
   **b.** Tanya: –$490
   **c.** Aaron: –$125
   **d.** Sean: –$79

**e.** Kim: –$53
**f.** Zoe: –$10
**g.** Devon: –$5
**h.** Lee: $0
**i.** Alice: $5
**j.** Sue: $142
**k.** Tad: $269
**l.** Cally: $1,000

**Mental Math Practice: Count Up and Down by 10's**

| –100 | –75 | –11 | 27 | 123 | 2,045 |
|------|-----|-----|-----|-----|-------|
| –90 | –65 | –1 | 17 | 113 | 2,035 |
| –80 | –55 | 9 | 7 | 103 | 2,025 |
| –70 | –45 | 19 | –3 | 93 | 2,015 |
| –60 | –35 | 29 | –13 | 83 | 2,005 |
| –50 | –25 | 39 | –23 | 73 | 1,995 |
| –40 | –15 | 49 | –33 | 63 | 1,985 |
| –30 | –5 | 59 | –43 | 53 | 1,975 |
| –20 | 5 | 69 | –53 | 43 | 1,965 |
| –10 | 15 | 79 | –63 | 33 | 1,955 |
| 0 | 25 | 89 | –73 | 23 | 1,945 |
| 10 | 35 | 99 | –83 | 13 | 1,935 |
| 20 | 45 | 109 | –93 | 3 | 1,925 |
| 30 | 55 | 119 | –103 | –7 | 1,915 |
| 40 | 65 | 129 | –113 | –17 | 1,905 |

## Extension: Sorry, Account Overdrawn

Dear Sir or Madam:

It has come to our attention that your account is now overdrawn for the amount of –$300. During the past weeks, you made several deposits, but also several withdrawals (reflecting the checks you wrote).

You had a balance of $500 in your checking account at the start of the month. You then made four deposits, each for $100, giving you a new balance of $900. However, you wrote 6 checks for $200 each, which means you made withdrawals totaling $1,200. This left you with a net balance of –$300 (the amount you are overdrawn).

It is our duty to inform you when you have overdrawn your account and show a negative balance. We are sure you are aware of bank policy regarding overdrawn accounts: We impose a one-time charge of $50 plus $15 for each check you bounce.

Therefore, because two of your checks bounced, we will be placing an additional total charge on your account of $80. Please note this deduction in your checkbook. We trust you will be making a deposit soon to cover these charges and the overdrawn amount.

Sincerely,

*Hedley Snobington*, Bank President

### Extension: Below Sea Level

1. 144′
2. 980′
3. 30,000′
4. 6; answers will vary.

### Test Practice

1. (4)
2. (3)
3. (3)
4. (2)
5. (5)
6. 221

## Lesson 6: Take Your Winnings

### Activity 1: How Do You Take Your Winnings?

1. Andrea: three $1,000 bills, eight $100 bills, four $10 bills and three $1 bills; Barbara: 38 $100 bills, four $10 bills and three $1 bills; Carla: 384 $10 bills and three $1 bills

2. Andrea: two $1,000 dollar bills, one $100 dollar bill, and five $1 bills; Barbara: 21 $100 dollar bills and five $1 bills; Carla: 210 $10 bills and five $1 bills

3. Andrea: 11 $1,000 bills, three $10 bills and five $1 bills; Barbara: 110 $100 dollar bills, three $10 bills and five $1 bills; Carla: 1,103 $10 bills and five $1 bills

### Activity 2: Concentration

Answers will vary. See *Activity 2*, p. 71, for some suggestions.

### Activity 3: Mystery Numbers

1. +30
2. −300
3. +2,000
4. +100
5. +600
6. +500
7. −20
8. −2,000
9. −400
10. +600

### Practice: True or False?

1. True
2. True
3. False
   Answer may vary. Sample statement:
   $6,503 = 6(1,000) + 5(100) + 3(1)$
4. False
   $666 + 40 = 706$
5. False
   $5,958 − 300 = 5,658$
6. False
   $92(10) = 9(100) + 2(10)$
7. True
8. True
9. False
   Answer may vary. Sample statement:
   $5(1,000) + 6(100) + 78(1) = 5,678$

### Practice: More Mystery Numbers

1. $543 \underline{+ 1,000} = 1,543$
2. $876 \underline{− 350} = 526$
3. $1,088 \underline{+ 2,000} = 3,088$
4. $1,077 \underline{− 370} = 707$
5. $21,156 \underline{+ 4,000} = 25,156$
6. $2,006 \underline{− 300} = 1,706$
7. $4,640 \underline{− 50} = 4,590$
8. $10,065 \underline{− 5} = 10,060$
9. $9,009 \underline{− 9,000} = 9$
10. $1,750 \underline{+ 600} = 2,350$

### Practice: Calculating with Money

1. $1.00    1 (or 100 if not using the decimal in front of 30 and 70)

2. $30.70    30.7

3. $3.07    3.07

4. $30.07    30.07

5. $307    307

6. $8.09    8.09

7. $80.90    80.9

8. $8.90    8.9

9. 98¢    0.98 (or 98 if not using decimal in front of 8 and 90)

10. $170    170

11. Answers will vary.

12. Answers will vary. Sample answers: The calculator leaves off the last 0 when it is to the right of the decimal. You have to be sure to add a decimal point when you are working with both dollars and cents.

## Practice: College Registration

1. Answers will vary. Sample answer: U.S. History, Math for Nonmajors, and Civil Engineering.

2. Answers will vary. Sample answer based on course selection above: $100 x 3 x 3 + $100(2) = 900 + 200 = $1,100.

## Mental Math Practice: Double Trouble

1. a. 24
   b. 19
   c. 88
   d. 59
   e. 18
   f. Answers will vary. Sample answer: The 1's digit will be a 9 because 9 + 9 = 18, putting an 8 in the 1's place. This is not always true because 4 + 4 = 8.

2. a. 174 lbs.
   b. 194 lbs.
   c. 214 lbs.
   d. 234 lbs.
   e. 254 lbs.
   f. All the digits in the 1's place are 4's.

3. a. 32
   b. 72
   c. 112
   d. Answers will vary. Sample answer: When you double 6, the number in the 1's place will be 2.

e. (1) 46
   (2) 48
   (3) 54

## Test Practice

1. (1)
2. (2)
3. (3)
4. (5)
5. (3)
6. 300

## Lesson 7: Patterns and Order

### Activity 1: Mental Math or Calculator?

1. 900
2. 30
3. 85
4. 85,000
5. 90,000
6. 30
7. 790
8. 79
9. 90,000
10. 79
11. Answers will vary. Sample answer: If it is a whole number, all I have to do is add a zero to the right of the number.
12. Answers will vary. Sample answer: If it is a whole number that ends in a zero, all I have to do is get rid of the last zero in the 1's place.
13. Answers will vary. Sample answer: If it is a whole number, all I have to do is add two zeroes to the right of the number.
14. Answers will vary. Sample answer: If it is a whole number that ends in at least two zeroes, all I have to do is get rid of the two zeroes in the 1's and 10's place.
15. Answers will vary. Sample answer: If it is a whole number, all I have to do is add three zeroes to the right of the number.
16. Answers will vary. Sample answer: If it is a whole number that ends in at least three zeroes, all I have to do is get rid of the three zeroes in the 1's, 10's, and 100's place.

**Activity 2: 3, 4, 5**

**Part 1**

1. Answers will vary. Sample answers:
   3(4) + 5 = 17; 3 + 4(5) = 23

2. Answers will vary.

**Part 2**

3. **a.** $1 + 9 \times 5 =$      46
   Multiply, then add

   **b.** $3 \times 7 + 2 =$      23
   Multiply, then add

   **c.** $12 \times 2 + 6 =$      30
   Multiply, then add

   **d.** $8 + 3 \times 4 =$      20
   Multiply, then add

   **e.** $10 \times 10 + 16 =$      116
   Multiply, then add

   **f.** $13 + 7 \times 3 =$      34
   Multiply, then add

4. $(1 + 9) \times 5$; $3 \times (7 + 2)$; $12 \times (2 + 6)$; $(8 + 3) \times 4$; $10 \times (10 + 16)$; $(13 + 7) \times 3$

5. **a.** 30
   **b.** 3
   **c.** Answers will vary.

**Practice: Just Like the Calculator**

1. $3 + 6 \times 5 =$    45    33
2. $7 \times 7 + 2 =$    51    51
3. $4 \times 12 + 2 =$    50    50
4. $18 - 3 \times 4 =$    60    6
5. $10 \times 10 + 10 =$    110    110
6. $15 - 7 \times 2 =$    16    1
7. Answers will vary.
8. Answers will vary.

**Practice: More or Less?**

1. More than 200. $50 \times 4 = 200$; 54 is more than 50, so $54 \times 4$ is more than 200.

2. Less than 800. $400 \times 2 = 800$; 370 is less than 400, so $370 \times 2$ is less than 800.

3. More than 1,000. $200 \times 5 = 1,000$; 203 is more than 200, so $203 \times 5$ is more than 1,000.

4. Less than 270. $90 \times 3 = 270$; 89 is less than 90, so $89 \times 3$ is less than 270.

**Mental Math Practice: Multiply and Divide with 10, 100, or 1,000**

1. $25 \times 10 = 250$
   $25 \times 100 = 2,500$
   $25 \times 1,000 = 25,000$

2. $205 \times 10 = 2,050$
   $205 \times 100 = 20,500$
   $205 \times 1,000 = 205,000$

3. $30 \times 10 = 300$
   $30 \times 100 = 3,000$
   $30 \times 1,000 = 30,000$

4. $360 \times 10 = 3,600$
   $360 \times 100 = 36,000$
   $360 \times 1,000 = 360,000$

5. $6,000 \div 10 = 600$
   $6,000 \div 100 = 60$
   $6,000 \div 1,000 = 6$

6. $100,000 \div 10 = 10,000$
   $100,000 \div 100 = 1,000$
   $100,000 \div 1,000 = 100$

7. $36,000 \div 10 = 3,600$
   $36,000 \div 100 = 360$
   $36,000 \div 1,000 = 36$

8. $306,000 \div 10 = 30,600$
   $306,000 \div 100 = 3,060$
   $306,000 \div 1,000 = 306$

**Extension: The Answer Is 24**

1. Answers will vary. Sample answer: $2(4 + 8) = 24$

2. Answers will vary. Sample word problem solved with b. By first adding and then dividing: Jon counted 200 cassettes in one crate and 40 in another. He packed cassettes 10 to a box. How many boxes did he need for all the cassettes? To solve: Add $200 + 40 = 240$ and then divide by $10 = 24$.

3. Answers will vary.

**Extension: Wrong Number!**

1. **a.** $4.00
   **b.** Answers will vary. Sample answer: The cashier rang up 40¢ as 40 instead of $0.40.

2. **a.** $7.25
   **b.** Answers will vary. Sample answer: Anton may have hit the subtraction key (−) instead of the division key (÷).

**3. a.** $49.90

   **b.** Answers will vary. Sample answer: Jorge probably hit the addition key (+) instead of the multiplication key (×).

## Test Practice

**1.** (2)

**2.** (3)

**3.** (5)

**4.** (4)

**5.** (2)

**6.** 10

## Lesson 8: Picture This

### Activity 1: Pictures and Numbers

Part 1

**1.** Answers will vary. Sample answer: There are 4 groups of 6 cans for a total of 24.

**2.** Answers will vary. Sample answer: There are 3 groups of 3 hands for a total of 9.

**3.** Answers will vary. Sample answer: There are 10 rows of 10 heads for a total of 100.

**4.** Answers will vary. Sample answer: There are 6 rows of 3 stamps plus 2 more for a total of 20.

**5.** Answers will vary. Sample answer: There are 6 groups of 3 candies, plus 1 more for a total of 19.

Part 2

**1.** b

**2.** d

**3.** c

**4.** a

**5. a.** 143

   **b.** Answers will vary. Sample answer:
$10 \times 13 = 130; 1 \times 13 = 13; 130 + 13 = 143$

**6.** Answers will vary. Sample answer: They all total 143.

### Activity 2: Counting Smart

Part 1

**1.** Answers will vary. Sample answer based on the following array:

   xxx   xxx xxx

   xxx   xxx xxx

**2.** Answers will vary. Sample answer based on the array above: $(3 \times 2) + (3 \times 4)$.

**3.** Answers will vary. Sample answer based on array above:

   xxxxx   xxxxx

   xxxxx   xxx

**4.** Answers will vary. Sample answer based on array above: $1(10) + 8$

Part 2

**1.**

   oooo    oo
   oooo
   oooo
   oooo
   oooo
   oooo
   oooo
   oooo
   oooo

**2.**

   ooooo
   ØØØØØ
   ØØØØØ
   ØØØØØ

**3.**

   ooo  ooo  ooo  ooo  ooo
   ooo  ooo  ooo  ooo  ooo
   ooo  ooo  ooo  ooo  ooo
   ooo  ooo  ooo  ooo  ooo

**4.**

   oo   ooo
   oo   ooo

   oo   ooo
   oo   ooo

   oo   ooo
   oo   ooo

**5.** Answers will vary.

### Activity 3: Garden Pathway

**1.** Answers will vary. Sample answer: $2(12)(2) + 2(10)$

**2.** Answers will vary. Sample answer: $2(14) + 2(10)(2)$

**Practice: Carton of Eggs**

1. 30

2. Answers will vary. Sample answer: 2(3)(5)

3. Answers will vary. Sample answer:
   There are 2 rows with 3 eggs each. That's 6 eggs.
   There are 5 sets of 6, so 5 × 6 = 30.

4. 6 × 5 or 3 × 5 × 2

**Practice: Expressions, Arrays, and Stories**

Part 1

1. 3 × 3 + 10

2. 3(10 + 3); 4 × 7 − 3

3. 5 × 5 + 5 + 5 + 5

Part 2

4. Array 3

5. Array 1

6. Array 2

**Practice: How Do You See It?**

1. a. Answers will vary. Sample answer:

   2(3) + 1

   b. Answers will vary. Sample answer:

   4(5) + 3

   c. Answers will vary. Sample answers:

   3(3)

2. Answers will vary. Sample answer:
   2(8) + 2(7); 2(9) + 2(6)

**Practice: Stone Paths**

1. a. 2(6) = 12

   b. 1(12) = 12

   c. 3(4) = 12

2. a.

```
XXXXXXXXXXXXXXXXXXXXXXX   1(23)

XXXXXXXXXXXXXXXXXXXXXXXX   1(24)

XXXXXXXXXXXX
XXXXXXXXXXXX   2(12)

XXXXX
XXXXX
XXXXX   4(6)
XXXXX

XXXXXXX
XXXXXXX   3(8)
XXXXXXX

XXXXXXXXXXXXXXXXXXXXXXXXX   1(25)

XXXXX
XXXXX
XXXXX   5(5)
XXXXX
XXXXX
```

   b. One array for 23: 1(23); four arrays for 24:
      1(24), 2(12), 3(8), 4(6); two arrays for 25:
      1(25), 5(5)

   c. Answers will vary. Sample answer:
      There are more ways to multiply numbers
      to get 24 than to get 23 or 25.

**Mental Math Practice: Square Numbers**

1. $n^2$

   | 0 | 1 | 4 | 9 | 16 | 25 | 36 |

   $n^2$

   | 49 | 64 | 81 | 100 | 121 | 144 |

2. a. 6 × 6 = 36

   b. 9 × 9 = 81

   c. $9 = 3^2$

   d. $8^2 = 64$

   e. $0^2 + 1^2 + 2^2 + 3^2 = 14$

**Extension: Missing Rolls of Film**

There are 36 rolls missing. Explanations will vary.
Sample explanation:
The rolls are stacked 3 deep. There are 2 rows that
have 6 rolls each missing: 3 × 2 × 6 = 36.

## Extension: Seeing Squarely

**1.**

```
X X X X X
X X X X X
X X X X X
X X X X X
X X X X X
```

**2.**

```
X X X X X    X X X
X X X X X    X X X
X X X X X    X X X
X X X X X
X X X X X
```

**3.**

```
X X X X X O O O
X X X X X O O O
X X X X X O O O
X X X X X O O O
X X X X X O O O
O O O O O O O O
O O O O O O O O
O O O O O O O O
```

**4.**

```
O O O O O
O O O O O
O O Ø Ø Ø
O O Ø Ø Ø
O O Ø Ø Ø
```

### Test Practice

**1.** (2)
**2.** (4)
**3.** (4)
**4.** (5)
**5.** (5)
**6.** 106

## Lesson 9: What's the Story?

### Activity 1: What's the Story?

Problem 1

Person A

1. All of the windows in one building. Sketches will vary. Sample sketch:

2. Answers will vary. Sample answer: $4(12 + 12 + 10) = 4(34)$

3. 136. Explanations will vary. Sample explanation:
Person A added $12 + 12 + 10$ to get a total of 34 windows in one building. Since there are four buildings, he then multiplied $4 \times 34$.

Person B

1. All of the windows on the first floor. Sketches will vary. Sample sketch:

2. Answers will vary. Sample answer: $4(12) + 4(12) + 4(10) = 48 + 48 + 40$

3. 136. Explanations will vary. Sample explanation:
Person B multiplied $4 \times 12$ to find the total number of windows on the first floor of all four buildings. She then multiplied $4 \times 12$ to find the total number of second-floor windows and $4 \times 10$ for the total number of third-floor windows.

Problem 2

Person A

1.

```
X X X X X X X X
X X X X X X X X
X X X X X X X X
X X X X X X X X
```

**2.** Answers will vary. Sample answer:
$4(9) \div 3 = 36 \div 3$

**3.** 12. Explanations will vary. Sample explanation: Person A multiplied 9 x 4 to figure out the total number of children. Then he divided the total by 3 because there were 3 shirts per pack.

Person B

**1.**

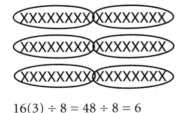

**2.** Answers will vary. Sample answer:
$9 \div 3 \times 4 = 3 \times 4$

**3.** 12. Explanations will vary. Sample explanation: Person B divided 9 x 3 to figure out the total number of shirts needed for one class. Then she multiplied that amount by 4 because there were 4 classes needing shirts.

## Activity 2: The Rose Problem

48. See *Lesson 9 in Action*, p. 117, for examples of how students solved the problem.

## Practice: Drawings and Equations

**1.** Answers will vary. Sample answer:

```
Ø Ø O O O O      Ø Ø Ø Ø O O
Ø Ø O O O O      Ø Ø Ø Ø O O
Ø Ø O O O O      Ø Ø Ø Ø O O
Ø Ø O O O O      Ø Ø Ø Ø O O
Ø Ø O O O O      Ø Ø Ø Ø O O
```

$5(6-2) + 5(6-4) = 5(4) + 5(2) = 30$

**2.** Answers will vary. Sample answer:

XXXXXXX XXXXXXX

XXXXXXX XXXXXXX

XXXXXXX XXXXXXX

$16(3) \div 8 = 48 \div 8 = 6$

**3.** Answers will vary. Sample answer:

```
X X X X X = $9
X X X X X = $9
X X X X X = $9
X X X X X = $9
X X X X X = $9
X X X X X = $9
```

$30 \div 5 \times 9 = 6 \times 9 = \$54$

**4.** Answers will vary. Sample answer:

```
C C C = $20      C C C = $8
C C C = $20      C C C = $8
C C C = $20      C C C = $8
C C C = $20      C C C = $8
C C C = $20   —  C C C = $8
C C C = $20      C C C = $8
C C C = $20      C C C = $8
C C C = $20      C C C = $8
C C C = $20      C C C = $8
C C C = $20      C C C = $8
```

$30 \div 3 \times (20 - 8) = 10 \times 12 = \$120$

## Practice: Equations and Word Problems

**1.** Answers will vary. Sample answer: $5(14) + 2$. There are five preschool classes. The director wanted to limit the class size to 14, but when a set of twins enrolled, the director allowed them to join one of the already full classes. How many children were there altogether?

**2.** Answers will vary. Sample answer: $5(2(4) + 3(4))$. There are two rows of shelves with four crates on each row across the top and three rows of shelves with four crates on each row on the bottom. If there are a total of five such sets of shelving, how many crates are there altogether?

**3.** Answers will vary. Sample answer: $4(10)$. Jane is building pyramids with sets of blocks. Each pyramid uses 10 blocks with four blocks used as the base. If she builds four pyramids, how many blocks does she need in all?

## Practice: The Answer Is _____

**1.** Answers will vary. Sample answer: 42

**2.** Answers will vary. Sample problem based on answer above: Seth earns $7 an hour. How much does he earn for working 6 hours? $\$7(6) = 42$

3. Answers will vary. Sample problem based on answer above:
   Tabitha has eight nickels and two pennies in her pocket. How much change does she have altogether?
   $8(\$0.05) + 2(\$0.01) = \$0.40 + \$0.02 = \$0.42$

## Practice: One Day, I . . .

Answers will vary.

## Mental Math Practice:

There are many patterns in the multiplication tables. Some, but certainly not all, follow:

The multiples of 10 end in zero.

The multiples of five end in zero or five.

Any number mutiplied by one is itself ($a \times 1 = a$).

Any number multiplied by zero is zero ($a \times 0 = 0$).

The square numbers run along the diagonal.

There is a mirror image along the diagonal of the squares ($a \times b = b \times a$).

The multiples of six are even.

## Test Practice

1. (2)
2. (2)
3. (3)
4. (3)
5. (2)
6. 90

## Lesson 10: Easy Payments

## Activity 1: Easy Payments

1. $9,600 over 4 months    $2,500   $2,400
2. $9,600 over 8 months    $1,250   $1,200
3. $9,600 over 12 months   $1,000   $  800
4. $9,600 over 24 months   $  375   $  400
5. Answers will vary. Sample answer:
   I estimated by rounding $9,600 to $10,000. To find the exact answer, I subtracted $400 ÷ 4 = 100 ($10,000 ÷ 4 = $2,500; $2,500 − $100 = $2,400).
6. Answers will vary. Sample answer:
   I estimated by rounding $9,600 to $10,000. To find the exact answer, I subtracted $400 ÷ 8 = 50 ($10,000 ÷ 8 = 1,250; $1,250 − $50 = $1,200).

7. Answers will vary. Sample answer:
   I estimated by rounding $9,600 to $12,000. To find the exact answer, I subtracted $2,400 ÷ 12 = $200 ($12,000 ÷ 12 = $1,000; $1,000 − $200 = $800).
8. Answers will vary. Sample answer:
   I estimated by rounding $9,600 to $12,000. To find the exact answer, I halved the amount for 12 months.
9. Answers will vary.

## Activity 2: The Payment Plan Game

Answers will vary.

## Practice: Four Ways to Write Division

| | | | |
|---|---|---|---|
| $8\overline{)56}$ | $56 \div 8$ | $\dfrac{56}{8}$ | 56 divided by 8 |
| $5\overline{)30}$ | $30 \div 5$ | $\dfrac{30}{5}$ | 30 divided by 5 |
| $6\overline{)180}$ | $180 \div 6$ | $\dfrac{180}{6}$ | 180 divided by 6 |
| $1\overline{)40}$ | $40 \div 1$ | $\dfrac{40}{1}$ | 40 divided by 1 |
| $7\overline{)2}$ | $2 \div 7$ | $\dfrac{2}{7}$ | 2 divided by 7 |
| $y\overline{)x}$ | $x \div y$ | $\dfrac{x}{y}$ | x divided by y |
| $10\overline{)m}$ | $m \div 10$ | $\dfrac{m}{10}$ | m divided by 10 |
| $\$0.50\overline{)\$10.00}$ | $\$10.00 \div \$0.50$ | $\dfrac{\$10.00}{\$0.50}$ | $10.00 divided by $0.50 |

## Practice: Which Is Not the Same?

1. c
2. a
3. a
4. b

## Practice: Those Monthly Payments

1. <
2. >
3. <
4. <

## Practice: 10's, 100's, and 1,000's

1. $10 \times 9 = 90$. Then: $2 \times 9 = 18$; $90 + 18 = 108$
2. $21 \times 10 = 210$. Then: $21 \times 1 = 21$; $210 + 21 = 231$
3. $25 \times 10 = 250$. Then: $2 \times 250 = 500$ and $3 \times 25 = 75$; $500 + 75 = 575$
4. $100 \div 5 = 20$. Then: $30 \div 5 = 6$; $20 + 6 = 26$
5. $1,000 \div 4 = 250$. Then: $200 \div 4 = 50$ and $72 \div 4 = 18$; $250 + 50 + 18 = 318$

## Mental Math Practice: Flowers by the Month

1. Join the Flower Club!
   12 months: 192.00
   10 months: $160.00
   6 months: $96.00
   2 months: $32.00
   Monthly: $16.00
2. Monthly Flower Club
   12 months: 456.00
   10 months: $380.00
   6 months: $228.00
   2 months: $76.00
   Monthly: $38.00
3. Flower Club of the Month
   12 months: $324.00
   10 months: $270.00
   6 months: $162.00
   2 months: $54.00
   Monthly: $27.00

## Test Practice

1. (2)
2. (4)
3. (2)
4. (5)
5. (3)
6. $4,788

## Lesson 11: String It Along

### Activity 1: String It Along

Part 1

1. a. 16
   b. 12
   c. 8
2. 48 inches. Answers will vary.
   Sample answer: $3'' \times 16 = 48''$
3.

4. Answers will vary. Sample answers:
   $3''(16) = 48''$; $48''/4'' = 12$; $48''/6'' = 8$

Part 2

1. a. 12
   b. 8
   c. 4
2. 72 inches. Answers will vary. Sample answer:
   $12 \times 6'' = 72''$
3.

4. Answers will vary. Sample answers:
   $72''/6'' = 12$; $9''(8) = 72''$; $18''(4) = 72''$

### Activity 2: Scales on Maps

1. a. 710 miles
   b. 2,840 miles
   c. 2,130 miles
2. a. 2,000 miles
   b. 1,200 miles
   c. 300 miles
   d. 1,250 miles
3. a. 0.21 inches ; 6 cm
   b. 0.42 inches; 12 cm
   c. 10.56 inches; 300 cm
4. Answers will vary.

**Practice: How Many Blanks in a Blank?**

1.  a.  3

    b.  $36 \div 12 = 3$

    c.

2.  a.  4

    b.  $60/15 = 4$

    c.

3.  a.  8

    b.  $128/16 = 8$

    c.

4.  a.  5

    b.  $10{,}000/2{,}000 = 5$

    c.

5.  a.  8

    b.  $24 \div 3 = 8$

    c.

6.  a.  Answers will vary.

    b.  Answers will vary.

    c.  Answers will vary.

**Practice: About How Many Times as Large?**

1.  10; Explanations will vary. Sample explanation: 72 is about 70. 70/7 = 10

2.  2; Explanations will vary. Sample explanation: 68 is about 70. 140/70 = 2

3.  100; Explanations will vary. Sample explanation: 197 is about 200. 200/2 = 100

4.  2; Explanations will vary. Sample explanation: 6 feet is 72 inches. 72 inches is about 70. 70/35 = 2

**Practice: Coin Rolling**

1.  a.  100

    b.  20

    c.  10

    d.  4

2.  24; 50¢ x 2 = $1; 12 x $1 = $12

3.  6; $12/$2 = $6

4.  2 rolls of $5 with 20 dimes left over; $12/$5 = 2 rolls with $2 left over.

5.  1 with 8 quarters left over; $12/$10 = 1 roll with $2 left over.

6.  Answers will vary. Sample answer: 1 roll of quarters ($10), 2 rolls of dimes ($10), 1 roll of nickels ($2), and 4 rolls of pennies ($2): $10 + $10 + $2 + $2 = $24

**Practice: Vacation Spots**

Answers will vary. Sample answers based on Los Angeles, CA.

1.  a.  40 hours; 2,000/50 = 40

    b.  26 hours and 40 minutes (26.67 hours); 2,000/75 = 26.66

    c.  30 hours and about 45 minutes (30.77); 2,000/65 = 30.77

2.  Answers will vary.

**Practice: Collecting Frequent Flyer Miles**

63 trips (one-way) or 32 round trips

60 trips (one-way) or 30 round trips

**Mental Math Practice: Factors**

1.  a.  1, 2, 4, 5, 10, 20

    b.  1, 23

    c.  1, 2, 3, 4, 6, 8, 12, 24

    d.  1, 5, 25

2.  a.  20, 25

    b.  24

    c.  20

    d.  23

    e.  24

**Test Practice**

1. (2)
2. (2)
3. (3)
4. (4)
5. (4)
6. 3

## Lesson 12: Making Do

### Activity 1: Party Favors

1. E
2. CS
3. E
4. SL
5. E
6. CS
7. CS
8. CS
9. CS
10. CS

### Activity 2: Making Do

Answers may vary based on personal experience.

1. Three feet of wire with 3 feet left over (or 3.75 feet each)
2. 60 feet of board
3. 67.5 feet of rope
4. About 50 screws each
5. Only three sites can have paint and one will have to do without; or 3/4 cans for each site.
6. 7.5 pounds of plaster
7. One bag each with two 40-pound bags left over
8. About 80 stones each

### Practice: Interpreting Remainders

1. h
2. d
3. j
4. f
5. i or l
6. i or l
7. e
8. k
9. c

10. b
11. a
12. g

### Practice: Pill Problems

1. 75 days
2. No. Explanations will vary. Sample explanation: 2 pills every 4 hours for 3 days is about 36 pills. Then she takes another 7–8 pills a day (if you consider a 24 hour cycle); $100 - 36 = 64$ total pills for 27 days. That would allow her to take only about 2 pills per day, not 7 or 8.
3. No
4. October 11

### Practice: Meaningful Remainders

1. 4; 100/22 = 4.5; she can't buy half a DVD.
2. 6; 175/30 = 5.8; 0.8 must become one more trip.
3. 30 inches, or 2.5 feet with no leftovers.
4. 8; 75/9 = 8.33; 0.33 feet is not enough for another jump rope.
5. 12; $25/$1.99 = 12.5; she can't buy half of a truck.
6. $370.60 each with no leftovers.
7. 1.5 feet with no leftovers.
8. Answers will vary. Sample answer: There are 29 children who are to be grouped into teams of 4 each. There would be 7 teams and 1 child who would become a helper.

### Mental Math Practice: Money in My Pocket

63

### Test Practice

1. (4)
2. (2)
3. (4)
4. (3)
5. (2)
6. 7.5 cookies

# Closing the Unit: Computer Lab

## Activity 1: Computer Lab Project
Answers will vary.

## Computer Lab Warm-Up 1:
## Mental Math Calculations for Paper Use

1.  a.  200; Explanations will vary. Sample explanation: 20 × 10 = 200

    b.  1,100; Explanations will vary. Sample explanation: 20 × 50 = 1,000 and 20 × 5 = 100

    c.  2,000; Explanations will vary. Sample explanation: 20 × 100 = 2,000

    d.  2,400; Explanations will vary. Sample explanation: 20 × 100 = 2,000 and 20 × 20 = 400

    e.  4,000; Explanations will vary. Sample explanation: 20 × 200 = 4,000

2.  a.  1,000; Explanations will vary. Sample explanation: 50 × 20 = 1,000

    b.  6,250; Explanations will vary. Sample explanation: 50 × 100 = 5,000, 50 × 20 = 1,000, and 50 × 5 = 250

## Computer Lab Warm-Up 2:
## How Much More for...?

1.  a.  $286

    b.  Answers will vary. Sample answer: $2,275 − $1,975 = $300; $1,989 is $14 more than $1,975, so $300 is $14 over estimate. $300 − $14 = $286.

2.  a.  $1,576

    b.  $2,275 − $700 = $1,575; $1,575 + $1 = $1,576

## Computer Lab Warm-Up 3: Inventory Count

1.  Answers will vary. Three possibilities are shown here:

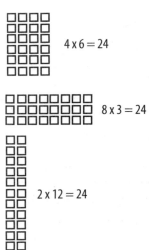

2.  a.  10 × 3 × 6 = 10 × 18 = 180

    b.  10 × (4 × 2 × 2) − 10(2) = 160 − 20 = 140

    c.  10 × (4 × 5 × 4) − 10(3) = 800 − 3 = 770

## Computer Lab Warm-Up 4: Item Costs

1.  a.  6
    $1,500 × 2 = $3,000;
    $3,000 × 3 = $9,000; 2 × 3 = 6

    b.  Yes

2.  a.  About $3,333

    b.  Answers will vary.

## Activity 2: Final Assessment

## Task 1: Mental Math Challenge

1.  $140
2.  $90
3.  $19
4.  $5,000
5.  $1.00
6.  $3,640
7.  $9,370
8.  $450
9.  $450
10. $3,300
11. 27
12. $80
13. No

**14.** Yes

**15.** Yes

**16.** No

## Task 2: Picturing the Math

**1. a.** Answers will vary. Sample answer:

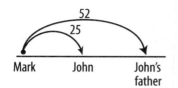

**b.** Answers will vary. Sample answer: How old was John's father when John was born? To solve it, I would subtract 25 from 52.

**2. a.** Answers will vary. Sample answer:

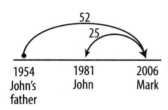

**b.** Answers will vary. Sample answer based on the two answers above: In the second picture, the positions of the people were reversed along the timeline.

**3.** Answers will vary. Sample answer: 4 × 5

**4.** Picture A

**5. a.** Answers will vary. Sample answer:

```
XX      XX
XX      XX
XX
XX
XX
```

**b.** Answers will vary. Sample answer:

```
XX      OOOO
XX      OOOO
XX      OOOO
XX      OOOO
XX      OOOO
```

**6.** Answers will vary. Sample answer:

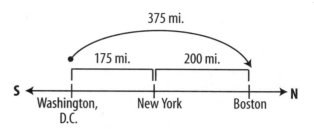

## Task 3: Four Problems

**1.** 646. Sample solution:
$(490 + 1) + (50 - 2) + (100 + 7) = (490 + 50 + 100) + (1 - 2 + 7) = 640 + 6 = 646$

**2.** 1,908. Sample solution:
$2,005 - 100 + 3 = 1,905 + 3 = 1,908$

**3.** 1,400. Sample solution:
$(50 + 6) \times 25 = 50(25) + 6(25) = 1,250 + 150 = 1,400$

**4.** 32. Sample solution:
$23 \times 10 = 230$, $23 \times 30 = 690$, $2 \times 23 = 46$, so there are <u>32</u> 23's in 736.

# Sources and Resources

## Mathematics Education

The National Council of Teachers of Mathematics (NCTM) publishes several excellent resources.

- *Principles and Standards for School Mathematics*. Reston, VA: NCTM, 2000.
- The NCTM journals: *Mathematics Teaching in the Middle Grades, Mathematics Teacher*, and *Journal for Research in Mathematics Education*.
- *Developing Number Sense in the Middle Grades, The Addenda Series, Grades 5–8*. Reston, VA: NCTM, 1991.
- *Historical Topics for the Mathematics Classroom*. Reston, VA: NCTM, 1989.
- http://www.nctm.org.

Fendel, D., D. Resek, L. Alper, and S. Fraser. *Interactive Mathematics Program*. Berkeley, CA: Key Curriculum Press, 1997.

Lappan, G., J. Fey, W. Fitzgerald, S. Friel, and E. Phillips. *Connected Mathematics Series*. Parsippany, NJ: Dale Seymour Publications, Division of Pearson Education, 1998.

Mokros, J., S.J. Russell, and K. Economopoulos. *Beyond Arithmetic: Changing Mathematics in the Elementary Classroom*. Palo Alto, CA: Dale Seymour Publications, 1995.

National Research Council. *Adding It Up: Helping Children Learn Mathematics*. J. Kilpatrick, J. Swafford, and B. Findell (Eds.). Mathematics Learning Study Committee, Center for Education, Division of Behavioral and Social Sciences and Education. Washington, DC: National Academy Press, 2001.

Russell, S.J. Developing Computational Fluency with Whole Numbers in the Elementary Grades in *New England Mathematics Journal*, 32, no. 2 (May 2000).

Russell, S.J., et al. *The Investigations in Number, Data, and Space Curriculum*. White Plains, NY: Dale Seymour Publications, 1998.

## Mathematics and Numeracy Education for Adults

Burns, M. *Math, Facing an American Phobia*. White Plains, NY: Math Solutions Publications, 1998.

Curry, D., M.J. Schmitt, and S. Waldron. *A Framework for Adult Numeracy Standards: The Mathematical Skills and Abilities Adults Need to Be Equipped for the Future*. Boston: World Education, 1996. (This framework was developed by members of the Adult Numeracy Network.) http://shell04.the world.com/std/anpn.

Evans, J. *Adults' Mathematical Thinking and Emotions: A Study of Adult Numerate Practices*. London: Routledge Falmer, 2000.

Massachusetts Department of Education. *Massachusetts Adult Basic Education Curriculum Frameworks for Mathematics and Numeracy*. Malden, MA: Massachusetts Department of Education, 2001. http://www.doe.mass.edu/acls/frameworks.

Northcote, M., and M. McIntosh. What Mathematics Do Adults Really Do in Everyday Life? *Australian Primary Mathematics Classroom*, 4(1), 1999.

Stein, S. *Equipped for the Future Content Standards: What Adults Need to Know and Be Able to Do in the Twenty-First Century*. ED Pubs document EX0099P. Washington, DC: National Institute for Literacy, 2000.

Tobias, S. *Overcoming Math Anxiety: Revised and Expanded*. New York: W.W. Norton & Company, 1994.

Zaslavsky, C. *Fear of Math: How to Get over It and Get on with Your Life*. Piscataway, NJ: Rutgers University Press, 1996.